Routledge International Handbook of Contemporary Racisms

The study of contemporary forms of racism has expanded greatly over the past four decades. Although it has been a focus for scholarship and research for the past three centuries, it is perhaps over this more recent period that we have seen important transformations in the analytical frames and methods to explore the changing patterns of contemporary racisms. The *Routledge International Handbook of Contemporary Racisms* brings together thirty-four original chapters from international experts that address key features of contemporary racisms.

The *Handbook* has a truly global orientation and covers contemporary racisms in both the western and non-western geopolitical environments. In terms of structure, the volume is organized into ten interlinked parts that include Theories and Histories, Contemporary Racisms in Global Perspective, Racism and the State, Racist Movements and Ideologies, Anti-Racisms, Racism and Nationalism, Intersections of Race and Gender, Racism, Culture and Religion, Methods of Studying Contemporary Racisms, and the End of Racism. These parts contain chapters that draw on original theoretical and empirical research to address the evolution and changing forms of contemporary racism. The *Handbook* is framed by a General Introduction and by short introductions to each part that provide an overview of key themes and concerns.

Written in a clear and direct style, and from a conceptual, multidisciplinary and international perspective, the *Handbook* will provide students, scholars, and practitioners with an overview of the most pressing issues of Racisms in our time.

John Solomos is Professor of Sociology at the University of Warwick. He has researched and published on questions about theories of race and racism, race in British society, multiculturalism and anti-discrimination policies, and on migration and social movements. He is co-editor of the journal *Ethnic and Racial Studies* and General Editor of *The Routledge Encyclopedia of Race and Racism*.

Routledge International Handbooks

Routledge International Handbook of New Digital Practices in Galleries, Libraries, Archives, Museums and Heritage Sites
Edited by Hannah Lewi, Wally Smith, Dirk vom Lehn and Steven Cooke

Routledge International Handbook of Human Trafficking
A Multi-Disciplinary and Applied Approach
Edited by Rochelle L. Dalla and Donna Sabella

The Routledge Handbook of Comparative Rural Policy
Edited by Matteo Vittuari, John Devlin, Marco Pagani and Thomas Johnson

Routledge International Handbook of Masculinity Studies
Edited by Lucas Gottzén, Ulf Mellström and Tamara Shefer

Routledge Handbook of European Welfare Systems, 2e
Edited by Sonja Blum, Johanna Kuhlmann and Klaus Schubert

Routledge International Handbook of Heterosexualities Studies
Edited by James Joseph Dean and Nancy L. Fischer

Routledge Handbook of Contemporary European Social Movements
Protest in Turbulent Times
Edited by Cristina Flesher Fominaya and Ramón A. Feenstra

The Routledge International Handbook of Military Psychology and Mental Health
Edited by Updesh Kumar

Routledge International Handbook of Green Criminology
Edited by Avi Brisman and Nigel South

Routledge International Handbook of Contemporary Racisms
Edited by John Solomos

For more information about this series, please visit: www.routledge.com/Routledge-International-Handbooks/book-series/RIHAND

Routledge International Handbook of Contemporary Racisms

Edited by John Solomos

LONDON AND NEW YORK

First published 2020 by Routledge

2 Park Square, Milton Park, Abingdon, Oxon OX14 4RN

605 Third Avenue, New York, NY 10017

Routledge is an imprint of the Taylor & Francis Group, an informa business

First issued in paperback 2021

Publisher s Note

The publisher has gone to great lengths to ensure the quality of thisreprint but points out that some imperfections in the original copies may beapparent.

British Library Cataloguing-in-Publication Data
A catalogue record for this book is available from the British Library

Library of Congress Cataloging-in-Publication Data
Names: Solomos, John, editor.
Title: Routledge international handbook of contemporary racisms / edited by John Solomos.
Description: Abingdon, Oxon ; New York, NY : Routledge, 2020. |
Series: Routledge international handbooks | Includes bibliographical references and index.
Identifiers: LCCN 2019051286 (print) | LCCN 2019051287 (ebook) |
ISBN 9781138485990 (hardback) | ISBN 9781351047326 (ebook)
Subjects: LCSH: Racism.
Classification: LCC HT1521 .R6869 2020 (print) | LCC HT1521 (ebook) |
DDC 305.8–dc23
LC record available at https://lccn.loc.gov/2019051286
LC ebook record available at https://lccn.loc.gov/2019051287

ISBN: 978-1-138-48599-0 (hbk)
ISBN: 978-1-03-217349-8 (pbk)
DOI: 10.4324/9781351047326

Typeset in Bembo
by Swales & Willis, Exeter, Devon, UK

Contents

Contents

Contents

Figures and tables

Figures

Tables

Preface and acknowledgements

Producing a *Handbook* on this scale is a long process and involves support and encouragement form a range of people. In particular this volume would not have been possible without the various scholars who have agreed to be part of the project. They have chosen to give generously of their time to see the volume come to fruition and have responded to my various requests with grace and humour. I hope they find the final product as a whole of interest to them. Second, various colleagues in my intellectual networks have been supportive of my endeavours over the years and have been kind enough to engage in on-going conversations that have helped me along the way, including: Claire Alexander, Leah Bassel, Alice Bloch, Eduardo Bonilla-Silva, Martin Bulmer, Patricia Hill Collins, Paul Gilroy, Clive Harris, Michael Keith, Marco Martiniello, Karim Murji, Yasmeen Narayan, Miri Song, Satnam Virdee and Aaron Winter. My colleagues in the Department of Sociology at the University of Warwick have been supportive by allowing me some valuable sabbatical time to focus on my research and writing after my period as Head of Department. My collaboration with Martin Bulmer over the past quarter of a century in editing the journal *Ethnic and Racial Studies* has provided me with a unique opportunity to learn about the changing preoccupations and paradigms that have helped to shape the study of race and racism in various disciplines and parts of the globe. I have learned much from that involvement and from the meetings that the journal has facilitated with both established and new generations of scholars. The administrative staff at the journal, Amanda Eastell-Bleakley and Celia Boggust, have been of immense help throughout this period. At Routledge the support of Gerhard Boomgaarden and Diana Ciobotea has been important in getting the project set up and in keeping it going.

At home the constant love and support of Christine, Nikolas, and Daniel has been important to me and I hope they don't mind too much the hours in the study. The last stages of producing the book have been helped along by long walks through North London, providing me with enjoyable moments to wonder at the richness of both the city that is my home and the nature that surrounds us. I have learned much about the Parkland Walk, Queen's Wood, Highgate Wood, and Hampstead Heath in the process and look forward to walking to new parts of the city. The various trips to watch West Bromwich Albion at the Hawthorns and all over England have been a different kind of distraction, mostly enjoyable, sometimes painful and often moving. Thanks to Max, Lana, Nikolas, Dave and Glenn for being such good company on these trips and tolerated the presence of an eccentric 'Prof' in their midst.

John Solomos
Crouch End, London
June 2019

Notes on the contributors

The editor

John Solomos is Professor of Sociology at the University of Warwick. He has researched and written widely on the history and contemporary forms of race and ethnic relations in Britain, theories of race and racism, the politics of race, equal opportunity policies, multiculturalism and social policy, race and football, and racist movements and ideas. His most recent books are *Race, Ethnicity and Social Theory* (forthcoming, Routledge) and *Race and Racism in Britain* (4th edition forthcoming, Palgrave Macmillan). His most recent edited book is *Theories of Race and Ethnicity: Contemporary Debates and Perspectives* (Cambridge University Press 2015, co-editor with Karim Murji). He is co-editor of the international journal *Ethnic and Racial Studies*, which is published in sixteen issues a year by Routledge. He is also co-editor of the book series on *Racism, Resistance and Social Change* for Manchester University Press and General Editor of *The Routledge Encyclopedia of Race and Racism*.

Contributors

Luis Manuel Hernández Aguilar is a postdoctoral researcher at the University of Amsterdam, working on the project *EnGendering Europe's Muslim Question*. He holds a PhD in Sociology from the Goethe-University Frankfurt am Main. His most recent publications include (2018) *Governing Muslims and Islam in Contemporary Germany: Race, Time, and the German Islam Conference*, and 'Institutionalisierung des anti-muslimischen Rassismus im Staat: Reflektionen über die Deutsche Islam Konferenz' in B. Uçar, & W. Kassis (Eds.) (2019) *Antimuslimischer Rassismus und Islamfeindlichkeit*.

Minoo Alinia is Associate Professor in Sociology and is currently working as Senior Lecturer at School of Social Sciences, Södertörn University in Stockholm. She has published on diaspora movements and identities, gender and violence, racism/nationalism and gender, and intersectionality.

Kristine Aquino is Lecturer in Global Studies in the Faculty of Arts and Social Sciences at the University of Technology Sydney, Australia. Her research is broadly concerned with migration, multiculturalism, race and racism. She explores these issues in the context of urban everyday life through the use of qualitative and ethnographic methods. She has published in international journals such as *Ethnic and Racial Studies* and *Journal of Intercultural Studies*. Her first book *Racism and Resistance among the Filipino Diaspora: Everyday Anti-racism in Australia* was published by Routledge in 2018 and explores how Filipino migrants in

Australia experience understand and negotiate racism in their everyday lives, grounding larger questions about race, citizenship, nationhood and anti-racism in lived experiences.

Jehonathan Ben is a doctoral candidate and researcher at Deakin University. His work focuses on racism, intercultural relations and migration. He currently conducts ethnographic research on experiences with work transformations and relationships among Eritrean migrants who live in Melbourne.

Sirma Bilge (PhD, Université Sorbonne Nouvelle-Paris III) is Full Professor of Sociology at Université de Montréal. She founded and directed the Intersectionality Research Unit at the Centre des études ethniques des universités montréalaises (CEETUM) from 2005 to 2010. Her current research looks at the neoliberal incorporation of minoritized knowledges and producers in the western academy. Her published works, in French, English and Turkish, include widely engaged articles such as 'Intersectionality Undone' (*Du Bois Review*, 2013) and 'Beyond subordination and resistance: an intersectional approach to the agency of veiled Muslim women' (Journal of Intercultural Studies, 2010), as well as her book *Intersectionality* (co-authored with Patricia Hill Collins, 2016).

Manuela Bojadžijev is Professor for Globalized Cultures at the Faculty of Cultural Studies at the Leuphana University of Lüneburg and vice-director of the Berlin Institute for Integration and Migration Research (BIM) at the Humboldt University of Berlin. The overall focus of her work is researching globalized and digitized cultures. She is interested in contemporary transformations of mobility and migration as well as of racism, in interplay with the current radical changes of work and life. Addressing these topics, she currently oversees four research projects (funded be the European research programmes H2020 and HERA, as well as the Volkswagen Foundation and the German Research Foundation). Additionally, she curates, together with the author Carolin Emcke, at Berlin's House of World Cultures an online archive on the history and presence of forced migration to Germany (funded by the Federal Cultural Foundation). Her more noteworthy publications include *Turbulente Ränder. Neue Perspektiven auf Migration an den Grenzen* Europas (2007; 2012; as part of Transit Migration Forschungsgruppe), *Die windige Internationale* (2008; 2012) and *Race, Nation, Class: Rereading a Dialogue for our Times* (2018; with Katrin Klingan).

Sarah Bracke is Professor of Sociology of Gender and Sexuality at the University of Amsterdam. Her fields of research include gender, religion (Islam and Christianity), the secular and secular governmentality, and multiculturalism in Europe, with a focus on questions of subjectivity and agency. She is the principle investigator of the *EnGendering Europe's Muslim Question* research project, funded by the Netherlands Organization for Scientific Research. She is an executive editor of journals *Ethnography* and *Religion and Gender*.

David Cook-Martín is Professor of Sociology and Program Head of New York University Abu Dhabi's Social Research and Public Policy (SRPP). His work focuses on understanding migration, race, ethnicity, law, and citizenship in an international field of power. His most recent projects examine temporary migration regimes in comparative and historical perspective, and the linkages between political and racial orders. Cook-Martín's 2013 book *Scramble for Citizens: Dual Nationality and State Competition for Immigrants* (Stanford 2013) won the Thomas and Znaniecki Prize of the American Sociological Association. *Culling the Masses: The Democratic Origins of Racism Immigration Policy in the Americas* (2014) – co-authored with David FitzGerald – won the ASA's Distinguished Scholarly Publication award in 2017.

Kevin Durrheim is a Professor of Psychology at the University of KwaZulu-Natal. His broad interests are in the field of social psychology of intergroup relations. He has a programme of research related to racism, segregation and social change which is embedded in the South African context in which he works and lives. His publications *Qualitative Studies of Silence* (Murray & Durrheim (eds) 2019), *Race Trouble* (Durrheim, Mtose & Brown, 2011) and *Racial Encounter* (Durrheim & Dixon, 2005, Routledge) have developed from this research programme.

Sean Elias studies racial and class group inequalities, imbalances, and injustices, such as examining ways racism operates in social science, identifying social and intellectual problems associated with the marginalization of critical black social thought, and exposing the dysfunctional social world of the contemporary power elite. He is lead author with Joe R. Feagin of *Racial Theories in the Social Sciences: A Systemic Racism Critique* (Routledge, 2016) and is now teaching at Colorado Mesa University while finalizing his ethnographic portrait and cultural critique of the power elite who frequent Aspen, Colorado (Routledge, forthcoming).

Umut Erel is Senior Lecturer in Sociology at the Open University, UK. She has widely published on the intersections of migration, ethnicity, citizenship, racism, gender, class. Her methodological interests are in creative and participatory methods for research and engagement. She was PI of Participatory Arts and Social Action in Research, exploring theatre and walking methods for research (http://fass.open.ac.uk/research/projects/pasar) and led the Open University's contribution to the 'Who are We?' Project at Tate Exchange, reflecting on migration, citizenship, participation and belonging across arts, activism and academia https://www.whoareweproject.com for recent publications, see http://www.open.ac.uk/people/ue27

Philomena Essed is professor of Critical Race, Gender and Leadership Studies at Antioch University's Graduate School of Leadership and Change and Affiliated Researcher at the University of Utrecht's Gender Graduate Program. She holds a PhD from the University of Amsterdam and Honorary Doctorate degrees from the University of Pretoria (2011) and Umeå University (2015). In 2011 she was honoured with a Knighthood in the name of the Queen of the Netherlands. Well known for introducing the concepts of *everyday racism* and *gendered racism,* Essed also pioneered in developing theory on *social and cultural cloning.* The now classical 1984 (in Dutch) *Alledaags Racisme* (English version, *Everyday Racism,* 1990) was republished in 2018 with additional chapters. Other books include *Understanding Everyday Racism, Diversity: Gender, Color and Culture,* and co-edited volumes: *Race Critical Theories; Refugees and the Transformation of Societies; A Companion to Gender Studies* ('outstanding' 2005 CHOICE award); *Clones, Fakes and Posthumans: Cultures of Replication, (2012), Dutch Racism* (2014), and *Relating Worlds of Racism: Dehumanisation, Belonging and the Normativity of European Whiteness* (2018). Her current focus is on humiliation, dehumanization, cultures of dignity and ethics of care as experience and practice in leading change.

Joe R. Feagin is Ella McFadden Professor and Distinguished Professor at Texas A&M University. Among his books are *Systemic Racism* (Routledge 2006); and (with Kimberley Ducey) *Racist America* (4th edition, Routledge 2019). He is the recipient of the American Association for Affirmative Action's Fletcher Lifetime Achievement Award and the American Sociological Association's W. E. B. Du Bois Career of Distinguished Scholarship Award, Cox/Johnson/Frazier Award, and Public Understanding of Sociology Award. He was the 1999–2000 President of the American Sociological Association.

Abby Ferber is a Professor of Sociology and Women's and Ethnic Studies at the University of Colorado, Colorado Springs, and Co-founder and Director of The Matrix Center for the Advancement of Social Equity and Inclusion, home of The Knapsack Institute: Transforming Teaching and Learning, and the international journal *Understanding and Dismantling Privilege*, the first and only journal dedicated to examining privilege. She is the author/editor of eight books, including *White Man Falling: Race, Gender and White Supremacy*; editor of *Home Grown Hate*; co-author of *Making a Difference: University Students of Color Speak Out, Privilege: A Reader*, and most recently, *The Matrix of Race: Social Construction, Intersectionality and Inequality*. Her work has been widely published in academic journals and mainstream news sources.

Genesis Fuentes is a doctoral student in the Department of Sociology and the Coordinator of the Lab for Applied Social Science Research (LASSR) at the University of Maryland, College Park. Her research interests are social psychology, identity, ethnic relations, and policing.

Charles A. Gallagher is professor and chair of the Sociology and Criminal Justice Department at La Salle University and a Senior Fellow at Yale University's Urban Ethnography Project. His research focuses on social inequality, race relations and immigration and he has published over fifty articles, reviews and books on these topics. A Fulbright Research Scholar, Professor Gallagher was housed at the University of Birmingham in the UK where he explored attitudes on immigration and Brexit. Professor Gallagher has given over sixty talks on these topics around the country, serves as an expert witness on civil rights cases, and is a frequent media source on these issues, appearing in the press, television and radio interviews over 150 times. He is currently writing a book on how institutions create self-reinforcing accounts of colour-blind egalitarianism that serve to maintain, normalize and reproduce racial inequality.

Yasmin Gunaratnam is a Reader in Sociology at Goldsmiths, University of London. She has an interest in critical race, disability, migration and feminist scholarship and in qualitative and participatory methods. Yasmin's publications include *Researching Race and Ethnicity: Methods, Knowledge and Power* (2003), *Death and the Migrant* (2013) and the co-authored book *Go Home?: The Politics of Immigration Controversies* (2017). Yasmin has edited nine collections and is an editor of *Feminist Review* and the writers of colour digital platform *Media Diversified*.

Natalie-Anne Hall is a doctoral candidate in Sociology at the University of Manchester. Her research focuses on the use of social media to find and share alternative information on controversial political topics. She has previously worked at HM Inspectorate of Prisons, the former Australian Department of Immigration and Citizenship, and UNESCO, and conducted research in Japan.

Laura Henneke is a PhD candidate in Visual Sociology at Goldsmiths, University of London. Her main research interests are the New Silk Road/Belt and Road Initiative, Chinese migration, and architectures of logistics and transportation. She studied Architecture and Urban Design at Technical University of Berlin and Tongji University Shanghai where she investigated the impacts of transnational traders from the Arab world on Chinese urban development in the case of Yiwu, a city famous for its wholesale market of small commodities. She is co-founder of Present Spaces, a collaborative unit at the intersection of research, design, sociology and urbanism, and an active member of the Centre of Urban and

Community Research at Goldsmiths where she teaches in visual urban sociology and co-convenes 'Infrastructural Explorations', a monthly walking event in different locations around London.

Matthew W. Hughey is Associate Professor of Sociology at the University of Connecticut (USA). He also holds affiliate positions at Nelson Mandela University (South Africa), the University of Barcelona (Spain), and the University of Cambridge (England). Professor Hughey's research examines the forms and functions of race and racism and has received wide support and honours, such as the National Science Foundation, Russell Sage Foundation, and the Fulbright Commission.

Marcus Anthony Hunter is the Scott Waugh Endowed Chair in the Division of the Social Sciences, Professor of Sociology, and Chair of the Department of African American Studies at UCLA. He is author of three books; *Black Citymakers: How the Philadelphia Negro Changed Urban America* (2013), *Chocolate Cities: The Black Map of American Life* (2018), co-authored with Zandria F. Robinson, and *The New Black Sociologists* (2018, Routledge).

Hannah Jones writes, researches and teaches about racism, migration control, belonging, and public sociology, and is an Associate Professor of Sociology at the University of Warwick. She is the author of *Negotiating Cohesion, Inequality and Change: Uncomfortable positions in local government* (2013) which won the British Sociological Association Philip Abrams Prize for best first and sole-authored monograph in UK sociology. She co-edited *Stories of Cosmopolitan Belonging: Emotion and Location* (2014, Routledge) with Emma Jackson, and co-authored *Go Home?: The Politics of Immigration Controversies* (2017) with Yasmin Gunaratnam, Gargi Bhattacharyya, William Davies, Sukhwant Dhaliwal, Kirsten Forkert, Emma Jackson and Roiyah Saltus. Hannah's next book, *Violent Ignorance,* is due out in 2020. On Twitter she is @uncomfy.

Tiffany Joseph is Associate Professor of Sociology and International Affairs Program at Northeastern University. Her research and teaching interests explore: race, ethnicity, and migration in the Americas; the influence of immigration on the social construction of race in the U.S., immigrants' health and healthcare access; immigration and health policy, and the experiences of minority faculty in academia. She is the author of *Race on the Move*: *Brazilian Migrants and the Global Reconstruction of Race* (2015) and her work has been published in various peer-reviewed journals.

Riva Kastoryano is a research director at the CNRS (National Center for Scientific Research), and Professor at SciencesPo Paris. Her work focuses on identity and minority issues and more specifically to their relations to states in France, Germany, the United States. She was a lecturer at Harvard University 1984–1987, a fellow at the Institute for Advanced Studies (Princeton), at Wissenschaftskolleg in Berlin, at the Radcliffe Institute for Advanced Studies (Harvard U.). She has been teaching as a visiting Professor at the New School for Social Research since 2005. Her last book *Burying Jihadis* (2018) treats the relationship between belonging and territory in globalization, built around the question of transnational nationalism. Her other recent books are *Negotiating Identities: States and Immigrants in France and Germany* (2002). She also edited *Quelle identité pour l'Europe? Le multiculturalisme à l'épreuve* (1998 and 2005 for the second edition); *Nationalismes en mutation en Méditerranée Orientale* (Changing Concept of Nationalism) (with A.Dieckhoff) Paris, Ed.du CNRS 2002; and *Les codes de la différence. Religion, Origine, Race en France, Allemagne et Etats-Unis* (Codes of Otherness. Religion, Ancester and Race in France, Germany and the United States) (2005) and *Turkey Between Nationalism and Globalization* (Routledge 2013).

David Kelly is a Research Fellow and Human Geographer at the HOME Research Hub, Deakin University. His research into housing-related issues seeks to promote indigenous rights and agendas, access and inclusion, and practices of commoning.

Caroline Knowles is Professor of Sociology at Goldsmiths, University of London and director of the British Academy *Cities and Infrastructure Programme*. She holds a Major Leverhulme Fellowship supporting her current research *Serious Money: A Mobile Investigation of Plutocratic London*. She is the author of many books and articles concerned with cities, space, ethnicity, migration and mobilities as well as visual and biographical research methods. Her most recent books involve collaboration with photographers: *Flip-Flop: A Journey Through Globalisation's Backroads* (2014) (www.flipfloptrail.com) and *Hong Kong: Migrant Lives, Landscapes and Journeys* (2009) with Douglas Harper.

Anna Korteweg is Professor and Chair of Sociology at the University of Toronto Mississauga. Her research focuses on the ways in which the perceived problems of immigrant integration are constructed in the intersections of gender, religion, ethnicity and national origin. From this critical vantage point, she has analysed debates surrounding the wearing of the headscarf, so-called 'honour-based' violence, and Sharia law. Current research projects focus on racialization and LGBTQ/gender rights construction in refugee politics, the criminalization of migrant status, and the citizenship implications of refugee sponsorship.

Tony Kushner is Professor in the Parkes Institute for the Study of Jewish/non-Jewish Relations and History Department at the University of Southampton. His most recent books are *The Battle of Britishness: Migrant Journeys since 1685* (2012) and *Journeys from the Abyss: The Holocaust and Forced Migration from the 1880s to the Present* (2017). He is currently working on a study of a Jewish triple murderer and, with Dr Aimee Bunting, *Co-Presents to the Holocaust*. He is co-editor of the journal *Patterns of Prejudice* and deputy editor of *Jewish Culture and History*.

Charles Leddy-Owen is Senior Lecturer in Sociology at the University of Portsmouth. Since 2014 he has written numerous journal articles and a book – *Nationalism, Inequalities and England's Political Predicament* – exploring racism and nationalism in contemporary England.

Nasar Meer is Professor of Race, Identity and Citizenship in the School of Social and Political Sciences at the University of Edinburgh. His publications include: *Islam and Modernity* (4 Volumes) (ed, 2017); *Interculturalism and Multiculturalism: Debating the Dividing Lines* (co-ed, 2016); *Citizenship, Identity and the Politics of Multiculturalism: The Rise of Muslim Consciousness* (2015, 2nd edition); *Racialization and Religion* (ed, 2014), *Race and Ethnicity* (2014) and *European Multiculturalism(s)* (co-ed, 2012). In 2016 he was awarded the Royal Society of Edinburgh (RSE) Thomas Reid Medal for excellence in the social sciences, and in 2017 he was elected as a Fellow of the Academy of Social Sciences.

Charles W. Mills is a Distinguished Professor of Philosophy at The Graduate Center, CUNY. He works in the general area of oppositional political theory as centred on class, gender, and race, and is the author of six books: *The Racial Contract* (1997); *Blackness Visible: Essays on Philosophy and Race* (1998); *From Class to Race: Essays in White Marxism and Black*

Radicalism (2003); *Contract and Domination* (co-authored with Carole Pateman) (2007); *Radical Theory, Caribbean Reality* (2010); and *Black Rights/White Wrongs: The Critique of Racial Liberalism* (2017). Together with Robert Gooding-Williams he co-edited a special issue of the *Du Bois Review*, 'Race in a "Postracial" Epoch' (Spring 2014), and together with Wulf D. Hund and Silvia Sebastiani, he co-edited *Simianization: Apes, Gender, Class, and Race* (2015).

Aurelien Mondon researches and teaches at the University of Bath. His research focuses predominantly on the impact of racism and populism on liberal democracies and the mainstreaming of far- right politics through elite discourse. His first book, *The Mainstreaming of the Extreme Right in France and Australia: A Populist Hegemony?* was published in 2013 and he recently co-edited *After Charlie Hebdo: Terror, Racism and Free Speech*.

Karim Murji is a Professor of Social Policy at the University of West London. His research focuses on race, culture, and policy and his latest book is *Racism, Policy and Politics* (2017). Some of his other books include, edited with Asma Sayed, *The Transnational Imaginaries of MG Vassanji* (2018); edited with John Solomos, *Theories of Race and Ethnicity: Contemporary Debates and Perspectives* (2015); and edited with Gargi Bhattacharyya, *Race Critical Public Scholarship* (Routledge 2014). With Sarah Neal, he is the Editor of *Current Sociology*. With Sarah Neal he edited the 2015 special issue of *Sociology* on 'Sociologies of everyday life'; and with Giovanni Picker and Manuela Boatca he co-edited a 2019 special issue of *Social Identities* on 'Racial Urbanities'

Sarah Neal is Professor of Sociology at the University of Sheffield. Sarah researches and writes in the fields of race, ethnicity, multiculture, community, belonging and place. Recent publications include *Friendship and Diversity: Class, Ethnicity and Social Relationships in the City* (with C. Vincent and H. Iqbal, 2018) and *Lived Experiences of Multiculture: The New Social and Spatial Relations of Diversity* (with K. Bennett, A. Cochrane and G. Mohan 2017, Routledge). Sarah is co-editor of *Current Sociology* and an editorial board member of *Ethnic and Racial Studies*.

Yin Paradies is Chair in Race Relations at Deakin University. He conducts research on the health, social and economic effects of racism as well as anti-racism theory, policy and practice across diverse settings, including on the Internet, in workplaces, schools, universities, housing, the arts, and healthcare settings.

Rashawn Ray is Associate Professor of Sociology and Executive Director of the Lab for Applied Social Science Research (LASSR) at the University of Maryland, College Park. He is also one of the co-editors of *Contexts Magazine: Sociology for the Public*. Formerly, Ray was a Robert Wood Johnson Foundation Health Policy Research Scholar at the University of California, Berkeley. Currently, he is David M. Rubenstein Fellow at The Brookings Institution in Washington D.C.

James Rhodes is a Lecturer in Sociology and a member of the Centre on Dynamics of Ethnicity (CoDE) at the University of Manchester. His research interests lie in the areas of racism and ethnicity, urban studies, and deindustrialization. His work has appeared in journals such as *Ethnic and Racial Studies, Journal of Ethnic and Migration Studies, Urban Geography*, and *Sociology*.

Michael L. Rosino is a PhD Candidate in Sociology at the University of Connecticut. His research centers the role of racial politics in parties; power; public debates; mass media; collective action; and social interactions. His work has appeared in *Social Currents, Sociology of Race and Ethnicity, Ethnic and Racial Studies,* and *Deviant Behavior.* His dissertation research examines how the participants of a progressive grassroots party in the Northeast engage with issues of racial and political inequality through their identities, habits, and political strategies. His first book, *Debating the Drug War: Race, Politics, and the Media,* is forthcoming with Routledge. It investigates mass and digital media in the debate over drug policy and demonstrates the influence of political ideologies and identities, the omission of racial justice concerns, the use of implicit racial meanings, and identity construction through racial discourse.

Graziella Moraes Silva is Assistant Professor in Anthropology and Sociology at the Graduate Institute of International and Development Studies. Between 2011 and 2016 she was at the Department of Sociology of the Federal University of Rio de Janeiro (UFRJ), Brazil and is still affiliated to the Graduate Program in Sociology and Anthropology (PPGSA) and to the Interdisciplinary Network for the Study of Inequality (NIED) at the same university. Graziella works at the intersection between inequality studies and cultural sociology. Her current research projects focus on comparative race relations and elite's perceptions of poverty and inequality. She is one of the authors of *Getting Respect: Dealing with Stigmatization and Discrimination in the United States, Brazil and Israel* (2016), and *Pigmentocracies: Ethnicity, Race, and Color in Latin America* (2014).

Sivamohan Valluvan is Assistant Professor of Sociology at the University of Warwick. Valluvan has written widely in the areas of racism and ethnicity, nationalism and cosmopolitanism, and social and cultural theory more broadly. His monograph, *The Clamour of Nationalism,* was published in 2019.

Peter Wade is Professor of Social Anthropology at the University of Manchester. He held a British Academy Wolfson Research Professorship (2013–2016). His publications include *Blackness and Race Mixture* (1993), *Race and Ethnicity in Latin America* (2010), *Race, Nature and Culture: An Anthropological Perspective* (2002) and *Race and Sex in Latin America* (2009), *Mestizo Genomics: Race Mixture, Nation, and Science in Latin America* (2014), and *Race: An Introduction* (2015). His most recent book is *Degrees of Mixture, Degrees of Freedom: Genomics, Multiculturalism and Race in Latin America* (2017). In 2017–2019, with Mónica Moreno Figueroa, he co-directed a project on *Latin American Antiracism in a 'Post-Racial' Age.*

Michel Wieviorka, is Professor at the Ecole des Hautes Etudes en Sciences Sociales, is the President of the Fondation Maison des Sciences de l'Homme (FMSH). From 2006 to 2010, he was President of the International Association of Sociology AIS/ISA, where he created the online encyclopedia Sociopedia. He has been a member of the ERC (European Research Council) Scientific Council since 2014. He heads the journal, SOCIO (with Laetitia Atlani-Duault), which he launched in 2013. His research has focused on conflict, terrorism and violence, racism, anti-Semitism, social movements, democracy and the phenomena of cultural difference. His more recent books are *Evil, Retour au sens* (éd. Robert Laffont), *Antiracistes* (éd. Robert Laffont) *Face au mal* (éd. Textuel). He is currently leading an international and multidisciplinary scientific program on violence and exiting violence.

Aaron Winter is Senior Lecturer in Criminology at the University of East London. His research is on the extreme/far right, with a focus on racism, violence and mainstreaming. He is co-editor of *Discourses and Practices of Terrorism: Interrogating Terror* (2010) and more recently, *Historical Perspectives on Organised Crime and Terrorism* (2018). He has published in the journals *Ethnic and Racial Studies*, *Identities: Global Studies in Culture and Power*, *Sociological Research Online* and *Women and Performance: A Journal of Feminist Theory*.

Ruth Wodak is Emerita Distinguished Professor of Discourse Studies at Lancaster University, UK, and affiliated to the University of Vienna. Besides various other prizes, she was awarded the Wittgenstein Prize for Elite Researchers in 1996 and an Honorary Doctorate from University of Örebro in Sweden in 2010. In 2011, she was awarded the Grand Decoration of Honour in Silver for Services to the Republic of Austria, and 2018, the Lebenswerk Preis for her lifetime achievements, from the Austrian Ministry for Women's Affairs. She is member of the British Academy of Social Sciences and member of the Academia Europaea. Recent books include: *The Routledge Handbook of Language and Politics* (2018, with B. Forchtner), *Europe at the Crossroads* (2019, with P. Bevelander), and *The Politics of Fear* (2015).

Zacharias Zoubir is a PhD student in philosophy at University Paris Nanterre (Sophiapol research center). His research focuses on race, social theory and the critique of political economy. With Abdellali Hajjat, he is also conducting empirical research on the experience of racism in the university space. His latest academic article in English is '"Alienation" and critique in Marx's manuscripts of 1857–58 ("Grundrisse")', The European Journal of the History of Economic Thought, no. 25 (5), October 2018.

General introduction

John Solomos

Thinking differently about contemporary racisms

At the end of his Du Bois Lectures delivered at Harvard in 1994 Stuart Hall sought to capture the challenge faced by scholars who were trying to understand the transformations in the new cultural politics of race, ethnicity and nation when he argued:

> The task of theory in relation to the new cultural politics of difference is not to think as we always did, keeping the faith by trying to hold the terrain together through an act of compulsive will, but to learn to *think differently*.
>
> *(Hall 2017: 174)*

Hall was, of course, writing in the aftermath of the intense debates about the cultural politics of race and ethnicity that had taken place during the 1980s and 1990s. He was particularly intrigued by the limitations of existing theoretical paradigms when it came to making sense of the new political formations around questions of difference such as race, ethnicity and nation (Henriques, Morley and Goblot 2017; hooks and Hall 2018). But more generally he wanted to explore more fully the relations of power that permeated these categories, both historically and in the present. It was on this basis that he used the Du Bois Lectures as an opportunity to explore both the opportunities offered by existing theories and the need to *think differently*.

Although Hall made this statement in its original form in the 1990s, it was interesting to read it again now that it has been published, some decades after the original lectures. In the period since Hall delivered his lectures there has been both a rapid expansion of research and scholarship in the field of race and racism and a flowering of new research perspectives and theoretical paradigms. New generations of scholars have emerged that have sought to broaden the boundaries of research, to question the dominant theoretical frames and to introduce new analytical and political frames (Collins and Solomos 2010; Emirbayer and Desmond 2015; Goldberg and Solomos 2002). Indeed, it can be argued without any exaggeration that a number of new generations of scholars have helped to shape and reshape this field of research both at the end of the 20th century and at the beginning of the 21st century. At the same time, scholarly debates about race and racism have expanded greatly just as these issues have come to the fore in key political and policy debates about racialised inequalities, migration and cultural and religious diversity. Yet, in many ways it seems curious that Hall's injunction to move beyond dominant research agendas and to learn to think differently remains as timely today as when Hall was seeking in his meticulous and reflective manner to outline a way of looking at race, ethnicity and nation through a different lens.

It is partly in response to Hall's challenge that we began thinking about putting together what has now evolved into the *Routledge International Handbook of Contemporary Racisms*. In particular, it seemed to us that there was still a need to question the ways in which research agendas on race and racism had evolved and changed over the past few decades, and to discuss the development of new areas of scholarship and research and to explore areas that had been relatively neglected by dominant research agendas. As the project developed it also became evident that there was a need for a volume that brought together both leading and emerging scholars to address key areas of research and to outline potential avenues for a conversation about where the study of race and racism is currently heading as well as to take a forward look and highlight lacunae and gaps in research. Before moving on to discuss the overarching concerns of the *Handbook* we want to explore some of the features of the historical background that have helped to shape the current conjuncture.

Looking forward

There seems little doubt as we survey developments over the past two decades that, both in terms of scholarly research agendas and political transformations, we are going through a period of important changes in the study of race and racism. This is, of course, not the first time that we have seen such a fundamental transformation in this field. Michael Banton, one of the foundational figures in the sociological study of race relations, famously argued that the early 1960s can be seen as a 'turning point' in the study of race and ethnic relations (Banton 1974). Banton linked this 'turning point' to the intellectual transformations that came to the fore in this period as well as the wider changes in social and political debates about race relations in societies such as the United States and the UK among others. More generally, Banton argued that the social and political struggles that helped to shape the Civil Rights Movement in the United States were creating a space for new perspectives to emerge, including more critical and radical paradigms. While this is not the place to discuss Banton's account of the early 1960s, one could argue that in the period since the 1980s we have seen another, and in many ways, more complicated 'turning point' in research agendas that has transformed both how we think about race and racism and how we develop conceptual and methodological tools that can address current realities. Certainly, the period since the 1980s can be seen as a highpoint in the development of both existing research agendas and the opening up of new areas of investigation and research (Back and Solomos 2009; Goldberg 2015; Meer and Nayak 2015).

This is even more the case in the current conjuncture, which has been marked by increasing recognition that questions about race and racism are central to social and political relations on a global scale. In the first two decades of the 21st century we have seen a resurgence of both more classical forms of racism and a growth of what some define as forms of new racism or cultural racism. As debates about immigration, refugees, terrorism and multiculturalism have become entangled with questions about racial difference and national identity there has been a growth of both extreme right political activism and more mainstream expressions of racialised ideologies (Elias and Feagin 2016; Meer and Nayak 2013; Murji and Solomos 2015). At the same time, we have seen a growth of avowedly anti-racist movements and ideas, both at national and more localised levels, that seek to provide alternative political and ideological frames for a discussion of how to counter racism in all its forms and to promote alternative modes of living together with difference (Hage 2015;

Lentin 2015; Nelson and Dunn 2016; Paradies 2016). In the case of refugees, we have seen both strong mobilisations against their arrival and counter-mobilisations that support providing them with humane treatment and support (see Chapter 7 by Kushner). Both of these developments have left their mark, and it is important to acknowledge the reality that both racism and anti-racism are helping to shape our experiences of the global environment as well as the everyday realities in specific societies. This is something of a recurrent theme throughout this volume and features as a key issue in a number of chapters (see in particular Chapter 15 by Bojadžijev, 32 by Wieviorka and 34 by Essed).

As a result of this evolving conjuncture, it can be argued that we have seen a new phase in the study of race and racism, particularly in the social sciences and humanities. This is evidenced in the growing bodies of scholarship and research in various geopolitical contexts, which have helped to push the boundaries of this field into new areas and disciplinary boundaries. These bodies of research have resulted in a wide range of monographs that have studied the impact of racism in specific national settings as well as from a comparative angle. There has also been a rapid expansion over the past four decades in the number of specialised journals covering questions about race and racism in the social sciences, as well as in more specific sub-fields such as gender, cultural studies and philosophy. There has, as a result, been a proliferation of articles about race, racism and ethnicity in many disciplines, including sociology, geography, politics and international relations, social policy, criminology and related fields. It is also worth noting that we have seen many of the mainstream journals in these fields open up much more to covering the latest research on race and racism.

While much of the research is carried out in specific national intellectual environments there is also at least some evidence that there are conversations developing among researchers that seek to bring about a greater awareness of the need for a comparative research focus as well as to give voice to cross-disciplinary research agendas. The need for more comparative research in this field has been clear for some time and has been the subject of both theoretical and empirically focused debate. Certainly, interdisciplinary initiatives have enabled scholars of race and ethnicity to draw upon knowledge bases and theoretical traditions both from pre-existing academic disciplines such as sociology, political science, history and anthropology, as well as from interdisciplinary areas such as women's studies, cultural studies, postcolonial studies, queer theory and similar areas of inquiry. This changing intellectual context has infused a new vitality into the field. We hope that this sense of vitality comes through in the contributions we have been able to include in the ten parts of the *Handbook*. However, it remains the case that whatever the success of efforts to generate more comparative research and to bring about more conversations that cross national and disciplinary divides, we still live in an environment where much of the core research in this field is carried out within quite limited intellectual and scholarly environments. While there are some hopeful signs of increasing dialogue and collaboration it remains a source of concern that the need for more of a comparative frame for research and scholarship remains more of a hope than a reality (see Chapter 4 by Joseph and 5 by Moraes Silva).

Overarching themes

Bearing this background in mind, it seems important to restate the overarching concerns that have helped to shape the *Handbook* and its ten component parts. The first of the concerns that helped to shape the *Handbook* was the need to provide an overview of key current debates and developments in this rapidly evolving field of scholarship and research. While there have been other efforts to produce such overviews that have helped to fill some of the gaps in research and knowledge, we felt that there was a need for a more comprehensive snapshot of this fast-changing area. Rather than focus on some of the main areas of scholarship we broadened the scope of the *Handbook* to include issues that have received relatively little coverage, and we have therefore invited contributions focusing more on issues such as nationalism, intersectionality, culture and religion and research methods. In doing so we very much hope we have been able to broaden both the scope of what we have been able to cover and to provide avenues that can be usefully explored in the future.

Second, we wanted to be open to developing a space to think about our key concepts and questions differently. This is something that we noted at the beginning of this Introduction was of some importance to us and we have therefore intentionally sought to include a range of perspectives that cover different conceptual strands in the study of race and racism, and it would be wrong to claim that all the different voices that are heard in the various chapters are in agreement about theory or approaches to empirical research. Rather than seek to include research that speaks from a particular perspective, we have intentionally sought out authors who can speak from a broad range of theoretical and methodological starting points. Indeed, a recurrent theme to be found in many of the chapters is a concern to explore a range of theoretical and methodological approaches in order to take the analysis of contemporary forms of racism beyond the dominant current analytical frames that have shaped research over the past few decades.

Third, we have also sought to highlight the need for on-going conversations about how we can develop more of a dialogue across the limits imposed by national scholarly traditions. Perhaps the most important site for such a dialogue to develop is the need for a fuller engagement between scholarship in the US and the emerging scholarly traditions in Europe, Latin America, Asia, Africa and other parts of the globe. Given the developments that we have seen over the past few decades we now have growing bodies of research that seek to provide new theoretical perspectives on key facets of both race and racism. Yet it is noticeable that there is still relatively little of a conversation between scholars based in the US and those working in European or other research contexts. The relative absence of a dialogue between these rapidly expanding bodies of scholarship and research is a feature of the current situation, and we hope that the various parts of this *Handbook* help to illustrate the possibilities for developing a conversation that can include scholars on both sides of the Atlantic and beyond.

By focusing on these overarching concerns together we hope that we have produced a volume that addresses the need for a more systematic account of the changing research agendas in this field and the emergence of new areas of interest. More importantly, of course, we have sought to bring together contributions from authors who have something to say on the basis of their scholarly research.

Contemporary racisms in perspective

One of the themes that runs through all the parts of the *Handbook* is the need to locate the more contemporary developments, on which many of the individual chapters are inevitably focused, in a more historical perspective that sees them as the product of historical processes that have helped to shape the present. In particular, the development of transatlantic slavery in the Americas, European colonialism and imperial expansion, the articulation of forms of racial thought, migration, racist and anti-racist mobilisations and the articulation of nationalism are all in different ways highlighted as playing an important role in shaping important features of the present situation (Crenshaw, Harris, HoSang and Lipsitz 2019; Molina,

HoSang and Gutiérrez 2019; Singh 2017). Part of the challenge faced by contemporary scholarship is how to balance the need to situate the present in a wider historical perspective without simply reducing the present to the past.

At the same time the need to broaden our vision towards a more nuanced historical perspective has been made more evident by recent trends. A case in point can be found in the efforts to make sense of the trends that have come to the fore in the first two decades of the 21st century, including research on ethno-nationalism and transnational religious mobilisation. If we take the case of ethno-nationalism, there seems little doubt that it has been the subject of much scholarly interest over the past two decades (see Chapter 13 by Wodak, 20 by Hughey and Rosino, and 21 by Rhodes and Hall). Partly as result of the re-emergence of new forms of ethno-racial and nationalist political discourses in this period, we have seen a growth of research on questions concerning the role of racist movements and ideologies, the rise of right-wing movements and the emergence of forms of exclusionary nationalism (Leddy-Owen 2019; Valluvan 2019). Much of this body of research has been focused on the need to make sense of what is new about these forms of mobilisation and to tease out their impact, both nationally and transnationally. This is particularly the case when it comes to the growing meshing together of forms of populism, from both the right and the left, and nationalism in the discourses of political and social movements.

A similar point can be made about the growing bodies of scholarship on the emergence of transnational forms of religious mobilisation and the growth of movements and networks within minority communities in the West. While there was a certain amount of research on religious and cultural identities in the decades at the end of the 20th century, there seems little doubt that in the aftermath of 9/11 there was a massive expansion of both funded and other scholarly research that focused on this phenomenon (Mahmood 2017; Sageman 2019; Selod 2018). Much of the emerging scholarship in this area has highlighted the need for a more systematic research-based understanding of the intersections between religious and racialised forms of identity and the development of new bodies of empirical knowledge and theoretical concepts that will allow us to make sense of the contemporary situation.

While it is beyond doubt that we have seen some important new research during these two decades that has been focused on making sense of these new trends, there is also an awareness that there remain important gaps in our knowledge of this new situation. In part, this is the result of the need to make sense of phenomena that are relatively new, or at least are expressed in new ways within the turbulence of the contemporary period. In this changing social, political and intellectual context, there are a number of issues that remain to be addressed more fully and it is to this issue that we now turn.

Rethinking the study of race and racism

Following on from the issues that we have discussed above it is also important to explore how we can rethink the study of race and racism and move it beyond the limitations that we have discussed thus far. In particular, we need to explore questions such as: how can we best develop the tools that we need to analyse the changing research agendas that have helped to shape this field of scholarship and research? What new theoretical tools will help us to understand new forms of racism and their expression in political and social environments? What methodological tools will help us to develop new research agendas that help to capture the complexities of the present situation? While it is beyond the scope of a single volume such as this to tackle all of these questions, there is much in the volume that helps us to address them, both at the level of theory and in terms of the empirical focus of research.

It is important to remember, however, that the questions that typically preoccupy scholars of race and ethnicity usually do not emerge solely or even primarily from scholarly literature. Rather, the political and social aspects of race and ethnicity across specific local, regional, national and increasingly global contexts catalyse much work in contemporary race and ethnic studies. When it comes to the study of race and ethnicity, it is impossible for the field to extract itself from the subject of its study; nor (some would say) should it. As a result, work in this field stands in a particular relationship to contemporary social and political realities. As many of the chapters in the *Handbook* explore in some detail it is precisely because political and policy agendas are always part of any discussion of contemporary racisms that we need to pay close attention to the links between research and socio-political processes.

There seems little doubt that one of the key questions we shall have to confront in the future is how to understand and tackle the social and political impact of racism, both as a set of ideas and as a form of political mobilisation. In broad terms we shall need to be able to explain both the roots of contemporary racist ideas, practices, organisational forms and social movements, as well as the source of their current appeal. Yet it is precisely on the issue of their contemporary appeal that current research seems to be least enlightening. Researchers have not, by and large, had much to say about the reasons why we have seen the persistence of racist ideas and practices in recent times. We shall also need to consider what kinds of counter-strategies can be adopted to challenge new types of racist mobilisation. Again, research on the historical trajectories of anti-racist mobilisation is enlightening, yet we do not as yet have a clear understanding of the reasons why certain anti-racist strategies work and others seem to fail to make much of an impact on expressions of racism (see Chapter 15 by Bojadžijev, 18 by Ray and Fuentes and 33 by Essed).

Perhaps what is striking about the current state of research on race and ethnic relations is that it is a field of scholarship that is still rapidly expanding. We have seen the growth of scholarship and research shaped by a range of conceptual frames, including critical race theory, postcolonial and decolonial theory and feminist theory. Indeed, the past two decades can be seen as a kind of high point in the establishment of ethnic and racial studies as a core theme across both the social sciences and humanities (Crenshaw, Williams, Charles, HoSang and Lipsitz 2019; Go 2018; Valdez and Golash-Boza 2017b). Much of this new research has helpfully pushed the boundaries of race and ethnic studies beyond the more limited research agendas of the second half of the 20th century.

Part of the challenge that we face in trying to make sense of the processes that are shaping the contemporary situation is the need to widen our field of vision and look forward to likely future trends. This is another recurring refrain that runs through the *Handbook*, with a number of authors noting that there is a need to link research focused on the present situation with questions about likely future trends, both in terms of substantive research issues as well as conceptual and theoretical frames of analysis. This is particularly important at a time when we are seeing the articulation of new forms of racist thought and movements that articulate an often messy and confusing mixture of nativist, populist and ethno-national ideology. All of these developments are the subject of discussion in different parts of the *Handbook* (see in particular Chapter 12 by Mondon and Winter, 14 by Ferber, 19 by Valluvan and 21 by Leddy-Owen).

It would be wrong to assume that we can understand these movements and ideas by using our existing theoretical and methodological tools. Rather, there seems to be an obvious need to push the boundaries of existing perspectives further by introducing new analytical frames into the discussion. Thus, we have seen a growing body of research on the need to bring in questions about intersectionality. Part of the complexity of analysing the historical impact of racism is that it is often intertwined with other social phenomena, and indeed it can only be fully understood if we are able to see how it works in specific social settings (Alexander 2006; Alexander and Knowles 2005; Duyvendak 2018; Salem 2017; Valdez and Golash-Boza 2017a). One interesting example of this process can be found in the ways in which modern racial and nationalist ideologies rely on a complex variety of images of race, sexuality and nationhood. Such images often emphasise questions about identity, both in relation to majority and minority communities. Because race and ethnicity are intrinsically forms of collective social identity, the subject of identity has been at the heart of both historical and contemporary discussions about these issues (Brubaker 2004; Calhoun 2007; Gilroy, Sandset, Bangstad and Høibjerg 2018; Leddy-Owen 2019; Malešević 2019).

Yet is also clear that if we aspire to develop our understanding of the social conditions that shape the role of race as a social phenomenon there is a need for more critical discussion about the changing boundaries of scholarship in this field. In the current environment there are a range of challenging and innovative research agendas about race and racism that need to be addressed by sociologists. Charles Gallagher has noted the following in relation to American sociology:

> A glance at any recent sociological annual meeting program reveals a wide range of scholarship where truly novel questions about race are being raised. Emerging areas of inquiry include research on intersections of race, class and gender, racial hybridity, identity formation, colorblind narratives of racism, growing racial inequality, pan-ethnic movements, race and religious intolerance and colorism.
>
> (Gallagher 2007: 553)

This is, in some ways, a reasonable description of the current state of play in the social sciences more generally. But it is also worth noting that even in the decade or so after Gallagher's overview the range of issues that have come to the fore have continued to evolve, with increasing attention to questions such as nationalism, ethnocentrism, anti-racism, whiteness, xenophobia and cultural racism. These issues have also become the subject of debate and analysis in the humanities, cultural studies, geography and related scholarly fields (Bulmer and Solomos 2019; Crenshaw, Williams, Charles, HoSang and Lipsitz 2019; Murji and Solomos 2015).

In the coming period it is perhaps through addressing questions such as these that we can hope to deliver on the promise to connect the study of race and racism with the wider social and political transformations that we are living through. Achieving this promise has not proved easy over the past few decades and it is likely to remain so in the coming period, but it is to be hoped that developments outlined in this *Handbook* provide a base for further research, innovation and reflection on the question of race and its role in our contemporary globalised social environment.

The intersections between race and religious identities among migrant and ethnic minority communities is a good example of the shifts in scholarship and research that we have seen at the beginning of the 21st century. While questions about religious and cultural diversity had begun to form a part of research agendas from the 1990s onwards it is only at the beginning of the 21st century that they have come to constitute an area of great significance for the field of race and ethnic studies. Religion seems in this context to have become more visible, both as a social and research issue, and also increasingly intertwined with race and ethnicity. As a result, the connections between race, ethnicity and religion have become an important arena for social and policy related research in the past decade or so. More importantly, it has become evident in the aftermath of events such as 9/11 (and subsequent terrorist attacks in a number of European countries) that contemporary research about race and ethnicity needs to look more rigorously at the role that religion plays in shaping racialised social relations in contemporary societies (see Chapter 28 by Meer and 29 by Kastoryano). The claims by some groups within minority communities to religious and cultural rights that are seen as outside of the common values of the West have become part of the current climate of public debate and are likely to shape both popular and policy agendas in the coming period. It is important in this context to explore more fully how race, ethnicity and racism increasingly form part of transnational processes, both in terms of movements and political mobilisation and more generally in terms of cultural and mediated flows (see Chapter 29 by Kastoryano).

It is also important to develop more fully conversations that take us beyond the bounds of national scholarly traditions. Given the increasingly global and transnational processes that have shaped contemporary expressions of racism, it is a great pity that we have at best very limited conversations that manage to engage scholars across national research agendas and scholarly traditions (see Chapter 5 by Moraes Silva). The most notable example of the limits on existing conversations can be found in the ways in which theoretical and empirical debates about race and racism in the US and in Europe rarely engage with each other in a substantial manner. There are some notable exceptions to this generalisation (Foner and Simon 2015; Hochschild and Mollenkopf 2009; Kelley and Tuck 2015), but there is still a tendency for researchers on each side of the Atlantic to carry out their research in relative isolation and to engage in little conversation about theory, methods and general research approaches.

As we look at the contemporary conjuncture it is important to address the question of what trends are likely to come to the fore in the coming period. We have argued above that the past few decades have seen the emergence of new forms of racial reasoning that have been shaped by the new politics of immigration and the mobilisation of racialised political agendas. This is not to say that what is at work is simply a process of linear evolution towards what is sometimes called new racism or cultural racism. For what is clear is that the framing of racialised discourses as new does not necessarily help us to understand the complex variety of arguments and ideas that are to be found within contemporary racist discourses. Nor for that matter does it tell us much about what is new and what is old in the racial politics that confronts us in the present environment.

While it is important to be clear about the differences between contemporary forms of racism and the traditional forms of racism, it does seem that some of the arguments about this issue do not really add much analytical clarity. From different perspectives other recent writings have talked of the emergence of meta-racism, new racism or more descriptively new cultural forms of racial discourse. While there is something valuable and important about these arguments, it seems important to emphasise that what some writers have called new racism is not a uniform social entity as such. There is strong evidence that racial discourses are increasingly using a new cultural and social language to justify their arguments, but the search for a uniform definition of new racism has proved intractable and has again emphasised the slippery nature of contemporary racisms (Bobo 2017; Singh 2017). A key problem is that in a very real sense what some writers today call new racism has in some sense always been with us. While it is true that in the nineteenth and early twentieth centuries there was an emphasis in much racial thinking on the biological superiority of some races over others, it is also the case that racial thinking has also always been about idealised and transcendent images of culture, landscape and national identity.

An important feature of racism over the years has been the various ways it has managed to combine different, and often contradictory, elements within specific social and political contexts. In this sense we would agree with Mosse that racism is not a coherent set of propositions that has remained the same in the period since the 18th century, but can best be conceived as a scavenger ideology, which gains its power from its ability to pick out and utilise ideas and values from other sets of ideas and beliefs in specific socio-historical contexts. There is, in other words, no essential notion of race that has remained unchanged by wider political, philosophical, economic and social transformations (Mosse 1995). The characterisation of racism as a scavenger ideology does not mean, however, that there are no continuities in racial thought across time and spatial boundaries. Indeed, it seems obvious that when one looks at the various elements of racial discourses in contemporary societies there are strong continuities in the articulation of images of the other as well as in the we-images which are evident in the ways in which racist movements define the boundaries of race and nation. The evident use of images of the past and evocations of popular memory in the language of contemporary racist and nationalist movements points to the need to understand the complex ways in which these movements are embedded in specific images of landscape and territory.

There seems little doubt that one of the key questions we shall have to confront in the future is how to understand and tackle the social and political impact of racism, both as a set of ideas and as a form of political mobilisation. In broad terms we shall (a) need to be able to explain both the roots of contemporary racist ideas and movements and the source of their current appeal, and (b) need to consider what kinds of counter-strategies can be adopted to challenge new types of racist mobilisation. Yet it is precisely on this issue that current research is least enlightening, since researchers have not had much to say about the reasons why we have seen a resurgence of racist ideas in recent times. Simplistic and monolithic accounts of racism will in the final analysis do little to enlighten us on why it is that is particular social and political contexts millions of people respond to the images, promises and hopes which are at the heart of mass racist movements. Additionally, they tell us little about the possibilities and limits of political strategies and policies that aim to challenge institutionalised racial inequalities. In relation to the long running debate about differentiated citizenship rights, we must be alert to the ways in which the effort to identify and respond to differences among people may turn into a process of reification, leading to a false imputation of essentialist qualities to the members of some group, ignoring important variations within groups. One of the limitations of anti-racist politics as it has developed is precisely this pattern of reifying minority communities as static and unchanging cultural and political collectivities. There is a need to confront the reality that in the present environment we have in one way or another to move beyond the certainties both of racism and simplistic multiculturalism and anti-racism.

It is essential to question deterministic and fixed notions about the relationship between race and racism and broader sets of social relations. We have to develop an analysis of contemporary racisms that is capable of understanding and explaining the power of the diverse racisms that have taken shape in the contemporary environment. In the current conjuncture of political turmoil and tension it has become easy in quite diverse societies, such as Germany, Britain and France, to see migrants and racial minorities as the principal threat to order and social stability. Before we can successfully challenge the hegemony of such ideas, we must be able to understand both why they have arisen at the present time and why it is that they have managed to attract sizeable political support. In order to do this, we must develop an analysis of racism in the present that is adequate to the task of telling us something about the future as well as the past, and in order to do this we need to investigate contemporary racisms in all their diverse forms.

Outlining the *Handbook*

The *Handbook* contains thirty-four chapters and is organised in ten interlinked parts that aim to provide a comprehensive and readable resource for scholars, researchers, students and general readers who would like to explore the changing forms of racism in contemporary societies. For a variety of reasons some parts are more extensive than others, but we hope that in their totality they will provide readers with many of the key issues that are part of both scholarly and everyday civil society debates about race and racism in the contemporary world. The various chapters that make up each part of the *Handbook* do not speak with one voice, and they use different conceptual and empirical points of reference. We hope, however, that when looked at in their totality they share the overarching concern of the volume as a whole to push the boundaries of current debates forward.

In order to facilitate the utility of the *Handbook* we shall begin each part with an introductory overview of the issues that are covered by the chapters they contain. But it is important to say something here about the overarching concerns of the various components of the *Handbook* and the common themes that help to tie them together. The various chapters in Parts I and II seek to provide an overview of theoretical and historical efforts to situate the analysis of contemporary racisms as well as to explore some facets of contemporary racisms in global perspective. Taken together, these two parts provide the starting point for readers who want to get a feel for some of the theoretical debates that have helped to shape the field of study as a whole. The focus of Part III shifts to an exploration of the state and political institutions in structuring contemporary expressions of racism. The chapters in Parts IV and V explore the role of racist and anti-racist movements and ideologies in a variety of national settings. There has been a noticeable expansion of both racist and anti-racist movements in the contemporary period and the chapters in these parts provide an insight into the evolution of these movements. The chapters in Part VI explore the linkages between racism and nationalism at both a conceptual level and through case studies of the mobilisation of nationalism. The research agendas on racism and nationalism have developed in somewhat different directions in recent times but there is much to be gained, as the various chapters in this part argue, from developing more of a dialogue between researchers in these discrete fields. Part VII brings together contributions from a number of leading scholars that focus on the intersections of race and gender. The focus in Part VIII moves on to the interrelationship between racism, culture and religion. Part IX takes up the question of the methodological challenges and dilemmas of doing research in this evolving field. Finally, Part X brings together reflective chapters that address the broad question of how we can think beyond the bounds of racism in the current conjuncture. The chapters in this part of the *Handbook* provide somewhat different perspectives to this question and suggest that there is a need to broaden our vision if we are to understand the complexities of racism in the contemporary period.

Returning to Stuart Hall's argument at the beginning of this Introduction, it seems clear that over the next period we shall face the challenge of how to move beyond the certainties of what we think we know and to *think differently* about race and racism. Rather than assume we know all that we should about the morphology of contemporary racisms, it seems important for us to remember that there are significant gaps in research and scholarly knowledge that need to be addressed, both from a conceptual and empirical angle. We are living through a period that has been characterised by the emergence of new forms of racism, the development of movements that articulate a mixture of xenophobic and anti-immigrant rhetoric, the resurgence of nativist ethno-nationalist populism, and the articulation of anti-Muslim ideologies. In this environment we need to be able to develop the necessary theories and research tools if we are going to be able to make sense of these developments and to develop political strategies that will tackle them in an effective manner. It would be a mistake to see these phenomena simply through the lens of the past and not make the effort to comprehend what is new about them (see Chapter 15 by Bojadžijev and 34 by Essed in this volume).

We hope that readers of the *Handbook* will find that it provides a useful guide to the changing research agendas in this field of scholarship and research.

References

Alexander, Claire E. (2006) 'Introduction: Mapping the Issues' *Ethnic and Racial Studies* 29, 3: 397–410.

Alexander, Claire E. and Knowles, Caroline (eds) (2005) *Making Race Matter: Bodies, Space, and Identity*, Basingstoke: Palgrave Macmillan.

Back, Les and Solomos, John (eds) (2009) *Theories of Race and Racism: A Reader*, London: Routledge.

Banton, Michael (1974) '1960: A Turning Point for the Study of Race Relations' *Daedalus* 103, 2: 31–44.

Bobo, Lawrence D. (2017) 'Racism in Trump's America: Reflections on Culture, Sociology, and the 2016 US Presidential Election' *British Journal of Sociology* 68, S1: S85–S104.

Brubaker, Rogers (2004) 'In the Name of the Nation: Reflections on Nationalism and Patrotism' *Citizenship Studies* 8, 2: 115–127.

Bulmer, Martin and Solomos, John (eds) (2019) *Why Do We Still Talk about Race?*, London: Routledge.

Calhoun, Craig J. (2007) *Nations Matter: Culture, History, and the Cosmopolitan Dream*, London: Routledge.

Collins, Patricia Hill and Solomos, John (eds) (2010) *The Sage Handbook of Race and Ethnic Studies*, London: Sage.

Crenshaw, Kimberlé, Williams, Harris, Charles, Luke, HoSang, Daniel Martinez and Lipsitz, George (eds) (2019) *Seeing Race Again: Countering Coloblindness across the Disciplines*, Oakland: University of California Press.

Duyvendak, Jan Willem (2018) 'Cultural Marxism and Intersectionality' *Sexualities* 21, 8: 1300–1303.

Elias, Sean and Feagin, Joe R. (2016) *Racial Theories in Social Science: A Systemic Racism Critique*, New York: Routledge.

Emirbayer, Mustafa and Desmond, Matthew (2015) *The Racial Order*, Chicago: University of Chicago Press.

Foner, Nancy and Simon, Patrick (eds) (2015) *Fear, Anxiety, and National Identity: Immigration and Belonging in North America and Western Europe*, New York: Russell Sage Foundation.

Gallagher, Charles A. (2007) 'New Directions in Race Research' *Social Forces* 86, 2: 553–559.

Gilroy, Paul, Sandset, Tony, Bangstad, Sindre and Høibjerg, Gard Ringen (2018) 'A Diagnosis of Contemporary Forms of Racism, Race and Nationalism: A Conversation with Professor Paul Gilroy' *Cultural Studies* 33, 2: 173–197.

Go, Julian (2018) 'Postcolonial Possibilities for the Sociology of Race' *Sociology of Race and Ethnicity* 4, 4: 439–451.

Goldberg, David Theo (2015) 'Racial Comparisons, Relational Racisms: Some Thoughts on Method' in Murji, K. and Solomos, J. (eds) *Theories of Race and Ethnicity: Contemporary Debates and Perspectives*, pages 251–262. Cambridge: Cambridge University Press.

Goldberg, David Theo and Solomos, John (eds) (2002) *A Companion to Racial and Ethnic Studies*, Oxford: Blackwell.

Hage, Ghassan (2015) 'Recalling Anti-racism' *Ethnic and Racial Studies* 39, 1: 123–133.

Hall, Stuart (2017) *The Fateful Triangle: Race, Ethnicity, Nation*, Cambridge, MA: Harvard University Press.

Henriques, Julian, Morley, David and Goblot, Vana (eds) (2017) *Stuart Hall: Conversations, Projects, and Legacies*, London: Goldsmiths Press.

Hochschild, Jennifer L. and Mollenkopf, John H. (eds) (2009) *Bringing Outsiders In: Transatlantic Perspectives on Immigrant Political Incorporation*, Ithaca: Cornell University Press.

hooks, bell and Hall, Stuart (2018) *Uncut Funk: A Contemplative Dialogue*, New York: Routledge.

Kelley, Robin D. G. and Tuck, Stephen G. N. (eds) (2015) *The Other Special Relationship: Race, Rights, and Riots in Britain and the United States*, New York: Palgrave Macmillan.

Leddy-Owen, Charles (2019) *Nationalism, Inequality and England's Political Predicament*, Abingdon: Routledge.

Lentin, Alana (2015) 'Racism in Public or Public Racism: Doing Anti-racism in 'Post-Racial' Times' *Ethnic and Racial Studies* 39, 1: 33–48.

Mahmood, Saba (2017) 'Secularism, Sovereignty, and Religious Difference: A Global Genealogy?' *Environment and Planning D: Society and Space* 35, 2: 197–209.

Malešević, Sinisa (2019) *Grounded Nationalism: A Sociological Analysis*, Cambridge: Cambridge University Press.

Meer, N. and Nayak, A. (2015) 'Race Ends Where? Race, Racism and Contemporary Sociology' *Sociology* 49, 6: NP3-NP20.

Molina, Natalia, HoSang, Daniel and Gutiérrez, Ramón A. (eds) (2019) *Relational Formations of Race: Theory, Method, and Practice*, Oakland, California: University of California Press.

Mosse, George L. (1995) 'Racism and Nationalism' *Nations and Nationalism* 1, 2: 163–174.

Murji, Karim and Solomos, John (eds) (2015) *Theories of Race and Ethnicity: Contemporary Debates and Perspectives*, Cambridge: Cambridge University Press.

Nelson, Jacqueline and Dunn, Kevin (2016) 'Neoliberal Anti-Racism: Responding to 'everywhere but Different' Racism' *Progress in Human Geography* 41, 1: 26–43.

Paradies, Yin (2016) 'Whither Anti-racism?' *Ethnic and Racial Studies* 39, 1: 1–15.

Sageman, Marc (2019) *The London Bombings*, Philadelphia: University of Pennsylvania Press.

Salem, Sara (2017) 'Intersectionality and Its Discontents: Intersectionality as Traveling Theory' *European Journal of Women's Studies* 25, 4: 403–418.

Selod, Saher (2018) *Forever Suspect: Racialized Surveillance of Muslim Americans in the War on Terror*, New Brunswick: Rutgers University Press.

Singh, Nikhil Pal (2017) *Race and America's Long War*, Oakland, California: University of California Press.

Valdez, Zulema and Golash-Boza, Tanya (2017a) 'Towards an Intersectionality of Race and Ethnicity' *Ethnic and Racial Studies* 40, 13: 2256–2261.

Valdez, Zulema and Golash-Boza, Tanya (2017b) 'U.S. Racial and Ethnic Relations in the Twenty-first Century' *Ethnic and Racial Studies* 40, 13: 2181–2209.

Valluvan, Sivamohan (2019) *The Clamour of Nationalism: Race and Nation in Twenty-First-Century Britain*, Manchester: Manchester University Press.

Part I
Theories and histories

Introduction

This first part of the *Handbook* focuses on the role of theoretical perspectives in framing the analysis of both contemporary and historical expressions of racism. In a way this is a recurrent theme in the volume as a whole, and many of the chapters in the following parts make important contributions in terms of theoretical and historical aspects of contemporary racisms. Nevertheless, the three chapters we have been able to include in this part address important aspects of contemporary debates.

In the first chapter Sean Elias and Joe R. Feagin outline the key ideas that have framed research in the United States from scholars who have focused on systemic racism and the white racial frame. The theoretical framework on which the chapter draws is most closely associated with accounts of the history of slavery and racial segregation in the United States and the evolution of contemporary forms of racial exclusion and division. But Elias and Feagin argue that their analytical frame can be used more broadly, particularly to examine the evolution of systemic racism in countries that have been shaped by European imperialism and colonialism generated by elite white men. In developing their core arguments, they make a number of suggestive analytical points about how this could be achieved.

In the following chapter, Zacharias Zoubir and Karim Murji shift their attention to an exploration of critical theories of racism and political action that have been influenced by theoretical debates within Marxism and cultural studies. They draw on examples from the history of the US and the UK to highlight how these theoretical perspectives have sought to make sense of political and social mobilisations such as political movements of migrant workers and Black Lives Matter. In exploring these historical and contemporary struggles, they suggest that it is important to understand political action as a product of a complex interplay between social and political processes rather than the product of structural processes. They suggest that it is important to explore in more detail the utility of both Marxist and cultural studies approaches to the study of contemporary forms of racialised political action and mobilisation.

The concluding chapter in this part is by Laura Henneke and Caroline Knowles. It takes a somewhat different approach to the other chapters by using the example of the evolution and development of Chinese London in order to illustrate the need to develop new theoretical frames to analyse cities and forms of racialised migrant ethnicity. They suggest that existing conceptions of Chinatowns are of somewhat limited utility in understanding contemporary forms of Chinese migration and settlement. They argue that Chinatowns are no longer residual inner-city neighbourhoods in which ethnic migrants take refuge in seeking familiarity, and that they are in practice more likely to be on the leading edge of urban development and regeneration. Henneke and Knowles argue that we need new theoretical frameworks that admit the simultaneous emerging dynamism of cities and migrant ethnicities as co-productions of some significance, and not the marginal inner-city markings of long-term ethnic occupation. They illustrate this through a detailed analysis of the ways in which Chinese London is a living and vibrant development, and argue that we need to develop new theoretical tools to allow us to make sense of contemporary processes of migration and settlement.

1

Systemic racism and the white racial frame

Sean Elias and Joe R. Feagin

Introduction

Systemic racism and its *white racial frame* are concepts essential for understanding contemporary racial group dynamics and racial group conflict in the United States and other countries developed through violent social histories of European imperialism and colonialism targeting peoples of color. These racist foundations have been further perpetuated and extended through whites' more recent racialized conquests, exploitations, and genocides targeting peoples of color. In probing the fundamental realities of contemporary societies, knowledge of the societal dysfunctionality of systemic racism and its white racial framing is necessary for conceptualizing well broader group dynamics, systemic power structures and inequalities, and group hierarchies and asymmetry in the US and other nation-states principally controlled by European invaders and their descendants. At the top of these societies, the decision-makers have largely been white men and from elite class (e.g. capitalistic) backgrounds.[1]

First, we provide background on the development of the concepts, systemic racism and the white racial frame, and their relation to other racial conceptualizations. These concepts emanate from a long-marginalized tradition of critical black social thought and are ideas that often run into conflict with mainstream racial analyses produced by whites. Next, we present a theoretical discussion of systemic racism and white racial framing in the US case, assessing the relationship between the two.[2] Our analysis then responds to significant criticisms of systemic racism theory and concludes with a call for challenging systemic racism and white framing in both racial analyses and the larger societal world.

Background

For more than four decades now, Joe Feagin and his colleagues have been refining conceptualizations of "systemic racism" in numerous works such as *Discrimination American Style: Institutional Racism and Sexism* (1978); *White Racism: The Basics* (1995); *Racist America: Roots, Current Realities, and Reparations* (2001/2019), *Systemic Racism: A Theory of Oppression* (2006); *White Party, White Government: Race, Class, and U.S. Politics* (2012); and *Systemic Racism: Making Liberty, Justice, and Democracy Real* (2017). Systemic racism refers to whites' historical and systemic oppression of non-European groups that manifests in the structures and operations of racist societies like the United States.

Rooted ultimately in an older critical black tradition, the need and demand for a systemic racism framework was reinvigorated during the 1950s and 1960s civil rights movements in the US, when black American protests and community uprisings made clear that the still conventional social science and policy concepts like prejudice, bias, and bigotry were far too individualistic to understand well the character of the societal conditions giving rise to these and other anti-racist uprisings by Americans of color. The renewed emphasis on institutional and systemic racism concepts emerged very substantially out of the speeches and writings of activists in the civil rights movements (e.g. Carmichael [Ture] and Hamilton, 1967) and soon spread to the field research and conceptual work of scientists and policymakers of diverse social backgrounds (e.g. Blauner, 1972; Feagin and Feagin, 1978).

Analysis of systemic racism is fundamental in explaining "the centuries-old foundation of American society" and the "racialized character, structure, and development of this society," specifically the "unjustly gained political-economic power of whites" and "continuing economic and other resource inequalities along racial lines" (Feagin, 2001, p. 6, 2006, p. 2).

A central component of systemic racism is the "white racial frame," an "organized set of racialized ideas, stereotypes, emotions, and inclinations to discriminate" that are part of the "color-coded framing of society," which includes a "positive orientation to whites and whiteness and a negative orientation to racial 'others' who are exploited and oppressed" (Feagin, 2001, p. 11; 2006, p. 25). This concept of the white racial frame presents an epistemological tool vital for explicating systemic racism, a concept that explicitly calls out self-identified "whites" as the racial oppressor group who devised and largely supported the social structures of western slavery and colonialism. They continue as the principal engineers and operators of contemporary systemically racist societies that developed out of these earlier oppressive societal realities.

As Feagin demonstrates in *The White Racial Frame: Centuries of Framing and Counter-Framing* (2009/2013), the systemic racism materially and socially constructed by whites was created by, is buttressed by, and is perpetuated through a complex process involving overt and covert white racial framing. Over several centuries, the subtle-to-obvious racialized ideas, narratives, interpretations, and emotions of the white racial frame have produced a broad worldview that permeates the minds and hearts of US citizens of all racial backgrounds, as well as the citizens of other systemically racist societies. Nearly a century ago, W.E.B. Du Bois (1920) perceived that "whiteness" had become the new civic religion in societies shaped by the color line and racial group hierarchies constructed by powerful whites. The white racial frame is central in the establishment, legitimation, and indoctrination of this "new religion of whiteness" and in the key structuring and functions of the socially constructed "white world."

Through the concerted ideas and subordinating practices of whites, the white racial frame upholds and legitimates the white supremacy and Eurocentrism so central to the development and continued operation of systemic racism. This highly consequential framing of social reality in the contemporary period justifies and enables the many aspects of systemic racism. It justifies and facilitates the racist system's unjust material gains benefiting whites and obstacles disadvantaging people of color and naturalizes the inegalitarian racial group hierarchy. And it valorizes, elevates, normalizes, and hegemonizes whites, while demonizing, stigmatizing, marginalizing, and devaluing people of color. For example, the white racial frame discounts or distorts the many societal contributions and profound acts of human agency exhibited by people of color in the face of everyday racial oppression, and it excuses or ignores recurring white mob and state violence and the exclusion or segregation of people of color from society's major societal institutions and opportunities.

Joe Feagin's published work, and that with colleagues and students, as well as writings of like-minded scholars who address white racism issues, reveals that systemic racism is very much alive in US society and across the globe. Much research systematically and empirically documents how whites have orchestrated a long-standing, deeply embedded societal racism through an ongoing white racial framing of social realities (see Thompson-Miller and Ducey, 2017). The central arguments of systemic racism analysis—that white racism is flourishing in plain sight and that whites are central in the construction of racist societies—counter positions of mainstream racial analyses that avoid investigating structural racism and avoid discussing whites' role in preserving systemically racist societies and advancing the socio-economic interests of whites as a group, especially those of the white male elite. As a primary starting point, systemic racism analysis identifies whites as architects of racist societies, societies segregated by a persistent construction of the color line that divides social worlds of whites and people of color. White-constructed societies routinely create hurdles and disadvantaged realities for people of color: disparate life chances and social opportunities; differences in access to important social institutions and networks; and status distinctions and different levels of access to basic rights of citizenship and human rights in general.

A systemic racism critique of mainstream racial analysis

Systemic racism analyses often present a different portrait of social reality and of human social interaction than mainstream racial analyses. As noted, they argue that well-institutionalized racism is an ever-present reality largely defining many aspects of certain societies. In contrast, most mainstream analyses of racial matters avoid or downplay discussion of systemic white racism, including indispensable subject matter like white supremacy, racial oppression, genocide, the racial hierarchy, enslavement, colonialism, and the white racial terror, inhumanity, and social pathologies that accurately describe the disquieting realities of systemic white oppression from its earliest days. Mainstream analysts have mostly been silent or diffident on these topics and often discourage or marginalize scholarship that addresses them (Elias and Feagin, 2006).

Not only have most mainstream racial analysts dismissed a deep racism analysis and discussion of whites' role as the responsible social actors, they have often, from the earliest days, promoted white-framed ideas and practices regarding the concept of "race." For example, early white social theorists constructed or espoused biological understandings of race that supposedly disclosed inherent intellectual, physical, and moral differences among different race groups. Today, the growing field of socio-genomics and offshoots of sociobiology have reinvigorated a new racial biologism that substantially mimics some earlier biologic understandings of racial group differences (though now differences are often internal and invisible, not external and visible).

Assimilation theory is another major approach in mainstream racial analysis that often imbeds troubling biases and presuppositions about racial matters. The assimilationist tradition is well-represented in the classic mainstream scholarship on racial matters, including analyses of Robert Park, Gunnar Myrdal, Milton Gordon and their current acolytes. The mainstream assimilationist perspective developed as a white-framed understanding of racial relations that assumes that a white-constructed, white-run society is the model society—and that all people should generally assimilate to its white-constructed norms, beliefs, and behaviors.

While assimilation theorists often attempt to skirt this white-racialized reality, nonetheless assimilation is a mostly one-way process of adaptation to a society which is white-controlled and where whites have highly privileged access to resources and power, relative to most people of color. Assimilation theory usually avoids serious discussion of the vivid discrimination and segregation—the systemic racism—that restricts many non-white individuals and groups from fairly accessing US society's institutions, networks, and opportunities, and thus from many of the socio-economic fruits of full societal membership.

In contrast, more critical social thinkers reflecting on assimilation have recognized that it has long meant one-way adaptation to white racial framing and white dominance and that systemic racism has been the major obstacle for full societal incorporation of most people of color. These analysts have asked such critical questions as: Exactly what are people assimilating toward? For what? And why? These critical questions have been addressed by perceptive black social theorists for centuries. Without question, the deep insights of critical black social thought are essential for understanding the systemic racism that has powerfully shaped US society and its human relations since its 17th-century founding.

The significance of critical black social thought in systemic racism analysis

To chart the centuries-long, social-historical progression of the systemic racism that developed across the globe, contemporary racial theorists ought to substantially ponder the writings of critical black social theorists who have exposed its inner workings and delineated its legitimating white racial framing over many decades now. In large part, the concepts of systemic racism and white racial framing ultimately derive from the critical black theorists' understandings and critiques of white racism, including understandings of the plight of people of color under racial oppression and of whites' position and activities as oppressors. Some of the most trenchant "counter-frames" of people of color deconstructing the white racial frame have been developed by critical black thinkers and activists (Feagin, 2006, 2015; Elias, 2009; Elias and Feagin, 2016). Challenging the dominant white frame demands intellectual and social-action counter-framing. Indeed, most critical black social thinkers were, and continue to be, social activists engaged in the practice of dismantling persisting white racism.

Reading the writings of historical black social thinker-activists—such as Benjamin Banneker, Maria Stewart, David Walker, Frederick Douglass, Anna J. Cooper, W.E.B. Du Bois, Ida B. Wells, Alexander Crummell, and Marcus Garvey, to name just a few—reveals the widespread and harsh racial realties of systemic racism, especially the horrific racist practices and crude racist framing of whites during the long slavery and Jim Crow eras. These black thinkers' critical take on racism as a well-organized structure of oppression and of whites' tyrannical actions propped up with an extensive white racist framing are usually forgotten or ignored, and thus underutilized, in contemporary studies of racial matters. The relevant critical black writings are extraordinarily perceptive in depicting the realities and operation of systemic racism and in their rigorous critiques of white propagandists who from the early days of the new republic aggressively promoted racist framing and subjugating racist actions flowing out of it (Elias and Feagin, 2016).

One of the earliest critics of whites' abusive racist beliefs and practices was the black abolitionist David Walker, a courageous thinker-activist who in the 1820s dared to advance scathing criticisms of the oppressive and hypocritical treatment of people of African descent by "white Christians." In his *Appeal to the Coloured Citizens of the World* Walker (1829) describes the destructiveness and immorality of white-imposed slavery, the façade of democracy and other western values, and the social pathologies of whites from an historical and sociological point of view of the oppressed. He offers evidence of whites' social misdeeds and concludes that whites who enslave and exploit fellow humans represent an "unjust, jealous, unmerciful, avaricious and blood-thirsty set of beings, always seeking after power and authority." His distributing the *Appeal* among free and enslaved black Americans signals a critical black theorist putting ideas into action. Walker, a social theorist and public sociologist, performs a necessary racial analysis of whites still missing in most mainstream racial analyses.

Other critical black social thinkers noted above also provide valuable perceptions of the key features of systemic racism and white tactics to maintain racial power over people of color. A pivotal figure is W.E.B. Du Bois (1896, 1915, 1945, 1947), whose critical writings not only address the African slave trade, African civilizations, and European colonialism but also more contemporary realities of systemic racism. Another important black thinker-activist is Ida B. Wells (1892, 1895), who documented well post-Reconstruction white terrorism, the realities of lynching and other violent brutalizing of black people as a means of maintaining a white supremacist racial order; she also developed some of the first critical analyses of racism in the criminal justice system.

Throughout the 20th century and up until today, critical black social theorists have often produced very thorough, theoretically erudite, and empirically rich analyses of US racial matters, analyses that disrupt much mainstream understanding of these matters. They provide deep critical assessments of the institutional and systemic nature of white racism, how the US state upholds systemic racism, the operation of European colonialism in subjugating peoples of color, white tactics to maintain racial power, and the connection between capitalism's growth and exploitation of people of color and their lands (see Ladner, 1973; Blackwell and Janowitz, 1974). They also were the first to critically examine the negative psycho-social effects of white racism on people of color and the connections among racial, class, and gender oppression (intersectionality) (see Collins, 1990). These crucial understandings of racial matters are just a few examples of critical black thought's contribution to understanding the racialized social phenomena later termed systemic racism.

Over time, critical black social scientists have developed a tradition of social thought and research that offers distinctive perspectives on social reality from the position of a marginalized and oppressed racial group. This counter-framed perspective often provides *heightened insights*, as Du Bois (1903, 1915) notes. It offers a raw and detailed portrait of the systemic subjugation of people of color over centuries and of the persisting reality of white-constructed racial group divisions. Building on these earlier analyses, during the peak of the most recent civil rights era (1960s–1970s) numerous critical black social scientists and other social thinkers researched and offered profound insights about US racist realities, including about the dysfunctionality of human relations and the white pathologies central to systemic white racism. Additionally, these critical social scientists presented penetrating critiques of white-framed mainstream social science generally, and of mainstream racial analyses most specifically. They questioned fundamental tenets of white-framed social scientific knowledge, including white social scientists' claims of objectivity, epistemological certainty, and value neutrality in social scientific research (Zuberi and Bonilla Silva, 2008). Indeed, professional associations like the Association of Black Sociologists (ABS) were formed in the 1970s, and continue today, because of the marginalization and alienation of many black social scientists and white resistance to their social science research in regard to black Americans and US racism.

Inside and outside academia, critical black social thinkers of the 1960s–1970s era advanced crucial and precise explanations of white racism. The especially influential 1967 book *Black Power: The Politics of Liberation,* written by black social thinker-activist Stokely Carmichael (later Kwame Ture) and black political scientist Charles Hamilton, in the midst of black community protests and uprisings, first outlined in contemporary detail the "institutional" nature of white racism. They delineated the well-designed organization of the "white power structure" that has been central in the racial colonization and oppression of people of color. While highly marginalized in academic circles, critical racial analyses like those of Carmichael and Hamilton and of critical black sociologists (for example, Joyce Ladner, Robert Staples, and James Blackwell) intellectually liberated a new generation of black social science analysts, as well as other social analysts of color and a few white social scientists (for example, Bob Blauner and Joe Feagin), who focused on institutional and systemic racism issues. Shortly thereafter, a related analytical tradition termed *critical race theory,* also drawing on the older tradition of critical black thinkers, emerged out of critical legal studies in US law schools (see Delgado, 1995).

As we now shift to a discussion of the theoretical understandings of systemic racism theory, we acknowledge that key observations of and approaches to contemporary systemic racism analysis are deeply informed by this centuries-old tradition of critical black social thought.

Theoretical understandings of systemic racism and the white racial frame

So how is systemic racism distinct from and related to other explanations of racism? Why is identification and delineation of the central white racial frame necessary for understanding the system-wide racism that structures racial group relations in contemporary societies like the US? And what are key features of the relationship between white racial framing and the ongoing white-orchestrated racial oppression against people of color that define systemic racism?

Systemic racism

In *Racist America* (2001), Feagin describes key features of systemic racism and the orientation of systemic racism analysis. "Begun some time ago by Frederick Douglass and W.E.B. Du Bois, a revolution in the analysis of American racism is slowly developing, one that views the U.S. social system as imbedding racism *at its very core.*" Systemic racism analysis "places the reality, development, and crises of systemic racism at the heart of U.S. history and society … as a centuries-old *foundation* of American society" and other societies shaped by European colonialism and slavery. Overall this

> systemic racism includes the complex array of [discriminatory practices directed at people of color], the unjustly gained political-economic power of whites, continuing economic and other resources inequalities along racial lines, and white racist ideologies and attitudes created to maintain and rationalize white privilege and power. Systemic here means that the core racist realities are manifested in each of society's major parts … Each major part of U.S. society—the economy, politics, education, religion, the family—reflects the fundamental reality of systemic racism.
>
> *(Feagin, 2001, pp. 5–6)*

In basic terms, systemic racism involves white-generated discrimination and other oppression directed at people of color that is spread throughout a society. This racism is *systemic* in that it embodies wide-ranging racist ideas and practices that infiltrate and thread through most societal institutions, organizations, and networks. White racism is deeply embedded in US social institutions, which reflect and shape racial group relations and positions in society's white-constructed racial hierarchy. In *Systemic Racism: A Theory of Oppression* (2006), Feagin further details these central characteristics of systemic racism. In addition to the central white racial frame, other critical concepts, issues, and themes are examined, including "racial oppression" ("the exploitative and other oppressive practices of whites"); the essential "inter-generational transmission of unjust enrichment [of whites] and unjust impoverishment [of people of color]"; and the great "centrality and injustice of white wealth, power, and privilege" (Feagin, 2006, pp. 2–4).

Unlike most mainstream understandings of racism, the systemic racism approach stresses the *foundational* nature of the white oppression that is grounded in long European and European American histories of slavery, genocide, and colonialism. That is, contemporary racial oppression still has deeply connected roots in past racial oppression. In contrast to most mainstream approaches that do address racism, systemic racism analysis highlights white Europeans' "predatory ethic (of conquering lands and people), ethnocentrism, and xenophobia" as key characteristics of past and present white racism. Most mainstream racial theory tiptoes around assessing the ugly predation and extensive social costs of racism, the enforced asymmetry and persisting imbalance of racial group relations, and the lasting effects of whites' socially constructed racial hierarchy that divides people according to perceived physical characteristics. Few mainstream approaches to discussing racism focus thoroughly and strongly on how present forms of color-coded discrimination regularly relate to those of the past in human destructiveness and social dysfunctionality, how whiteness has become hegemonic in intellectual thought and social practice, and how racism is aggressively and regularly resisted by people of color.

Mainstream analyses of racism tend to focus on studying micro- and meso-level racial "attitudes" and "biases" of individuals and groups, not on the macro-level foundational, institutional, and systemic features of white racist practices and framing. Additionally, many mainstream racial analyses bypass or downplay white racism and stress the social "assimilation" process without assessing the commonplace racial exclusion, segregation, and discrimination of people of color in regard to this process. Frequently, when it is considered by mainstream analysts, racism is individualized and viewed as just one of many "social problems" in an otherwise healthy social system. In contrast, analyses of systemic racism focus on demonstrating its structural, institutional, and systemic characteristics, as well as its operation at the micro- and meso-levels. These analyses are, thus, critical of white-framed assimilation theories of racial relations that do not address white control over the norms of, and pathways to, substantial societal assimilation and incorporation for racialized individuals and groups.

In addition, current systemic racism analyses, like those of earlier institutional and structural racism analyses, problematize certain basic ideas rhetorically articulated by mainstream social scientists, such as freedom, democracy, human rights, racial progress, and civilization. They also question the assumed sanctity, preeminence, and idealization of western beliefs, values, and knowledges. Like the aforementioned black social theorists, systemic racism analysts also question key principles of white-framed social scientific knowledge (e.g. scientific objectivity) and the damaging applications of much white-designed research. A systemic racism approach to understanding racial realities recognizes that:

Much of the social terrain of this society is significantly racialized. Most major institutional and geographical space, acceptable societal norms, acceptable societal roles, privileged language forms, preferred sociopolitical thinking, and favored understandings of history are white-generated, white-shaped, white-imposed, and/or white authenticated. All people, whether they are defined socially as white or not white, live largely within a substantially white-determined environment.

(Feagin, 2006, p. 47)

The white racial frame

A substantial focus on the social history and ongoing mechanisms of systemic racism and its central white racial frame (worldview) is very useful for developing a more exact comprehension of contemporary patterns of white racial oppression. This approach contrasts sharply with numerous mainstream analyses of racial matters that take the white discriminators and related white actors out of the analytical picture or de-emphasize whites' primary and continuing role in the creation and maintenance of racist societies like the US. Such mainstream analyses often imply or claim that "any person or group can be racist."

In contrast, from a systemic racism perspective whites—especially powerful whites—are the primary actors in the construction and maintenance of white racist societies. Specifically, whites' construction and utilization of a legitimating white racial frame has been fundamental in the creation and perpetuation of other aspects of systemic racism (Feagin, 2006, 2010).

Central to the persistence of systemic racism has been the development of a commonplace white racial frame—that is, an organized set of racialized ideas, stereotypes, emotions, and inclinations to discriminate ... the frame and associated discriminatory actions are consciously or unconsciously expressed in the routine operation of racist institutions ... this white framing of society has strongly buttressed anti-Indian genocide, African American slavery, legal segregation, and contemporary incarnations of racial oppression. Today, as in the past, this frame provides an encompassing conceptual and interpretive scheme that shapes and channels assessments of everyday events and encounters with other people.

(Feagin, 2006, pp. 25–26)

An essential function of this white racial framing involves aggressively promoting narratives depicting "a positive view of white superiority, virtue, and moral goodness." This view has become

hegemonic in [U.S.] society—that is, it has been part of a distinctive way of life that dominates all aspects of this society ... the white racial frame is more than just one significant frame among many; it is one that has routinely defined a way of being, a broad perspective on life, and one that provides the language and interpretations that help structure, normalize, and make sense of society.

(Feagin, 2010, p. 11)

Thus, the white racial frame operates in societal mores, religious beliefs, political views, and ideas of beauty, morality, and intelligence; in the dominant culture, including in music, sports, and mainstream media; and across political, economic, educational, and other major institutions.

Reaching into all walks of life, the white racial frame is prominent or just beneath the surface in most social interaction, social thought, and social practices in white racist societies. It follows that "those with the greatest power, white Americans in the US case, have the greatest control over society-wide institutional memories, including those recorded by the media and in most history books, organizational histories, laws, textbooks, films, and public monuments" (Feagin, 2010, p. 15). Because of their position atop the racial hierarchy in society, whites have the greatest power to determine what society's collective memories are and what gets forgotten, specifically the collective forgetting of inconvenient, less flattering social and historical truths regarding systemic racism, particularly whites' oppressive mistreatment and associated mis-framing of people of color for centuries.

Establishing and steering the dominant white frame requires constant activity, a process of white racial framing. More specifically, "white racial framing involves the explanation and construction of social reality from the perspective of the dominant whites, one normally steeped in Eurocentrism" (Elias and Feagin, 2016, p. 7). Successfully propping up the white racial frame requires accenting the racial superiority of whites and whiteness; it also requires delegitimizing, distorting, and marginalizing the perspectives of people of color and their counter-frames. Stated differently, a major aspect of this racial framing involves a general mis-framing of people of color that misrepresents and demeans their character, intelligence, value, and contributions to society.

Negative and false frames of people of color produced by whites have historically been challenged by people of color, including in the intellectually rich historical tradition of critical black social thought. Since the first European colonialist rampages, indigenous genocides, and enslavement of peoples of color, the latter's counter-framing has presented very "different understandings, practices, visions of socio-racial arrangements of society, and the innovative means of realizing that vision … the counter-framing of people of color challenges the status quo and dominant narratives of white racial framing" (Elias and Feagin, 2016, p. 7). Previously, we identified critical black social thought as among the most developed counter-frames to the white frame, but we do not have the space here to adequately discuss the importance of other people of color's counter-frames to that still dominant white racial frame.

In our view, attaining a historically, empirically, and theoretically accurate understanding of the ways that racial oppression developed since early European colonization of people of color requires acknowledging and highlighting the centrality of this legitimating white racial framing. Importantly, explications of systemic racism and its powerful racial frame are necessary for addressing whites' current, still extensive oppression of people of color. This also aids in better understanding and researching the reproduction and reframing of the color line, racial hierarchies, white societal supremacy, and the ongoing unjust enrichment for whites and unjust impoverishment of people of color.

Response to criticisms of systemic racism analysis

As indicated earlier, mainstream racial analyses (e.g. assimilation theory) tend to ignore, de-emphasize, critique, or eliminate racial analyses exposing the everyday workings of systemic white racism. Indeed, some analysts of racial matters—such as Mara Loveman, Andreas Wimmer, Loïc Wacquant, Rogers Brubaker, and Shelby Steele—wish to do away with or severely deconstruct studies of racial meanings, racial groups, and white racism (see Elias and Feagin, 2016). Some of these analysts reject racial analysis entirely and posit theories of post-raciality and colorblindness that contradict the most basic and observable empirical evidence of the historical and contemporary racial oppression still entrenched in systemically racist societies like the United States.

Furthermore, mainstream social scientists who do address contemporary racial matters often do with little epistemological rigor or with predictable white-framed research methods that avoid serious analyses of critical issues like the dominant white elite's role in racial oppression, white racism's well-institutionalized and systemic nature, and the serious societal dysfunctionality and human destruction created by a white racist society. Various mainstream racial analysts have been critical of systemic racism-based theory and methods, which is unsurprising given that these systemic racism studies often address and illuminate the significance of many issues of white-imposed racism that these mainstream racial analysts downplay or bypass (see Elias and Feagin, 2016).

The emphasis of systemic racism analysts on the centuries-old racist framing and enduring racist practices of elite and ordinary whites, the principal maintainers of racist societies like the US, has also been criticized by more progressive race theorists like Michael Omi and Howard Winant (Omi and Winant, 2013). They contend, for example, that systemic racism analyses are not optimistic enough about the positive racial changes over US history. However, investigations of US racism like those of Omi and Winant become problematical when they ignore or downplay the foundational and systemic continuities of US racial oppression, including the continuing role of elite and ordinary whites as central framers and facilitators of contemporary racism (Feagin, Vera, and Batur, 2000; Feagin, 2006; Feagin and Ducey, 2019).

Another criticism of systemic racism analysis is that it has addressed the US context and does not provide understandings of racism beyond the United States. It is true that systemic racism analysis has heavily focused on unraveling the operation of systemic white racism in the US, but that does not mean there have been no significant applications elsewhere. In numerous articles and books Feagin and his colleagues (Batur and Feagin, 1996, 2004; Feagin, 2006; Feagin and Ducey, 2017, 2019) have given substantial attention to global aspects of systemic racism, including many connections and impacts created by US corporations and government agencies overseas. Indeed, systemic racism theory has recently been applied by Feagin's students to several Global South nations, including to explain anti-Haitian framing in the Dominican Republic (Liberato and St. Jean, 2017, pp. 309–332) and to assess climate crises facing numerous island nations, occupied by once or currently colonized people of color (considered disposable by white elites), in the Pacific Ocean (Batur and Weber, 2017). Currently, Ducey and Feagin (2021) are analyzing systemic British racism.

For decades, institutional and systemic racism analysts have made clear that many overseas societies connected to centuries of white European imperialism and colonialism—for example, "settler colonies" like South Africa, Brazil, India, the Philippines, and Australia—have been greatly shaped by systemic white racism and its white rationalizing frame. The countries above (and many others)—as well as the home countries of white colonizers such as Great Britain, Spain, the Netherlands, also among others—have long histories steeped in systemically racist white framing and its racially exploitative practices.

Other recurring criticisms are that systemic racism analyses depict an overly pessimistic vision of racial matters, that systemic racism theory does not perceive adequately the "flexibility" and "transformations" occurring in racial group relations and in the "racial formations" of society (Omi and Winant, 2013). However, this critique is inaccurate in that major changes in US oppression—such as the US move from slavery (after 246 years), to Jim Crow (another 92 years), to contemporary racial oppression (about 50 years so far)—are concretely and thoroughly examined in key systemic racism texts, such as Feagin's *Systemic*

Racism (2006) and *Racist America* (2001, 2019), and in numerous articles in the edited collection of Thompson-Miller and Ducey (2017). While the racialized social world is in flux and does change in some significant ways over time, certain foundational social structures—including systemic racial discrimination and the rationalizing white racial frame—have demonstrably persisted in their US operations for four centuries now. Although the dominant white frame does periodically get reworked and refurbished with some new racist ideas, and even though systemic racism's oppressive practices do sometimes shift, new and reimaged racist ideas and practices are part of centuries-old processes of promoting white supremacy and perpetuating white dominance (Feagin, Vera, and Batur, 2000; Feagin, 2001; Feagin and Ducey, 2017). In addition, systemic racial analyses document that racial progress is typically fueled by the protest and resistance actions of people of color, but that is usually met with new, rehabilitated, or revised forms of white oppression, and that ideas about racial democracy and racial group equality are far-off ideals in the contemporary racial climate (Elias and Feagin, 2017; Feagin and Ducey, 2019). To empirically and theoretically address the actual negative state of US and global racial oppression and consequent inequalities is thus not pessimistic, but indeed quite realistic.

Conclusion: addressing systemic racism in racial analyses and real-world change

Today, systemic white racism still plays a central role in the organization of society and social interactions of racial groups divided according to a white-constructed racial hierarchy. Developing theoretical and empirical insights about systemic racism assists in better understanding past and present social realities in the US and other white racist societies and is a necessary step in dismantling that systemic racism. Yet, not only are mainstream analyses of systemic racism usually lacking, there is an active move away from such analysis. Class-based, ethnicity-based, culture-based, and nationality-based understandings of group relations and social formations, while important for understanding the range of group relations, have sought to eclipse or eliminate white racism analyses, thereby avoiding the serious study of still racialized societies.

In addition to this trend, a more disturbing movement among certain mainstream social scientists is the resurgence of biological explanations of race, namely sociobiology and socio-genomics. This approach to understanding matters of "race" (i.e. supposed "races" sorted through DNA analysis) is riddled with theoretical and scientific research problems (see Morning, 2014). Problematical, too, is the resurgence of popular sociobiological explanations for white supremacy in society (e.g. Herrnstein and Murray, 1994). Serious theoretical and empirical analyses of foundational and systemic racism and white racial framing provide useful correctives to much of this problematical mainstream racial thought.

The 2016 election of Donald Trump created a powerful US president who has intentionally incited racial divisions and manipulated many beliefs, images, and emotions of a very reactionary version of the white racial frame. This demonstrates that proclamations, including from mainstream race scholars, of a post-racial US society being signaled by Barack Obama's past presidency have proven overly optimistic and unfounded. Trump has emboldened many overt racist acts of white nationalist groups, openly displayed white racist ideas and actions toward various racial groups, and enacted government policies very damaging to people of color and beneficial for whites, especially for fellow white elite men. Trump's election signals that white racial framing and other elements of systemic racism are still operative and central in major US institutions. Whereas most mainstream racial analyses offer few or no conceptual tools for addressing the current Trump-era social realities of overt white racism, and of whites' actions as continuing architects and controllers of racially oppressive societies, systemic racism analyses provide very useful intellectual and empirical tools that ultimately will be needed in the practical dismantling of this still foundational white racism.

Notes

1 Systemic racism is interwoven with systemic sexism (patriarchy) and capitalist exploitation, demonstrating that white-framed socially constructed divisions between different racial groups are strengthened and perpetuated through gender group and class group divisions. For a better understanding of this intersectionalist understanding of race-class-gender power, see bell hooks (1984) and Feagin and Ducey (2017).
2 We do not have space here to list and discuss the many empirical studies of systemic racism and white racial framing that Joe Feagin and his colleagues have performed over many years, including current ongoing studies.

References

Batur, P. & Feagin, J.R. 1996, "Racism in the post-colonial world," *International Policy Review*, vol. 6, pp. 10–40.
Batur, P. & Feagin, J.R. 2004, "The global color line: systems of racial oppression in comparative perspective," in G Ritzer (ed.), *Handbook of international social problems*, Sage, Thousand Oaks, CA, pp. 121–138.
Batur, P. & Weber, K. 2017, "Water connects it all," In R. Thompson-Miller and K. Ducey (eds.), *Systemic Racism: Making Liberty, Justice, and Democracy Real*, Palgrave Macmillan, New York, pp. 333–356.
Blackwell, J. & Janowitz, M. (eds.) 1974, *Black Sociologists: Historical and Contemporary Perspectives*, University of Chicago Press, Chicago.
Blauner, B. 1972, *Racial Oppression in America*, Harper-Collins, New York.
Carmichael, S. & Hamilton, C. 1967, *Black Power: The Politics of Liberation in America*, Vintage Books, New York.
Collins, P.H. 1990, *Black Feminist Thought: Knowledge, Consciousness, and the Politics of Empowerment*, Unwin Hyman, Boston.
Delgado, R. (ed) 1995, *Critical Race Theory: The Cutting Edge*, Temple University Press, Philadelphia.
Du Bois, W.E.B. 1896/1986, "Conservation of the races," In N Huggins (ed), *WEB Du Bois writings*, Literary Classics, New York.
Du Bois, W.E.B. 1903/1995, *The Souls of Black Folk*, Penguin, New York.
Du Bois, W.E.B. 1915/2007, *The Negro*, Cosimo Classic, New York.
Du Bois, W.E.B. 1920/2003, "The souls of white folk," In W.E.B. Du Bois (ed), *Darkwater: Voices Behind the Veil*, Prometheus, New York, pp. 17–18.
Du Bois, W.E.B. 1945/2007, *Dusk of Dawn*, Oxford University Press, New York.
Du Bois, W.E.B. 1947/1979, *The World and Africa*, International Publishing Co, New York.
Ducey, K. & Feagin, J. R. 2021, *Royal Racism: White Racial Framing and Counterframing of Meghan Markle*, Routledge, New York.
Elias, S. 2009, *Black and White Sociology: Segregation of the Discipline*, PhD thesis, Texas A&M University, College Station.
Elias, S. & Feagin, J.R. 2016, *Racial Theories in Social Science: A Systemic Racism Critique*, Routledge, New York.
Feagin, J. & Vera, H. 1995, *White Racism: The Basics*, Routledge, New York.
Feagin, J.R. 2001, *Racist America: Roots, Current Realities, and Future Reparations*, Routledge, New York.
Feagin, J.R. 2006, *Systemic Racism: A Theory of Oppression*, Routledge, New York.
Feagin, J.R. 2010/2013, *The White Racial Frame: Centuries of Racial Framing and Counter-Framing*, Routledge, New York.
Feagin, Joe 2012, *White Party, White Government: Race, Class, and U.S. Politics*, Routledge, New York.

Feagin, J.R. & Ducey, K. 2017, *Elite White Men Ruling: Who, What, When, Where, and How*, Routledge, New York.

Feagin, J.R. & Ducey, K. 2019, *Racist America: Roots, Current Realities, and Future Reparations*, Routledge, New York.

Feagin, J.R. & Feagin, C.B. 1978/1986, *Discrimination American Style: Institutional Racism and Sexism*, Kreiger, Malabar, FL.

Feagin, J.R., Vera, H. & Batur, P. 2000, *White Racism: The Basics*, 2nd edn, Routledge, New York.

Herrnstein, R. & Murray, C. 1994/1995, *The Bell Curve: Intelligence and Class Structure in American Life*, Free Press, New York.

hooks, b 1984, *Feminist Theory: From Margin to Center*, South End Press, Boston.

Ladner, J (ed) 1973, *The Death of White Sociology*, Vintage Books, New York.

Liberato, A.S.Q. & St. Jean, Y. 2017, "Systemic racism and anti-Haitian racism," In R. Thompson-Miller and K. Ducey (eds.), *Systemic Racism: Making Liberty, Justice, and Democracy Real*, Palgrave Macmillan, New York, pp. 309–332.

Morning, A. 2014, "And you thought that we had moved beyond all that: biological race returns to social science," *Ethnic and Racial Studies*, vol. 37, no. 10, pp. 1676–1685.

Omi, M. & Winant, H. 2013, "Resistance is futile?: A response to Feagin and Elias," *Ethnic and Racial Studies*, vol. 36, no. 6, pp. 961–973.

Thompson-Miller, R. & Ducey, K. (eds.) 2017, *Systemic Racism: Making Liberty, Justice, and Democracy Real*, Palgrave Macmillan, New York.

Walker, D. 1829/1997, *Appeal to the Colored Citizens of the World*, Black Classic Press, Baltimore.

Wells, I.B. 1892/1996, In J.J. Royster (ed), *Southern Horrors and Other Writings*, 2nd edn, Bedford/St. Martin Press, New York.

Wells, I.B. 1895/2011, *The Red Record: Tabulated Statistics and Alleged Causes of Lynching in the United States*, Tredition, Hamburg.

Zuberi, T. & Bonilla-Silva, E. (eds.) 2008, *White Logic, White Methods*, Rowman & Littlefield, Lanham, MD.

2

Beyond Marxism versus cultural studies

Critical theories of racism and political action from migrant workers to Black Lives Matter

Zacharias Zoubir and Karim Murji

Across many parts of the world there are intensifying mobilisations, often expressed through forms of ethno-nationalisms that are realised in some electoral success and indeed even in government in some nations. This "populist" revival has led to warnings about the "return of fascism" in Europe, while others argue, in a more down-to-earth way, that it makes the task of anti-racism more urgent and demanding. Yet, at a time when the so-called "migration crisis" has led to many deaths at the borders of Europe, and when the precarity of black lives, especially men, in the USA, has become more evident, the question of what anti-racism could or should look like remains as fraught as it has been in some decades. While the span and depth of such debates is too large a subject for present purposes, in this chapter we focus on one area or question in particular: are the resources for anti-racist action, both in theory as well as in practical politics, to be found in drawing on or using the idea of race itself? Or, to develop a subsidiary question to this one, to what extent is anti-racism a matter of autonomous and identitarian social and political movements based around group identity, or better founded in a "wider" politics of class struggle and opposition to capitalism? While these questions are not new, we suggest the answer to them is not given in theory. Rather it will be configured differently in specific moments and conjunctures. In order to frame an outline response to the contemporary "race first" or "class first" dichotomy, we draw on and revisit a classic debate from the 1980s to see the ways the debate was framed then, what we can draw from it now, and what this means for political action against racism.

A contemporary instance where similar oppositions are being played out is the Black Lives Matter campaign. Now a well-known hashtag on social media as well as a social movement, Black Lives Matter (BLM) started around 2013 from protests at the death of an African American teenager, Trayvon Martin, in Sanford, Florida. The protests were against the acquittal of George Zimmerman who had shot Martin after an altercation between the two of them. Later some of the leading BLM protestors also took part in demonstrations in Ferguson, Mississippi following the fatal shooting of Michael Brown, another African American teenager, by a white police officer. The Black Lives Matter Network and the Movement for Black Lives came out of these events (Rickford, 2016) which also included widespread rioting or protests across cities in the US that led some to see the events as a global crisis of policing (Camp and Heatherton, 2016). While we are going to focus only on the race/class debate that has occurred around BLM, it is important to register that there are other tensions and divergences within it, such as how to engage mainstream politicians. While stating a number of policy demands the Movement for Black Lives tended to reject working with mainstream political parties or elected politicians, while other groups have adopted a more pragmatic approach (see Rickford, 2016).

While there have been pro-police counterblasts to BLM such as Blue Lives Matter, there are also reactions such as All Lives Matter that maintains that it is more than just black people who are at risk from police violence, and that the focus on race or blackness is too narrow to build political coalitions. This "false universal" (Rickford, 2016: 38) is also highlighted by Yancy and Butler (2015) who suggested that if black people cannot be regarded as being included in "all lives", this race-blind proposition actively deracialises and obscures the precarity of black lives. (Agozino, 2018 makes a similar point.) This takes us to the nub of the race/class and political action issue this chapter considers. While it is undeniable that BLM began in response to black deaths, particularly from contact with the police, and the riots across the USA in 2014–15 can all be linked primarily to the deaths of black men, there are arguments that BLM is both too narrowly as well as incorrectly framed. In highlighting just black lives it misses, it is argued, that the core issue is poverty and class inequalities, often geographically evident in US cities. More generally, by focusing on race it fails to address capitalist social relations themselves.

It is notable that more nuanced versions of this line of argument emerge from Marxist writers who are to an extent sympathetic to BLM, but think it is misguided or underdeveloped in some ways. There are various aspects to this claim; we focus only on those that relate explicitly to the relation between race politics and class politics, and their intersections. John Clegg (2016), for instance, recognises the insurgency that drives BLM and the protests across the USA as based in police violence, as well as worsening levels of racial inequality in the US from the financial crisis of 2008 onwards. Yet in seeing racial inequalities as being based on long-standing or "baked-in" material inequalities over generations, Clegg casts a dubious lens on the impact of policies such as affirmative action and police reform programmes to challenge decades of "inherited black disadvantage" that can "only be overcome by challenging the basic working of capitalist markets". Although previous generations of black radicals did consider that anti-racism requires a critique of capitalism, his argument is that while "capitalism plays an even greater role in reproducing racial inequality, the most visible activists of Black Lives Matter rarely adopt an anti-capitalist stance". Part of the reason for this, Clegg argues, is that BLM activists have different social origins – more educated, more middle class – than the victims of police violence. They are part of what he regards as a "new black elite" where activism has become a "professional option". Such elites "may seem like allies" in the fight against racism but only up to the point "at which their own interests in social order [and] political patronage … come into conflict with demands from the street".

While Clegg recognises that the present condition of black lives in poverty is too severe to wait for white workers to move beyond a kind of bureaucratised trade union consciousness to form "black and white unite and fight" politics, the main point underlying his argument is a class-based view of the struggle against racism. Rickford (2016), while appearing more sympathetic to BLM, drives in the same direction also. He recognises that BLM aims to remain autonomous from the Democratic party's establishment, as well as the older generation of black leaders, and that the tactics of BLM derive from "independence and militancy" (p. 36). Yet the challenges he sees for BLM are questions of its ambiguous view of electoral politics, and of police reform. Moreover, while "leaders of the movement have displayed signs of a race-class analysis that acknowledges the inseparability of economic justice and black liberation ... the movement has yet to articulate a clear analysis of the economic underpinnings of white supremacy" (p. 39).

So, generally speaking, where BLM and its allies insist upon the much higher degree of exposure of blacks to racist discrimination and violence, their critics argue that the driving force behind such racist practices is in fact the reproduction of material inequality. The BLM stance highlights the irreducibly specific precarity of "black lives", whereas its class-based critique contends that today, the primary cause of this precarious situation is not racism but the persisting concentration of disadvantage in certain social groups. These two analyses go hand in hand with two different practical strategies which, although not opposed in every aspect, do imply a different focus. On the one hand, it is the mobilisation of blacks against, first and foremost, structural racism, and on the other hand, the emphasis on a more general struggle waged by workers against material inequality.

In Britain in the 1980s we can find an echo of these "race and/or class" debates. This took the form of an opposition between the Marxist sociologist Robert Miles and various people associated with the Race and Politics Group at the Birmingham Centre for Contemporary Cultural Studies (CCCS), particularly Pratibha Parmar and Paul Gilroy. This "Miles–CCCS debate" as it has come to be known has been discussed before (e. g. Back and Solomos, 2000; Virdee, 2014). This has been and still can be broadly characterised as "Marxist sociology *versus* cultural studies". For Miles the key issue was to criticise the "sociology of race relations" as it had developed in the UK, and which Miles argues lacked an understanding of the status of migrant labour and the effects of colonialism in capitalist labour markets. For the CCCS group, influenced by the work of Stuart Hall, the focus was instead the ways in which black and anti-racist struggles had developed in the climate of new right conservative ideology and state restructuring in post-war Britain. In returning to this debate here our purpose is to draw out some key features as they provide insights that are important for contemporary debates.

On a theoretical level, the sharpest difference between Miles and the CCCS was in their respective conceptions of race. The dividing line here is not Marxism in itself, since both currents drew upon Marx and Marxists in different ways. The CCCS group, following Hall (1980), were influenced primarily by Gramsci and Althusser, as well as theories of "new racism". As for Miles, he was actually one of the first to develop a systematic theory of racialisation against the sociological current of "race relations" that presented racism as the result of the conflicts of "ethnic" or "racial" groups (Miles, 1982). Instead of presupposing the existence of such "ethnic" or "racial" differences, Miles proposed a research program focusing on the social constitution of the very idea of such differences. He wondered: what are the processes – material, political and ideological – that make us perceive and act upon social relations through the lens of racial signifiers, that is, through the representation of certain characteristics understood as inherent to the bodies of different human groups? Miles understood these processes in terms of "racialisation" and studied them empirically in numerous publications most notably on the history of the relation between migrant workers and British working class organisations, often co-written and researched with Annie Phizacklea (e.g.

Phizacklea and Miles, 1979, 1987), as well as on the contemporary conditions of the racialised "fractions" of the working class (Phizacklea and Miles, 1980).

During the 1980s, the work emerging from CCCS was certainly not anti-Marxist, although some of the associated researchers were later to take their distances with the concepts of class or class struggle (e.g. Gilroy, 1987, 1993). Still, in the early 1980s the CCCS was developing a different analysis. For them, mobilisations in the US such as *black power* and the civil rights movement had developed rhetorics and practices distinguished from those of the trade union movement of the first half of the 20th century. In a similar fashion, migrant workers from former British colonies had histories, cultures and political strategies of their own (CCCS, 1982). For the CCCS, those workers' particular experiences as colonial and postcolonial subjects meant that they could not be considered as just low-qualified "class fractions", as Phizacklea and Miles (1979, 1982) had suggested. Hence, for the CCCS, the problem was not so much that Miles theorised society in terms of relations of production and class struggle. Instead, the trouble with his approach was its neglect of the irreducibly specific living conditions and experiences of migrant workers.

What is at stake in this debate are two key points. First, what is meant in using "race", and second, as a corollary of that, what are the forms of political action and alliances required to combat racism. It is here that we can see the divergences between Miles and CCCS. Drawing upon a certain reading of Marx, Miles suggested that "race" is a "form of appearance" of relations of production, in the sense that the access of certain social groups to material resources or political rights can be barred due to the persistent and institutionalised belief in racial differences between social groups (1982, pp. 31–32). For the likes of Gilroy and Parmar, "race" was not just this distorted representation of social relations. As conceptualised in influential theoretical work by Stuart Hall, "race" had a reality of its own, not as a biological distinction but as a set of materialised relations between bodies, racist ideas and social positions (Hall, 1980). This is something we ought to bear in mind in order to frame our own take on the contemporary "race first" or "class first" debate. When delving deeper into this opposition it becomes clear that at issue is how to determine precisely the relationship between racism and class relations. Rather than an alternative between race and class, the Miles–CCCS debate can thus be seen as a confrontation between two ways of addressing these two questions: what, exactly, is the impact of race upon the material conditions and political organisation of workers? And what are the consequences of that in terms of antiracist and anti-capitalist movements?

The CCCS approach to these questions centred the idea of an experience specific to a certain position *within* the class. Drawing upon authors like Frantz Fanon and Selma James, their exploration sought to make room for the lived history of migrant workers within the study of racism, and to place that within colonial and postcolonial relations. "Experience" here is not to be understood as passive impressions of society but in terms of what Hall et al. conceptualised when viewing race as "the modality through which class is lived" (1978, p. 394). In other words, race is the lens through which a group interprets, thinks of and acts upon its social conditions. Since the latter are differentiated by one's position within or on the margins of the so-called "majority population", so are the interpretations, the ideas and the actions. This is why, for example, the authors of the seminal *Policing the Crisis* argued that for many blacks in Britain, police repression and violence could be more important, at least on a symbolic level, than issues such as unemployment or working conditions (Hall et al., 1978, p. 387).

For Miles, this way of conceptualising experience was deeply problematical in its tendency to separate political and cultural questions from class relations. Theoretically, he argued, it gave up the question of the social constitution and reproduction of racism (1982, pp. 176–177). On a practical level, it over-interpreted the effects of racism by asserting and supposing such a stark divide between white and non-white workers that the conditions for any struggles beyond specific group identities seemed impossible (1982, pp. 177–178). That point was reinforced in *Labour and Racism* (Phizacklea and Miles, 1980): the affirmation of racial identities, be they black or otherwise, is a step toward a polarisation of society along a white nationalist/black immigrant divide (Phizacklea and Miles, 1980, pp. 231–232). For Miles, as we will see later on, struggles waged by white and black workers together were by contrast the most efficient way to oppose racism.

It is precisely this theorised version of the "black and white unite and fight" perspective that the CCCS attacked in the collective work *The Empire Strikes Back: Race and Racism in 70s Britain* (1982), a critique which Gilroy (1987) later reinforced. For Parmar, to conceive of labour and British working class institutions as fundamentally neutral, as if any worker, white or black, could relate to them in the same way, was in fact to generalise that which was specific to white workers, understood as those already integrated to the social, political and cultural norms of the nation (Parmar, 1982, pp. 262–263). Obviously, the long Grunwick strike of 1976–1978 was led by female workers at a film factory in North-West London. However, even while organising as workers, demanding better wages and working conditions, there was always more to the struggle than that, as Pearson, Anitha, and McDowell (2010) indicate in their intersectional understanding of the strike. Parmar (1982) considered Miles' and Phizacklea's outlook as Eurocentric insofar as it neglected the specific forms of these women's struggle. Many of them had emigrated from India and could thus draw upon representations and modes of organisation inherited from the mobilisation against the British colonial power, as well as from the severe repression it had faced (p. 261). Characteristically, one of the strike leaders, Jayaben Desai, had taken part in some historical Indian demonstrations involving Gandhi (Ahmed and Mukherjee, 2012, p. xvi).

For Parmar, what caused Miles' and Phizacklea's neglect of these specificities was their limited conceptual framework. They presupposed that it was enough to measure migrant workers' politicisation by collecting data on labour union participation, thus excluding alternative forms of workplace organisation (Parmar, 1982, p. 262). Such questionnaires were thus not adapted to the kind of wider forms of cooperation that developed during strikes like the one at the Leicester Imperial Typewriters factory in 1974, where workers benefited from financial support coming from both entrepreneurs and religious organisations linked to the South Asian communities (p. 264). On Parmar's view, such phenomena could not be estimated by means of Miles' and Phizacklea's questionnaires, as they relied upon a more traditional understanding of working class organisation. Politically, the lack of a critique of institutions inherited from the historical workers' movement implied that the authors of *Labour and Racism* failed to question the ways in which British unions treated whites and non-whites differently, through racist discrimination as well as through the management of wage gaps between the one and the other group. To put it simply, against Miles and some of his collaborators, CCCS authors like Parmar were developing the idea that non-white workers are not just workers like any others, with reference to both their living conditions and the struggles they wage. Therefore, even apparently self-evident political concepts like those of "struggle" and "class politics" could no longer be taken for granted or assumed to carry the meaning they did for Marxists like Miles.

In his responses to these critiques, Miles did admit that some of his sociological inquiries into the relationship between labour and racism suffered from a Eurocentric bias (1984, p. 231). Later, in "Racism, Marxism and British Politics" (1988) he stressed that the problem with the CCCS approach remained its belief in a new revolutionary subject, namely the "black masses" which were said to comprise all non-white groups in the UK that had now become relatively superfluous with regard to capital's needs of labour power. First, statistically speaking, in 1980s UK, non-whites were more affected by unemployment, although Miles added that most Asian and Caribbean migrants were actually employed and therefore inserted into class relations (p. 442). Second, historically speaking, there was nothing new about unemployment. It had always been a structural characteristic of the capitalist mode of production (p. 443). And third, there was nothing intrinsically revolutionary in the struggles waged by unemployed non-white people. For example, the 1980 Bristol riots in response to a police raid in a café with a mainly black crowd did not give rise to any long-term political organisations, other than calls for reform or the integration of some activists into the parliament and local city structures (p. 444).

Hence, Miles' answer to the CCCS is an internal critique of their project. If the point is to practically overcome racism, it is a mistake to present the opposition between the "black masses" and state racism as *the* most important antagonism, because class belonging shared by whites and non-whites is the only available actual means to this end. Miles (1984) made clear that he was mainly referring here to struggles waged by both blacks and whites together such as those for a minimum wage in the National Health Service, as well as to the leading role played by non-whites with the lowest wages in the public sector during the 1970s up until the early 1980s (pp. 224–225). According to this view, the only way to fight racist distinctions is to unite through the fight against a common enemy, material inequality, and for a common cause, social justice. From any perspective that sets out to criticise racism, it is of course difficult to reject these goals. For us, the problem is rather that Miles simply substitutes an immediate class unity to the CCCS's somewhat idealised vision of the "black masses". Indeed, for Miles, all workers, be they white or black, share "a universality of experience and interest" (1988, p. 447). It is as if an objective political potential was inscribed into the workers' conditions, while the shared experience and interest of racialised groups could only gain legitimacy by somehow adapting to that potential.

This leads us back to the central issues at stake in the debates outlined here: how does race impact upon workers' conditions and organisation and what are the implications for political action of different conceptualisations of this race-class relationship? For Miles the precise material and political impact of race on the lives of workers is, through the process of racialisation as defined above, to influence what kind of occupational niches non-white workers are to fill in the labour market (1982, pp. 184–185). In other words, his view suggests that racialisation does not fundamentally constitute the conditions of the racialised, which are already there in the relations of production. However, in the work of the CCCS, from the fact that class positions can in theory be said to be the basis of (the experience of) racism, it does not follow that in practice class is paramount or can be conceived without any other mediations. And one of those mediations is precisely race, understood as a social stigma that can, however, be contested by minorities in their cultural or political resistance.

Gilroy's (1987) later contribution was key in framing this practical – perhaps even pragmatic in the philosophical sense – understanding of race as a "basis for action" (1987, p. 27). This does not mean that the groups in question necessarily use the terminology of "race", as in the "Inter-Racial Solidarity Campaign". Instead, as indicated in a 1980s leaflet about the 1984–85 British miners' strike that Gilroy (1987) cites, "race" may refer to a broader definition of shared social stigma or subjugation: "The experience of Irish people, Black People and The Miners are Same [*sic*]" (quoted in Gilroy, 1987, p. 40). The point, then, is to consider blacks not only as the passive objects of a process of racialisation, but also as the conscious protagonists of economic, political and cultural struggles that form and change their experiences and living conditions. In the CCCS account, race is neither a free-floating idea disconnected from class, nor just the allocator of one's occupation. Rather, it shapes the kind of collective political representation that a certain group might reach. Class, then, is not a pre-given universal identity opposed to the narrowness of race. To the contrary, it is differentiated by the degree to which one is exposed to material and symbolic disadvantage, or, in other words: it is composed by different relations to capitalist markets and nation-state institutions.

Returning to BLM and the contemporary US "race first" or "class first" debate, this historical detour provides us with some theoretical tools to think of the articulation between material inequality and racism rather than their opposition. In spite of the theoretical sophistication evident in some of these debates, it is clear that there is still a noticeable tendency to articulate race and class as a dichotomy, or to place the latter as primary or as "above" the former due to implicit, unreflected presuppositions. From this it is a short step to seeing movements such as BLM as undermining class solidarity (as in Lilla, 2017, and also, in a different context but to the same end, in; Winlow et al., 2015). These social movements and class politics are posed as antithetical or at least as not combinable. While Marxists such as Virdee (2014) adopt a more nuanced position, refusing to see race and class as dichotomy, echoes of this way of thinking are still evident, as made clear in Adolph Reed Jr.'s brief intervention in a recent exchange on the Verso blog (Reed Jr., 2018).

Drawing from the Miles–CCCS debate of the 1980s we think there are three main lessons we can take from it. First, we can note that, to a large extent, Miles and the CCCS seemed to be talking past each other, insofar as their respective contributions were actually of a different nature or operating on distinct levels (Solomos and Back, 1995). When dealing with the material and political significance of race, Miles raised the question in terms of a systematic Marxian social theory. His point of departure was thus the capitalist relations of production in general: what effect does racialisation have upon the latter? Miles' answer was that the impact of racialisation is limited to the allocation of groups into positions already constituted by the relations of production. The CCCS, for their part, did not set out to provide such a general theory of the status of racialisation within the capitalist mode of production. Following Hall (1980), Gilroy even dismissed this as a vain effort due, precisely, to the ideological, i.e. distorted, nature of the idea of race (1982, p. 281). Instead, he suggests, race should be approached by limiting its scope to specific conditions, to see how the struggles of the racialised against both capitalists and state institutions are played out. At that time, the CCCS (1982) saw Britain as being in an organic crisis that, as also developed in Hall et al. (1978), entailed a new right orientation under the Thatcher premiership that combined capitalist restructuring as well as different forms of social and political repression or authoritarian populism. It is this conjunctural specificity of race that cultural studies more than Marxism brought to the fore.

Second, by highlighting this difference, partly outlined by the CCCS authors, between the level of social theory and the level of historical inquiry, we want to stress the importance of not conflating epistemological questions with political ones. Indeed, at the level of knowledge, as Miles often pointed out, race and class cannot be granted the same value. Race is an idea of common sense which attributes certain supposedly corporeal, hereditary and unchangeable properties to human groups. Class, on the other hand is, in Marxist terms, an "analytical concept" insofar that it serves to describe a process that actually determines one's position in society (Miles, 1984, pp. 232–233). However, as Parmar (1982) and Gilroy

(1987) pointed out, what Miles seems to neglect is that both with regard to present conditions and to political history, be it as an idea of common sense or as the theme of an outright racist ideology, race is irreducibly ingrained in that process. More generally, we would argue that it provides not only tropes of discourses, but also a rationale for discrimination in various spheres as well as for nationalist and authoritarian state policies or political mobilisations "from below". This, we suggest, is something that many Marxist critics of BLM (e.g. Haider, 2018) either miss or underestimate. By distinguishing the rational-theoretical inquiry into the *validity* of the idea of race from the political-practical question of the *uses* of race as such a trope and rationale, we see that race does not merely allocate individuals into pre-existing class positions, but does actually take part in the "*social and discursive practice* of the *construction* of these groups" (Müller-Uri, 2014, p. 64). More specifically, by marking out certain groups as essentially incapable, unassimilable, or detrimental, this trope and rationale serves to defend the material and symbolical advantages of the "majority population" against non-whites.

Third, this analysis in turn has implications for the way we think politically. Through a thought experiment, Clegg (2016) argues that under present US conditions, "even if racial discrimination were completely eradicated, racial inequality would persist" because "under capitalism poverty is a heritable condition". The BLM movement's focus on discrimination thus occludes broader tendencies in the US labour market since the 1970s, characterised by strong segmentation, i.e. blockages to intra- and inter-class mobility. Undoubtedly, anti-black racism does not have the same impact today as it had during slavery and Jim Crow, and contemporary racial inequality rests in large part upon differentiated segmentation of this kind. However, historically, one cannot separate intergenerational material disadvantage on the one hand, and more or less institutionalised forms of racist discrimination and segregation in labour, housing and education on the other. Also, today, from the point of view of capitalist social relations in the US, such particular forms of racist discrimination and segregation do not have the same status as general tendencies of capitalist markets. Still, to varying degrees in space and time, *racist discrimination and segregation are integral parts* of these markets. This implies that class relations and race as a trope and rationale for discrimination, segregation and political mobilisation can only be separated analytically, not in reality – unless racism has actually been wiped out completely from a particular social formation and its history. So, without falling into the rather indeterminate "both-and" perspective of "we must fight both material inequality *and* racism", we may argue that, from determinate positions and circumstances, material inequality is actually fought by taking on racist forms of discrimination, segregation and mobilisation as well as their intergenerational, coagulated effects. This does not mean that the struggle against racist discrimination or racism should simply replace the one against material inequality, but neither can it just be collapsed into the latter. Writing about 1970s Birmingham (UK), Hall et al. did indeed argue that the primary focus should be not so much on discrimination per se as on the differentiated positions of groups on the labour market (Hall et al., 1978, pp. 339–340). A struggle waged by blacks against the specific forces to which they are exposed is thus a moment of the struggle against material inequality, aiming at one of its particular mediations.

Both when looking back on past struggles and when engaging with those that unfold as we speak, what makes this perspective relevant is its ability to point at the specificity of particular forms of inherited disadvantage without losing sight of broad tendencies of capitalist markets. From this standpoint, we can go beyond seeing either race and class, or Marxism and cultural studies, as dichotomously as they are framed in historical and contemporary debates. In the US, racist discrimination and segregation has taken part in shaping and perpetuating the particularly precarious conditions of many African-Americans in such a way that, for them, even today, "improved class position might at any moment fall subject to a racist veto" (Fields and Fields, 2012, p. 267). In the UK, the struggles of the working class from the mid-19th to the mid-20th century took part in creating a national identity through which "class as a representational form and as a material relation was indelibly nationalized and racialized" (Virdee, 2014, p. 5). Through processes that are political, legal and ideological in nature, material disadvantage can thus be ingrained in certain populations while social and political citizenship is polarised along imagined in- and out-groups. Rather than conflating race into a "relation of production" (Backer, 2018), it is the workings of those processes within relations of domination and exploitation that must be explored (Singh and Clover, 2018). For instance, many participants in the spate of riots ignited by the police killings of Trayvon Martin and Michael Brown were poor, either unemployed or working in low-wage sectors. However, because of their particular forms of intergenerational material disadvantage and the social stigma of race attached to them, many of those participants acted not so much upon labour relations *per se* – from which they tended to be excluded. Rather, they reacted to the state institutions designed to manage them, most notably the police, as well as those characteristic, ubiquitous outlets of capital that even the long-term unemployed can reach: stores, malls, fast-food chains, etc. (for an analysis of rioting in Britain that offers a similar analysis see Millington, 2016). Here again, the conjunctural specificity of race explored by the CCCS comes to the fore, not as something given, but as the combined effect of contemporary capitalist markets and the historical weight of past segregation and discrimination.

References

Agozino, B., 2018. "Black Lives Matter Otherwise All Lives Do Not Matter," *African Journal of Criminology and Justice Studies: AJCJS*, vol. 11, no. 1, pp. I–XI.

Ahmed, R. and Mukherjee, S., 2012. *South Asian Resistances in Britain, 1858–1947*, A&C Black.

Back, L. and Solomos, J., 2000. "Introduction: Theorising Race and Racism" in Back, L. and Solomos, J, eds, *Theories of Race and Racism: A Reader*. London: Routledge, pp. 1–33.

Backer, D. I., 2018. "Race and Class Reductionism Today." www.versobooks.com/blogs/4068-race-and-class-reductionism-today

Camp, J.T. and Heatherton, C. eds., 2016. *Policing the Planet: Why the Policing Crisis Led to Black Lives Matter*. London: Verso Books.

Centre for Contemporary Cultural Studies, 1982. *The Empire Strikes Back: Race and Racism in 70s Britain*. Routledge.

Clegg, J., 2016. "Black Representation After Ferguson," https://brooklynrail.org/2016/05/field-notes/black-representation-after-ferguson.

Fields, K. E. and Fields, B. J., 2012. *Racecraft: The Soul of Inequality in American Life*. London and New York: Verso Books.

Gilroy, P., 1982. "Steppin' out of Babylon – race, class and autonomy" in Centre for Contemporary Cultural Studies, *The Empire Strikes Back: Race and Racism in 70s Britain*. London: Routledge, pp. 275–315.

Gilroy, P., 1987. *"There Ain't No Black in the Union Jack": The Cultural Politics of Race and Nation*. Unwin Hyman.

Gilroy, P., 1993. *The Black Atlantic: Modernity and Double Consciousness*. London: Verso Books.

Haider, A., 2018. *Mistaken Identity: Race and Class in the Age of Trump*. London: Verso Books.

Hall, S., 1980. "Race, articulation and societies structured in dominance" in UNESCO ed., *Sociological Theories: Race and Colonialism*. Paris: UNESCO, pp. 305–345.

Hall, S., Critcher, C., Jefferson, T., Clarke, J. and Roberts, B., 1978. *Policing the Crisis: Mugging, the State and Law and Order*. London: Macmillan.

Lilla, M, 2017. *The Once and Future Liberal: After Identity Politics*. New York: Harper.

Miles, R., 1982. *Racism and Migrant Labour*. London: Routledge & Kegan Paul.

Miles, R., 1984, "Marxism versus the sociology of 'race relations'?" *Ethnic and Racial Studies*, vol. 7, no. 2, pp. 217–237.

Miles, R., 1988. "Racism, Marxism and British politics," *Economy and Society*, vol. 17, no. 3, pp. 428–460.

Millington, G., 2016. "'I Found the Truth in Foot Locker': London 2011, Urban Culture, and the Post-Political City," *Antipode*, vol. 48, no. 3, pp. 705–723.

Müller-Uri, F., 2014. *Antimuslimischer Rassismus*. Mandelbaum.

Parmar, P., 1982. "Gender, race and class: Asian women in resistance" in Centre for Contemporary Cultural Studies, *The Empire Strikes Back: Race and Racism in 70s Britain*. London: Routledge, pp. 236–275.

Pearson, R., Anitha, S. and McDowell, L., 2010. "Striking issues: from labour process to industrial dispute at Grunwick and Gate Gourmet." *Industrial Relations Journal*, vol. 41, no. 5, pp. 408–428.

Phizacklea, A., and Miles, R., 1979. "Working Class Racist Beliefs in the Inner City" in Miles, R., and Phizacklea, A. eds, *Racism and Political Action in Britain*. London: Routledge & Kegan Paul.

Phizacklea, A., and Miles, R., 1980. *Labour and Racism*. London: Routledge & Kegan Paul.

Phizacklea, A., and Miles, R., 1987. "The British Trade Union Movement and Racism" in Leeand, G. and Loveridge, R. eds, *The Manufacture of Disadvantage: Stigma and Social Closure*. Buckingham: Open University Press.

Reed Jr., A., 2018. "Response to Backer and Singh." www.versobooks.com/blogs/4073-response-to-backer-and-singh.

Rickford, R., 2016. "Black lives matter: Toward a modern practice of mass struggle." *New Labor Forum*, vol. 25, no. 1, pp. 34–42.

Singh, N. and Clover, J., 2018. "The Blindspot Revisited," www.versobooks.com/blogs/4079-the-blindspot-revisited.

Solomos, J. and Back, L., 1995. "Marxism, racism, and ethnicity." *American Behavioral Scientist*, vol. 38, no. 3, pp. 407–420.

Virdee, S., 2014. *Racism, Class and the Racialized Outsider*. London: Macmillan.

Winlow, S., Hall, S., Treadwell, J. and Briggs, D., 2015. *Riots and Political Protest: Notes from the Post-Political Present*. London: Routledge.

Yancy, G. and Butler, J., 2015. "What's Wrong With 'All Lives Matter'?" https://opinionator.blogs.nytimes.com/ 192015/01/12/whats-wrong-with-all-lives-matter/.

3

Conceptualising cities and migrant ethnicity

The lessons of Chinese London[1]

Laura Henneke and Caroline Knowles

Introduction: new departures

On 10 April 2017 the first UK to China export train pulled out of the newly constructed London Gateway port to a set piece political send-off with a full cast of Chinese officials and a wave from Greg Hands, the then Minister of State for the Department of International Trade, who called the departure 'another boost for global Britain' as he proclaimed the new (post-Brexit) era. The railway terminal is a component of 'one of the biggest privately funded infrastructure projects the UK has ever seen'.[3] The departing freight train connects London and the Chinese city of Yiwu with 7,500 miles of rail track through the Channel Tunnel, France, Belgium, Germany, Poland, Belarus, Russia, Kazakhstan, and China. The route makes part of the China-Europe rail corridor, a fast-growing network of railway connections and a poster child for China's Belt and Road Initiative (BRI)[4].

The departure of the train signals the need for another departure – a departure from imagining that Chinese London is a clearly marked neighbourhood in Soho's Chinatown, or that it is simply inscribed in bodies and businesses that bear its iconic markers. A departure in how to think about the ways in which (Chinese) ethnicities, migrations and other circulations co-compose cities on the scale suggested by the infrastructure developments implicated in the BRI's route through London and its emerging consequences.

This chapter sketches in some of the realities on the ground when it comes to the emerging cartographies of Chinese London. We argue that it is no longer appropriate just to focus research and analysis on the small-scaled migrant-led ethnic marking of *places* that currently hold sway, such as in London's Chinatown, not least because this has a bigger context in large-scaled capital-intensive Chinese infrastructural projects in construction that *connect* places. Urban, migration and ethnicity scholars alike have paid little attention to these often subtle, less visibly ethnically marked, but ultimately, as we will argue, more dramatic manifestations of Chinese ethnicities embedded in large-scale infrastructure projects. We describe what happens when classic tropes of migrant bodies moving small-scale capital to create Chinatowns (Anderson, 1919) are recalibrated, and large volumes of capital instead move migrant bodies and enterprise into a highly networked version of place making. This paper explores the implications of a vastly different scale of Chinese influence on the ways in which we think about cities, ethnicity and migration. It speculates on the consequences for London of becoming part of the complex dynamics of Chinese economic growth (The Economist, 2015), processes which are not necessarily confined to London and Chinese influence, but which may have broader resonance in our understanding of the ways in which ethnicity and migration produce cities.

Thinking through ethnicities and migration

Migrants to the UK, and, by extension the migration processes landing them on the shores of the island nation, have always been made conceptually and empirically visible through the interconnected social categories of race and ethnicity. Thereby race, ethnicity and migration have become inextricably intertwined in UK academic, policy and political discourse over the last half century (Alexander and Knowles, 2005; Bloch and Solomos, 2009; Gilroy, 1982; Rex, 1981; Rex and Moore, 1967; Solomos, 2003; Solomos and Wrench, 1995). This is at best an uneven process. Academic research and policy intervention have rendered some migrant ethnicities hyper-visible, while obscuring others[5] (Knowles, 2013; Vertovec, 2007). The Chinese,[6] one of the world's great diasporas (Skeldon, 2011), were excluded from the racialised anxieties that problematised African, Caribbean and South Asian migrants in the UK, conceptualising the Chinese instead as a small and successful minority, and thereby revealing the 'social problem' framework within which migrant ethnicities are understood as socially underachieving, failed examples of integration.[7]

While Chinese sailors, predominantly from Hong Kong and the Chinese Province of Fujian have lived in London, Liverpool and Cardiff for over a hundred years, in 1945 there were only 5,000 Chinese people in the UK. By the time of the 2011 census the recorded UK Chinese population had risen to 379,530, equivalent to a city the size of Bristol today, with London forming the centre of Chinese Britain. This increase coincides with a shift in the character of the migrant population itself (Pharoah, 2009); in the past it was predominantly the result of colonial connections with Hong Kong and long settled. Two thirds of Chinese people in the UK today are new, mainland-born migrants, with the resources to navigate the new architectures of immigration control, which favour 'exceptionally skilled' and 'investor' migrants.[8] Visa applications by aspiring Chinese migrants over the last few years have massively increased. This coincides with the rising significance of China as a global force and the eagerness of successive UK governments to do business with China – the biggest single export market on the planet – and, as we will argue, an important source of foreign direct investment (FDI).

City-thinking

While cities have long been recognised as de facto territories of ethnic migrant habitation, they are predominantly seen as microcosms of larger scales of activity generated by states (Alexander and Knowles, 2005). A clearer focus on urban scales offers new insights into the co-construction of ethnically marked migration and city life, in the context of an emerging framework in which the agency of cities in generating the processes they also ground is increasingly acknowledged. More than points of entry, exit and transit, more than places of long and short-term residence (Smith and Eade 2008:5–7), cities are key social spaces grounding transnational practices routing connected mobile subjects. Translocal migrant ethnicities are imbricated in urban space through everyday bodily encounters (Amin and Thrift, 2002; Swanton, 2010) and through personal urban cartographies (Knowles and Harper 2009). To paraphrase Swanton, (2010:450) this takes migration into the very fabric of the city and its visual economy, making a more fluid, emergent and provisional mapping of new migrant ethnicities and cities possible. Cities condense the challenges we face in ethnicity and migration sociology: as places where lives are generated; where traces of elsewhere are registered in architectural and other surfaces of emergence, as well as in bodies in motion on the journeys of everyday life. Human and non-human trajectories converge on cities; and tracing these reveals ethnic-migrant lives, journeys and activities. These factors make cities the appropriate scale at which to develop an analysis of migration.

Acknowledgements of the agency of cities stress continuous city making, emergence and composition (Amin and Thrift, 2002; Swanton, 2010); interactions between (migrant and ethnic) material and human fabrics (Boutros and Straw, 2010; Ingold, 2000) and the understanding that cities are constituted in the multiple mobilities (of ethnic migrants and materials) that converge upon them (Amit, 2007; Clifford, 1997; Ingold, 2004); making cities best conceptualised as junction-points in a shifting matrix of local and translocal routes, plied everyday by people (sometimes as migrants), materials and objects (Knowles, 2014). Quite how these more fluid conceptions of cities work alongside migration and ethnicity remains to be fully explored. Thinking about this constellation of concepts through infrastructure might provide some leads.

Cities and ethnicities

When it comes to understanding the connections between cities and ethnicity it is difficult to keep pace with emerging realities of contemporary urban life on the ground: people are inherently mobile, albeit on different scales, and cities are always expanding, remade and reconfigured. Lived versions of ethnicity on the ground are equally motile, hybridised and emergent, especially around youth cultures as Parker and Song (2006) show in relation to the young Chinese online presence. The Chinese character of London in particular challenges the ways in which we might think about Chinese ethnicities co-composing urban landscape. Chinese London may hold wider ramifications for other migrant ethnicities and the cities they help make. London, of course, is not just a Chinese city, it is a Middle Eastern city, a Russian city and many other cities too, but these insights involve excavating beyond the visible optics of race and ethnicity and its more obvious inscriptions in urban space (Massey, 1994, 2004)[9] in order to establish sources of capital investments and materials.

Despite recent developments in thinking about cities that acknowledge their fluid and emergent properties, consideration of ethnicity and urban landscape remains dominated by classic conceptions of ethnic enclaves (Farrar, 1997). This is derived through empirical studies dating from the early years of the 20th century in the Chicago School of urban sociology, which identified ethnicities in spatial terms as, for example, Chinatowns and Little Italys (Burgess, 1967). These formulations and their contemporary derivatives are underpinned by visibly marked commercial surfaces, in the case of Chinatown iconic images of Chineseness in red lanterns, Chinese food, the presence of Chinese people and (maybe) waving cats, staples in marking Chinatowns worldwide as well as in London.

But these essentialised and static versions of ethnic place-making are not only challenged by the more fluid conceptions of cities outlined above, they are disrupted by the heave of everyday city life as Chinese people make their way through London on myriad journeys with different intentions and outcomes, and, crucially, they are challenged by rising rents, rates and property values, forcing Chinese businesses to move from London's (Soho) China-town. Chinatown – as an indoor-outdoor museum commemorating Chinese London – remains visible in its stereotypical rendering, which many young Chinese people find objec-tionable (Knowles, 2015). But much of its commercial and residential vitality has moved to other parts of the city and a great deal of it is hidden. The dynamism co-composing cities' ethnic texture is poorly captured by these static mappings of space. While cities are now conceptualised in more dynamic, mobile and emergent terms, little thought is given to how ethnicities – which are equally dynamic, mobile and emergent – are configured through these changes and through the routes that populations marked by ethnicity tread through them as they go about their everyday lives and business.

There are further complications too, complications which shift the analytic focus from places, even from emergent conceptions of places, to *particular kinds* of connections *between* places. We refer to infrastructure – something that is, we argue, particularly important in thinking about Chinese London. Little consideration is given to these subtler, less visibly ethnically marked and ultimately, as we will show, more dramatic manifestations of Chinese ethnicities embedded in large-scale infrastructure projects. What happens when the classic formulas of migrant bodies moving small-scale capital (Anderson, 1919) are reversed and large volumes of capital instead move migrant bodies and enterprise into place-and-connection-making? This paper focuses on thinking about urban ethnicity with a different scale of Chinese influence and the consequences of this. It is about what happens when London becomes a part of the complex dynamics of state and private sector Chinese eco-nomic growth (The Economist, 2015). How then should we think about the relationship between cities, ethnicity and migration?

Urban infrastructure

Ethnic migration, while still an active agent in city making, co-exists with large-scale capital movements, sometimes accompanied by the bodies of migrants, sojourners, temporary resi-dents, distant and visiting investors, interlocutors, students and those who are passing through the city in the slipstream of Chinese capital from various private and state sources and its invisible as well as its visible manifestations (Knowles and Burrows, 2018). What happens when we shift the focus from the visible ethnic character of city making – in architecture, commercial surfaces, ethnic residence and so on – to include the city's main arteries, the conduits through which people, objects and materials navigate movement within and through cities? What happens to thinking about ethnicities, migration and cities when infra-structure becomes a central analytic focus?

Amin and Thrift, (2017) note the essential and machine-like character of the 'infrastructural entanglements' that allows cities to stay in working order. Infrastructures constitute the loose vectors along which materials and objects move, forming complex assemblages with ethnic migrants bodies, capital and its human agents, also elements of infrastructure and vital compo-nents in city making. Infrastructure is what holds cities against the fragilities of collapse; infra-structure makes cities work – albeit often in ad hoc and circumscribed ways; infrastructure grinds a lens onto cities' multiple possibilities. Of course we intend infrastructure in its broadest sense. Infrastructures are a matrix of urban fabrics – material, virtual, human – often combined in unexpected and creative ways in meeting everyday needs. Infrastructures are a fast emerging set of technical possibilities that interface with human ingenuity and creativity. Infrastructures are a practical tool in city making which at the same time provides a way of thinking about cities and the relationship between cities and the ethnicities co-composing them.

Departures – the train

On 10 April 2017 the first UK to China export train pulled out of the newly constructed London Gateway freight terminal, 'one of the biggest privately funded infrastructure projects the UK has ever seen'[10] and yet it is *unseen* – described by one journalist as a megaport 'you didn't know existed'. Much urban infrastructure lies hidden beneath the surface of cities as pipes and cables but a megaport is hard to conceal. Its underpinning – in all of its giant sky scraping crane materiality and its 230 hectare business park, silt dredging that has refashioned the three kilometres of the Essex coastline near Stanford-le-Hope and the financial structures on which these giant construction stands – is hardly concealed. What are concealed are associations with other nation states and ethnicities' financial and other city-making interests. That this £1.5 billion infrastructural investment was built by a Dubai company called DP World *is* invisible. Capital does not necessarily declare its national and ethnic associations explicitly; these must be excavated through registers of commercial interests and land ownership. No one looks at London's Shard, for example, and intuits that it is a congealed pile of oil – the Qatar Sovereign Wealth Fund – but it doesn't take long to work this out.

The freight train is part of the China-Europe rail corridor – sometimes called the New Silk Road in order to establish its long historical antecedents – that connects Yiwu in the eastern Chinese province of Zhejiang with 7,500 miles of rail track through Kazakhstan, Russia, Belarus, Poland, Germany, Belgium, France and now London. Trains departing from Yiwu head for nine different destinations across the Eurasian continent, including Teheran, Riga, and Madrid. Madrid perhaps provides a glimpse of London's future, deeply textured with imported pound shop styled Chinese products and traders, a vibrant hive of commerce on the edge of the Spanish capital. More of this later.

The Belt and Road Initiative

The Belt and Road Initiative (BRI) is China's grand strategy to expand its influence by means of ambitious infrastructure projects across its border and into territories beyond (CPC, 2015, 2016; Leverett and Wu, 2017; Summers, 2016; World Bank, 2016). By establishing alternative trade routes, stabilising China's border regions, increasing trade with neighbouring countries, integrating them into quickly evolving Asian value chains, and by promoting economic development in BRI countries, the intention of this initiative is to create a more connected, wealthier Asia (Kratz, 2017). London is just a small part of a grander plan. This interconnected Asia will have China as its core and have stable links to Africa and Europe. The increase of Chinese outward FDI has been observed for several years but only recently did China's president Xi Jinping brand this as the 'Belt and Road Initiative'. In this he folded a number of existing or planned schemes into the grand narrative while claiming it to be his contribution in the quest of rejuvenating the 'empire' (Miller, 2017, p. 34).

The BRI has two main prongs: one is called the 'Silk Road Economic Belt' (the Belt) and the other the '21st Century Maritime Silk Road' (the Road)" (CPC, 2015). Contrary to what the metaphor suggests, the expansion of 'the Belt' is not limited to China's neighbouring countries. It reaches as far as to South East Asia, West Africa and Europe, criss-crossing Central Asia, which forms a focus of the initiative. The region was largely neglected by international investors after the Soviet Union fell apart and today, Central Asian governments are especially open to contracts with Chinese developers who want to build highways, transport hubs and other supporting infrastructure to enable the circulation of goods in the most remote areas of the Eurasian continent. 'The Road' on the other hand, refers to a sea route linking China's southern coast to East Africa and the Mediterranean mainly in terms of investment in geostrategic harbours such as the Greek port of Piraeus, the Gate to Europe, purchased by Chinese state-owned COSCO[11,12] when Greece privatised many of its assets as austerity measures in 2016.[13]

The BRI is financed through a complex funding mechanism. To begin with, Beijing established the $40 billion 'Silk Road Fund' in December 2014 to support investments as part of the initiative, gathering resources from the State Administration of Foreign Exchange, the China Investment Corporation, the Export-Import Bank of China, and the China Development Bank (Guluzian, 2017, p. 136). Another important funding body is the $100 billion China-initiated Asian Infrastructure Investment Bank (AIIB). This is a development bank allocating funds for infrastructure construction projects as part of the New Silk Road and is constituted of 57 members including the United Kingdom, Germany, France, and Russia, but not the United States. However, the estimated price tag of the Belt and Road Initiative is $1 trillion. To bridge the gap, international and regional development banks (such as the European Bank for Reconstruction and Development, the Asian Development Bank, and the World Bank), host governments, and private-sector actors are also providing financing (ibid.).

A dense infrastructure network

According to the Chinese government, the BRI will run through 67 countries; however, a clear definition of what it is is not provided. It is commonly agreed, however, that BRI is a network of trading routes influenced by the competing demands of geography, commerce and geopolitics (Frankopan, 2018; Macaes, 2018; Miller, 2017; Nolan, 2017; Summers, 2016). Chinese firms will build new roads and railway tracks, linking mines with power plants, factories, wholesale markets, and new mushrooming cities wherever they can find willing partners (Miller, 2017, p. 31). London is but a small node in a vast networked infrastructure project centred on China – the new, fast emerging Chinese London.

At a summit in Beijing on 15 May 2017, China was hoping to give global legitimacy to Xi's signature initiative through the endorsement of all participating countries. However, the European Union refused to back a statement on trade because several EU member states raised concerns about the lack of commitments to social and environmental sustainability and transparency.[14] Thereby the EU made it clear that it would not be the willing partner of Xi Jinping (yet). The UK, however, on its way out of the European Union, will (Henneke, 2017, p. 118). Processes that began under the Cameron premiership continued under May, and were repeatedly emphasised by the then Chancellor of the Exchequer, Philip Hammond; the strengthening of economic ties with China stands at the forefront of the current UK strategy on its global reach. From the summit in Beijing Hammond tweeted 'Britain is ready to work with all OBOR [One Belt One Road] Partners' (Hammond, 2017).

The royal albert dock – large scale urban remaking

A little to the West of the London Gateway port another giant building project at the Royal Albert Dock, adjacent to London City Airport, is keen to be seen as part of the Belt and Road Initiative.[15] The Royal Albert Dock Development is in the hands of a China-based property group called ABP. ABP announced that the Royal Albert Dock is London's 'new business heart'[16], and at the time of accepting ABP's bid in 2013, the then Mayor of London Boris Johnson proclaimed that 'creating a third financial district in the capital, this development will act as a beacon for eastern investors looking west, bringing with it tens of thousands of jobs and billions of pounds of investment for the UK economy'.[17]

Completed in 2019, phase one of this £1.7 billion development was built by Chinese state contractor Citic Construction and Multiplex, comprising public realm, roads, infrastructure and a total of 460.000 square feet of office space.[18] ABP's CEO Nancy Xu's vision for the entire 4.7 million square feet development of the Royal Albert Dock includes a cyber park attracting the best Chinese high tech companies with ABP operating as 'an agent between China and the UK' in what is intended as an 'Asian business port'[19] in the heart of London's Eastwards extension. This is no ethnic enclave! It is a reconfiguration of the commercial vitality of the city, its continued eastwards extension and the opening of new rail and air routes between London and China.

Compared to numerous other Chinese investments in London's property and infrastructure, the Royal Albert Docks present a novel scenario with uncertain, yet exciting and potentially far reaching outcomes. Aimed at Chinese small- and medium-sized enterprises, it goes beyond the monetary level of capital investments, possibly marking the beginning of a new, giant, highly networked Chinatown. Time will tell. Most likely it will be accompanied by an indispensable transnational migration of Chinese entrepreneurs who may eventually transform the social and material fabric of London's East (Henneke, 2017).

As Ms Xu's aspiration hit the ground, the local professionals at the ABP East London office, including some from the Greater London Authority who are in charge of the project, seemed to know little about Chinese business, how the development of the site would actually unfold, and what the impact of this giant Asian business port on the neighbourhood might be.[20] However these processes of urban remaking unfold, they seem a long way from the history of Chinese London; Royal Albert Dock, of course, is near Limehouse and London's first Chinatown in East London before it moved to Soho in the central London borough of Westminster. There are, of course, many East Londons and this is only one of them. And yet these Chinese infrastructure developments also align perfectly with recent transformations in this part of London.

Building on the past

In the 1980s East London's Docklands, now the site of the new heart of London with Asian business properly at its centre, was emblematic of 'the physical decline of the inner city' according to Michael Heseltine, a minister in the Thatcher government.[21] Physical decline was a deliberate and highly visible argument for this area's redevelopment, away from its historical image as a place of dock labour unloading the spoils and military hardware of empire. As Schwarz, (1991:85) points out, London's East End had always been an imperial international enclave linking the Atlantic economies to the Indian subcontinent, a connection that only became visible in the 1950s and 1960s when Indians and West Indians came to live in the area. In the 1880s Chinese businessmen started to settle here because of the convenient maritime connection (Seed, 2006, p. 59), and by the 1920s Limehouse had become London's first Chinatown. Limehouse became 'the most cosmopolitan district of the most cosmopolitan city of Britain' (ibid.). In fact, ever since goods circulated globally by locomotives and steamboats, the London Docks became an 'arrival quarter' for migrating entrepreneurs (Gidley, 2017). During the late 19th and beginning of the 20th century 'migrants were not just immigrants but rather part of larger networks of circulation. Arrival quarters were not just gateways to particular nations but nodes in these larger circuits' (ibid.). Such quarters are described to 'provide social networks, mutual aid and linguistically accessible economic niches as a way of integrating people into the city' (Saunders, 2011). Aerial bombing during World War II mostly destroyed the Limehouse Chinatown and its population was dispersed further west. In the 1960s the once-prosperous Docklands were allowed to decay as they outlived their original purpose. Freight transport was containerised and larger vessels were demanding more accessible ports further downstream on the River Thames.

The London Docklands Development Corporation (LDDC) was set up in 1981 by a Conservative government to usurp plans already underway by three London boroughs – Tower Hamlets, Newham and Southwark – to develop the area (Schwarz, 1991:84). The LDDC appropriated public land and sold 5,000 acres and 55 miles of waterfront property to the speculative capital of private developers, with the Toronto-based company Olympia and York, who had successfully regenerated large areas of New York, initially taking a leading role before it went bankrupt. The state funded Docklands Light Railway (DLR) – another railway albeit on a smaller scale – underwrote the all-important publicly funded infrastructure investment in the area, which both expanded the geographically constricted square mile of the City of London to its eastward riverside extension as London's financial institutions and deregulation opened it up to global capital on a more speculative and profitable basis than ever before. The infrastructure investments of ABP are perfectly consistent with this area's recent history and its direction of development. Its Chinese credentials are not visibly marked. Local people would have no means of identifying the source of its capital and even its building process is only subtly marked as Chinese.

While the impact of this massive Chinese infrastructure project on East London is yet to unfold, earlier infrastructure projects associated with Chinese investment and which are now included in the narrative of the Belt and Road Initiative are already impacting other European cities and may serve as a harbinger for what is to come in London (Henneke, 2017, p. 122).

Will London resemble Fuenlabrada?

One is Fuenlabrada, a municipality at the southern fringes of Madrid, where Chinese traders from Zhejiang Province have settled since the 1990s (Nieto, 2003) transforming the adjacent business park, Cobo Calleja, into one of the biggest and most important distribution centres for Chinese imported small commodities in the European Union. When small businesses around Spain faced bankruptcy during the aftermath of the 2008 financial crisis, Chinese entrepreneurs kept busy. Their low-cost commodities were in higher demand than ever and the influx of new traders arriving from China continued due to relaxed visa regulations designed to attract foreign investment. In the 2016 census, Madrid's Chinese community accounted for 55,784 people, signalling the highest influx of new arrivals compared to any other migrant group (Communidad Communidad de Madrid, 2016). Many of the Chinese migrants live in the southern fringes of the city, perhaps unsurprisingly close to the warehouses that belong to the economic zone of Cobo Calleja (Henneke, 2017).

Just as we expect for East London, the recent formation of Madrid's China Pequeña in the city's south is not marked by red lanterns or other stereotypical decorative and architectural features. Yet, Chinese migrants have gained visibility due to their concentration in specific neighbourhoods where Chinese restaurants as well as supporting services in Mandarin flourish and events such as the Chinese New Year are celebrated publicly (Henneke, 2017, p. 119). Furthermore, urban development projects such as Plaza de Oriente, an addition to the existing industrial zone of Cobo Calleja with 40.000m^2 exclusive to Chinese entrepreneurs[22] show the municipality's support for Chinese businesses and the people who arrive with them.

Fuenlabrada's ongoing effort to endorse Chinese businesses by implementing supporting infrastructure was rewarded in 2014 when the first freight train from Yiwu reached Madrid, laden with products destined for the warehouses in Cobo Calleja.[23] In fact, the business park is a mini version of Yiwu's wholesale market and serves as a distribution centre for low-cost commodities such as shoes, textiles, toys and household goods which are sold in bulk and distributed around the country to shops of different types, but all informally called El Chino: one type sells everything imaginable, the other type are typical corner shops with long opening hours run by Chinese migrants. The establishment of the Yiwu-Madrid rail connection is the result of reciprocal business interests between China and Spain. Since the Chinese middle class has developed a taste for Mediterranean cuisine, the containers that bring the small commodities from Yiwu to Madrid return to China filled with crates of wine, olive oil, and Spanish *jamón*. The connection between producers in Spain and bulk buyers in China's Zhejiang Province is made through the dense networks and strong family ties the Chinese migrants of Fuenlabrada keep with their home towns.[24]

Or Tbilisi?

The other city that showcases a possible scenario for the future of London's Royal Albert Dock is Tbilisi in Georgia (Henneke, 2017, p. 119). This is a major location for Chinese investment from one source in particular: the Hualing Group, which has its headquarters in Urumqi, Xinjiang Province. The Hualing Group became involved in Georgian infrastructure projects during the preparations of the 2015 European Youth Summer Olympic Festival, where shortly before the start of the games accommodation was still missing. Coming to help at the last minute, the Hualing Group provided an immaculate Athletes' Village situated between Tbilisi's city centre and the airport. Once the Youth Games were over, the buildings were returned to the investor's real estate portfolio (Shepard, 2016). The master plans as well as the architectural features of the so-called 'Hualing Tbilisi Sea New City' strikingly resemble modern neighbourhoods in China. The greenfield development site consists of about 20 ten-storey-high apartment blocks. The apartments have richly ornamented facades and roofs, which imitate a mix of European styles and respond to current Chinese tastes. Clustered in a gated community, the buildings are connected through neat greenery, walkways, and ponds. They could not differ more from the adjacent grey-on-grey neighbourhood (Henneke, 2017, p. 120). Hualing's successful project has whetted Georgia's appetite for more. Within sight of the former Athletes' Village, which is now inhabited by well-to-do homeowners, the Chinese investor is building a wholesale market that will serve as distribution centre for Chinese imported commodities. The goods arrive by train through the China-Turkey corridor operated by DHL and launched in late 2015.[25] Additionally, the 'Hualing Kutaisi Free Industrial Zone' is built near the city of Kutaisi to facilitate imports from China. Hualing Group is not only leaving a footprint with distinct architecture but also naming the developments after the company (Henneke, 2017, p. 120). These are all potential scenarios for East London.

Manifestations of economic uncertainty

These projects – the Royal Albert Docks in London, Cobo Calleja near Madrid and the Hualing developments in Georgia – have at least two things in common: First, the Chinese investments were accepted in a moment of economic uncertainty. Like most Western European countries, the UK used to stop Chinese developers from building large infrastructural projects locally. This changed when local investors pulled out of ongoing projects in the aftermath of the 2008 financial crisis. In the case of the London Docklands, the almost ten years of stand-still in the highly-valued stretch of land prompted the City of London to finally agree to Chinese investment to transform the urban landscape between the O2 Arena and London City Airport. The next step – to agree on plans for a Chinese business park – is a good example of the UK's increasing interest in strengthening economic ties with China and what are now described as 'post-Brexit trade deals'.[26]

Secondly, in all three cases Chinese FDI is finding its way through large infrastructure projects on locations along the newly established train routes. These projects inevitably expand the transportation networks on the Eurasian continent in favour of spreading Chinese influence and soft power based on goods and the means by which they circulate (Henneke, 2017, p. 120). As in the South of Madrid, traders and entrepreneurs migrate to where the goods go, bringing new, expanded hyper-Chinatowns on a scale previously unknown. As in the times of the ancient Silk Road, they bring not only merchandise but also their cultures, languages and architectural designs. Even though remarkable parallels can be found in the cities of Madrid, Tbilisi and London, we acknowledge the vagueness of anticipating the outcomes of future projects such as the Royal Albert Docks through a simple comparison. Each case of Chinese investment encounters very diverse preconditions and local regulations. The impact of the large infrastructure projects on sociospatiality also depends on the collaboration of the investor and the receiving municipality. After all, it is migrating individuals animating the area that we assume will have the biggest impact on everyday life in the city of investment – London – in the long run.

With the plans to erect a business park for Chinese entrepreneurs on the site of the Royal Albert Docks – within a stone's throw of the former Limehouse Chinatown – it could be that a new arrival quarter is underway. Of course, the type of businesses that are expected to operate in the Chinese business hub at the Royal Albert Docks are different to the importers of small commodities in Fuenlabrada or Tbilisi. We argue that the type of businesses is of secondary importance for the emergence of new Chinatowns. Following Massey's idea that the formation of the ethnic character of a place is a product of interactions (Massey, 1994), we expect that individual entrepreneurs will establish dense social networks within a globally connected urban structure that combines work with living and leisure. Surrounding neighbourhoods will likewise see an influx of Chinese migrants as well as supply services and facilities such as kindergartens, schools, medical institutions or homes for the elderly operating in Mandarin. Having all those services locally available will make the Chinese entrepreneurs independent from the inner city and thereby contribute considerably to the budget of the surrounding areas (Henneke, 2017, p. 121).

Conclusions

Returning to conceptual dimensions of these new departures in how we might think about ethnicity, migration and cities, it is apparent that what we describe is on a massively bigger scale than anything hitherto imagined either for Tbilisi, Madrid or London. The emerging cartographies of Chinese London exceed the imagination of even those who are intimately involved in their development. Instead of an emphasis on ethnic place we propose a framework that stresses connections between places as the engines of ethnic place making. Infrastructure is one of these generative connections, a conduit that is intimately connected with large scale circulations of Chinese capital on the one hand, and, potentially, circulations of Chinese bodies on the other. Crucial questions then arise: which Chinese bodies, materials and objects will circulate through London with Chinese capital? How will those ethnic migrant bodies, lives and objects operate as part of the emerging city?

On what conditions will they operate as part of a dense transnational network of infra-structural mobilities? And in what ways will they become instantiated into the fabrics of this city-in-the-making?

We suggest that in future Chinatowns will take on new meaning and heightened significance in their impact. No longer residual inner city neighbourhoods in which ethnic migrants take refuge in seeking familiarity; Chinatowns will be on the leading edge of urban development and regeneration. Unmarked, or subtly marked infrastructure projects only reveal their national and ethnic alignments with probing efforts. They may in fact be the bridgeheads of substantial ethnically marked commerce and occupation. Or not. Either way, we need new frameworks that admit the simultaneous emerging dynamism of cities and migrant ethnicities as co-productions of some significance, and not the marginal inner city markings of long-term ethnic occupation. Chinese London is a living and vibrant development, which may be in the process of radically transforming a neighbourhood near you and the city as a whole.

Notes

1 A small part of this chapter was published in: Laura Henneke (2017) 'Belt and Road Initiative: China's Rising Impact on Socio-Spatiality in European Cities' *Mapping China Journal* 1(1): 116–123.
2 Kay Anderson's (1919) *Vancouver's China Town: Racial Discourse in Canada 1875–1980* McGill-Queens University Press is an exemplary and serious study of anti-alien agitation and the urban forms resulting. But it addresses an earlier era of Chinese migration and city-making activities.
3 Oliver Wainwright 'Inside the London Megaport you didn't know existed' Guardian 15/09/2015.
4 BRI is China's grand strategy to invest in infrastructure projects across Eurasia, Africa and beyond to build an interconnected trade network with China as its core.
5 See Caroline Knowles (2013) for a fuller discussion.
6 We understand that the term Chinese is contentious and use it here to refer to Hong Kong and Taiwanese Chinese who are engaged in an ongoing struggle for autonomy from the Chinese mainland, to people from the Chinese mainland and to the substantial Chinese populations in Malaysia and Singapore.
7 For an expanded account of this see Knowles and Burrows (2018) and Knowles (2017).
8 These (2008) changes were fully implemented in 2011. They prioritise wealth and elite connection and close traditional avenues of migration, for example into the restaurant trades, leaving migrants with fewer resources with only illegal channels of entry, often with disastrous consequences.
9 Doreen Massey's work, especially *World City*, is exemplary in this regard.
10 Oliver Wainwright 'Inside the London Megaport you didn't know existed' Guardian 15/09/2015
11 China Ocean Shipping Company (COSCO) is a Chinese state-owned shipping and logistics services supplier company
12 This acquisition also illustrates how in fact, China expands the transportation networks also in favour of spreading influence and soft power based on goods. In the year following the strategic purchase of Piraeus, Greece used its veto to prevent the European Union from officially condemning China's human rights records at the UN – a procedure that was common practice in precedent years (Smith, 2017).
13 Kerin Hope 'Greece picks China's Cosco in port deal' Financial Times 21/01/2016.
14 Tom Philips 'Philip Hammond calls China a "natural partner" as he seeks post-Brexit trade deals' in Guardian 04/11/2017.
15 Laura Henneke's field notes from a visit and interview at ABP Offices 07/04/2017.
16 http://www.abp-london.co.uk/
17 Reuters 'Chinese firm to develop London's third financial district in US$1.5b deal' South China Morning Post 30/05/2013.
18 http://https://www.building.co.uk/buildings/projects-royal-albert-dock-london/5102109.article

19 http://www.abp-london.co.uk/assets/Media/NEWS-COVERAGE/2018.06/2018.06.28-The-Wharf-Interview-with-ABP-London-CEO-Nancy-Xu-Creating-a-smart-destination.pdf
20 Laura Henneke's field notes from a visit and interview at ABP Offices 07/04/2017.
21 Bill Schwarz (1991) 'Where horses shit a hundred sparrows feed: Docklands and east London during the Thatcher Years' in John Corner and Sylvia Harvey eds *Enterprise and Heritage: Crosscurrents of National Culture*, London and New York: Routledge pp. 76–92
22 'Blanco acuede a la aperture de Plaza de Oriente, un macroproyecto chino' El Mundo 16/02/2011
23 Stephen Burgen 'The Silk Railway: freight train from China pulls up in Madrid' The Guardian 11/12/2104
24 Laura Henneke's field notes from visits and interviews at Yiwu Futian Market District 5 (07/08/2017 and 06/01/2019).
25 https://postandparcel.info/70168/news/dhl-announces-inaugural-service-on-new-china-turkey-rail-corridor/
26 Simon Tisdall 'UK's need for post-Brexit trade deals will trump human rights concerns' The Guardian 04/04/2017.

References

Alexander, C. and Knowles, C. Eds. (2005) *Making Race Matter*, London: Palgrave.
Amin, A. and Thrift, N. (2002) 'Guest Editorial, Special Issue: Cities and Ethnicities', *Ethnicities*, 2(2), pp. 291–300.
Amin, A. and Thrift, N. (2017) *Seeing Like a City*, Cambridge: Polity.
Amit, V. (2007) 'Structures and Dispositions of Travel and Movement' in V. Amit (ed) *Going First Class? New Approaches to Privileged Travel and Movement*, Oxford: Berghahn, 1–14.
Anderson, K. (1919) *Vancouver's China Town: Racial Discourse in Canada 1875–1980*, Montreal: McGill-Queens University Press.
Bloch, A. and Solomos, J. Eds. (2009) *Race and Ethnicity in the 21ˢᵗ Century*, London: Palgrave.
Boutros, A. and Straw, W. (2010) *Circulation and the City: Essays on Urban Culture*, Montreal: McGill Queens University Press.
Burgen, S. (2014) 'The Silk Railway: freight train from China pulls up in Madrid', *The Guardian*, 11 December. Available at: https://www.theguardian.com/business/2014/dec/10/silk-railway-freight-train-from-china-pulls-into-madrid (Accessed: 19 April 2016).
Burgess, E. (1967) 'The Growth of the City: An Introduction to a Research Project' in Burgess, E. et al. (ed) *The City*, Chicago: University of Chicago Press [originally published 1925].
Clifford, J. (1997) *Routes: Travel and Translation in the Late Twentieth Century*, Boston: Harvard University Press.
Communidad de Madrid (2016) *Informe de Poblacion de Origen Extranjero Empadronada en la Comunidad de Madrid*.
CPC (2015) 'Vision and Actions on Jointly Building Silk Road Economic Belt and 21st-Century Maritime Silk Road'. Central Committee of the Communist Party of China (CPC).
CPC (2016) '13th Five-Year Plan for Economic and Social Development of the People's Republic of China (2016 – 2020)'. Central Committee of the Communist Party of China (CPC).
The Economist (26 September 2015) 'The Osborne Doctrine: Britain is sleepwalking into a much closer relationship with China'.
Farrar, M. (1997) 'Migrant Spaces and Settlers' Time' in S. Westwood, and J. Williams (eds) *Imagining Cities*, London: Routledge, 104–126.
Frankopan, P. (2018) *The New Silk Roads: The Present and Future of the World*, London: Bloomsbury Publishing.
Gidley, B. (2017) 'Arrival Quarters: Diasporic Cartographies and Migrant Urbanism' in *Migrant Cartographies: Cities, Circuits and Circulations* (conference), Goldsmiths College, University of London.
Gilroy, P. (1982) 'Police and Thieves' in Centre for Contemporary Cultural Studies (CCCS)' in CCS *The Empire Strikes Back*, London: Hutchinson, 143–184.
Guluzian, C. R. (2017) 'Making Inroads: China's New Silk Road Initiative', *Cato Journal; Washington*, 37 (1), pp. 135–147.
Hammond, P. (2017) 'In China for @OBORCHINA ★One Belt and One Road★ Britain is ready to work with all OBOR partnerspic.twitter.com/F5oTvjysyL', *@PhilipHammondUK*, 11 May. Available at: https://twitter.com/PhilipHammondUK/status/863642713568268288 (Accessed: 4 November 2017).

Henneke, L. (2017) 'Belt and Road Initiative: China's Rising Impact on Socio-Spatiality in European Cities', *Mapping China Journal*, 1(1), pp. 116–123.

Hope, K. (2016) 'Greece picks China's Cosco in port deal', *Financial Times*, 20 January. Available at: https://www.ft.com/content/d65aa7c4-bfb1-11e5-846f-79b0e3d20eaf (Accessed: 22 January 2016).

Ingold, T. (2000) *The Perception of the Environment: Essays in Livelihood, Dwelling and Skill*, London: Routledge.

Ingold, T. (2004) *Being Alive: Essays on Moevment, Knowledge and Description*, London: Routledge.

Kratz, A. (2017) 'Panel 2: Foreign policy and security landscape' in *YCW-Lau China Institute Conference: 'China in 2050: The World Through Beijing's Eyes'*, King's College London.

Knowles, C. (2013) 'Nigerian London: remapping space and ethnicity in superdiverse cities', *Ethnic and Racial Studies*, 36(issue 4), pp. 651–659.

Knowles, C. (2014) *Flip-Flop: A Journey Through Globalisation's Backroads*, London: Pluto.

Knowles, C. (2015) *London's Young Chinese Migrants*, London: Runnymede Trust.

Knowles, C. (2017) 'Reframing Sociologies of Migration in Encounters with Chinese London', *British Journal of Sociology*, 68(Issue 3), pp. 454–473.

Knowles, C. and Burrows, R. (2018) 'Reimagining Chinese London' in Suzanne Hall and Ricky Burdett (eds) *The Sage Handbook of the 21st Century*, London: Sage, 87–103.

Knowles, C. and Harper, D. (2009) *Hong Kong: Migrant Lives, Landscapes and Journeys*, Chicago: University of Chicago Press.

Leverett, F. and Wu, B. (2017) 'The New Silk Road and China's Evolving Grand Strategy', *The China Journal*, 77(1), pp. 110–132.

Macaes, B. (2018) *Belt and Road: A Chinese World Order*, London: C Hurst & Co Publishers Ltd.

Massey, D. (1994) *Space, Place and Gender*, London: Polity.

Massey, D. (2004) 'The Responsibilities of Place', *Local Economy*, 19(2), pp. 97–101.

Miller, T. (2017) *China's Asian Dream: Quiet Empire Building along the New Silk Road*, London: Zed Books.

Mundo, El (2011) 'Blanco acude a la apertura de Plaza de Oriente, un macroproyecto chino', *El Mundo*, 16 February. Available at: http://www.elmundo.es/elmundo/2011/02/16/madrid/1297882310.html (Accessed: 12 May 2016).

Nieto, G. (2003) 'La inmigración china en España. Definiciones y actuaciones sobre integración social', *Revista CIDOB d'Afers Internacionals*, (63), 167–189.

Nolan, P. (2017) 'State, Market and Infrastructure: The New Silk Road', *Croatian International Relations Review*, 23(78), 7–18.

Parker, D and Song, M. (2006) 'New Ethnicities Online: Reflexive Racialization and the Internet', *The Sociological Review*, (54), 575–594. https://doi.org/10.1111/j.1467-954X.2006.00630.x.

Pharoah, R. (2009) *Migration, Integration, Cohesion: New Chinese Migrants to London*, London: Chinese in Britain Forum.

Rex, J. (1981) 'Urban Segregation and Inner City Policy in Great Britain' in C. Peach, V. Robinson and S. Smith (eds) *Ethnic Segregation in Cities*, London: Croom Helm, 25–42.

Rex, J and Moore, R. (1967) *Race, Community and Conflict*, Oxford: OUP.

Saunders, D. (2011) *Arrival City: How the Largest Migration in History is Reshaping Our World*, London: Windmill Books.

Schwarz, B. (1991) 'Where horses shit a hundred sparrows feed: Docklands and east London during the Thatcher Years' in John Corner and Sylvia Harvey (eds) *Enterprise and Heritage: Crosscurrents of National Culture*, London and New York: Routledge, 76–92.

Seed, J. (2006) 'Limehouse Blues: Looking for "Chinatown" in the London Docks, 1900-40', *History Workshop Journal*, 62(1), 58–85.

Shepard, W. (2016) *Silk Road Impact: Chinese Company Turns Old Soviet Factory Into Free Industrial Zone*, Forbes.

Skeldon, R. (2011) *China: An Emerging Destination for Economic Migration*, Sussex: Migration Policy Institute. Vol. 6. 1024–1105.

Smith, H. (2017) 'Greece blocks EU's criticism at UN of China's human rights record', *The Guardian*, 18 June.

Smith, M. P. and Eade, J. Eds. (2008) *Transnational Ties: Cities, Migrations and Identities*, New Brunswick: Transaction Books, 3–14.

Solomos, J. (2003) *Race and Racism in Britain*, London: Palgrave.

Solomos, J. and Wrench, J. (1995) *Racism and Migration in Western Europe*, Oxford: Berg.

Summers, T. (2016) 'China's "New Silk Roads": Sub-National Regions and Networks of Global Political Economy', *Third World Quarterly*, 37(9), pp. 1628–1643.

Swanton, D. (2010) 'Flesh, Metal, Road: Tracing the Machinic Geographies of Race', *Environment and Planning D: Space and Society*, 28(3), pp. 447–466.

Tisdall, S. (2017) 'UK's need for post-Brexit trade deals will trump human rights concerns', *The Guardian*, 4 April.

Vertovec, S. (2007) 'Superdiversity and its Implications', *Ethnic and Racial Studies*, 30, 1024–1054.

World Bank (2016) Europe and Central Asia Economic Update, April 2016: The Impact of China on Europe and Central Asia. The World Bank.

Websites

www.abp-london.co.uk/

www.abp-london.co.uk/assets/Media/NEWS-COVERAGE/2018.11/2018.11.09-Property-Week-Agents-appointed-for-offices-at-ABPs-1.7bn-Royal-Albert-Dock.pdf

www.abp-london.co.uk/assets/Media/NEWS-COVERAGE/2018.06/2018.06.28-The-Wharf-Interview-with-ABP-London-CEO-Nancy-Xu-Creating-a-smart-destination.pdf

Part II

Contemporary racisms in global perspective

Introduction

The chapters in this part of the *Handbook* link up with the accounts in Part I by focusing on discussing the evolution of contemporary racisms from a more global perspective.

The first chapter by Tiffany Joseph uses recent developments in the U.S. and Europe to explore the development of contemporary accounts of race, ethnicity and migration status. Joseph argues that recent developments in both the United States and Europe illustrate the need to explore the linkages between both regions in the contemporary period. In particular, Joseph argues that the presumption of citizenship being synonymous with whiteness reflects both explicit and implicit boundaries drawn around citizens racialized as white, separating them from citizens and non-citizens of color who are racialized as domestic and foreign outsiders. She utilises the notion of "whitening citizenship" to explore developments over the past two decades in both the U.S. and Europe and to outline the benefits of using a comparative analytical frame to make sense of current developments.

The next chapter by Graziella Moraes Silva takes a somewhat broader look at the question of the comparative analysis of race and racism. Her key argument is that the comparison of race and racisms is central to unpacking the different ways that race is socially constructed and how racisms work across different contexts. She argues that developing a comparative analytical frame is essential if we are to show how race is a social construct, in opposition to essentialist understandings of race that are still relatively commonplace. In the concluding part of the chapter she argues forcefully that a comparative analytical frame is important for understanding the development of new antiracist alliances, both through formal and informal antiracist associations.

The chapter by Peter Wade explores the forms of racism that have evolved in Latin America and the way they have been shaped by ideologies and practices of *mestizaje*. The chapter traces the historical process of mixture that produced mestizos and also underpinned the idea of the mestizo nation, seen as founded on racial difference, but as having overcome racism through mixture. Wade also explores how the notion of racial democracy has been used to describe the situation in Brazil, despite the evidence that racial disadvantage and racism were an important feature of its social and political relations. He argues that ideas of racial mixture continued to obfuscate the operation of racism, by generating real experiences of racial conviviality. In the concluding section of the chapter Wade explores the transformations in perspectives that we have seen over the past three decades and their impact in challenging dominant ideologies about race and racism in Latin America.

The concluding chapter in this part is by Tony Kushner and it tackles the subject of hostility and fear of refugees. Given the wider international conjuncture this is a very topical subject, particularly at a time when fear of persecution and genocidal violence have led to refugee movement on a scale that has not been witnessed since the Second World War. Kushner seeks to outline both the broader historical context of hostility to refugees and the more recent debates about how states should respond to the position of refugees. His critical account of the ways in which hostility to refugees helps to make their precarious existence even more difficult is all the more timely at a time when the borders of many nation–states have been mobilized in order to accentuate a hostile environment for refugees.

4

Whitening citizenship

Race, ethnicity, and documentation status as brightened boundaries of exclusion in the U.S. and Europe

Tiffany Joseph

Introduction

The resurgence of overtly racist, nationalistic, and anti-immigrant sentiment in the United States and Europe demonstrates that these societies are no longer as solidly democratic and socially progressive as they were once perceived to be. As the world's largest immigrant-receiving country, the U.S. has grappled with its contentious race relations alongside being considered a "welcoming" nation to immigrants (Feagin 2000; Foner and Alba 2015). European countries like Great Britain, France, and Germany have also seen a substantial increase of immigrants, especially refugees, to their predominantly white countries amid the Syrian Civil War, other Middle Eastern crises, and the global recession (Foner and Alba 2015; Tyler 2018; Wrench and Solomos 1993). In both regions, immigration and subsequent more ethno-racially and religiously diverse societies have yielded increasing xenophobia towards individuals perceived not to be American, British, or more broadly white European (DeGenova 2018; Gupta and Virdee 2018). These societal struggles also entail determining who legally belongs to the nation, has rights to public benefits, and contributes to the nation socially, economically and politically. This chapter examines how race, ethnicity, and documentation status have stratified and continue to stratify populations in the U.S. and Europe. Such a comparative examination is important now, as both regions receive the world's largest number of immigrants – from predominantly non-white Global South countries – amid intensifying economic inequality, socio-political conflicts, and climate change. Drawing on boundaries and citizenship scholarship, I argue that the presumption of citizenship being synonymous with whiteness reflects both explicit and implicit boundaries drawn around citizens racialized as white, separating them from citizens and non-citizens of color who are racialized as domestic and foreign outsiders. To demonstrate these boundaries, I incorporate scholarly accounts and events of racialized anti-immigrant discrimination in policies, interpersonal interactions, and institutional structures in both regions. This chapter contributes to scholarship on race, ethnicity, immigration, boundaries, and citizenship by highlighting how race, ethnicity, and documentation status brighten boundaries between white citizens and citizens and immigrants of color.

To make this argument, I first provide an overview of the ethno-racial demographics related to immigration in the U.S. and Europe. I then review relevant literature comparing immigrant integration in both regions. Next, I demonstrate my argument about stratification on the basis of race, ethnicity, and documentation status in both regions using recent scholarly accounts and events, namely the: (1) racialization of immigrants and citizens of color as foreign others; (2) retrenchment of immigrants' public benefits; and (3) increased securitization of borders, detention, and incarceration of people of color. To conclude, I briefly discuss the social implications of this increased intersectional stratification for both regions.

Literature review

Migration and shifting ethno-racial demographics

Economic recessions, the shifting demand for global labor, environmental changes due to climate change, and political conflicts have facilitated significant migration from the Global South to the Global North (IOM 2018). As of 2015, there were an estimated 244 million international migrants, which is three percent of the global population (International Organization for Migration (IOM) 2018). This number includes an estimated at 22.5 million refugees, one million of whom sought refuge in Western Europe in 2015 alone, generating a refugee crisis (International Organization for Migration (IOM) 2018; Holmes and Castañeda 2016). Countries receiving the most migrants are the U.S., Canada, Germany, the United Kingdom, France, Italy, and Spain with a sizable number of migrants being unauthorized and refugees. The U.S. has the highest number, with an estimated 11 million unauthorized immigrants, while the European Union (EU) had an estimated eight million (International Organization for Migration (IOM) 2018). This has created debates regarding pathways to citizenship and immigrants' eligibility for obtaining social services like health care and welfare (Cappelen and Peters 2018; Fox 2016; Joseph 2016). In response to backlash and anti-immigrant sentiment, legislators in the U.S. and Europe have implemented policies limiting the number of refugees and restricting non-citizens' access – both authorized and unauthorized – to social safety nets (Cappelen and Peters 2018; Fox 2016; Joseph 2016).

Migrants to the U.S. and Europe have diversified over time, with the majority coming from Latin America, Asia, and Northern Africa (International Organization for Migration (IOM) 2018). Differences in religion and national security concerns have sparked anxiety about how these immigrants are transforming the ethno-racial, religious, and cultural fabric of these host nations (Foner and Alba 2015; Virdee and McGeever 2018). Despite being a nation with predominantly immigrant origins, the U.S. legally restricted migration and naturalization for people of color until 1965 with an immigration act that removed explicitly racist immigration quotas (Feagin 2000). The country's troubled history with its legal citizens of color (i.e. African Americans, Mexican Americans, and Native Americans) continues to shape contemporary discussions of race and immigration (Feagin 2000; Flores-Gonzalez 2017). This has elicited concerns about how the "browning" of America will transform the longstanding racialized social order (Flores-Gonzalez 2017; Tavernise 2018). Scholars argue that white racial anxiety about shifting demographics aided Donald Trump's election to the presidency (Bobo 2017; Lamont et al., 2017; Strolovitch et al., 2017).

Unlike the U.S., European nations have been predominantly white and racially homogenous for most of their history. Many of these nations' ties to people of color were consequences of colonization (Bosworth and Trumbull 2015; DeGenova 2018; Virdee and McGeever 2018). Decolonization efforts and resulting economic destabilization in newly independent nations (previous colonies), in the Caribbean and Africa facilitated waves of migration to Western Europe in the 1950s and 1960s (Bosworth and Trumbull 2015; Virdee and McGeever 2018). Subsequent conflicts in the Middle East pushed migrants first to Eastern and then Western Europe (Foner and Alba 2015; Wrench and Solomos 1993). Most recently, the Syrian Civil War has yielded the highest number of displaced individuals since the Second World War (International Organization for Migration (IOM) 2018). This also sparked debates about the "assimilability" of Syrian refugees and other migrants and if they would drain social safety nets and transform Europe into a Muslim state (Cheliotis 2017; International Organization for Migration (IOM) 2018; Virdee and McGeever 2018). Rising anti-immigrant sentiment, nationalism, and fiscal concerns have also produced anti-democratic, fascist, and far-right political candidates and elected officials promising to stop immigration and targeting citizens who are ethno-racial, religious, and LGBTQ minorities (DeGenova 2018; Gupta and Virdee 2018; Schierup et al., 2018).

Immigration integration in the U.S. and Europe

Amid shifting ethno-racial demographics in these regions, scholars have conducted various studies to assess the integration of immigrants. Foner and Alba (2015) define integration as the ways in which immigrants (and their children) obtain similar socioeconomic status and inclusion in various societal institutions as the native-born population. Some studies have primarily examined the U.S. post-1965 migration wave and their U.S.-born children (Foner and Alba 2015; Portes and Rumbaut 2014). Others focus primarily on Europe after the Cold War and into the present (Crawley and Skleparis 2018; Wrench and Solomos 1993). Increasingly, scholars from both regions have conducted comparative studies yielding insights into how contexts facilitate different incorporation experiences (Foner and Alba 2015; Imoagene 2017). One primary difference between the U.S. and European countries is divergent immigrant integration policies. These policies fall into three categories: (1) differential exclusion – immigrants are excluded based on certain characteristics (i.e. Germany); (2) assimilation – immigrants take on cultural and social characteristics of the host society (i.e. Great Britain) and (3) multiculturalism – immigrants may retain aspects of their culture while acquiring those of host society (i.e. U.S.) (Freeman 2004; Joppke 2007). The U.S. has "laissez-faire integration" where immigrants are expected to utilize their own resources, social networks, and ties to local community organizations to adapt to the country (Foner and Alba 2015). Conversely, Western European countries have taken more explicit approaches to integration by investing in language acquisition and other integration programs for immigrants (Freeman 2004; Joppke 2007).

Research suggests that race – specifically being racialized as non-white – in the U.S. and religion – specifically Islam – in Europe presents integration barriers in socioeconomic stability, educational attainment, and interracial marriage (Foner and Alba 2015). In the U.S., integration outcomes vary by race and ethnicity, with Asian-descended Americans demonstrating high integration tied to socioeconomic status with more limited gains experienced by Americans of Latino and black immigrant heritage (Foner and Alba 2015). In Europe, conflicts in the Middle East and African nations spurring non-white immigration to Europe, have made race, ethnicity, and religion highly visible in European socio-political discourse.

Boundary-making in societies

In the U.S. and Europe, social scientists have developed the concept of boundaries to better understand how distinctions are made and perpetuate inequality between individuals (Alba 2005; Crawley and Skleparis 2018; Lamont and Molnar 2002; Wimmer 2013). There are two types of boundaries: (1) symbolic boundaries which are used to categorize individuals and (2) social boundaries that yield unequal access to the distribution of resources among those individuals. In some cases, symbolic boundaries can become so salient in vindicating social boundaries that they eventually replace them.

Lamont and Molnar (2002) also posit that individuals are aware of the social and symbolic boundaries which stratify society and that institutions are important in creating and perpetuating boundaries. Wimmer's (2013) study of ethnic boundary-making argues that governments, as state institutions, have the power to determine who is a citizen and also use laws to differentiate the rights of citizens and non-citizens. Thus, governments use citizenship status as a symbolic boundary to categorize and stratify their populations (Lamont and Molnar 2002; Wimmer 2013). Such rights are social boundaries because governments allocate resources based on one's citizenship status. The reification of citizenship status categories perpetuates social and symbolic boundaries that stratify U.S. and European societies. In recent years, scholars have highlighted the increasing social and symbolic boundaries separating immigrants from citizens and whites from people of color, generating stratification and inequality along those boundaries (Flores-Gonzalez 2017; Waters and Kasinitz 2015). Thus, the concept of social and symbolic boundaries is ideal for examining how race, ethnicity, and documentation status shape perceptions of citizenship and belonging in the U.S. and Europe.

Citizenship and belonging

Much scholarship on the social, political, and civic construction of citizenship argues that differentiated forms of citizenship exist in most nation-states, where factors such as race, ethnicity, proximity to immigration, gender, social class, and sexual orientation stratify citizenries (Bloemraad et al., 2019; Flores-Gonzalez 2017; Smith 2015). *Legal, state, or political citizenship* is the legal recognition of an individual as formally belonging to a particular nation-state. Legal citizenship formally entitles citizens to benefits and privileges (i.e. voting, welfare) from which non-citizens are excluded (Marback and Kruman 2015; Smith 2015). However, all legal citizens may not be *social* or *cultural citizens* who are fully socially, culturally, and civically included within a nation-state (Bloemraad et al., 2019; Flores-Gonzalez 2017; Smith 2015). Ngai (2014) uses the term "alien citizen" to describe birthright citizens whose immigrant ancestry physically marks them as racialized foreigners, diminishing their status as citizens. Thus, race and ethnicity become important for shaping social citizenship and belonging to the nation-state. In both regions, the racialization of U.S. and European citizenship and national identity are socio-politically constructed as white (Bloemraad et al., 2019; DeGenova 2018; Flores-Gonzalez 2017). Individuals marked as ethno-racially different are not regarded as full social citizens, regardless of their legal citizenship status.

In the U.S. and Europe, public policy has played an important role in facilitating de jure *and* de facto differentiated citizenship. In the late 20th century, Soysal (1994) and Hollifield (1992) argued that formal citizenship was becoming less significant in Europe, as immigrants gained more civil and legal rights. Interestingly, at the same time, the U.S. was beginning to curtail immigrants' (of various documentation statuses) access to public benefits and increase border security, particularly with 1996 immigration and welfare reforms under President Bill

Clinton (Fox 2016). In the 21st century, both regions' public policies have become less generous to immigrants and also some formal citizens perceived as less deserving amid fiscal and security concerns (Bloemraad et al., 2019). Some policy changes have been tied to perceptions that "othered" legal citizens and non-citizens of color did not fully belong to the nation and were undeserving of access to public benefits like white citizens (Bloemraad et al., 2019; Crawley and Skleparis 2018; Fox 2016).

Discussion

To illustrate how citizenship and belonging have become more explicitly synonymous with whiteness through brightening social and symbolic boundaries between whites and people of color in the U.S. and Europe, I examine three specific phenomena, drawing from scholarly and accounts and recent events. First, I discuss the racialization of immigrants and citizens of color as foreign others in both regions. Second, I examine government retrenchment policies that reduce immigrants' access to public benefits. Finally, I consider legislators' efforts to increase government funds for the securitization of national borders amid the detention, deportation, and/or incarceration of immigrants and citizens of color.

Racialization of immigrants and citizens of color as foreign others

Recent events in Europe and the U.S. reveal the increasing racialization of immigrants and citizens of color as "foreign others," who do not fully belong to the envisioned nation. Each event demonstrates how the symbolic boundaries categorizing legitimate members of these regions have brightened to separate them from illegitimate members. This boundary brightening also highlights distinctions between legal and social citizens whereby legal citizens of color are not perceived as social citizens and are sometimes treated like immigrants. While race and ethnicity have been central in establishing boundaries in the U.S., religion – particularly being Muslim – has been a marker of difference in Europe, although increasingly so in the U.S. (Foner and Alba 2015; Selod 2018). The recent events I assess from the lens of boundary-making and citizenship are: (1) the United Kingdom's Brexit Vote; (2) the political campaigns of current U.S. president Donald Trump; and (3) the political rise of extreme right leadership in various European countries.

Regarding the June 2016 Brexit vote, scholars have argued that the UK's referendum vote to leave the EU was tied to the politics of racism against a backdrop of the global recession, terrorism concerns, and migration woes from the Syrian refugee crisis (Gusterson 2017; Inglehart and Norris 2016; Virdee and McGeever 2018). Virdee and McGeever (2018) posit that the "politics of Englishness" were an invisible driver of the vote: the relationship between English national feeling and longing for Empire was racialized concretely through whiteness. Britain's structural decline globally caused downward mobility that facilitated a "politics of nationalist resentment" among Britain's white working class (Virdee and McGeever 2018). Concerns about ethnically diverse EU migration to the UK generated campaign rhetoric about protecting the UK from vilified undesirables who would destroy the nation (Bhambra 2017; Virdee and McGeever 2018). Such rhetoric also highlighted anti-immigrant sentiment towards Jewish, Caribbean, and Asian multigenerational citizens, who lacked social citizenship because they were not Christian or white (Virdee and McGeever 2018). Collectively, these factors brightened symbolic racial and social citizenship boundaries between white Britons – "the true Brits" – and brown and black Britons while simultaneously separating white British legal citizens from non-citizens. The Brexit vote aftermath accentuated these brightened boundaries amid increased racist rhetoric and hate crimes against black and brown (citizen) Britons who were told to leave (Komaromi 2016; Virdee and McGeever 2018). The Brexit vote and aftermath highlighted the true belonging of "Englishness" in terms of legal and social citizenship as racially white and exclusive to immigrants and citizens of color.

On the other side of the Atlantic Ocean, another event demonstrating significant boundary brightening in the United States was the political ascendancy of current U.S. President Donald Trump in 2016. Identifying as a political outsider and self-made billionaire, he crafted an unorthodox and socio-politically divisive campaign that drastically transformed the political landscape. He began his campaign by threatening to build a wall on the U.S.-Mexico border and vilified Mexican (and other Latino) immigrants as criminals and rapists who threaten national security (Lamont et al., 2017). Throughout his campaign, individuals perceived as "others" were targeted, derided, and ridiculed as criminals (African Americans), threats (Muslims), and not conforming to hegemonic sexist gender standards ("nasty women") (Bobo 2017; Lamont et al., 2017; Strolovitch et al., 2017). Yet, Trump's campaign slogan "Make America Great Again," implying the U.S. had lost its greatness, appealed to many less educated white Americans who felt they had been left behind in a rapidly changing and more ethno-racially diverse world (Inglehart and Norris, 2016; Lamont et al., 2017).

Scholarly analysis of Trump's divisive rhetoric reveals that he successfully used an overt "us-them" strategy to stoke the fears of his political base who perceived foreigners as competition and threats to hegemonic (white) American life (Gusterson 2017). Trump's rhetoric also indicates how race, ethnicity, and citizenship have been reconfigured to distinguish "real Americans" from outsiders. Trump's strategy relied on redrawing symbolic and social boundaries between "us" and "them" to exclude Americans of color, immigrants, Muslims, LGBTQ individuals, and other minorities from social *and* legal citizenship. His tough "law and order" stance regarding policing and immigration enforcement represents a clear distinction between social and legal citizenship in two ways. For African Americans who are disproportionately overrepresented in the criminal justice system and likely to be shot while unarmed by police officers, their legal citizenship does not entail full social citizenship. Trump's support of racial profiling alongside other denigrating remarks about African Americans demonstrates that he does not view them as social citizens. Relatedly, for immigrants of various documentation statuses, Trump's anti-immigrant rhetoric has become draconian immigration policy, resulting in record deportations, reduced work visas and refugee/asylum seekers, and limiting who can receive legal permanent residency (Pierce et al. 2018). He has also ended protected status for certain nationalities, is removing pathways to legal citizenship for immigrants, and minimizing social citizenship for legal citizens of color. Overall, Trump's rhetoric and policy initiatives have hardened boundaries between his predominantly white citizen supporters and everyone else, as evidenced by 2016 presidential election exit polls and the 2018 midterm elections (Beauchamp 2018; Tyson and Maniam 2016).

While Trump's U.S. election seemed unlikely, he has joined the ranks of an increasing number of elected and would-be populist politicians in Europe (Gusterson 2017; Inglehart and Norris 2016).[1] Politicians like Marine Le Pen (France), Norbert Hoffer (Austria), Nigel Farage (UK), and Geert Wilders (Netherlands) have run on similar platforms for increasingly populist political parties (Inglehart and Norris 2016). Similar to the U.S., anxieties about a shifting economic order and related inequality, increasing migration, and concerns that ethno-racially homogeneous societies no longer exist influenced the shift to populist leaders. Research suggests that populist support is strong among individuals who are older, male, less educated, religious, and ethno-racial majorities (Gusterson 2017; Inglehart and Norris 2016;

Virdee and McGeever 2018). Anti-immigrant attitudes, mistrust of national governance, and support for authoritarian values also influenced populist support (Inglehart and Norris 2016). Similar to the UK Brexit vote, concerns about racialized and foreign others increased support for populist candidates expressing explicit xenophobia and racism. These candidates tapped into ethnic majorities' resentments by highlighting racialized symbolic boundaries between "us" and "them" and between legal and social citizens in Europe.

Government retrenchment of public benefits for immigrants

European and American legislators have also curtailed non-citizens' access to public benefits like health care and welfare (Baldi and Goodman 2015; Fox 2016). This process began in the 1970s and has continued into the present due to economic downturns, increasing costs of benefits for aging populations, and attempts to reduce immigration over concerns that generous welfare systems attract lower-class immigrants (Baldi and Goodman 2015; Fox 2016). Recent retrenchment measures have been austerity responses to the 2008 global recession and rising immigration (Cappelen and Peters 2018; Hiam 2018). Studies have shown that increasing ethno-racial diversity, whether of native-born or immigrant populations, is associated with lower support for social welfare spending in both regions (Alesina and Glaeser 2004; Xu 2017). Such legislative changes demonstrated brightened social boundaries between white Americans and Europeans and those of color, and, also between legal citizens and non-citizens.

In the U.S. before 1972, there were no legal distinctions or social boundaries determining eligibility for benefits between citizens and non-citizens. However, between 1972 and 1996, the U.S. Congress passed legislation barring unauthorized immigrants from receiving various public benefits (i.e. social security Medicaid), representing a restrictive shift that brightened social boundaries between unauthorized immigrants and everyone else. In 1996, passage of immigration and welfare reforms curbed unauthorized immigration, reduced eligibility for welfare benefits for nearly all immigrants and further securitized the U.S.-Mexico border (Fox 2016; Park 2011). These 1996 reforms brightened social boundaries between citizens and long-term residents and immigrants of other documentation statuses. These reforms remain in effect and are why most immigrants are ineligible for healthcare benefits under the 2010 Affordable Care Act, which aimed to increase health coverage for most Americans (Joseph 2016).[2] Despite most immigrants' ineligibility for public benefits, the general public believes the contrary – that immigrants are reaping public benefits while hardworking Americans struggle to survive (Haynes, Merolla, and Karthick Ramakrishnan 2016). This falsehood has fueled anti-immigrant sentiment, with scholars arguing that harsher policies signify a more hostile and exclusive context towards immigrants of various statuses (Fox 2016). These shifts represent brighter social boundaries between legal citizens and non-citizens of different documentation statuses.

In Britain, beginning in the 1970s, legislation passed requiring all newcomers to demonstrate the ability to support themselves without state assistance. Policies passed in 1994, 1999, and 2009 implemented further requirements on immigrants to obtain public benefits such as: (1) proving UK residency for a required length of time; (2) being ineligible for certain benefits if subject to immigration control; (3) increasing residency requirement to eight years for progression from residence to citizenship; and (4) requiring that residents applying for citizenship demonstrate self-sufficiency. In 2017, the UK government issued a Memorandum of Understanding in which the National Health Service would begin charging different health service rates for those not deemed "ordinarily residents" – those "not living on a lawful, voluntary, and properly settled basis" (Hiam 2018, 108). To enforce this policy – informally referred to as the "hostile environment" – healthcare providers were required to obtain documentation status information from patients. Consequently, undocumented immigrants stopped seeking medical treatment. Cumulatively, such policies represent government retrenchment, which reduces immigrants' access to public benefits, drawing social boundaries around immigrants and brightening social boundaries between immigrants and citizens when allocating resources.

In Germany, as the country received one million refugees in 2015, there have been debates about the deservingness of, fiscal responsibilities for, and integration of refugees and migrants (Holmes and Castañeda 2016). In recent years, legislators have shifted the country's naturalization policy to become more inclusive while at the same time implementing civic integration requirements (Baldi and Goodman 2015). Up until the 2000s, acquiring German citizenship was very difficult for immigrants given the country's jus sanguinis policy. Starting in 1999 and with successive laws in 2004 and 2005, Germany reduced the residency duration required for naturalization and introduced jus soli for children who could obtain citizenship if one parent was a long-term resident. German language proficiency and civic integration were also required for residency. But naturalization applicants also had to demonstrate self-sufficiency without public benefits. While the German government sought to extend legal citizenship to immigrants, the conditions for citizenship were tied to retrenchment of public benefits for immigrants and requirements that immigrants demonstrate social membership (i.e. German proficiency). Thus, like the U.S. and Britain, Germany's policies represent a brightening of social boundaries between citizens and immigrants that make obtaining legal citizenship and public benefits more difficult for immigrants.

Increased securitization of borders, detention, and incarceration of people of color

Symbolic and social boundaries are also drawn between white citizens and people of color (citizens and non-citizens) in the U.S. and Europe via border securitization, immigrant detention, and incarceration (Abrego et al., 2016; Alexander 2012; Bosworth and Trumbull 2015; Cheliotis 2017). In both regions, immigration has been racialized as an ethno-racial minority issue, where people of color or ethnic minorities not perceived to "belong" to the nation are considered threats (Abrego et al., 2016; Bosworth and Trumbull 2015; Cheliotis 2017). Thus, policies regarding national security and securitization of borders from racialized foreign (and domestic) others have been implemented since the 1990s (Abrego et al., 2016; Bosworth and Trumbull 2015; Cheliotis 2017). Consequently, boundaries separating citizens and non-citizens of color from white citizens have brightened considerably, generating diminished formal and social citizenship for people of color (Abrego et al., 2016; Flores-Gonzalez 2017).

The U.S.'s troubled history of race relations has meant that the implementation of law and order through local police departments and federal agencies (FBI and CIA) have disproportionately harmed communities of color (Abrego et al., 2016; Alexander 2012; Golash-Boza 2015). Racial profiling of black and Latino Americans and increasingly those with Middle Eastern or Muslim phenotypes usually leads to escalated encounters with law enforcement (Golash-Boza 2015; Selod 2018). Such encounters can result in eventual incarceration, part of a huge corporate regime known as the prison industrial complex (Alexander 2012; Golash-Boza 2015). Despite having four percent of the global population, the U.S. has the largest incarcerated population at 22 percent of the global population, the majority being black and brown bodies (Alexander 2012; Kuhn 1996). U.S. citizens convicted of felony crimes are legally disenfranchised, losing their right to vote and access to public benefits even after serving their sentences (Alexander 2012). The prison industrial complex has also expanded into the immigration detention regime, intimately connecting the immigration, criminal justice, and penal systems (Golash-Boza 2015). Growth of the immigrant detention and incarceration regimes – via the legal and social disfranchisement of immigrants and citizens of color – demonstrates diminished citizenship and hardened social boundaries between them and white Americans.

In Europe, the criminal justice system is less punitive compared to the U.S. (Kuhn 1996). But, more resources have also been allocated to border security and detaining immigrants (Bosworth and Trumbull 2015). This trend has been followed in the UK, which established "Immigration Removal Centers" (IRCs) in 2001. Although immigration detention is "geared toward the ejection of unwanted citizens from British soil," it is not legal punishment (Bosworth and Trumbull 2015, 50). However, immigrants detained in IRCs experience their detention as punitive because IRCs are structured like prisons, with immigrants detained alongside criminal offenders. As in the U.S., multinational prison corporations operate prisons and immigrant detention centers in the UK, with white men guarding a disproportionate number of detainees and prisoners who are young men of color (Bosworth and Trumbull 2015). However, detainees' non-citizen status is brightened by their ability to be detained indefinitely without legal recourse, to which British citizen prisoners are entitled. IRCs also operate with fewer legal mechanisms than criminal prisons. Detainees are typically from countries where the UK had an active military presence, highlighting the impacts of post-colonialism and imperialism (Bosworth and Trumbull 2015). Bosworth and Trumbull (2015) argue that "detention is one among many techniques that maintain the whiteness of the nation by separating those who 'belong' in Britain from those who do not" (62). Thus, the UK's IRC system does the legal work of brightening boundaries between (white) citizens and (non-white) non-citizens.

Conclusion

Race, ethnicity, and documentation status have become crucially important for establishing social and symbolic boundaries, and legal and social citizenship in the 21st century U.S. and Europe. These distinguishing factors are also the bases for de jure and de facto exclusion primarily for citizens and non-citizens of color compared to white counterparts in both regions. Those who are not ethno-racially perceived as "belonging" are likely to be targeted and mistreated for not being legitimate members of their respective countries. This chapter has outlined recent socio-political events that demonstrate brightened social and symbolic boundaries that make whiteness synonymous with legal and social citizenship. In response to global economic disorder and increasing migration, explicitly racist and anti-immigrant rhetoric and politicians have become part of our current socio-political discourse. Subsequently, public policies have become more restrictive towards non-citizens and citizens of color, reducing their access to public benefits, and making them more subject to detention, deportation, or incarceration. People of color's marginalization has increased in these regions and legal citizenship does not guarantee social citizenship. But rather, being a person of color or immigrant makes an individual more likely to experience de jure and de facto discrimination from the state and white citizens. These recent events reveal that one must be racially white to be fully socio-politically included, experience the full rights of formal citizenship, and perceived as belonging to the U.S. or Europe. Unless the U.S. and Europe can blur brightened boundaries based on race, ethnicity, and documentation status, extend social citizenship to legal citizens of color, and treat non-citizens as members of their nations, the divisiveness of recent years will intensify. The consequence will be persistent inequality, social disparities, and conflict and hardened boundaries between white citizens and everyone else.

Notes

1 Populism is a philosophy that accentuates the wisdom of ordinary people over establishments, engenders cynicism of existing authority, has authoritarian leanings, and usually emphasizes xenophobia nativism (Inglehart and Pippins 2016).
2 Amid legislative battles between the conservative and liberal parties in government, the ACA was not fully implemented in all U.S. states, resulting in some formal citizens not benefiting from the policy (Joseph 2016).

References

Abrego, L., Coleman, M., Martínez, D., Menjívar, C., and Slack, J. (2016). Making Immigrants into Criminals: Legal Processes of Criminalization in the Post-IIRIRA Era. *Journal on Migration and Human Security*, 5(3), pp. 694–715.
Alba, R. (2005). Bright vs. Blurred Boundaries: Second-Generation Assimilation and Exclusion in France, Germany, and the United States. *Ethnic and Racial Studies*, 28(1), pp. 20–49.
Alesina, A., and Glaeser, E. (2004). *Fighting Poverty in the US and Europe: A World of Difference*. Oxford: Oxford University Press.
Alexander, M. (2012). *The New Jim Crow: Mass Incarceration in the Age of Colorblindness*. New York: New Press.
Baldi, G., and Goodman, S. (2015). Migrants into Members: Social Rights, Civic Requirements, and Citizenship in Western Europe. *West European Politics*, 38(6), pp. 1152–1173.
Beauchamp, Zach. 2018. The Midterm Elections Revealed that America is in a Cold Civil War. November 7. Available at www.vox.com/midterm-elections/2018/11/7/18068486/midterm-election-2018-results-race-surburb. [Accessed 7 Nov. 2018.].
Bhambra, G. (2017). Brexit, Trump, and 'Methodological Whiteness': On the Misrecognition of Race and Class. *British Journal of Sociology*, 68, pp. 214–232.
Bloemraad, I., Kymlicka, W., Lamont, M., and Hing, L. (2019). Membership without Social Citizenship? Deservingness and Redistribution as Grounds for Equality. *Daedalus*, doi:10.1162/DAED_a_01751.
Bobo, L. (2017). Racism in Trump's America: Reflections on Culture, Sociology, and the 2016 US Presidential Election. *British Journal of Sociology*, 68, pp. S85-S104.
Bosworth, M., and Trumbull, S. (2015). Immigration, Detention, and the Expansion of Penal Power in the United Kingdom. In K. Reiter and A. Koenig eds., *Extreme Punishment*. London: Palgrave McMillan, pp. 50–65.
Cappelen, C., and Peters, Y. (2018). Diversity and Welfare State Legitimacy in Europe. The Challenge of Intra-EU Migration. *Journal of European Public Policy*, 25(9), pp. 1336–1356.
Cheliotis, L. (2017). Punitive Inclusion: The Political Economy of Irregular Migration in the Margins of Europe. *European Journal of Criminology*, 14(1), pp. 78–99.
Crawley, H., and Skleparis, D. (2018). Refugees, Migrants, Neither, Both: Categorical Fetishism and the Politics of Bounding in Europe's Migration Crisis. *Journal of Ethnicand Migration Studies*, 44(1), pp. 48–64.
DeGenova, N. (2018). The "Migrant Crisis" as Racial Crisis: Do *Black Lives Matter* in Europe? *Ethnic and Racial Studies*, 41(10), pp. 1765–1782.
Feagin, J. (2000). *Racist America: Roots, Current Realities, and Future Reparations*. New York: Routledge.
Flores-Gonzalez, N. (2017). *Citizens But Not Americans: Race and Belonging Among Latino Millennials*. New York: New York University Press.
Foner, N., and Alba, R. (2015). *Strangers No More: Immigration and the Challenges of Integration in North America and Western Europe*. Princeton, NJ: Princeton University Press.
Fox, C. (2016). Unauthorized Welfare: The Origins of Immigrant Status Restrictions in American Social Policy. *Journal of American History*, 102(4), pp. 1051–1074.

Freeman, G. (2004). Immigrant Incorporation in Western Democracies. *International Migration Review*, 38(3), pp. 945–969.

Golash-Boza, T. (2015). *Deported: Immigrant Policing, Disposable Labor and Global Capitalism*. New York: New York University Press.

Gupta, S., and Virdee, S. (2018). Introduction: European Crises: Contemporary Nationalisms and the Language of "Race". *Ethnic and Racial Studies*, 41(10), pp. 1747–1764.

Gusterson, H. (2017). From Brexit to Trump: Anthropology and the Rise of Nationalist Populism. *American Ethnologist*, 44(2), pp. 209–214.

Haynes, C., Merolla, J., and Karthick Ramakrishnan, S. (2016). *Framing Immigrants: News Coverage, Public Opinion, and Policy*. New York: Russell Sage Foundation.

Hiam, L. (2018). Creating a "Hostile Environment for Migrants": The British Government's Use of Health Service Data to Restrict Immigration is a Very Bad Idea. *Health Economics, Policy and Law*, 13, pp. 107–117.

Hollifield, James. (1992). *Immigrants, Markets, and States: The Political Economy of Postwar Europe*. Cambridge: Harvard University Press.

Holmes, S., and Castañeda, H. (2016). Representing the "European Refugee Crisis" in Germany and Beyond: Deservingness and Difference, Life and Death. *American Ethnologist*, 43, pp. 12–24.

Imoagene, O. (2017). *Beyond Expectations: Second-Generation Nigerians in the United States and Britain*. Berkeley, CA: University of California Press.

Inglehart, R., and Norris, P. (2016). *Trump, Brexit, and the Rise of Populism: Economic Have-Nots and Cultural Backlash*. Paper presented at 2016 Annual Meeting of the American Political Science Association, Philadelphia.

International Organization for Migration (IOM). (2018). World Migration Report 2018. The UN Migration Agency.

Joppke, C. (2007). Beyond National Models: Civic Integration Policies for Immigrants in Western Europe. *West European Politics*, 30(1), pp. 1–22.

Joseph, T. (2016). What Healthcare Reform Means for Immigrants: A Comparison of the Affordable Care Act and Massachusetts Health Reforms. *Journal of Health Policy, Politics, and Law*, 41, pp. 101–116.

Komaromi, P. (2016). Post-referendum Racism and Xenophobia: The Role of Social Media Activism in Challenging the Normalisation of Xeno-racist Narratives. Available at www.irr.org.uk/news/post-ref erendum-racism-and-the-importance-of-social-activism/. [Accessed 20 Nov 2018.].

Kuhn, A. (1996). Incarceration Rates: Europe versus USA. *European Journal on Criminal Policy and Research*, 4(3), pp. 46–73.

Lamont, M., and Molnar, V. (2002). The Study of Boundaries in the Social Sciences. *Annual Review of Sociology*, 28, pp. 167–195.

Lamont, M, Park, B., and Ayala-Hurtado, E. (2017). Trump's Electoral Speeches and His Appeal to the American White Working Class. *British Journal of Sociology*, 68(S1), pp. S153-S180.

Marback, R., and Kruman, M. (2015). Introduction. In R. Marback and M. Kruman, eds., *The Meaning of Citizenship*. Detroit, MI: Wayne State University Press, pp. 1–11.

Ngai, M. (2014). *Impossible Subjects: Illegal Aliens and the Making of Modern America*. Princeton, NJ: Princeton University Press.

Park, L. (2011). *Entitled to Nothing: The Struggle for Immigrant Health Care in the Age of Welfare Reform*. New York: New York University.

Pierce, S., Bolter, J., and Selee, A. (2018). U.S. Immigration Policy under Trump: Deep Changes and Lasting Impacts. *Migration Policy Institute*. Accessed at www.migrationpolicy.org/research/us-immigra tion-policy-trump-deep-changes-impacts [Accessed 1 February 2019.].

Portes, A., and Rumbaut, R. (2014). *Immigrant America: A Portrait [4th Edition]*. Berkeley, CA: University of California Press.

Schierup, C., Ålund, A., and Neergaard, A. (2018). Race and the Upsurge of Antagonistic Popular Movements in Sweden. *Ethnic and Racial Studies*, 41(10), pp. 1837–1854.

Selod, S. (2018). *Forever Suspect: Racialized Surveillance of Muslim Americans in the War on Terror*. New Brunswick: Rutgers University Press.

Smith, R. (2015). The Questions Facing Citizenship in the 21st Century. In R. Marback and M. Kruman, eds., *The Meaning of Citizenship*. Detroit, MI: Wayne State University Press, pp. 12–23.

Soysal, Y. (1994). *Limits of Citizenship: Migrants and Postnational Membership in Europe*. Chicago: University of Chicago Press.

Strolovitch, D., Wong, J., and Proctor, A. (2017). A Possessive Investment in White Heteropatriarchy? The 2016 Election and the Politics of Race, Gender, and Sexuality. *Politics, Groups, and Identities*, 5(2), pp. 353–363.

Tavernise, S. (2018). Why the Announcement of a Looming White Minority Makes Demographers Nervous. November 22. *New York Times*.

Tyler, I. (2018). The Hieroglyphics of the Border: Racial Stigma in Neoliberal Europe. *Ethnic and Racial Studies*, 41(10), pp. 1783–1801.

Tyson, A., and Maniam, S. (2016). Behind Trump's Victory: Divisions by Race, Gender, Education. Nov 9. Available at www.pewresearch.org/fact-tank/2016/11/09/behind-trumps-victory-divisions-by-race-gender-education/[Accessed 20 Nov 2018.].

Virdee, S., and McGeever, B. (2018). Racism, Crisis, Brexit. *Ethnic and Racial Studies*, 41(10), pp. 1802–1819.

Waters, M., and Kasinitz, P. (2015). The War on Crime and the War on Immigrants: Racial and Legal Exclusion in the Twenty-First Century United States. In N. Foner and P. Simon, eds., *Fear, Anxiety, and National Identity: Immigration and Belonging in North America and Western Europe*. New York: Russell Sage Foundation, pp. 115–144.

Wimmer, A. (2013). *Ethnic Boundary Making: Institutions, Power, Networks*. New York: Oxford University Press.

Wrench, J., and Solomos, J. (1993). *Racism and Migration in Western Europe*. Oxford: Oxford University Press.

Xu, P. (2017). Compensation or Retrenchment? The Paradox of Immigration and Public Welfare Spending in the American States. *State Politics & Policy Quarterly*, 17(1), pp. 76–104.

5

Race and racisms

Why and how to compare?

Graziella Moraes Silva

Introduction

This chapter outlines recent debates in the literature on comparative race and racisms, with a particular emphasis on empirical, cross-national comparisons. Due to the exponential growth of this field, an exhaustive review of all works produced in the past decades is beyond the scope of this chapter. Instead, this chapter focuses on three key issues: (1) the conceptual justifications for the proliferation of comparative studies on race and racism; (2) the historical development, and limitations posed by, studies of comparative race thus far; and (3) the emergence of new strategies for comparing race and racisms, with a focus on conceptual and methodological choices. The chapter concludes by discussing remaining challenges to, and potential opportunities for, the advancement of a comparative approach to studies of race and racism.

Why compare race and racisms?

The central claim of this chapter is that the comparison of race and racisms is central to unpacking the different ways that race is socially constructed and how racisms work across different contexts. Given the high frequency with which versions of the statement "race is a social construct" can be found in the footnotes and introductions of academic papers dealing with race and racism, one might be tempted to claim further examination of this topic is unnecessary. Yet, there is much less consensus about the meaning of this statement within academia. Analyzing school textbooks, surveying college students, and interviewing university professors across disciplines, Morning (2011) finds that the idea of race as a social construct is more elusive than its frequent mention might lead one to believe. The author argues that, although the social construction of race is a widely accepted notion in social sciences, most scholars have a hard time explaining what it means beyond a vague rejection of essentialist understandings of race. It is also a less accepted notion in other disciplines, such as biology. In fact, across most disciplines, college students generally rely on essentialist understandings (both biological and cultural) when explaining racialized outcomes (e.g., why blacks are more frequently professional athletes or the causes of lower birth weight among African American or Asian infants). Beyond academia, the growing popularity of genetic tests in search of "racial origins" serves as a tangible reminder that understanding of race as a social construct is not as prevalent as most social scientists might assume (Roth and Ivemark, 2018).

According to Suzuki (2017), one obstacle to the diffusion of the idea of race as socially constructed could be that most studies on race and racism still rely on a definition of race that is specifically relevant to the United States context and assume this national understanding of race as universal. If Omi and Winant's (1994) concept of racial formation—and other similar concepts—have been important in pushing forward scholarly understanding of the social construction of race, such concepts might also have unintentionally generalized from the historical experience of the United States. This is partially due to the fact that, after World War II, social scientific theorizing about race and racism developed much more consistently in the United States than elsewhere. The consequence has been that, although race has been studied in the UK, South Africa, and Brazil, the United States experience is often taken as paradigmatic in studies about race and racialization.

The growth of comparative studies has been, in part, a response to the perceived ethnocentrism of the United States literature. According to Van den Berghe (1970), one of the pioneers of comparative sociology of race and ethnicity, the only way to overcome the provincialism of the American literature on race and ethnicity is to rely on a comparative approach. Similarly, Fredrickson's (1989) comparative studies of slavery and race were also largely inspired by the need to put the American alleged exceptionalism in perspective. By contrasting the American context to that of other countries, we can better understand the multiple ways in which racialization processes work across these contexts and illuminate the shortcomings and national assumptions of existing theories and concepts. What are the limits of what can be considered as "race" and "racism"? And what types of comparisons can be made with such multifaceted concepts?

The historical development of comparative race relations as a field of study

Throughout the 20th century, the cross-national, comparative study of race and racisms was dominated by historians. According to Frederick Cooper (1996), comparisons of slavery and discourses of racial difference can be found as early as 1910. One exemplary work is Frank Tannenbaum's (Tannenbaum, 1992 [1946]) comparison of slavery in the United States and Latin America. First published in 1946, in the aftermath of World War II and escalating attention to race issues in the form of a growing civil rights movement, today the book reads as an attempt to find a solution to what the author perceived as the problems in the United States. Indeed, Tannenbaum found a solution in Latin America.

Comparing moral discourses about slavery across the Americas, Tannenbaum argued that in English-speaking colonies—namely the United States—the status of the slave was that of non-human, subject of neither Church nor State. In contrast, in Latin America, the slaves, even if exploited, retained an element of humanity as subject of the crown and the church. Because of that, according to Tannenbaum, after abolition, "the integration of the ex-slave into society and polity posed no fundamental problem in Latin America but a very basic one in the United States." (Cooper, 1996, p. 1123). In order to explain this basic difference, Tannenbaum relied on a broader discourse of "Iberian culture," similar to that mobilized in Gilberto Freyre's (1934) argument for the existence of racial democracy in Brazil (which can also be considered—even if not explicitly—a comparative work between the United States and Brazil).

Although today such an argument seems overly simplified, if not irrelevant, we should not underplay its political and academic consequences. Politically, works like those of Tannenbaum and Freyre have encouraged UNESCO to conduct studies in Latin America and have been mobilized in nation-building narratives based on racial-exceptionalism (or claims of lack of racism) throughout the region. Academically, the comparison between the United States and Latin America (in particular Brazil) became one of the most influential in comparative race research, but criticisms of this approach created resistance within, and against, the field.

Criticisms unfolded on multiple fronts. Historians such as Charles Boxer (2002) have relied on empirical data based on social indicators (e.g. the higher mortality rates of Brazilian slaves) to denounce the idealized version of Latin American history and slavery. Others, such as Eugene Genovese (1969), have focused on similarities across countries—in particular, Marxist explanations for race and slavery that center on global capitalism. More recently, historians such as Frederick Cooper (1996) have denounced the underlying essentialism of race and culture that has served as the basis for these comparisons—"a willingness to draw direct inferences from the era of slavery to the present, leapfrogging over a messy history that lay in between" (p. 1123).

Focusing on differences or exceptionalisms, such comparisons commonly make moral judgments about what comprises better or worse race relations. If most early studies echoed Pierre van den Berghe (1976, p. 532) question, "Why is the United States a more racist society than the Latin American republics?", explicit and implicit comparisons in the post-civil-rights era increasingly became concerned with the failure of Latin American racial minorities to organize successfully to fight racism (Hanchard, 1998). The underlying assumption was one of a similar moral hierarchy of racialization processes across nations that still echoes in more recent works focusing on normative evaluations of nation-building ideologies, multicultural strategies, and resistance strategies.

These shortcomings have been addressed, in part, in later more systematic and less normative comparative studies and a shift in focus from "nations" as cultural entities to "nation-states" with institutions and political conflicts. Anthony Marx's (1998) *Making Race and Nation* is exemplary of this turn. First, Marx proposes a reframing of the research question driving comparison of processes of racialization between Brazil, the United States and South Africa. The question no longer seeks to explain *why* there are racial tensions or racism in Brazil but why Brazil lacks a history of formal segregation, such as Jim Crow or apartheid, and what are the consequences of this difference. Second, Marx's explanation for the differences does not rely on abstract cultural differences—which are explicitly denied in the first section of the book—but on institutions, actions, and power. For example, the author argues that conflicts between white elites were absent in Brazil yet central to the shaping of political alliances in the United States and South Africa. Third, Marx focuses not only on formal and legal practices but also on the unintended consequences of these practices. In particular, he argues that a lack of segregation policies created obstacles for the political mobilization of black Brazilians around anti-racist movements.

While *Making Race and Nation* is exemplary of a new approach to the comparison of race and racisms, its criticisms reflect the continuing challenges of this field. Loveman (1999) argues that, even if Marx clearly states that race is a social construction, the author still largely takes for granted the existence of "whites" and "blacks" across the three sites, making the book less about how race is made and more about how states manipulate race. Nation-states are also largely taken for granted as the unit of analysis, underplaying the importance of transnational processes and repertoires about race. Finally, despite taking seriously the possibility that racisms can be mobilized differently, Marx still evaluates different strategies based on the assumption that they should look the same in all contexts or, even more egregiously, develops a normative argument about national anti-racism strategies (as discussed in the justification of the project of Moreno Figueroa and Wade, (n.d.)).

New approaches to comparing race and racisms

Recent works comparing race and racisms have taken these issues seriously. In order to address them, they have proposed new methods of comparison, including innovative macro-historical approaches, survey strategies and ethnographic approaches.

Comparing race-making in state institutions and through transnational processes

Several scholars have followed the path of macro-historical approaches, focusing on institutions—especially the state—as the key actors of race-making. Yet they also incorporate the idea that racial boundaries are themselves created by the state. The institutional focus ranges from formal categorization to more informal networks, but, regardless of the object of analysis, they all analyze historical and changing processes that transform the meanings and consequences of these categories across time and space.

Comparative research on the history of census serves as an excellent example of the potential of these approaches. In pathbreaking work on census racial categories in Brazil, the United States, and South Africa, Nobles (2000) has shown how counting (or not) race is a political process that creates and negotiates race as a political category. Several authors have examined how laws create race indirectly—beyond official segregation policies and openly discriminatory practices. The focus on racial effects of race-blind laws (or a racism without races) has been particularly prolific in Europe, where immigration has brought a wave of non-white residents but the language of race is still largely resisted (Simon, 2017). Comparisons have been made regarding how countries design and implement policies to promote equality and fight discrimination against racialized, and mostly immigrant minorities (e.g. Kastoryano, 2002; Bleich, 2003). The growth of anti-Muslim sentiment has also opened a new comparative agenda about the different ways in which racism is defined by states and by policies for responding to it (e.g. Bleich, 2011; Kastoryano, 2015).

Beyond the central role of nation-states, contemporary comparisons have also taken seriously a broader understanding of race as a global experience extending from histories of colonization, slavery, and immigration (e.g. Gilroy, 1993; Winant, 2001; Reid Andrews, 2004; Goldberg, 2006). In fact, recent studies have been much more attentive to transnational processes, in particular new scientific ideas about race and frameworks of multiculturalism. For example, Stepan (1991) and Wade et al. (2014) have focused on how national ideas about race enter into and are affected by transnational scientific practices such as old theories eugenics and contemporary debates on genomics. Loveman (2014) shows that Latin American censuses are shaped by transnational ideas of scientific practices and transnational repertoires about race, while Paschel (2016) analyzes how the wave of new anti-racism policies in Latin America has been shaped by alliances between local and transnational social movements in Brazil and Colombia. Focusing on Asia, Goh (2008) investigates the impact of racialist policies adopted by colonial powers on current understandings of multiculturalism in Malaysia and Singapore. Together these works highlight the importance of incorporating these transnational movements into research, yet without losing sight of variation in their enactment across different contexts.

This body of research on transnational processes has also pushed the scope of the literature beyond the Western experience and revealed a paradox: Transnational processes are, in large part, studied in non-Western (or Global South) racialization experiences. In contrast, racialization processes in Europe and North America are more often understood as shaped by domestic and national contexts. In fact, the processes through which race is negotiated within international organizations and through international relations have remained largely understudied (Lauren, 2018; Galonnier and Simon, forthcoming).

Comparing race and racisms as the independent and the dependent variable

Macro-historical and institutional comparisons provide us important insights into how nation-states and transnational processes construct race, but they tend to focus on top-down approaches, telling us little about the actual impact of race and racism in shaping unequal outcomes across different countries. Since the 2000s, the growth in the number of countries collecting ethnoracial data in their national censuses—itself a transnational transformation (Morning, 2008; Loveman, 2014)—presents an opportunity to compare how racialization shapes socioeconomic outcomes across different contexts.

Such types of comparisons are more common, if not widespread, in economics. These studies largely converge in identifying statistically significant inequalities across national contexts, even if in different degrees and diverse associations. For example, in a recent analysis relying on national household surveys in Brazil, the United States, and South Africa, Gradín (2014, p. 90) finds,

> [E]ven if blacks [operationalized as *pretos* and *pardos* in Brazil, African black in South Africa and African American in the United States] had the same observed characteristics as whites in these three countries, a substantial (conditional) differential would still persist in average incomes.

The author shows how racial income inequalities are related to different observed demographic characteristics in the three countries. While educational gaps and regional concentration are the most important drivers of racial inequalities in Brazil, type of household (e.g. female-headed households) and performance of household members in the labor market play a more important role in the United States. In South Africa, Gradín found the strongest association between racial and household characteristics, especially the educational level. Considering these findings from a sociological perspective, one can conclude that racialization is happening through different institutional mechanisms, an agenda that could be pursued further by social stratification scholars interested in how institutions shape racial inequalities (e.g. Telles, 1992; Moraes Silva et al, under review; Carter, 2012).

Nevertheless, relying on official data collected through varied methods and with differently constructed categories may create a problem of comparability (Wrench, 2011). This is especially consequential in the case of comparisons of attitudes towards race, racisms and discrimination, in which the framing of the question can have a strong impact on the patterns of response. Cross-national surveys—although rare due to their high cost—have opened a new path for comparison. Comparison that relies on publicly available surveys (e.g., Eurobarometer, LAPOP) and include questions about ethnoracial identification or perceptions of racism and discrimination have shown how attitudes about the salience of racism and discrimination vary across countries (e.g. Quillian, 1995; Bail, 2008; Staerklé et al., 2010;

Canache et al., 2014). In Europe in 2008, the EU-Midis, financed and conducted by the European Agency for Fundamental Rights, surveyed 23,500 ethnic minorities and immigrant groups throughout the 27 EU member states, as well as 5000 majority people across ten member states (EU-MIDIS, 2009). The survey asked respondents about their experiences of discrimination, their experiences of criminal victimization (including racially motivated crime), the extent of any involvement of the security forces in these encounters, their aware- ness of their rights, and their reasons for reporting (or not) these encounters. In its official report (EU-MIDIS, 2009), the study primarily compares across different ethnoracial groups (Roma, Muslims, North Africans, Sub-Saharan Africans, etc) within each country and, due to sampling limits, refrains from comparing across countries.

But beyond collecting comparable data, comparing race without taking it seriously as a theoretical concept may conflate different dimensions and meanings of the term (see Roth, 2017) and reproduce an essentialized notion of race. Aware of this risk, surveys have also been used to compare different understandings of race or compare race as a dependent variable (Suzuki, 2017). The Project on Ethnicity and Race in Latin America (PERLA), for example, has focused on how racial self-identification can vary depending on the categories proposed to respondents. The survey analyzes divergence between the self-identification of respondents and the interviewer's classification of them. It also attempts to disentangle racial categories from skin color, ideas that are frequently conflated. Telles and PERLA (2014) asked interviewers to rate the skin color of interviewees based on a color palette and concluded that, when compared to racial categories, skin color rankings better captured the dynamics of racism in Brazil, Colombia, Mexico, and Peru. Bailey, Saperstein, and Penner (2014) advanced the analysis of racial categories and skin color by using data from the Latin American Public Opinion Project (LAPOP), which relied on the same color palette designed by PERLA to expand the measurement of color and racial hierarchies across Latin America. The authors also added the case of the United States, where a different but comparable skin color measure has been used in the 2012 General Social Survey. As in the case of PERLA, they find that racial categories and color do not always overlap, but they also show that income inequality can best be understood in some countries by using racial categories alone and in others by using skin color. In a few countries, including the United States, a combination of skin color and self- identified race best explains income variation. They conclude that the different ways in which racial categories (and skin color) are understood impact inequality, complicating cross-national comparisons of racial inequalities within Latin America as well as between Latin American and the United States.

Comparing cultural repertoires of race and racisms

Comparative studies relying on ethnographic and in-depth interviews propose a different alternative to understanding how people experience race and racism. By focusing on narrated experiences and observed interactions, these methods can be more appropriate for analyzing how race and racism work across different settings. An exemplary approach is Essed's (1991) study of everyday racism based on 55 in-depth interviews with black women in the Netherlands and United States. Analyzing these narratives, Essed shows how everyday micro-processes are linked to distinct macrosocial racialized structures. Although the author's explicit goal is not to make a systematic comparison between the Netherlands and United States—rather she uses the United States as a frame of reference for analyzing the Netherlands—Essed points to a number of factors that cause race and racism to be interpreted differently in these two national contexts.

The comparative goal is more clearly at the heart of the collectively authored book, *Getting Respect*, (Lamont et al., 2016). Based on 500 in-depth interviews with working-class and middle-class African Americans, black Brazilians, and Arab Palestinians, Ethiopian and Mizrahi citizens of Israel, the study seeks to systematically compare how racism—conceptualized as experiences of assault on worth and discrimination—is experienced in the United States, Brazil, and Israel. Conceptually, the authors propose that these experiences can be better understood by focusing on similarities and differences across contexts and along three dimensions: historical, socioeconomic, and institutional structures (such as those analyzed in the macro-historical comparative studies previously discussed); national and transnational cultural repertoires (such as national myths and empowering ideologies); and groupness (defined as the mix of self-identification and symbolic boundaries towards outgroups, in terms of both race and class). The detailed comparison of narratives of stigmatization experiences illustrates how specific experiences are perceived as discriminatory (i.e. as having consequences on access to certain resources) in certain contexts but not in others. This explains, for example, why in survey studies perception of discrimination among black Brazilians is much lower than among African Americans, despite experiencing similar, or even higher, levels of socioeconomic racial inequalities. In addition, the authors explore why different ideal and actual responses to racism are chosen, despite a widespread recognition of racial stigmatization across all cases. Finally, adding the case of Israel to the traditional Brazil versus United States comparison highlights how understanding race as skin color, ethnicity, national identity or religion can change the way racism is interpreted and resisted. The exclusion through blackness—as in the case of African Americans, black Brazilians and Ethiopian citizens of Israel—has a long shared history and a vast repertoire of interpretation and resistance. In contrast, the exclusion through ethnicity or culture may be perceived as localized, specific or naturalized through the often elusive goal of integration, as illustrated by the case of Mizrahi citizens of Israel. The case of Palestinian citizens of Israel evidences racialization, coupling religion and national identity, in which ethnoracial boundaries are perceived as more rigid and hard to cross or question. The growing importance of nationality and religion coupled with a context of growing securization of national borders and restriction of citizenship may make the Palestinian case particularly illustrative of new forms of exclusionary racialization.

While *Getting Respect* identifies the importance of transnational narratives in shaping national experiences of race, particularly in Brazil and Israel, other recent studies have focused more explicitly on the growing transnational dimension of race. Roth's (2012) comparison of the racial schemas of Dominicans and Puerto Ricans who migrated to the United States versus those who stayed in their home countries shows how these schemas migrate from one country to another. The author finds that these "race migrations" have transformed understandings of race not only in the home countries but also in the United States. Along the same lines, Joseph's (2015) detailed account of changes in the racial repertoires of Brazilian immigrants in their comings and goings from the United States shows how changing understandings of race transform the way racism (and anti-racism) are experienced.

More conceptually, recent works comparing national repertoires of race brought "culture" back into the study of racialization processes but abandon essentialized and nationalistic understandings of culture. Instead, such works analyze "culture in action," focusing on how different cultural repertoires frame both the social construction of race and resistance to racialization and racisms.

Concluding remarks

Although not exhaustive, this chapter has presented a broad review of multiple comparative approaches to the study of race and racisms in social science research. It has argued that comparison of race and racisms has a long history in the social sciences, but it has often been accused of falling short in its conceptualization of race and national differences.

As reviewed in this chapter, recent works on comparative race relations have relied on diverse conceptual and methodological approaches that have addressed prior shortcomings in multiple ways. Macro-historical comparisons have taken seriously the idea of how race is constructed differently by state institutions and transnational processes. Statistical models and surveys have been mobilized to examine how race and racisms shape socioeconomic stratification across different contexts and, as concepts, are perceived differently across countries. Finally, in-depth interview studies and multi-site ethnographies have analyzed how race and racism are shaped by everyday interactions and boundary-making, which are themselves shaped by national and transnational cultural repertoires. Despite the abundant literature, a number of challenges and opportunities remain for future research.

First, and perhaps most importantly, the comparative study of race and racisms always carries with it the risk of essentializing race. Although a degree of analytical abstraction is necessary to define a comparative unit of analysis, we should be careful not to take racial categories as proxies for racial groups (for an important discussion on this topic see Loveman, 1999). The groupness of racialized groups is itself a key variable to understanding how race and racisms work across different societies (Lamont et al., 2016). Recent works comparing how these boundaries are challenged, for example, through different understandings about multiracial or mixed-race identities (e.g. Thompson, 2012), multiracial relationships (Osuji, 2013), or the experiences of those converted to Islam (Galonnier, 2015) open an interesting line of inquiry about how racial boundaries work in different ways across different contexts.

The second challenge is the flipside of the reification of race—the risk of constructing comparisons between apples and oranges. The idea of racism without race contributes to the understanding that race is not inherently linked to any specific characteristic, such as skin color or phenotype. It also creates the challenge of drawing the limits of what constitutes racialization. Does it make sense to compare groups based on their language, immigrant status, religion or phenotype? The answer, of course, depends on the types of research questions proposed in the comparison. More attention to comparative studies of dominant identities, for example—such as experiences of whiteness and white privilege—might help us find a common unit of analysis across different cases.

Third, there is always risk of relying on comparisons to emphasize the exceptionality of traits, groups, or countries, and to create moral hierarchies among them. For example, the growing focus on skin color in the Americas has advanced an argument that racial categories such as black, mestizo, and indigenous have limited explanatory power (Telles and PERLA, 2014; Monk, 2014). Focusing on skin color as a more objective measure, however, also risks reducing racialization to phenotype, without developing a clear conceptual understanding of what skin color tells us about race or acknowledging the relationality through which skin color is experienced. When it comes to the "groups" analyzed, the focus of comparative research has been largely on the experiences of people of African-descent, and more recently Muslims. This focus risks overgeneralizing these experiences and underestimating other experiences of racialization or the multiple intersectionalities that shape them. Finally, the continuous emphasis on the United States as a paradigmatic—or, alternatively, exceptional—comparative case threatens to bias our understanding of how race and racisms work. In fact, most of the work on comparative race and racism is still produced in the United States, although a growing number of transnational collective projects have been produced in recent years (e.g. Lamont et al., 2016; Moreno Figueroa and Wade, (n.d.); Telles and PERLA, 2014).

In spite of these risks, comparative studies on race and racism remain an important tool to unpack the different ways that race is constructed. As shown in this review, recent studies have proposed interesting ways to conduct comparative research that take stock of these challenges and address them through creative research strategies. This is certainly a growing and resourceful field of research "in the making" not only through emerging analytical approaches but also new empirical developments. Race and racism are currently being transformed through transnational processes that not only reproduce racism but also create new anti-racist alliances. Transnational formal and informal anti-racist associations and forums as well as international migrations are interesting points of reference to empirically analyse those issues. In addition, it is important to take into account how these transnational processes are experienced and translated in local disputes not only to recognize discriminated identities but also to make visible dominant (and usually invisible) ones. In other words, comparing race and racism also means comparing the different ways in which racial privilege is constructed, reproduced and challenged. Finally, in comparing race and racisms studies can also be more attentive to how these concepts are transformed through different and localized intersectionalities with class, gender and sexuality. In fact, comparing the different ways these categories interact across different contexts, as well as the different political alliances they perform, would be a great tool to move forward processual and dynamic understandings of race and intersectionality. In short, the best way to deal with the perils of comparative research on race and racism is comparing more and in creative ways.

References

Bail, C.A. (2008). The Configuration of Symbolic Boundaries against Immigrants in Europe. *American Sociological Review*, 73 (1), 37–59.

Bailey, S.R., Saperstein, A., and Penner, A.M. (2014). Race, Color, and Income Inequality across the Americas. *Demographic Research*, 31, 735–756.

Bleich, E. (2003). *Race Politics in Britain and France: Ideas and Policymaking since the 1960s*. Cambridge: Cambridge University Press.

Bleich, E. (2011). What is Islamophobia and How Much is There? Theorizing and Measuring an Emerging Comparative Concept. *American Behavioral Scientist*, 55 (12), 1581–1600.

Boxer, C.R. (2002). *O império marítimo português, 1415-1825*. São Paulo: Editora Companhia das Letras.

Canache, D., Hayes, M., Mondak, J.J., and Seligson, M.A. (2014). Determinants of Perceived Skin-Color Discrimination in Latin America. *The Journal of Politics*, 76 (2), 506–520.

Carter, P.L. (2012). *Stubborn Roots: Race, Culture, and Inequality in US and South African Schools*. New York: Oxford University Press.

Cooper, F. (1996). Race, Ideology, and the Perils of Comparative History. *The American Historical Review*, 101 (4), 1122–1138.

Essed, P. (1991). *Understanding Everyday Racism: An Interdisciplinary Theory*. Newbury Park: Sage Publications.

EU-MIDIS (2009). *EU-MIDIS at a Glance: Introduction to the FRA's EU-Wide Discrimination Survey*. [online] European Union Agency for Fundamental Human Rights. Available at: http://fra.europa.eu/en/publication/2011/eu-midis-glance-introduction-fras-eu-wide-discrimination-survey (Accessed 26 November. 2018).

Fredrickson, G.M. (1989). *The Arrogance of Race: Historical Perspectives on Slavery, Racism, and Social Inequality*. Hanover: Wesleyan University Press.

Freyre, G. (1934). *Casa-grande & Senzala: Formação Da Familia Brasileira Sob O Regimen De Economia Patriarchal*. Rio de Janeiro: Maia & Schmidt.

Galonnier, J. (2015). The Racialization of Muslims in France and the United States: Some Insights from White Converts to Islam. *Social Compass*, 62 (4), 570–583.

Galonnier, J. and Simon, P. (eds). Forthcoming. « La question raciale dans les organisations internationales : un dilemme persistant (1945–2019) » Special Issue of *Critique internationale*.

Genovese, E.D. (1969). "The Treatment of Slaves in Different Countries: Problems in the Application of the Comparative Method." In L. Foner and E. Genovese (eds.), *Slavery in the New World*. NJ: Englewood Cliffs, 202–210.

Gilroy, P. (1993). *The Black Atlantic: Modernity and Double Consciousness*. Cambridge: Harvard University Press.

Goh, D.P.S. (2008). From Colonial Pluralism to Postcolonial Multiculturalism: Race, State Formation and the Question of Cultural Diversity in Malaysia and Singapore. *Sociology Compass*, 2 (1), 232–252.

Goldberg, D.T. (2006). Racial Europeanization. *Ethnic and Racial Studies*, 29 (2), 331–364.

Gradín, C. (2014). Race and Income Distribution: Evidence from the USA, Brazil and South Africa. *Review of Development Economics*, 18 (1), 73–92.

Hanchard, M.G. (1998). *Orpheus and Power: The Movimento Negro of Rio de Janeiro and São Paulo, Brazil 1945-1988*. Princeton: Princeton University Press.

Joseph, T.D. (2015). *Race on the Move: Brazilian Migrants and the Global Reconstruction of Race*. Palo Alto: Stanford University Press.

Kastoryano, R. (2002). *Negotiating Identities: States and Immigrants in France and Germany*. Vol. 12 Princeton: Princeton University Press.

Kastoryano, R. (2015). *Que faire des corps des djihadistes?: territoire et identité*. Paris: Fayard.

Lamont, M., Moraes Silva, G., Welburn, J., Guetzkow, J., Mizrachi, N., Herzog, H., and Reis, E. (2016). *Getting Respect: Responding to Stigma and Discrimination in the United States, Brazil, and Israel*. Princeton: Princeton University Press.

Lauren, P.G. (2018). *Power and Prejudice: The Politics and Diplomacy of Racial Discrimination*. New York: Routledge.

Loveman, Mara. (1999). Making "Race" and Nation in the United States, South Africa, and Brazil: Taking Making Seriously. *Theory and Society*, 28 (6), 903–927.

Loveman, Mara. (2014). *National Colors: Racial Classification and the State in Latin America*. New York: Oxford University Press.

Marx, A.W. (1998). *Making Race and Nation: A Comparison of South Africa, the United States, and Brazil*. Cambridge: Cambridge University Press.

Monk, Jr, Ellis, P. (2014). Skin Tone Stratification among Black Americans, 2001–2003. *Social Forces*, 92 (4), 1313–1337.

Moreno Figueroa, M. and Wade, P. n.d. *Latin American Anti-Racism in a Post Racial Age*. University of Cambridge. Available at: www.lapora.sociology.cam.ac.uk/(Accessed 18 November. 2018).

Morning, A. (2008). Ethnic Classification in Global Perspective: A Cross-National Survey of the 2000 Census Round. *Population Research and Policy Review*, 27 (2), 239–272.

Morning, A. (2011). *The Nature of Race: How Scientists Think and Teach about Human Difference*. Berkeley: University of California Press.

Nobles, M. (2000). *Shades of Citizenship: Race and the Census in Modern Politics*. Palo Alto: Stanford University Press.

Omi, M. and Winant, H. (1994). *Racial Formation in the United States: From the 1960s to the 1990s*. New York: Routledge.

Osuji, C.K. (2013). Racial 'Boundary-Policing': Perceptions of Black-White Interracial Couples in Los Angeles and Rio de Janeiro. *Du Bois Review: Social Science Research on Race*, 10 (1), 179–203.

Paschel, T.S. (2016). *Becoming Black Political Subjects: Movements and Ethno-Racial Rights in Colombia and Brazil*. Princeton: Princeton University Press.

Quillian, L. (1995). Prejudice as a Response to Perceived Group Threat: Population Composition and Anti-Immigrant and Racial Prejudice in Europe. *American Sociological Review*, 60 (4), 586–611.

Reid Andrews, G. (2004). *Afro-Latin America, 1800–2000*. New York: Oxford University Press.

Roth, W. (2012). *Race Migrations: Latinos and the Cultural Transformation of Race*. Palo Alto: Stanford University Press.

Roth, W. (2017). Methodological Pitfalls of Measuring Race: International Comparisons and Repurposing of Statistical Categories. *Ethnic and Racial Studies*, 40 (13), 2347–2353.

Roth, W. and Ivemark, B. (2018). Genetic Options: The Impact of Genetic Ancestry Testing on Consumers' Racial and Ethnic Identities. *American Journal of Sociology*, 124 (1), 150–184.

Simon, P. (2017). The Failure of the Importation of Ethno-Racial Statistics in Europe: Debates and Controversies. *Ethnic and Racial Studies*, 40 (13), 2326–2332.

Staerklé, C, Sidanius, J., Green, E. G.T., and Molina, L.E. (2010). Ethnic Minority-Majority Asymmetry in National Attitudes around the World: A Multilevel Analysis. *Political Psychology*, 31 (4), 491–519.

Stepan, N. (1991). *"The Hour of Eugenics": Race, Gender, and Nation in Latin America*. Ithaca: Cornell University Press.

Suzuki, K. (2017). A Critical Assessment of Comparative Sociology of Race and Ethnicity. *Sociology of Race and Ethnicity*, 3 (3), 287–300.

Tannenbaum, F. (1992 [1946]). *Slave and Citizen*. New York: Beacon Press.

Telles, E. (1992). Residential Segregation by Skin Color in Brazil. *American Sociological Review*, 57 (2), 186–197.

Telles, E. and the Project on Ethnicity and Race (PERLA). (2014). *Pigmentocracies: Ethnicity, Race, and Color in Latin America*. Chapel Hill: University of North Carolina Press.

Thompson, D. (2012). Making (Mixed-) Race: Census Politics and the Emergence of Multiracial Multiculturalism in the United States, Great Britain and Canada. *Ethnic and Racial Studies*, 35 (8), 1409–1426.

Van Den Berghe, P.L. (1970). *Race and Ethnicity: Essays in Comparative Sociology*. New York: Basic Books.

Van Den Berghe, P.L. (1976). The African Diaspora in Mexico, Brazil and the United States. *Social Forces*, 54 (3), 530–545.

Wade, P., López Beltrán, C., Restrepo, E., and Ventura Santos, R. (eds) (2014). *Mestizo Genomics: Race Mixture, Nation, and Science in Latin America*. Durham: Duke University Press.

Winant, H. (2001). *The World is a Ghetto: Race and Democracy since World War II*. New York: Basic Books.

Wrench, J. (2011). Data on Discrimination in EU Countries: Statistics, Research and the Drive for Comparability. *Ethnic and Racial Studies*, 34 (10), 1715–1730.

6

Latin American racisms in global perspective

Peter Wade

Introduction

An enduring feature of Latin American racial formations is *mestizaje* (*mestiçagem* in Portuguese). Translatable as mixture, the term refers to the processes of sexual and cultural interactions between Europeans, Africans and indigenous Americans that started in the sixteenth century and gave rise to substantial populations of "mestizos" – an umbrella term for people categorised as neither European, nor African nor *indio* (the Spanish colonial term for indigenous Americans), but something in between. Mestizo originally referred to the products of sexual interactions that mixed together *razas* (races), understood not so much as categories of people, but rather as lines of ancestry or "blood" (Banton 1987). But the term quickly acquired connotations of cultural mixture, with mestizos perceived to have inherited a combination of European, African and indigenous American habits.

Due to the colonial context, in which Europeans conquered, exploited and enslaved indigenous and African people, hierarchy always structured these interactions: "blood" and cultural traits perceived to be of African and indigenous origin were seen by the colonial powers as inferior to those considered as European: blackness/Africanness was strongly associated with enslavement; indigeneity was a vassal status; both were linked to barbarism and religious heterodoxy. *Mestizaje* was also structured by gender hierarchy, both in the sense that the European colonists were predominantly men who had sex with indigenous and African women, and in the ideological sense that nineteenth- and twentieth-century nationalist discourses highlighted masculine dominance in what was seen as the foundational creation of the populations that eventually formed nation-states.

In a global context, although colonialism everywhere gave rise to sexual and cultural mixture, only in Latin America did the process come to characterise a whole region in racial terms, and from the mid-nineteenth century to be widely – although not uniformly – adopted as national self-image, said by elites to differentiate the region's countries from other areas of the world, especially the Atlantic world. It is in relation to *mestizaje* that – still today – we have to grasp racism and the struggle against it.

Processes of mixture

Estimates are vague but, over the colonial period, probably less than 2 million Europeans arrived in Latin America; of these, under 30% were women. Some 6.5 million enslaved

Africans were forcibly brought to the region, with men in the great majority. Once there, many of these Europeans and Africans mixed with each other and with indigenous peoples whose original numbers are uncertain, but who, by 1650, numbered about 6 million, having been depleted by disease and abuse (Marcílio 1984; Newson 1993; Sánchez-Albornoz 1984). By the late colonial period, a heterogeneous category of legally free people had emerged, recognised as intermediate between enslaved people, *indios* and whites. These people – many of whom were mestizos of diverse kinds – formed between a quarter (e.g. Mexico, Peru), a third (e.g. Brazil) and a half (e.g. Colombia) of the total population. Within a racial hier-archy dominated by whites, with enslaved and indigenous people at the bottom, the mestizo population was stratified according to multiple criteria, including occupation, wealth and racialised ancestry and appearance; complex nomenclatures attempted to organise this stratifi-cation. Historians have debated the role played in the stratification by what we might now call "race" (see Wade 2010: 28–29), but ideas about a person's "blood", often inferred from phenotype, were very important (Martínez 2008; Twinam 2015).

Between independence (which in most places occurred 1810–1830) and the mid-twentieth century, more than 15 million European immigrants entered the region – of which 12 million went to Argentina and Brazil. There were much smaller numbers of immigrants from China, Japan and the Middle East. All over Latin America, governments and elites encouraged European immigration, while restricting non-white immigrants (and often Jews too), frequently through covert means. These policies obeyed both a colonially-derived ideology, which valued whiteness, and late nineteenth- and early twentieth-century eugenic thinking, which saw Europeans as biologically and culturally superior and able to offset the supposedly deleterious effects of African and indigenous contributions to the national mix (Appelbaum, Macpherson, and Rosemblatt 2003; FitzGerald and Cook-Martín 2014).

The colonial period had created regional patterns of racialised demography, with regions where the indigenous population remained an important presence and source of labour (the Andes, much of Meso-America) and regions where that population had declined and been mostly replaced by African and mestizo labour (Brazil, lowland Colombia, Venezuela, much of the southern cone). The independence period reshaped the regional racial demography somewhat by vastly expanding the white populations of Argentina and Brazil, creating in the former country a dominant image of whiteness and, in the latter, a sense of a society that, for all its mixture, was underlain by a division between coloured (black and brown) and white (Alberto and Elena 2016; Hofbauer 2006; Skidmore 1974).

Ideologies of mixture

Colonial and republican Latin American societies were highly racist. It is arguable that colo-nial Latin America formed the crucible for the ideas about "race" that came to dominate the Atlantic world. In fifteenth-century Iberia, concepts of *limpieza de sangre* (cleanliness of blood) were developed as a way to police the social order, keeping people who supposedly had *raza de judío o moro* (Jewish or Moorish "race", in the sense of blood or ancestry) out of certain occupations and subjecting them to the possibility of Inquisitorial investigation for religious heterodoxy. In the Americas, these ideas embraced African and indigenous ancestry and were used to police the emerging mixed social strata, both formally – not allowing people with such ancestry into certain occupations and regulating marriages involving them – and informally – discriminating against them in social and especially family circles (Martínez 2008; Wade 2009: 67–71, 88–94). In the republican era, nation-building elites saw black, indigenous and dark-skinned mestizo populations as a drag on the nation's progress, due to their "inferior" *raza*, understood as a biocultural whole combining "blood" and "civilisation" (Stepan 1991).

Despite this, from the mid- to late-nineteenth century, elites began to make claims about the inherent links between mixture and democracy. In 1861, Colombian writer and politician José María Samper wrote of the "marvellous work of the mixture of races", believing it "should produce a wholly democratic society, a race of republicans, representatives simultaneously of Europe, Africa and Colombia, and which gives the New World its particular character" (Samper 1861: 299). In 1920, asking a conference audience "What is the result of this variety of races?", the Colombian medic Jorge Bejarano answered that it would bring "the advent of a democracy", because it was known that "the promiscuity of races, in which the element socially considered inferior predominates, results in the reign of democracies" (Jiménez López et al. 1920: 198). In Mexico, especially after the 1910 Revolution, the link between mixture, democracy and harmony was elevated into a national ideology, with the writer and politician José Vasconcelos as its chief proponent, lauding the advent of a universal "cosmic race", of which the Latin American mestizo was a precursor, embodying "the equality of all men by natural right [and] the social and civic equality of whites, blacks and *indios*" (Vasconcelos 1925: 16). In 1933, Mexico's Foreign Ministry, attempting to counteract complaints from China about Mexican legislation seen to be anti-Chinese, declared that the government did not have "any racial or class prejudice", because "the great Mexican family comes from the crossing of distinct races" (FitzGerald and Cook-Martín 2014: 236). In Brazil, the idea of "racial democracy" was explicitly developed during the populist dictatorship of Getúlio Vargas (1939–1945) and subsequently. It drew on the depiction of Brazil as a harmonious mixture of European, African and indigenous heritages, which had first been propounded by the writer Gilberto Freyre in the early 1930s (Burke and Pallares-Burke 2008; Freyre 1933). Freyre believed that "miscegenation and the interpenetration of cultures – chiefly European, Amerindian and African culture … have tended to mollify the interclass and interracial antagonisms developed under an aristocratic economy"; this meant that "perhaps nowhere is the meeting, intercommunication, and harmonious fusion of diverse or, even, antagonistic cultural traditions occurring in so liberal a way as it is in Brazil" (Freyre 1986: xiv, 78).

These claims were being made – explicitly or implicitly – on a global stage. The Mexican Foreign Ministry was, in the case cited, talking directly to China, but the main audience was the rest of the Americas and Europe. Contrasts were often made between Latin American countries and the United States, which, especially during the period under discussion, was seen as the home of racism, understood as involving violent racial hatred, clear segregation and taboos on racial mixture. Until about the 1920s, the United States and north-western Europe were also seen as the home of "hard" eugenics, embracing policies of sterilisation (which persisted until later in Nazi Germany). In contrast, Latin American "soft" eugenics generally advocated policies of social hygiene (Stepan 1991; Stern 2011). Latin American "racial democracy" was constructed in relation to North American "racial hatred". The Cuban independence hero, José Martí, in his celebrated essay, "Nuestra América" – first published in *La Revista Ilustrada de Nueva York*, addressing an international Spanish-speaking readership on the need for Latin Americans to counter the threat posed by "the formidable neighbour who does not know us" – said that in Latin America "there is no hatred between races, because there are no races" (Martí 1891). This oppositional counterpoint, in which Latin American elites took the moral high ground in the democracy stakes, helped to gloss over the racism that existed in their countries (Guimarães 2007; Seigel 2009).

Racism re-discovered?

The reputation of Brazil as a racial democracy was sufficiently strong that, in the wake of the Second World War, it attracted the attention of UNESCO, which in 1949 had formed a committee to deliberate on the race concept. The committee had been set up by UNESCO's social science division, then headed by the Brazilian Arthur Ramos, who recruited, among others, a Brazilian sociologist, Luiz de Aguiar Costa Pinto, and a Mexican physical anthropologist, Juan Comas. Other members of the first committee meeting included the black US sociologist Franklin Frazier and French anthropologist Claude Lévi-Strauss, who had both worked in Brazil. Although several committee members had inklings that all might not be rosy in Brazil's racial garden, the country was chosen because it seemed to have lessons to teach the rest of the world about racial conviviality (Maio 2001). UNESCO then coordinated a series of studies of race relations in urban and rural areas of the country. The focus was squarely on blackness and black–brown–white relations. Texts included *Race Relations Between Blacks and Whites in São Paulo* and *The Integration of the Black in a Class Society* (Bastide and Fernandes 1955; Fernandes 1964). Indigenous Brazil was only occasionally included (Wagley 1952) and questions of racism were almost entirely confined to the black–white context.

The upshot of the UNESCO studies was that racial democracy was a "myth" (Fernandes 1964) and that racism existed. Yet while the research provided lots of examples of racist stereotyping and plenty of anecdotal evidence from black people attesting to the impact of these stereotypes on their self-esteem and life chances, racism as a set of structures that shaped inequality and distributed privilege was less clearly documented. Fernandes got close with his depiction of a system of "accommodation", in which most black and brown people had been placed in the lowest social strata by slavery and colonialism and, post-abolition, were trapped there by racial stereotypes and discrimination and by traditional paternalist relations with – mostly whiter – people in the strata above them. Racism was dissimulated and obfuscated by the limited individualistic upward mobility allowed by paternalism: many black and brown people denied the existence of racism, while whites also denied it or were indifferent to questions of racial difference. However, Fernandes also optimistically believed that a shift in Brazil away from paternalism towards a "competitive social order" (i.e. free market capitalism) would bring greater racial equality as black people became integrated into a class society.

This claim tapped into a key feature of the racial formation found in Brazil and other Latin American countries, which also obfuscates the role of racism: the fact that class and race tend to coincide. This allows evident racial inequality to be explained away by saying it is a matter of class not racial discrimination and that black (and indigenous) people are poor because of the legacy of slavery (or other past oppressions and neglect), not because of current racism. In Brazil (and in some other countries), the existence of a significant number of poor whites (or light-skinned mestizos) is also used to reinforce the "class not race" argument. Fernandes aligned himself with these arguments in assuming that, if class dynamics were to be liberated from the constraints of paternalism and allowed free rein in the capitalist market, black people would increasingly become upwardly mobile into the middle and upper classes, leaving behind the legacies of slavery and neglect.

But, post-UNESCO, research in Brazil from the 1970s began to demonstrate the structural dimensions of racism using census and survey data, which had traditionally included self-ascribed "colour" categories (the main ones being black, brown and white). Social scientists deployed the data to show that, while brown people (in the 1970s around 40% of the total) were intermediate between black (under 10%) and white (about 55%), in statistical terms it made sense to put black and brown together as a single category, which was systematically disadvantaged compared to whites. The data also showed that racism had an independent and ongoing effect. For example, black university graduates earned less than white ones ten years after graduation. More broadly, racial differences in income-earning could not be fully explained by a combination of non-racial variables such as occupation, education, migrant status, age, etc.: racism had to be playing a role (Hasenbalg 1985; Lovell 1994, 2006; Silva 1985; Telles 2004).

Similar data are emerging from other countries, such as Colombia (Barbary and Urrea 2004; Urrea Giraldo and Viáfara López 2007) and Mexico (Flores and Telles 2012) and from region-wide studies, including ones that correlate social status with skin colour (rather than self-ascribed identities) (Telles and Project on Ethnicity and Race in Latin America 2014; Telles, Flores, and Urrea-Giraldo 2015). Fernandes' optimism about the competitive social order seems very misplaced: the structural disadvantage bequeathed by slavery and past neglect is not only very hard – perhaps impossible – to shake off, but is also inseparable from ongoing racism, which naturalises the link between racialised difference and structural disadvantage.

Racism and *mestizaje*

Fernandes did not link the features he identified in the Brazilian system of accommodation to the role played by mixture in the society – for him, black and brown people were in the same position. Another UNESCO researcher, Marvin Harris, argued in the 1960s and 70s that pervasive mixture in Brazil had created a society in which racial identities were ill-defined and ambiguity was maximised (Harris 1964, 1970). For him, this meant that "the issue of racial discrimination is scarcely a vital one" (1964: 63). Harris over-stated the case, but he put his finger on something that Fernandes passed over, which was the role of *mestizaje* in the racial formation. In Brazil and in Latin America more widely, *mestizaje* shapes racial formation in important ways: racism operates through it, but in a way that makes racism hard to recognise as such (Da Costa 2016; Moreno Figueroa and Saldívar 2016).

On the one hand, *mestizaje* is powerfully structured by ideas about the inferiority of blackness and indigeneity – associated with low status, backwardness and poverty – and the superior value of whiteness or, often, a light-skinned, not-quite-white mestizo-ness – associated with wealth and modernity. These racialised hierarchies pervade the social order and structure people's behaviour and relationships. They correlate with inequalities in occupation, education, income, security, health and life expectancy, as shown by data from Brazil and elsewhere that document the position of black, indigenous and dark-skinned people.[1] They underlie racist stereotypes and associated acts of stigmatisation (Lamont et al. 2016). They structure ideas about beauty, especially for women who are particularly marked by and sensitive to the negative values attached to the skin tones, hair textures and facial features associated with black and indigenous people (Edmonds 2007; Gordon 2013; Nichols 2013; Rahier 1999). They enter into the intimate domains of the family, where they can guide decisions about romantic relationships and reproduction, and can differentiate in a fine-grained way between darker and lighter siblings (Hordge-Freeman 2015; Moreno Figueroa 2012; Roberts 2012). Numerous studies attest to these patterns across Latin America.[2]

On the other hand, *mestizaje* creates a lived experience in which many people live in families and contexts where everyone is more or less "brown"; levels of racial segregation are relatively low, compared to the United States (Barbary and Urrea 2004; Telles 2004); and there is some flexibility in racial classifications, in that, while most people can agree on what a typical "black", "white" or "indigenous" person looks like and where they are likely to fit in the social structure, things are much more uncertain on the middle ground of brownness. *Mestizaje* creates a context in which, for many people, racial difference is a fact of life, but not a very salient one compared to what they perceive as the greater role played by differences of class and gender. Some scholars have characterised this situation by distinguishing between social realms in which race is more and less important. Describing a low-income neighbourhood of Salvador, Brazil, Sansone (2003: 52–53) argues that the residents perceive a "soft" domain of social relations, where "color is seen as irrelevant in the orientation of social and power relations" (street corners, parties, the neighbourhood, sports, and religion), and a "hard" domain, where it is considered important (interactions with the police, the world of work, and of marriage and dating). Telles (2004) likewise characterises Brazil in terms of the coexistence of "horizontal" and "vertical" social relations. The realms of friendship, the family, and the neighbourhood are marked by the strong presence of horizontal or convivial relations of interaction, mixture, and fairly equal exchange. In contrast, vertical relations of hierarchy and inequality are more obvious in the realms of work, education, health, housing, and politics. Interestingly, Sansone describes family as a hard area, while Telles says it is a domain of horizontality. This suggests that it is not easy to distinguish domains of interaction in this way and that, instead, hierarchy and conviviality are in tension in all domains, albeit with different balances in different contexts. For example, family relations are intimate sites where racial conviviality and racial hierarchy coexist (Wade 2009). Both aspects are immanent in *mestizaje* and in each other.

In sum, *mestizaje* has created in Latin America a long-standing example of what scholars of other regions have been identifying as new, neoliberal conjunctures of "post-raciality" (Goldberg 2015; Lentin 2014), "racism without racists" (Bonilla-Silva 2003), or "raceless racism", in which racism has been "buried alive" (Goldberg 2008). In Latin America, people have long lived with situations in which racism, racial hierarchy and inequality exist hand-in-glove with the denial and, more often, the *minimisation* of these hierarchies and their *delegitimation* as matters unworthy of sustained attention, especially in terms of government policy, because they supposedly lead to counter-productive outcomes for society by focusing on "divisive" differences and thus causing more racism (often labelled as "racism in reverse" because these concerns challenge white and mestizo privilege). While in North America and Europe these minimisations and delegitimations are coinciding with neoliberalisation, Latin America shows us that they are actually deeply embedded in liberalism more generally, which has a constitutive tension between equality and hierarchy (Wade 2017).

Racism, multiculturalism and anti-racism

Since the 1990s, Latin American nations have apparently disrupted the dominance of regimes centred on *mestizaje* by undertaking legislative reforms that assert the multicultural or pluriethnic character of the nation. Driven by an uneasy combination of indigenous and Afro-descendant activism (drawing on long-standing traditions of resistance and invigorated by global decolonisation and anti-racist movements) and state agendas of co-optation and governance (guided by global redefinitions of democracy as including respect for difference), these reforms have given unprecedented recognition to indigenous and Afro-descendant minorities. Reforms have accorded minorities rights pertaining to land, education, prior consultation about development projects, and political and juridical autonomy; these rights have been uneven both across different countries and in terms of rights being more widely recognised for indigenous than Afro-descendant people (Hale 2005; Paschel 2016; Rahier 2012; Sieder 2002; Speed 2005).

This cultural recognition opens debates about the symbolic and socio-economic status of "cultural" minorities and thus might be thought to address issues of racism and racialised inequality. However, the discussion has more often focused on the need to recognise cultural difference and "diversity", mirroring familiar tensions in global debates about multicultural-ism, which has been criticised as a co-optative top-down policy that divides subordinate groups and distracts attention from the structural racialised inequalities that affect them all (Hale 2018; Lentin and Titley 2011; Saldívar 2018). In some Latin American cases, similar neighbouring communities have mobilised as either "black" or "indigenous" to claim land rights, depending on contingent factors (French 2009); in other cases, indigenous and black people who in the past had collaborated over land claims have found it necessary to work separately to fit into state frameworks (Ng'weno 2007). The "multicultural turn" has resulted in some changes to racialised inequality – at least on paper. For example, legally constituted indigenous reserves in Colombia now account for about 30% of the national territory, while, on the basis of a 1993 law, Afro-Colombian communities had by 2014 obtained legal title to more than half the area of the country's Pacific coast region (Salinas Abdala 2014). But such changes have done little to shift the entrenched patterns of racialised inequality outlined earl-ier. Indeed, a backlash against land titling processes may be one reason why Afro-Colombians and indigenous people from the Pacific region are suffering massive and violent displacement: members of these communities figure disproportionately among Colombia's many internally displaced people and murder victims (Oslender 2007; Wade 2016).

From about 2010, there have been signs of a greater willingness to talk about racism, not only in state circles but also among social movements, many of which had avoided such talk, preferring to focus on cultural difference – a tendency particularly noticeable among indigen-ous activists, who see cultural differences as constitutive of their identities and claims to autonomy. There are indications that some indigenous activists are willing to adopt a discourse of racism, in the context of intensifying extractivist and agro-industrial economic enterprises, which, backed by neoliberal state policies, threaten indigenous lands and lives. Indigenous protest tends to provoke state and popular violence targeting indigenous bodies, which can elicit an indigenous discourse about racism as a systemic feature of the society. For example, the recent attempt by indigenous female leader María de Jesús Patricio (a.k.a. Marichuy) to become a presidential candidate for Mexico provoked a storm of abuse on social media that was so clearly racist in tone that anti-indigenous racism could hardly be ignored as an issue (Marini 2018).[3]

Still, the incipient emergence of racism as a topic of public debate has tended to centre around anti-black racism, partly because it has been led by Brazil, where racism had long been a central focus for the country's mostly urban – and culturally not very distinctive – black population. In 1995, the state officially recognised racism as a problem, sparking a series of reforms that from the early 2000s led to race-based affirmative action measures in higher education admissions and later in federal employment, which provoked debates about "fairness" familiar from US and other contexts (Lehmann 2018). In Colombia, the state sup-ported the National Campaign Against Racism (2009) and later, as part of the UN's Inter-national Decade of Afrodescendants (2015–2024), the Face Up to Racism campaign (2016). Several countries passed anti-discrimination legislation (Hernández 2013) and in a few cases this led to high-profile cases, such as that which saw an Ecuadorian army officer found guilty of racial hate crime for abusing a black recruit.[4]

These media campaigns and legal battles, while symbolically significant, are short-lived and arguably tokenistic, but they complement affirmative action measures that, following the Brazilian lead, aim to address structural issues of education and employment. For example, Ecuador's Ministry of External Relations has instituted policies to increase ethnic minority recruitment in the lower ranks of the diplomatic service. The jury is out on the long-term effects of these policies, which are partly a product of Latin America's "pink tide" – a region-wide shift to the left from 1998. Given the signs of a reverse tide heralded since 2015 by the election of several important right-wing leaders, who seem to be less open to policies of racial reparation, the future is looking precarious. For example, in 2018 Brazil elected right-wing president Jair Bolsonaro, who had declared that indigenous land rights are an obstacle to agri-business and pledged to cut back affirmative actions favouring black people.

Conclusion

Recent changes in the Latin American panorama – the multicultural turn, the incipient naming of racism – seem to have dislodged *mestizaje* from its dominant position. However, these changes can be seen as modifying *mestizaje* regimes rather than displacing them. *Mestizaje*, although apparently a project of homogenisation, always had a subordinate space for blackness and indigeneity, whose existence, along with whiteness, is necessary for *mestizaje* to exist conceptually in the first place. So adapting to multiculturalism was not, in fact, too much of a stretch. Racism has always been an absent presence in *mestizaje*: there, but not there at the same time; always in operation, but obfuscated by class hierarchies, blurred racial identifications and middle ground conviviality. So even the incipient calling out of racism can be accommodated to this dynamic to some extent. A fundamental destabilisation of *mestizaje* regimes would require a much more radical recognition of the pervasive and structural effects of racism. But this recognition has to be fought for, against more tokenistic acknow-ledgements and the tendency – seen in Mexico's national agency for the prevention of dis-crimination, CONAPRED – to relativise racism as just one more form of discrimination, alongside sexism, ableism, ageism, heterosexism, etc. (Lentin 2011). While it is paramount to grasp the intersectional dimensions of racism – particularly notable in *mestizaje*'s reliance on sexist constructions of mixture – it is also necessary to comprehend racism's particular modes of operation, driven by colonial histories of conquest and enslavement.

Notes

1 On inequalities of occupation, income and education, see the references cited earlier in the main text; see also CEPAL (2017), Del Popolo (2017). On security, see Amnesty International (2015), Vargas (2018), Wade (2016).
2 For overviews, see de la Fuente and Andrews (2018), Hernández (2013), Wade (2010).
3 See also www.jornada.com.mx/2018/02/27/opinion/019a2pol.
4 See www.lapora.sociology.cam.ac.uk/michael-arce-case-first-ruling-hate-crime-ecuador.

References

Alberto, Paulina, and Eduardo Elena, eds. 2016. *Rethinking Race in Modern Argentina*. New York: Cambridge University Press.
Amnesty International. 2015. "You killed my son": homicides by military police in the city of Rio de Janeiro. London: Amnesty International.

Appelbaum, Nancy P., Anne S. Macpherson, and Karin A. Rosemblatt, eds. 2003. *Race and Nation in Modern Latin America*. Chapel Hill, NC: University of North Carolina Press.

Banton, Michael. 1987. *Racial Theories*. Cambridge: Cambridge University Press.

Barbary, Olivier, and Fernando Urrea, eds. 2004. *Gente negra en Colombia, dinámicas sociopolíticas en Cali y el Pacífico*. Cali, Paris: CIDSE/Univalle, IRD, Colciencias.

Bastide, Roger, and Florestan Fernandes. 1955. *Relações raciais entre negroes e brancos em São Paulo*. São Paulo: Editora Anhembí.

Bonilla-Silva, Eduardo. 2003. *Racism Without Racists: Color-Blind Racism and the Persistence of Racial Inequality in the United States*. Lanham, MD: Rowman & Littlefield.

Burke, Peter, and Maria Lúcia G. Pallares-Burke. 2008. *Gilberto Freyre: Social Theory in the Tropics*. Oxford: Peter Lang.

CEPAL. 2017. *Situación de las personas afrodescendientes en América Latina y desafíos de políticas para la garantía de sus derechos*. Santiago: CEPAL.

Da Costa, Alexandre Emboaba. 2016. Confounding anti-racism: mixture, racial democracy, and post-racial politics in Brazil. *Critical Sociology* 42(4–5):495–513.

de la Fuente, Alejandro, and George Reid Andrews, eds. 2018. *Afro-Latin American Studies: An Introduction*. Cambridge: Cambridge University Press.

Del Popolo, Fabiana. 2017. *Los pueblos indígenas en América (Abya Yala): desafíos para la igualdad en la diversidad*. Santiago: CEPAL.

Edmonds, Alexander. 2007. Triumphant miscegenation: reflections on beauty and race in Brazil. *Journal of Intercultural Studies* 28(1):83–97.

Fernandes, Florestan. 1964. *A integração do negro na sociedade de classes*. São Paulo: Universidade de São Paulo.

FitzGerald, David Scott, and David Cook-Martín. 2014. *Culling the Masses: The Democratic Origins of Racist Immigration Policy in the Americas*. Cambridge, MA: Harvard University Press.

Flores, René, and Edward Telles. 2012. Social stratification in Mexico: disentangling color, ethnicity, and class. *American Sociological Review* 77(3):486–494.

French, Jan Hoffman. 2009. *Legalizing Identities: Becoming Black or Indian in Brazil's northeast*. Chapel Hill, NC: University of North Carolina Press.

Freyre, Gilberto. 1933. *Casa-grande & senzala: formação da família brasileira sob o regime de economia patriarcal*. Rio de Janeiro: Maia & Schmidt.

———. 1986. *The Masters and the Slaves: A Study in the Development of Brazilian Civilization*. Berkeley, CA: University of California Press.

Goldberg, David Theo. 2008. *The Threat of Race: Reflections on Racial Neoliberalism*. Malden, MA: Wiley-Blackwell.

———. 2015. *Are We All Postracial Yet?* New York: John Wiley.

Gordon, Doreen. 2013. A beleza abre portas: beauty and the racialised body among black middle-class women in Salvador, Brazil. *Feminist Theory* 14(2):203–218.

Guimarães, Antonio Sérgio. 2007. Racial democracy. In *Imagining Brazil*, edited by Jessé Souza and Valter Sinder, 119–140. Lanham, MD: Lexington Books.

Hale, Charles R. 2005. Neoliberal multiculturalism: the remaking of cultural rights and racial dominance in Central America. *PoLAR: Political and Legal Anthropology Review* 28(1):10–28.

———. 2018. When I hear the word culture …. *Cultural Studies* 32(3):497–509.

Harris, Marvin. 1964. *Patterns of Race in the Americas*. New York: Norton Library.

———. 1970. Referential ambiguity in the calculus of Brazilian racial terms. *Southwestern Journal of Anthropology* 27:1–14.

Hasenbalg, Carlos. 1985. Race and socioeconomic inequalities in Brazil. In *Race, class and power in Brazil*, edited by Pierre-Michel Fontaine, 25–41. Los Angeles, CA: Center for Afro-American Studies, University of Califonia.

Hernández, Tanya Kateri. 2013. *Racial Subordination in Latin America: The Role of the State, Customary Law, and the New Civil Rights Response*. Cambridge: Cambridge University Press.

Hofbauer, Andreas. 2006. *Uma história do branqueamento ou o negro em questão*. São Paulo: Editora UNESP.

Hordge-Freeman, Elizabeth. 2015. *The Color of Love: Racial Features, Stigma, and Socialization in Black Brazilian Families*. Austin, TX: University of Texas Press.

Jiménez López, Miguel, Luis López de Mesa, Calixto Torres Umaña, et al. 1920. *Los problemas de la raza en Colombia*. Bogotá, CO: El Espectador.

Lamont, Michèle, Graziella Moraes Silva, Jessica Welburn, et al. 2016. *Getting Respect: Responding to Stigma and Discrimination in the United States, Brazil, and Israel*. Princeton, NJ: Princeton University Press.

Lehmann, David. 2018. *The Prism of Race: The Politics and Ideology of Affirmative Action in Brazil*. Minnesota: University of Michigan Press.

Lentin, Alana. 2011. What happens to anti-racism when we are post race? *Feminist Legal Studies* 19(2):159–168.

———. 2014. Post-race, post politics: the paradoxical rise of culture after multiculturalism. *Ethnic and Racial Studies* 37(8):1268–1285.

Lentin, Alana, and Gavan Titley. 2011. *The Crises of Multiculturalism: Racism in a Neoliberal Age*. London: Zed Books.

Lovell, Peggy A. 1994. Race, gender and development in Brazil. *Latin American Research Review* 29(3):7–35.

———. 2006. Race, gender, and work in São Paulo, Brazil, 1960–2000. *Latin American Research Review* 41(3):63–87.

Maio, Marcos Chor. 2001. UNESCO and the study of race relations in Brazil: regional or national issue? *Latin American Research Review* 36(2):118–136.

Marcílio, Maria Luiza. 1984. The population of colonial Brazil. In *The Cambridge History of Latin America: Volume 2: Colonial Latin America*, edited by Leslie Bethell, 37–64. Cambridge: Cambridge University Press.

Marini, Anna Marta. 2018. *La normalidad racista del discurso público en México y el caso de Marichuy*. Iberoamérica Social [cited 5 February 2019]. Available from https://iberoamericasocial.com/la-normalidad-racista-del-discurso-publico-en-mexico-y-el-caso-de-marichuy/.

Martí, José. 1891. Nuestra América. *La Revista Ilustrada de Nueva York*, 10 January.

Martínez, María Elena. 2008. *Genealogical Fictions: Limpieza de Sangre, Religion, and Gender in Colonial Mexico*. Stanford, CA: Stanford University Press.

Moreno Figueroa, Mónica. 2012. "Linda morenita": skin colour, beauty and the politics of mestizaje in Mexico. In *Cultures of Colour: Visual, Material, Textual*, edited by Chris Horrocks, 167–180. Oxford: Berghahn Books.

Moreno Figueroa, Mónica, and Emiko Saldívar. 2016. "We are not racists, we are Mexicans": privilege, nationalism and post-race ideology in Mexico. *Critical Sociology* 42(4–5):515–533.

Newson, Linda A. 1993. The demographic collapse of native peoples of the Americas, 1492–1650. In *The Meeting of Two Worlds: Europe and the Americas 1492–1650*, edited by Warwick Bray, 247–288. London: British Academy.

Ng'weno, Bettina. 2007. *Turf Wars: Territory and Citizenship in the Contemporary State*. Stanford, CA: Stanford University Press.

Nichols, Elizabeth Gackstetter. 2013. "Decent girls with good hair": beauty, morality and race in Venezuela. *Feminist Theory* 14(2):171–185.

Oslender, Ulrich. 2007. Violence in development: the logic of forced displacement on Colombia's Pacific coast. *Development in Practice* 17(6):752–764.

Paschel, Tianna S. 2016. *Becoming Black Political Subjects: Movements and Ethno-Racial Rights in Colombia and Brazil*. Princeton, NJ: Princeton University Press.

Rahier, Jean. 1999. Body politics in black and white: señoras, mujeres, blanqueamiento and Miss Esmeraldas 1997–1998, Ecuador. *Women and Performance: A Journal of Feminist Theory* 21:103–119.

———, ed. 2012. *Black Social Movements in Latin America: From Monocultural Mestizaje to Multiculturalism*. New York: Palgrave Macmillan.

Roberts, Elizabeth F. S. 2012. *God's Laboratory: Assisted Reproduction in the Andes*. Berkeley, CA: University of California Press.

Saldívar, Emiko. 2018. Uses and abuses of culture: mestizaje in the era of multiculturalism. *Cultural Studies* 32(3):438–459.

Salinas Abdala, Yamile. 2014. Los derechos territoriales de los grupos étnicos: ¿un compromiso social, una obligación constitucional o una tarea hecha a medias? *Punto de Encuentro* 67:1–39.

Samper, José María. 1861. *Ensayo sobre las revoluciones políticas y la condición social de las repúblicas colombianas (hispano-americanas): con un apéndice sobre la orografía y la población de la Confederación Granadina*. Paris: Imprenta de E. Thunot y Cia.

Sánchez-Albornoz, Nicolás. 1984. The population of colonial Spanish America. In *The Cambridge History of Latin America: Volume 2: Colonial Latin America*, edited by Leslie Bethell, 1–35. Cambridge: Cambridge University Press.

Sansone, Livio. 2003. *Blackness Without Ethnicity: Constructing Race in Brazil*. Basingstoke: Palgrave Macmillan.

Seigel, Micol. 2009. *Uneven Encounters: Making Race and Nation in Brazil and the United States*. Durham, NC: Duke University Press.

Sieder, Rachel, ed. 2002. *Multiculturalism in Latin America: Indigenous Rights, Diversity and Democracy*. Basingstoke: Palgrave Macmillan.

Silva, Nelson do Valle. 1985. Updating the cost of not being white in Brazil. In *Race, Class and Power in Brazil*, edited by Pierre-Michel Fontaine, 42–55. Los Angeles, CA: Centre of Afro-American Studies, University of California.

Skidmore, Thomas. 1974. *Black into White: Race and Nationality in Brazilian Thought*. New York: Oxford University Press.

Speed, Shannon. 2005. Dangerous discourses: human rights and multiculturalism in neoliberal Mexico. *PoLAR: Political and Legal Anthropology Review* 28(1):29–51.

Stepan, Nancy Leys. 1991. *"The Hour of Eugenics": Race, Gender and Nation in Latin America*. Ithaca, NY: Cornell University Press.

Stern, Alexandra Minna. 2011. "The Hour of Eugenics" in Veracruz, Mexico: radical politics, public health, and Latin America's only sterilization law. *Hispanic American Historical Review* 91(3):431–443.

Telles, Edward, René D. Flores, and Fernando Urrea-Giraldo. 2015. Pigmentocracies: educational inequality, skin color and census ethnoracial identification in eight Latin American countries. *Research in Social Stratification and Mobility* 40:39–58.

Telles, Edward E. 2004. *Race in Another America: The Significance of Skin Color in Brazil*. Princeton, NJ: Princeton University Press.

Telles, Edward E., and Project on Ethnicity and Race in Latin America. 2014. *Pigmentocracies: Ethnicity, Race and Color in Latin America*. Chapel Hill, NC: University of North Carolina Press.

Twinam, Ann. 2015. *Purchasing Whiteness: Pardos, Mulattos, and the Quest for Social Mobility in the Spanish Indies*. Stanford, CA: Stanford University Press.

Urrea Giraldo, Fernando, and Carlos Viáfara López. 2007. Pobreza y grupos étnicos en Colombia: análisis de sus factores determinantes y lineamientos de políticas para su reducción. Bogotá, CO: Departamento Nacional de Planeación.

Vargas, João H. Costa. 2018. *The Denial of Antiblackness: Multiracial Redemption and Black Suffering*. Minneapolis, MN: University of Minnesota Press.

Vasconcelos, José. 1925. *La raza cósmica: Misión de la raza iberoamericana. Notas de viajes a la América del Sur*. Madrid: Agencia Mundial de Librería.

Wade, Peter. 2009. *Race and Sex in Latin America*. London: Pluto Press.

———. 2010. *Race and Ethnicity in Latin America*. 2nd ed. London: Pluto Press.

———. 2016. Mestizaje, multiculturalism, liberalism and violence. *Latin American and Caribbean Ethnic Studies* 11(3):323–343.

———. 2017. Liberalism and its contradictions: democracy and hierarchy in mestizaje and genomics in Latin America. *Latin American Research Review* 52(4):623–638.

Wagley, Charles, ed. 1952. *Race and Class in Rural Brazil*. Paris: UNESCO.

7

Hostility to refugees and asylum seekers

Tony Kushner

Human history is the story of migration, both voluntary and forced (albeit that these two categories of movement have never been self-contained). In reality there has always been a mixture of positive and negative stimuli – on the one hand, seeking material and other opportunities, sheer wonderment and the desire to explore what is out of sight, and, on the other, economic necessity to escape poverty and starvation, war and persecution. All these factors have intersected and underlie each individual decision to become a migrant, and taking the longue durée, more recently within and outside the nation state (Manning, 2013). The term 'refugee' dates only to the late seventeenth century and was self-coined by the Huguenots to explain their status as deserving recipients of asylum in receiving countries within the Protestant world. The absence of terminology, however, should not disguise the reality that refugees have been a constant feature of history. And recent attempts to create a 'myth of difference' between those coming from Europe and the 'Third World' are, as B. S. Chimni argues, 'self-serving and refugee studies has done little to combat this' (Chimni, 1998: 357, 360, 368). Refugees, across time and place, have something in common as have attitudes and responses to them.

Refugee studies is a recent academic pursuit. The *Journal of Refugee Studies* was first published in 1988 (Zetter, 1988), and this interdisciplinary field is still in its infancy. Dominated by law and the social sciences, the focus has been on contemporary issues including the legal status of refugees and asylum seekers and the problems they are facing in transit, temporary and permanent settlement. Earlier generic studies dating from the work of John Hope Simpson (Simpson, 1938, 1939), Jacques Vernant (Vernant, 1953) and Malcolm Proudfoot (Proudfoot, 1957) were equally concerned with the *now* of refugee crises of the Nazi era and the early Cold War.

What typified these early studies was a belief that refugees were a temporary and ultimately solvable problem. As Hope Simpson somewhat optimistically wrote in 1939 before the outbreak of the Second World War, if it was successfully dealt with at its root cause, 'the refugee problem in Europe would reduce itself to that minor feature of international life which it ought to be' (Simpson, 1939, p. 546). Simpson had in mind the mid-nineteenth century when refugees were relatively few in number and confined to prominent individuals (such as Karl Marx) or small groups of political exiles (Kushner, 2017:10). Sadly the refugee crisis has had a longer life than Simpson, Vernant and Proudfoot anticipated. At the end of

2018, the global number of refugees stood at 70.8 million, up over two million from the previous year. It consisted of 41.3 million internally displaced people; 25.9 million 'formal' refugees and 3.5 million asylum seekers, according to the United Nations High Commissioner for Refugees (UNHCR) in June 2019. This is the highest level ever recorded, exceeding (indeed over double) that at the end of the Second World War when the figure stood at over 40 million, itself a record total (Proudfoot, 1957: 32; Marrus, 1985: 297).

With a recognition that refugees, the internally displaced and asylum seekers are here to stay (indeed, with a world in increasing crisis and instability, including climate change, the numbers are likely to increase even further in the twenty first century), there is a growing move to historicise their existence (Gatrell, 2013; Noiriel, 2012 [1991])). There is still much to be done, especially as refugee studies tends to relegate history to a footnote. There is, as Jessica Reinisch and Matthew Frank argue, 'an overwhelming presentism within the field of refugee studies' (Frank and Reinisch, 2017: 8). Historians, however, are equally at fault. As anthropologist, Liisa Malkki has stated, the refugee 'remains curiously, indecently, outside of history' (Malkki, 1996: 398). More prosaically, Peter Gatrell, who has written by far the most geographically comprehensive history of the modern refugee, highlights how 'Refugees have been allowed only a walk-on part in most histories of the twentieth century, and even then as subjects of external intervention rather than actors in their own right' (Gatrell, 2013: 283).

The enforced liminal characteristic of the refugee – homeless, stateless and hard to define – is at the heart of antagonism towards them. This is in spite of, or even because of, the 1951 United Nations Convention relating to the Status of Refugees which limited those under its scope geographically to Europe and chronologically to the Nazi era. Since then Gil Loescher notes that 'International law seeks to define the minimum that should be offered to refugees' (Loescher, 1989: 9; Tuitt, 1996). Refugees themselves have internalised this marginality and have often rejected the label. Hannah Arendt, a refugee two times over (first from Nazi Germany and then from Vichy France), wrote from her new place of refuge in wartime America, 'we don't like to be called "refugees". We ourselves call each other "newcomers" or "immigrants"'. She added that in pre-war France 'we were even more sensitive about being called refugees. We did our best to prove to each other people that were just ordinary immigrants' (Arendt, 2007 [1943]: 264).

Vernant, a decade later, and using the gendered language that was utilised in the 1951 Convention and the use throughout of 'he', also noted that

> What stamps the refugee as a man apart, justifying his classification in a special social category, is his *inferiority*, he is inferior both to the citizens of the country which gave him shelter and to all other foreigners, not refugees, living in that country.
>
> *(Vernant, 1953: 13)*

The difficulty in *placing* refugees in the nation state (and in the historical archive given their temporary, fluid status where their impermanence has often left only the faintest of marks) has led to specific attitudes towards them which in turn has impacted on their treatment.

As with attitudes and responses to most if not all oppressed groups, the 'refugee' is regarded with ambivalence rather than sheer hatred. Hostility, in theory, is mitigated by belief in the concept of asylum with its classical origins and presence in the foundations of all major religious faiths. In practice, however, it has often been articulated in the modern world in the form of virtue-signalling to show the liberality, decency and tolerance of liberal or emerging democracies without a full commitment to offering a permanent home to the persecuted. There has been a huge gap between the rhetorical commitment to the right of asylum and the actual granting of it. If 'history' is turned to for those who want to have a 'usable past' to endorse more generous policies today, it is likely to lead to disappointment. As refugee historian Lyndsey Stonebridge warns: 'We're on shaky ground indeed if we think we simply need to retrieve a lost humanitarian impulse' (Frank and Reinisch, 2017: 6).

On a symbolic level, however, the commitment to asylum has been key in constructing the identity of first Revolutionary France in the late eighteenth century (Noiriel, 2012 [1991])), then the United States of America (as with the Statue of Liberty, erected in 1886 and its ambiguous claim to welcome 'Your huddled masses yearning to breathe free. The wretched refuse of your teeming shore' (Higham, 1978 [1955]): 23), and the United Kingdom (Kushner and Knox, 1999) and more recently post-war West Germany/unified Germany (Schuster, 2003a). Occasionally, when other factors have come into play (for example, France after the First World War when it was short of manpower), pragmatic factors allowed the commitment to asylum to have substance in terms of significant refugee entry, including in this case hundreds of thousands of Armenians and White Russians (Cross, 1983), or Germany in the second decade of the twenty-first century, when a deep sense of its shameful recent past prompted Chancellor Angela Merkel to let in 890,000 mainly Syrian refugees in 2015, following the outcry over the death of three-year-old Alan Kurdi, washed up on a Turkish beach.

Even then, it has not followed that the refugees themselves have been given a universally warm welcome. The case of Karl Marx in Victorian England is revealing. He was allowed in because of a xenophobic belief that Britain was intrinsically better than the 'dangerous' continent, with the arrogant assumption that his diseased, revolutionary world view would be effectively neutralised in a stable democracy. In practice, he and other refugees were regarded with disdain and often treated negatively (Porter, 1979). Still, it would be wrong to dismiss the neglected and often brave work of organisations and individuals in the modern era who have fought for refugee rights whether as a whole or for specific groups trying to find asylum. There is thus a secret history of the largely undocumented worked to *help* refugees on a practical level whether in the global north or south.

Alongside such ambivalence towards refugees through the racialised and hierarchical application of asylum where the 'right' individual or group was helped and allowed entry (for example, bourgeois German Jews during the 1930s who were regarded as cultured as against the mass of poverty stricken East European Jews who were viewed as uncivilised, racially unfit, ill-disciplined and a revolutionary menace) (London, 2000), was outright hostility towards them. Recognising the potential sympathy that might be evoked by the term 'refugee', they have been re-labelled as 'undesirable aliens' at the fin de siècle and 1930s, 'displaced persons' after the Second World War and then in the last decades of the twentieth century and into the new millennia as 'bogus asylum seekers' or 'illegal immigrants', the last term shortened to one word in racist populist discourse: 'illegals' (Kushner, 2006: 5–7).

And as Arendt noted, the word 'refugee' itself has often been loaded and negatively received. In *memory*, refugees from Nazism are amongst the most validated and celebrated in the history of forced migration. *At the time*, they were treated with deep suspicion in places of refuge such as Britain. There in 1938 the Jewish Refugee Committee became the German Jewish Aid Committee because 'refugee' had developed negative connotations (Kushner, 2006: 6). There thus remains a (particularly western) tradition of anti-refugee political movements, newspapers and later media, articulated in politics and culture as well by ordinary people, that remains under-researched as a specific topic in its own right.

Indeed, there is often only passing reference in more general works on xenophobia, populism, fascism and neo-fascism, and other forms of racial, ethnic and religious intolerance to a discrete and continuous anti-refugee discourse. An example is John Higham's magisterial and pioneering study of American nativism, *Strangers in the Land*, originally published in 1955 and covering the period from the mid-nineteenth century through to the 1920s. Focusing on anti-Catholicism, antisemitism, anti-Irish and anti-German sentiment as well as white supremacy, specific animosity to refugees (or support of them) was absent from Higham's narrative. The treatment of refugees in academic literature reflects their marginality on an everyday level.

Regarded as, at best, a temporary phenomenon (in spite of all historical evidence to the contrary), they add complications to the study of migration as well as that of racism and prejudice. Chimni notes that 'every refugee differs from another in the circumstances which force her to flee' (Chimni, 1998: 360) which does not mean that they have nothing in common – including in their treatment. Inevitably they will vary in terms of politics, class, wealth, education, age, gender, sexuality, place of origin, religion, ethnicity, skin colour and so on – as, accordingly, will their treatment. It is this complexity that perhaps explains their general absence from consideration in the study of intolerance where boundaries (for example between the study of antisemitism and anti-black racism) are rarely overcome, in spite of the pioneer efforts of scholars such as Paul Gilroy, Bryan Cheyette and Michael Rothberg (Cheyette, 2013; Gilroy, 2000; Rothberg, 2009) in the sphere of cultural and literary studies and Colin Holmes, Panikos Panayi and myself in history (Holmes, 1988; Kushner, 2006; Panayi, 2010) and John Solomos in Sociology (Solomos, 2003 [1989])). As Rothberg argues, there is a politics of collective memory involved. Aiming to overcome it, he asks 'When memories of slavery and colonialism [for example] bump up against memories of the Holocaust in contemporary multicultural societies, must a competition of victims ensue?' (Rothberg, 2009: 2). But in the case of scholars confronting anti-refugee politics and sentiment, there is perhaps an even greater challenge: refugees come in all shapes, sizes and colours. What unites them is their refugeedom viewed positively, negatively and ambivalently. They do not 'fit' into classic theories of racism, Marxist or otherwise, but are still frequently victims of racialisation.

Refugees do not themselves, it must be stressed, cause a 'problem'. Revealingly, the politicisation of anti-refugee sentiment is more often articulated in countries or localities where refugee numbers are extremely low. Warnings against the menace posed by refugees has been uttered on an almost daily basis by Viktor Orbán, the extreme nationalist Prime Minister of Hungary, and its dominant political force in the new millennia. In 2018 Hungary, which has amongst the lowest refugee population in Europe, admitted just 670 applications for asylum. Asylum seekers have been kept at bay by the erection of a 100-mile plus fence stopping any crossings on its southern border with Serbia and Croatia.[1] According to UNHCR statistics, 84% of the world's refugee population are located in the developing world. Whilst there are exceptions, these much greater numbers have not been negatively politicised as they have been in the global north.

It remains that the words 'refugee' and 'problem' are incessantly and almost automatically coupled. 'Refugee' has become, like many other minority groups, but in a peculiarly all-embracing way, an outlet for fears and frustrations of real problems in culture, society and politics such as unemployment and job security, housing, crime, health, terrorism and international instability. The ease with which populist and other political parties have mobilised against them in the early twenty-first century (in both liberal and illiberal countries, including in sections of the left and progressive world – the ruling Social Democrats in Denmark in 2019 are, for example, pushing through harsh restrictive measures) is an indication that hostility towards them needs to be taken with the utmost seriousness, including in academic work on intolerance.

As David Goldberg has insisted, racism is not singular. Indeed, the title and contents of this volume insists upon its plurality (Goldberg, 1994). In this light, Liza Schuster has argued that the treatment of asylum seekers (and I would add refugees as a whole), can be defined as racist (Schuster, 2003b: 244). She follows a definition of racism that it is based on 'any argument which suggests that the human species is composed of discrete groups in order to legitimate inequality' (Miles, 1989: 49).[2] Schuster defends her position by arguing that 'asylum seeker' is no longer simply an (almost exclusively western, post-1980s) legal category for those awaiting a decision on their application for refugee status. Instead it is now 'a term that is used unambiguously, and immediately conjures up cheat, liar, criminal, sponger – someone deserving of hostility by virtue not only of any misdemeanour, but simply because he or she is an "asylum seeker"'. It is, she adds, 'a figure that has by now become a caricature, a stereotype, in the way that "Blacks", "Jews" and "Gypsies" have been and still are' (Schuster, 2003b: 244).

The label 'refugee', as emphasised here, has much more ambiguity associated with it than the 'asylum seeker' which is almost always regarded with hatred and suspicion. But if the former can evoke pity (which in turn can lead to patronising treatment of refugees and the removal of their agency and even voice), the figure of the refugee is also associated, as Vernant perceptively noted as early as 1953, with producing 'an element of anxiety' (Vernant, 1953: 12). Vernant's analysis of why this was the case still holds validity over half a century later. The crux is, as he underlined, is that 'The refugee is, in the first place, a symbol of *instability*' (Ibid).

For some postmodern writers, the state of exile is a place of freedom, spared from the tyranny of the nation state and the imaginative limitations of restrictive borders. But for the less rarefied, those 'whose homeland is nowhere' are seen as a potential threat (Vernant, 1953: 13). It explains the speed with which refugees desire and our encouraged to integrate, often being at the forefront of attempts to define their country of adoption in the cultural realm. Arendt, writing critically in the middle of this process, stated 'We were told to forget; and we forgot quicker than anybody could imagine … after four weeks in France or six weeks in America, we pretended to be Frenchmen or Americans'. She added that 'The more optimistic among us would even add that their whole former life had been passed in a kind of unconscious exile and only their new country now taught them what a home really looks like' (Arendt, 2007 [1943]: 265). The Hungarian refugee and satirist of English mores, George Mikes, relayed a joke doing the rounds in London during the late 1940s: 'A German refugee was offered naturalisation but he indignantly exclaimed: "What? Without India?!"' (Mikes, 1986 [1984]: 190).

Vernant adds that alongside being a living embodiment of a world in flux, 'the refugee is the *unknown*'. Immigrants, even if disliked, have a clear homeland from where they chose to leave, but the refugee no longer has a country, 'he has been cast out by his *group*' (Vernant, 1953, 13). 'He' is thus both inferior to other foreigners, but potentially more dangerous. 'His' lack of paperwork, or the perception that it is unreliable, leads to a first contact, in Vernant's analysis, that 'provokes an inevitable conflict' (Vernant, 1953: 14). The refugee or asylum seeker is thus put into a placeless place – a camp or reception centre that reinforces her/his liminal status and most recently geographical anomalies such as the Italian island of Lampedusa where they can be processed remotely (Zolberg, 1999: 73; Cuttitta, 2014; Mazzara, 2019).

Schuster highlights how 'Just as there is a hierarchy among migrants who may be included, so too is there a messy and complex hierarchy among asylum-seekers, a hierarchy of the excluded' (Schuster, 2003b: 245). She emphasises class and gender as complicating factors, noting especially how in state asylum processes in many western countries, there is an 'unequal and particular treatment of women' (Ibid). Indeed, as has become clear, the language of the 1951 Convention and of early studies of refugees assumed that refugees – essentially political dissidents in the writers' minds - were exclusively *male*.

What is complicated about anti-refugee discourse is that it combines at different times and different places with a variety of other 'isms' and 'phobias'. In the late-nineteenth century through to at least the 1940s, it was heavily influenced by antisemitism (or more accurately, antisemitisms), a hostility that came from all parts of the political spectrum. More recently, Islamophobia has been a major feature of attacks on refugees, as has in more specific movements, anti-Gypsy racism. Racisms with imperial and post-imperial origins have been employed against those coming from Africa and Asia, skin colour being an important factor in hostility to refugees coming from the developing world. Indeed imperial thinking has deeply influenced both hostility *and* humanitarian impulses towards refugees, just as the rise and especially the decline of empires has led to massive refugee movements (Panayi and Virdee, 2011; Shaw, 2015). And yet refugees constructed as 'white' – for example those from former Yugoslavia in the 1990s – were also racialised, revealing again the essentially complex nature of anti-refugee racism (van Selm, 2000). Alongside sexism, homophobia has played a role in the treatment of refugees in relation to gender and sexuality.

It is, however, the power of nationalism and national exclusivity and concomitant xenophobia (which then collectively influences international responses to refugees) that has singled out refugees for special treatment from the nineteenth century onwards. The 'good' refugee (following the narrative of deserving status – that is one escaping from a regime hated by the receiving society – then gratitude, loyalty and contribution) might be included within the national story, but unlike migrants recruited for work purposes, the refugee is often perceived as at best a burden and at worst, a threat to the stability of society. Thus an analysis of what the refugee or asylum seeker is accused of is a good guide to the anxieties, both domestic and international, of each particular age. Within the histories produced of particular refugee groups – Huguenots, Jews and East African Asians are classic examples – an apologetic tradition emerges that emphasises only contribution and downplays any animosity faced, whether from state or populace (Gwynn, 1985; Medawar and Pyke, 2000; Nasar, 2018).

What then does this suggest about future research directions? There is a need for those working in many different fields to recognise that animosity to refugees complicates understanding of responses to broader categories of the excluded. Thus, for example, whilst refugees might be regarded with within wider migration studies, despite their huge and growing numbers, as a relatively small group (and one that do not always fit broader trends in movements), reactions and responses to them are both part of and apart from wider categories of migrants.

Indeed, the study of anti-refugee racism is valuable because it forces connections to be made in scholarship that is still too often divided by specialisms, groups studied and rigid ideology. The argument of Harry Goulbourne relating to Britain that

> whilst relations between different European groups or between different groups of white people gave rise to patterns of discrimination, the emergence of racial differentiation and the subsequent race relations… arose out of the dramatic contact and integration of Africans and Asians

still holds great sway (Goulbourne, 1998: ix-x, 26–9). In contrast, the fundamental argument here is that the ambiguous status of the 'refugee', and other racialised migrant groups, suggests strongly that the 'colonial/imperial past' (Goulbourne: ix) is not always the only factor determining whether racism is present or not. And as is the case with refugee studies as a whole, rather than be subsumed in other fields, the analysis of anti-refugee racism has its own internal dynamics within traditions of intolerance (Kushner and Lunn, 1989).

There is something in what is perceived as the unsettling nature of refugeedom (and even more so in the recent legal construct of asylum seeker) which deserves to be studied in its own right. This includes the long bureaucratic restrictionist history (moving from the creation of 'paper walls' in the 1930s through to real ones as in Hungary or demanded by President Trump in America's border with Mexico in the twenty-first century), as well as the deep and uneasy social, cultural and political engagement with the figure of the refugee. The need for this specific focus, ironically, extends to the so-far largely ahistorical field of refugee studies.

What I am advocating is far from studying anti-refugee racism in isolation or as a static, unchanging phenomena. Instead, an inclusive approach will enable an understanding of the strength of anti-refugee hostility (and the limitations of pro-refugee sentiment and action, reassuring and important though these are) *and* greater understanding of how racisms and other intolerances mutate throughout history and geography. Through this we can begin to understand how, since the turn of the millennia, in a world of constant and ubiquitous surveillance close to 50,000 refugees have been allowed to drown in one of the world's most busy shipping waters – the Mediterranean – desperately trying to find safety and a chance to rebuild lives in 'Fortress Europe'.[3]

Notes

1 Figures from https:asylumineurope.org, accessed 26 June 2019.
2 Schuster links this definition to Robert Miles but it is critiqued by this sociologist of racism who attributes it more to John Rex.
3 Figures from the Missing Migrants project run by the International Organization for Migration. See missingmigrants.iom.int, accessed 26 June 2019.

References

Arendt, H. (2007 [1943]). 'We Refugees' in J. Kohn (ed), *The Jewish Writings. Hannah Arendt*. New York: Schocken Books, pp. 264–274.

Cheyette, B. (2013). *Diasporas of the Mind: Jewish and Postcolonial Writing and the Nightmare of History*. New Haven: Yale University Press.

Chimni, B.S. (1998), 'The geopolitics of refugee studies: A view from the South'. *Journal of Refugee Studies* 11, 4: 350–374.

Cross, G. (1983). *Immigrant Workers in Industrial France: The Making of a New Laboring Class*. Philadelphia: Temple University Press.

Cuttitta, P. (2014), 'Borderizing the Island: Setting and narratives of the Lampedusa "Border Play".' *ACME* 13/2: 196–219.

Gatrell, P. (2013). *The Making of the Modern Refugee*. Oxford: Oxford University Press.

Gilroy, P. (2000). *Between Camps: Nations, Cultures and the Allure of Race*. London: Allen Lane.

Goldberg, D. (1994). *Racist Culture*. Oxford: Blackwell.

Goulbourne, H. (1998). *Race Relations in Britain Since 1945*. Basingstoke: Macmillan.

Gwynn, R. (1985). *Huguenot Heritage: The History and Contribution of the Huguenots in Britain*. London: Routledge.

Higham, J. (1978 [1955]). *Strangers in the Land: Patterns of American Nativism 1860-1925*. New York: Atheneum.

Holmes, C. (1988). *John Bull's Island: Immigration & British Society, 1871-1971*. Basingstoke: Macmillan.

Kushner, T. (2006). *Remembering Refugees: Then and Now*. Manchester: Manchester University Press.

Kushner, T. (2017). *Journeys from the Abyss: The Holocaust and Forced Migration from the 1880s to the Present*. Liverpool: Liverpool University Press.

Kushner, T. and Knox, K. (1999). *Refugees in an Age of Genocide: Global, National and Local Perspectives During the Twentieth Century*. London: Frank Cass.

Kushner, T. and Lunn, K. (eds) (1989). *Traditions of Intolerance: Historical Perspectives on Fascism and Race Discourse in Britain*. Manchester: Manchester University Press.

Loescher, G. (1989). 'Introduction: Refugee Issues in International Relations' in Gill Loescher and Laila Monahan (eds), *Refugees and International Relations*. Oxford: Oxford University Press, pp. 1–33.

London, L. (2000). *Whitehall and the Jews 1933-1948: British Immigration Policy and the Holocaust*. Cambridge: Cambridge University Press.

Malkki, L. (1996), 'Speechless emissaries: Refugees, humanitarianism and dehistoricization.' *Cultural Anthropology* 11, 3: 377–404.

Manning, P. (2013). *Migration in World History*. Abingdon: Routledge.

Marrus, M. (1985). *The Unwanted: European Refugees in the Twentieth Century*. Oxford: Oxford University Press.

Mazzara, F. (2019). *Reframing Migration: Lampedusa, Border Spectacle and the Aesthetics of Subversion*. Oxford: Lang.

Medawar, J. and Pyke, D. (2000). *Hitler's Gift: Scientists Who Fled Nazi Germany*. London: Richard Cohen Books.

Mikes, G. (1986 [1984]). *How to be a Brit: A George Mikes Minibus*. Harmondsworth: Penguin.

Miles. R. (1989). *Racism*. London: Routledge.

Nasar, S. (2018). 'We Refugees? Re-defining Britain's East African Asians' in Jennifer Craig-Norton, Christhard Hoffmann and Tony Kushner (eds), *Migrant Britain – Histories and Historiographies: Essays in Honour of Colin Holmes*. London: Routledge, pp. 138–148.

Noiriel, G. (2012 [1991]). *Réfugiés et sans-papiers. La République face au droit d'asile, XIX-XX siecle*. Paris: Pluriel.

Panayi, P. (2010). *An Immigration History of Britain: Multicultural Racism since 1800*. London: Longman.

Panayi, P. and Virdee, P. (eds) (2011) *Refugees and the End of Empire: Imperial Collapse and Forced Migration in the Twentieth Century*. Basingstoke: Palgrave Macmillan.

Porter, B. (1979). *The Refugee Question in Mid-Victorian Politics*. Cambridge: Cambridge University Press.

Proudfoot, M. (1957). *European Refugees 1939-52: A Study in Forced Population Movement*. London: Faber and Faber.

Reinisch, J. and Frank, M. (eds) (2017) *Refugees in Europe 1919-1959: A Forty Year Crisis?*. London: Bloomsbury Academic.

Rothberg, M. (2009). *Multidirectional Memory: Remembering the Holocaust in the Age of Decolonization*. Stanford: Stanford University Press.

Schuster, L. (2003a). *The Use and Abuse of Political Asylum in Britain and Germany*. London: Frank Cass.

Schuster, L. (2003b), 'Common sense or racism? The treatment of asylum-seekers in Europe.' *Patterns of Prejudice* 37, 3: 233–255.

Selm (J.) (ed) (2000) *Kosovo's Refugees in the European Union*. London: Pinter.

Shaw, C. (2015). *Britannia's Embrace: Modern Humanitarianism and the Imperial Origins of Refugee Relief*. Oxford: Oxford University Press.

Simpson, J. (1938). *Refugees: Preliminary Report of a Survey*. London: Royal Institute of International Affairs.

Simpson, J. (1939). *Refugees: A Review of the Situation Since September 1938*. London: Royal Institute of International Affairs.

Solomos, J. (2003 [1989]). *Race and Racism in Britain*. Basingstoke: Palgrave Macmillan.

Tuitt, P. (1996). *False Images: The Law's Construction of the Refugee*. London: Pluto Press.

Vernant, J. (1953). *The Refugee in the Post-War World*. London: George Allen & Unwin.

Zetter, R. (1988). 'Refugees and refugee studies: A label and an agenda.' *Journal of Refugee Studies* 1, 1: 1–6.

Zolberg, A. (1999). 'Matters of State: Theorizing Immigration Policy' in Charles Hirschman, Philip Kasinitz and Josh DeWind (eds), *The Handbook of International Migration*. New York: Russell Sage Foundation, pp. 71–93.

Part III
Racism and the state

Introduction

The role of the state and political institutions in shaping both historical and contemporary forms of racism has been an important feature of both historical and contemporary accounts of racism. The notion of the racial state has been used to talk about the Nazi racial state, but in more recent times it has also been widely utilised to talk about more contemporary racialised political orders.

The opening chapter of this part, by Charles W. Mills, provides an overview of the concept of the racial state. Mills argues that in many ways the racial state can be traced back to Western antiquity, although he then goes on to argue that the transition to modernity was still significant because of the way it helped to globalise what he calls the "Euro/white racial state", as compared to more localised and heterogeneous premodern racial states. Mills then goes on to argue that race needs to be to be centred as determinant of the West's trajectory from the start, and that it is important in this context to explore the notion of the racial state and its utility in analysing the contemporary situation.

This is followed by Marcus Hunter's chapter, which outlines the dynamics that shape how the state maintains and manifests racialised power. Hunter's chapter explores the processes that shape the meanings of Blackness and its relationship to the state. He argues that it is important to develop the tools that can help us to understand Blackness as a global social fact and epiphenomenon. He suggests that politics and state institutions play a central role in shaping everyday and politicised ideas about Blackness. Although much of his focus is on the situation in the U.S., Hunter also seeks to argue that this frame can be utilised more globally.

The following chapter by David Cook-Martín focuses on the linkages between political and racial orders. In particular he seeks to investigate the relationship between racial and political orders and how it has evolved and changed. Cook-Martín engages with political sociology, racial and ethnic studies, and with the empirical instance of immigration and nationality policy in the Americas in order to provide an overview of this relationship. A key part of his analysis focuses on the ways in which states have relied on ideas of race to determine political membership and how racial orders have relied on state institutionalisation processes. He develops this line of analysis through some illustrative examples.

In the concluding chapter of this part Charles Gallagher focuses more specifically on the mechanisms through which non-white spaces are framed in colour-blind narratives. Drawing on illustrative examples he argues that when non-white or mixed-race spaces increase in real or potential value, they can become majority white spaces through racial gentrification or white power brokers using legal means to re-whiten these spaces. The chapter draws on a case study of a city in the U.S. Midwest and the processes that led to the shutting down of twelve minority bars and restaurants. Gallagher argues that although they were shut down through ostensibly race-neutral, colour-blind legal procedures, in practice white officials enforced code violations against non-white establishments while ignoring similar violations in white-owned establishments. This analysis underpins the core argument of the chapter, namely that colour-blind narratives can be and are used by political actors to engage in racist actions and maintain white spaces.

8

The racial state

Charles W. Mills

The concept of a "racial state" both draws upon and challenges the official lexicon of Western political theory. In the conventional genealogy that traces Western political thought's intellectual origins to ancient Greece, theorizations of the state can be found from the start. Plato and Aristotle offer us a range of characterizations, both descriptive and normative (good/bad), most of which are still in use today: monarchy, tyranny, aristocracy, oligarchy, and democracy. Of course, the exclusions taken for granted in the premodern period mean that there was no pretense that the state was anything but a minoritarian institution. Women, slaves, and foreigners were not even conceivably full members of the Athenian polis, while patricians and plebeians in the early Roman Republic were sharply demarcated in status and rights. So, the state in the classical world was not bound by popular democratic will, if the *demos* are conceived of inclusively. Nor, of course, would medieval monarchies place on the same scale of political consideration the interests and demands of the feudal nobility and the humble serf. It was government of the people, but certainly not by and for any but a small privileged segment of them.

It is really only with the advent of liberal modernity, then, that the crucial transition from the world of ascriptive status and hierarchy to the world of contract and consent begins, and even then the transition is very partial. As exemplified most clearly in social contract theory's 1650-1800 "golden age" (Thomas Hobbes: *Leviathan*, 1651; John Locke: *Two Treatises of Government*, 1689; Jean-Jacques Rousseau: *The Social Contract*, 1762; Immanuel Kant: *The Metaphysics of Morals*, 1797), democratic government—albeit heavily qualified—was now to be the new norm. Even Hobbes's endorsement of absolutism rests not on traditionalist hierarchical premises but modernist egalitarian ones: it is by popular contractarian consent and fear of others' non-compliance that the mighty Leviathan is brought into existence. And for his successors, Locke, Rousseau, and Kant, the contract metaphor would be used to justify "egalitarian" (as in white male, though sometimes just propertied white male) rule, whether in the constitutionalist commonwealth, the direct democracy of the "general will," or the republican *Rechtsstaat*. It is against this background of *advertised but unrealized* universalism—a polity consensually based on the equal rights of all "men"—that the indictment as actually exclusionary of a state pretending to be representative thereby gains its demystificatory force. Thus, the accusation, the political exposé, that the supposedly inclusive liberal democratic state is really a bourgeois state/a patriarchal state/a racial state (Goldberg, 2002; MacKinnon, 1989; Macpherson, 2011; Miliband, 2009; Mills, 1997; Pateman, 1988).

By comparison with the extensive Marxist literature, though, the "racial" state is comparatively under-investigated and under-theorized. I suggest that the two crucial questions for us are the following: (1) *Conceptualization:* what is a racial state? How should it be essentially characterized? (2) *Periodization and Scope:* when do racial states come into existence and what is their scope?

Conceptualization

The conceptualization of the racial state will obviously be determined by competing conceptions of race, racism, and what kinds of policies essentially constitute racial governance. Consider, as an ostensive starting point and useful foil, historians Michael Burleigh and Wolfgang Wippermann's well-known study of Nazi Germany, *The Racial State* (1991), in which they declare (p. 23) that "the Third Reich became the first state in world history whose dogma and practice was racism." On this analysis, the racial state is virtually unique. Thus, there is no problem of under-theorization except perhaps as lack of investigation of this particular regime's racist workings. Yet a decade earlier, historian George Fredrickson's *White Supremacy* (1981), a detailed comparativist treatment of the United States and South Africa, had concluded (p. xii) that both nations should be regarded as "*Herrenvolk* societ[ies] in which people of color … [were] treated as permanent aliens or outsiders." This certainly sounds like a "racial state" characterization and indeed, more recently, James Whitman's *Hitler's American Model* (2017, p. 7, 5, 160) reveals that the Nazis used American Jim Crow legislation as their juridical model for the anti-Semitic 1935 Nuremberg Laws. The two countries' "shared commitment to white supremacy" made the United States at the time "the innovative world leader in the creation of racist law" and thus "the natural first place to turn for anybody in the business of planning a 'race state.'"

So, while the Third Reich is undoubtedly demarcated in various ways, for example by the modern "industrial" character of its horrific racial genocidal program, it would still be theoretically mistaken to make it the sole member of the category. The real defining characteristic, I suggest, is systemic racial subordination (that may be manifest in policies other than genocide, for example racial slavery, expropriation, or colonial forced labor), and on this basis, let us attempt a more conceptual approach to the question.

To begin with, the idea of a racial state presupposes, at a minimum, the intersubjective belief in races, Rs, in the society in question. It could be, however, that only one race, R, is deemed to exist in the given society. So, a racial state, in the sense of a state privileging R1s over R2s, is not possible: if some people are advantaged over others, it cannot be on "racial" grounds. At least two Rs, R1s and R2s, need to exist, though there could be more, R3s and R4s. But again, this condition is necessary rather than sufficient, for it could be that no race is currently discriminated against, nor is there any legacy of previous discrimination that has shaped the overall social structure in a way that unfairly benefits, say, the RXs.

Obviously, then, what is required is (1) the existence of at least two races, R1 and R2, in the society in question, and (2) the differential privileging of the R1s over the R2s, whether in terms of ongoing patterns of system-wide transactional discrimination or structural disadvantaging or both, on the basis, (3), whether exclusively, or at least significantly, of R-membership. The last stipulation is necessary to eliminate situations where, through accidental correlation, the privileging/disadvantaging of the respective Rs is not based on race but on some other identity they happen to have, for example their being simultaneously Q1s and Q2s (such as members of dominant and subordinate classes), or possessors of some other set of intersectional traits that, by happenstance, has produced this particular outcome of overlap with R-identity. So, R-membership has to play some appropriate *causal* role for the characterization to be apt.

Now "state" is ambiguous between nation-state (that is, the polity as a whole) and a particular complex of apparatuses of government/governance (that is, the state as a ruling entity). To be sure, depending on one's background theory of sociopolitical causation, the line between the two may be drawn in radically different places. Contrast, for example, the classic Marxist view of the "bourgeois" state as a centralized organ of ruling-class power with the more decentered Foucauldian vision of power as "capillary," permeating the social order as a whole. But bracket these differences. Then a "racial state" could refer both broadly to the society in general (cf. class society for Marxism, patriarchy/patriarchal society for feminism) and to the governing apparatus of that society (cf. the "bourgeois" state as a variety of class state, and the "patriarchal" state as a variety of gender state). In general, we would expect them to be in sync, that is, a racial polity privileging R1s over R2s would be governed by an apparatus reproducing that privileging. But just as Marxism envisaged a transitional "socialist" state (classically, if unhappily, termed "the dictatorship of the proletariat") whose mission it would be to dismantle the capitalist class order and prepare the groundwork for "communism," a classless order, so one could imagine the term "racial state" also being applied to a racially reformist state apparatus trying in the name of R2 emancipation to end R1 domination. This would then be a politically transformative "racial state," one seeking to undermine illicit inherited R1 racial advantage and the social-structural hegemony of the R1 racial *ancien régime* in the larger nation-state.

Ideally, of course, the goal would be a society of racial equality and justice, where race, R, is no longer linked with unfair advantage and disadvantage, or even disappears altogether. But it could transpire that the actual outcome is a new kind of racial rule, in which the R2s now oppress the R1s. Needless to say, this has precisely been the fear that has historically haunted the actual white-dominant orders of modernity: the regional terror ignited across the slaveholding Caribbean and the Americas by the 1791-1804 Haitian Revolution; the panic at the prospect of "Negro Rule" in postbellum 1865-77 Reconstruction in the United States; the 1980s' warning that an ANC (African National Congress) "terrorist" victory in apartheid South Africa would lead to a bloodbath of whites. The contemporary version is the fearmongering in white nationalist, alt-right, and neo-Nazi circles about the prospect of "white genocide" and being "replaced" by people of color and/or Jews.

So, the four key ideas—as illustrated in the homologous notions of a bourgeois or patriarchal state—are *system-wide* differential group *advantage* that is causally linked to differential group *power* and is morally *unjust*. That is, one or more races, R1 … will be differentially and unfairly privileged vis-à-vis one or more other races, R2, R3 … and this privileging will be the result of coordinated action on the part of some subset of R1 … to institutionalize structures, policies, and practices that have this effect, and/or to resist the dismantling of these structures, policies, and practices once they have been established.

For the "racial state" characterization to be apropos, then, such privileging has to be *systemic*, not a matter of isolated individual occurrences, or particular flawed social institutions, and either actively created and maintained by the pertinent state agencies, or not challenged and corrected by these agencies (for example in patterns of individual, group, and corporate action) when such intervention would seem to be called for on grounds of racial equity and the norm of governmental protection of people's legitimate interests. "Privileging" is being conceived of in a very broad way that can encompass economic benefit, political input, cultural influence, juridical status, moral standing, and many others. Without such differential R1 *advantage*, it would be odd to speak of a racial state, since state power would not be invidiously serving R1 interests. On the other hand, without the exercise of differential R1 *power* in creating and maintaining the social order, it would likewise generally be odd to speak of a racial state, since in this case, by hypothesis, that order arose from and is being perpetuated by other causes. But the crucial point is that by norms of racial moral equality the advantage is somehow *morally unjust*, involving invidious discrimination and/or the perpetuation of the legacy of past invidious discrimination against the subordinated race(s). (It is necessary to specify "invidious" since policies of corrective racial justice—for example, affirmative action and reparations—will arguably also require racial discrimination, in the sense of demarcating members of some R group for special treatment over other Rs in ameliorative public policy.) Thus, all four elements are required. While for racists, a racial state is a praiseworthy sociopolitical institution (assuming it favors them), from a non-racist perspective it is, of course, one to be condemned, so the phrase is a pejorative one (with the possible exception noted earlier).

The point of putting things in this very abstract way has been to try to get at the essence of a racial state without being tied down to specific historical manifestations. In other words, one wants a conceptualization broad enough that it can accommodate not only (what I will claim are) the many different varieties of actually existing and historically existent racial states, but possible future incarnations not yet anticipated. It needs to be borne in mind, for example, that the R1s need not be white. Because of the actual history of European domination in modernity, it has been natural—to the extent that there has been literature in this area—to focus on racial states that privilege whites, or at least a subset of the population counted as such. The racial state has generally been the white state, the white-supremacist state. But there is no necessity about this. If race has a premodern history (see discussion below), whether in the West or elsewhere, then racial states in which some other group counted as the dominant R1s might have existed, not just in the West, but for example in Asia, or Africa, or the Americas. And in possible future worlds, whether evolving from our own timeline or alternative timelines, other racial states might privilege particular non-white groups ruling over other non-white groups, or, as mentioned, even over whites.

Periodization and scope

Let us now turn to the linked questions of periodization and scope. As emphasized, the racial state cannot exist without race in some sense. But what sense is that exactly? Class and gender are uncontroversial social categories and social realities, taken for granted as legitimate by sociological theory. But race is different, given its dominant biologistic conceptualization in modernity. In fact, should we even still be working with such a category?

Appropriately enough, this issue—the correct "metaphysics" of race—has been investigated in greatest detail by philosophy, in what has come to be called "critical philosophy of race." Five basic anti-racist metaphysical positions have been demarcated. (1) *Realism/biologism/naturalism:* biological races do indeed exist after all, though not as "racially" determined by this biology in their behavior and not ranked in the cognitive/characterological/spiritual hierarchies assumed by classic racist thought but positioned as equals (Spencer, 2018a, 2018b). (2) *Eliminativism:* races exist in no sense, neither as biological nor social entities (Appiah, 1992). (3) *Anti-eliminativist social constructionism:* races do not exist biologically, but they do exist as social constructs (Haslanger, 2012). (4) *Hybrid unified social-naturalism:* races exist in a unitary way as entities *both* socially constructed and naturally based (Kitcher, 2012). (5) *Hybrid bifurcated social-naturalism:* races exist as both biological and social entities, not necessarily coincident with each other, so that one's biological race could be different from one's social race (Hardimon, 2017). For example, by the American "one-drop rule" for determining blackness, many black Americans are "socially" black while being "biologically" largely white (Davis, 1991).

Now it might initially seem that any given metaphysical position automatically determines the periodization of racial states. But I would claim that this is not actually so, since for our purposes what counts is the intersubjectivist *uptake* of "races" as socially significant entities: race as a central category of self- and other-identification. Thus, even if realism is correct, what will matter is not the mere existence of race (since by hypothesis it has no significant causal power), but people's (largely fictive) beliefs about race and their actions based on those beliefs, which might long postdate the evolution of biological race. On the other hand, even if eliminativism is correct, people could still believe there are races and on that basis create, through custom, institutional policy, ideology, value judgment, behavioral pattern, legal prescription and proscription, structural positioning, etc., racialized social groups, which would effectively be "races" for our political purposes (Blum, 2010). Even for realism and eliminativism, then, it is social endorsement and social causality that are ultimately crucial, as they obviously are for social constructionism and social-naturalism in its two versions. Sociality is thus the key element throughout, whether in literally making race or at least in creating entities believed to be races (racialized social groups) or in making (pre-existing biological) race intersubjectively salient. In this respect—counterintuitively—the politics (the racialization of the polity) may be independent of the metaphysics. Racial states could exist even if actual races did not ("races" would just be racialized social groups), and races could exist (as biological entities) without there being racial states organized around them.

The crucial prerequisite for the creation of a racial state, then, will be the existence of "social" race, and "race" should henceforth be read that way. After World War II, in the aftermath of the Holocaust, and with the acceleration of the global decolonial movement, "scientific" biological racism (natural hierarchy) had been largely discredited in mainstream academic circles (Barkan, 1992). So, the important question became: when in the West did social race become intersubjectively recognized/constructed? (I will focus on the West, since it is here that race has been most thoroughly researched, not—as emphasized above—because I am ruling out the possibility of racial states in the pre-colonial non-Western world.) As David Theo Goldberg asks in his book *The Racial State* (2002), what is the "time" of racial states? Two main competing "times" of "social" race would develop in the postwar literature, a majority "short periodization" view (race as modern) and a minority "long periodization" view (race as ancient). More recently, they have been joined by a compromise third position that sees race as originating in the medieval period.

On the short periodization, the emergence of race dates back only to early modernity. George Frederickson (2015) and others (Hannaford, 1996) argue that while, of course, you have ethnocentrism, religious bigotries, and xenophobia in the ancient and medieval worlds, race does not appear till later. Hence the racial state, if it exists, would have to be modern; there is no premodern (social) race and so no premodern racial state. The influential work of black classicist Frank Snowden, Jr., for example, declared this to be a period "before color prejudice" (Snowden, Jr., 1970; Snowden, Jr., 1983). In this spirit, Goldberg (2002) confidently asserts that the "time" of racial states is modernity.

But a cohort of revisionist classicists (Eliav-Feldon et al., 2009; Isaac, 2004; McCoskey, 2012) has for the past decade and a half contended that race can indeed be found in the ancient world, once "race" is de-linked from familiar definitions in terms of color and continental origins (that is, the usual polychrome cast of white Europeans, black Africans, red Amerindians, brown and yellow Asians). In fact, a crucial premise of their argument is that defenders of the short periodization have defined "race" in a question-begging way, essentially requiring that all varieties of race need to conform to the modern kind. But this makes the periodization of race a matter of definitional truth rather than empirical discovery. No wonder, then, that with this tacit stipulation, race turns out to be distinctively modern. As Benjamin Isaac insists in his *The Invention of Racism in Classical Antiquity* (2004), a starting point for such a debate must be a non-tendentious conception, that can be accepted by all reasonable parties to the discussion, one that does not presuppose the desired conclusion.

Further complicating the picture, some scholars are now claiming that on such a conception, the correct dating actually turns out to be premodern but medieval, as announced in the contrasting title of Geraldine Heng's recent book: *The Invention of Race in the European Middle Ages* (2018). Debra Higgs Strickland's *Saracens, Demons, & Jews* (2003) had earlier argued that in the iconography of medieval Christendom's "monstrous races" (inherited from Pliny the Elder's *Natural History*) we find a bestiary of grotesques that groups together the clearly nonhuman—one-legged Sciopods, dog-headed Cynocephali, headless Blemmyae—with more familiar enemies of the faith—sinister Jews, threatening Saracens, invading Mongols, diabolical Ethiopians—thereby raising questions about the latter's equal humanity. Heng (2018) adds "Skrælings" (Native Americans) and Romani to the list, and concludes, contra the conventional narrative, that on this evidence we can indeed speak of medieval race. Indeed, she goes further to claim—in a second book published next year, *England and the Jews: How Religion and Violence Created the First Racial State in the West* (Heng, 2019)—that it is actually in medieval England's treatment of its Jewish population that we find the first example in the West of the racial state (see also Heng [2018, ch. 2]). So, this is obviously a very different storyline from the orthodox one.

The most important neighboring concept from which race would have to be demarcated is, of course, ethnicity. Whereas "race" would in the post-World War II period become a controversial category, "ethnicity" is far more respectable, without the theoretical baggage "race" is standardly taken to have. Hence the recommendation to simply drop "race" in favor of "ethnicity." Moreover, given the centrality of ethnocentrism to human, or maybe more generally hominin, history, the idea of an ethno-state—the polity of the tribe, writ large and institutionalized—is already well-established, and indeed of resurgent applicability, with the ominous development across the globe in recent years of an illiberal exclusionary right-wing nationalism. Michael Hanchard's *The Spectre of Race* (2018), for example, makes the case that the ancient Athenian polis, proudly claimed as the political fountainhead of the Western democratic political tradition, was itself an ethno-state, so that modern instantiations of this pattern in countries like Britain, France, and the United States, far from betraying the classical lineage, are in fact affirming it.

But short periodization scholars would retort that the link between present and past can be affirmed without blurring the crucial differences between ethnicity and race. Race is indeed distinctively modern, and we should not dilute its peculiar specificities by sloppy theoretical generalizations that gloss over the discontinuities between radically different historical epochs.

Yet the difficulty of drawing a clear line between the two is, ironically enough, manifest in the coinage by Goldberg himself of the term *ethnorace*, a recognition of their frequent reciprocal conceptual osmosis through a permeable boundary. If the shorthand contrast has traditionally been ethnicity/ethnocentrism as culture/cultural prejudice versus race/racism as imputed biology/biological determinism, the formal recognition of "cultural racism" as a possibility blurs this once clear-cut opposition. Moreover, while cultural racism (originally termed the "new" racism) is generally taken to be the variety of racism that only becomes hegemonic in the postwar epoch, long periodization scholars would insist that it is actually the *modal* variety in the history of racism. "Scientific" biological racism is the outlier, only a century and a half or two in duration: late eighteenth century to mid-twentieth century. Before and after, it is cultural racism (sometimes fused with theological racism, the appeal to supernatural causation) that held/holds sway. (However, the rise of the alt-right has stimulated a rebirth of old-fashioned biological racism [Saini, 2019], so this situation may change in coming years.)

The issue should thus be regarded as the subject of an ongoing scholarly debate rather than a resolved one. In addition, apart from uncertainty in determining the "time" of race, controversy also besets the conceptualization of a racial state, as indicated in the preceding section. Fredrickson (2015, 100-3), for example, draws another important contrast, that between what he calls "overtly racist regimes" (e.g., the U.S. South under Jim Crow, Nazi Germany, apartheid South Africa) and "racialized societies" (e.g., the U.S. North, Latin America, the colonial world).

The crucial demarcators of the former are: (1) an official racist ideology (2) racial "purity" as an ideal (3) mandatory de jure segregation (4) prohibitions on the political activity (voting, holding public office) of the subordinated race(s) and (5) deliberate impoverishment of the subordinated race(s). So, should we limit the "racial state" designation to such societies? Obviously, while more expansive than Burleigh and Wippermann's (1991) view, much of the modern world would still be excluded on this conception.

How to decide? In large measure, the division of opinion here tracks rival political commitments. What are conventionally characterized as "radical" scholars—sympathetic, for example, to Marxism, post-structuralism, or postcolonial theory—are generally more open than mainstream theorists to endorsing a more inclusive conception. For them, the reluctance of mainstream liberal sociopolitical scholars to recognize the broad applicability of the concept is merely another manifestation of the general postwar Western whitewashing of the historical record of Western colonial racial domination. (Indeed, another of Whitman's [2017, p. 8, 36, 51, 141] startling revelations is that for the Nazis, the runner-up candidate model for juridical racial exclusion was the British Empire.) From this perspective, the "overtly racist" vs. "racialized" distinction is secondary to the question of the existence or not of the systemic structural advantaging of whites (R1s), and it is this feature that the proposed conceptualization in the first section was meant to capture. Racialized societies would then actually be the fundamental category, with overt and non-overt variants then being different species of the larger genus. In fact, a case can be made that—at least for non-genocidal states, where the subordinated R-population continues to exist—a system of racial domination *that does not present itself as such*, characterized by de facto rather than formal R1 privileging, may well be more stable and enduring than an overtly racist one.

Michael Omi and Howard Winant's classic *Racial Formation in the United States*, for example, now in its third edition (Omi and Winant, 2015), had argued from its original 1986 version that we should see the U.S. as a whole, not just the U.S. South, as a "racial state" (ch. 5), given its constitution on the basis of racial domination, even if the mechanisms of domination evolve over time. Earlier statements of this position, if not always focusing specifically and in a detailed way on the theorization of the state as such, can be found in such "radical" texts as Stokely Carmichael (later Kwame Ture) and Charles V. Hamilton's 1967 (1992) *Black Power*, the book that first introduced the concept of "institutional racism." Then of course we have the longstanding black American radical tradition, going back to the nineteenth century, such as the work of W.E.B. Du Bois (1996) and his predecessors, and diagnosing white supremacy as the actual system of government in the United States, no matter what its liberal pretensions. Or, more generally, the global nineteenth- and twentieth-century anti-colonial tradition, of which Frantz Fanon's 1961 *The Wretched of the Earth* (2005), with its vision of a planet divided between dominant and subordinate races, is perhaps the most famous example. So, it is important to appreciate that the "racial state" characterization has a history in global oppositional ("underground") activist anti-racist scholarship that long predates tentative mainstream admission of the validity of the concept. Insofar as the modern state presides over—initiating, facilitating, consolidating—Euro-colonial and Euro-imperial and Euro-settler rule, including racial slavery, it can be contended that it is ineluctably formed as a racial state, given that rulers and ruled are constituted of differentially racialized populations, and remains such insofar as this legacy is not dismantled in the "postcolonial"/"post-civil rights" epoch (Goldberg, 2002; Mills, 1997).

Finally, some specific examples. On the broader conception, the modern racial state is created in relation to the gradual establishment of a pan-European "whiteness" (Bacchetta, Maira, and Winant, 2019; Lake and Reynolds, 2008; Winant, 2001; Wolfe, 2016), though of course more fine-grained internal distinctions need to be registered between colonial rule, as in large parts of Africa (Mamdani, 2018), and white settler colonialism, for example in the Americas, Australia and New Zealand, and South Africa (Cavanaugh and Veracini, 2017; Coulthard, 2014; Pateman, 2007), not to mention between the "Anglosphere," the globally hegemonic Anglo-American empire (Vucetic, 2011; Atkinson, 2017) and the other competing Euro-empires. Detailed in-depth studies of particular racial states, synchronically and diachronically, have already been undertaken, most notably of the United States (Bateman, Katznelson, and Lapinski, 2018; Jung, Vargas, and Bonilla-Silva, 2011; King, 2007; Omi and Winant, 2015), and the significance there of a juridical "whiteness" (Crenshaw et al., 1995; Davis, 1991; López, 2006), sometimes in comparison with South Africa (Fredrickson, 1981), and also Brazil (Marx, 1998), or with Canada and Australia (Pateman, 2007; Vickers and Isaac, 2012), or Canada and Great Britain (Thompson, 2016). Latin American nations have traditionally represented themselves as racial democracies characterized by an inclusionary *mestizaje* rather than the segregationist white supremacy of the United States. But a growing body of work over the past few decades has undermined this self-serving set of illusions, documenting the long history of Afro-Latin and Indo-Latin oppression, the role (contra official denials) of the Latin state and the legal system in this subordination, and the ways in which the structure of "pigmentocracies" safeguards a subtler form of white domination (Andrews, 2004; Dixon and Johnson, 2019; Hernández, 2013; Telles, 2014). By contrast, Australia's history of unabashed and overt racism against both its indigenous population and would-be Asian immigrants made it harder from the start to sustain such myths, given the explicit advertised ideal of a "White Australia" (Hage, 2000; Carey and McLisky, 2009; Atkinson, 2017; Maddison, 2019).

The Western European nations themselves, despite being the headquarters of empire and Atlantic slavery, and the original source of modern (and perhaps premodern) racial theory, would in the postwar period begin to erase their role in establishing this global racial system. In some cases (as in "republican" France) the very legitimacy of race as a social category was denied—in fact, it was deleted from the constitution in 2018—let alone "white supremacy" as a defensible overarching characterization. In Britain, however, with its long black activist history, this amnesia was contested from the beginning (Centre for Contemporary Cultural Studies, 2016; Gilroy, 2002), while a newly emergent body of revisionist scholarship on global race and global "whiteness" has begun to challenge this exculpatory whitewashing in other European nations also (Garner, 2007; McEachrane, 2014; Fleming, 2017; Hund, 2017; *Modern Italy*, Nov. 2018). Racism's inconsistency with official communist ideology, not to mention the difficulties of access to accurate data, originally shielded these nations (when they existed) from the desirable investigative scrutiny, but research is beginning to be done here as well (Law, 2012; Sawyer, 2010). Finally, race has seemed to many scholars to be an obviously non-illuminating category by comparison with religion in trying to understand the Middle East and its conflicts. But Bakan and Abu-Laban (2019) argue for its importance, both locally and in relation to global power dynamics, thereby possibly opening up a new paradigm of inquiry for the region.

It can be appreciated, then, how dramatically our pictures of Western history, and our corresponding conceptual framings, would have to change if the "racial state" categorization is academically vindicated even just for the modern period alone. And if race can be shown to be premodern, some medieval states might count also, as Heng (2019) contends. But if Hanchard's (2018) ethno-state analysis of ancient Athens is brought into dialogue with Isaac's (2004) recommended revisionist re-reading of "race," then the backdating of the concept would have to be even more far-reaching. The racial state would indeed go back to Western antiquity, and perhaps be coeval with the development of the West itself. (Though as earlier emphasized, the transition to modernity would still be of revolutionary significance in its *globalization* through European expansionism of the Euro/white racial state, as against more localized and heterogeneous premodern racial states.) It would mean that the inherited taxonomy cited at the beginning of this entry would at a minimum have to be radically supplemented with the concept of racial polities, rule not just by oligarchies, monarchs, the people, or dictators, but racial groups. Race would have to be centered as determinant of the West's trajectory from the start, with all the sweeping repercussions (across multiple disciplines) such a rethinking of that trajectory would imply. In both the descriptive realm studied by the social sciences (the sociopolitical) and the normative realm analyzed by ethics and political philosophy (social justice, national and global: see Bell, 2019), conventional analyses would therefore need drastic reconsideration and re-evaluation. The intellectual and political stakes are thus very high indeed.

References

Andrews, G.R. (2004). *Afro-Latin America, 1800-2000.* New York: Oxford University Press.

Appiah, K.A. (1992). *In My Father's House: Africa in the Philosophy of Culture.* New York: Oxford University Press.

Atkinson, D.C. (2017). *The Burden of White Supremacy: Containing Asian Migration in the British Empire and the United States.* Chapel Hill, NC: University of North Carolina Press.

Bacchetta, P., Maira, S., and Winant, H., eds. (2019). *Global Raciality: Empire, Postcoloniality, Decoloniality.* New York: Routledge.

Bakan, A., and Abu-Laban, Y. (2019). *Israel, Palestine and the Politics of Race: Exploring Identity and Power in a Global Context.* New York: I.B. Tauris/Bloomsbury.

Barkan, E. (1992). *The Retreat of Scientific Racism: Changing Concepts of Race in Britain and the United States between the World Wars.* New York: Cambridge University Press.

Bateman, D.A., Katznelson, I., and Lapinski, J.S. (2018). *Southern Nation: Congress and White Supremacy after Reconstruction.* Princeton, NJ: Princeton University Press.

Bell, D., ed. (2019). *Empire, Race and Global Justice.* New York: Cambridge University Press.

Blum, L. (2010). "Racialized Groups: The Sociohistorical Consensus." *Monist,* 93, no. 2: 298–320.

Burleigh, M., and Wippermann, W. (1991). *The Racial State: Germany 1933-1945.* New York: Cambridge University Press.

Carey, J., and McLisky, C., eds. (2009). *Creating White Australia.* Sydney: Sydney University Press.

Cavanagh, E., and Veracini, L., eds. (2017). *The Routledge Handbook of the History of Settler Colonialism.* New York: Routledge.

Centre for Contemporary Cultural Studies, eds. (2016). *The Empire Strikes Back: Race and Racism in 70s Britain*. New York: Routledge.

Coulthard, G.S. (2014). *Red Skin, White Masks: Rejecting the Colonial Politics of Recognition*. Minneapolis, MN: University of Minnesota Press.

Crenshaw, K., Gotanda, N., Peller, G., and Thomas, K., eds. (1995). *Critical Race Theory: The Key Writings That Formed the Movement*. New York: New Press.

Davis, F.J. (1991). *Who Is Black? One Nation's Definition*. University Park, PA: The Pennsylvania State University Press.

Dixon, K., and Johnson, O.A., eds. (2019). *Comparative Racial Politics in Latin America*. New York: Routledge.

Eliav-Feldon, M., Isaac, B., and Ziegler, J., eds. (2009). *The Origins of Racism in the West*. New York: Cambridge University Press.

Fanon, F. (2005). *The Wretched of the Earth*. Trans. R. Philcox. New York: Grove Press.

Fleming, C.M. (2017). *Resurrecting Slavery: Racial Legacies and White Supremacy in France*. Philadelphia: Temple University Press.

Fredrickson, G.M. (1981). *White Supremacy: A Comparative Study in American and South African History*. New York: Oxford University Press.

Fredrickson, G.M. (2015). *Racism: A Short History*. Princeton, NJ: Princeton Classics.

Garner, S. (2007). *Whiteness: An Introduction*. New York: Routledge.

Gilroy, P. (2002). *There Ain't No Black in the Union Jack*. London: Routledge Classics.

Goldberg, D.T. (2002). *The Racial State*. Malden, MA: Blackwell.

Hage, G. (2000). *White Nation: Fantasies of White Supremacy in a Multicultural Society*. New York: Routledge.

Hanchard, M.G. (2018). *The Spectre of Race: How Discrimination Haunts Western Democracies*. Princeton, NJ: Princeton University Press.

Hannaford, I. (1996). *Race: The History of an Idea in the West*. Baltimore: Johns Hopkins University Press.

Hardimon, M.O. (2017). *Rethinking Race: The Case for Deflationary Realism*. Cambridge, MA: Harvard University Press.

Haslanger, S. (2012). *Resisting Reality: Social Construction and Social Critique*. New York: Oxford University Press.

Heng, G. (2018). *The Invention of Race in the European Middle Ages*. New York: Cambridge University Press.

Heng, G. (2019). *England and the Jews: How Religion and Violence Created the First Racial State in the West*. New York: Cambridge University Press.

Hernández, T.K. (2013). *Racial Subordination in Latin America: The Role of the State, Customary Law, and the New Civil Rights Response*. New York: Cambridge University Press.

Hobbes, T. (1996). *Leviathan*. Ed. R. Tuck. New York: Cambridge University Press.

Hund, W.D. (2017). *Wie die Deutschen Weiss Wurden: Kleine (Heimat) Geschichte des Rassismus*. Stuttgart: J.B. Metzler.

Isaac, B. (2004). *The Invention of Racism in Classical Antiquity*. Princeton, NJ: Princeton University Press.

Jung, M-K., Vargas, J.H.C., and Bonilla-Silva, E., eds. (2011). *State of White Supremacy: Racism, Governance, and the United States*. Stanford, CA: Stanford University Press.

Kant, I. (2017). *The Metaphysics of Morals*. Rev. ed. Ed. L. Denis. Trans. M. Gregor. New York: Cambridge University Press.

King, D. (2007). *Separate and Unequal: African Americans and the US Federal Government*. Rev. ed. New York: Oxford University Press.

Kitcher, P. (2012). "Does 'Race' Have a Future?." In Taylor, P., ed *The Philosophy of Race*. pp. 106–125. New York: Routledge. Vol. II.

Lake, M., and Reynolds, H. (2008). *Drawing the Global Colour Line: White Men's Countries and the International Challenge of Racial Equality*. New York: Cambridge University Press.

Law, I. (2012). *Red Racisms: Racism in Communist and Post-Communist Contexts*. New York: Palgrave Macmillan.

Locke, J. (1988). *Two Treatises of Government*. Ed. P. Laslett. New York: Cambridge University Press.

López, I.F.H. (2006). *White by Law: The Legal Construction of Race*. Rev. 10th anniversary ed. New York: New York University Press.

MacKinnon, C.A. (1989). *Toward a Feminist Theory of the State*. Cambridge, MA: Harvard University Press.

Macpherson, C.B. (2011). *The Political Theory of Possessive Individualism: Hobbes to Locke*. New York: Oxford University Press.

Maddison, S. (2019). *The Colonial Fantasy: Why White Australia Can't Solve Black Problems*. London: Allen & Unwin.

Mamdani, M. (2018). *Citizen and Subject: Contemporary Africa and the Legacy of Late Colonialism*. Princeton, NJ: Princeton University Press.

Marx, A.W. (1998). *Making Race and Nation: A Comparison of the United States, South Africa, and Brazil*. New York: Cambridge University Press.

McCoskey, D.E. (2012). *Race: Antiquity and Its Legacy*. New York: Oxford University Press.

McEachrane, M., ed. (2014). *Afro-Nordic Landscapes: Equality and Race in Northern Europe*. New York: Routledge.

Miliband, R. (2009). *The State in Capitalist Society*. London: Merlin.

Mills, C.W. (1997). *The Racial Contract*. Ithaca, NY: Cornell University Press.

Modern Italy 23, no. 4 (Nov. 2018). Special Issue: Nation, 'Race', and Racisms in Twentieth-Century Italy.

Omi, M., and Winant, H. (2015). *Racial Formation in the United States*. 3rd ed. New York: Routledge.

Pateman, C. (1988). *The Sexual Contract*. Stanford, CA: Stanford University Press.

Pateman, C. (2007). "The Settler Contract." In Pateman, C., and Mills, C.W., *Contract and Domination*. pp. 35–78. Malden, MA: Polity.

Rousseau, J-J. (1997). *The Social Contract and Other Later Political Writings*. Ed. and trans. V. Gourevitch. New York: Cambridge University Press.

Saini, A. (2019). *Superior: The Return of Race Science*. Boston: Beacon.

Sawyer, M.Q. (2010). *Racial Politics in Post-Revolutionary Cuba*. New York: Cambridge University Press.

Snowden, Jr., F.M. (1970b). *Blacks in Antiquity: Ethiopians in the Greco-Roman Experience*. Cambridge, MA: Harvard University Press.

Snowden, Jr., F.M. (1983). *Before Color Prejudice: The Ancient View of Blacks*. Cambridge, MA: Harvard University Press.

Spencer, Q. (2018a). "Racial Realism I: Are Biological Races Real?." *Philosophy Compass*, 13, no. 1: e12468.

Spencer, Q. (2018b). "Racial Realism II: Are Folk Races Real?." *Philosophy Compass*, 13, no. 1: e12467.

Strickland, D.H. (2003). *Saracens, Demons, & Jews: Making Monsters in Medieval Art*. Princeton, NJ: Princeton University Press.

Sundquist, E.J., ed. (1996). *The Oxford W.E.B. Du Bois Reader*. New York: Oxford University Press.

Telles, E.E. (2014). *Pigmentocracies: Ethnicity, Race, and Color in Latin America*. Chapel Hill, NC: University of North Carolina Press.

Thompson, D. (2016). *The Schematic State: Race, Transnationalism, and the Politics of the Census*. New York: Cambridge University Press.

Ture, K. (Carmichael, S.) and Hamilton, C.V. (1992). *Black Power: The Politics of Liberation*. New York: Vintage.

Vickers, J., and Isaac, A. (2012). *The Politics of Race: Canada, the United States, and Australia*. 2nd ed. Toronto: University of Toronto Press.

Vucetic, S. (2011). *The Anglosphere: A Genealogy of a Racialized Identity in International Relations*. Stanford, CA: Stanford University Press.

Whitman, J.Q. (2017). *Hitler's American Model: The United States and the Making of Nazi Race Law*. Princeton, NJ: Princeton University Press.

Winant, H. (2001). *The World is a Ghetto: Race and Democracy Since World War II*. New York: Basic Books.

Wolfe, P. (2016). *Traces of History: Elementary Structures of Race*. New York: Verso.

9

Blackness everywhere

How the state maintains and manifests racialized power

Marcus Anthony Hunter

Introduction

Recent projections by global organizations (e.g. the United Nations and World Health Organization) suggest that by the year 2050 nearly 85% of the world's population will live in an urban or near-urban area. The U.S. Census indicates that upwards of 85% of Black Americans live in urban or near-urban areas, suggesting that the urban Black experience is ripe for examining and forecasting this global broader trend towards urbanization. Across a range of disciplines that consider the social and political realities of predominantly Black communities, there has been some debate as to the larger causes with a specific focus on the role of socio-economic factors and state-authorized patterns of racial segregation.

Arguing that structural economic changes, in particular the shift away from a goods-producing to a service-producing economy, have led to increased concentrations of poverty especially in Black enclaves, some scholars have pointed to socio-economic forces as primary causes for the current and persistent disparities within and across Black enclaves. Positing a larger theory of social isolation, Wilson (1996) for example, offered the classic argument that dramatic socio-economic shifts and the out-migration of Whites from urban areas leave behind an urban Black population with limited educational levels, job skills, and social networks. To be sure, Wilson's claims have not gone unchallenged. In effect, these challenges have pointed to domestic and global patterns of racial residential segregation as emblematic of causes unaddressed by Wilson.

Additionally, explicit and implicit focus on issues of residential segregation has encompassed much of the continued attention to the social and political realties and histories of Black life. Continued debates about the causes and continuance of urban Black neighborhoods, and the changes thereof, have been situated along two complementary perspectives: (1) spatial assimilation and (2) place stratification (Charles, 2003). Focusing more directly on the link between socio-economic opportunity and status and cross-racial difference in wealth accumulation and returns to education, the spatial assimilation perspective privileges understandings of mobility.

Within this perspective scholars have argued that the continued social isolation of Black urban dwellers is the result of constrained socio-economic opportunities, dwindling job prospects, and low educational levels. Here, then the persistence of poverty in urban Black neighborhoods is directly linked to economic opportunities and larger trends of urban disinvestment. Black neighborhoods continue to decline because opportunities for low-skilled work in particular, and economic and educational opportunities in cities more broadly, continue to decline. In essence, works within this perspective have argued that patterns of residential segregation generally, and the socio-political realities of urban Black enclaves "is simply the logical outcome of these differences in status and the associated differences in lifestyle" (Oliver and Shapiro, 1995; Clark, 1989; Charles, 2003:176).

Challenging the focus on socio-economic status and opportunities (or the lack thereof) as primary, research within the place stratification perspective has focused sharply on issues of residential segregation, racial attitudes, and discriminatory practices as fundamentally linked to the rise and fall of urban Black neighborhoods. Key to this perspective is the focus and serious attention to institutional and individual-level actions as fundamentally connected to the isolation of and persistence of poverty in urban Black neighborhoods in particular, and global racial residential segregation.

Spurred on by the analysis of racial residential segregation patterns across cities as presented in Massey and Denton's *American Apartheid* (1993), scholars in this perspective point to the attitudes of whites, restrictive covenants, and persistent racism as key. For instance, Alba and Logan argue that a racial "group's relative standing in society" is key to the opportunities for spatial mobility and key to understanding the racial residential segregation patterns across cities (Alba and Logan, 1993: 1391). Others demonstrating the direct effects of individual-level actions have highlighted the implications of White attitudes and sheer reluctance about interracial neighborhoods and having racial minorities as neighbors (see e.g. Gans, 1982; Rieder, 1985). In addition, scholars highlighting practices such as restrictive covenants, redlining and discriminatory mortgage procedures of real estate agencies and the Federal Housing Administration have further pointed to the connection between the rise, and persistent decline of and in urban neighborhoods and institutional-level actions and behaviors (Massey and Denton, 1993; Sharkey, 2013). Ultimately, the place stratification perspective takes more seriously the role of racial prejudice in determining the spatial mobility of Blacks and the economic viability and stability of urban Black enclaves and the residents therein.

Taken together, all of these perspectives highlight the socio-political and economic climate in which Blackness, urbanity, the state, and place are intertwined and mutually constitutive. Centering the subjectivity of Black residents and the internal divisions within the larger Black population has helped elucidate the role of individual-level actions and state racial logics about place and policy (Pattillo, 1999, 2010; Hunter, 2013, 2017, 2018; Rothstein, 2017; Hunter and Robinson, 2018). While some researchers have highlighted the role of internal divisions within the larger Black population, this work has focused on national origin as the key internal division, evidenced in the analysis of the emergent distinction between African Americans, Africans and Afro-Caribbeans. This chapter instead will amplify other divisions, particularly those around global Blackness and region, which will in turn add to the larger discussion and theorization of the role of individual-level actions in the creation, maintenance, and collapse of Blackness in and through state action.

Race has been an effective tool with which the state has determined where to show its best and worst manifestations. It is through racism that the state can simultaneously deny and weaponize its mirroring systems of justice/injustice and inequality/equality. As a range of scholars have demonstrated, the reach of the global effects of race and racism extends beyond the confines of the Western Hemisphere. Colonization has had a nearly totalizing effect on the globe, carrying with it a range of racial logics to effectively disaggregate "us" from "them"—be they indigenous (to Australia, Africa, the Caribbean, North or South America, and all the places in between) and/or of color (non-White, Black, Arab, Latinx, Chicanx) (see e.g. Said, 1979; Appiah, 1991; Alexander, 1996; Pierre, 2012; Ahmed, 2013; Smith, 2013; Moraga and Anzaldúa, 2015; Hudson, 2017). As critical geographers (Wynter, 2003; McKittrick, 2006; McKittrick and Woods, 2007; Hunter and Robinson, 2018) demonstrate, our current maps are the products of the purposeful manifest destiny and capitalist conquests of European nations.

As a result, Blackness has traveled. Blackness arrived unanticipated in some places, nestled alongside and surrounding White supremacy in other places, and even in other places still Blackness burst into a pigmentocracy (Telles, 2014)—a spectrum of browns, blacks, oranges, neutrals and reds (see e.g. Telles and Ortiz, 2008; Omi and Winant, 2014; Beaman, 2017; Hunter, 2017). Blackness has stayed, even as many would proclaim its death and flight from the geographies and places it helped sustain and produce purposefully, inadvertently, and proactively. Indeed, nation states dispensing with anti-Blackness has solidified and rendered visible other sustaining locations of disempowerment amidst supposed states of freedom.

This chapter explores and demonstrates these aforementioned features of Blackness and its relationship to the state. In each of the subsequent three sections, the chapter draws on the experience and insights we can gain from attending to Blackness as a global social fact and epiphenomenon. That Blackness has traveled, arrived, and stayed is at the heart of the discussion. So, too, are the racial logics of the state whereby racism becomes obdurate and indispensable.

Exploring the consequences of the social fact of Blackness, this chapter draws on key insights from a range of disciplines, implicitly highlighting its transdisciplinary and global nature. Centering and building out from critical insights of Steve Biko, Derrick Bell and Audre Lorde, this chapter looks across many socio-political landscapes and intersections to underscore the obdurate contours of race and racism. The chapter concludes by suggestion that future scholarship, research and understandings of race and racism benefit from a continued expansion of notions and practices of Blackness.

What if Steve Biko and Derrick Bell were right?

Blackness is everywhere as a consequence of White supremacy, quests for manifest destiny, colonization, European and Arab slave trades, and racial capitalism (see e.g. Feagin, 1991; Gilroy, 1993; Rodney, 1972; Robinson, 2000; Hall, 2006; Pierre, 2012; Hudson and McKittrick, 2014; Hudson, 2017). With each addition to the empire, a new place and group had to be folded in so as to count in favor for but never against the status quo. There is no place in the world perhaps more primed to demonstrate the importance and consequences of this insight than South Africa.

Where America's brand of racism and race may be a source of overgeneralization, the Black South African experience provides a generative way to look at race and racism through the continued entanglements of the colonization of Africa, African independence movements, Pan-Africanism and state sanctioned racialized violence via the Apartheid regime (Marx, 1998; Veracini, 2010). Where Jim Crow would seem effective yet limited and finite, Apartheid made racialized logics laws, manifesting them in passbooks, racially disparate health and wealth outcomes, and a national practice (Brubaker, 2004; Marx, 1998).

Blackness in this context is perhaps even more visible, with national mandates enforced at all levels to limit the lives and outcomes of Black and Coloured South Africans.

Coming of age amidst this context, freedom fighter and scholar Steve Biko's work is especially generative here. Bantu-educated and a Black South African of Xhosa origin, Biko was a product of South Africa's educational racial segregation practice and policy. 1971 had been a difficult year in the anti-Apartheid struggle. Passbooks were the necessary accessories to the survival of Black South Africans (see e.g. Wolpe, 1972; Lipton, 1986). While an average White South African might find their lives deeply insulated from the daily horrors of the Apartheid system, those deemed Black, Coloured or even adjacent to Blackness went without the courtesy of ignorance of Apartheid.

During that same year, Biko was key in the founding of the Black People's Conference, which set to work to draw together the range of anti-Apartheid activists with an emphasis on raising Black consciousness. Over that year, Biko had delivered and written critical and racially radical remarks that aimed to demonstrate that those not a part of the dominant power elite comprised a larger and potentially more politically powerful constituency of underdeveloped allies and comrades. "Black people—real black people—" a direct and impassioned Biko professed, "are those who can manage to hold their heads high in defiance rather than willingly surrender their souls to the white man" (Biko, 2017: 52).

Blackness is everywhere as a consequence of anti-Blackness—the product of a steady diet of messages of racial stereotypes, danger, and violence (see e.g. Feagin, 1991; Pierre, 2012; Hudson and McKittrick, 2014). Though, as scholars have demonstrated, this proposition applies globally, it is in the United States that we find a generative and perhaps most evident in America's hypermedia culture. Despite the promises of Civil Rights legislation (e.g. the Civil Rights Act of 1964, Fair Housing Act of 1968), by the late 1980s it had become clear that Reaganomics was not trickling down but up. Key in this debate, at the time and for some time thereafter, was whether the local, state and federal policies better known collectively as Affirmative Action were of use, working and constitutional (see e.g. Forman, 2017; Rothstein, 2017).

While many fought such policies of the unfounded arguments of embedded racial favoritism, Critical Race scholars have shown that not only does Whiteness operate legally as property but also that Affirmative Action was an always already handicapped policy. While it may help to bring historically underrepresented populations into previously racially segregated professional and education spaces, it had become clear by the early 1990s that these policies were limited in their impact, favoring White women, leaving many with a certain racial reality where racism was obdurate, ever more buoyant despite state interventions. Aware and insightful on this point, pioneering scholar Derrick Bell did not mince words. "*Black people will never gain full equality in this country,*" Bell powerfully observes, "*Even those herculean efforts we hail as successful will produce no more than temporary 'peaks of progress,' short-lived victories that slide into irrelevance as racial patterns adapt in ways that maintain white dominance*" (Bell, 1992:12, emphasis in the original). Bell's provocation would prove prescient then and now. Just a few years later, state sanctioned practices of racism and Blackness, like South Africa, in Los Angeles were on the global stage.

A man is dragged from his seat. A group of police officers congregate around him as the recording continues. By the end of the ordeal the man, hospitalized and humiliated, becomes a siren song for resistance and uprising. A half-hearted apology is issued by those responsible. Sounds familiar? You may be thinking of the 2017 United Airlines ordeal. Yet twenty-five years earlier, the scene was a traffic stop in Los Angeles. The man was not a doctor and not of Asian descent, but instead a Black resident of Los Angeles named Rodney King.

The verdict "not guilty," rang out across the Los Angeles's Black belt like acid on old wounds. By 1992, Black migration from the American South had over the twentieth century manifested as an entire Black region, South-Central Los Angeles. Neighborhoods like Leimert Park and Baldwin Hills were built on a history of black artists and entertainers great enough to make millions but too Black for Beverly Hills and Bel-Air. Separate water fountains and bathrooms had been replaced with separate communities and regions of the city. So when the brutal beating of Rodney King hit the television and airwaves, the graphic images and tale were an all too familiar reminder that Black migrants had not escaped the chokehold of the Jim Crow South. The South had followed them to California, refracted back in a video of a Black man being savagely beaten by police officers. Never before had a recording so captured the experience. Never before had there been such clear indisputable evidence of the tendency for police officers to be forgetful of the humanity of Black citizens. Even still, hearts would be crushed, tears shed and storefronts damaged after word of the "not guilty" verdict spread through South-Central.

From late April until early May, the Rodney King verdict reverberated across the city and nation in waves of protests, unrest and heavy police presence. Stores and buildings burned with the fury of a population that had escaped the South only physically. The commonly unheard voices of the city's Black and Latino residents roared just beyond the gates and palm tree-lined campus of the University of Southern California (see e.g. Hunt, 1997; Hunt and Ramón, 2010).

Twenty-five years later many things have changed. On the site of the 1992 rebellions, now sits a construction site accompanied by the noise and scaffolding of new light rail construction. Built on the future of Los Angeles, the site—packed with steel and concrete—will create a vast transportation intersection between South-Central and the rest of the city by 2020. As predominantly white runners' clubs jog along the blocks that burned after the verdict, the spectacle of twenty-five years ago is merely a distant memory (Hunter and Robinson, 2018).

The name of the region of the city has changed too. No longer "South-Central", the area is called South LA and Mid-City now. Newly built light rail traverses back and forth between downtown and the Santa Monica promenade, as young White families and residents have discovered how convenient the area is. Where there was once an isolated set of Black neighborhoods, there are gentrifying blocks. Many displaced Black residents have gone back to the South to states like Texas and Louisiana and cities like Atlanta and Houston. Those who are poor, homeless and unemployed move about the city's shrinking residential choices, as the cost of living continues to price them out.

Twenty-five years later many things remain deeply consistent too. Tinseltown continues to draw Black people West in search of fame, fortune and freedom. Los Angeles still reflects the unrealized aspirations of the some of the oldest Americans, Black people. Indeed, UCLA's recent reports confirm that diversity in Hollywood remains relatively non-existent. Hollywood, like the famous sign affixed to Laurel Canyon, is still White. Black actresses, like almost all of the Black LA workforce, are forced to live out their dreams in a highly segmented and segregated labor industry. Although the median household income of Black households in Los Angeles has historically outpaced the national average, Black homeownership and Black employment levels remain low and are declining.

Historically, Black communities and the various neighborhoods to which they belong are contracting. Across the world there has been a relative decline in the urban Black population —from Los Angeles's South-Central, New York City's Harlem, to Manchester's Moss Side, to London's Brixton, to Guangzhou, China (just to name a few). Los Angeles's Black Belt, for example, bears this fact out especially well. South Los Angeles comprises seven neighborhoods along the forthcoming Crenshaw/LAX light rail transit line: (1) West Adams, (2) Jefferson Park, (3) Baldwin Hills/Crenshaw, (4) Leimert Park, (5) View Park-Windsor Hills, (6) Hyde Park, and (7) Inglewood. Based upon decennial census records, the aggregate population in these neighborhoods grew from 280,488 to 321,734 between 1970 and 2010. Despite the growth in the area's overall population, the Black population in particular has seen an extended decline, falling from 180,960 in 1980 to just 151,476 in 2010. This equates to a drop in the Black share of the population from 63.8% to 48.2%. Over the same period of time, the white non-Hispanic population has also declined from 16.3% to 4.2%, and the Asian-Pacific Islander population also declined from 3.8% to 3%. However, the Hispanic population has increased from 14.7% to 43.9%, an increase of 100,230 residents. Finally, by immigration status, the fraction of individuals who were foreign-born grew from 8.6% to 27.5%.

As a result, new all-White residential zones are forming. Police helicopters fly above, while their patrols increase in their surveillance strategies of poor and working class, ethnic and racial communities. And shiny new trains traverse old racial boundaries. The city emerges from the ashes of the uprising, while long-standing Black residents fend for themselves. The makings of a classic movie about the South or country western, this, however is just a slice of Black life in LaLa Land twenty-five years after the verdict.

What if Audre Lorde was right?

Blackness is everywhere as a consequence of categories and the relations thereof to power. Focused in particular on the Global South in her perspective, scholar and Black feminist Audre Lorde's insights allow us to see how the entanglements of race and sexuality inform a particular kind of Blackness, one that is circumscribed by state policies that often target LGBTQ people and Black women in particular in the U.S. and abroad. "For the master's tool will never dismantle the master's house," Lorde notably reminds us, "They may allow us to temporarily beat him at his own game but they will never enable us to bring about real change … Racism and homophobia are real conditions of all our lives in this place and time" (Lorde, 1984: 112–114). Here the site and practice of state policies via incarceration and criminal justice are especially generative to extend out from Lorde's provocation.

Lorde's prescience highlights the limits of models and theories that rely only on master narratives about marginalized and oppressed peoples. The tools of state repression, such as anti-Blackness, even if reframed, will not secure the end of racism or homophobia. For example, when Black transgender people are incarcerated, many are forced to serve their time based upon a gender designation not of their choosing (Richie, 2012). Of course, this makes for additional stressors and may likely increase the importance of familial support. Where cisgender Americans may have this support from their biological families, oftentimes the opposite is true for those who are transgender; thus making fictive family members as important, if not more important, in overall successful reintegration of formerly incarcerated transgender Americans.

Research has illustrated that there is a vibrant global Black LGBT population living under equally, if not more, dire constraints relative to their heterosexual counterparts (Richie, 2012). Black LGBT individuals convicted of crimes are incarcerated alongside their heterosexual counterparts, often without proper adjustments to account for the needs of black transgender inmates (Richie, 2012). It is often the case that the gender indicated on birth certificates dictates where the inmate is assigned, leaving many black transgender prisoners misplaced and vulnerable to the gender practices and constraints of the facilities in which they serve their time.

Furthermore, Lorde's provocation illustrates that systemic shifts require intersectional methodological frameworks. That is, the impact of race, class, sexual orientation, and socio-economic status shapes the experience and outcomes of individuals and is also critically reflected in the composition of familial networks. Black LGBT Americans' familial networks often predominantly comprise other members of the Black LGBT community. Intersectional analyses anticipate this reality and as a result, must be sensitive to the experiences of those impacted by both racism and homophobia. Oppression and prejudice are reinforced by state sanctions structures and institutions like prisons, rendering the Black LGBT experience especially potent for helping to identify and eliminate the mechanisms of inequality deeply embedded in systems of justice and incarceration. Despite the overlapping oppressions of racism and homophobia, in our research and models we often miss the key experiences of transmen and transwomen (of all backgrounds) because our working conceptions of incarceration and punishment are heteronormative and gendered.

While we know that LGBT men and women are not immune from mass incarceration, emphasis on their treatment, support, and reentry would help better identify latent and explicit mechanisms of oppression and inequality impacting the world's prison population. For example, incarcerated transwomen and transmen are most likely to be assigned based upon normative gender assumptions and assignments per their birth certificate. Added to this is the role of sexual orientation and its impact on the experience and imprisonment of sexual minorities. As scholars have demonstrated, alongside racial logics the prison industrial complex, in architecture and practice, is built upon regressive, suppressive, and normative assumptions about gender and sexuality (Davis, 2011; Haley, 2016; Richie, 2012). Questions examining the experiences of Black LGBT inmates and former felons would provide a powerful intersectional lens that would identify critical gaps in the reentry and probation programs that contribute to high rates of recidivism and programmatic failures. Black feminism and Black LGBT scholarship remind us that some of the best and most profound strategies to correct systems and patterns of inequality and oppression are within the voices and experiences of minorities (see Davis, 1981; Hull, Scott, & Smith, 1982; Combahee River Collective, 1983; Moraga, 1983; Smith, 1983; Hooks, 1984; Moraga & Anzaldúa, 2015; Glenn, 1985; Anzaldua, 1990; Mohanty, 1988; Spelman, 1988; Collins, 1989, 1990; Crenshaw, 1989, 1991; Sandoval, 1991; King, 1988; Carbado, 1999; Cohen, 1999, 2005; Walcott, 2003; Battle & Bennett, 2005; Johnson & Henderson, 2005).

Conclusion

While the global Great Recession (2008–2010) has yielded fruitful debates and research regarding the reach of Blackness, racism, and inequality such as banking crises and their impact, sub-prime mortgage lending, unemployment, and health care, retirement has received less attention, particularly among sociologists. In much of the existing research on labor, wealth, and the world of work, the focus most often has been exclusively upon pre-retirement workers, glass ceilings along lines of race and gender, and general racially disparate outcomes in labor force (see e.g. Halle, 1984; Kanter, 1977; Oliver and Shapiro, 1997; Conley, 1999).

A report from the U.S. Census Bureau (2005: 641), for example, reported: "In 1999, 8.2%, 12.3%, 19.6% and 23.5% of White, Asian American, Hispanic/Latino and Black persons age 65 and above, respectively, lived below the poverty level." According to

Rockeymoore and Maitin-Shepard (2010: 1), "African Americans (95%) and Hispanics (85%) … are more likely than whites (80%) to assert that Social Security is or will be an important part of their retirement income." Such reports indicate racial differences in retirement practices, poverty rates for senior citizens, and reliance upon federal welfare entitlement programs.

Racial differences in life expectancy and mortality rates further amplify the implicit and explicit effects of state sanctioned practices of race and racism. That is, although Black workers contribute to long-term retirement benefit systems, globally Black workers do not live as long as their White counterparts due to health disparities and violence; thus Black workers, globally, are structurally situated to benefit less than their white counterparts from the welfare policies such as retirement and other entitlement systems, such as state-based healthcare.

As a recent report from the Urban Institute (2011: 5) indicates, there are also important racial disparities in income distribution among U.S. workers:

> Among men age 50 to 61 employed full time, 2009 median annual earnings totaled $56,100 for non-Hispanic whites, compared with $40,800 for African Americans, $35,700 for Hispanics, and $50,000 for Asians … The earnings gap between men of color and non-Hispanic whites did not change much after 62.

It follows, then, that if non-Whites generally and Black people more specifically, have worse health outcomes and lower incomes over the life course than most other demographic groups, then it is likely that the limited outcomes and access to employment, full citizenship and welfare programs are a reflection of how race and racism, vis-a-vis Blackness in particular, travel, stay and are deployed to delimit the fates of some and amplify the wealth and outcomes of the dominant power majority.

References

Ahmed, S. 2013. *Strange Encounters: Embodied Others in Post-Coloniality*. London: Routledge.

Alba, R.D. and Logan, J.R. 1993. Minority Proximity to Whites in Suburbs: An Individual-level Analysis of Segregation. *American Journal of Sociology*, 98(6), pp. 1388–1427.

Alexander, C. E. 1996. *The Art of Being Black: The Creation of Black British Youth Identities: The Creation of Black British Youth Identities*. Oxford: Clarendon Press.

Anderson, E. 1990. *Streetwise: Race, Class and Change in an Urban Community*. Chicago, IL: University of Chicago Press.

Anzaldúa, G. 1990. Bridge, Drawbridge, Sandbar or Island: Lesbians-of-color hacienda alianzas. In *Bridges of Power: Women's Multicultural Alliances*, pp. 216–231.

Appiah, K. A. 1991. Is the Post-in Postmodernism the Post-in Postcolonial? *Critical Inquiry*, 17(2), pp. 336–357.

Battle, J.J. and Bennett, N.D. 2005. Striving for Place: Lesbian, Gay, Bisexual, and Transgender (LGBT) People. In *A Companion to African American History*, edited by Alton Hornsby Jr. New York: Blackwell Press, pp. 412–445.

Beaman, J. 2017. *Citizen Outsider*. Berkeley, CA: University of California Press.

Bell, D. 1992. *Faces at the Bottom of the Well*. New York: Basic Books.

Biko, S. 2017. *I Write What I Like: Selected Writings*. London: Picador Africa.

Brubaker, R. 2004. *Ethnicity without Groups*. Cambridge, MA: Harvard University Press.

———. 1925. The Growth of the City. In *The City*, edited by R. Park, E. Burgess and R. D. McKenzie. Chicago, IL: University of Chicago Press.

Carbado, D. ed., 1999. *Black Men on Race, Gender, and Sexuality: A Critical Reader*. New York: NYU Press.

Charles, C.Z. 2003. The Dynamics of Racial Residential Segregation. *Annual Review of Sociology*, 29(1), pp. 167–207.

Cohen, C.J. 1999. *The Boundaries of Blackness: AIDS and the Breakdown of Black Politics*. Chicago: University of Chicago Press.

Cohen, C.J. 2005. Deviance as Resistance: A New Research Agenda for the Study of Black Politics. *Du Bois Review: Social Science Research on Race*, *1*(1), pp. 27–45.

Collins, K. E. 1980. *Black Los Angeles: The Maturing of the Ghetto, 1940–1950*. Saratoga, CA: Century Twenty One Pub.

Collins, P.H. 1989. The Social Construction of Black Feminist Thought. *Signs: Journal of Women in Culture and Society*, *14*(4), pp. 745–773.

Collins, P.H. 1990. *Black Feminist Thought: Knowledge, Consciousness, and the Politics of Empowerment*. New York: Routledge.

Conley, D. 1999. *Being Black, Living in the Red*. Berkeley, CA: University of California Press.

Crenshaw, K. 1989. Demarginalizing the Intersection of Race and Sex: A Black Feminist Critique of Antidiscrimination Doctrine, Feminist Theory and Antiracist Politics. *u. Chi. Legal f.*, pp. 139–174.

Crenshaw, K. 1991. Race, Gender, and Sexual Harassment. *s. Cal. l. Rev.*, *65*, pp. 1467–1521.

Davis, A. 1981. Reflections on the Black Woman's Role in the Community of Slaves. *The Black Scholar*, *12*(6), pp. 2–15.

Davis, A. Y. 2011. *Are Prisons Obsolete?* New York: Seven Stories Press.

Feagin, J. R. 1991. The Continuing Significance of Race: Antiblack Discrimination in Public Places. *American Sociological Review*, *56*(1), pp. 101–116.

Flamming, D. 2005. *Bound for Freedom: Black Los Angeles in Jim Crow America*. Berkeley, CA: University of California Press.

Forman, Jr, J. 2017. *Locking Up Our Own: Crime and Punishment in Black America*. New York: Farrar, Straus and Giroux.

Gans, H. J. 1982. *The Levittowners: Ways of Life and Politics in a New Suburban Community*. New York: Columbia University Press.

Gilroy, P. 1993. *The Black Atlantic: Modernity and Double Consciousness*. London: Verso.

Glenn, E.N. 1985. Racial Ethnic Women's Labor: The Intersection of Race, Gender and Class Oppression. *Review of Radical Political Economics*, *17*(3), pp. 86–108.

Haley, S. 2016. *No Mercy Here: Gender, Punishment, and the Making of Jim Crow Modernity*. Chapel Hill: UNC Press Books.

Hall, S. 2006. What is This "Black" in Black Popular Culture? In *Stuart Hall* (pp. 479–489). London: Routledge.

Halle, D. 1984. *America's Working Man*. Chicago, IL: University of Chicago Press.

Hudson, P. J. 2017. *Bankers and Empire: How Wall Street Colonized the Caribbean*. Chicago: University of Chicago Press.

Hudson, P. J. and McKittrick, K. 2014. The Geographies of Blackness and Anti-Blackness: An Interview with Katherine McKittrick. *The CLR James Journal*, *20*(1/2), pp. 233–240.

Hull, G.T., Bell-Scott, P. and Smith, B. 1982. *All the Women are White, All the Blacks are Men, but Some of Us are Brave: Black Women's Studies*. New York: Feminist Press.

Hunt, D. and Ramón, A. C. eds., 2010. *Black Los Angeles: American Dreams and Racial Realities*. New York: NYU Press.

Hunt, D. M. 1997. *Screening the Los Angeles' Riots': Race, Seeing, and Resistance*. Cambridge: Cambridge University Press.

Hunter, M. A. 2013. *Black Citymakers: How the Philadelphia Negro Changed Urban America*. New York: Oxford University Press.

Hunter, M. A. 2017. Racial Physics or a Theory for Everything That Happened.

Hunter, M.A. ed. 2018. *The New Black Sociologists: Historical and Contemporary Perspectives*. New York: Routledge.

Hunter, M. A. and Robinson, Z. 2018. *Chocolate Cities: The Black Map of American Life*. Oakland: University of California Press.

Johnson, E.P. and Henderson, M. 2005. *Black Queer Studies: A Critical Anthology*. Durham, NC: Duke University Press.

Kanter, R. M. 1977. *Men and Women of the Corporation*. New York: Basic Books.

King, D.K. 1988. Multiple Jeopardy, Multiple Consciousness: The Context of a Black Feminist Ideology. *Signs: Journal of Women in Culture and Society*, *14*(1), pp. 42–72.

Lorde, A. 1984. *Sister Outsider: Essays and Speeches*. Toronto: Crossing Press.

Lipton, M. 1986. *Capitalism and Apartheid: South Africa, 1910–1986*. Cape Town: New Africa Books.

Marx, A.W. 1998. *Making Race and Nation: A Comparison of South Africa, the United States, and Brazil.* Cambridge: Cambridge University Press.

Massey, D.S. and Denton, N.A. 1993. *American Apartheid: Segregation and the Making of the Underclass.* Cambridge, MA: Harvard University Press.

McKittrick, K. 2006. *Demonic Grounds: Black Women and the Cartographies of Struggle.* Minneapolis: University of Minnesota Press.

McKittrick, K. and Woods, C. A. eds., 2007. *Black Geographies and the Politics of Place.* Boston: South End Press.

Mohanty, C. 1988. Under Western Eyes: Feminist Scholarship and Colonial Discourses. *Feminist Review,* *30*(1), pp. 61–88.

Moraga, C. 1983. *Loving in the War Years: Lo que nunca pasó por sus labios.* Boston: South End Press.

Moraga, C. and Anzaldúa, G. eds., 2015. *This Bridge Called My Back: Writings by Radical Women of Color.* Albany, NY: Suny Press.

Oliver, M. and Shapiro, T. 1995. *Black Wealth/White Wealth: A New Perspective on Racial Inequality.* New York: Routledge.

Oliver, M. L. and Shapiro, T. M. 1997. *Black Wealth/White Wealth: A New Perspective on Racial Inequality.* New York: Routledge.

Omi, M. and Winant, H. 2014. *Racial Formation in the United States.* New York: Routledge.

Pattillo, M. 1999. *Black Picket Fences: Privilege and Peril among the Black Middle Class.* Chicago: University of Chicago Press.

Pattillo, M. 2010. *Black on the Block: The Politics of Race and Class in the City.* Chicago: University of Chicago Press.

Pattillo, M. 2017. *Black on the Block.* Chicago: University of Chicago Press.

Pierre, J. 2012. *The Predicament of Blackness: Postcolonial Ghana and the Politics of Race.* Chicago: University of Chicago Press.

Richie, B. 2012. *Arrested Justice: Black Women, Violence, and America's Prison Nation.* New York: NYU Press.

Rieder, J. 1985. *Canarsie.* Cambridge, MA: Harvard University Press.

River, C. 1983. The Combahee River Collective Statement. In *Home Girls: A Black Feminist Anthology.* New Brunswick, NJ: Rutgers University Press.

Robinson, C. J. 2000. *Black Marxism: The Making of the Black Radical Tradition.* Chapel Hill: University of North Carolina Press.

Robinson, Z. F. 2014. *This Ain't Chicago: Race, Class, and Regional Identity in the Post-Soul South.* Chapel Hill: UNC Press Books.

Rockeymoore, M. and Maitin-Shepard. 2010. Tough Times Require Strong Social Security Benefits: Views on Social Security among African Americans, Hispanic Americans, and White Americans. *Social Security Brief,* pp. 32.

Rodney, W. 1972. *How Europe Underdeveloped Africa* (Vol. 239). London: Bogle-L'Ouverture Publications.

Rothstein, R. 2017. *The Color of Law: A Forgotten History of How Our Government Segregated America.* New York: Liveright Publishing.

Said, E. W. 1979. *Orientalism.* New York: Vintage.

Sandoval, C. 1991. US Third World Feminism: The Theory and Method of Oppositional Consciousness in the Postmodern World. *Genders* (10), pp. 1–24.

Sharkey, P. 2013. *Stuck in Place: Urban Neighborhoods and the End of Progress toward Racial Equality.* Chicago: University of Chicago Press.

Smith, L. T. 2013. *Decolonizing Methodologies: Research and Indigenous Peoples.* London: Zed Books Ltd.

Spelman, E.V. 1988. *Inessential Woman: Problems of Exclusion in Feminist Thought.* New York: Beacon Press.

Telles, E. 2014. *Pigmentocracies: Ethnicity, Race, and Color in Latin America.* Chapel Hill: UNC Press Books.

Telles, E.E. and Ortiz, V. 2008. *Generations of Exclusion: Mexican-Americans, Assimilation, and Race.* New York: Russell Sage Foundation.

U.S. Census Bureau. 2005. U.S. Census Bureau, Statistical Abstract of the United States: 2004–2005, Income, Expenditures, and Wealth. Washington, DC: U.S. Census Bureau. Retrieved August 12, 2018 from: www.census.gov/prod/www/statistical-abstract-2001_2005.html

Veracini, L. 2010. *Settler Colonialism.* Basingstoke: Palgrave Macmillan.

Walcott, R. 2003. *Black Like Who?: Writing Black Canada.* London: Insomniac Press.

Wilson, W. J. 1996. *When Work Disappears: The World of the New Urban Poor*. New York: Vintage.

Wolpe, H. 1972. Capitalism and Cheap Labour-Power in South Africa: From Segregation to Apartheid. *Economy and Society*, *1*(4), pp. 425–456.

Wynter, S. 2003. Unsettling the Coloniality of Being/Power/Truth/Freedom: Towards the Human, after Man, Its Overrepresentation—An Argument. *CR: The New Centennial Review*, *3*(3), pp. 257–337.

10

Cui bono? Linking political and racial orders

David Cook-Martín

José de San Martín, a prominent Latin American independence figure, observed in 1821 that in the future people native to the Americas would be called children and citizens of Peru, Peruvians, rather than "Indians" or natives (Santos de Quirós 1831). Discursively, at least, Latin American independence elites included all inhabitants in the emerging nations. The inclusionary rhetoric would not last and by the early 20th century most countries in the Americas formally excluded prospective immigrants and citizens by race or showed preference for European immigration. By then, the general sentiment among political elites in the hemisphere resembled that of then Assistant Secretary of the U.S. Navy Theodore Roosevelt's view that "the whole civilization of the future owes a debt of gratitude … to that democratic polity which has kept the temperate zones of the new and the newest worlds a heritage for the white people" – even if "white" meant something different in their respective contexts. Democracies had seen the "race foe" and had kept out the dangerous aliens (Roosevelt 1897).

Yet Roosevelt's discursive expression about who belongs in a democratic polity would not have been effective without organizations to implement it. The key point of this chapter is that, as an organization faced with the challenge of determining membership, the state has relied on, institutionalized, and legitimated ideas of race. Racial orders have, in turn, been shaped by official institutions and mechanisms of regulation and enforcement. The agenda is to systematically explore an explicit theorization of the relationship between political and racial orders. To that end, the following sections define political and racial orders, examine the state as a multi-level, variegated organization that encompasses a range of actors with disparate interests, and propose domains in which to examine the interconnectedness of political and racial orders. Connections among these orders are especially salient in the policy domain of immigration and nationality. The Americas is a fruitful region in which to observe these linkages because of the variation in regimes[1] and types of racial orders over time.

Why racism and politics?

A rich literature describes how states made nationals of individuals they considered their own – whether or not these individuals lived within the relevant state's borders (Choate 2008, Cook-Martín 2013, Fitzgerald 2009, Torpey 1998, Weber 1976). Imagining nations as deep horizontal comradeships was a common trope among political elites (Anderson 2006).

Yet the evidence shows that origins mattered a great deal in determining who could participate in that comradeship and on what terms. Choosing citizens and prospective citizens by perceived origins, has not been anomalous or exceptional, but rather the persistent trend, especially among major migrant receiving countries (Fitzgerald and Cook Martín 2014, Zolberg 2006). The selective impulse suggests the need for a sustained exploration of the relationship between the political orders in which states are embedded, and the ethnic orders prevalent especially since the advent of European colonial expansion and subsequent mass migration.

Political and racial orders

To understand the relationship between political and racial domains, it is useful to do some basic conceptual spadework. The following sections offer working definitions and theoretical perspectives on politics, states, ethnicity and race, the social fields in which these concepts play out, and the orders or configurations into which they crystallize. The conclusions reached are necessarily provisional, and not prescriptive, but suggestive of the analytic work to be done if we are to theorize the empirical relationship between state organizations and systems of social organization premised on ideologies of naturalized difference and sameness.

By politics I mean the exercise of influence to get one's way (Dahl 2003, Jasper 2008; Lukes 2004). The players that vie to get their way in our analysis are organizational actors in the government, market and public spheres as well as individuals who engage in these spheres to maximize their life chances. From a Bourdieuan perspective, the "game" or competition happens on a field wherein the relationship between players has a particular quality and dynamic by virtue of who is there or may get their way (Bourdieu and Wacquant 1992). For example, in the field in which entry to and membership in a political jurisdiction are at stake, government bureaucrats from sending and receiving states, employers, domestic workers, prospective and actual migrants, migration industry actors,[2] politicians, and policy makers vie to achieve their conflicting goals. The dynamic at point X in time affects what happens at point X + 1, but does not fully determine outcomes which are susceptible to contingent events and innovative actors.

Relations among social actors and organizations in a field can take on particular patterns that endure over repeated interactions primarily because of institutionalization – the process by which rules regulating interactions in a field become formalized. By "orders", then, I mean the arrangement of social actors and institutions in a particular pattern by virtue of the influence they exert over each other, their ideological underpinnings, and the effects of these patterns in a given time and place (cf. Emirbayer and Desmond 2015, Hochshild et al. 2012). Political order refers to a relational pattern or configuration resulting from a struggle over the exercise of the legitimate means of violence in a particular jurisdiction. The dynamic underlying that pattern is a field in the Bourdieuan sense. A field is an arena of social struggle, orders are the resulting configurations or systems that take shape within it. The dynamics of a field shape these orders which can take on a life of their own. Who belongs in a city, for instance, may have historically been determined by existing city dwellers with different interests, potential citizens and their attributes or capabilities (e.g. could they act in defense of the city or could they bring other resources to bear?), and external threats. Making formal rules about the eligibility requirements of citizens and developing a body of legal interpretations of these rules gives social struggles around the determination of citizenship a particular shape which in turn affects future struggles over belonging.

In the Americas and elsewhere, political orders have varied by the relationship between ruling elites and "the people". In Robert Dahl's well-known scheme, political orders range on a spectrum from polyarchies to non-polyarchies depending on the extent to which they allow for open contestation by or inclusion of people outside the ruling elite (Dahl and Stinebrickner 2003). Contestation refers to citizens' unimpaired opportunities to formulate their preferences and to signify their preferences for fellow citizens and the government (Dahl 1971, 2). Inclusiveness refers to "the proportion of the population entitled to participate on a more or less equal plane in controlling and contesting the conduct of the government" (Dahl 1971, 4). Liberal democracies like the United States and Canada are presumed to allow political subjects within the national territory to contest or influence government decisions. The government is conceptualized as by and for the people. Non-polyarchies or authoritarian regimes like those of Argentina in the 1930s or late 1970s may purport to protect the nation but do not include citizens in the political process and repress expressions of contestation. At a midpoint on this spectrum are regimes that purport to rule on behalf of the people (perhaps to protect them from exploitative elites) through corporatist organizations and allow for little or no contestation outside authorized means like those organizations. When it comes to ethnoracial discrimination, a conventional expectation is that polyarchies are inclusive and that non-polyarchies are comparatively more discriminatory and exclusive. Empirically that has not been the case, but for the purposes of this essay, what matters is that political orders must determine who is an actual or eligible member of the political community. Who are "the people"?

Whatever the type of political order, relies on states to be effective in the world. The state can be thought of as an organization that exercises the legitimate means of violence over a political jurisdiction (Mann 1993). It is the organization that will execute the will of political leaders over a territory and its people. The state is not only a territorial organization, however, but also a membership association (Brubaker 1992, 22–23). One of its key roles is to determine who belongs, to vet claims to membership, and to monitor and enforce membership rules.

The critical domain of membership determination and oversight reveals an important characteristic of state institutions and organizations. Rules and schema of governance are not implemented mechanistically or unilaterally in a top-down manner. The state as an organization has, to borrow Morgan and Orloff's imagery, many hands that work at micro, meso, and macro levels (Morgan and Orloff 2017). Moreover, there is a back and forth between state actors and the governed: states exert governance, people respond, states respond to people's reactions, and so on (Bayat 2013, Chatterjee 2004).

Consider the sphere of immigration and nationality policy. In it, legislative and/or executive actors devise rules for entry and permanence as well as for citizenship in contexts of national and international politics. Judiciary actors may adjudicate among interpretations of these rules. Ministries or departments may be charged with implementing these rules, a responsibility which may in turn be delegated to smaller organizational subunits. These subunits devise administrative rules or guidelines about how to implement often vague charges. Ministries and subunits compete for scarce resources and recognition by high level decision-makers or simply against peers in other administrative entities. Implementers may receive a charge that cannot be carried out with the personnel or resources allocated. Front line bureaucratic actors who deal directly with people affected by immigration and nationality rules have discretion that may be affected by all of the factors named, as well as their own social prejudgments and orientations. In turn, civil actors respond to governance efforts by means of workarounds, violations of legal norms, or fraud. Bureaucrats respond to these evasive efforts with new initiatives, or by relaxing enforcement of existing initiatives. In this iterative process, interactions at a given point in time are affected by past exchanges and affect future ones.[3]

Political orders and states change over time in levels of legitimacy and infrastructural power. Typically, state-making elites and bureaucrats assert that they have the legitimate right to exercise their functions until such claims become a natural and taken for granted fact of life. In addition, state organizations accrue over time the practical means to exercise authority over a territorial jurisdiction and its inhabitants. In the domain of population governance, for instance, states have developed ways to count and individuate people, certify their "identities" through paperwork, surveil and control the execution of people's obligations toward the state, and manage their movement across borders (Cook-Martín 2008, Torpey 1998).

Whatever the combination of inclusiveness and openness to contestation that define a particular political order, it faces the challenge of determining the subjects of its governance. Historically, states have determined who is to be governed by examining a range of behavioral, religious, and moral attributes. Especially in the age of nation-states and mass migration – where the nationalist presumption has been that every individual belongs to a state and, preferably, inhabits its territory – ethnicity, and in particular, race, has been a widely used means of determining the relationship of states to actual or prospective subjects. For instance, ethnic selectivity has operated within national borders to determine who has access to public goods (Fox 2012). The policies of major immigrant receiving countries during the 19th and first half of the 20th century – Argentina, Australia, Canada, Cuba, and the United States, among others – used ethnicity to show preference toward or discrimination against prospective immigrants and citizens. Even states with low levels of immigration such as Mexico selected among prospective immigrants by race (Fitzgerald and Cook Martín 2014). After World War II, states have also acted to create a deracialized order through civil rights offices, deracialization of immigration and nationality policies, and affirmative action among other domains. The following section examines more closely how ideas about and institutionalizations of race have interacted in the determination of subjecthood.

Racial orders

Ideas about ethnicity and race have been key means of determining eligibility for membership in a range of political orders. Analytically, race can be conceptualized as a special case of ethnicity.[4] If ethnicity is a long-standing and ubiquitous mode of social classification by people's perceived and felt origins, race and nation are relatively modern categories linked to the emergence of capitalism and colonial forms of exploitation in particular contexts. In Weberian terms, ethnicity and its special cases of race and nation are ways of effecting closure around valued material and symbolic resources (Stone 1995). By "special" I mean that race and nation capture phenomena with particular historical characteristics and outcomes that merit distinct consideration. Racism is an ideology of hierarchically categorizing humans into immutable groups – typically by phenotype – as a justification for the unequal distribution of resources and treatment (see Fields and Fields 2014). Immutability implies the mistaken belief that membership in a racial category cannot be changed because it is rooted in biology or nature. The assumption of immutability distinguishes the idea of race, and the proto-racisms discussed below, as a special case of ethnicity.

Race as a way of distinguishing among humans is a relatively modern construct institutionalized by governments and legitimated by science. Counting people and sorting them into categories has been a key feature of modern state-making. Population *statistics* enumerate inhabitants based on governance goals – for instance, institutionalizing racial domination in the case of the United States prior to 1965 or the redistribution of public goods – and/or on the perception that modernity calls for counting. In the Americas and elsewhere, classifying people by ethnoracial categories has been common (Loveman 2014). In the United States, the institutionalization of ethnoracial categories and their legitimation by science and by the implication of the state was central to legal racial domination (Marks 1995). As Loveman (2014) notes, while Latin American countries did not create an architecture to institutionalize legal racial domination as in the United States, they did engage in some form of ethnoracial classification. Sometimes countries engaged in the development of such systems for purposes of appearing modern (modern nations must have censuses) and sometimes with redistributive ends (public goods are to be distributed equitably to underprivileged categories of people).

The modernity of race as a construct does not mean, however, that it came out of the blue. There were precursors to the modern notion of race dating to antiquity (Dikötter 2015, ix). A notion from past proto-racisms that resonates with contemporary racisms is that belonging to a racial category is unchangeable (FitzGerald 2017, Isaac 2006). Racial categories that became prevalent after the mid-19th century resonated with proto-racist ideas. Still, the implication of states and science in forging, consolidating, and institutionalizing modern racisms makes these ideologies distinct from their precursors.

A variant that emerged in the late 19th century and remained in effect into the 1940s, scientific racism viewed biological origins, among other axes of distinction, as a means of social categorization. Scientists in this period inferred social differences from visible expressions of biological variation even if mechanisms of heredity were largely a black box for anything other than Mendelian traits wherein genotype and phenotype are strongly correlated. For instance, eugenicists in the first four decades of the 20th century filled in gaps in their knowledge of heritability mechanisms with either the logic of how mendelian traits are expressed or with common sense notions of heredity – for example, from animal husbandry. They had no clear understanding of how complex traits were inherited and certainly not of additive and interactive genetic effects. If positive and negative behavioral and moral traits could be inherited like eye color or height, and these traits could be grouped with bodily appearance, then it was a small step to inferring these complex traits from categorical group membership. Scientists and health professionals expressed and promulgated these notions authoritatively and policymakers conferred on them official recognition, especially when science reinforced existing racial classification systems.

Since World War II, the idea that race has a biological reality has been largely discredited by biologists and anthropologists. Yet the racial logic of deeply rooted cultural difference persists in institutions and in spaces where state agents have discretion. The advent of genomics, especially the massive amounts of data and studies generated over the last decade, has also contributed to a resurgence of claims that race does indeed have a biological reality (e.g. Reich 2018). To be clear, these claims do not deploy, and explicitly reject, the racist rhetoric of one putative group's superiority over others as was the case in the age of eugenics. However, given the power of institutionalized racial categorizations and easy conflations of social categories and populations defined by shared genetic variations, there is at least a potential for the return to a scientific racism that is progressively minded but exclusionary in effects. I take up this point again in the conclusion.

Race in the Americas

An analysis of race across the Americas suggests that this idea of how to parse humanity is characteristic of (though not exclusive to) the region, its colonization, and exploitation. While there are ancient precursors to the idea of race as deployed in racism, some authors argue that it emerged in its modern form in the Americas (Isaac 2006, Quijano 2000, 534). The encounter of Europeans with indigenous populations and the forced movement of Afro-origin slaves to the hemisphere provided the backdrop to ideologies that legitimated the ranking of people by perceived natural and biological differences and into powerful categories. Those at the top of the hierarchy – primarily ruling liberal elites in the early independence period – assigned desirable qualities and capacities to those with whom they shared the top rungs and less desirable ones to those on the bottom ones. In the Americas, European-identified elites consistently inferred moral and civic capacities from categorical membership which was in turn inferred from phenotype.

Racial orders are configurations of social actors and institutions which result from a struggle to sort people into hierarchically arranged categories by perceived origins. Social actors misperceive these categories as natural and relatively unchanging. Basic historical knowledge of how racial categories have been used in struggles over who could be a member of the polity and who could rule suggest that the racial order is a separate configuration within the political order. While it is true that *demos* have since antiquity been interpreted through the lens of *ethnos*, the historical particularity of race as an idea, and its legitimation by states and science call for special consideration. Moreover, racial orders span multiple fields of symbolic and material struggle – another reason to avoid the reduction of such orders to epiphenomena of the political. If political and racial orders are distinct, but closely linked, what have been the specific connections among them?

Boundaries or hierarchies?

Current conceptual debates among sociologists of race and ethnicity are hampered by a theoretically unproductive contraposition of analytic approaches that stress hierarchy and those that emphasize boundaries. Rogers Brubaker and Andreas Wimmer are often credited with (or accused of, depending on standpoint) drawing attention to how boundaries are constructed through social interaction and away from groups as things in the world (Brubaker, Loveman and Stamatov 2004, Brubaker 2004, Wimmer 2008a, 2008b). Emirbayer and Desmond (2015) characterize scholars in this camp as "cognivists" – a designation which obscures the extent to which institutions and history play a role in their view of racial ideology formation (e.g. Loveman, 2014). Eduardo Bonilla-Silva (1997), and Omi and Winant (Omi and Winant 2014), are cast in the role of stressing "hierarchy": that racial categories have historically been ranked with the purpose of including some and excluding others from access to resources (Omi and Winant 2014:106 ff.). Scholars in this camp are likely to underscore the historical particularity of race in the Americas, and to show how racial hierarchies are entwined with political, particularly state struggles.

A comprehensive understanding of racial and political orders requires both approaches. Understanding the formation of ethnic and racial categories calls for analytic attention to the bounds of categories, their negotiation and contestation in different settings, as well as their permeability. How racial categories have been used in mundane encounters and/or for purposes of determining access to resources and of governance suggests the hierarchical dimension is no less important and goes a long way to explaining the hardness or immutability of categories. Conceptually, we need a focus on boundaries to understand the genesis, persistence, and mutability of social categories, not to be confused analytically with groups of actual people, and an understanding of how the hierarchical arrangement of categories has excluded people from resources in a political community (Brubaker 2004). Scholars of Latin American history have already moved in this direction (see Pérez Vejo 2015, Yankelevich 2015).

An approach that assumes a range of classificatory phenomena at different levels would shift attention to linkages between racial and political orders by examining how states adopt racial categories prevalent among intellectual and political elites and/or advanced by science. Moreover, if the idea of race has provided a means of determining membership in the polity, states have also served a role for racial orders: they institutionalize ideas about biological differences, enforce boundaries among social categories, and at times redistribute resources accordingly. In the next section, I sketch the contours of political and racial orders in the Americas over the long run and illustrate how these orders were linked by scientific cultural entrepreneurs before and after World War II.

The interconnection of orders in the Americas

The independence movements that began in the late 18th century with the United States and extended throughout the Americas resulted in the establishment of some form of polyarchic configuration in most of the newly formed republics – mostly with a liberal flavor. Political orders in this country oscillated between polyarchy and non-polyarchy in the decades after independence. Most of the newly independent republics looked to the United States, but also to France and Spain (e.g. the *Declaration of the Rights of Man and of the Citizen*, and the *Constitución de Cádiz*) for constitutional models as well as for other accoutrements of modern nationhood. Many of the republics faced the issue of populating and protecting from imperial threats vast territories.

Liberal elites undertook the work of creating extractive, military, educational and social institutions through which to make state organizations and to advance ideas of nationhood among inhabitants of national territories. As Miguel Centeno and others have demonstrated, the "wars make states" model that has been used to explain the rise of European states does not work well in Iberian America (Centeno 2002: Centeno and Ferraro 2013). Weak as states may have been south of the United States, they did adopt models from other latitudes and grew state capacity in particular domains like population and migration control (Cook-Martín 2008).

Political orders across national jurisdictions have faced the challenge of determining who its members were and could be. Pronouncements by independence leaders, constitutions, and immigration and nationality policies reveal a range of criteria for determining who could belong to the political community, and, by implication if not explicit statement, who could not. Religion, nationality, moral character and socioeconomic characteristics were among some of the most commonly cited criteria in constitutions of the region.[5]

Ethnicity and race figured prominently in constitutional texts, but especially in immigration and nationality policy. In the early independence period, the United States and Haiti were on one end of the spectrum with explicit racial preferences and exclusions, though for very different reasons. The United States constitution defined slaves as only counting for three-fifths of free (white) persons for purposes of determining electoral apportionment and restricted naturalization to free whites (1790 Uniform Rule of Naturalization, 1 Stat. 103, Sec. 1). The Act of Feb, 28, 1804 (ch. 10, 2 Stat. 205) restricted black immigration. Haiti was exceptional in giving preference to any black person or to Amerindians who came to Haiti, and in banning citizenship for whites unless they were already Haitians.[6] Some form of preference for the naturalization of people of African descent remained until 1987. Ethnic selection in Haiti's nationality and immigration policies, however, did not come from a sense of racial superiority. Rather Haitian leaders intended to secure the gains of an unprecedented and successful slave rebellion against French oppressors and to assert sovereignty in the face of European and U.S. hostility (C.L.R. James 1963).

On the other end of the spectrum, early Latin American liberal leaders dismantled colonial racial distinctions in formal law. Most countries in Latin America also banned slavery at or shortly following independence (Andrews 2004, 57). Leaders of newly independent Latin American republics viewed nationality as the bases for political membership. South American independence leader Simón Bolívar extolled the "sovereignty of the people, the division of powers, civil liberty, the proscription against slavery, the abolition of monarchy and privileged classes" (Bolívar 2003, 40). In his view, liberal republicanism and slavery could not coexist: "Can there be slavery where equality reigns? Such a contradiction would demean not so much our sense of justice as our sense of reason" (Bolívar 2003, 62). The Venezuelan Constitution of 1811, heavily influenced by Bolívar, abolished slave trade and ownership.[7]

Post-independence liberal elites, including South American independence hero José de San Martín, strongly opposed the ethnic categorizations on which the Spanish Crown had built its extractive policy towards the colonies. Like Bolívar, San Martín saw the extraction of tribute from "Indians or natives" as a shameful demonstration of tyranny by the Spanish government, which went against the rights of reason and justice (e.g. San Martín, Supreme Decree of August 27, 1821). Even if Creole elites continued to discriminate against the indigenous, black, and mixed populations in practice, they discursively sought to include their entire populations in the construction of the nation. An exception is in the treatment of Spaniards, who were for a time banned from nationality in a number of Latin American countries who had gained independence from Spain and worried about allowing a constituency of nationals who would support former imperial rulers.

Once the threat of a return to Spanish rule subsided, however, Latin American liberal elites restricted any meaningful political participation by indigenous or black populations. Racial distinctions became important in official domains like national censuses. Loveman (2014) has shown how Creole elites in Latin America initially renounced colonial racial categories in efforts to construct independent nations, only to recover these categories when trying to enumerate like other modern countries. Elites who aspired to whiteness began to promote ethnic selectivity in immigration law soon after independence. Indeed, most countries in the Americas began negative ethnic discriminations in their immigration policies after the United States introduced restrictions on Asian labor in 1856, a full ban on "coolie trade" in 1862, and outright Chinese labor exclusion in 1882. By 1905, seventeen Latin American countries had adopted racialized preferences or exclusions in their immigration policies.

FitzGerald and Cook-Martín (2014) have examined the close link between liberal and populist political orders and racism, but the key point here is that by the 20th century political orders had converged on race as fundamental means of assessing the suitability of prospects for full membership or for entry as immigrants. A large body of historical work shows how the racial conceptions of political elites and policymakers were expressed in a number of policy domains (Hsu 2000, McKeown 2008, Ngai 2014, Putnam 2013). This work suggests the need to carefully trace the connection among policymakers, the science on which they relied to legitimate notions about race, heredity, and the moral worth of actual and prospective citizens and immigrants.

By way of illustration, the corpus of literature on eugenics as well as new archival research on immigration and nationality policy formation in the Americas may throw light on the interstitial or connective role of scientific experts and especially advocates. Such actors linked political and racial orders by fashioning biologically distinguishable categories of people, the hierarchical arrangement of which could be justified on authoritative scientific grounds. Policy makers and state bureaucrats were eager to adopt scientifically informed means of constituting populations and these ambassadors of science provided legitimacy and acceptable justifications. The archives contain many examples of scientific ambassadors who were interstitial actors, bridging state imperatives of distinguishing and governing actual and prospective members. Before World War II, the role of these actors was to advance scientific rationales for a racial hierarchy to which policies should adjust. After World War II, a number of key scientific actors played a key role in dismantling scientific legitimations for racist systems of social classification.

Directions for future research

The central claim advanced in this chapter has been that the state – as a complex organization that operates at multiple levels and encompasses a range of actors with disparate interests – has relied on and institutionalized ideas of race to determine who could be a political subject. Across policy domains – from migration and membership, to population enumeration, to health and welfare – race has been a key notion that allowed state actors to determine the position of individuals in a polity. The relationship between racial and political orders has not received sustained theoretical attention or has become mired in debates about the relative importance of boundaries or hierarchical arrangements of racial categories. Scholars who cluster around competing claims have much to teach us about the analytical importance of understanding how people make boundaries and how the categories created in social interaction become institutionalized and used for political purposes. A focus on the linkages among political and racial orders and, specifically, of interstitial organizations and actors does not reconcile these positions. It is instead a strategy to recognize the importance of both at different analytical moments and the involvement of social and other scientists in the very object of study.

The type of approach suggested in this chapter has important analytical, policy, and ethical implications. One important analytical takeaway is that the relationship between racial and political orders may be opaque to those of us embedded within them. These relations have become so naturalized and taken for granted that it is difficult to see, much less analyze them. Paying close attention to the categories advanced in the work of experts, in public discourse, and in state practices is a starting point. Identifying the criteria by which human beings are distinguished and sorted for the purposes of resource allocation or distribution is a step in understanding how categories are arranged into hierarchies. Identifying non-state actors that link the political and racial orders is yet another important step to throw light on otherwise unclear mechanisms.

In the realm of contemporary population and especially migration governance, the absence of explicitly racial criteria for sorting actual or potential immigrants is a serious analytic challenge. It is a challenge to uncover, catalogue, and explain categorical distinctions mediated through ostensibly neutral language (sometimes even adopting the language of public good), and/or operating in official spaces less visible to public and scholarly scrutiny and in which bureaucratic discretion creates an opening for all manner of prejudices and discrimination. For instance, immigration policies in many western countries are facially neutral but may disproportionately affect people of a particular origin. The actions and logic of bureaucrats who adjudicate entry or citizenship are often hidden from public scrutiny.

Another challenge is how new and complex knowledge about human genetic variation shapes ideas about racial categories and hierarchies. The state of the art clearly demonstrates that humans are more similar as a species than any other primate (e.g. Conley and Fletcher 2017; Marks 1995). Yet scholars, policymakers, and the public have fixated on our differences. These differences, some of them significant from a health perspective, tend to cluster in populations of different geographic regions. The discursive move of conflating these regional "populations" – defined by biologists along very specific dimensions of interest – and "races" – defined in a long and messy historical process of state and nation making – is imperceptible but underlies the reemergence of the argument that there are "real races". "Races" are real in their consequences because people think they are real, to draw on Thomas and Swain's sociological maxim (Thomas and Dorothy Swaine 1928). They are not real as biological phenomena. Yet the discursive conflation of "race" and "populations" in the work of experts can have serious policy consequences, such as associating complex negative traits with ethnoracial categories particular to a specific political context rather than regional populations. In the domain of biomedical research, Epstein (2008) has shown that even well-intentioned policies of inclusion in biomedical research can have unanticipated and sometimes negative consequences. The unexpected challenges of analyzing linkages between political and racial fields are more relevant than ever. How are policy makers understanding very complex genetic science and to what uses will they put such knowledge in governance and with what unanticipated consequences?

The stakes in understanding connections among political and racial orders are high, both analytically and practically. Future work should strive to make advances in three areas. First, scholars may want to deepen historical research on the role of interstitial actors both for the sake of understanding the empirical pattern, and also to see if this suggests dynamics to which we should be alert in contemporary contexts. Second, analysts should focus on bureaucratic spaces in which ideas of race result in categorizations and hierarchies for the purposes of allocating material and symbolic resources. To the extent that bureaucratic spaces are inaccessible to social scientific scrutiny, such efforts will require creative methodological approaches. Finally, social scientists should move beyond condemnations of spurious claims made about the biological bases of race to understand the science of contemporary genomics, its implications, and the role of genomic experts who span social, economic, and political fields.

Notes

1 By regime I mean "basic patterns in the organization, exercise, and transfer of government decision-making power" (Higley and Burton 1989, 18). As noted below, I follow Dahl in distinguishing regimes by the combination of contestation and inclusion which they express.

2 On migration industries see Hernandez-Leon (2013) and Andersson (2014).

3 The many hands and levels of the state are illustrated in a number of studies of immigration and nationality bureaucracies and their interactions with immigrants and would-be citizens. Anthropologist Anna Tuckett (2018) has demonstrated how street-level bureaucrats in Italy make law in their interactions with immigrants in search of a legal status. Historian Deborah Kang (2017) has meticulously documented how US immigration officers have used administrative discretion at the micro level that then became national policy. My own work shows how Latin Americans seeking an ancestral homeland state nationality in Europe navigate discretionary spaces managed by bureaucrats who make decisions about nationality (Cook-Martín, 2013).

4 In this chapter, race refers to an idea that varies, yet preserves common features across contexts. It does not refer to biological differences across groups. For a useful overview of how race and ethnicity have been conceptualized across Latin America, see Wade (2010, 4–23). The definitional work done here is not without its politics or effects on the racial field of which it is a part. Still, it seems heuristically and theoretically useful to maintain some analytical distance from race as an idea.

5 Preliminary analysis by the author of positive preferences and negative discriminations in constitutional texts of the Americas between 1804 and 1999.

6 1816 *Constitution of Haiti*, Art. 39, 44. Decree of November 6, 1984 on Nationality, Art. II; 1987 Constitution of Haiti.

7 Although Bolívar was not unprejudiced, especially against so-called mulattoes (Helg, 2003).

References

Anderson, B. 2006. *Imagined Communities: Reflections on the Origin and Spread of Nationalism*. New York: Verso Books.

Andersson, R. 2014. *Illegality, Inc.: Clandestine Migration and the Business of Bordering Europe*. Oakland: Univ of California Press.

Andrews, G.R. 2004. *Afro-Latin America: Black Lives, 1600-2000*. Cambridge, MA: Harvard University Press.

Bayat, A. 2013. *Life as Politics: How Ordinary People Change the Middle East*. Amsterdam: Amsterdam University Press.

Bolívar, S. 2003. *El libertador: Writings of Simón Bolívar*. New York: Oxford University Press.

Bonilla-Silva, E. 1997. "Rethinking racism: Toward a structural interpretation." *American Sociological Review*, 62 (3), pp. 465–480 www.jstor.org/stable/2657316.

Bourdieu, P. and Wacquant, L.J. 1992. *An Invitation to Reflexive Sociology*. Chicago: University of Chicago Press.

Brubaker, R. 1992. *Nationhood and Citizenship in France and Germany*. Cambridge, MA: Harvard University Press.

Brubaker, R. 2004. *Ethnicity without Groups*. Cambridge, MA: Harvard University Press.

Brubaker, R., Loveman, M. and Stamatov, P. 2004. Ethnicity as cognition. *Theory and Society, 33* (1), pp. 31–64.

Caplan, J., Torpey, J.C. and Torpey, J. eds., 2001. *Documenting Individual Identity: The Development of State Practices in the Modern World*. Princeton, NJ: Princeton University Press.

Centeno, M.A. 2002. *Blood and Debt: War and the Nation-State in Latin America*. New York: Penn State Press.

Centeno, M.A. and Ferraro, A.E. eds., 2013. *State and Nation Making in Latin America and Spain: Republics of the Possible*. Cambridge: Cambridge University Press.

Chatterjee, P. 2004. *The Politics of the Governed: Reflections on Popular Politics in Most of the World*. New York: Columbia University Press.

Choate, M.I. 2008. *Emigrant Nation: The Making of Italy Abroad*. Cambridge, MA: Harvard University Press.

Conley, D. and Fletcher, J. 2017. *The Genome Factor: What the Social Genomics Revolution Reveals About Ourselves, Our History, and the Future*. Princeton, NJ: Princeton University Press.

Cook-Martín, D. 2008. Rules, red tape, and paperwork: The archeology of state control over migrants, 1850-1930. *Journal of Historical Sociology*, 21 (1), pp. 82–119.

Cook-Martín, D. 2013. *The Scramble for Citizens: Dual Nationality and State Competition for Immigrants*. Stanford: Stanford University Press.

Dahl, R.A. 1971. *Polyarchy: Participation and Opposition*. New Haven: Yale University Press.

Dahl, R.A. and Stinebrickner, B. 2003. *Modern Political Analysis*. Englewood Cliffs, NJ: Prentice-Hall.

Dikötter, F. 2015. *The Discourse of Race in Modern China*. New York: Oxford University Press.

Emirbayer, M. and Desmond, M. 2015. *The Racial Order*. Chicago: University of Chicago Press.

Epstein, S. 2008. *Inclusion: The Politics of Difference in Medical Research*. Chicago: University of Chicago Press.

Fields, K.E. and Fields, B.J. 2014. *Racecraft: The Soul of Inequality in American Life*. Verso Trade. New York: Verso [strike "Trade"].

Fitzgerald, D. 2009. *A Nation of Emigrants: How Mexico Manages its Migration*. Los Angeles: University of California Press.

FitzGerald, D. 2017. The history of racialized citizenship. *The Oxford Handbook of Citizenship*, 103 (1), p. 129.

Fitzgerald, S. David, and David Cook Martín 2015. *Culling the Masses: The Democratic Origins of Racist Immigration Policy in the Americas*. Cambridge, MA: Harvard University Press.

Fox, C. 2012. *Three Worlds of Relief: Race, Immigration, and the American Welfare State from the Progressive Era to the New Deal*. Princeton, NJ: Princeton University Press.

Fredrickson, G.M. 2002. *Racism: A Short History*. Princeton, NJ: Princeton University Press.

Helg, A. 2003. Simon Bolivar and the spectre of pardocracia: Jose Padilla in post-independence Cartagena. *Journal of Latin American Studies*, 35 (3), 447–471.

Hernández-León, R. 2013. "Conceptualizing the migration industry." In *The Migration Industry and the Commercialization of International Migration*. New York: Routledge, pp. 42–62.

Higley, J. and Burton, M.G. 1989. "The elite variable in democratic transitions and breakdowns." *American Sociological Review*, 54 (1), pp. 17–32.

Hochschild, J.L., Weaver, V.M. and Burch, T.R. 2012. *Creating a New Racial Order: How Immigration, Multiracialism, Genomics, and the Young can Remake Race in America*. Princeton, NJ: Princeton University Press.

Hsu, M.Y. 2000. *Dreaming of Gold, Dreaming of Home: Transnationalism and Migration Between the United States and South China, 1882-1943*. Stanford: Stanford University Press.

Isaac, B.H. 2006. *The Invention of Racism in Classical Antiquity*. Princeton, NJ: Princeton University Press.

James, C.L.R. 1963. *The Black Jacobins: Toussaint L'Ouverture and the San Domingo Revolution*. New York: Vintage Books.

Jasper, J.M. 2008. *Getting Your Way: Strategic Dilemmas in the Real World*. Chicago: University of Chicago Press.

Kang, S.D. 2017. *The INS on the Line: Making Immigration Law on the US-Mexico Border, 1917-1954*. New York: Oxford University Press.

Loveman, M. 2014. *National Colors: Racial Classification and the State in Latin America*. USA: Oxford University Press.

Lukes, S. 2004. *Power: A Radical View*. London: Palgrave Macmillan.

Mann, M. 1993. *The Sources of Social Power: Volume 1: A History of Power from the Beginning to AD 1760*. Cambridge: Cambridge University Press.

Marks, J. 1995. *Human Biodiversity: Genes, Race, and History*. New York: Aldine de Gruyter.

McKeown, A.M. 2008. *Melancholy Order: Asian Migration and the Globalization of Borders*. New York: Columbia University Press.

Morgan, K.J. and Orloff, A.S. eds., 2017. *The Many Hands of the State: Theorizing Political Authority and Social Control*. New York: Cambridge University Press.

Ngai, M.M. 2014. *Impossible Subjects: Illegal Aliens and the Making of Modern America*. Updated edition. Vol. 105. Princeton, NJ: Princeton University Press.

Omi, M. and Winant, H. 2014. *Racial Formation in the United States*. New York: Routledge.

Pérez Vejo, T. 2015. "Extranjeros interiores y exteriores: la raza en la construcción nacional mexicana." In Pablo Yankelevich *Inmigración y racismo: Contribuciones a la historia de los extranjeros en México*. México, DF: El Colegio de México, 89–124.

Putnam, L. 2013. *Radical Moves: Caribbean Migrants and the Politics of Race in the Jazz Age*. Chapel Hill: UNC Press Books.

Quijano, A., 2000. Coloniality of power and Eurocentrism in Latin America. *International Sociology*, 15 (2), pp. 215–232.

Reich, David. 2018. "How Genetics is Changing our Understanding of 'Race'" New York Times, Opinion, March 23, 2018.

Roosevelt, T. 1920 [1897]. *American Ideals*. New York: G.P. Putnam's Sons.

Santos de Quirós, Mariano. 1831. *Colección de leyes, decretos y órdenes pub- licados en el Perú desde su independencia en el año de 1821 hasta 1854*. Lima: José Masías.

Stone, J. 1995. Race, ethnicity, and the Weberian legacy. *American Behavioral Scientist*, 38 (3), pp. 391–406.

Thomas, W.I. and Dorothy Swaine Thomas 1928. *The Child in America*. New York: Alfred Knopf.

Torpey, J.C. 1998. *The Invention of the Passport: Surveillance, Citizenship and the State*. London: Cambridge University Press.

Tuckett, A. 2018. *Rules, Paper, Status: Migrants and Precarious Bureaucracy in Contemporary Italy*. Stanford: Stanford University Press.

Weber, E. 1976. *Peasants into Frenchmen: The Modernization of Rural France, 1870-1914*. Stanford: Stanford University Press.

Wimmer, A. 2008a. The making and unmaking of ethnic boundaries: A multilevel process theory. *American Journal Of Sociology*, 113 (4), pp. 970–1022.

Wimmer, A. 2008b. Elementary strategies of ethnic boundary making. *Ethnic And Racial Studies*, 31 (6), pp. 1025–1055.

Yankelevich, P. 2015. *Inmigración y racismo.: Contribuciones a la historia de los extranjeros en México*. Mexico DF: El Colegio de Mexico AC.

Zolberg, A.R. and Zolberg, A.R. 2009. *A Nation by Design: Immigration Policy in the Fashioning of America*. Cambridge, MA: Harvard University Press.

11

"Re-whitening" non-white spaces through colorblind narratives

Charles A. Gallagher

As an expert witness I was retained in a legal case that involved the racial targeting and closing of twelve minority owned bars and restaurants over the course of three years in Rivertown, a fictionally named city in the US Midwest. The plaintiffs in this case alleged that the closing of these establishments was a racially motivated, orchestrated effort by white city leaders to remove non-white entrepreneurs from a part of the city that was targeted for urban waterfront redevelopment plan. White political and business leaders had undertaken a state and federally funded waterfront development project whose goal was to make the downtown river front district a middle class tourist destination. These minority owned restaurants and bars that were shuttered fell within the footprint of the city's proposed riverfront redevelopment zone. These minority owned establishments were ostensibly closed because of code violations like underage drinking, drugs on the premises and drunk and disorderly citations. Given these rather serious infractions, a reasonable person would conclude that it was legally justifiable that these bars and restaurants should be closed. The race of the owners or the minority customers they served was irrelevant; these establishments were in violation of the law, putting their liquor licenses and hence their businesses in jeopardy.

The legal question here was not if these minority owned restaurants had broken the law. They did. The constitutional and legal issue that was raised was one of equality. White owned bars and restaurants, some on the very same block as these minority owned establishments, had the same exact violations in the city's police blotter but none of these white establishments were subject to harsh injunctions, fines nor did any of the white owned establishments lose their liquor licenses. In violation of the equal protection clause of the Fourteenth Amendment, these non-white restaurants and bars were treated differently by state agents because of the race of their owners compared to similarly situated white owned establishments. The race of the owners or animus directed at these owners because of the color of their skin cannot be why these groups were targeted for what was differential treatment relative to white owned establishments.

The plaintiffs contend that what white city elites wanted was to "re-whiten" the downtown by removing establishments owned by racial minorities and the non-white racial clientele these establishments brought to the downtown riverfront area. In his insightful article on how space is raced within a black and white frame, sociologist Elijah Anderson notes that "as demographics change, public spaces are subject to change as well, impacting not only how a space is occupied and by whom but also the way in which it is perceived" (Anderson p. 11, 2015). If these non-white establishments constituted a short lived "cosmopolitan canopy," that is "an island of racial and ethnic civility in a sea of segregated living" (Anderson p. 19, 2015), it was small and temporary. What transpired in Rivertown was not a case of racialized gentrification where working class black or Asian establishments were displaced by wealthier white businesses. What happened in the mid-size city of Rivertown was in effect a hostile takeover of non-white spaces by elite whites in order to re-segregate and "re-whiten" a space these leaders wished to reclaim because of the huge profits that could be realized through redevelopment of the riverfront. What makes these racist and illegal actions all the more pernicious was how the political and legal institutions of the city were used to "re-whiten" this downtown space by using tactics that on the face of it appeared to be colorblind and race neutral.

As part of this civil rights case I was given 1000s of documents to review, including police blotters, emails of city hall workers, government employees, business leaders and police officers, minutes from city council meetings and the depositions of those named in the suit. What became abundantly clear was that white city officials hyper-policed minority owned bars, used racist and ethnocentric language to describe racial minorities in their work as government officials, enforced a zero tolerance policy for minority bars but not white owned bars and worked in concert with city council to target bars whose owners were racial minorities with the intent of shutting down these minority owned establishments. When the minority owned restaurateurs realized that white owned bars and restaurants had committed the same violations, but had not been subject to the same legal sanctions, they sued the city of Rivertown. The initial response by the city was to claim that race had nothing to do with the sanctions leveled against the minority owned businesses.

The defendants were a group of white elected politicians, city employees and business leaders who represented this majority white city in the Midwest. Like many rustbelt cities in the Midwest, by 2015 the city's manufacturing base had been decimated by decades of deindustrialization. The city's population has been shrinking year after year since 1990. The city faces a scenic river and a master plan for development was conceived and voted on by city council to reinvent this sleepy, ex-manufacturing town into a quaint, hip tourist destination where couples from several large, vibrant cities just a few hours away could visit. The idea was that young, urban, educated couples with high levels of disposable income would "weekend" to this quaint soon-to-be hip town and spend money on the trendy restaurants and chic art galleries was part of the master plan. The fifty million dollar federal and state funded development plan would set in motion a riverfront revival that would bring the city back to its post-World War II glory days. The problem, however, as many white city planners and white politicians saw it, was that over the years, when the downtown city's retail abandonment rates were high and rents were relatively cheap, many non-white entrepreneurs open restaurants and bars on the riverfront, which attracted a growing African-American, Asian, and Latino clientele. For most of the city's history the population and retail establishment owners were almost entirely white. While small in number, the non-white restaurateurs were able to create sustainable businesses at a time when the city appeared to be in an economic death spiral by bringing in a significant number of young non-whites to the downtown district to eat, drink and dance. A master revitalization plan conceived by white consultants, white business leaders and the overwhelmingly white city council and aided by state and federal money changed how the white power structure viewed the downtown river front area. If this part of the downtown had once been written off by white elites as a "no-go zone" or stigmatized because it now housed minority owned establishments, that was no longer the case. The economic and cultural transformation that was being planned would mean a waterfront renaissance where residential and commercial property values could potentially skyrocket.

There was, however, a problem. The white political and business leaders that controlled or owned virtually every commercial business in the city felt that the bars and restaurants owned by non-whites and the racial minorities that patronized these establishments not only devalued these formerly all-white public spaces, but city leaders felt a non-white presence in the development zone would scare off the middle class whites they were trying to lure to the waterfront development area. This fear of the "racial other" is an established part of the race relations literature. Research suggests that the perceived size of the non-white population has strong influence on anti-black prejudice by whites and their perceived threat to their social status. A national study examining the link between racial group size, racial attitudes and perceptions of threat found that whites feel threatened by blacks as whites perceive blacks' group size increasing and whites are forced to share social space with blacks. This research indicates that prejudice towards blacks varies with the size of the black population; as the size of the black population increases so too does anti-black prejudice by whites (Fossett and Jill Kiecolt 1989; Alba, 2009; Gallagher 2014). The positive relationship between group size means that the "the greater the percentage of blacks in an environment, the more racially antagonistic whites tend to be" (Oliver and Mendelberg 2000, p. 575). Rivertown has experienced a significant growth in the black, Latino and to a lesser extent Asian populations over the last two decades, but for most of Rivertown history whites did not "share social space with blacks." Non-whites constitute about a third of the non-white population and the overwhelming majority of non-whites live in the city limits. Rivertown County, which includes the suburbs of the city, is overwhelmingly white. One city hall worker said whites from the majority white suburbs called Rivertown "Raysheen-town," a reference to what is assumed to be a stereotypical name associated with African Americans.

Whiteness as property ⟵ // Stoler.

Herbert Blumer identified four feelings or perspectives that encourage race motivated discriminatory behavior. The dominant group sees themselves as superior and views the subordinate group as different or alien, the dominant group feels entitled to valued social and economic resources, and finally the dominant group is fearful that the subordinate group will encroach upon those resources the dominant group believes is rightfully theirs (Blumer 1958). Use of stereotypical traits as the basis for seeing a group as being fundamentally different from the dominant group is conducive to aversion and antipathy directed at the subordinate group. Defining one's group as superior and a minority group as "being of a fundamentally different stock" creates the feeling that the dominant group is entitled to "certain control and decision-making as in government and law, [and] the right to exclusive membership in given institutions such as schools, churches and recreational institutions" (Blumer 1958 p. 118). What sets in motion race based discriminatory behavior is the belief by the dominant group that the subordinate or minority group harbors designs on those resources, hence threatening the social and material status of the dominant group. The dominant group organizes and responds when a resource they believe is their own "property" is threatened with loss or devalued by sharing this resource with a subordinate group. These threats to white economic, political, and social standing are thought to be most acute when whites find themselves competing over resources and the various social structures that control their allocation (Gallagher 2003a; Bobo 2001; Bonilla-Silva 2001; Lopez 2012). Blumer argued that when a minority group intrudes into the dominant groups "sphere of group exclusiveness, or an encroachment on their area of proprietary claim" the result is race motivated prejudice and discrimination in order to maintain and control the resources whites believe is their "property." All the conditions that give rise to and are predictive of race based discriminatory treatment against non-white bar owners were in place in Rivertown: defining racial minorities as being different from and inferior to the whites; the use of disparaging language to demean non-whites and justify different treatment; a sense of entitlement to resources by white elites and a concern that the subordinate group was encroaching on those resources that the dominant group believed were the prerogative of their group. These circumstances in Rivertown were not only grounded in the dynamics of race relations in Rivertown but also socioeconomic and demographic changes that have taken place in Rivertown's recent history.

The discriminatory treatment of non-white restaurateurs needs to be understood in its historic and sociological context. For the last 75 years, a long and established record of social science research on racial attitudes in the United States has been amassed (Schuman et. al 1997; Massey and Denton 1993). While the research shows a liberalizing of whites' attitudes on some social issues (interracial marriage, voting for a black president), negative racial stereotypes of racial minorities by whites are still quite commonplace (AP 2012; Bobo 2011; Charles 2000; Gallagher 2003a, Gallagher 2003b; Bonilla-Silva 2003; Feagin 1995). Stereotypes are exaggerated beliefs associated with an entire category of people where it is believed that all or almost all members of that category share a common, typically negative, trait, behavior, propensity or characteristic. These stereotypes become the basis to prejudge or be prejudiced toward a group based on faulty generalizations (Allport 1974) and can form the basis for race based discrimination.

While large strides in race relations have been made, it is still the case that a sizable part of the white population continues to believe various stereotypes about African Americans, including that they are less intelligent, more prone to violence, less hardworking, more criminal, and more willing to live off welfare than whites. A nationally-representative study found that over two-thirds of whites believe that blacks were more likely to prefer to live off welfare, while 50% of whites rated blacks as less intelligent and more prone to violence than whites (Markus and Moya 2010). In 2008, a General Social Survey found that 45% of whites rated blacks as less hardworking than whites. A 2014 study found 44% of whites believed that whites were more intelligent as a group (American National Election Study 2014). In 2014, 43% of whites agreed that social inequality was due to a lack of motivation or will power rather than other structural explanations like lack of access to quality schooling, living-wage jobs, or poverty (Krysan and Bader 2009).

Research has also demonstrated that one of the most pernicious stereotypes about African Americans is an assumption of criminality. Examining how "being black" is synonymous with "being a criminal," researchers found that the "stereotypes of blacks as criminals is widely known and is deeply embedded in the collective consciousness of Americans, irrespective of level of prejudice or personal beliefs" (Quillian and Pager 2001 p. 722). Researchers have found that

> whites are more fearful of encounters with blacks than those with whites and that this fear of blacks was independent of the age and gender of the persons encountered, the context in which the encounter takes place, and the age and gender of the individual experiencing the encounter.

> *(St. John and Hearld-Moore 1996 p. 277)*

These continued stereotypes result in ongoing prejudice and stereotyping against African Americans more generally. A 2012 poll conducted by the Associated Press with the assistance of researchers from Stanford University and University and Michigan found that there has been an increase in anti-black attitudes since 2008. The researchers found that "51% percent of Americans now express explicit anti-black attitudes, compared with 48% in a similar 2008 survey" (Associated Press 2012). A study of Los Angeles County found that there was a greater average level of hostility towards blacks by non-blacks compared to any other racial group (Bobo and Smith 1998).

Non-white spaces as polluted

Now that these non-white spaces had the potential for significant profit, they came to be viewed by the white power structure as stigmatized spaces that were, to borrow from Erving Goffman, "polluted" (Goffman 1963). The influx of non-white establishments to the downtown had "spoiled" this formerly white space whose racial "blemish" could only be removed, and the downtown be "cleaned up" as the mayor put it, by re-whitening these once white spaces. The narrative emerged that minority businesses were an obstacle to a downtown economic revival in what was once, and needed to be once again, a white space where white tourists could eat, drink and stroll in an environment unthreatened by the presence of young non-whites. In the end, this is exactly what the city was able to do. Using licensing and inspection codes and zoning ordinances all twelve establishments were eventually forced to close their doors. The case was a pyrrhic victory for the plaintiffs as the city settled the suit before going to a jury trial. The lawsuit resulted in all twelve plaintiffs receiving a token settlement from the city, but the loss of revenues when the restaurants closed and the cost of the lawsuit put them out of business. These restaurants are now almost all-white owned establishments and the fifty million dollar riverfront development project broke ground in the spring of 2018.

Re-whitening white spaces and racial laundering

Sociologist Elijah Anderson defines a "white space" where

> the wider society is still replete with overwhelmingly white neighborhoods, restaurants, schools, universities, workplaces, churches, and other associations, courthouses, and cemeteries, a situation that reinforces a normative sensibility in settings in which black people are typically absent, not expected, or marginalized when present.
>
> *(Anderson p. 10, 2015)*

When white flight, urban restructuring or demographic transitions take place, white spaces become mixed or majority non-white, at which point these communities may be stigmatized as a "black space" or a "ghetto" by the dominant group. Black or non-white spaces can, however, can be taken back and reappropriated as white spaces in various ways. While gentrification often involves wealthier whites pushing lower income whites out of a particular neighborhood it is not uncommon for wealthier whites to displace working class non-whites from neighborhoods that have become desirable. Anderson describes one such West Philadelphia neighborhood in the article cited earlier and such gentrification that involves both displacement around race and class is happening in large cities throughout the country.

Philadelphia's Point Breeze and parts of NYC's Harlem are other examples of wealthy whites displacing working and lower middle class blacks.

Gentrification often leads to creating or reclaiming white spaces where the result is typically increased property values over time and the establishment of amenities that serve a wealthier clientele. However, in the case of Rivertown, the white leaders in city hall, the business community and their city council, which oversees the licensing and inspection of bars and restaurants, colluded to reestablish a white space by using ostensibly race neutral legal measures to target, shut down and push out non-white establishments. In my eight hour deposition with defense lawyers I was asked detailed questions about the report I wrote explaining how the city's concerted effort to "clean up" the downtown, as the mayor put it, of non-white bars and their majority non-white clientele was consistent with an established body of social science research on how the dominant group, in this case the white controlled power structure of the city, sought to further racially monopolize the city's assets and resources and do so in a fashion that appeared race neutral. The defendants insisted that their enforcement of the laws was done in a race neutral, colorblind fashion.

"Professor, do white people drink Hennessy?" "Yes, Councilor"

Police reports documenting illegal behavior on the part of these minority owned establishments was objective proof that race had nothing to with city council's actions to close these establishments. This everything-but-race defense was a common theme throughout these proceedings. My report detailed how in one effort to discourage black customers from patronizing non-white owned bars a non-white bar owner was instructed not to sell Hennessey cognac. When a bar or restaurant is alleged to have violated some type of ordinance (underage drinking, for example) council members can require bar owners into "side agreements," where in order to keep their food or liquor operating license they agree to conditions and prohibitions which would remedy what city council members perceived to be a problem. Prohibitions or conditions placed on restaurant owners by law must be race neutral but under investigation these proscriptions were racially biased and discriminatory. In this case the prohibition was serving Hennessy cognac. Hennessy is the largest manufacturer of cognac in the world and became associated with hip-hop and rap because this brand (and others) had been featured in a significant number of rap and hip-hop videos, starting with *Pass the Courvoisier, Part II* by Busta Rhymes and P. Diddy in 2002. According to a spirits industry publication in 2011, young African Americans accounted for 75% of *all* cognac sales. It was the position of various city employees and members of city council that restrictions on certain types of alcohol, clothing, music, and jewelry would enhance the stature of bars and have a calming effect on these establishments, all of whom happened to be minority owned bars with minority clientele. Asking a bar, and in this case a minority owned bar, to ban the sale of Hennessy was one such request made of non-white owned bars that was not made of white bars. Hennessy has the same proof alcohol (80%) as Jim Beam and Jack Daniels yet these whiskeys were never asked to be taken off the shelves of white bars. The larger point is that Hennessey is associated with black hip-hop and as such is devalued by many whites and viewed as a way to control the behavior of blacks who frequent these establishments.

It is not, however, just the association of Hennessy cognac with hip-hop or black culture that has been the target of the city's demands on minority owned bars who serve a minority clientele. Indeed, city council has utilized almost every black associated symbol as a way to target minority owned bars and exclude their minority patrons. Even white owned and patronized bars were encouraged by the city council to make an effort to dissuade minority clientele from entering their premises. Responding to two incidents that took place at bar on Main Street, the owner appeared before city council and was presented with this list of proposed restrictions which appeared in the meeting's minutes:

> Everyone under 30 has an ID check
> All male patrons are scanned for metals
> Rap and R/B have been removed from the Juke Box
> No Hats, doo rags or bandanas allowed to be worn on premises
> No White T-Shirts or Tank allowed to be worn on premises
> No Baggy pants allowed to be worn on premises
> No Long gold chains allowed to be worn by customers

In response, the city council members "complimented him on his changes and encouraged him to continue in this direction." In other words, this government body praised a restaurateur for creating a set of restrictions that overwhelmingly and disproportionately would keep black and Latino customers out of his bar. The restriction list is a coded way to disproportionality exclude black and Latino patrons and achieve this in an ostensibly race neutral fashion.

One might argue that checking a customer's age or using a metal scanner to allow admittance to a bar are race neutral. However, a reasonable person with a basic understanding of fashion trends associated with blacks and Latinos might conclude that taken together the last five items would disproportionally affect non-white customers. The last five items on this list are racially coded and taken in total amount to targeting certain racial and ethnic groups from exclusion from this establishment. The restrictions above, however, were not viewed by the defendant's lawyers as racially coded or racially motivated actions that would disproportionately impact non-white customers. In deposition the defendant's lawyers asked pointed questions where I was to respond:

"Professor Gallagher, do white people drink Hennessy?" "Yes, councilor."

> "Professor Gallagher, do white people wear baggy pants?" "Yes, Councilor."
> "Professor Gallagher, do white people wear white tee shirts?" "Yes, Councilor."
> "Professor Gallagher, do white people wear gold chains?" "Yes, Councilor."

This technique of "stopping the video" and reframing a racist incident, much like what was done at the Rodney King trial, first atomizes events, then takes them out of context, and then reconstructs a racist action or event so an alternative race neutral, colorblind narrative can be presented as a reasonable, plausible or justifiable explanation of a thoroughly racist act. Rivertown city council members put seven conditions on entering a bar, four of which were dress codes that taken together most individuals would see were racially loaded. These questions are rendered race neutral by taking each of these dress code requirements individually and out of their overarching racial context. If some white people wear gold chains, hats, baggy pants, white tee shirts and drink Hennessy, just like black people do, how could this city council-imposed restriction on dress or certain types of beverages be racist? This is how institutional colorblindness operates: establish that certain behaviors or preferences are not exclusive to one group and racism as an explanatory variable or cause for behavior can be discarded (Moore 2008, Mueller 2015; Gallagher 2015).

Laundering racism and whitewashing a city

In effect what these lawyers are doing is akin to how "dirty" money is laundered by criminals. Laundering racism is taking an act that is illegal, in this case city council members targeting minority owned restaurants because of their race and through a sequence of placement, layering and integration takes a patently racist act and scrubs it clean of racist intent. An explicitly racist act is "placed" into the legal system by lawyers who for large fees "layer," that is conceal and reframe, racist acts through race neutral legalese, sophistry, specious counter claims, false equivalents or appeals to common sense stereotypes. What is taking place are linguistic legal tricks where the now sanitized, non-racist explanations are presented, that is integrated into the court of public opinion as a plausible counter narrative to what is an irrefutably racist act.

Another bar owner was able to circumvent any punitive measures as a consequence of citation regarding a bar fight by agreeing to block rap music from his juke box and discontinuing the use of a DJ who was bringing in, as a council person put it, a "diverse" crowd. In other words, these restrictions that were pleasing to the city council members had the effect of whitening the clientele of these bars by imposing restrictions that discourage black and Latino customers from patronizing these establishments.

Many of the requirements placed on minority owned bars by city council and various other city employed actors were motived by race. To say a restriction on rap or hip-hop or the removal of Hennessy from the bar shelves or a ban on baggy pants, gold chains or white T-shirts is race neutral is extremely disingenuous and strains all credibility. By enforcing these restrictions, the city was using its authority to reclaim and re-whiten these once all-white places and spaces. The re-whitening of these spaces occurred in three ways. The first was to hyper-police these establishments which allowed city council to impose costly fines on these establishments and call them in for a hearing thus setting them up to have the legal justification to revoke their liquor licenses. Second, the requirements, which can easily be construed as race based harassment, made these establishments less desirable to the racial minorities who typically frequent these places while symbolically signaling that how they dress and the beverages they might wish to consume are devalued. Finally, creating an environment so hostile to non-whites through dress code and beverage restrictions and a constant police presence resulted in pushing non-whites out of the downtown area. Who wants to enter an area where the police routinely harass you, your style of dress is effectively outlawed and there are restrictions on the music and beverages you like? The coordinated efforts of city council and police to rid the downtown of black and brown faces was successful. Within three years the vibrant small pocket of non-white owned establishments in the downtown disappeared to be replaced by white owned establishments that catered to majority white customers. Rivertown had been whitewashed.

Privileging white spaces

The disparagement, disrespect and racial bias directed at racial minorities in Rivertown created the environment that made the mistreatment and discrimination of minority owned bars possible. Similarly situated white bars—bars that had the same type of issues regarding noise violations, underage drinking, fights, violence or crowd control—were treated quite differently than bars owned by racial minorities. What we found when reviewing the log of police reports was that white owned bars with exactly the same license and inspection violations as minority owned bars were treated differently by city employees because of racial bias. A number of white owned bars serving a white clientele had numerous incidents involving shootings, underage drinking, guns on the premises and fights but had never been subject to the hyper-scrutiny, ongoing police surveillance and onerous side agreements to which minority owned bars have been subject. These bars have never been called in for a due process hearing nor have they ever had their licenses revoked.

The colorblind narrative was used by invoking laws and statutes on the books that were in principle race neutral. Violations of license and inspection codes applied equally to all establishments regardless of the race of the owner. However, what became obvious upon reviewing the minutes from city council meetings was that the councilmen engaged in behaviors of code enforcement that were extremely selective and subjective. White restaurant and bar owners were typically not called in to city council for mandatory hearings to have fines leveled against them or impose various restrictions on their establishment, even though police reports would warrant such action. This was not the case for minority owned establishments. Non-white restaurateurs were routinely brought in for all violations which set in motion ever increasing fines and restrictions which culminated in a loss of one's food and liquor license. There existed no standard about when or under which circumstances restaurant owners should be brought in front of city council to face fines nor were there any guidelines about what type of violation would result in restrictions being placed on their establishments. There was no metric or checklist about what violations triggered the process that would result in the loss of one's operating license. Almost all of these decisions regarding the treatment of bar owners were made at the discretion of the members of city council. Where standards like a point system for alcohol violations exist (there is a state-wide system in place where this city is located) the ability for subjectivity and racial bias to creep into the decision-making process is minimized. In Rivertown, no such point system or checklist or metric exists that guarantees that minority bar owners are treated in the same way as white bar owners. The result is that racial bias, stereotypes, and prejudice became the foundation and starting point from which city officials made decisions about when, where and whom to police, who should get a ticket or citation, where to place police resources like cameras, squad cars and their SWAT unit. This institutional bias was also evident in what areas get framed as those that need to be "cleaned up," which groups are inherently loud, rowdy, violent or criminal and which groups are worthy of a verbal warning when there is a violation and which groups are dealt with in the harshest and most punitive ways.

In every one of these potential decision trees, the law and the public servants, empowered to enforce the law equally, privileged white bar owners over minority bar owners because of the color of their skin and the color of the clients they served. The custom of discrimination that permeated every level of Rivertown was persistent and widespread. The result was that racial minorities were effectively shut out of the downtown bar business while whites now enjoy a virtual monopoly on this industry and have reclaimed this area as a white space.

Monopolizing white spaces

Race scholars maintain that whites, as the dominant group in an established racial hierarchy, seek to monopolize and control public and private resources they believe are their exclusive or proprietary property. Throughout our nation's history, neighborhoods, parks, lunch counters, schools, pools, unions and jobs were once viewed by whites as their own form of private property—an entitlement sanctioned by social norms, enforced by law and kept by force (Moore 2008; Blumer 1958, Bobo 1998). In his seminal work linking stereotypes, racial attitudes and racism to one's sense of "group position," Herbert Blumer (1958) explained that whites view public resources (neighborhoods, pools, schools, jobs, restaurants) as their own private property because the established racialized hierarchy places whites above blacks. Social scientists working in this field view the sense of white entitlement and the monopolization of social, political and economic resources as a reflection of a group's perceived and relatively privileged placement in a social system based on a racial hierarchy. This positioning of whites over blacks within this racial hierarchy justifies, as members of this group see it, the exclusive right to preferred social and economic resources. These actions serve to maintain white privilege and reestablish, reframe or recreate the existing racial hierarchy. Historically, segregated public spaces and criminalizing individual interactions between whites and blacks was a matter of law, which guaranteed that whites would seldom have to compete for resources or share social space with blacks. This was a form of white supremacy in its clearest manifestation; desired social amenities like quality housing stock, high performing schools, and parks or restaurants were under the control of and solely available to whites because racist ideology defined whites as being socially and biologically superior to blacks. Historically, that blacks could not own housing and were segregated in "ghettoes" in Rivertown while whites had access to all of the city's amenities is one such example of how whites monopolize public and private resources. The fact that whites control entities like the city of Rivertown's City Council, Rivertown Hospitality League (an all-white restaurant association) or large corporations in the city, are further examples of how whites control public and private resources. What is different today is that the overt, legally sanctioned Jim Crow racism of the past is illegal yet whites still wish to own, control and monopolize and keep white the white spaces they see as their own property as well as non-white spaces that have potential value (see Moore's 2008 work on institutionalized white spaces).

Drawing on Blumer's insights into the situation in Rivertown, the increased concentration of minority owned bars along Main Street was an encroachment into what had historically been a white space. These non-white bars and non-white clientele were viewed by whites as devaluing and diminishing the quality of life—or as a Councilman put it, that Rivertown was "turning into a Detroit" even though this city is 65% white. For a point of comparison Detroit is 85% black, 40% of the population lives in poverty and has one of the highest murder and violent crime rates in the country. That the Main Street part of the city of Rivertown would need to be "cleaned up," as the mayor announced, suggests that non-white establishments and their clients are somehow qualitatively different and deficient compared to white bars and restaurants in the immediate area. The research discussed earlier which found that whites associate non-whites with "negative characteristics" is typified in a comment by the Executive Director of Downtown Rivertown Corporation that the non-white establishments in the downtown area had "not added any value to the neighborhood." The concept of "value" here is critical in understanding the subjective nature of how black spaces are devalued by whites and provides a window into what white business leaders thought about non-white establishments in the downtown area. As an objective measure the owners of these establishments have created many forms of "value" in the downtown—they pay their rent and utilities, pay wages to their employees, purchase food and beverages for their establishments, materials for their daily operations, provide entertainment for their customers and bring people into the downtown area where they spend additional money patronizing other establishments. Clearly these businesses brought financial and social value to the downtown. What is suggested by the Executive Director's comment is that there could be little or no value added to the neighborhood by non-white establishments because, as the social science literature makes clear, whites devalue, denigrate and disparage black and non-white spaces. It is economically irrational to claim from a business perspective that no value was brought to the city by these non-white establishments, but the nature of racism is not based on logic, objectivity or rationality but a viscerally prejudiced predisposition towards a group that results in bias directed at that group which results discriminatory behavior.

Whites' denigration of minority owned bars and the majority non-white customers they serve was evident in a large number of public comments and email exchanges. While testifying at a hearing of a minority owned establishment, one of the city of Rivertown's witnesses, Mary, described "black" and "Mexican" customers as being abnormally loud. Specifically, Mary testified,

> I think that is just their normal talk. They are screaming, they are loud, they are in groups. It must be the normal way they talk. I don't get it … If they didn't do that and would leave the bar like normal people do …

Apparently the "normal talk" of Mexicans and Blacks is to scream. They do not conduct themselves as "normal people."

The construction of the "racial other" and the highlighting of race based differences was on display when the former mayor explained to a black businessman, "I'm trying to keep *you people* out of Town Square." The term "you people" to describe racial minorities is typically understood as a pejorative indicative of racism or racial marginalization. At a minimum it constructs an "us versus them" dichotomy where whites are on one side and racial minorities are on the other. In this us/them binary it is important to remember which group has institutional power. Another of the city's witnesses at a city council hearing testified that he perceived the non-white customers on Main Street as uniformly hurting the city's image, explaining, "I do care about clientele [which was mostly non-white] because they are a detriment to the city of Rivertown."

Conclusion

Given the sordid history of race relations in Rivertown, its racially tense and economically challenged environment and the overtly racist, ethnocentric and stereotypical language used by defendants to describe racial minorities, it is extremely implausible, if not impossible, for any reasonable person to read the emails, depositions, City Council meeting minutes and supporting materials in this case and *not* conclude that the racial animus of the defendants contributed to and ultimately caused the minority bar owner's establishments to be shut down. What is important to note here is that the actions taken against these non-white owned businesses was accomplished by public institutions working in a coordinated way to frame racist intent and actions within the context of a race neutral colorblind narrative. This everything-*but*-race, colorblind approach has become thoroughly embedded in our nation's institutions. This particular case is unique only because the city of Rivertown closed so many restaurants in such a short amount of time that it was impossible for the plaintiffs not to see the role race played in closing their businesses. The challenge we now face is to locate and uncover how the embeddedness of institutional colorblindness serves to maintain white supremacy.

References

Alba, Richard. *Blurring the Color Line: The New Chance for a More Integrated America*. (Cambridge, MA: Harvard University Press, 2009).

Allport, Gordon. *The Nature of Prejudice*. (Reading, MA: Addison Wesley, 1974).

American National Election Studies and Stanford University. 2014. ANES Time Series Cumulative Data File. Inter-university Consortium for Political and Social Research.

Anderson, Elijah. 2015. "The White Space." *Sociology of Race and Ethnicity*. 1 1: 10–21.

Associated Press Racial Attitudes Survey (October 29, 2012).

Blumer, Herbert. 1958. "Race Prejudice as a Sense of Group Position." *The Pacific Sociological Review*. 11: 3–7 Spring.

Bobo, L. and Smith, R. (1998). "From Jim Crow Racism to Laissez Faire Racism: The Transformation of Racial Attitudes." In Katlin, W. (ed.), *Beyond Pluralism: The Conception of Groups and Group Identities in America*, Chicago: University of Illinois Press: 198–212.

Bobo, Lawrence. (2001). "Racial Attitudes and Relations at the Close of the Twentieth Century." In Smelser, N. (ed), *Amercia Becoming: Racial Trends and Their Consequences*, Washington, DC: National Acedmy Press: 262–299.

Bobo, Lawrence. (2011). "Somewhere between Jim Crow & Post-Racialism: Reflections on the Racial Divide in America Today, Daedalus." The Journal of the American Academy of Arts and Sciences, 140 2 Spring 2011.

Bonilla-Silva, E. *White Supremacy and Racism in the Post-Civil Rights Era*. (Boulder, CO: Lynne Rienner, 2001).

Bonilla-Silva, Eduardo. *Racism Without Racists: Color-Blind Racism and the Persistence of racial Inequality in the United States*. (New York: Rowman and Littlefield, 2003).

Charles, Camille Zubrinsky. 2000. "Neighborhood Racial Composition Preference: Evidence from a Multiethnic Metropolis." Social Problems, 47.

Feagin, Joe and Hernan Vera. *White Racism: The Basics*. (New York, NY: Routledge, 1995).

Fossett, Mark and K. Jill Kiecolt. 1989. "The Relative Size of Minority Populations and White Racial Attitudes." *Social Science Quarterly*. 70 4: 820–835.

Gallagher, C.A. 2003a. "Color-Blind Privilege: The Social and Political Functions of Erasing the Color-Line in Post-Race America." *Race, Gender Class*. 10 4: 22–37.

Gallagher, C.A. 2003b. "Miscounting Race: Explaining Whites' Misperceptions of Racial Group Size." *Sociological Perspectives*. 46 3: 381–396.

Gallagher, C.A. (2006). "Color Blindness: An Obstacle to Racial Justice?" In Brunsma, D. (ed.), *Mixed Messages: Multiracial Identities in the "Color-blind Era"*, Lynne Rienner Publishers: 103–116.

Gallagher, C.A. "Blacks, Jews, Gays and Immigrants Are Taking Over": How the Use of Polling Data Can Distort Reality and Perpetuate Inequality Among Immigrants" *Ethnic and Racial Studies Review* March, 2014, pp. 731–738.

Gallagher, C.A. (2015). "Color-blind Egalitarianism as the New Racial Norm." In Karim Murji and John Solomos (eds.), *Theories of Race and Ethnicity: Contemporary Debates and Perspectives*, Cambridge, UK: Cambridge University Press: 40–56.

Gilens, Martin. 1996. "Race and Poverty in America: Public Perceptions and the American News Media." *Public Opinion Quarterly*. 60: 515–541.

Goffman, Erving. *Stigma: Notes on the Management of Spoiled Identity*. (Englewood Cliffs, N.J.: Prentice-Hall, 1963).

Krysan, Maria and Michael Bader. 2009. "Racial Blind Spots: Black-White-Latino Differences in Community Knowledge." *Social Problems*. 56: 677–701.

Lopez, I.H. 2012. *Intentional Blindness*, 87 N.Y.U. L. Rev. 1779 (2012).

Markus, Hazel Rose and Paula Moya. *Doing Race: 21 Essays for the 21st Century* (W.W. Norton and Company, 2010).

Moore, Wendy. *Reproducing Racism: White Space, Elite Law Schools and Racial Inequality*. (New York: Rowman and Littlefield Publishers, 2008).

Mueller, Jennifer C. 2015. "The Undeserving Rich: American Beliefs about Inequality, Opportunity, and Redistribution (by Leslie McCall)." *Contemporary Sociology*. 44 4: 537–539.

Oliver, J. Eric, and Tali Mendelberg. (2000). "Reconsidering the Environmental Determinants of White Racial Attitudes." *American Journal of Political Science*. 44 3: 574–589.

Public Policy Forum: Race Relations Survey and Overview November 2006.

Quillian, Lincoln and Devah Pager. 2001. "Black Neighbors, Higher Crime? The role of Racial Stereotypes in Evaluations of Neighborhood Crime." *American Journal of Sociology*. 107 3: 717–767 November.

Schuman, Howard, Charlotte Steeh, Lawrence Bobo and Maria Krysan. *Racial Attitudes in America: Trends and Interpretations*. (Boston, MA: Harvard University Press, 1997).

St. John, Craig and Tamaera Hearld-Moore. 1996. "Race Prejudice and Fear of Criminalization." *Sociological Inquiry*. 66 3: 267–284.

Part IV

Racist movements and ideologies

Introduction

In the contemporary conjuncture the role of racist movements and their associated ideologies has been the subject of increasing attention, both by scholars and researchers and by civil society activists. We have seen a growing body of scholarship that has focused on both the history of these movements and, perhaps more importantly, on the ways they have evolved and changed in the contemporary period.

The opening chapter by Aurelien Mondon and Aaron Winter provides an account of the complex ways in which racist movements and the far right have sought to become part of the mainstream. Mondon and Winter begin by outlining the variety of contemporary racist movements, their diverse manifestations and ideological and historical roots. From this starting point they move on to discuss the key concepts that have been used to make sense of the range of movements that are part of this phenomenon. The chapter then explores the position of racist movements in the post-racial era, where they stand in for racism itself, and the impact of such positionality. In the concluding section of the chapter Mondon and Winter explore the ways in which the far right adapt to liberal contexts by seeking to mainstream their arguments and portray them as part of everyday political discourse.

The following chapter by Ruth Wodak approaches the question of racist ideologies through a discussion of how the language of walls is based on the racialisation of space. Wodak's focus is on the securitisation and moralisation of borders and the way they articulate ideologies of exclusion of the other. By way of illustration the chapter explores Donald Trump's argumentation for building a wall in order to keep Mexican and more generally Latin American migrants out of the US. In the concluding part of the chapter Wodak reflects on current discourses about exclusion via borders and walls, and the ways these discourses help to articulate a politics of fear.

The concluding chapter of this part, by Abby L. Ferber, is focused on the evolving role of the white supremacist movement in the US. Ferber uses the first part of the chapter to outline the analytical value of the *Matrix of Race* theory, which she sees as crucial for any rounded understanding of white supremacism. This theory uses an intersectional lens to examine both the narratives and institutions of oppression. Individuals and social identity groups are all shaped by a range of social identities, both privileged and oppressed, and interact within specific institutional, historical and geographical locations. It is on the basis of this theory that Ferber discusses the intertwined history of white supremacy and the organised white supremacist movement in the US. She then shifts her focus to the discussion of the contemporary movement. She argues that the current movement is both well organised and bolstered by a strong foundation of financial support and a wider political context that legitimates hate speech and has given rise to high levels of hate crime and far-right domestic terrorism.

12

Racist movements, the far right and mainstreaming

Aurelien Mondon and Aaron Winter

We have recently witnessed a resurgence and mainstreaming of the far right across much of the west, but also in countries like Brazil. In the UK, we have seen the deep influence of UKIP on mainstream politics, the street activism of the English Defence League (EDL) and Britain First, and wider support for anti-immigrant and anti-Muslim politics and their role in the Brexit victory. In the US, we have witnessed the election of Donald Trump, whose campaign and nativist, anti-immigrant and anti-Muslim policies have been endorsed and supported by the white nationalist alt-right and wider racist extreme right, including David Duke, the Ku Klux Klan and Stormfront. There have also been strong electoral performances in France by the Front National, Alternative für Deutschland (AfD) in Germany, Dansk Folkeparti (DF) in Denmark and Jobbik in Hungary, while Freiheitliche Partei Österreichs (FPÖ) in Austria, Lega in Italy and Fiddesz in Hungary entered government as coalition partners.

Beyond parties, new anti-immigrant and anti-Muslim protest movements such as Generation Identity, the EDL and PEGIDA have developed in Europe. These movements often have ties with parties, but provide different avenues for recruitment and allow for more radical approaches, which could prove alienating to voters for parties involved in a more mainstream strategy. In addition, there has also been a rise in hate crimes in many of these contexts. This all occurs in liberal democracies that have, since the Second World War, seen themselves as having defeated and expunged fascism, and self-righteously 'post-racial'. That is not to say that far right activity had disappeared, but that in many cases the far right came to be seen as both an unacceptable remnant of the illiberal pre-war period and embodiment of racism in the post-race context.

As Eduardo Bonilla-Silva and Victor Ray (2015) pointed out, this is not surprising as racism is commonly thought of today as 'individual-level animosity or hatred towards people of colour', and associated primarily with its most explicit and historical manifestations or representations, such as 'Klan rallies or overt racial behaviour like hanging a noose from a tree' (Bonilla-Silva with Ray 2015: 59). This perspective or take on racism not only conveniently misses ongoing structural and institutional racism and racial inequality that were not defeated with the Nazis or the Klan (before the latter's many revivals), but the discursive reconstruction of the far right in ways that displaced or concealed their racism under a liberal veneer. Following from this, it is important to note that despite the far right being widely seen as the form in which racism takes place in the post-war and post-race context, research and scholarship on what we refer to as 'racist movements', tends to occur in political science and looks at them as part of the 'extreme', 'far', 'radical' or 'populist' right, as opposed to racism proper. Racism and xenophobia are often viewed as characteristics in a terminological framework or taxonomy, as opposed to constitutive. The focus of such work tends to be where they sit on the political spectrum. Furthermore, in such studies, they are often constructed as a threat to post-war liberal democracy rather than racialised people who they target, as if liberal democracy was a safeguard in itself rather than a potential enabler of racist practices. While this is a specific analytic formulation and approach, as opposed to the traditional survey or overview, we believe it is necessary to understand the contemporary landscape of racist movements, how they emerged in particular forms, including the denial of racism and white victim narratives, and their mainstreaming.

In this chapter, we examine contemporary racist movements. In the first section, we look at what and who 'racist movements' are. In the second section, we look at a range of approaches to defining and researching racist movements, often under other labels which can sometimes sideline focus and analysis of racism. In Section 3, we look at the concept and position of racist movements in the post-racism era, where they stand in for racism itself. Finally, in the fourth section, we will look at the adaptation of the far right to liberal contexts, and mainstreaming, which challenges concepts such as 'extremist' and the function of racist movements as the embodiment of racism.

Racist movements

When considering 'racist movements', one's thoughts often turn to a series of historical and contemporary notables: The Ku Klux Klan, alt-right, Nazis, Oswald Mosley's British Union of Fascists, the National Front, British National Party (BNP), EDL, Britain First, PEGIDA, Front National, Lega and others. Yet, when the phenomenon is studied, it is often labelled instead 'extreme', 'far' or 'radical' right, and more recently and perhaps most incorrectly 'populism', with racism de-emphasised or even removed. According to Kathleen Blee (2013),

> Racist movements are organized, collective efforts to create, preserve, or extend racial hierarchies of power and privilege. Such movements explicitly espouse the ideologies of white supremacism and/or anti-Semitism (anti-Judaism or hatred of Muslims or Arabs) that were consolidated in the Western world in the eighteenth and nineteenth centuries.

While this is a good starting point, it is worth noting here that the point of reference is now discarded historical ideas. Moreover, the historical roots of such ideas do not limit their continuing transmission, legacy and structural impact, and the representation of the far right as their contemporary manifestation is a construction that distracts from that legacy, as well as systemic and liberal racism.

Although this is far from exhaustive, the types of organisations we define as racist movements include political parties, social movements (protest and street activists), violent and paramilitary, media and intellectual platforms. It may also be the case that there is overlap or duel functions and repertoires, such as in the cases of the British National Party (BNP) and Britain First which have engaged in street activism and elections, with the latter also engaging in paramilitary training and harassment during street protests. There are also larger networks and subcultures, and linked to these, (new) media platforms, such as The Daily Stormer, The Right Stuff and Gab, that allow movements, affiliated and non-affiliated individuals to participate and engage.

Within these formations are specific ideological types including fascists and neo-Nazis, white supremacists, white separatists, neo-confederates, Identitarians, anti-Muslims, anti-immigrants and combinations of these. These also contain diverse variations, such as a white supremacy or fascism founded upon specific theologies or ideologies, such as Christian Identity. They may also be regionalist, nationalist (including separatist) and/or imperialist in their identity, location or political orientation, and system or state supportive and hegemonic or oppositional and counter-hegemonic, although they are typically hegemonic in terms of race even when claiming, for example, that whites are marginalised and victimised.

It is also important to recognise the role of the individual and the ways in which racism within society allows and produces individualisation in cases of white extremism. In recent years, the 'lone wolf' trope has become increasingly popular to describe extreme right attacks, leading to some commentators lamenting on the double standards within analyses of terrorism. Attacks seemingly conducted in the name of Islam are usually treated as terrorist in nature, both by politicians and the media, while extreme right attacks, even those with clear and avowedly terrorist intent, have been portrayed as the acts of mad or bad individuals or aberrations. Yet research shows that more often than not the individual is linked to a movement or radicalised by one. This was made particularly obvious in the wake of the attack conducted by Anders Breivik on 22 July 2011 when he bombed a government building in Oslo, killing eight people, and committed a gun attack on a youth Labour Party gathering on Utøya, killing 69. He was widely described as a 'lone wolf', despite having been part of Norway's powerful far right Progress Party for a number of years. A similar kind of individualisation took place in the case of Thomas Mair who murdered UK Labour MP Jo Cox in Birstall at the height of the EU Referendum campaign. Despite clear links to a number of organisations and their programmes and ideologies, Mair was widely described as a mentally unstable loner by UKIP and Leave.EU leader Nigel Farage ('one man with serious mental health issues'); *Spiked!*'s Brendan O'Neill ('warped killer'); and *The Daily Mail* ('loner' seeking counselling) (Winter 2017).

The relationship between the extreme right, individualisation and racial privilege come together in the case of Timothy McVeigh who bombed the Murrah Federal Building in Oklahoma City on 19 April 1995, killing 168. In the *Time* magazine issue on the bombing, the cover image was of McVeigh's mugshot with the headline 'The Face of Terror'. In the related article, Elizabeth Gleick argued that 'a sense of guilty introspection swept the country when the FBI released the sketches of the suspects, distinctly Caucasian John Does one and two'. Mike Hill argued that more than guilt and introspection, the image and headline were terrifying to *Time*'s implied white readers because they rendered whiteness distinct or particular, as opposed to universal, as it became directly implicated in the terror (Hill 1997). Yet, this was wishful thinking. The hegemonic universalism that renders whiteness invisible and non-racialised (to itself) is not challenged by the act of an individual (or even a suspicious pattern of individuals, who happen to be aligned with a movement), because the opposite of white universalism is not particularism, but individualism (Winter 2010). This occurred despite his links to the wider anti-government extreme right that had been active throughout the 1980s and 1990s.

Defining and researching racist movements

While we have Blee's definition of 'racist movements', as noted, within the literature terms such as extreme, far and radical right have been used over the years, at times interchangeably, to describe a myriad of movements and parties that have racist identities and hold racist ideologies, from more mimetic iterations of fascism and Nazism to nationalist parties with no ties to historical ideologies. There is a lack of consensus, not only on the appropriate terminology, but also on which features should be used to define such a disparate ideological family, and racisms are typically only part of the picture. According to Cas Mudde in 2007:

> Without claiming to be exhaustive, titles of (comparative) books and articles in various languages on the topic include terms like extreme right, far right, radical right, right, radical right-wing populism, right-wing populism, national populism, new populism, neopopulism, exclusionary populism, populist nationalism, ethno-nationalism, anti-immigrant, nativism, racism, racist extremism, fascism, neofascism, postfascism, reactionary tribalism, integralism, antipartyism. The terminology chaos is not the result of fundamental difference of opinion over the correct definition; rather, it is largely the consequence of a lack of clear definition.

The term used depends on a variety of factors, including context, politics (of the movement and scholar) and discipline. Literature on these comes primarily from Political Science and Politics, and includes country and movement case studies, electoral analysis, organisation analysis, ideological (type) analysis, as well as work on (and long-standing debates about) definitions themselves.

Throughout the 1990s and until the late 2000s, the term extreme right was probably the most commonly used to describe the resurgence of parties such as the Front National or the Freedom Party of Austria (FPÖ). Mudde (1997) has listed at least fifty-eight possible characteristics which identify and define the extreme right, including racism, anti-Semitism, xenophobia, anti-communism, nationalism, patriotism, libertarianism or authoritarianism, paramilitarism, violence, terrorism and conspiracism. Such taxonomic definitions allow for the identification and inclusion of new phenomena, although they are typically based on manifestations in different historical, political and geographical contexts. Where new characteristics are encountered these can be included and the category can be expanded. As such, taxonomic definitions can be either analytically reductionist in their application, historically presentist in their use or apply to characteristics that exist across the political spectrum, including the mainstream at times. It should also be noted that there was also an uptake in uses of and scholarship on 'fascism' (and varieties thereof) applied to contemporary movements at the same time, highlighting the shadow cast by Nazism on the recognition and analysis of later movements and parties (see Griffin 1993, 1995).

The use of the term extreme right changed with the influential work carried by Mudde on the populist radical right in the mid-2000s, which he defined as having three main characteristics: nativism, authoritarianism and populism. More recently, we have also witnessed the revival (and hype) of the term populism in response to Brexit, Trump and so-called radical right populist parties in Europe (Glynos and Mondon 2016). We have also seen the rise of new terminology, such as the alt-right, coined by leader Richard Spencer, which has not only added to the number of terms used, but led to debates over the use of movement self-definition by the media, researchers and analysts, particularly as this one conceals the movement's extremism, racism, white supremacism/white nationalism and fascism under the more acceptable and edgy 'alt'/alternative moniker. Moreover, it is also a looser network of activists than traditional movements, and operates on diverse online and offline platforms. In a sense though, these characteristics may also be key to understanding media interest and the movement's success mainstreaming racist extreme right ideas (Winter 2019).

These issues are complicated further by attempts to position these parties and movements on the political spatial spectrum, and what status their defining characteristics, such as racism, have in contemporary society. For example, Minkenberg (1997: 84–85) argues that these parties and movements 'are "extreme" not in terms of being against or outside the existing constitutional order but in terms of being extreme within it'. They abide by 'a belief system that does not share the values of the political order within which it operates'. Martin Durham (2000: xii) has attempted to establish clear taxonomic definitions and boundaries between the mainstream, extreme, far and radical right. Those committed to white suprem- acy and anti-Semitism are best defined as extreme right, while non-racist conspiracists are best defined as radical right. Where there is ambiguity, indecision or overlap, Durham makes use of the term far right.

In our definition and approach, we foreground racism and have decided to reserve the use the term extreme right for those movements and activists who express illiberal articulations of racism and may engage in violence. We use the term far right to describe movements and parties that espouse a racist ideology, but do so in an indirect, coded or even covert manner, by focusing notably on culture and/or occupying the space between illiberal and liberal racisms, between the extreme and the mainstream. This can be witnessed in what we call the reconstructed far right. Such movements and parties may challenge mainstream parties and be more explicit in their ideologies and agendas, but these differences are exaggerated by the mainstream to establish its liberal self-image and hegemony.

If anything, all of this tells us that how we understand and define such phenomena is not fixed across different historical and political contexts and disciplines. These differ- ences can reflect changes to the movements in question, their relationship to the main- stream or centre, what is acceptable political discourse, and the function of such terminology (or the scholars' analysis or objectives). It is worth noting here that the term 'radical right' was coined by Seymour Martin Lipset (1955), to describe movements, organisations and actors, including the Ku Klux Klan, John Birch Society and McCarthy- ism, that sought 'far-reaching changes in American institutions', rejecting tolerance, establishment conservatism and democratic procedures, such as lobbying and the ballot box, in favour of agitation and practices which threatened 'to undermine the social fabric of democratic politics'. While Lipset identified the rejection of tolerance as a characteristic, the conceptualisation can be seen as a normative defence of the main- stream liberal democratic system and order, which was racist and anti-communist, and its accepted procedures, which were also used to express and maintain these. Crucially, these new movements, and associated typologies, coincided with the emergence of the post-war liberal order, the second phase of the Cold War (both following the defeat of the Nazis) and the American battle over desegregation and civil rights. Paul Hainsworth's framing of his book *The Politics of the Extreme Right: From the Margins to the Mainstream*, a central concern of the early 2000s literature, is telling here:

> historians and political commentators will look back upon a century of extremism, in which fascism and intolerance figured prominently, and to devastating effect. Total war, Holocaust, ethnic cleansing and scapegoating of 'the Other' have marked the past hun- dred years of Western civilization. The mid-point of the century, of course, witnessed the defeat of Nazi and fascist forces and signalled – in the West – the victory of liberal democratic ideas, rooted in pluralism, multi-partyism, a renewed assertion of dignity of the individual and a respect for human rights.
>
> *(Hainsworth 2000: 1)*

While fascism and Nazism cast a shadow over the definitions and analysis, and for Lipset and Raab *The Politics of Unreason: Right Wing Extremism in America, 1790–1970* (1970), desegregation and civil rights provide the context, it is notable that racism is not foregrounded or prioritised in work on the extreme, far or radical right. This is partly because of the dominance of political scientists working on the topic. There is also work in other disciplines that addresses race and racism more prominently, particularly in Sociology, Social Psychology, Criminology, History, Anthropology and Politics. The terms used for the movements in question include racist movements, hate groups, and, to a lesser extent, extreme and far right. Notable examples include Michael Billig's *Fascists: A Social Psychological View of the National Front* (1979), Raphael Ezekiel's *The Racist Mind: Portraits of American Neo-Nazis and Klansmen* (1996), Jessie Daniels' *White Lies: Race, Class, Gender, and Sexuality in White Supremacist Discourse* (1997), Jeffrey Kaplan and Tore Bjorgo's edited collection *Nation and Race: The Developing Euro-American Racist Subculture* (1998), Kathleen Blee's *Inside Organized Racism: Women in the Hate Movement* (2002) and more recent *Understanding Racist Activism: Theory, Methods, and Research* (2018), and Sindre Bangstad's *Anders Breivik and the Rise of Islamophobia* (2014). There are also studies of movements, that focus more on racism, in terms of a range of sub-themes and issues, utilising a range of methods and theoretical approaches. A non-exhaustive list with a small selection of examples includes: activism (Dobratz and Shanks-Meile 2000; Klandermans and Mayer 2006; Simi and Futrell 2015); gender (Blee 2002; Daniels 1997; Ferber 1998; Sanders-McDonagh 2018); online (Back, Keith and Solomos 1998; Daniels 2009; Perry and Scrivens 2016; Winter 2019); history (Berlet and Lyons 2000; Chalmers 1965; Copsey and Richardson 2015; Copsey and Worley 2018; Macklin 2007; Webb 2010; Winter 2018); class (Rhodes 2011; Rydgren 2012); popular culture (King and Leonard 2014; Miller-Idriss 2017); terrorism and violence (Adamczyk, Gruenewald, Chermak and Freilich 2014; Winter 2010, 2018); mainstreaming (Mondon 2013; Winter 2017, 2019), and specific country-based cases (e.g. Mondon 2014 on France); and a wealth of work on the alt-right in the current context (Hawley 2017; Neiwert 2017; Wendling 2018). There is also work (including amongst these examples) that focus on movements and organisations or individuals, particular contexts or comparative analysis, while some are critical analyses and others more practical problem solving in function (e.g. deradicalisation, security and policing). There is also some work in the field of race and racism studies, that addresses racist movements, but they are positioned as a minor aspect or part of the landscape of contemporary racism that is largely defined and determined by structural and institutional forms (e.g. Anderson 2016; Bonilla-Silva 2001; Omi and Winant 1994; Solomos 2003; Wieviorka 1995) This is something that needs to be highlighted as racist movements can often stand in for and/or distract from racisms more broadly.

Racist movements and post-racial

Just like the fact that when racist movements are studied, their racism can be de-emphasised, in some cases when they are the focus of study or when racism is discussed in the media and wider society, ironically, such racist movements come to stand in for and embody racism itself. We can see this in past and current panics about the far right bringing racism back into the mainstream, or the denial of systemic and everyday racism that is based on a comparison to 'real' racism from the past or in extreme forms, which we call illiberal. Often, these are based on the notion that racism has been defeated, because the Nazis or the Klan have, and paradoxically, that mimetic acts are the only remaining forms, thus foreclosing on recognition of systemic and contemporary mainstream forms and manifestations.

Examples of this could be seen particularly in responses to Obama's election. In one editorial image, 'Obama and resigned KKK member', by Riber Hansson (2008), Obama is shown walking up the White House passing a Klansman looking downcast and leaning on his cross. Of the election, Richard Cohen (2008), of the *Washington Post*, wrote 'it is not just that he is post-racial; so is the nation he is generationally primed to lead', and quoting Lyndon Johnson, 'we have overcome'. The image used is of police attacking voting rights marchers at the Edmund Pettus Bridge, which was still named after the former Senator and Grand Dragon of the Alabama Klan, in Selma on 'Bloody Sunday', 7 March 1965.

In the UK, following the post-Brexit rise in hate crimes, Brendan O'Neill (2016), the editor of far right libertarian *Spiked!* argued in *The Spectator*:

> there is a great disparity between the handwringing over hate crime and what Britain is actually like. The open racism even I can remember in the 1980s has all but vanished … The likes of the BNP and EDL have withered due to lack of interest.

UKIP founder and former leader Nigel Farage (2016) claimed that:

> I destroyed the British National Party – we had a far right party in this country who genuinely were anti-Jew, anti-Black, all of those things, and I came along, and said to their voters, if you're holding your nose and voting for this party as a protest, don't. Come and vote for me – I'm not against anybody, I just want us to start putting British people first, and I, almost single-handedly, destroyed the far right in British politics.

This occurred despite, or perhaps because of, the fact that UKIP is widely seen as the inheritor of the BNP's politics and a mainstreaming version, something we will return to in the section on discursive reconstruction. In France, Jean-Marie Le Pen was for a long time used as a scarecrow, and regularly described as the 'filthy beast' (*la bête immonde*), a direct reference to Nazism and fascism. This in turn facilitated the ignorance of racism within mainstream politics in France, particularly expressed towards Muslim communities, but also allowed Marine Le Pen to pitch herself as moderate compared to her father, while being literally the heir of the old order.

It is often an effect or product of historical narratives that celebrate victory over historical enemies. This can be seen in post-war celebrations of the defeat of Nazism across the liberal democratic west, as well as more specifically in the more recent case of Winston Churchill, whose racism is defended with recourse to both being a man of his time and having defeated the Nazis (no comment on Empire and colonial racism which continued) (Burrows 2018; Sky News 2019). This narrative would be replayed for all of Britain following the defeat of post-war fascists such as the National Front in the 1980s and the BNP in early 2000s, as the O'Neill quotation illustrated. Whereas in the US, the ability to conflate racism and the extreme (as well as far) right separates them both from the mainstream, and sees them as defeated, a discursive construction that furnishes the post-racial narrative and mythology that accompanied Obama's election was the product of a series of developments in the 1960s. These were the FBI COINTELPRO White Hate Groups Programme from 1964 and HUAC hearings into the Activities of the Ku Klux Klan Organization from 1965, which condemned the group as terrorists and un-American, which greatly diminished the organisation just as Civil Rights and Voting Rights had passed (Winter 2018), paving the way for post-race.

The notion that racism is defined by the extreme or far right is part of the construction of what we term 'illiberal racism'. This is racism defined by extreme and historical movements, such as Nazism, the Klan or National Front, as well as corresponding beliefs and ideologies such as biological racism, white supremacy and blood and soil nationalism, and practices such as slavery, colonialism, and segregation, which were once part of the mainstream, but have been cast out as illiberal and unacceptable in the liberal post-war and post-civil rights eras. This is evident when Hainsworth refers to Nazism in his analysis of the mainstreaming of the extreme right and Blee defines racist movements in terms of racist ideologies of the eighteenth and nineteenth centuries. Yet, this ignores systemic racism and inequality in favour of the illusion (and defence) of colourblindness and perpetuation of colourblind or liberal racism.

This echoes Bonilla-Silva's 'racism without racists' (2006), and particularly, his two frames of abstract liberalism and cultural racism. The former is 'an abstract manner to explain racial matters' and even celebrate racial progress (as a liberal achievement): with each person being now equal in rights and opportunity, proof of which is based on individual achievement universalised, white people can righteously claim that barriers have been lifted and the onus in on the (liberal) individual to make their own life, ignoring thus the structural and systemic racial inequalities still in place.

According to Tim Wise, commenting on this liberal post-racial frame being used in reference to Obama, the election did not signify the death of racism, but the usurpation of 'Racism 1.0,' the 'old-fashioned bigotry … that has long marked the nation's history: the kind that, in its most extreme moments has precipitated racist murder, lynching, and terror' (illiberal racism in our terms) by 'Racism 2.0.' (Wise 2009: 26). That is, 'enlightened exceptionalism a form that allows for and even celebrates the achievements of individual persons of color' (abstract liberalism in Bonilla-Silva's terms and liberal racism in ours). Yet, as Wise points out supports, 'Racism 1.0' persists and 'animates hate groups and hate crimes' (Wise 2009: 26), something we saw in the racist extreme and far right backlash to Obama's election and resurgence under Trump.

The second frame, cultural racism, shifts the focus from race to culture (and religion in the case of Muslims) and blame that for the inferior standing of minorities (see also Balibar and Wallerstein 1997; Barker 1982). We see this in movements and discourses that deny their racism and articulate it through liberal causes, such as women's rights, LGBTQ+ rights, free speech and democracy (Mondon and Winter 2017a), which has been central to what we term 'discursive reconstruction' and one of the keys to mainstreaming.

Discursive reconstruction, the liberal turn and mainstreaming

If the war marked a shift in how racism was perceived, so too did the social upheaval of the 1960s and 1970s. The extreme right would play the functional role of illiberal scarecrow for the liberal mainstream to distract from the liberal racism. While some embraced this extremism, others attempted to reshape their discourse and strategy to adapt to their new context in a more counter-hegemonic fashion. In the post-war period, the Klan very much played the functional boogieman in the US. Yet, what is often ignored is just how embedded in the mainstream they were. While the American far right moved from the mainstream to the extreme in the post-civil rights era, abandoning the state for political insurgency, white supremacy for white separatism, Protestantism for Christian Identity and Odinism and the Klan for more overtly fascist movements such as Aryan Nations and National Alliance, in Europe the picture would be different (at least until the Trump era and emergence of the alt-right).

The response to the post-war and post-1960s consensus involved a process of discursive reconstruction to ensure electoral credibility. While the process has been uneven and has very much depended on context, some trends have become common in the reshaping of extreme right politics into more moderate far right politics. The impetus towards discursive reconstruction really took shape in the 1980s, when groups of intellectuals devised ways for the extreme right to escape the position it had been forced in after the defeat of fascism in the Second World War. The illiberal nature of extreme right discourse, based on biological racism and fascist nostalgia, was further marginalised by the rise of progressive counter-movements in the 1960s based on second-wave feminist, civil rights, anti-colonial and anti-racist ideas. As extreme right support reached a nadir and as conservative mainstream parties on the right were forced to give way to a number of progressive measures, it became necessary for the more strategically-minded actors on the right-wing fringe of politics to seek a way out of the margins without diluting their ideological roots. For this to be possible, the extreme right needed to engage in a process of discursive reconstruction which would provide it with a way into the mainstream by separating it from the more illiberal forms of right-wing politics. This manifested in their discursive rejection of the extreme right, although links between both would remain alive, albeit concealed. Biological racism was increasingly replaced by the cultural racism referred to by Bonilla-Silva, mostly targeted against Muslim communities, and populism became central to their discourse.

In France, this would see the Front National (see amongst others, Crépon, Dézé and Mayer 2015; Mondon 2013, 2014) initiated by neo-fascist Ordre Nouveau in 1972 and led by fascist, anti-Semite Jean-Marie Le Pen, their first president, move away from crude racism, and instead focus on 'culture' and Islam as a convenient scapegoat. This would be something which proved particularly effective in France where the concept of *laïcité* (secularism) had already turned into a reactionary tool to push racist agendas (Mondon 2015). In the 21st century, and even more so under the new leadership of Marine Le Pen, who embraced liberal tropes of free speech and women's rights, as well as philosemitism, against Muslims and the illiberal fascism of her father's party.

In the UK, the story was again different. Pre-war, the extreme right was represented by Oswald Mosley's British Union of Fascists and post-war by the National Front. Yet, the place occupied by the nation as the last standing bulwark against Nazism and fascism in the Second World War has given a particular twist to the way the extreme and far right have organised This was made particularly clear when Nick Griffin tried to use Spitfires in one of his BNP campaign posters, and faced near universal condemnation as he was automatically linked to the enemy of this national emblem of the fight against the Nazis. The BNP, formed in 1982, proved similarly unsuccessful at shedding its extreme right image decisively despite a few breakthroughs in the 2000s. It was UKIP's lack of ties to the traditional extreme right and Euroscepticism as opposed to open racism that has allowed supporters of a more reconstructed approach.

Of particular interest is the way UKIP followed an almost inverted trajectory to that of the FN. Farage's UKIP moved beyond traditional Euroscepticism, found in large swathes of the Conservative party, adding a more targeted fear of the other in the form of Brussels, immigrants and Islam. At the same time, the UK experienced the EDL, whose founder Stephen Yaxley-Lennon (a.k.a. Tommy Robinson) styled the organisation as both a voice of the working class and champion of free speech, women's and LGBT rights against Islam and Muslims. As the climate became increasingly polarised and far right (and to a lesser extent more extreme right) issues mainstreamed, what Robinson would say in the late 2010s was no longer as shocking to elite discourse, as when he said it a decade prior from the confines of the extreme right. In fact, like Farage, Robinson was feted by the media and given a frequent platform by the BBC and other outlets (Mondon and Winter 2017b).

Many books and articles have focused on the ways the discourse of parties and movements once considered toxic has evolved or been adapted: 'From the margins to the mainstream' has become a popular refrain since the early 2000s (see for example Akkerman, de Lange and Rooduijn 2016; Hainsworth 2000). Recent events such as Brexit, Trump's election, and the strong performance of a number of far-right parties across Europe have made it an ever more debated issue. This was compounded by a rise in everyday racism and hate crimes, extreme and far right marches and rallies, and mainstream establishment parties legitimising the anti-immigrant and anti-Islam discourse. (see Mondon and Winter 2019). We argue that mainstreaming is indeed very much a two-way process and that it cannot take place with the far right as sole agent (e.g. merely moderating): no matter how hard a far right party tries to reform itself, if the broader political system is not open to welcoming it and/or its ideas, it is bound to remain at the margins. The breakthrough of far-right politics has thus necessitated the help of mainstream actors such as politicians of course, but also the media and academics to legitimise, if not their cause, their presence in the political debate. A sense of crisis and urgency is essential for far-right ideas to make their way into the mainstream as they require a derogation from the current (and contingent) norms. This is almost always related to the perceived pressure created by the other, whether they are internal (and even citizens at times such as Muslims, Jews or 'second/third-generation immigrants') or external (refugees, asylum seekers, immigrants). While we are now seeing fascists marching, it is worth noting that the soft liberal racism, which had once denounced the illiberal racism or the far right, also allowed them back in the mainstream through media platforming (e.g. Richard Spencer and Tommy Robinson), free speech, moderation, populist hype and more.

In the UK, we have seen the normalisation of anti-immigrant and anti-Muslim ideas and discourses within the mainstream in ways that legitimise and even mainstream the ideas of the far right, as well as embolden them. Sometimes this is done by mainstream political parties to fend off the alleged threat by the far right (such as the BNP after their electoral success in the early 2000s), but other times this is merely used as justification. This includes the Tory Party's 'Go Home' vans, the 'hostile environment' and Prevent, which have all been used as dog-whistle politics to appease far right voters, emboldening the extreme and far right and ignoring the impact this has had on immigrants, refugees and Muslims and the mainstreaming of certain discourses. In France, this is epitomised by the positioning of Islam and Muslim communities as the other to the concept of *laïcité*, increasingly understood in reactionary terms. The ban of the hijab in schools in 2004, the burqa in 2010 and more recently the burkini affair in 2016 have all entrenched ideas which were once found on the margins, within the extreme right. In the US, it took Trump's rhetoric about Muslims and Mexicans in the campaign (and even-tually office) to bring the extreme and far right in from the cold of the post-civil rights era, but he did not do this alone. It took the influence of Breitbart editor and later Trump advisor Steve Bannon, the emergent alt-right and alt-lite with their white identitarianism and social media savvy, and endorsements from Spencer, Duke and the wider racist extreme right. The mainstreaming process does not only take place through far right and politicians' actions, but the mainstream media and academics have also played a key role in normalising and legitimis-ing liberal Islamophobia and the notion that the 'people' or 'white working class' are in revolt against immigration and Islam in the UK, US and France, and more widely, in ways that make these politics appear democratic as opposed to extreme right (see Mondon and Winter 2018, 2019). What is worth noting is that the mainstreaming process that was founded upon the liberal turn emboldened fascists and white supremacists (and in some cases allowed them back in the fold), but also racist and authoritarian policies from liberal states that used to define themselves in opposition to racist, extremist movements.

Conclusion

This chapter provides an overview of the literature, definitions and debates about racist movements, particularly focused on the ways in which racism is constructed, ignored or displaced within these. We also offer an analysis of the ways in which racist movements (particularly historical manifestations) have stood in for racism in the post-war and later post-racial contexts. We argue that this has made it more difficult to see racism in its deeper, more entrenched systemic forms, but also to understand how such movements have adapted, transformed and mainstreamed, and undergone a resurgence in both liberal and more traditional fascist forms. As a number of parties and movements have reached the gates of power, whether themselves as in the case of the FPÖ in Austria and the Lega in Italy by means of coalition, or through infiltration and radicalisation as was the case for Trump and Orban in Hungary, understanding the role of racism and its impact in our societies is urgent. To do this, it is essential that we move beyond the impact and actions of these parties and movements, but also engage with the role of mainstream actors in the hype and normalisation of certain discourses. Without such a holistic approach, we believe that any victory against the rise of the far right and continuation of racism as a structural and systemic issue will be shortlived.

References

Adamczyk, Amy, Gruenewald, Jeff, Chermak, Steven, and Freilich, Joshua 2014. 'The Relationship between Hate Groups and Far-Right Ideological Violence'. *Journal of Contemporary Criminal Justice*, 30(3): 310–332.

Akkerman, Tjitske, de Lange, Sarah L., and Rooduijn, Matthijs eds. 2016. *Radical Right-Wing Populist Parties in Western Europe: Into the Mainstream?* London: Routledge.

Anderson, Carole. 2016. *White Rage: The Unspoken Truth about Our Racial Divide*. New York: Bloomsbury.

Back, Les, Keith, Michael, and Solomos, John 1998. 'Racism on the Internet: Mapping Neo-Fascist Subcultures in Cyberspace'. *Nation and Race: The Developing Euro-American Racist Subculture*, eds. Jeffrey Kaplan and Tore Bjorgo. Boston: Northeastern University Press, pp. 73–101.

Balibar, Etienne and Wallerstein, Immanuel. 1997. *Race, Nation, Classe; les identités ambiguës*. Paris: la Découverte.

Bangstad, Sindre. 2014. *Anders Breivek and the Rise of Islamophobia*. London: Zed Books.

Barker, Martin. 1982. *The New Racism: Conservatives and the Ideology of the Tribe*. Frederick: Aletheia Books.

Berlet, Chip and Lyons, Matthew N. 2000. *Right-Wing Populism in America: Too Close for Comfort*. New York: The Guilford Press.

Billig, Michael. 1979. *Fascists: A Social Psychological View of the National Front*. London: Academic Press.

Blee, Kathleen. 2002. *Inside Organized Racism: Women in the Hate Movement*. Berkeley: University of California Press.

Blee, Kathleen. 2013. 'Racist Social Movements'. *The Wiley-Blackwell Encyclopedia of Social and Political Movements*, eds. David A. Snow, Donatella della Porta, Bert Klandermans and Doug McAdam. doi: 10.1002/9780470674871.wbespm443.

Blee, Kathleen. 2018. *Understanding Racist Activism: Theory, Methods, and Research*. New York: Routledge.

Bonilla-Silva, Eduardo. 2001. *White Supremacy & Racism in the Post-Civil Rights Era*. Boulder: Rienner.

Bonilla-Silva, Eduardo. 2006. *Racism without Racists: Color-Blind Racism and the Persistence of Racial Inequality in the United States*. New York: Rowman & Littlefield.

Bonilla-Silva, Eduardo with Ray, Victor. 2015. 'Getting over the Obama Hope Hangover: The New Racism in "Post-racial" America'. *Theories of Race and Ethnicity: Contemporary Debates and Perspectives*, eds. Karim Murji and John Solomos. Cambridge: Cambridge University Press, pp. 57–73.

Burrows, Thomas. 2018, 9 Oct. 'Why Live in a Country You Loathe?'. The Sun. www.thesun.co.uk/news/7452049/piers-morgan-in-extraordinary-gmb-row-with-professor-who-branded-winston-churchill-a-racist-after-astronaut-was-forced-to-delete-tweet-praising-wartime-leader/

Chalmers, David. 1965. *Hooded Americanism: The First Century of the Ku Klux Klan 1865–1965*. Garden City: Doubleday.

Cohen, Richard. 2008. 'The Election That LBJ Won'. Washington Post. 4 November.

Copsey, Nigel and Richardson, Nigel eds. 2015. *Cultures of Post-War British Fascism*. Abingdon: Routledge.

Copsey, Nigel and Worley, Matthew eds. 2018. *Tomorrow Belongs to Us: The British Far Right Since 1967*. Abingdon: Routledge.

Crépon, Sylvain, Dézé, Alexandre, and Mayer, Nonna eds. 2015. 'Les faux-semblants du Front National'. Les Presses de Sciences Po.

Daniels, Jessie. 1997. *White Lies: Race, Class, Gender, and Sexuality in White Supremacist Discourse*. New York: Routledge.

Daniels, Jessie. 2009. *Cyber Racism: White Supremacy Online and the New Attack on Civil Rights*. Lanham: Rowman & Littlefield.

Dobratz, Betty A. and Shanks-Meile, Stephanie L. 2000. 'The White Separatist Movement in the United States: "White Power, White Pride!"'. Baltimore: Johns Hopkins University Press.

Durham, Martin. 2000. *The Christian Right, the Far Right and the Boundaries of American Conservatism*. Manchester: Manchester University Press.

Ezekiel, Raphael S. 1996. *The Racist Mind: Portraits of American Neo-Nazis and Klansmen*. London: Penguin.

Farage, Nigel via Press Association. 2016. 'Nigel Farage: I Destroyed Far-Right in British Politics'. The Daily Echo.

Ferber, Abby L. 1998. *White Man Falling: Race, Gender, and White Supremacy*. London: Rowman & Littlefield.

Glynos, Jason and Mondon, Aurelien. 2016. 'The Political Logic of Populist Hype: The Case of Right-Wing Populism's 'Meteoric Rise' and Its Relation to the Status Quo'. *Populismus Working Paper Series* No. 4.

Griffin, Roger. 1993. *The Nature of Fascism*. London: Routledge.

Griffin, Roger. 1995. *Fascism*. Oxford: Oxford University Press.

Hainsworth, Paul. 2000. *The Politics of the Extreme Right: From the Margins to the Mainstream*. London: Pinter.

Hansson, Ribor. 2008. 'Obama and Resigned KKK Member'. Cagle Cartoons.

Hawley, George. 2017. *Making Sense of the Alt-Right*. New York: Columbia University Press.

Hill, Mike. 1997. 'Can Whiteness Speak? Institutional Anomies, Ontological Disasters, and Three Hollywood Films'. *White Trash: Race and Class in America*, eds. Annalee Newitz and Matt Wray. New York: Routledge, p. 172.

Kaplan, Jeffrey and Bjorgo, Tore eds. 1998. *Nation and Race: The Developing Euro-American Racist Subculture*. Boston: Northeastern University Press.

King, C. Richard and Leonard, David J. 2014. *Beyond Hate: White Power and Popular Culture*. Farnham: Ashgate.

Klandermans, Bert and Mayer, Nonna. 2006. *Extreme Right Activists in Europe*. Abingdon: Routledge.

Lipset, Seymour Martin. 1955. 'The Sources of the "Radical Right"'. *The New American Right*, ed. Daniel Bell. New York: Criterion Books, pp. 166–234.

Lipset, Seymour Martin and Raab, Earl. 1970. *The Politics of Unreason: Right Wing Extremism in America, 1790–1970*. New York: Harper & Row.

Macklin, Graham. 2007. *'Very Deeply Dyed in Black': Oswald Mosley and the Resurrection of British Fascism after 1945*. London: IB Tauris.

Miller-Idriss, Cynthia. 2017. *The Extreme Gone Mainstream: Commercialization and Far Right Youth Culture in Germany*. Princeton: Princeton University Press.

Minkenberg, Michael. 1997. 'The New Right in France and Germany: Nouvelle Droite, Neue Rechte, and the New Right Radical Parties'. *The Revival of Right-Wing Extremism in the 90s*, eds. Peter Merkl and Leonard Weinberg. London: Frank Cass, pp. 65–90.

Mondon, Aurelien. 2013. *The Mainstreaming of the Extreme Right in France and Australia: A Populist Hegemony?* Farnham: Ashgate.

Mondon, Aurelien. 2014. 'The Front National in the Twenty-First Century: From Pariah to Republican Democratic Contender?'. *Modern and Contemporary France*, 22(3): 301–320.

Mondon, Aurelien. 2015. 'The French Secular Hypocrisy: The Extreme Right, the Republic and the Battle for Hegemony'. *Patterns of Prejudice*, 49(3): 392–413.

Mondon, Aurelien and Winter, Aaron. 2017a. 'Articulations of Islamophobia: From the Extreme to the Mainstream?'. *Ethnic and Racial Studies*, 13(40): 2151–2179.

Mondon, Aurelien and Winter, Aaron. 2017b. 'Normalized Hate'. Jacobin. https://jacobinmag.com/2017/08/islamophobia-racism-uk-far-right

Mondon, Aurelien and Winter, Aaron. 2018. 'Whiteness, Populism and the Racialisation of the Working Class in the United Kingdom and the United States'. Identities, Online first.

Mondon, Aurelien and Winter, Aaron. 2019. *Reactionary Democracy: Racism, Populism, the Far Right and 'the People'*. London: Verso.

Mudde, Cas. 1997. *The Extreme Right Party Family: An Ideological Approach. Leiden University.* Leiden, Netherlands: Leiden University is the Publisher.

Mudde, Cas. 2007. *Populist Radical Right Parties in Europe*. Cambridge: Cambridge University Press.

Neiwert, David. 2017. *Alt-America: The Rise of the Radical Right in the Age of Trump*. London: Verso.

O'Neill, Brendan. 2016. 'Britain's Real Hate Crime Scandal'. The Spectator. 6 August.

Omi, Michael and Winant, Howard. 1994. *Racial Formation in the United States: From the 1960s to the 1990s.* New York: Routledge.

Perry, Barbara and Scrivens, Ryan. 2016. 'White Pride Worldwide: Constructing Global Identities Online'. *The Globalisation of Hate: Internationalising Hate Crime?* eds. Jennifer Schweppe and Mark Austin Walters. London: Oxford University Press, pp. 65–78.

Rhodes, James. 2011. 'It's Not Just Them, It's Whites as Well': Whiteness, Class and BNP Support'. *Sociology*, 45(1): 102–117.

Rydgren, Jens. 2012. *Class Politics and the Radical Right*. Abingdon: Routledge.

Sanders-McDonagh, Erin. 2018. 'Women's Support for UKIP: Exploring Gender, Nativism, and the Populist Radical Right (PRR)'. *Gendering Nationalism: Articulating Nation, Gender and Sexuality*, eds. Jon Mulholland, Erin Sanders-McDonagh and Nicola Montanga. London: Palgrave MacMillam, pp. 203–219.

Simi, Pete and Futrell, Robert. 2015. *American Swastika: Inside the White Power Movement's Hidden Spaces of Hate.* Lanham: Rowman & Littlefield.

Sky News. 2019, 14 Feb. 'Was Winston Churchill a "Racist" or "Man of His Time"?'. https://news.sky.com/video/was-winston-churchill-a-racist-or-man-of-his-time-11637578

Solomos, John. 2003. *Race and Racism in Britain*. London: Palgrave-Macmillan.

Webb, Clive. 2010. *Rabble Rousers: The American Far Right in the Civil Rights Era*. Athens: University of Georgia Press.

Wendling, Mike. 2018. *Alt-Right: From 4chan to the White House*. London: Pluto Press.

Wieviorka, Michel. 1995. *The Arena of Racism*. London: Sage.

Winter, Aaron. 2010. 'American Terror: From Oklahoma City to 9/11 and after'. *Discourses and Practices of Terrorism: Interrogating Terror*, eds. Bob Brecher, Mark Devenney and Aaron Winter. Abingdon: Routledge, pp. 156–176.

Winter, Aaron. 2017, 2 Apr. 'Brexit and Trump: On Racism, the Far Right and Violence'. Institute for Policy Research (IPR) Blog. http://blogs.bath.ac.uk/iprblog/2017/04/03/brexit-and-trump-on-racism-the-far-right-and-violence/

Winter, Aaron. 2018. 'The Klan is History: A Historical Perspective on the Revival of the Far-Right in "post-Racial" America'. *Historical Perspectives on Organised Crime and Terrorism*, eds. John Morrison, Andrew Silke, James Windle and Aaron Winter.. Abingdon: Routledge, pp. 109–132.

Winter, Aaron. 2019. 'Online Hate: From the Far-Right to the "Alt-Right", and from the Margins to the Mainstream'. *Online Othering: Exploring Violence and Discrimination on the Web*, eds. Emily Harmer and Karen Lumsden.. London: Palgrave MacMillam, pp. 39–63.

Wise, Tim. 2009. *Between Barack and a Hard Place: Racism and White Denial in the Age of Obama*. San Francisco: City Lights Books.

13

The language of walls

Inclusion, exclusion, and the racialization of space

Ruth Wodak

Introduction: some functions of walls[1]

In his important book *Steinzeit. Mauern in Berlin* (2011), the cultural theorist Olaf Briese describes the multi-layered foundations—including various remains of walls—on which the city of Berlin has been built over the centuries. Walls, he claims, have many functions: First and most importantly, walls protect the citizens inside from invaders trying to destroy the walls and capture the respective cities during wartimes (ibid. 316ff.). Briese thus traces the protective intention behind the construction of walls from the fortresses of ancient times to the castles and citadels of the Middle Ages. Second, walls also serve to protect cities and villages from floods and other natural catastrophes (ibid. 69ff.). Third, they allow trading while regulating the access of people and goods. In this way, *walls function as distinct borders* though the latter are, however, not set in stone, as they can be renegotiated, closed, and opened according to various political interests (De Chaine 2012; Lehner 2019). As Vollmer (2017b) rightly argues, borders (and walls) distinguish those people who are considered to be *deserving* to enter cities and countries from those who are—usually quite arbitrarily—defined as not deserving.

The fall of the Berlin Wall in 1989 and the subsequent advent of an international system whereby the principle of state sovereignty seemed bound to wane "left little reason to expect a return of the wall" (e.g. Briese 2011: 369ff; Vallet & David 2012: 111). However, the 9/11 terrorist attacks and the huge migration flows since 2013 and 2014 sparked a dramatic surge in wall-building around the world, mostly undertaken by liberal democratic governments which have employed and continue to employ a range of legitimation strategies to substantiate their ever stricter politics of exclusion. Thus, it appears as if wall-building has been re-established and sanctioned as a legitimate strategy to control state borders. As Sicurella (2018: 60) maintains in his analysis of Croatian and Bosnian debates about borders and walls in 2015:

> although current deterritorialization discourses have enabled us to interpret borders in a less deterministic way than in the past, it has become clear that the "hard" and

often coercive nature of their material embodiment cannot and should not be under-estimated; […] an epistemological shift has taken place in the way borders are theorized.

Borders can be conceptualized as social constructions, historically contingent, embedded in their sociopolitical contexts; they express power relations and have a material reality—potentially resemiotized as walls—as well as a symbolic meaning (Paasi 2012). Unlike previous conceptualizations of walls and borders as historical, factual, stable, and material entities, recent approaches highlight their various (in)visible manifestations (Konrad 2015) and their capacity to (re)produce social orders, inequalities, inclusions, and exclusions as well as differentiations. Following Van Houtum (2010), processes of differentiation and constructions of a dangerous Other are crucial to imaginations of symbolic and material walls and borders, regulating who is allowed to enter a given territory and who is not (Bickham Mendez and Naples 2015a: 24). Walls in their function as borders are material *and* social constructions; thus, bordering must be understood as a practice involving those who decide on and implement exclusionary and inclusionary practices (e.g. politicians, border guards, or soldiers) (Bickham Mendez and Naples 2015b: 375).

In ancient times, walls defined and preserved important sites of public discussion for some and not for others (for example, slaves and women were excluded from democratic deliberations and decision-making in the ἀγορά (agora; *market-place*); e.g. Camp 1989; Briese 2011: 29). City walls also used to protect the healthy from the ill (e.g. leper colonies constructed outside of city walls, ibid. 139ff). Walls surrounding cemeteries guard the dead and separate them from the living, i.e. the "pure" space from the "impure" (in Judaism for example), in ritualized ways as prescribed in a range of religions (ibid. 293–295). Moreover, walls encircling prisons and prison camps (such as labor camps, the Stalinist gulags, the Nazi concentration camps, and the US high security prison Guantanamo) served and continue to serve to keep prisoners inside and to make them invisible for citizens living outside of these walls.

Hence, walls exist inside cities, outside and around cities; they define specific areas where distinct groups and communities are allowed to live or choose to live. As the anthropologist Setha Low (2001: 46) illustrates through her extensive fieldwork in US cities, the rich and wealthy sometimes choose to live in *gated communities* which provide security from unwanted outsiders:

> Adding walls, gates, and guards produces a landscape that encodes class relations and residential (race/class/ethnic/gender) segregation more permanently in the built environment.
>
> *(ibid, 45)*

Borders (and walls understood as materially resemiotized borders) have thus become the contingent manifestation of highly dynamic processes and institutions that need to be constantly managed, maintained, and socially reproduced. This chapter elaborates and discusses the revitalization of walls and borders in the many hegemonic debates in EU member states and the US in spite of our ever more globalized and globalizing world and the communication channels and options which necessarily transcend borders and walls. As Newman and Paasi (1998: 201) maintain:

> The study of narratives and discourse is central to an understanding of all types of boundaries, particularly state boundaries. These narratives range from foreign policy discourses, geographical texts and literature (including maps), to the many dimensions of formal and

informal socialization which affect the creation of sociospatial identities, especially the notions of "us" and the "Other," exclusive and inclusive spaces and territories.

Processes of inclusion and exclusion, of racialization and culturalization, therefore often involve conflicting discourses, narratives, and related identities about bordering, about access and rejection, that are consistent with fundamental claims of critical discourse studies (CDS)—that is, that discourses and social realities are mutually constitutive and that discursive practices may have major ideological effects, helping to produce and reproduce unequal power relations (Wodak and Meyer 2016) and legitimize inclusion and exclusion, particularly in regard to ethnic and religious minorities, refugees, immigrants, and asylum seekers.[2]

In the next section, I discuss the *securitization and moralization* of borders via specific discursive forms of *argumentation and legitimation* of exclusion, and then turn to one example: I briefly summarize Donald Trump's argumentation for building a wall in order to keep Latin American (primarily Mexican) migrants out of the US. In the conclusion, I reflect on the resemiotization of discourses about exclusion via borders and walls, and their continuous reinforcement via a *politics of fear*.

Walls, ghettos, and borders: inclusion and exclusion

The view that borders have social, cultural, and political significance has become a central tenet within critical scholarship focusing on the ambivalences underlying border (and bordered) subjects and identities. More generally, there is now widespread agreement among geographers, sociologists, political scientists, anthropologists, and discourse analysts alike that borders (and walls) are inevitably loaded with (often contested) symbolic, cultural, historical, political, and ideological meanings and that such meanings may arise from a variety of social practices, discourses, and narratives.[3]

As mentioned above, migration is increasingly constructed as a "problem" that needs to be regulated, whereby "'the border' has become a key discursive icon and manifestation of controlling migration" (Vollmer 2017a: 3). Similar meanings are attributed to walls, for example in the US context (see Section 3, below). Border controls and their fortification are discursively linked to national security and the control of movement (see *economization* and *securitization* in Rheindorf and Wodak 2018). Concomitantly, borders are being increasingly militarized (Schwenken and Ruß–Sattar 2014: 6), with huge and insurmountable walls symbolizing inaccessible borders, with people being prevented from climbing over them via different technical means such as barbed wire and broken glass (Paasi 2012: 2306). In addition to fortification, we observe restrictive *border regimes* which, inasmuch as they are proposed or implemented in the EU, are controversial and discussed under the label of "Fortress Europe." Indeed, the term "Fortress Europe", which was once used by the Nazis and since 1945 has carried a negative meaning, has been recontextualized since the refugee movement in 2015 (i.e. "protecting the European Union *from* refugees") (Pinos 2009; Wodak 2018).

Moralization, mediatization, and securitization

Increasing processes of securitization and militarization can be noticed not only at political levels but also at normative levels in what Vollmer (2017a: 4) terms the moralization of bordering.

Moralization of bordering takes place when considering the balancing act of excluding a selection of people but at the same time standing on the high moral ground for which the EU and its Member States stand for. This exclusionary practice has been morally legitimized over the years by an array of policy frames […] but also by a narrative of deservingness, that is, by following the principle that "some people do not deserve to be treated equally or in the way we (the 'host' society) treat human beings."

The moralization of borders thus requires a range of *legitimation strategies* (e.g. Van Leeuwen and Wodak 1999: 104; Wodak 2018; see below). Territorial borders have become more than a means of providing security and control, moreover symbolizing social meanings that cut to the core of human life (e.g. Lamont and Molnar 2002). In this vein, most migration control regimes were transformed—especially in the so-called age of terrorism—into *securitization regimes* and attended by debates about distinctions between who is a migrant and who is a refugee and, even more significantly, about who is a "genuine" asylum seeker and who is a "bogus asylum seeker" (e.g. Wodak 2015). These developments have caused migration- and border politics to be increasingly framed as *body politics*, constructing nation states as bodies that have to be protected from "invasion, penetration, infection or disease" (Musolff 2004: 437–438). In close connection with mediatization effects (Forchtner, Krzyżanowski, and Wodak 2013; Rheindorf and Wodak 2018; Triandafyllidou, Krzyżanowski, and Wodak 2018), a "securitization of migration" in relation to terrorism has been observed in post-9/11 migration policies and in the Schengen agreements and the gradual dismantling of national borders within the European Union (Bigo 2002; Scheibelhofer 2012: 325). In this context, mediatized politics can be understood as politics that actually depends upon the mechanisms and reach of mass media, which is therefore ineffective without them (Strömbäck 2008; Preston 2008). Hence, migration is being constructed as a "risk to the liberal world […] normalizing the view that immigrants are a threat" (Ibrahim 2005: 163). These meanings are captured in the notion of securitization.

Securitization occurs when an issue is presented as posing an existential threat to a designated referent object—that is, the state, incorporating government, territory, and society. According to Buzan, de Wilde, and Waever (1998: 21), a state representative can traditionally, by declaring a state of emergency, claim the right to use whatever means are necessary to counter a threatening development; in the US case, this actually implied categorizing migration in the same way as—for example—a natural catastrophe such as Hurricane Katrina when Donald Trump sent troops to the Mexican border in October 2018.[4] The special nature of security threats can be invoked to justify the use of extraordinary measures to handle them (ibid. 21–24)—that is, governmental acts of power such as forced registration of refugees, militarization, use of police and military force, constructing walls, and so on. This is a securitizing move insofar as threats are discursively constructed in the sense that they do not simply "exist" independently of our knowledge and representations of them (Peoples and Vaughan-Williams 2010: 5–6). Securitization, moralization, legitimation, and mediatization are thus all interlinked in intricate ways when political actors depend on mass media to construct a referent as an existential security threat.

Walls and segregated spaces

Debates about walls are, as mentioned in the first section, not new. The history of the Jewish ghetto is a case in point. Jews in early-modern Europe were for the most part not allowed to own land and were often forced to live in specific areas surrounded by walls—ghettos—and had to pay rent to landowners who lived outside the ghetto. In the oldest European ghetto in Venice (dating back to 1516), Jews would leave behind the world of the ghetto each morning—their clothing marked with a yellow (!) circle (for men) or yellow scarf (for women)—to work or to shop among gentiles and then return to the ghetto each evening before sundown. The enclosure of the Jews came, it is reported, after an outbreak of syphilis assumed to be linked to the arrival of the so-called *Marrano* Jews from Spain. With an act of the Venetian Senate on March 29, 1516, some 700 Jewish households were forced to move into the Ghetto Nuovo, with entry controlled by two gates that were locked at sundown. At that time, while the ghetto developed as an urban space isolated from the outside world, it also provided the Jewish community with some protection from regularly occurring pogroms. Thus, Hayley (2008: 348) maintains that

> we must view the ghetto as a space between expulsion (in Spain and France) and incorporation (in the Muslim world). While segregation from the outside world brought an oppressed community together, it also turned the oppressed inward in new ways.

This example relates to *the racialization of urban space* across many dimensions. Racialization in this instance began with the forced relocation of a group of persons distinguished as (morally) different and identified by a particular ethnic feature—their religion—to a physical space that was isolated from other areas of the city. Indeed, this very space of the city became identified with the stigmatized Jews and was instrumentalized for many stereotypes against Jews. As Sennett (1994: 248) argues, "the space of the Ghetto reinforced such beliefs about the Jewish body: behind the Ghetto's drawn bridges and closed windows, its life shut off from the sun and the water, crime and idolatry were thought to fester". Of course, during the Nazi era and the Shoah, the specifically created ghettos in many cities and villages in occupied Poland became sites of forced exclusion, preparing deported Jews from across Europe for extermination in the Nazi concentration and extermination camps.

The racist rhetoric employed by the Austrian extreme-right populist Freedom Party (FPÖ), the junior partner in the national conservative government coalition since the beginning of 2018, provides a salient current example of such exclusionary practices which most probably draw on the Nazi nativist discourses: Their slogans recontextualize antisemitic and racist appeals of the 1930s which excluded Jews from council housing and other apartments, schools and professions. For example:

> The slogan must be: No more Muslim migrants in municipal housing in Döbling [the nineteenth district of Vienna, a wealthy area, RW][5,6]

> *(SOS Mitmensch 2019: 34)*

Such blatant anti-Muslim racism entails much danger for any pluralist and liberal democracy because it is hugely divisive, excludes specific people on the basis of their religion, and is instrumentalized to trigger nativist movements. Extensive historical research illustrates that such proposals and appeals have not been seen or heard in Vienna and Austria since Nazi times (SOS Mitmensch 2019: 4). In such rhetoric, migrants are dehumanized (Charteris-Black 2006: 569), their number exaggerated to suggest an invasion by an alien and dangerous culture which will subsequently destroy the "pure" Christian Austrians, a process which subsequently legitimizes the moralization of borders and walls (see Figure 13.1).

FPÖ-Döbling fordert: Keine weiteren muslimischen Migranten in Döblings Gemeindebauten!

Wien (OTS) - Wie den aktuellen Daten von wien1x1.at zu entnehmen ist, haben Döblings Gemeindebauten mit einem zunehmenden Ausländer-Anteil zu kämpfen. Besonders dramatisch ist die Lage im berühmten Karl-Marx-Hof: Bereits über 50% (!) der Bewohner sind nicht in Österreich geboren. Der Anteil von Personen mit Migrationshintergrund im Karl-Marx-Hof und anderen Gemeindebauten in Döbling liegt dementsprechend noch weit höher.

„Die Willkommenspolitik der rot-grünen Stadtregierung hat auch auf Döbling Auswirkungen. Die Beschwerden österreichischer Gemeindebaubewohner über Probleme mit muslimischen Nachbarn, von denen ein nicht unerheblicher Teil, fundamentalen Werten folgen, häufen sich. Die SPÖ ist gefordert, dieser Entwicklung endlich einen Riegel vorzuschieben!" so der aus Döbling stammende Wiener Gemeinderat und Landtagsabgeordnete Michael Eischer.

Der Zuwachs von Migranten in Döblings Gemeindebauten ist laut dem Döblinger FPÖ-Klubobmann Klemens Resch kein Zufall: „Die SPÖ kümmert sich schon seit Jahren nicht mehr um die Döblinger. Nun versucht man Wähler anzusiedeln, indem man Gemeindewohnungen bevorzugt an muslimische Migranten vergibt. Das einzig verbliebene Wählerklientel der SPÖ. "Die FPÖ-Döbling wird sich weiterhin um die Döblinger kümmern und nimmt sich jenen Problemen an, welche muslimische Migranten in die Siedlungen gebracht haben. „Die Devise muss lauten: Keine weiteren muslimischen Migranten in Döblings Gemeindebauten!", so Eischer und Resch abschließend. (Schluss) akra

Figure 13.1 Press Agency message from the Austrian Freedom Party about social housing for Muslim Viennese

City planner and legal scholar Peter Marcuse (1997: 228) distinguishes between "enclaves", "citadels", and "ghettos", i.e. various guarded spaces defined in respect to their functions in distinguishing insiders and outsiders. The "black ghetto" in US cities, he claims, is an outcast ghetto; those within are subject to exclusion from the mainstream economic, political, and social life of the city. These ghettos are not necessarily surrounded by visible walls, but are rather defined by other spatial and semiotic characteristics such as street names, district names, visual signs of poverty, worse infrastructure such as bad roads, more unemployment, crime, and so forth. An "enclave", however, houses cultural communities of migrants and differs from outcast ghettos. Finally, Marcuse states that citadels were and are established by higher-income groups, and thus differ both from ghettos and enclaves. Hence, space, class, ethnicity, religion, and race play decisive roles in organizing cities and urban wealth or poverty in neo-liberal economies. Walls may divide such areas but they need not; moreover, borders can be visible but need not be. Indeed, as Ono (2012) states, the "others" *internalize borders* emotionally and cognitively, even if having accessed the areas populated and owned by the insiders.

Legitimizing exclusion: discourse, argumentation, and legitimation

Usually, in liberal democracies, politicians must seek the approval of the population for severe policy changes, appeals which obviously also depend on the mass media to convince the electorate. The discursive practices used to reach this aim thus have a strong strategic aspect and have been studied as strategies of *legitimation*.

As a sociopolitical act, legitimation is characteristically accomplished through discourse using persuasive and sometimes manipulative means. Regarding the linguistic realization of legitimizing acts, Rojo-Martin and van Dijk (1997: 531–32) distinguish between pragmatic, semantic, stylistic, interactional, and social dimensions. Importantly, the propositions employed in legitimation are commonly organized by complex argumentative schemes, including premises that concern the nature of the proposed action and the phenomena it relates to (usually presented or established in descriptive or narrative modes) as well as conclusions that concern said action's social, moral, or political acceptability (e.g. Rheindorf and Wodak 2019; Wodak 2018).

Given its sociopolitical nature, it follows that legitimation routinely draws on recurring *argumentation* schemes in order to persuade the public of the acceptability or necessity of a specific action or policy. Van Leeuwen (2007) and Van Leeuwen and Wodak (1999) distinguish between four broad types: authorization, moralization, rationalization, and mythopoeias. *Legitimation by authorization* depends on reference to personal, impersonal, expert, or role model authority, but may also appeal to custom in the form of tradition or conformity. *Legitimation qua moralization* is based on abstract moral values (religious, human rights, justice, culture, and so forth), straightforwardly evaluative claims, or analogy to ostensibly established moral cases. *Legitimation through rationalization* references either the utility of the social practice or some part of it (i.e. instrumental rationalization by way of goals, means, or outcomes) or to assumed "facts of life" (i.e. theoretical rationalization by way of definition, explanation, or prediction). Rationalization may be established as "common sense" or by experts in the domains of knowledge used for legitimation, e.g. economics, biology, or technology. In *legitimation through mythopoeias*, the proponents of the policy in question will rely on telling stories that may serve as exemplars or cautionary tales (see Table 13.1).

Table 13.1 Types of legitimation (adapted from Wodak 2018)

Authorization	
Authority	*Personal authority*: based on institutional status of individuals/groups
	Impersonal authority: originating from laws, policies, regulations, etc.
	Expert authority: academic, scientific, or other type of credible expertise
	Role model authority: popularity and acceptability of positions held by role models or opinion leaders
Custom	*Authority of tradition*: acceptability of what is claimed to have always been done
	Authority of conformity: acceptability of what everyone or most people do
Moralization	
	Abstraction: abstract depiction of practices that links them to moral values
	Evaluation: legitimation of positions and practices via evaluative adjectives
	Analogy: legitimation relying on comparisons and contrasts
Rationalization	
Instrumental Rationalization	*Goal orientation*: focused on goals, intentions, purposes
	Means orientation: focused on aims embedded in actions as means to an end
	Outcome orientation: focused on outcomes of actions as if already known
Theoretical Rationalization	*Definition*: characterizing activities in terms of already moralized practices
	Explanation: characterizing people as actors because the way they do things is appropriate to the nature of these actors
	Prediction: foreseeing outcomes based on some form of expertise
Mythopoeias	
	Moral tales: narrating rewarding decisions and practices of social actors
	Cautionary tales: linking nonconformist practices to undesirable consequences

In the formal analysis of argumentation, which relies on a functional model of argumentation, the three basic elements investigated are *argument*, *conclusion rule*, and *claim* (Reisigl 2014: 75). Conclusion rules (also referred to as *topoi*) are central to the premise inasmuch as they justify the transition from argument to conclusion (see Wodak 2015: 51–54 for an extensive discussion). A key strategy of discourse analysis is to make tacit or implicit *topoi* explicit in the form of conditional or causal paraphrases (Reisigl and Wodak 2001: 69–80). While *topoi* are often "shortcuts" and not explicated in discourse, they are not necessarily fallacious. In the context of legitimation, the analysis of *topoi* may reveal flawed logic and manipulative or erroneous conclusions inasmuch as what they ignore or sidestep can be fallacious.

Most recently, Lehner and Rheindorf (2018)—analyzing political discourse in Austria—identified the following *topoi* in relation to arguing for or against inclusion/exclusion of refugees and asylum seekers (e.g. Rheindorf and Wodak 2018; Wodak 2018):

It becomes apparent that overlaps exist between some legitimation strategies and related *topoi* (see Tables 13.1 and 13.2); "authorization", for example, frequently makes

Table 13.2 Topoi in Austrian media during the "refugee crisis" (Drawing on Wodak 2018 and, with permission, on Lehner and Rheindorf 2018)

Topos	Warrant
Topos of abuse/definition	Most of the people arriving at the moment are not in danger of being persecuted; therefore, they are not refugees but (economic) migrants
Topos of burden	Providing for so many refugees places an inordinate burden on Austria and Austrians; therefore, Austria should only accept a limited number
Topos of culture/burden	The people arriving at the moment are mostly uneducated and/or illiterate; therefore, they are an inordinate and unacceptable burden on the welfare state
Topos of culture/burden	The people arriving at the moment do not share "our" values and are therefore difficult/impossible to integrate; therefore, Austria should only accept a limited number
Topos of culture/male nature and burden	The people arriving at the moment are mostly young men who have never learned to or cannot exercise restraint; therefore, they are a danger to Austrian women
Topos of economic resource limitation	Austria does not have the resources (money, housing) to provide for so many refugees; therefore, Austria should only accept a limited number
Topos of historical dissimilarity/conditionality	The Geneva Convention was designed for a different (historical) situation and does not apply to the current situation; therefore, Austria should not be bound by it
Topos of law and order	According to international treaties (Dublin II, Geneva Convention), refugees must apply in the first safe state they reach; therefore, most of the people arriving at the moment are not eligible to apply for asylum in Austria

(Continued)

Table 13.2 (Cont.)

Topos	Warrant
Topos of national borders	Austria has a natural right to control its borders and know the identity of everyone who is in the country; therefore, borders must be closed entirely and strictly policed
Topos of national responsibility	If the EU does not control its external borders, Austria must take national measures
Topos of reality	The universal human right to asylum is a theoretical ideal, not a reality, unlike limited resources; therefore, granting this right is optional for Austria
Topos of solidarity (within the group/ charity begins at home)	Because they are Austrian (like us), homeless or poor Austrians deserve our help more than refugees; therefore, Austria should help them instead
Topos of (potential) threat/danger	Some of the people arriving at the moment are/could be/may in the future become radicalized and commit acts of terrorism; therefore, Austria should close its borders and police them strictly

use of the *topos of authority*, or the "authority of tradition" is linked to the *topos of history*. Indeed, the *topos of history* plays a significant role in this context as many political parties, NGOs, and politicians allude to past dealings with refugees and migrants, such as in World War II or during the Yugoslav Wars in the 1990s. The *topos of comparison* integrates well with moralization by analogy; mythopoesis (using anecdotes and stories as a legitimation strategy) is related to the *argumentum ad exemplum*, and so forth. In this way, the interdependence of legitimation strategies and argumentation schemes becomes explicit. In my brief example below, I will refer to both legitimation strategies and topoi when tracing Donald Trump's arguments for building walls to keep "illegal migrants" out.

Debating the building of walls

States and transnational organizations are developing policies and promoting practices in different directions: on the one hand, these policies are enhancing the free movement of labor and persons, e.g. in the European Union; on the other, billions are being spent to erect new and highly "technologized" effective barriers, electrified walls, and surveillance apparatuses to control and reduce the free movement of "unwanted", "illegal" migrants. US President Donald Trump is leading the anti-immigrant war with wall-building as *rearguard action*, drawing on Israel's wall to contain the Palestinians in the West Bank, as obsessive restrictions on migration and asylum are spreading throughout the world to divide us in an "age of walls" (Marshall 2018). This has also started a war of protectionism, turning the world upside down as the Chinese government under Xi Jinping is paradoxically becoming the supreme defender of free trade across the globe (Trimikliotis 2019).

In a similar vein, Rheindorf and Wodak (2018) investigated the Austrian debates about erecting fences and/or walls during the refugee movement of 2015/16. Major policy and frame shifts could be observed in this quantitative and qualitative study (see also Wodak 2018, 2019): overall, a discourse of empathy with and pity for the thousands of refugees fleeing from Syria and Iraq in August and September 2015 changed to a rhetoric of exclusion after the terrorist attacks in Paris in November 2015 and the sexual harassment case on New Year's Eve 2015 in Cologne. This significant frame shift implied viewing strangers primarily as threatening and not as needy or suffering. This frame shift also implied the use of different strategies of legitimation (moralization, mythopoesis) and topoi (focus on topoi of culture, crime, and threat). Rheindorf and Wodak (2018: 34) thus succeed in tracing and documenting the step-by-step normalization of walls, fences, and borders: "borders are 'moral,' then, also in the sense that politicians can thus make a claim to be acting responsibly, using cost-and-benefit analyses in an effort to protect social security and cohesion." Because of such frame shifts and related policy changes, it is also possible to reformulate the interdependence between borders and boundaries (Kinnvall and Nesbitt-Larking 2013: 346):

> The fact that borders are politically constructed means they have to find their legitimacy in *boundaries*, i.e. the cultural and political narratives about a society, its culture, territory and history; about who is a member of that society and, consequentially, who is an outsider.

In an extensive study, Demato (2019: 276ff) analyses several speeches by Donald Trump in which he promised—as one of his most important electoral pledges—to build a wall along the border between the US and Mexico. As Demato argues, while Trump promises to "Make American Great Again" by building a wall to stem the flow of immigration, he is merely resurrecting the divisive politics of nativism that has a long historical precedent in American politics. Thus, Demato (2019: 291) states:

> Trump's anti-immigration rhetoric reinforces a vision of the nation and of its borders which is based on a power which is realized through the legitimization of the identity of some subjects and the alienization or exclusion of others: in Trump's nationalist narrative the alienized subject is marginalized and kept out of the space of the US homeland. Through his wall proposal, which is instrumental in providing social actors with certain (negative) roles, Trump exploits a prevalent narrative which views the US-Mexico border as a gateway to the nation from unwanted and threatening enemies. Trump wants to "make America great again" through immigration reform because, by demarcating borders, both geographically, physically and socially, and by excluding the "alien" element, he can draw the rhetorical outlines of group identity, and specifically of who should be, and who should not be, American.

When Trump announced his candidacy for president on 16 June 2015, the "them" in this specific speech consisted of foreign countries that were apparently taking advantage of America by sending them immigrants who were inferior social outcasts. To Trump, the former great nation had thus become a *victim* (a well-known demagogic strategy labeled as *victim-perpetrator reversal*). Thus, he asked: "When do we beat Mexico at the border?" He then continued to disparage the entire Mexican nation, accusing the country of not sending their best people to the US, but of exporting a host of social problems onto American soil. His solution: build a big wall to protect Americans from the Mexicans. At the end of this speech, after disparaging all other candidates in both parties and severely criticizing former presidents,

Trump proclaimed that he alone could save America from its ostensibly downtrodden position:

> Sadly, the American dream is dead. But if I get elected president, I will bring it back bigger and better and stronger than ever before, and we will make America great again.
>
> *(Time staff, 2015)*

In this way, Trump depicted America as a crumbling, declining country, a victim of losses to foreign competitors, and a nation that had failed to protect its people and their problems. His answer to this dystopic vision was to restore greatness by negotiating advantageous trade deals for Americans, by promising to create new jobs, by repairing the decaying infrastructure, *and by constructing a wall on the southern border of the US to curb illegal immigration*, thus employing rational and moral legitimation, substantiated by *topoi* of numbers, burden, law and order, and criminality (e.g. Table 13.2).

Obviously, many argumentative moves which occurred in the Austrian debates and other European debates are apparent in this rhetoric, albeit in this case directed against the so-called "illegal Mexicans" and "all illegal migrants coming from South America", and not against the refugees coming from the Middle East. The Italian author Roberto Saviano (2019), however, provides the empirical facts about the metaphorically framed so-called "caravans" or "floods" of immigrants in an extensive and carefully researched essay; these migrants which are perceived as threatening the US-Mexican border are mostly refugees, fleeing from torture, slavery, and death in their countries of origin, including some of the most dangerous and crime-plagued countries in the world, such as Columbia, El Salvador, Honduras, Mexico, and Venezuela:

> In recent months, some have said of the migrants, "Instead of running away, they should try to change the situation in their country!" Only those unfamiliar with the Honduran situation could say such a thing. Anyone who opposes it, anyone who criticizes it or tries to change it, risks death. Between 2010 and 2016, more than 120 environmental and human rights activists were killed in Honduras. Freedom of the press is also under siege, as Reporters Without Borders has documented [...] President Trump talks about the migrant caravan as if it were an attempted invasion. In reality, Honduras and Central America have paid an enormous price precisely because of US policies. The dire market in Honduras right now is shaped by the drug market, and the world's largest consumer of cocaine is the United States.
>
> *(Saviano 2019: 2)*[7]

In all his speeches, Trump promises to build a "big, fat, beautiful wall" to prevent Mexicans and others from illegally crossing the border, thus discursively constructing and presenting himself as "the savior" of the US—a strategy employed by all far-right populists in their attempt to present themselves as the speakers for the "true people" (Wodak 2015, 2017). Such leaders necessarily claim to speak and act on behalf of *the people*, who are in turn arbitrarily defined as a unified homogenous whole, which supposedly constitute the majority of the state and represent the *will* of the nation. Along this vein, Milbank (2019) maintains—quite sarcastically—that

> [t]he trouble with the wall isn't that it's evil, but that it's medieval [...] To turn the 2000-mile border into a walled fortress Trump desires, my experts suggest a medieval

arms race as terrifying as the plague. Not only will we need a 30-foot 'glorious wall' (Trump will like that term) with towers rising to 50 feet, but we'll also need two more 'curtain' walls, a moat and an earthen berm to keep away the invading migrants' siege towers, ladders, battering rams and pole axes.[8]

Of course, there is much opposition to Trump's plan, especially in Congress since the Democratic Party succeeded in winning the majority in the November 2018 mid-term election (Riotta 2018). Internationally and nationally, Trump triggered an enormous scandal when dozens of parents were being split from their children each day—the children being labeled "unaccompanied minors" and placed in government custody or foster care, the parents being labeled criminals and sent to jail, in August 2018. Indeed, as Lind (2018) elaborates:

> Between October 1, 2017 and May 31, 2018, at least 2,700 children have been split from their parents. 1,995 of them were separated over the last six weeks of that window—April 18 to May 31—indicating that at present, an average of 45 children are being taken from their parents each day.[9]

However, this is not the first time in recent decades that the US rejected unaccompanied adolescents and children from applying for asylum in the US. As Lind (2017) elaborates, the US (and other countries in the Western Hemisphere) could have saved thousands of Jews from the Nazis in the 1930s and 1940s but instead they closed their borders. The US even rejected a proposal to allow 20,000 Jewish children to come to the US for safety. Of course, many politicians and people did not know at that time how terrible the Holocaust would become. But, Lind states,

> Americans did know that Nazis were encouraging vandalism and violence against Jews—many Americans had been alarmed by Kristallnacht in 1938, and President Franklin D. Roosevelt had issued a statement condemning it. But America didn't feel strongly enough about the mistreatment of Jews to allow them to find a safe harbor in the US. That is a moral stain on the nation's conscience, and it's what led the US and other countries, after the war, to create a way for persecuted people to seek and find refuge.[10]

However, such historical facts do not influence Trump's decision-making in any way. He intentionally triggers and substantiates *fear*, which draws on the historically recurring theme of criminal foreigners who attempt to invade the country to take jobs away from law-abiding citizens and which evokes the image of Mexicans as illegal aliens, rapists, and criminals.[11]

In the following, I present the argumentative moves distilled from four of Trump's speeches (from New York 21/11/15; Birmingham 8/12/15; Iowa 16/6/16; Las Vegas 11/7/16):

1. "We have illegal immigrants who are being taken care of better than our incredible veterans." "People flow through like water."
2. "When Mexico sends its people, they're not sending their best … They're sending us not the right people." "They're sending people they don't want." "When Mexico sends its people … they're sending people that have lots of problems." "[they] take our jobs, and then we pay them interest." "It's going to get worse and worse."

3. "ISIS authorizes such atrocities as murders against non-believers; beheadings and unthinkable acts that pose great harm to Americans, especially women." "They want to kill us." "These are people [who] don't want our system. They don't want our system and lead a normal life."

First, Trump depicts a dangerous situation in which, he claims, the US presently finds itself: He employs the almost universally used metaphor of *migrants as floods* which implies that there is no way to defend oneself against such a natural catastrophe. Americans, thus, have to be defined as victims. Moreover, he appeals to resentment by employing the *topos of comparison*, setting veterans against "illegal immigrants" who, he claims, receive more support than veterans, a highly respected group in the US. His second move then depicts Mexican migrants as criminals and enemies, unworthy to enter the US. They threaten the "true and pure" Americans as they would, he further claims, take their jobs away. Finally, in these first moves, he mentions ISIS (which is of course not connected to Mexico) but serve as enforcing the danger created by strangers. Maybe, via analogy, listeners might see similarities between radical fundamentalist ISIS warriors who kill, rape, and murder innocent people, and "illegal immigrants" from Mexico. After all these claims, Trump continues with the "data", the evidence for the alleged danger.

1. "We're out of control. We have no idea if they love us or hate us. We have no idea if they want to bomb us." "And it's got to stop and it's got to stop fast."
2. "We have to be vigilant." "We have tremendous eyes and ears." "We have millions and millions and millions of eyes and ears." "Database is OK and watching them is OK and surveillance is OK." "I want to know who they are."
3. "To make the country strong, we have to stop the border." "We have to establish borders and we have to build a wall." "We have to and we will."
4. "You can't be great if you don't have a border."

Here, Trump claims that the government is out of control and has to win back control in order to protect the US and its people. Trump does not provide any evidence for his claims. However, this move is reinforced by the *topos* of urgency as otherwise a catastrophe is to be expected. Urgency implies that decisions have to be taken quickly. And, as is presupposed throughout this argumentation scheme, only he as leader of the American people would be able to take these decisions and promise to implement more security. In this way, the discursive construction of fear and resentment is linked to the promise of hope, of a savior protecting the American people. Law and order, Trump argues, would have to be strengthened via more surveillance and, finally, borders would then be better controlled—specifically if a wall is built. Only then, he concludes, will America be great again!

It is a simple argumentation scheme (e.g. Toulmin 1958) which is employed here: Crisis and dystopia are presented as immediate dangers which can only be prevented if a wall is built which would keep the "illegal immigrants" out—who are claimed to be the cause of all social and economic problems in the US. This is a typical scapegoating strategy, coupled with the evocation of fear and—in a second step—hope, with the promise of a savior—Trump—who will urgently implement all necessary steps to make all problems disappear and guarantee safety and wealth, i.e. will "make America great again" (see Figure 13.2).

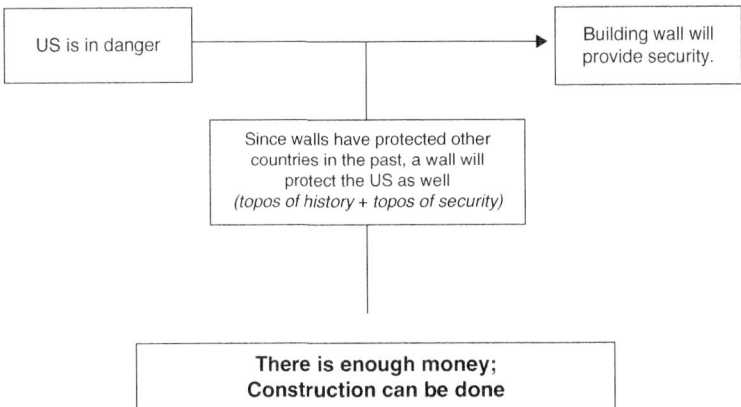

Figure 13.2 Simple Toulmin argumentation scheme: 'If the US is in danger, a wall will provide security'

Conclusions

The *revitalization of debates about borders and walls* and their mediatization in Europe, the European Union member states, and beyond since 2014 could be regarded as a response to the mounting influx of refugees from war zones in Iraq, Syria, Sudan, and so forth (Triandafyllidou, Krzyżanowski, and Wodak 2018). These debates reflect a worldwide tendency—i.e. the *fortification and securitization* of borders, the building of fences and walls, as a way to protect state sovereignty against globalized phenomena such as migration and terrorism—that began in the early 2000s (Sicurella 2018), or as Briese (2011) legitimately argues, much earlier.

The social scientist and essayist Ivan Krastev argues in his essay *Twilight in Europe* (2017) that the experience of demographic decline should be awarded a central role in explaining the rise of the far-right populist vote and the political agenda to keep "strangers" out. (Krastev has developed his argument mostly in light of East European experiences and particularities. However, his observations may also apply to more general developments and therefore merit consideration.)

Thus, we might ask: what actually happened *after the fall* of the Iron Curtain in 1989? After 1989, most East European countries have indeed seen their populations reduced: Poland has lost 2.5 million people, Romania 3.5 million, Bulgaria and East Germany each around 10% of their previous populations. This is why, Krastev argues, the remaining population, mostly older, less educated, and less mobile, suffers from "demographic panic": the "fear that a country and its population ceases to exist" (Krastev 2017: 50–51). This fear, he continues, might explain why these people are unable to consider migrants and immigration as a solution to fill the demographic gap: They fear being overwhelmed, that their "culture" will become extinct.

Also, in receiving countries after 1989, xenophobia and antisemitism began rising—against the influx of migrants from the former Eastern bloc (Matouschek, Wodak, & Januschek 1995). Austrians, for example, felt threatened by East Europeans and employed similar exclusionary rhetoric as in 2015, however without at first focusing on religion and Islam. These experiences provide much evidence that emigration and immigration can be instrumentalized; scapegoats are easily created to explain the alleged causes of huge economic and social problems which obviously have their roots elsewhere.

Thus, economic problems, specifically after the financial crisis 2008, "the demographic argument", and fears of acceleration/globalization emphasize the serious disruptions of the social fabric and cohesion of the life world and civil society in late capitalist societies. The racialized exclusionary rhetoric of "our land", "*Heimat*", and the wish to protect "our country" from outside influences and attracts many who harbor such fears and simultaneously hope that far-right populist leaders might be able to turn back the clock to an imagined homogenous society which is nostalgically believed to be safe. In this way, debates about walls signal a massive tension between different ideologies and visions (Bauböck 2019: 14): the anachronistic vision of "the homeland" in the midst of turmoil, insecurity, and loss of stability on the one hand, and the importance of defending democratic values and human rights against authoritarian governments that would rather watch refugees and migrants drown than open the borders of their countries on the other.

Notes

1 I am very grateful to the Institute for Human Sciences (IWM, Vienna) for inviting me as a senior fellow in 2018/2019. The many stimulating discussions have been hugely inspiring for the writing of this chapter. I would also like to thank Dr Tim Corbett who edited my English language writing and gave me some very constructive comments. Of course, I am solely responsible for the final version.

2 See Delanty, Wodak, and Jones 2011; KhosraviNik 2010; Krzyżanowski and Wodak 2009; Pohl and Wodak 2012; Reisigl and Wodak 2001; Sicurella 2018; Wodak 2015, 2017).

3 See Andersen, Klatt, and Sandberg 2012; Bhabha 1990; Newman and Paasi 1998; Paasi 1999.

4 See www.independent.co.uk/news/world/americas/us-politics/us-mexico-border-troops-migrant-caravan-donald-trump-midterms-2018-republicans-ploy-a8643111.html (accessed January 4, 2019). Here, Trump instrumentalized this measure before the US midterm elections in November 2018 in order to evoke fear of migrants and, therefore, to enhance his image of protecting America from "an invasion."

5 See "Die Devise muss lauten: Keine weiteren muslimischen Migranten in Döblings Gemeindebauten!" The translation necessarily neglects the rhyme in this slogan. www.ots.at/presseaussendung/OTS_20181113_OTS0187/fp-eischerresch-spoe-steuert-zuwanderung-gezielt-nach-doebling (accessed February 14, 2019)

6 Translation: "Freedom Party Councilors Eischer/Resch: Social Democratic Party [SPÖ] Deliberately Steering Migration to Döbling! The FPÖ in Döbling demands: No more Muslim migrants in municipal housing in Döbling! Vienna—As the latest data from wien1x1.at reveals, the municipal housing blocks in Döbling are struggling with an increasing proportion of foreigners. *The situation is especially dramatic in the famous Karl-Marx-Hof: By now, over 50% (!) of the inhabitants were not born in Austria.* The proportion of inhabitants with a migration background in the Karl-Marx-Hof and other municipal housing in Döbling must therefore be much higher still. 'The welcome policy of the red-green city government is also having an impact on Döbling. *The number of complaints by Austrian municipal housing residents about problems with Muslim neighbors, of whom a not insignificant number have fundamental [sic] values, is rising. The SPÖ must put a stop to this development!*', so the Viennese city councilor Michael Eischer, who is from Döbling. The increase of migrants in Döbling's municipal housing is no coincidence, according to the local FPÖ party whip Klemens Resch: 'For years now, the SPÖ has not been taking care of the people of Döbling. *Now they are trying to plant voters by giving Muslim migrants preference in the allocation of municipal housing, who form the only remaining voting base of the SPÖ.* The FPÖ in Döbling will continue to take care of the people of Döbling and will address the problems brought into municipal housing by the Muslim migrants. *The slogan must be: No more Muslim migrants in the municipal housing in Döbling!*', so Eischer and Resch concluded."(italics inserted by RW) Via emphasizing the allegedly high number of migrants who are said to receive such housing and by claiming that the "real Viennese" thus might not have access to municipal housing, the FPÖ appeals to resentment and envy, and attacks the Viennese "red-green" government.

7 See www.nybooks.com/articles/2019/03/07/migrant-caravan-made-in-usa/(accessed February 20, 2019)

8 www.washingtonpost.com/opinions/trumps-wall-isnt-evil-its-medieval/2019/01/09/80dfa20a-1458-11e9-90a8-136fa44b80ba_story.html?noredirect=on&utm_term=.2723f5e2d526 (accessed February 20, 2019)

9 For details of numbers, security measures, consequences, arguments, and justifications, see the extensive report by Vox (August 14, 2018) www.vox.com/2018/6/11/17443198/children-immigrant-families-separated-parents (accessed February 20, 2019)

10 www.vox.com/policy-and-politics/2017/1/27/14412082/refugees-history-holocaust (accessed February 20, 2019)

11 It is impossible to cover and present the entire debate about walls during Trump's presidency in detail in this chapter; moreover, the debate is on-going during the time of writing, and a range of conflicts between the democratically led Congress (since the mid-term elections in November 2018) and the White House dominate the US media and public sphere. In this chapter, I primarily deconstruct the macro-argument and have to refer readers to other detailed studies of Trump's rhetoric and speeches (e.g. Montgomery 2017; Kreis 2017; Demato 2019).

References

Andersen, Dorte J., Klatt, Martin and Marie Sandberg (Eds.) (2012) *The Border Multiple: The Practicing of Borders Between Public Policy and Everyday Life in a Re-scaling Europe*. Farnham: Ashgate.

Bauböck, Rainer (2019) Mare nostrum: the political ethics of migration in the Mediterranean. *Comparative Migration Studies* 7:4, doi:10.1186/s40878-019-0116-8

Bhabha, Homi (1990) Introduction: Narrating the nation. In Homi Bhabha (Ed.) *Nation and Narration* London: Routledge, 1–7.

Bickham Mendez, Jennifer and Nancy A. Naples (2015a) Border politics: contests over territory, nation, identity, and belonging. In Nancy Naples and Jennifer Bickham Mendez (Eds.) *Border Politics: Social Movements, Collective Identities, and Globalization* New York and London: New York University Press, 1–32.

Bickham Mendez, Jennifer and Nancy A. Naples (2015b) Creating a dialogue between border studies and social movements. In Nancy Naples and Jennifer Bickham Mendez (Eds.) *Border Politics: Social Movements, Collective Identities, and Globalization* New York and London: New York University Press, 357–379.

Bigo, Didier (2002) Security and immigration: toward a critique of the governmentality of unease. *Alternatives: Global, Local, Political* 27, 63–92.

Briese, Olaf (2011) *Mauern in Berlin*. Berlin: Matthes & Seitz.

Buzan, Barry, de Wilde, Jaap H. and Ole Weaver (1998) *Security: A New Framework for Analysis*. London: Lynne Rienner.

Camp, John M. (1989) *Die agora von Athen*. Mainz: von Zabern.

Charteris-Black, Jonathan (2006) Britain as a container: immigration metaphors in the 2005 election campaign. *Discourse & Society* 17:5, 563–581.

De Chaine, D. Robert (Eds.) (2012) *Border Rhetorics: Citizenship and Identity on the US-Mexico Frontier*. Tuscaloosa: University of Alabama Press.

Delanty, Gerard, Wodak, Ruth and Paul Jones (Eds.) (2011) *Migration, Identity, and Belonging*. Liverpool: Liverpool University Press.

Demato, Massimiliano (2019) "A great and beautiful wall": Donald Trump's populist discourse on immigration. In Andreas Musoff (Ed.) *Public Debates on Immigration* Amsterdam: Benjamins, 274–294.

Forchtner, Bernhard, Krzyżanowski, Michał and Wodak, Ruth (2013) Mediatisation, right-wing populism and political campaigning: the case of the Austrian Freedom Party (FPÖ). In Mats Ekström and Andrew Tolson (Eds.) *Media Talk and Political Elections in Europe and America* Basingstoke, UK: Palgrave, 205–228.

Haynes, Bruce (2008) The *ghetto*: origins, history, discourse. *City & Community* 7:4, 347–352.

Ibrahim, Maggie (2005) The securitization of migration: a racial discourse. *International Migration* 43:5, 163–187.

KhosraviNik, Majid (2010) The representation of refugees, asylum seekers and immigrants in British newspapers: a critical discourse analysis. *Journal of Language and Politics* 9:1, 1–28.

Kinnvall, Catarina and Paul Nesbitt-Larking (2013) Securitising citizenship: (b)ordering practices and strategies of resistance. *Global Society* 27:3, 337–359.

Konrad, Victor (2015) Toward a theory of borders in motion. *Journal Borderlands Studies* 30:1, 1–17.

Krastev, Ivan (2017) *Europadämmerung. Ein Essay*. Frankfurt: Suhrkamp.

Kreis, Romana (2017) The "tweet politics" of president Trump. *Journal of Language and Politics* (special issue, eds. Ruth Wodak & Michal Krzyżanowski). 16:4, 607–618.

Krzyżanowski, Michał and Ruth Wodak (2009) *The Politics of Exclusion: Debating Migration in Austria.* New Brunswick, NJ: Transaction.

Lamont, Michelle and Virag Molnar (2002) The study of boundaries in the social sciences. *Annual Review of Sociology* 28, 167–195.

Lehner, Sabine (2019) Diskurs und Grenze. In Dominik Gerst, Hannes Krämer and Maria Klessmann (Eds.) *Handbuch zur Grenzforschung.* Berlin: De Gruyter.

Lehner, Sabine and Markus Rheindorf (2018) "Fortress Europe": The construction of borders in Austrian media and EU press releases. In Giovanna Dell'Orto and Irmgard Wetzstein (Eds.) *Covering Europe's Refugee Crisis: Journalistic Practices, News Discourses and Public Debates in Austria, Germany and Greece.* London: Routledge, 40–55.

Lind, Dara (2017) "How America's rejection of Jews fleeing Nazi Germany haunts our refugee policy today". www.vox.com/policy-and-politics/2017/1/27/14412082/refugees-history-holocaust (accessed February 20, 2019).

Lind, Dara (2018). "The Trump administration's separation of families at the border, explained." www.vox.com/2018/6/11/17443198/children-immigrant-families-separated-parents (accessed February 20, 2019).

Low, Setha M. (2001) The edge and the center: gated communities and the discourse of urban fear. *American Anthropologist* 103:1, 45–58.

Marcuse, Peter (1997) The enclave, the citadel, and the ghetto. *Urban Affairs Review* 33:2, 228–264.

Marshall, Tim (2018) *Divided: Why We Are Living in an Age of Walls.* London: Elliot and Thompson.

Matouschek, Bernd, Wodak, Ruth and Franz Januschek (1995) *Notwendige Maßnahmen gegen Fremde? Genese und Form von Rassistischen Diskursen der Differenz.* Vienna: Passagen.

Milbank, Dana (2019) "Trump's wall isn't evil. It's medieval". *Washington Post* www.washingtonpost.com/trumps-wall-isnt-evil-its-medieval/2019/01/09/80dfa20a-1458-11e9-90a8-136fa44b80ba_story.html?utm_term=.9b4c4cf9983a (accessed February 20, 2019).

Montgomery, Martin (2017) Post-truth politics? Authenticity, populism and the electoral discourses of Donald Trump. *Journal of Language and Politics* (special issue, eds. Ruth Wodak and Michał Krzyżanowski). 16:4, 619–639.

Musolff, Andreas (2004) The heart of the European body politic: British and German perspectives on Europe's central organ. *Journal of Multilingual and Multicultural Development* 25, 437–452.

Newman, David and Annsi Paasi (1998) Fences and neighbours in the postmodern world: Boundary narratives in political geography. *Progress in Human Geography* 22:2, 186–207.

Ono, Kent A. (2012) Border that travel: matters of the figurative border. In Robert De Chaine (Ed.), *Border Rhetorics: Citizenship and Identity on the US-Mexico Frontier.* Tuscaloosa: University of Alabama Press.19-32.

Paasi, Annsi (1999) Boundaries as social practice and discourse: the Finnish-Russian border. *Regional Studies* 33:7, 669–680.

Paasi, Annsi (2012) Commentary. Border studies reanimated: going beyond the territorial/relational divide. *Environment and Planning* 44, 2303–2309.

Page, Susan (2015) "This time, Donald Trump says he's running". *USA TODAY*, June 17, 2015, https://eu.usatoday.com/story/news/politics/elections/2015/06/16/donald-trump-announcement-president/28782433/ (accessed November 13, 2019).

Peoples, Columba and Nick Vaughan-Williams (2010) *Critical Security Studies: An Introduction* (2nd ed.). London: Routledge.

Pinos, Castan J. (2009) "Building fortress Europe? Schengen and the cases of ceuta and melilla." *Centre for International Border Research* (CIBR)-WP18, 1–29.

Pohl, Walter and Ruth Wodak (2012) The discursive construction of "migrants" and "migration.". In Messer, Mischa, Renee Schroeder and Ruth Wodak (Eds.) *Migrations: Interdisciplinary Perspectives.* Berlin: Springer, 205–212.

Preston, Pascal (2008) *Making the News: Journalism and News Cultures in Europe* (London: Routledge).

Reisigl, Martin (2014) Argumentation analysis and the discourse-historical approach: a methodological framework. In Chris Hart and Piotr Cap (Eds.) *Contemporary Critical Discourse Studies.* London, UK: Bloomsbury, 67–96.

Reisigl, Martin and Ruth Wodak (2001) *Discourse and Discrimination: Rhetorics of Racism and Antisemitism.* London: Routledge.

Reisigl, Martin and Ruth Wodak (2016) The discourse-historical approach (DHA). In Ruth Wodak and Michael Meyer (Eds.) *Methods of Critical Discourse Studies* (3rd ed.). Los Angeles: Sage, 23–61.

Rheindorf, Markus and Ruth Wodak (2018) Borders, fences and limits – protecting Austria from refugees. Metadiscursive negotiations of meaning in the current refugee crisis. *Journal of Immigrant & Refugee Studies* org/10.1080/15562948.2017.1302032.

Rheindorf, Markus and Ruth Wodak (2019) Building "Fortress Europe": legitimizing exclusion from basic human rights. In Markus Rheindorf and Ruth Wodak (Eds.) *Sociolinguistic Perspectives on Migration Control: Language policy, Identity, and Be-longing.* Bristol: Multilingual Matters, 116–141.

Riotta, Chris (2018) "US troops at Mexican border returning home to start "returning home" two weeks after midterm elections". *Independent,* www.independent.co.uk/news/world/americas/us-politics/us-mexico-border-troops-migrant-caravan-donald-trump-midterms-2018-republicans-ploy-a8643111.html. (accessed 4 January 2019).

Rojo-Martín, Luisa and Teun A. van Dijk (1997) "There was a problem, and it was solved!" Legitimating the expulsion of "illegal" migrants in Spanish parliamentary discourse. *Discourse & Society* 8:4, 523–556.

Saviano, Roberto (2019) The migrant caravan: made in USA. *The New York Review of Books* 2019/03/07.

Scheibelhofer, Paul (2012) From health check to muslim test: the shifting politics of governing migrant masculinity. *Journal of Intercultural Studies* 33:3, 319–332.

Schwenken, Helen and Sabine Ruß-Sattar (2014) New Border and Citizenship Politics. An introduction. In Helen Schwenken and Sabine Ruß-Sattar (Eds.) *New Border and Citizenship Politics.* Basingstoke: Palgrave Macmillan, 1–13.

Sennett, Richard (1994) *Flesh and Stone: The Body and the City in Western Civilization.* New York: W.W. Norton.

Sicurella, Federico Giulio (2018) The language of walls along the Balkan Route. *Journal of Immigrant & Refugee Studies* 16:1-2, 57–75.

SOS Mitmensch (2019) "Antimuslimischer rassismus hat in spitzenpolitik fuß gefasst. www2.sosmitmensch.at/antimuslimischer-rassismus-in-der-spitzenpolitik" (accessed January 31, 2019).

Strömbäck, Jesper (2008) Four phases of mediatization: an analysis of the mediatization of politics. *International Journal of Press/Politics* 13:3, 228–246.

Toulmin, Stephen (1958) *The Uses of Argument.* Cambridge: Cambridge University Press.

Triandafyllidou, Anna, Krzyżanowski, Michał and Ruth Wodak (Eds.) (2018) The Mediatization and the politicization of the "Refugee Crisis" in Europe (special issue). *Journal of Immigrant & Refugee Studies* 16: 1-2.

Trimikliotis, Nicos (2019) *The European Migration and Refugee Dissensus in Europe: Borders, Security and Austerity.* London: Routledge.

Vallet, Elisabeth and Charles-Philippe David, (2012) Introduction: the (re)building of the wall in international relations. *Journal of Borderland Studies* 27:2, 111–119.

Van Houtum, Henk (2010) Human blacklisting: the global apartheid of the EU's external border regime. *Environment and Planning D: Society and Space* 28:6, 957–976.

Van Leeuwen, Theo and Ruth Wodak (1999) Legitimizing immigration control: a discourse-historical analysis. *Discourse Studies* 1:1, 83–118.

Van Leeuwen, Theo (2007) Legitimation in discourse and communication. *Discourse & Communication* 1:1, 91–112.

Vollmer, Bastian A. (2017a) A hermeneutical approach to European bordering. *Journal of Contemporary European Studies* 25:1, 1–15.

Vollmer, Bastian A. (2017b) Security or insecurity? Representations of the UK border in public and policy discourses. *Mobilities,* 1–16.

Wodak, Ruth (2015). *The Politics of Fear: What Right-Wing Populist Discourses Mean.* London, UK: Sage.

Wodak, Ruth (2017) The "Establishment," the "Élites," and the "People." Who's who? (special issue, eds. Ruth Wodak and Michał Krzyżanowski) *Journal of Language and Politics* 16:4, 551–565.

Wodak, Ruth (2018) The revival of numbers and lists in radical right politics. *CARR: Center for the Analysis of the Radical Right*: www.radicalrightanalysis.com/2018/06/30/the-revival-of-numbers-and-lists-in-radical-right-politics/ (accessed June 1, 2019).

Wodak, Ruth (2019) Entering the "Post-Shame era" – the rise of illiberal democracy, populism and neo-authoritarianism in EU-rope: the case of the turquoise-blue government in Austria 2017/2018. In Russell Foster and Jan Grzymski. (Eds.) The Limits of EU-rope. Special issue Global discourse doi:10.1332/204378919X15470487645420.

Wodak, Ruth and Michael Meyer (Eds.) (2016) *Methods of Critical Discourse Studies* (3rd ed.). London, UK: Sage.

14

The white supremacist movement in the U.S. through the lens of the matrix of race

Abby L. Ferber

The matrix of race

This chapter will examine the "matrix of race" theoretical and analytical lens, discuss its history and contours, and then apply it to one specific case: the white supremacist movement in the U.S. Using the matrix of race framework provides an intersectional analysis that bridges individual and systemic approaches, while focusing on the centrality of white privilege to the maintenance of white supremacy. Additionally, it draws direct connections between systemic white supremacy built into the fabric of the nation and institutionalized throughout society, with the more narrowly identified white supremacist movement that arose later as a defense of slavery and the system of white supremacy it saw as threatened.

The matrix of race analytical lens builds upon a range of advancements in sociological thinking about race, and brings them together into a coherent approach. Institutional and structural approaches to understanding race, research on intersectionality, narrative approaches, including those that focus on color-blindness, white privilege studies, anti-racism studies, and socio-geographical analyses of race, place and space are all brought together here to create a dynamic, historical, multi-level framework for making sense of race and racial inequality (Coates, Ferber, and Brunsma 2018). This comprehensive and fully developed theory distinguishes it from earlier references to racial matrices, and it is the most fully developed iteration of a model that has been developed over time by multiple groups of scholars (Coates, Ferber, and Brunsma 2018, Ferber et al. 2007, 2008).

Coates, Ferber and Brunsma have created this visual depiction of the matrix of race (Figure 14.1).

The inner ring centers the socially constructed category of race. The next ring includes many of our other constructed and hierarchical social identities that intersect with race, producing various forms of racialized identities, both self-defined and ascribed, experience, interpersonal relations, and positionality within the next ring. In the third ring, we see the many overlapping institutions that we live in. They reproduce and advance racism and constructs of race, but also provide spaces where race can be challenged, evolve, and restructured. The outer layer

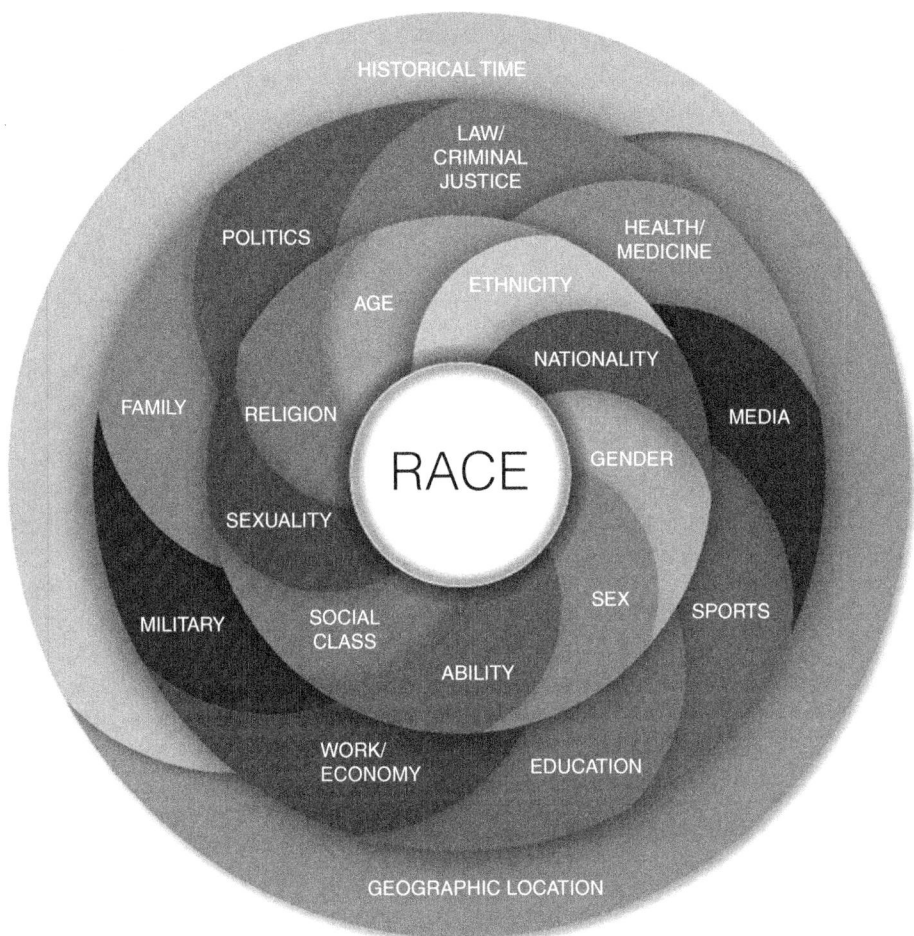

Figure 14.1 Visual depiction of the matrix of race

emphasizes the larger context of history, location, and culture. When and where we are located shapes the specific structures and manifestations of race. The various dominant and alternative cultural narratives produced at that historical moment in that specific setting provide the essential context for shaping, determining, acting, and structuring all of the inner circles. This model connects the micro and macro levels, centering micro level experiences and interactions within macro-level structures.

In this matrix of race, race is centered within the context of our many shifting social identities and systems of inequality. However, this is only one way in which to look at the social matrix. It was created to examine any system of inequality. Gender, religion or any other of the social identities structured by dominance may be placed in the middle. Alternatively, one could simply place "the individual" in the center.

The basic assumptions of this model are that:

1. Race is inherently social
2. Race is a narrative and can also be interpreted through endless narrative lenses
3. Race is relational and intersectional
4. Race is institutional and structured
5. People are active agents in the matrix.

Race is inherently social

Scholars across social sciences, humanities, and sciences have demonstrated the constructed nature of race (Desmond and Emirbayer 2010; Ferber 1998; Omi and Winant 2015; Smedley 2016). Race is a product of racism. The creation of "races" occurred at a specific point in time, to further advance specific relations of oppression and privilege already secured by colonialism and Christian dominance. These included both the near genocide of Indigenous people and the theft of their land and resources, as well as the extraction of free labor via the system of chattel slavery. Those who came to be defined as white created the classification systems, which have varied over time, while keeping white superiority intact.

The widely held assumption that race is a biological reality, and that people are born into specific racial groups which do not change over the life course, remains generally intact. Anthropologist Audrey Smedley (2007) identified these key features of the construction of racial classifications: race consists of visible physical differences that reflect inherent internal ones (such as intelligence, morals, work ethic and more); race is inherited and unchanging, determined by nature and/or God; and races are ranked and valued hierarchically (in terms of superiority, beauty, degree of civilization, capacity for moral reasoning, and more). This generally accepted ideology justified white supremacy, and was written into the foundations of our nation and enshrined by our "Founding Fathers" (Feagin 2010, 2013; Painter 2010; Roediger 2008).

Race is a narrative

The construction of race required a justifying narrative. The invention of racial groups developed alongside the growing abolitionist movement and threats to the future of the institution of slavery. The myth of race requires a strong cultural belief system to remain unquestioned. Joe Feagin (2010) identifies this as the "white racial frame" which provides a "comprehensive orienting structure or took kit by which dominant racial groups and others are understood, interpreted and act within social settings" (Feagin 2010:13).

Lee Anne Bell (2010) provides a framework for interpreting different narratives of race. She classifies these narratives, or stories as she calls them, into four categories:

1. Stock stories: the predominant stories. They reinforce hierarchy and the status quo.
2. Concealed stories: these have been excluded and hidden from the dominant stories. History is filled with concealed stories, often the voices and experiences of the marginalized, as well as the data and research that challenges stock stories.
3. Resistance stories: these are narratives that directly challenge stock stories in some way. They are rooted in struggles for social justice change.
4. Transforming stories: these are alternative and imaginative stories which can support resistance and guide the construction of a different and equitable future.

Our stock stories of race change over time depending upon the political and economic circumstances (Feagin 2013; Irons 2010; Roediger 2008).

Other scholars have focused on specific racialized narratives. After the Civil Rights Movement, as public attitudes shifted and racism was no longer being publicly embraced, a "new racism" took hold (Hill Collins 2004; Irons 2010) Sociologists have dubbed this new racism "covert racism" (Coates 2011) and "color-blind racism" (Bonilla-Silva 2010).

Color-blindness is the view that one does not see race or ethnicity, only humans, and it informs many of our most prevalent stock stories today (Bonilla-Silva 2010; Gallagher 2003). According to this ideology, if we each embrace a color-blind attitude and just stop "seeing" race it can finally become a relic of the past. This approach argues that we should treat people as simply human beings, rather than as racialized beings because we now live in an equitable society. As a result of this narrative, whites are more likely to believe African Americans are as well off or better off than whites (Bush 2011; Pew 2016).

Bonilla-Silva identifies (2010) four components of color-blind ideology:

1. *Abstract liberalism*: based on abstract concepts of equal opportunity, rationality, free choice, and individualism; argues that discrimination is no longer a problem; and any individual who works hard can succeed.
2. *Naturalization*: interprets inequity and inequality as the result of natural group differences, rather than social relations. Segregation is explained as the result of people's natural inclination to live near others of the same race.
3. *Cultural racism*: inherent cultural differences serve to separate racialized groups.
4. *Minimization of racism*: we now have a level playing field, everyone has equal opportunities to succeed, and racism is no longer a real problem.

Color-blind racism maintains and reproduces the subtle and institutional racial inequality that pervades the U.S. Examining color-blind ideology intersectionally, and identifying similar strategic narratives shaping stories about gender and religious inequity, this framework has been enlarged, and coined "oppression-blindness" (Ferber 2012).

While oppression-blindness has remained intact, a loud and growing overt white supremacist voice began to emerge as a backlash to the election of Barack Obama, and has only continued to gain momentum ever since. Donald Trump's campaign drew out large numbers of white supremacist group members to his campaign events. White supremacist organization gatherings actually decreased during that time because Trump rallies took their place and provided a space for self-declared white supremacists to gather. At the same time, these events brought together not only overt white supremacists, but white people all along the conservative spectrum, and overt racism and other forms of oppressions were given greater legitimacy among a growing segment of the population. This pattern has intensified throughout Trump's presidency, as he makes racist, sexist, ableist statements, and more. His anti-immigrant rhetoric, policies and practices have spread white supremacist views, and enabled and encouraged people to become much bolder in expressing their own prejudices. This has also opened many white people's eyes to how much racism lay just below the surface and ready to erupt when unleashed. Nevertheless, color-blind views are maintained at the same time, and reduce the problem of contemporary overt white supremacy to the level of the individual racist.

Race is relational and intersectional

Race and other social identities based on systems of oppression and privilege intersect and shape each other; they are relational and intersectional (Crenshaw 1990; Ferber 1998, 2012; Hurtado and Sinha 2008; Ken 2010; Romero 2017; Vivar 2016). Intersectional theory moved both race and gender scholarship beyond the silo approach which treated each social identity as its own distinct system of oppression and privilege.

Intersectional theories argue that race, gender, and other salient social identities are intertwined and inseparable, and cannot be comprehended on their own (Ken 2010, Case et al. 2012, Ferber 1998). The term "intersectionality" was coined by Kimberle Crenshaw (1990); however, intersectional theory has a long history, dating back to at least the abolitionist and suffrage movements, and rooted in the work of black women. Many women of color, and some men of color, recognized multiple oppressions, and the inherent limitations of social movements that focused on only one social identity (Combahee River Collective 1986; Cooper 1988; Lemons 2009; Lorde 1984; Robnett 1996; Ruiz 2008; Ruiz 2017; Terrell 1940; Truth 1851).

There is a common misconception that intersectionality means focusing on all social identities at the same time (race, gender/gender identity, sexuality, class, nationality, ability, age, religion, etc.). Instead, intersectional theorizing examines those identities most salient in any given context. Even when examining a specific subject like race, an intersectional lens provides breadth and depth that makes it fully inclusive, more nuanced, and more accurate. For example, simplistic statements about Asian American levels of education and income reinforce the myth of the "model minority". However, bringing national origins into the analysis provides different insight. Asians from India and Japan are far more successful than those originating from Thailand or Vietnam. And the preference for marriage partners reveals that Asian women are more highly desired by whites than are Asian men.

Another misconception is that an intersectional approach focuses only on multiple oppressions. While early works focused on the "double jeopardy" faced by women of color, scholars have moved beyond that starting point to examine all lives as intersectional, taking into account not only oppressed but privileged identities (Hurtado and Sinha 2008). The matrix of race theory applies to studying intersecting privileged identities as well. There is a growing body of research on white privilege and its interactions with masculinity, Christianity, heterosexuality and more (Hurtado and Sinha 2008). While it is essential to know the history of the concept of intersectionality and its roots in the experiences of African American women's work, it also proves essential to understanding why organized white supremacist movement is overwhelmingly made up of white Christian men (Blee 2002, 2009; Daniels 1996; Ferber 1998, 2004).

Race is institutional and structural

The sociology of race as a field generally takes for granted that race is rooted in institutional structures. The substantial bodies of scholarship on race, racism and inequity within healthcare, primary and secondary education, higher education, workplaces, families, television and movies, social media, the criminal justice system and more, all examine pieces of the picture of the institutionalization of racial inequity. Everyone lives in and among social institutions. Race fundamentally structures and organizes our lives within society in and amongst overlapping and interconnected institutions. Research documents the ways white supremacist assumptions and white privilege imbue every social institution (Boulware et al. 2016; Coates, Ferber, and Brunsma 2018; Dominelli 2017; Sleeter 2016; Tilley and Shilliam 2018). Within these institutions, dominant racial narratives also structure how they are built and organized, as well as their practices and policies. Institutions foster and reproduce inequity, discrimination, unequal outcomes, and the system of white supremacy as natural and often invisible.

We are active agents

Racial constructs shape our identities, and we continuously reproduce them. Stock stories are often internalized, even by those they fail to benefit. They are processed and made sense of by individuals and groups. Human beings, as active agents, have the potential to question inherited and ever-present narratives. Narratives guide our behaviors and can support the status quo, guide our search for concealed stories, produce resistance, and inspire transformative stories that might produce a more equitable society. If race is socially constructed, it follows that we are active agents that can also construct race differently (Coates, Ferber, and Brunsma 2018; Michael and Conger 2009; Tochluk 2010; Warren 2010).

Understanding how dominant discourses are framed and reproduced by our institutional practices and policies helps us to understand how these patterns are not only maintained or advanced, but also how they can be restructured (Bell 2010, 2014; Bush 2011).

The organized white supremacist movement through the lens of the matrix of race

Utilizing the matrix of race theory to understand the organized white supremacist movement in the U.S. provides a fuller and less simplistic understanding of the movement. First, it situates the organized white supremacist movement in a larger cultural and historical context. The U.S. is both a white supremacist nation, and possesses an organized white supremacist movement, or collection of groups, that become more vocal and visible at specific points in history when white supremacy may feel to be threatened or under attack. The white supremacist movement literally arises from the broader white supremacist culture and society that it exists within. It is the tip of the iceberg – sometimes it is the only visible manifestation of racism that many people see; however, it rests upon a much larger and deeper foundation. Continuing the metaphor – the tip is pointed, and may appear dangerous and deadly like the tip of a knife. However, without the entire apparatus of systemic white supremacist history holding it up, it would not exist. How large the tip appears to be varies at specific points in time, depending upon how deep the iceberg is. It is always there, but at times like now, the bulk of the iceberg has been strengthened and the tip is now larger.

Oppression and privilege predated the construction of race. When slaves and abolitionists began revolting and posing a serious threat to the system of slavery, early efforts to divide human beings into classifications called "races" quickened. An ideology of white supremacy congealed, defining whites as superior in a multitude of ways, including intelligence, work ethics, civics, beauty, and more (Smedley 2016; West 1982). Throughout the history of the census, the only category that has remained constant is "whites", because the construction of race was about defining who is white and has the power to vote, make law, run for office, buy property, accumulate resources, and more. It was about the distribution of privilege. In defining who counts as white, boundaries were established between whites and all others, who were denied these privileges. The U.S. has always been a white supremacist nation that endows all white people with some degree of white privilege. White privilege is the product of white supremacy. The daily operations and benefits of white privilege helps to ensure that white people protect the system of white supremacy.

The organized white supremacist movement overtly fights to protect white supremacy and privilege. When it appears to be threatened, their numbers and activity increase. The Ku Klux Klan was birthed by confederate veterans after the Civil War, afraid of the political power of newly freed blacks. During Reconstruction, whites felt their privilege threatened by the enfranchisement of black men and civil rights granted to all blacks. Approximately 2,000 African Americans were elected to public office during this time. Small Klan groups terrorized the African American community, and white supremacy was again enshrined more deeply in law and policy by the Black Codes, which limited and cut short Reconstruction. Taking land away from African Americans, denying them access to jobs and the vote, and segregating public and private spaces frequently resulted in their total exclusion from existing institutions including schools and hospitals (Du Bois 2017; Holt 1977).

In the 1920s, a widespread white supremacist movement bloomed, no longer limited to the South (Blee 2008). This expansion was fueled by the large numbers of European immigrants that did not already have much presence in the U.S. (for example, the Irish, Italians, Jews and Catholics). These groups were initially identified as non-whites. African Americans were most likely to face rioting white mobs, lynching, and banishments of entire populations from many towns across the U.S., forcing people to abandon any property they had accumulated. These are only some of the examples of what should be rightly labeled domestic terrorism. This second wave of the Klan counted approximately five million members, including many elected officials, with a minority now in the South. Even whites who did not perpetuate violence generally legitimated it. Crowds of white families attended lynchings and officers of the law were complicit. Klan groups no longer had to operate in secrecy.

Kathleen Blee's (2008) groundbreaking work in *Women of the Klan* introduced an intersectional approach and was the first to really examine gender differences in the Klan. She focused specifically on the very different ways in which wives supported the movement. The role of women was ignored by scholars up until that point, yet women played an important role in sustaining the work of the Klan through their reproductive and domestic labor.

The third wave of increased movement activity occurred in the 1950s–1970s. During the Civil Rights and Black Power Movements, the KKK and other organized white supremacist groups like the neo-Nazis became more visible again to defend against threats to institutionalized white supremacy. The growth in other movements, including the women's movement, further fanned their flames, and writing and publications of white supremacist groups became more hostile towards women, depicting them either as ideal white mothers reproducing white children for the movement, or race traitors involved in interracial relationships with non-whites. The controlling image of white women being raped or "stolen away" by oversexualized black men was a constant theme. The threat many men felt was posed by the women's movement was clear in the white supremacist appeal to white men to "reclaim their women" and "reclaim their nation" (Ferber 1998).

The white supremacist narrative remained largely unchanged at its core, but reflected the country's shift in expanding the category of whites to embrace the immigrants of the previous wave, with the exception of Jews. Jews are defined as the masterminds behind the plot to eliminate whites. This belief has deep, historical roots preceding the creation of the U.S., and remains a core belief in the white supremacist movement. The white supremacist narrative also evolved again as immigration policy did. In 1965, the very tiny quotas limiting immigrants from non-European countries was lifted. Thus, non-white immigrants, and immigration in general, grew as a significant focus for white supremacist groups. Immigrants were added to the list of enemies trying to wipe out whites and take control.

The white supremacist movement today

This brief historical overview has highlighted the importance of an intersectional perspective, a focus on the role of narratives, and changing constructions of race and who counts as white. All of these facets of the matrix of race play an essential role in making sense of the organized white supremacist movement, and its relationship to the larger white supremacist system.

The rise of the current phase of white supremacist movement activity has arisen as a result of many factors. At the top of that list is the explosion of social media and Presidential politics. In 2000 555 hate groups were identified; in 2018 1,020 were identified (a small number are not white supremacist) (SPLC 2019).

This movement consists of a wide range of groups that may give themselves or be given other labels, such as white nationalists, alt-right, militias, etc. The varied organized groups lumped together under this label still share the common historical narrative that white people are inherently superior, should be running the nation, and must protect themselves from threats to their power and privilege. They continue to focus on non-white immigrants, especially those coming across the Southern border, as a threat to the white race and white people's wellbeing. The image of white women being raped by dark men was invoked by President Trump to further his narrative about dangerous throngs of non-white men crossing the border. The second relatively new villain is the Muslim, another addition to the list of threats to the white race. All Muslims are depicted as terrorists, despite the fact that the vast majority of domestic terrorism is carried out by men with connections to white supremacist groups and/or ideology. The white supremacist stock story does not depict violent extremists as terrorists.

> 268 right-wing extremists prosecuted in federal court since 9/11 were allegedly involved in crimes that appear to meet the legal definition of domestic terrorism. Yet the Justice Department applied anti-terrorism laws against only 34 of them, compared to more than 500 alleged international terrorists.
>
> *(Aaronson 2019)*

The recent steep rise in visible racism

From the highest levels of our government, vocal attacks as well as policy changes are rolling back rights and threatening the safety of many oppressed groups, including women and transgender people, the disabled, immigrants, people of color and anyone falling under the queer umbrella.

There has been a dramatic rise in hate speech in schools and on college campuses. The alt-right has targeted college campuses in various ways, including leafleting, posting hate filled flyers and posters, funding alt-right speakers, and the creation of alt-right student clubs. For example, Turning Point U.S.A. boasts a presence at 1300 high schools and colleges, with 300 chapters. This is the organization behind Professor Watch, a website created to target and expose faculty that they believe "advance leftist propaganda in the classroom".

Both hate speech and hate crime have skyrocketed. In the one month period following the 2016 election, over 1000 hate crimes were reported. The greatest number of incidents targeted immigrants, followed by blacks, and then Muslims. In 2016, hate crimes reached a five year high. In the FBI's recently released annual report, 2017 saw a 17% increase above 2016 (U.S. Department of Justice 2017; SPLC 2018). The number of hate groups rose 7% in 2018, reaching an all time high of 1,020 (Southern Poverty Law Center 2019). The number of killings tied to white supremacists also rose in 2018. The movement growth tied to the election of Trump has also prompted more vocal and blatant vitriol against women, and LGBTIQ/queer people on top of the continuing anti-Muslim, anti-Semitic and anti-immigrant obsessions (Southern Poverty Law Center 2018).

Large numbers of white men feel like they are losing their white and male privilege. are increasingly attracted to the belief that white people are losing control of the country, and losing out. They see themselves as victims. Masculinity in the U.S. is very narrowly defined – real men are supposed to be tough, powerful, and in control, a stock story also embedded in white supremacist ideology. Since the legal successes of the Civil Rights, women's liberation, LGBT, and disability rights movements, in conjunction with the relatively recent vicious vilification of immigrants and Muslims, the Black Lives Matter movement, the rise of MeToo and fear of becoming a minority in the U.S. have all intensified the fears of white men who look at the world as a zero-sum game.

Institutions: social media and the economy

Social media

Social media and the economy are two of the most important institutions necessary to understand today's white supremacist movement, and its relationship to white supremacy broadly.

Social media has become an essential tool for the movement. Before then, most organized white supremacist groups were isolated, disconnected, and disorganized. They and their members were more easily identifiable as "extremist". The web provides the security of anonymity while also allowing for greater participation. It allows people to simply read and embrace the ideology. People no longer have to know someone else in the movement, nor wait to receive their latest organizational newsletter in the mail. Online dialogue is 24/7. Now that participants engage and organize online, it is difficult to tell how far their reach has grown. It is common for individuals to be followers of and participate in the dialogues of various websites and varieties of groups even if they do not see themselves as "members".

The web has also facilitated an increase in white supremacist organizations and is the most powerful recruitment tool. Today one only needs to create a website and start posting. The many websites that serve as aggregators allow stories to be reposted and spread quickly and far. There are now specialized, very well funded websites and YouTube channels such as EAG, College Fix, and Campus Reform that, like Professor Watch, target higher education with the goal of silencing faculty that teach about racism, white supremacy and white privilege (among other topics, such as climate change). The right-wing social media continuum moves stories from these amateur college sites that invent stories, to sites like the Drudge Report, The Blaze and Breitbart, where they then may be picked up by Fox news or other right wing media considered "mainstream".

The white supremacist movement has traditionally been seen as a fringe movement, which has allowed significant numbers of whites to see themselves as non-racist and to ignore the structures of racial inequality they participate in daily. Manifestations of white supremacy have always existed along a continuum. The fringe is part of the larger fabric. Narratives along the continuum have reproduced the same foundational ideology of race as rooted in nature. More than any other factor, social media today is making visible this narrative continuum.

Many major hate crimes and acts of white supremacist terrorism are carried out by people who follow or contribute to white supremacist social media. In October 2018, a man opened fire in a Pittsburgh synagogue, murdering 11 people. He previously posted anti-Semitic comments on social media. The March 2019 murderous rampage in New Zealand, carried out by a white man targeting Muslims at a mosque, was also connected to white supremacist beliefs and organizations. The white man charged with the murder of at least 50 people flashed a white power hand signal when he first appeared in court. The manifesto he published online is filled with white supremacist rhetoric, and he also chose to stream his rampage on the internet. Social media allows for the free exchange of white supremacist ideology in a public context where it is available to all, and hard to ignore.

Despite their many differences, white supremacist groups have been joining together, along with the (not so) new "alt-right" (white supremacists who perform under a new, less threatening name, and aim to attract young members). It is the basic white supremacist narrative that works to "unite the right" (one of the reoccurring chants at the far-right Charlottesville march in August of 2017, in response to the planned removal of a statue of Robert E. Lee). The shared ideology is so strong that it brought together skinheads, neo-Nazis, neo-confederates, alt-righters, neo-fascists, and militia and Klan members. This kind of joint effort had not been seen before and was facilitated by the broader political and cultural context where white supremacist views are becoming increasingly common in public, by people with no association or affiliation with white supremacist groups. We are seeing another era of close convergence between the organized white supremacist movement, and visible manifestations of systemic white supremacy. Not coincidentally, the marchers were almost entirely men.

The economy

Despite *feeling* victimized, white men continue to rule. They overwhelmingly fill the top seats of power in the government, finance and business worlds. Why do so many white men feel powerless, then? White men *feel* powerless because they *have* been losing ground – economically. All but the wealthy white elites are worse off today financially than they were in the past. The USA has the greatest levels of income inequality among all G7 nations (UK, Italy, Canada, Japan, Germany and France, in that order), and wealth inequality is at its highest point since the great depression, with the top 1% controlling 22%. Between 1970 and 2016, overall incomes for those in the top 10% more than doubled, compared with those in the bottom 50%. Since 2000, incomes for the 50th percentile decreased 2% and for the lowest 10% income declined by 11%,

The crash in the housing and financial markets during the Great Recession contributed further to declining wealth accumulation. The recession damaged the net worth of all families, across race. Given the lower assets of African American and Hispanic families prior to the recession, however, these groups suffered the most and were more likely to lose their homes. Despite the fact that we have recovered from the recession, the recovery actually widened both the class and racial wealth gaps.

During the first two years of recovery, 100% of gains went to the wealthiest 7% of people, who saw their net worth, as a group, grow from $19.8 trillion to $25.4 trillion (a rise of 28%). For the remaining 93%, their combined net worth decreased 4%, from $15.4 trillion to $14.8 trillion. In terms of race, just after the recession, the wealth of white households was eight times that of black households, and increased to 13 times the amount of wealth by 2013. The amount of income concentrated in the pockets of the top 1% has reached levels not witnessed since the 1920s (Stone et al. 2018).

The majority of whites lost ground financially, and has contributed to white people's perception that their economic, and therefore many other forms of wellbeing, are in decline.

However, when we bring in an intersectional approach, we see that whites have fared much better than African Americans and Latinx. The majority of whites are not seeing the kind of income growth they could expect in the past, but they still reap the benefits of white privilege. Further, adding in the variable of gender, white men out earn women of every racial group, even when controlling for education and job (Coates, Ferber, and Brunsma 2018).

The overall losses or stagnation faced by the majority of whites are real, but the defenders of white supremacy direct their anger towards people of color, women in the labor market, and immigrants "stealing their jobs", rather than the tremendous wealth gap in the U.S. Both an *intersectional* and *institutional* approach contribute to our understanding of white men's increasing rage and their readiness to defend white supremacy publicly, and/or to ally with organized white supremacist groups.

At the same time, the white supremacist movement has become extremely well funded, with many alt-right organizations and websites funded by major foundations with names like Devos, Coors and Koch. This money has facilitated the growth of professional looking websites, and very well organized and strategic organizations, like Turning Point USA.

Conclusion

The white supremacist movement is just one manifestation of the white supremacist nation. Movement activism and the daily exercise and defense of white privilege have helped maintain white supremacy and interconnected forms of oppression. From colonization forward, an underlying narrative has been relied upon to justify centuries of violence, terrorism, and the maintenance of extreme inequality. In both numbers and tactics, the movement today is stronger than perhaps at any previous time. As the continuum shortens in length, we witness a range of voices along the spectrum becoming increasingly united, well funded, and highly strategic.

The matrix of race theoretical approach provides a map of key factors necessary for a more complex and comprehensive understanding of both the movement, and its historical relationship to the white supremacist society it is a part of. Many of these characteristics, for example, the essential role of gender and the appeal to masculinity went unrecognized until the 1990s, and is only very recently appearing in analyses and research conducted by male scholars (Ferber 1998, 2004). Combining an intersectional approach with a focus on privilege, probing the social construction of race with other social identities, taking narratives seriously while also exploring the role of specific institutions at specific points in history in specific locations, provides a deeper and more nuanced analysis than many of the past.

References

Aaronson, T. (2019) Terrorism's double standard. [Online] Available from: https://theintercept.com/2019/03/23/domestic-terrorism-fbi-prosecutions/ [Accessed 12th April 2019].

Bell, J. M. (2014) *The Black Power Movement and American Social Work*. Columbia: Columbia University Press.

Bell, L. A. (2010) *Storytelling for Social Justice: Connecting Narrative and the Arts in Antiracist Teaching*. New York: Routledge.

Blee, Kathleen M. (2009) *Women of the Klan: Racism and Gender in the 1920s*. Second Edition. Berkeley: University of California Press.

Blee, K. M. (2002) *Inside Organized Racism: Women in the Hate Movement*. Berkeley: University of California Press.

Bonilla-Silva, E. (2010) *Racism Without Racists: Color-blind Racism and Racial Inequality in Contemporary America*. Lanham, MD: Rowman & Littlefield Publishers, Inc.

Boulware, L. E., Cooper, L. A., Ratner, L. E., LaVeist, T. A. & Powe, N. R. (2016) Race and trust in the health care system. *Public health reports*.

Bush, M. E. L. (2011) *Everyday Forms of Whiteness: Understanding Race in a "Post-racial" World*. Second Edition. Lanham, MD, Rowman & Littlefield Publishers, Inc.

Case, K. A., Iuzzini, J. & Hopkins, M. (2012) Systems of privilege: Intersections, awareness, and applications. *Journal of Social Issues*. [Online] 68 (1), 1–10. Available from: doi: 10.1111/ j.1540-4560.2011.01732.x [Accessed 15th December 2018].

Coates, R.D., 2011. Covert racism in the US and globally. In *Covert Racism*. BRILL. pp. 239–265.

Coates, R. D., Ferber, A. L. & Brunsma, D. L. (2018) *The Matrix of Race: Social Construction, Intersectionality, and Inequality*. Thousand Oaks, California: SAGE Publications, Inc.

Collins, P.H. & Bilge, S., 2016. *Intersectionality*. Hoboken, NJ: John Wiley & Sons.

The Combahee River Collective. (1986) *The Combahee River Collective Statement: Black Feminist Organizing in the Seventies and Eighties*. Albany, New York, Kitchen Table, Women of Color Press.

Cooper, A. J. (1988) *A Voice from the South*. Oxford: Oxford University Press.

Crenshaw, K. (1990) Mapping the margins: Intersectionality, identity politics, and violence against women of color. *Stanford Law Review*. 43, 1241.

Daniels, J. (1996) *White Lies: Race, Class, Gender and Sexuality in White Supremacist Discourse*. New York: Routledge.

Desmond, M. & Emirbayer, M. (2010) *Racial Domination, Racial Progress: The Sociology of Race in America*. New York: McGraw-Hill Higher Education.

Dominelli, L. (2017) *Anti-racist Social Work*. New York: Macmillan International Higher Education.

Du Bois, W. E. B. (1999). *Darkwater: Voices from within the Veil*. New York: Courier Corporation.

Du Bois, W. E. B. (2017) *Black Reconstruction in America: Toward a History of the Part which Black Folk Played in the Attempt to Reconstruct Democracy in America, 1860-1880*. New York: Routledge.

Feagin, J. R. (2010) *Racist America: Roots, Current Realities, and Future Reparations*. Second Edition. New York, Routledge.

Feagin, J. R. (2013) *The White Racial Frame: Centuries of Racial Framing and Counter-framing*. New York: Routledge.

Ferber, A. L. (1998) *White Man Falling: Race, Gender, and White Supremacy*. Lanham, MD: Rowman & Littlefield Publishers, Inc.

Ferber, A. L. (ed.) (2004) *Home-grown Hate: Gender and Organized Racism*. New York, Routledge.

Ferber, A. L. (2012) The culture of privilege: color-blindness, postfeminism, and christomormativity. *Journal of Social Issues*. 68 (1), 63–77.

Ferber, A. L., Herrera, A. O. R. & Samuels, D. R. (2007) The matrix of oppression and privilege: theory and practice for the new millennium. *American Behavioral Scientist*. 51 (4), 516–531.

Ferber, A. L., Jimenez, C., Herrera, A. & Samuels, D. (eds.) (2008) *The Matrix Reader: Examining the Dynamics of Oppression and Privilege*. New York, McGraw-Hill.

Gallagher, C. A. (2003) Color-blind privilege: the social and political functions of erasing the color line in post race America. *Race, Gender & Class*. 22–37.

Hill Collins, P. (2004) *Black Sexual Politics: African Americans, Gender, and the New Racism*. New York: Routledge.

Holt. (1977) *Black over white: Negro political leadership in South Carolina during reconstruction*. Vol. 82 Urbana and Chicago, University of Illinois Press.

Hurtado, A. & Sinha, M. (2008) More than men: Latino feminist masculinities and intersectionality. *Sex Roles: A Journal of Research*. [Online] 59 (5-6), 337–349. Available from: doi:10.1007/s11199-008-9405-7 [Accessed 15th December 2018].

Irons, J. (2010) *Reconstituting Whiteness: The Mississippi State Sovereignty Commission*. Nashville: Vanderbilt University Press.

Ken, I. (2010) *Digesting Race, Class, and Gender: Sugar as a Metaphor*. New York: Palgrave McMillan.

Lemons, G. L. (2009). *Womanist Forefathers: Frederick Douglass and WEB Du Bois*. SUNY Press.

Lorde, A. (1984) *Sister Outsider*. New York: Quality Paperback Book Club.

Michael, A. & Conger, M. C. (2009) Becoming an anti-racist white ally: how a white affinity group can help. *Perspectives on Urban Education*. 6 (1), 56–60.

Omi, M. & Winant, H. (2015) *Racial Formation in the United States*. Third Edition. New York, Routledge.

Painter, N. I. (2010) *The History of White People*. New York: WW Norton & Company.

Pew Research Center. (2016). *On Views of Race and Inequality, Blacks and Whites Are Worlds Apart.* [Online] Available from: www.pewsocialtrends.org/2016/06/27/on-views-of-race-and-inequality-blacks-and-whites-are-worlds-apart/ [Accessed 26th March 2019].

Robnett, B. (1996) African-American Women in the Civil Rights Movement, 1954–1965: Gender, Leadership, and Micromobilization. *American Journal of Sociology.* 101 (6), May 1661–1693.

Roediger, D. R. (2008) *How Race Survived US history: From Settlement and Slavery to the Obama Phenomenon.* New York: Verso Books.

Romero, M. (2017). *Introducing Intersectionality.* Hoboken, NJ: John Wiley & Sons.

Ruiz, E. (2017) Framing Intersectionality. In Taylor, Paul C., Alcoff, Linda Martin & Anderson, Luvell (eds.) *The Routledge Companion to the Philosophy of Race.* New York: Routledge. pp. 335–348.

Ruiz, V. L. (2008) *From Out of the Shadows: Mexican Women in Twentieth-Century America.* Oxford: Oxford University Press.

Sleeter, C. (2016) Wrestling with problematics of whiteness in teacher education. *International Journal of Qualitative Studies in Education.* 29 (8), 1065–1068.

Smedley, A. (2016) *Race in North America: Origin and Evolution of a Worldview.* New York: Routledge.

Southern Poverty Law Center. (2018) *Weekend read: the FBI is massively undercounting hate crimes.* [Online] Available from: www.splcenter.org/news/2018/11/16/weekend-read-fbi-massively-undercounting-hate-crimes [Accessed 26th March 2019].

Southern Poverty Law Center. (2019). *Hate map: in 2018 we tracked 1,020 hate groups across the U.S.* [Online] Available from: www.splcenter.org/hate-map [Accessed 26th March 2019].

Stone, C., Trisio, D., Sherman, A. & Taylor, R. (2018) A guide to statistics on historical trends in income inequality. Center on Budget and Policy Priorities. [Online] Available from: www.cbpp.org/research/poverty-and-inequality/a-guide-to-statistics-on-historical-trends-in-income-inequality [Accessed 26th March 2019].

Terrell, M. C. (1996) *A Colored Woman in a White World.* 1940. New York: GK Hall.

Tilley, L. & Shilliam, R. (2018) Raced markets: An introduction. New Political Economy. 23, 5.

Tochluk, S. (2010). *Witnessing Whiteness: The Need to Talk About Race and How to Do it.* Lanham, Maryland: R&L Education.

U.S. Department of Justice, Federal Bureau of Investigation. (2017) 2017 Hate crime statistics. [Online] Available from: https://ucr.fbi.gov/hate-crime/2017 [Accessed 26th March 2019].

Vivar, M. T. H. (2016) *Framing Intersectionality: Debates on a Multi-faceted Concept in Gender Studies.* New York: Routledge.

Warren, M. R. (2010) *Fire in the Heart: How White Activists Embrace Racial Justice.* Oxford: Oxford University Press.

Watson, V. T. (2013) *The Souls of White Folk: African American Writers Theorize Whiteness.* Jackson: University Press of Mississippi.

Wells-Barnett, I. B. (2014). *On Lynchings.* New York: Courier Corporation.

West, C. (1982) *Prophecy Deliverance!: An Afro-American Revolutionary Christianity.* Louisville, Kentucky: Westminster John Knox Press.

Wildman, S. M. (1996) *Privilege Revealed: How Invisible Preference Undermines America.* New York: New York University Press.

Zinn, M. B. & Dill, B. T. (1994) Difference and domination. In Zinn, M. B. & Dill, B. T. (eds.) *Women of Color in US Society.* Philadelphia: Temple University Press. pp. 3–12.

Part V
Anti-racisms

Introduction

We noted in earlier parts of the *Handbook* that any rounded analysis of contemporary racisms needs to address the role of anti-racism, both in terms of its ideological forms and political practices. This is the focus of the three chapters that we have included in this part.

The opening chapter by Manuela Bojadžijev serves as a good starting point because it begins by outlining a broad overview of the history and contemporary forms of anti-racism. Bojadžijev begins her account by discussing historical struggles against racism, particularly in the context of labour history, in the colonial context, and in migration struggles. The chapter then moves on to discuss the changing role contemporary anti-racisms, focusing particularly on the ways that an understanding of anti-racism can help us to make sense of the complex expressions of racism in the contemporary global environment. In the concluding part of the chapter Bojadžijev argues that theoretical discussions about racism must therefore not only include anti-racist practices in theoretical analysis and critique, but also include conflicts that go beyond resistance to racism in which struggles and critiques are not necessarily articulated as anti-racist.

This is followed by the chapter by Jehonathan Ben, David Kelly and Yin Paradies that explores what we know about effective practice for combating racism, racial prejudice and racial/ethnic discrimination. The core part of the chapter examines interventions that have resulted in measurable reductions in racism and related outcomes, with a focus on intergroup contact. The chapter then moves on to discuss what it sees as the key issues in ensuring effective practice, namely training and education, communications and media campaigns and organisational development. The chapter then discusses what it sees as 'backlash effects', where anti-racism approaches can unintentionally increase racism. It then concludes with an overview of emerging anti-racism strategies and recommendations for future research directions.

The following chapter, by Kristine Aquino, seeks to explore the role of anti-racism within everyday life. This chapter draws on research on anti-racism in everyday life and highlights how it contributes to broader anti-racism theory and praxis. Aquino provides a discussion of research on micro dimensions of historical social movements and epochs, doing anti-racism in organisational contexts, negotiating cultural difference and countering racism in spaces of encounter and victims developing cultural repertoires to cope with racism. The chapter then highlights some of the central objectives of this scholarship which involve enhancing understandings of how the everyday is an integral part of processes that configure and challenge racism.

The concluding chapter is by Rashawn Ray and Genesis Fuentes and is focused more specifically on anti-racist activism and its changing role. The chapter aims to provide a framework for theoretically informing, empirically evaluating, and practically approaching anti-racism activism. The chapter draws upon critical race theory and the public health critical race praxis. Ray and Fuentes seek to establish what they see as a racially-inclusive sociological imagination framework to better formulate a typology for engaging in anti-racism activism. The chapter then uses policing in the United States as a case to illuminate the pervasive ways that structural racism permeates a social institution such as the criminal justice system. It suggests that the racially-inclusive sociological imagination framework to show to how to reduce implicit biases, identify trust points, and create brave spaces. The broad objective of the chapter is to provide a theoretical, empirical, and practical template to engage in scholar-activism from a comprehensive perspective that is theoretically-driven and empirically informative.

15

Anti-racism as method

Manuela Bojadžijev

Racism as episteme and the global condition

The editors of the journal *Ethnic and Racial Studies*, founded in 1978, Martin Bulmer and John Solomos, produced a special issue in 2018 looking back on 40 years of publishing about race and racism that provocatively asked: 'Why do we still talk about race?' (Bulmer and Solomos 2018). Emphasising the Anglophone, primarily US and UK context, in a few paragraphs they outlined the development of racism scholarship in the United States from the early twentieth century to the present before finally diagnosing a changed research land-scape. Here they searched for a current, historically specific form of racism, of 'the produc-tion and reproduction of an episteme' (ibid., 7) which structures – and here I generalise their statement – 'the ideological production of categories relating to oneself and the consti-tution and comprehension of the Other' (ibid.). This ideological production, they claimed, must at the same time be continuously instituted and maintained in order to persist.

In my view, foregrounding the role of institutions and the maintenance of *racism as episteme* hints at a deeper insight into contemporary formations of racism. *Racism as episteme* refers to more than a set of knowledges, for an episteme must be understood as the very historical grounding of knowledge and the conditions of its possibility, or as Michel Foucault writes in *The Order of Things*, 'expressed in a theory or silently invested in a practice' (Foucault 2002 [1966], 183). He would later elaborate on the episteme in 'Truth and Power' as 'the strategic apparatus which permits of separating out from among all the statements which are possible those that will be acceptable' (Foucault 1980, 197). Bulmer and Solomos thus emphasise the necessity of a 'historical reflexivity about the historical background to the emergence of modern racism', reaching a rather drastic diagnosis of our times when speaking of our 'failure to come to terms with the transformations of racial ideologies and practices over time and space' (Bulmer and Solomos 2018, 8). To be clear: in my understanding, 'over time and space' refers to the global scale of racism(s). I would suggest that we also need to speak of a variegated global space in which racism operates and produces and reproduces at the same time, one we are still struggling to research and understand in its full scope and variety. In speaking of a variegated global space, I borrow from urban geographers Neil Brenner, Jamie Peck, and Nick Theodore (2010) to stress the relational dimension of racist diversity, maintain-ing the heterogeneity of racist articulations and practices as an uneven process across the world.

Alongside such geographies, racism as an episteme also refers to temporalities of racisms, i.e. the periodisation of racist discourses that itself constitutes a contested field of scholarly debate in terms of to what extent we can make plausible generalising accounts of trending conjunctures of racism. Take, for example, the current inflation of the concept when it comes to different manifestations of racisms in different parts of the world (anti-Muslim racism, anti-Roma, anti-Semitism, xenophobia, hatred towards refugees or migrant labour, racism against indigenous people). Talking about xenophobia, for example, and continuing to use ethnicity, if not as a given empirical then as an analytical category, aims at an understanding of ethnicity as a social construction, of why a belief in the existence of ethnicity persists and why people organise their lives and relationships accordingly. But this also means that ethnicity continues to function as a signifier, albeit in inverted form, leading to some discretion in the interpretation of racism. During the era of biologically grounded racism (which as we know is not over) it still appeared as if ethnicity could theoretically unify various racisms like anti-Semitism and 'colonial racism' – as if they were subject to a hierarchical and spatially organised pattern of different cultures, a linearly determined notion of progress, a preference for purity over hybridity, etc. Such certainty has grown more complicated with the analysis of 'differential' or 'neo-racism' since the 1950s, and with the global variegated scale on which racisms operate. The loss of analytical sharpness in understanding the essence of racism, I would argue, has to do with the influence of the critique of racism and anti-racist practice.

We know that knowledge of racism (as can be found, for example, in anti-racist practices) is trans-disciplinarily informed in that it is knowledge established across fields and struggles. Moreover, it has developed different sets of problematisation, formulating questions which are meaningful and therefore possible within a certain organisation of discourse, and, correlatively, identifying objects which are either visible or invisible for a certain 'experience' informed by this discourse. Perhaps more importantly, the episteme always has another side, if you will, in which it is questioned as a set of theories and practices, signalling the conflictual dimension of any given knowledge/episteme. This is to say that every episteme – even racism – has its limits. This is where I think transgression lies, even if it means that racism does not dissolve but rather becomes something else, something transformed in comparison to what we 'knew' up to that point.

When we try to understand such morphologies, I argue, it is precisely because practical forms of resistance to racism have gained strength and work on different memories, on different histories of racism, and anti-racism has brought the differences between various politics and experiences of racism to the fore. It is at this historical moment that the controversies about whether one form of racism has alternated with another in the past and present or will alternate in the future become acute, as Etienne Balibar appropriately remarked. The question of racism's essence and the unity of the term thus arises (see Balibar 2005, 22). Bulmer's and Solomos's diagnosis of the 'failure to come to terms with the transformations of racial ideologies and practices over time and space', which I share and believe is widely shared, may then have to do with the fact that why we even call racism 'racism' in the first place has been contested. Along these lines Balibar, in his article 'Difference, Otherness, Exclusion' (2005), rightly noted that it is precisely the numerous uses, denunciations, and critiques of racism – the current transformations of social conditions in which racism develops into practices and discourses and changes into other formations – which have made the term so ambiguous that its origin, its unity, its ability to summarise various phenomena and manifestations is called into question. In theoretical terms such an approach presents us with an epistemological paradox: we do not presuppose racism, but we must state that it has existed for a very long time. Therefore, if we focus our investigation on a specific understanding of the constitution of racism, analysing the reasons why racism persists and appears so resistant to critique, then arguments often blur into an area where it is no longer clear whether we are theorising racism at all. That is why I take this diagnosis and predicament as an invitation to think of an epistemological way, a method, to come to terms with transformations of 'ideologies and practices'.

In this contribution I attempt to delineate and critically assess the contributions made to anti-racism, yet it would be impossible to truly do so given the vast histories and stories of anti-racist practices across the world, or the theoretical knowledge that has organically developed from them. Rather, my turn to method is motivated by a desire to unravel the variety, renewal, and overall mixed profile of new and persisting forms and practices of racism. Therefore, while we can say that the foundations of anti-racism are being renewed through globalising processes, the struggle is waged on an extremely wide and varied front and scale, in microforms, and is yet to be further theorised. Confusion over method of inquiry is widespread in this context. The following question must then be posed: method of inquiry for what and for whom, and why is the question of method so urgent today? I would suggest that the answers can be found in the realities of the conflicts that racism constitutes and that emerge in anti-racist practices. The implications of such assumptions are deep, as they signify the need to bring historical and political experiences back into consideration in order to draw methodological conclusions for our times, when racism appears ever on the rise. The question of method may help to ask: how do we effectively encounter racism? How can our studies be guided towards that purpose? What experiences can we draw on today? Where are those deposits where experiences are contained in congealed form? How can we find them? How do we detect those insurgent ideas and experiences, the 'minor knowledges' (Foucault), so to speak, among the layers of social archives and memory? The overall aim of this contribution is to foreground the advantages of an analysis of global racism formations to investigate resistance, flight paths, and return to where anti-racism has effectively encountered racism.

By insisting on such an approach I am aware that these have already existed in the genealogy of racism scholarship, but suggest that we should return to them in times when it may no longer suffice to only add another crisis analysis, explaining to each other the secrets of this specific domination (Hage 2016, 126) – although I still consider this intellectual practice to be absolutely necessary. Rather, I argue that in times of transformation we must return to the archives of previous encounters of anti-racism. Anti-racism as method therefore suggests two simultaneous moves: drawing on such archives helps to learn from historical experiences of success and defeat, and moreover may open a perspective in which we develop our knowledge and analysis of racism from concrete conflicts constituted through racism.

Racism as social relation

Relational approaches to understanding racism (Fanon 1952, 1965 [1959], 1961, 1969; Balibar 1988; Goldberg 2009; Hall 2016; Hage 2016, 2017) have been helpful in understanding racist conditioning in its complexity and as it travels across the globe, and not only because they state that racism is not a question of individual racist subjects (Balibar 1988). Theo Goldberg more fully elaborates on the topologies and linkages, 'causally or symbolically, ideationally or semantically', of a relational understanding of racism when he points out, firstly, that the way we know and institutionalise racism, how it is expressed and conceptualised, is not only local, and therefore cannot be understood in comparative perspective, but rather relational, as racism 'circulates in wider circles of meaning and practice' (Goldberg 2009, 174). He also reminds us of the historical and material process underlying the constitutive connections in-built into racism when he writes: 'The globalization of the racial is predicated on the understanding that racial thinking and its resonances […] racial ordering, racist institutional arrangement and racial control were key instruments of colonial govern-mentality and control' (Goldberg 2009, 1275). He aims for a 'cartography of reiterative impacts, of their transformations and redirections' (ibid., 1279). Secondly, he claims we must understand the globalisation of the racial in terms of its inter-local pervasion, i.e. when 'racial thinking and racism "here" gets (support) from "there"'. Drawing on this line of argu-ment allows for a conception of how historical conditions led to the emergence of our global racialised world in the first place, and reminds us of the desire to understand the unfinished decolonisation process that intensified in many parts of Europe and the US through anti-racist conflicts.

Three aspects strike me as central to understanding the globalisation of the racial: firstly, racism must be seen as a mutually dependent process in tandem with the expansion of the capitalist world market through colonialism, marked until today by deep inequalities, uneven development, and incessant economic extraction as well as cultural hybridisation that con-tinually produces new cultural differentiations. Secondly, this history is as much an integral part of world history and the present as it is of Europe. It is an ambivalent story in which the conceivable unity of the world was always linked to intellectual projects seeking to inte-grate the tendencies of world-ing and localising practices, while at the same time linked inseparably to the constellations of a post-colonial situation. Finally, as Goldberg points out when he speaks of the constitutional conditions of colonialism, this development was and is always characterised by a material practice, to which I would like to add both the forced and the more or less voluntary mobility of people who have been described by quite a few com-mentators – among them Aimé Césaire – in relation to migration to Europe after the Second World War as a 'retorsion effect' of colonialism, and finally and decisively by the very processes of decolonisation that created the one world in which we live today.

Building on this, conjunctures of racism as determined in relation to social struggles thus, and most importantly, require an understanding based on struggles against racism rather than on subjects constituted by racism (Bojadžijev 2008). For a relational theory of racism I believe that three more aspects must be combined. Firstly, we need to do more than just emphasise the strategic effect of the relationship inherent in racism, i.e. its functionality in the relations of power. Secondly, it will not suffice to understand the reorganisation of racism, i.e. the effects of struggles against racism on each historically specific formation of racism. Thirdly, it is in fact always a matter of also working out the institutional and main-taining modes of regulating these struggles, which in turn have an effect on the determin-ation, i.e. the subjectivation, of those subjected to racism. In short, racism does not exist outside the history of its constitution and reproduction, and like all ideological formations is based, to borrow a phrase from Louis Althusser, on an interplay of a double constitution, constituting and constituted at the same time (Althusser 1971).

An analysis of racism therefore cannot fail to consider the historical process of how, when, and why racism transforms. Analysing this has been the task of historiographies of social struggles framed by racism. Such historiographies provide accounts of the forms of racist subjectification. They do so, I would say, in a double sense of reconstructing the per-severance and tenacity of those resisting racism who constitute themselves as subjects in the social conflicts, but also offering a sense of the history of their subjugation. The deep insight such accounts provide is that racialised subjects exist as a group for as long as they exist under conditions that make them one. This invites a reverse assumption: that as long as they exist, there will be conflict. Such a relational theory of racism would prove that struggles repeatedly force racism to reorganise itself, sometimes with the aim of ultimately removing the basis of its reinstitution and maintenance.

History has always been an important resource and terrain of anti-racist imagination and action for relational accounts, which is why I now turn to historiographies of labour, migration, and racism. Such accounts usually provide the grounds for a conversation across time and space, reading racialised politics in different parts of the world through the history of a whole variety of social struggles such as anti-colonial struggle, labour politics, or struggles of migration. They help constitute a way of thinking about politics and its subjects that is radically different from essentialising conceptions of these issues, for they strictly limit the scope of strategic essentialism to historical instances.

'Singular histories' of anti-racism

First, I discuss three international histor(iograph)y cases. The first is part of the US labour history tradition and deals with the slavery era. The second is the seminal work of Frantz Fanon, whose understanding of anti-racism in the colonial context was decisive for many who followed. The last case turns to post-war European history, specifically France, the UK, and Germany. Combining these approaches enables me to gain an overview of social struggles against racism in different social formations, all of which were influential in developing relational concepts of racism, provided insights into historical conjunctures of racism, and were influential in understanding racism from the perspective of struggles against it.

Labour history, racism, and class

The social labour history field in both the US and Europe exhibits a number of studies focused on racism and class (cf. among others Tabili 1994; Ignatiev 1995; Mills 1997; Jacobson 1998; Roediger 1999, 1994, 2005, 2017; Bojadžijev 2008; Virdee 2014). At least historically, it makes sense to link the theme of racism with the question of struggles against exploitation. David R. Roediger's contribution to this field is particularly noteworthy. In the introduction to his most recent book, *Class, Race, and Marxism* (2017), Roediger takes up the current debate's fundamental problem when discussing the political intersections between anti-capitalist movements such as Occupy Wall Street and struggles against racism, as currently manifested in the protests against police violence within the framework of the Black Lives Matter movement. Roediger's political positions reject the ongoing polarisation between arguments for or against the political primacy of anti-capitalist struggles over 'identity-related' ones. Even if they do not directly formulate anti-capitalist goals, identity-related struggles must, according to Roediger, be understood as part of the class struggle because they both attack the fundamental logic of social inequality in capitalist societies and offer the possibility of innovatively combining different forms of political struggle. This argumentation is not new, but has in fact been repeated remarkably often. We need only think of Stuart Hall's (1980) earlier work in line with investigations that studied race and class in articulation. In 'Race, articulation and societies structured in dominance' he elaborated a concept seeking to develop an integrated analysis of the structuring and manufacturing of racialised social divisions with economic, political, ideological, and cultural dimensions. Hall developed a materialist approach to understanding racism with a historically concrete analysis of distinctive racial aspects (Hall 1980, 336).

Building upon this vast literature, I would like to highlight one particular contribution that stands out for its analysis of the relationship between class and racism, dealing with it in the context of the transformation of capitalism and its inherent history of forced migration: the transatlantic history of slavery. It offers me the opportunity to discuss a methodological and analytical framework for anti-racism as method. The work in question is Theodore W. Allen's two-volume study *The Invention of the White Race* (1997), in which he conducts a historical comparison between the colonisation of Catholic Ireland from the sixteenth to eighteenth centuries and the enslavement of black workers on Virginia's tobacco plantations.

A number of works in the line of Allen attempt to determine the functioning of racism for the conditions of exploitation they examine in the struggles of slaves and indentured labour in Atlantic colonial history. This was a time when industrialisation asserted itself, and historically coincided with the effective restitution of the plantation economy in the transition to cotton cultivation. Allen's work is chosen for typological reasons and as an example of a historiography that successfully puts struggles of labour, everyday life, racism, and forced migration into context and describes significant historical moments. In reflecting on these contributions, I focus not so much on reconstructions of the struggles themselves as on the methodology, foregrounding how the constellation of racism, migration, and class struggle is conceptualised in the work.

Allen's work is indicative here in that it provides a historical analysis of struggles in the context of racist oppression and exploitation, implying a critical theory of racism. In particular, Allen's investigation and analysis of historical documents is influenced and informed by the civil rights movements of the twentieth century (cf. Allen 1997). As Allen demonstrates in his analogy of Irish and American history, racism cannot simply be traced back to the workings of phenotypic characteristics or an analysis thereof. Rather, he emphasises that a deconstructivist analysis *or* a historical view alone is not enough to prove this. What is so fascinating in his investigation is that he links back to moments when the institutional differentiation and definition of 'white' and 'black' begins in US history. Allen's concept of social control is based on a socio-theoretical consideration that analyses racist oppression in the context of class struggle and the struggles of slaves and indentured labour. In this way, it becomes clear how the relationship that generated this system of oppression is built, instituted, and maintained. Furthermore, Allen's analysis supports a relational theory of racism according to which racism organises and intermittently reorganises itself in relation to struggles against racist oppression. He shows how state measures and institutions constitute racism in everyday life by issuing various decrees that themselves can be read as a response to rebellions. His work's strength is that he abandons simplistic comparisons and blurs contradictions when tracing the existence of class solidarity where barriers of 'white' and 'black' were transgressed *before* they were legally codified in response to such collective action. This turn to investigating historical solidarity *avant la lettre* does not, as a common line of doubt claims, give priority to the class struggle or a presupposed unity of the working class. The opposite is rather the case, for Allen's intention is specifically to understand how racist oppression takes on an intrinsic form that cannot be eliminated by reflecting on the class struggle, but requires solidarity. It is only in the precise historical description of this development that it becomes possible to show how the forces of power shift historically and makes drastically clear that from the moment of legal distinction between 'black' and 'white' struggles can no longer side-step making structural and institutional (in this case racist) lines of division their starting point if they are to succeed at all.

Moreover, what becomes clear in these historical accounts is that there can be no general theory of racism. Rather, according to Allen it can only be understood as a fundamental system of rule whose economic and political constitutional conditions must be precisely specified. He thus chooses a form of analysis that could be described as the 'singular history' of racism (cf. Balibar 1988, 40) in order to determine the conjuncture.

Temporalities of anti-racism in the context of colonialism

The notion that racism has assumed new historical configurations since roughly the mid-twentieth century has been emphasised many times. Frantz Fanon was one of the first to identify this shift in his lecture 'Racism and Culture' at the First Congress of Black Writers and Artists in Paris in 1956:

> Racism has not managed to harden. It has had to renew itself, to adapt itself, to change its appearance. It has had to undergo the fate of the cultural whole that informed it. [...] These old-fashioned positions tend in any case to disappear. This racism that aspires to be rational, individual, genotypically and phenotypically determined, becomes transformed into cultural racism.
>
> *(Fanon 1967, 32)*

In addition to his theoretical reflections on racism as a sociogeny, influenced by his psychiatric practice and participation in anti-colonial struggles as a member of the Algerian National Liberation Front (FLN) and editor of its journal, Fanon also provided historical-theoretical considerations in the context of the Algerian anti-colonial liberation movement conceptualising the relationship between racism and anti-racist practices. Proceeding from French colonialism, Fanon distinguished between three phases particularly with regard to the practices of colonised intellectuals and in terms of racist subjectification, which he ideal-typically identified in *The Wretched of the Earth* (originally published in French in 1961 as *Les damnés de la terre*) and elaborated in other writings.

In *Aspects of the Algerian Revolution*, first published in 1966 as *Sociologie d'une révolution*, Fanon makes changes in everyday conditions the starting point of his analysis and gives an idea of how quotidian practices can be conceived of in the context of racism and decolonisation. Fanon depicts the 'self-consciousness of the people' transcending the colonial situation, their subjectivity as changing and changed social practice which at the same time questions power relations among the colonised themselves. The possibility of this arises between the layers of time from which colonialism is composed. Fanon shows what liberation could look like under colonisation and in this sense demands that 'people' have to change at the same moment 'in which they change the world', because their liberation struggle ultimately aims at 'a fundamental reorganization of the relations between people' (Fanon 1969, 14). Liberation, we can conclude, lies in liberation from subjectification. Towards the end of *Black Skin, White Masks* he reminds us that 'the real leap consists in introducing invention into existence. [...] I am a part of Being to the degree that I go beyond it' (Fanon 2008 [1952], 179).

Thus, Fanon's work combines many relevant aspects for anti-racism as method: firstly, his insistence on what today would be called a trans-disciplinary approach by operating historically, socially, culturally, and psychologically at the same time. Secondly, the question of the possibilities and limits of a reference to history permeated by racism for those who want to free themselves from it. Thirdly, the problem of not thinking of history as mere progress, thus, the non-timelessness of his or anyone's writings. And finally, the question of how change is possible under such conditions of colonial violence, without creating an abstract statement but analysing the material practices of de-subjectification in history.

The reception of Fanon's work is quite ambivalent in the sense that he was a theoretical role model for highly diverse projects over the course of history. Although Fanon's influence on Cultural Studies and Post-Colonial Studies has been enormous, here it is precisely his theoretical ambivalence, the rejection of clear-cut attributions and pure categories that are deployed – or, as Paul Gilroy put it, his 'reparative humanity' (2011, 14). Interestingly, Gilroy (2010) recently returned to the writings of Fanon (and Améry), attacking their domestication 'by timid, often parochial fields like "critical race theory" and "postcolonial theory"' (ibid., 17). He reminded readers of the changed political situation as a result of the 'war on terror' in tandem with the 'uneven effects' of the financial and debt crisis post-2008, as well as the impact of technological innovations in warfare, suggesting: 'It may be greater if his [Fanon's, MB] ideas can be reapplied carefully to managing challenges that are tied up in the lives of the often traumatized incomers (migrants) who are expected to bring the global insurgency alive on the fertile soil of their racialized exclusion from the dreamscapes of indentured consumerism' (2010, 21).

Migration struggles

I will pick up on this reference to the 'incomers' and go to a very different example that takes us to Europe and the crisis of Fordism to examine traditions and efforts in the self-organisation of migrants across Europe. This section is dedicated to the analyses of Mogniss Abdallah and Abdelmalek Sayad in France, Satnam Virdee's analysis of 'racialised outsiders' in the UK (2014), and some reference to my own (2008) and Serhat Karakayali's work in Germany. All of these works investigate conditions and struggles of migration. They deal with important stages in conflicts arising through migration and serve as exemplary points of orientation both methodologically and in terms of substance. The history of mobile populations receives a different rhythm and nuanced understanding if read as the history of its struggles and not focused solely on changes to immigration legislation and regulations. All contributions tell this story from the perspective of migrants and their political and everyday struggles, which is particularly important given how common the erasure of those conflicts from labour history narratives is. They deserve special attention in that they address migrant forms of self-organisation, i.e. those that were formed autonomously rather than within existing trade unions, organisations, or parties.

For France, Abdallah's book *J'y suis, j'y reste! Les luttes de l'immigration en France depuis les années soixante* ('I'm here, I'll stay! The struggles of immigration in France since the 1960s', 2001) provides a good understanding of the different currents, themes, and debates of migrant politics in France. Abdallah sums up historical developments in terms of political engagement and emphasises the collective force that emerges from self-organisation that is capable of social transformation. Like in Germany, many associations were initially founded on the basis of national origins (Bojadžijev 2008) to meet the social and cultural needs of 'immigrant workers' and offered legal, material, and moral support. They concentrated their activities on their countries of origin, whose regimes they often opposed. In their public self-representation they often committed themselves to political neutrality and entrenched themselves behind cultural activities. However, it should not be underestimated – and this must be objected to a culturalist historiography of migration – that cultural orientation was sometimes used (especially since the cultural awakening marked by the revolts in May 1968) to circumvent the prohibition of migrant politics as regulated by law. Around the same time in both France and Germany, the late 1960s and early 1970s, new migrant activities came to the fore which in France were very much about politics, the question of citizenship, and the right to vote in particular. Working closely with Pierre Bourdieu, Sayad's posthumously published volume *The Suffering of the Immigrant* (2004) emphasises the conditions of migration mainly under this aspect, the provisional and legal status of migrants and their children, as was also the aim of Karakayali's study (2008) on the historical genealogy of illegal immigration to Germany. While Sayad focused on the permanent deprivation of rights in migration and used the term 'immigrants of the interior' for the generation born in France, Karakayali's work renders the autonomy of migration historically visible without the claim to control inherent in the governance of migration (ibid., 258).

Abdallah's perspective on self-organisation also captures the conflicts of quotidian life. From 1974 to 1980 the residents of the apartment buildings managed by the *Société nationale de construction de logements pour les travailleurs* (Sonacotra) went on one of the longest national tenant strikes in France. As in many European countries at the time, in 1972 the Marcellin-Fontanet decrees subjected immigration to strict controls aimed at stopping official labour migration and at the same time called for integration of those considered integrable. Politically active migrants could thus be tied to the union; trade-union sections for migrants emerged, but overall the policy sought to integrate immigrants into the homogenously depicted French workforce (cf. Abdallah 2001, 113). Abdallah speaks of a very close connection between French workers' struggles and migrants' struggles; they were repeatedly able to place so-called 'specific demands' into a broader social context of growing ethnification of power relations as a whole. Virdee (2014) observed something similar for the UK:

> By reading that history through the lens of race, through the eyes of racialized minorities who were present in every one of those moments, we find that race and class were mutually constitutive in the making of the English working class.
>
> *(Virdee 2015, 226f)*

Racism itself could thus be understood in all of these studies as a form of social confrontation in which racism renews itself and contributes to a certain form of social reproduction – instead of reducing it to the subjects it produces (foreigners vs. French; racialised outsiders vs. English).

All mentioned authors' assessments refer to their knowledge of historical migration struggles. In this respect they are in agreement with the reflections of Allen or Roediger: they all investigate the fields of conflict. What Allen describes as the concept of social control, by which he means constructing a system of rule that enables effective control of the labour force through social stratification, is reflected in trade-union and state integration policies which others (Abdallah 2001; Bojadžijev 2008; Virdee 2014) in turn describe. These works evidence that politics in its dominant form functions recuperatively: it responds to demands made in struggles by isolating some of them and integrating others. This must not necessarily be understood as a historical defeat but can be reversed in a historical analysis, for social disputes are in fact inscribed in the reorganisation of racism, politics, and production. This reorganisation can only be understood with a view to conflict.

Conclusion and possible developments

Following the notion of anti-racism as method, in conclusion we could ask how racism can be analysed without adopting a perspective in which those affected by racism are seen merely as victims. To bring these considerations into the present, we need only think of the countless workers who are referred to as the 'shadow workforce' of the tech industry. All those who work for shiny, global monopolists like Google, Facebook, Apple, Amazon, or Microsoft as contract workers or in subcontracted firms, and who inhabit a number of different roles across the industry, including content moderation, serving meals, driving as bike and package couriers across cities, cleaning offices, providing security, writing code, and performing click work. First studies show that this workforce is highly mobile and flexible, and that historically-driven race, class, and gender-based orders and relationships with gentrification and growing inequality exist in tech industry contexts (Altenried, Bojadžijev, and Wallis 2017). Additionally, workers tend to become an atomised unit, dispersed across space, their labour spatially and temporarily reconfigured according to employer's needs. The end of the factory as a spatial unity, the introduction of the 'digital factory' (Altenried 2017), means for the individual contractors, that the burden of responsibility for their livelihoods is placed merely on them. As a result, labour becomes more fragmented, disempowered, and made to accept lower wages despite intensifying exploitation. Such workers are stereotyped in gendered and racialised ways by their employers, which creates an ambivalent space for both resistance and at the same time such discrimination prevents them from officially organising. Employers will attempt to recuperate the worker's social and cultural customs as assets to the flexible workplace and process, for example in content moderation (Altenried and Bojadžijev 2017). Many of the women working in electronics manufacturing that Karen Hossfeld (1995) interviewed already in the 1980s and 1990s in Silicon Valley were resistant to traditional labour unions and generally wary of collective organising. But they did have strategies for dealing with unreasonable, sexist, and racist superiors. In her analyses she concludes:

> For immigrant women workers, a successful organizing movement will be one that addresses the intersections of class, gender, race, and nationality in their lives, a movement recognizing that for women [...] a work life means not only wage work but household and community labor, and often includes the struggles associated with being undocumented. What is needed is an interethnic labor and community movement that challenges gender and racial oppression as well as dangerous, unstable working conditions in the high-tech industry. And because of the global scope and mobility of the industry, such a movement must also have an international component.
>
> *(Hossfeld 1995, 429–430)*

We can learn from such studies that the variegated global spaces of racism and labour that I have been investigating for this chapter are sometimes encapsulate in local images of the world. Thus, researching racism under global conditions may lead us back to anti-racism as method in that we can learn how such space does not only 'hit the ground' in concrete struggles but also teaches us how to understand racism and its morphologies. Those subjected to racism were and are never only objects and victims, but have defended themselves against it in various forms and practices. Resistance has historically emerged in direct or indirect, collective or individual confrontations following certain patterns of identity (as leftists, according to their origin/religion/racial or ethnic identities, as internationalists). Only in the rarest of cases did they articulate the question of social change as a question of identity or of change itself within the respective power relations. They are to be understood as a search for change in which the conditions for a better life in and against racist situations are found again and again.

Taking the disquiet in racism scholarship diagnosed at the beginning of this chapter as a motive and drawing conclusions from the theoretical considerations discussed above, I dare to put forward a far-reaching thesis for a relational theory of racism: conjunctures of racism determine, organise, and reorganise themselves in struggle – in social and political confrontations that produce, reproduce, and transform their opponents (which can be manifold) in their identity and formation. Consequently, and this point has certainly been made by many but also questioned by others, one of the constant efforts in undermining racism is to dissolve positions of identity. The conjunctures of racism do not depend only on its internal reproductive capacity – racism's reorganisation and development is shaped decisively by those who defend themselves against it. The fight against racism can thus be taken as the methodological starting point. Racism itself is a form of social confrontation in which it renews itself and contributes to capitalist development's complex forms. A theory of racism must therefore not only include anti-racist practices in theoretical analysis and critique, but also include conflicts that go beyond resistance to racism in which struggles and critiques are not necessarily articulated as anti-racist (cf. Bojadžijev 2008). We must therefore always ask and define: what is the concrete conflict?

References

Abdallah, M. (2001). *J'y suis, j'y reste ! Les luttes de l'immigration en France depuis les années soixante*. Paris: Éditions REFLEXes.

Allen, T. W. (1997). *The Invention of the White Race. The Origin of Racial Oppression in Anglo-America*. London and New York: Verso.

Allen, T. W. (1998). 'An interview with Theodore W. Allen by Jonathan Scott and Gregory Meyerson'. In: *Cultural Logic*, 1(2). Available at: http://eserver.org/clogic/1-2/1-2index.html

Altenried, M. (2017). 'Die Plattform als Fabrik. Crowdwork, Digitaler Taylorismus und die Vervielfältigung der Arbeit'. *PROKLA. Zeitschrift für kritische Sozialwissenschaft*. pp. 175–192.

Altenried, M. and M. Bojadžijev (2017). 'Virtual migration, logistics, and the multiplication of labour'. In: *Spheres. Journal for Digital Cultures*, 4. Media and Migration, Available online: http://spheres-journal.org/virtual-migration-racism-and-the-multiplication-of-labour/

Altenried, M., M. Bojadžijev and M. Wallis (2017) Researching Labour Mobility in Digital Times. Border Criminologies Blog. Faculty of Law, University of Oxford. Available at: www.law.ox.ac.uk/research-subject-groups/centre-criminology/centreborder-criminologies/blog/2018/05/researching

Althusser, L. (1971). 'Ideology and ideological state apparatuses'. In: *Lenin and Philosophy and Other Essays*. London: New Left Books, pp. 121–176.

Balibar, E.(1988). 'Racism and nationalism'. In: *Race, Nation, Class. Ambiguous Identities*. London and New York: Verso, pp. 37–68.

Balibar, E. (2005). 'Difference, otherness, exclusion'. In: *Parallax*, 11(1), pp. 19–34.

Bhabha, H. (1987). 'Remembering Fanon'. In: *New Formations*, 1, pp. 118–124.

Bhabha, H. (1994). *The Location of Culture*. London and New York: Routledge.

Bojadžijev, M. (2008). *Die windige Internationale. Rassismus und Kämpfe der Migration*. Münster: Westfälisches Dampfboot.

Brenner, N., J. Peck and N. Theodore (2010). 'Variegated neoliberalization: geographies, modalities, pathways'. In: *Global Networks*, 10(2), pp. 182–222.

Bulmer, M. and J. Solomos (2018). 'Why do we still talk about race today?'. In: *Ethnic and Racial Studies*, 41(6), pp. 997–1013.

Césaire, A. (1972). *Discourse on Colonialism*. New York and London: Monthly Review Press.

Fanon, F. (2008 [1952]). *Black Skin, White Masks*. New York: Grove Press.

Fanon, F. (1961). *The Wretched of the Earth*. New York: Grove Weidenfeld.

Fanon, F. (1965 [1959]). *A Dying Colonialism*. New York: Grove Press.

Fanon, F. (1967). *Toward the African Revolution*. New York: Grove Press.

Foucault, M. (1980). 'Truth and power'. In: C. Gordon (ed.), *Power/Knowledge. Selected Interviews & Other Writings 1972–1977 by Michel Foucault*. Brighton: Havester, pp. 109–133.

Foucault, M. (2002 [1966]). *The Order of Things: An Archaeology of the Human Sciences*. London and New York: Routledge.

Gilroy, P. (1997). 'Diaspora and the detours of identity'. In: K. Woodward (ed.), *Identity and Difference*. London: Sage, pp. 301–343.

Gilroy, P. (2010). 'Fanon and Améry. Theory, torture and the prospect of humanism'. In: *Theory, Culture & Society*, 27(7–8), pp. 16–32.

Gilroy, P. (2011). 'Fanon and the value of the human'. In: *The Salon*, 4. Available at: http://jwtc.org.za/volume_4/paul_gilroy.htm

Goldberg, D. T. (2009). 'Racial comparisons, relational racisms: some thoughts on method'. In: *Ethnic and Racial Studies*, 32(7), pp. 1271–1282.

Hage, G. (2016). 'Recalling anti-racism'. In: *Ethnic and Racial Studies*, 39(1), pp. 123–133.

Hage, G. (2017). *Is Racism an Environmental Threat?* Cambridge: Polity.

Hall, S. (1980). 'Race, articulation and societies structured in dominance'. In: United Nations Educational Sociological Theories: Race and Colonialism (ed.), *Scientific and Cultural Organisation*. Paris: UNESCO, pp. 305–345.

Hall, S. (2016). *Cultural Studies 1983: A Theoretical History*. Durham, NC: Duke University Press.

Hossfeld, K. (1995). 'Why aren't high-tech workers organized? Lessons in gender, race, and nationality from silicaon valley'. In: D. Conford (ed.), *Working People of California*. Berkeley, Los Angeles, Oxford: The Regents of the University of California, pp. 406–432.

Ignatiev, N. (1995). *How the Irish Became White*. London: Routledge.

Jacobson, F. (1998). *Whiteness of all Colors: European Immigrants and the Alchemy of Race*. Cambridge: Harvard University Press.

Karakayali, S. (2008). *Gespenster der Migration: Zur Genealogie illegaler Einwanderung in der Bundesrepublik Deutschland*. Münster: transcript.

Lentin, A. (2016). 'Racism in public or public racism: doing anti-racism in "post-racial" times'. In: *Ethnic and Racial Studies*, 39(1), pp. 33–48.

Mauss, M. (2000 [1925]). *The Gift: Forms and Functions of Exchange in Archaic Societies*. New York: W. W. Norton & Company.

Mills, C. W. (1997). *The Racial Contract*. Ithaca, NY: Cornell University Press.

Mukherjee, R. (2016). 'Antiracism Limited'. In: *Cultural Studies*, 30(1), pp. 47–77.

Roediger, D. (1994). *Towards the Abolition of Whiteness: Essays on Race, Class and Politics*. New York and London: Verso.

Roediger, D. (1999). *The Wages of Whiteness: Race and the Making of the American Working Class*. Revised ed. London: Verso.

Roediger, D. (2005). *Working Toward Whiteness: How America's Immigrants Became White. The Strange Journey from Ellis Island to the Suburbs*. New York: Basic Books.

Roediger, D. (2008). *How Race Survived US History: From Settlement and Slavery to the Obama Phenomenon*. New York and London: Verso.

Roediger, D. (2017). *Class, Race, and Marxism*. New York and London: Verso.

Sayad, A. (1999). *La double absence. Des illusions de l' emigréaux souffrances de l'immigré*. Paris: Seuil.

Sayad, A. (2004). *The Suffering of the Immigrant*. Cambridge: Polity Press.

Tabili, L. (1994). *'We Ask for British Justice': Workers and Racial Difference in Late Imperial Britain*. Ithaca, NY: Cornell University Press.

Virdee, S. (2010). 'Racism, class and the dialectics of social transformation'. In: P. Hill-Collins and J. Solomos (eds.), *Handbook of Race and Ethnic Studies*. London: Sage, pp. 135–165.

Virdee, S. (2014). *Racism, Class and the Racialized Outsider*. Basingstoke: Palgrave.

Virdee, S. (2015). 'Opening a dialogue on race, class and national belonging'. In: *Ethnic and Racial Studies*, 38(13), pp. 2259–2266.

16

Contemporary anti-racism

A review of effective practice

Jehonathan Ben, David Kelly, and Yin Paradies

Introduction

Anti-racism can be minimally defined as 'forms of thought and/or practice that seek to confront, eradicate and/or ameliorate racism' (Bonnett, 2000, p. 4) and as 'ideologies and practices that affirm and seek to enable the equality of races and ethnic groups' (Bonnett, 2006, p. 1099). Anti-racism practice has expanded remarkably over the past decades (Paradies, 2016; Pettigrew & Tropp, 2006). At the same time, evidence as to what works in confronting, eradicating and ameliorating racism, or, complementarily, how to enable and affirm racial/ethnic equality, remains limited. Paluck (2016, p. 147), for example, asks, 'What do social scientists know about reducing prejudice in the world?' before concluding that we know 'very little'. And indeed, relative to the amount of anti-racism work underway, few evaluations have discerned interventions' causal effects, limiting our understanding of interventions' effectiveness. Real-world field experiments with longitudinal bearings (Paluck & Green, 2009; Paluck, Green, & Green, 2018) are especially well placed to answer questions about the extent and manners by which racism may be curbed, but remain particularly uncommon.

In this chapter, we examine research on anti-racism practice, focusing on effective approaches to tackling racism and interrelated phenomena like prejudice and racial/ethnic discrimination. In focusing on effectiveness, we examine the extent to which interventions produce measurable, positive changes. We draw especially on recent meta-analyses, reviews, and experimental (field- and laboratory- based) studies. First, we briefly summarise four central approaches to tackling racism, and synthesise key findings concerning effective anti-racism practices per approach as well as across approaches. We then consider the possibility that hindrance to anti-racism efforts may come from initiatives themselves, resulting in counterproductive 'backlash effects', and we discuss how these may be avoided. The chapter concludes with a broader discussion of current knowledge and implications for future research directions.

Approaches to anti-racism

Anti-racism approaches are highly diverse, spanning everything from prejudice reduction to conflict resolution to collective action (Paradies, 2016); and from reducing the incidence of racism to empowering racialised subjects to fostering a radical indifference to race (Hage,

2015). This includes examples such as virtual reality experiments (Banakou, Hanumanthu, & Slater, 2016) and participatory theatre projects (Sonn et al., 2015). Here we focus on some of the most commonly used anti-racism approaches and their effectiveness in addressing racism, namely: (1) intergroup contact; (2) training and education; (3) communications and media campaigns; and (4) organisational development. These approaches sometimes overlap or can be used in combination to reinforce one another; organisational development may, for instance, feature a component of diversity training, while diversity training and media campaigns may involve a degree of intergroup contact.

Intergroup contact

Intergroup contact is a broad anti-racism approach that has been extensively implemented and studied, and has arguably become the most important approach for reducing prejudice (Paluck, Green, & Green, 2018). Grounded in Gordon Allport's (1954) intergroup contact theory, it is predicated on five 'optimal contact conditions' for successfully reducing intergroup conflict and increasing harmony: (1) equal status between interacting groups; (2) common goals between groups; (3) intergroup cooperation; (4) support from authorities, law, or custom; and (5) situations that allow for developing personal acquaintance and friendships through meaningful, repeated contact (Al Ramiah & Hewstone, 2013; Pettigrew & Tropp, 2006). Contact may take direct (face-to-face) or indirect forms (i.e. as imagined, extended, vicarious or virtual) that can both be effective in reducing prejudice (Brown & Paterson, 2016). Educational settings like schools and universities are the most popular sites for intergroup contact interventions, followed by workplaces and organisations, and a host of other settings (Kalinoski et al., 2013; Pettigrew & Tropp, 2006).

Intergroup contact reduces prejudice through various mechanisms. Some of the best-studied and most important mechanisms include affective processes that decrease intergroup threat, anxiety and symbolic threat (i.e. anticipating harmful consequences), enhance self-disclosure, increase empathy and perspective taking, and alter group norms and social categorisations (Dovidio et al., 2017). The impact of intergroup contact on attitudes can generalise beyond the individual out-group members encountered and towards their greater group (Lemmer & Wagner, 2015; Pettigrew & Tropp, 2006). The extent to which the individuals encountered (whether directly or indirectly) are perceived as typical members of the out-group makes generalisation more likely (Al Ramiah & Hewstone, 2013; Brown & Paterson, 2016; Dovidio et al., 2017). Meta-analyses have shown that programme effects can persist after the programme has ended (Beelmann & Heinemann, 2014; Lemmer & Wagner, 2015).

Research demonstrates that the quality/favourability of contact has a stronger effect on attitudes than contact quantity, while the duration of contact also matters, with sustained contact becoming more positive over time, up to a point of diminishing returns (Dovidio et al., 2017). A balanced ratio of majority to minority group members in contact situations makes contact more effective in reducing prejudice, as it can maximise opportunities for interaction and reduce perceived intergroup threat (Al Ramiah & Hewstone, 2013). As to participants, college-aged students are more strongly impacted compared to adults (Pettigrew & Tropp, 2006), and participants who are highly prejudiced and/or for whom contact experiences are relatively novel may be more strongly impacted as having ample room for attitudinal change (Al Ramiah & Hewstone, 2013). While meeting Allport's conditions for optimal contact is associated with greater prejudice reduction, not all conditions may be required to reduce prejudice, and contact may not always lead to positive attitudes, whereas the attitudes of majority group members toward minority group members are often more strongly affected than vice versa (e.g. Dovidio et al., 2017; Pedersen et al., 2011; Ülger et al., 2017).

Anti-racism training and education

Various anti-racism initiatives use forms of education and training to enhance cultural competency or challenge discrimination, often at workplaces and schools. The most common intervention is diversity training, which draws on programmes that aim to increase positive intergroup behaviours and decrease prejudice or discrimination towards (perceived) out-group members (Pendry, Driscoll, & Field, 2007, p. 29). Training can decrease discriminatory attitudes and beliefs among most participants, but disturbingly can also *increase* them for a small, yet sizeable group (Paradies et al., 2009).

A meta-analysis of curricular and co-curricular diversity-related activities found they had moderate effect in reducing racial bias, where effects were stronger for white students compared with non-white students (Denson, 2009). Another meta-analysis of diversity training programmes, of which over a third focused on race, ethnicity, culture and/or religion, found considerable effects on cognitive-based and skill-based outcomes, and somewhat smaller effects on affective-based outcomes (Kalinoski et al., 2013). Other reviews have been less supportive of diversity training. A recent review suggests that training 'can lead to both positive and negative social justice outcomes', including studies that find that training can both reduce and increase discrimination (Alhejji et al., 2016, p. 5). A review of the impact of diversity training on management composition in private organisations found that it was generally ineffective in increasing the share of black American managers (Kalev, Dobbin, & Kelly, 2006).

Discussing effective manners of training and education, several studies stress the importance of explicitly discussing racism, within a safe space for open and frank dialogue (Paradies et al., 2009; Pedersen et al., 2011). Bezrukova, Jehn, and Spell (2012) point to effective aspects of diversity training such as using multiple instruction methods, and integrating training as part of systematic, planned organisational development rather than as standalone components. Focusing on participants from a range of racial/ethnic/cultural/religious backgrounds was deemed more effective than focusing on a specific group (Bezrukova, Jehn, & Spell, 2012; Paradies et al., 2009). In workplaces, engaging managers in promoting diversity, propelling them to increase their contact with members of different out-groups and encouraging their accountability are effective in reducing bias and increasing workplace diversity (Dobbin & Kalev, 2016). Both voluntary and compulsory training may be effective under certain situations. Although both have been subject to critique, for example for 'preaching to the converted' when voluntary, or for inducing resistance when forced (Bezrukova, Jehn, & Spell, 2012; Dobbin & Kalev, 2016).

To be effective, training should be neutral and informal, and provide accurate information about the out-group based on multiple disciplines, preferably using multiple instruction methods (e.g. readings, audio-visuals, small group discussion and role plays) (Pedersen et al., 2011; Torino, 2015). Training should be tailored to each organisation, linked to operational goals, and specifically address behaviour, while trainers should engage participants respectfully and interactively, build and invoke social norms, enhance awareness, attitudes and skills, and encourage intergroup contact where appropriate. They preferably should be 'insiders', from various racial/ethnic/cultural backgrounds, and with experience and/or qualifications in organisational change (Paradies et al., 2009).

Communications and media campaigns

Communications and media campaigns against racism usually consist of large-scale initiatives drawing on various media forms and platforms, sometimes use social marketing techniques, and are frequently assessed via experiments (naturalistic and lab-based). Media and communications can aggravate stereotyping, prejudice and discriminatory behaviour towards different racial/ethnic groups (Willard, Isaac, & Carney, 2015), but they can also raise awareness of race-based discrimination, impact attitudes and behaviours, and help develop or strengthen positive social norms (Paluck & Green, 2009; Paradies et al., 2009).

Although many 'real-life' campaigns exist, their impact has rarely seen rigorous assessment (Donovan & Vlais, 2006). A review of 13 media interventions addressing different forms of prejudice that used field experiments, noted that interventions were mostly conducted in schools and showed 'suggestive' results in their impact on empathy, perspective taking and social norms, as well as on using narratives for persuasive purposes (Paluck & Green, 2009). Other reviews have portrayed a similarly mixed picture of the effectiveness of anti-racism campaigns using communications and social marketing approaches to reduce discrimination and support diversity (Aboud et al., 2012; Donovan & Vlais, 2006; Rankine, 2014).

Popular racism-reduction methods that rely on audio-visual media (e.g. television and film) are vicarious and imagined intergroup contact (i.e. observing or imagining other people in intergroup contact situations) (Cadenas et al., 2018; Murrar & Brauer, 2018). Vicarious contact may produce constructive perceptions of the out-group and positive emotional responses towards them. It may capitalise on exposure to typical, favourable and salient counter-stereotypical media exemplars, and on identification with in-group characters that engage in positive contact. Other initiatives provide new information to challenge existing stereotypes and norms, or invoke emotions that are conducive to tackling prejudice (e.g. empathy). Studies assessing the impact of such media forms, often in laboratory contexts demonstrate mixed findings (e.g. Castelli et al., 2012; Igartua & Frutos, 2017; Vittrup & Holden, 2011).

Communications campaigns have stronger effects when they address specific negative beliefs rather than focus on generating positive feelings, and when focusing on various individuals from one ethnic/racial group at the time rather than promote broad purposes like 'diversity' and 'multiculturalism' (Donovan & Vlais, 2006). To increase their effectiveness, campaigns should identify beliefs that underlie expressions of racism, challenge racism and promote anti-racism as a prescriptive norm, and highlight perceived, appreciated similarities between groups, especially where negative beliefs are based on ignoring such similarities (Donovan & Vlais, 2006). Campaigns should involve the affected group as a visible part of the campaign, engage media personnel to change media representations, use advocacy and activism to generate wider support and impact policy, provide opportunities for discussion and interaction across groups and aim to pre-emptively address counterarguments (Donovan & Vlais, 2006). Finally, lab experiments suggest that nonverbal behaviours (in audio-visual representations) carry strong impact and need to be considered (Castelli et al., 2012), and that messages' content should be explicated (Vittrup & Holden, 2011).

Organisational development

Organisational development has been the least reviewed of the approaches we discuss here. Its projects typically use development and change processes to assess or 'audit' organisational functions in order to address discrimination and endorse diversity (Paradies et al., 2009, p. 52).

Such projects may implement new organisational policies, plans or operational processes, model and enforce non-discriminatory standards, and work to impact social norms and wider societal change. They may use the three aforementioned approaches, as well as develop resources (e.g. teacher professional development, journalist guides), draw on organisational leadership and deploy conflict resolution approaches (Paradies et al., 2009, pp. 52–53). Multiple studies have documented the effects of individual initiatives, suggesting promising results in relation to organisations in areas such as healthcare (Weech-Maldonado et al., 2018), education (Hagopian et al., 2018) and workplaces (Ferdinand, Paradies, & Kelaher, 2017; Trenerry, Franklin, & Paradies, 2012).

Practices considered effective include development of a shared organisational vision, clear goals, measurable outcomes, and organisational accountability, as well as customisation based on local social, political and other contexts (Paradies et al., 2009; Trenerry, Franklin, & Paradies, 2012). Initiatives are more impactful when cultivating transparency, trust and the exchange of information (Ferdinand, Paradies, & Kelaher, 2017; Paradies et al., 2009). Organisational development tends to involve multiple layers and elements and large-scale public institutions. Although such complexity is important, it may also introduce inherent challenges to organisational development that must be engaged with (Ferdinand, Paradies, & Kelaher, 2017; Spaaij et al., 2016). Using a 'whole of organisation' approach (Trenerry, Franklin, & Paradies, 2012), and a detailed strategic plan addressing multiple aspects of organisational functioning are also considered effective practices (Trenerry, Franklin, & Paradies, 2012, and see discussion in Abramovitz & Blitz, 2015).

Effective practice across approaches

Various practices have demonstrated effectiveness across two or more of the approaches we discussed. At the outset, interventions should be carefully planned, mapped, and well developed, attending to areas like their objectives and materials, while involving a management group and various stakeholders (Donovan & Vlais, 2006; Paradies et al., 2009). Interventions that are theory-driven or based on solid theoretical foundations have been considered more effective in curbing prejudice (Aboud et al., 2012; Pettigrew and Tropp, 2006). The significant place of evaluation research throughout interventions' lifespan has been reiterated across approaches, involving the use of formative research, preliminary testing of objectives and methods (Aboud et al., 2012; Donovan and Vlais, 2006), allocation of sufficient resources for planning and implementation (Paradies et al., 2009; Rankine, 2014), and preferably using evaluations that consist of pre- and post- testing, randomisation, and delayed outcome measures (Paradies et al., 2009; Pedersen et al., 2011).

Strong support from organisational leaders and champions has been considered crucial for programme effectiveness (Paradies et al., 2009; Trenerry, Franklin, & Paradies, 2012). There is usually an advantage to longer programmes and to programmes that consist of many sessions (Aboud et al., 2012; Kalinoski et al., 2013; Paradies et al., 2009; Pedersen et al., 2011), and wide support for programmes that emphasise invoking empathy (Dovidio et al., 2017; Mazziotta et al., 2011; Paluck & Green, 2009; Pedersen et al., 2011). Last, some have recommended that these approaches work best when integrated and that initiatives are more impactful when collaborating with other organisations involved in anti-racism work (Bezrukova, Jehn, & Spell, 2012; Paradies et al., 2009). The use of multiple, multi-level (e.g. state authorities, organisations), reinforcing approaches, can render interventions more effective (Paradies et al., 2009; and see; Ferdinand, Paradies, & Kelaher, 2017; Johnson, Antle, & Barbee, 2009; Weech-Maldonado et al., 2018 for effective combinations of organisational development and training).

Within the scope of this chapter, we are unable to discuss in detail real-world examples of practices that embody many of these recommended approaches previously. For further reading, refer to exemplary work on intergroup dialogue (Rodríguez et al., 2018); training (Johnson, Antle, & Barbee, 2009); organisational development (Weech-Maldonado et al., 2018); and media campaigns (Paluck, 2009, 2010).

Backlash effects

Anti-racism practice can have unintended consequences that may deter its effectiveness. The possibility of such backlash should be considered and pre-empted. Backlash towards anti-racism programmes, policies or practices, denotes forms of resistance that have the potential to strengthen prejudiced attitudes and negative relations between in-groups and out-groups. It can occur everywhere, from small-scale training to national populations, in relation, for example, to multicultural policies (Hewitt, 2005). Backlash works in ways that range from affective-based measures such as negative emotions, through to cognitive forms such as attitudes and perceptions, and is expressed in behaviours that negatively affect the outcomes of programmes, policies or practices (Kidder et al., 2004, p. 77). Anticipating backlash can itself become a form of backlash, by precluding the initiation or implementation of anti-racism initiatives, which can manifest as a refusal or withdrawal of basic resources and services (Bakan and Kobayashi, 2004, 2007a, 2007b).

Research on perspective taking demonstrates that imagining one's 'self' increases the potential to negatively evaluate oneself which can entrench racial prejudice (Vorauer & Sasaki, 2014). Perceived threat to notions of 'self' in interpersonal contexts (e.g. because of high dissimilarity with others) may also provoke backlash effects (Sassenrath, Hodges, & Pfattheicher, 2016). Backlash is always a risk in intergroup encounters that confront negative behaviours (Focella, Bean, & Stone, 2015). Some studies have explored how intergroup encounters, where minority groups seek to reduce harm and prejudice by confronting perpetrators, can produce backlash effects that increase prejudiced attitudes (Vorauer & Sasaki, 2009). Studies on confronting prejudice report various forms of backlash, including dislike for the person and their perceived in-group (Czopp, Monteith, & Mark, 2006), while racial discrimination reported by African American participants in educational settings resulted in the stigmatisation of them as complainers (Kaiser & Miller, 2001). Other studies found that out-group members who confronted discriminatory behaviour were more likely to be negatively assessed (or have negative attitudes of them reinforced) by in-group members who were being discriminatory (Gulker, Mark, & Monteith, 2013; Rasinski & Czopp, 2010). This is especially true when persons who hold strong views of meritocracy are confronted, where evaluations of the 'confronter' are particularly negative (Schultz & Maddox, 2013), and likewise for those who adopt a colour-blind perspective (Zou & Dickter, 2013).

Forms of framing in anti-racist interventions play a significant role in manifestations of backlash. Framing diversity as 'good' within organisations (and not as 'fair') may broaden definitions of diversity to include axes of difference beyond race, which can lead, unintentionally, to deprioritising hiring applicants from racial minority backgrounds (Trawalter, Driskell, & Davidson, 2016). The colour-blind approach may often be seen as remedy to such paradoxical framings, although it can reinforce exclusive institutions that maintain unequal power structures in society (Smith & Mayorga-Gallo, 2017). In institutions where cultural diversity is widespread, multicultural policies are generally likely to reduce stereotyping and prejudice, whereas colour-blind practices and policies (ignoring or avoiding race and racial categories) may enhance stereotyping and prejudice, and may leave discrimination undetected (Plaut, 2014). Also, while a focus on multiculturalist frameworks produces a higher rate of success in reducing biases than colour-blind frameworks, negative outcomes routinely occur, and multiculturalist frameworks can ironically produce higher instances of racialised essentialism, reproducing beliefs that race is biologically determined and fixed (Wilton, Apfelbaum, & Good, 2019).

When diversity inclusion frameworks are imposed upon – or topped-down from within – organisations, research has also found paradoxical outcomes. Dobbin, Schrage, and Kalev (2015) examined the effects of workplace innovations like training, on managerial diversity in 816 U.S. workplaces over 30 years. Accountability in the implementation of such innovations, such as monitoring the impact of hiring reforms through 'diversity managers', improved outcomes and reduced the potential for workplace backlash. However, compulsory accountability frameworks often backfired, suggesting that frameworks should in such contexts be willingly implemented. Using data on approximately 500 high-profile employment discrimination lawsuits resolved in U.S. federal courts between 1996 and 2008, Hirsh and Cha (2017) found that court-mandated policy changes to reduce bias expanded opportunities for white women but not for other demographic groups, while policies to increase awareness of rights were associated with declines in managerial diversity. Verdicts with the most costly monetary payouts did not expand managerial diversity compared to more modest payouts, and can further a lack of diversity.

Rutchick and Eccleston (2010) show that when minority groups invoke shared identity characteristics with the majority group during diversity training, this may lead to negative outcomes. The level of backlash exhibited in these experimental studies is predominantly determined by the strength of relationship and identification that groups have with a (perceived) larger homogenous whole, like the nation. The extent to which groups identify as being emblematic of such an overarching whole determines the degree to which messages that invoke dominant-group diversity will be received as intended (Falomir-Pichastor & Frederic, 2013; Steffens et al., 2017).

Discussion

Assessments of intergroup contact, training and education, communications and media campaigns and organisational development have varied in their approaches and conclusions. Intergroup contact interventions have been frequently evaluated, resulting in a broad evidence base that suggests that contact can often reduce racism, especially prejudice. Training and education initiatives, and particularly cultural diversity/competence programmes, have been widespread, yet not much is known about the extent to which, and circumstances under which, they effectively address racism. Concerns about null and adverse effects have made diversity training a particularly contentious area, as suggested by several study titles, like 'Why diversity programs fail' (Dobbin & Kalev, 2016) and 'Pointless diversity training' (Noon, 2018). Other areas of anti-racism practice have seen far less evaluation. Communications and media campaigns show promise but also mixed findings, and have been scarcely evaluated outside the lab. Organisational development initiatives have been discussed individually (or as part of education/training initiatives), but to our knowledge have yet to be collectively reviewed or assessed regarding their effects.

Anti-racism's limited evidence base calls for further comprehensive, fine-grained analysis. Field experiments are clearly a priority in this field because of the dynamic, real-life nature of many anti-racism initiatives and the change they seek to instigate. In addition to using randomisation and control, there remains a strong need for assessments to go beyond pre- and immediate post- test measures. Given that intervention effects may transform post-intervention (for example diminish, or show delayed improvement) it is crucial that we develop better understanding of what happens long after initiatives end. Systematic reviews and meta-analyses of the relationship between training, communications and organisational development initiatives (and initiative components) and the reduction of racial prejudice, discrimination, and contingent outcomes pertaining to racism are also much-needed.

Recently, several studies have emerged that constitute promising future directions in anti-racism practice and research. Examples of innovative, effective methodologies include reading popular books (e.g. Harry Potter) to reduce prejudice that capitalise on processes like identification and perspective taking (Vezzali et al., 2015), embodiment of another racial/ethnic group's (e.g. black) virtual body to reduce implicit racial bias (Banakou, Hanumanthu, & Slater, 2016; Peck et al., 2013), and exposure to extreme racist audio-visual content which can, paradoxically, lead individuals to reassess their current (less extreme) racist attitudes and beliefs (Hameiri, Bar-Tal, & Halperin, 2019; Hameiri et al., 2014, 2016).

Based on available research, anti-racism initiatives are particularly effective when they are carefully developed, theory- and evidence- based, longer-term, draw on clear objectives and explicit messages, and include rigorous, ongoing evaluation research (e.g. Johnson, Antle, & Barbee, 2009; Paluck, 2009, 2010; Rodríguez et al., 2018; Weech-Maldonado et al., 2018). Reviews also repeatedly stress, and successful initiatives demonstrate, the significance of collaboration, support from and ongoing engagement with and between stakeholders, from institutional leadership to affected groups. There are indications that the integration of various approaches, initiative components, methods and materials is effective in addressing racism. Emerging scholarship cautions us against ways in which anti-racism initiatives may do more harm than good and have led to efforts to understand how we can best avoid backlash. Key suggestions include avoiding negations, given that injunctions to '*do not*' create unintended associations between subjects (Gawronski et al., 2008), enhancing participants' self-affirmation (Stone et al., 2011; Watt et al., 2009), and being wary of framing diversity within an overriding identity category (e.g. 'the nation') that the dominant in-group is protective of (Falomir-Pichastor & Frederic, 2013; Steffens et al., 2017).

References

Aboud, F. E., Tredoux, C., Tropp, L. R., Brown, C. S., Niens, U., Noor, N. M.Una Global Evaluation Group. 2012. Interventions to reduce prejudice and enhance inclusion and respect for ethnic differences in early childhood: A systematic review.. *Developmental Review, 32* (4), pp. 307–336.

Abramovitz, M. & L. V. Blitz 2015. Moving toward racial equity: The undoing racism workshop and organizational change. *Race and Social Problems, 7* (2), pp. 97–110.

Al Ramiah, A., & Hewstone, M. 2013. Intergroup contact as a tool for reducing, resolving, and preventing intergroup conflict: Evidence, limitations, and potential. *American Psychologist, 68* (7), pp. 527–542.

Alhejji, H., Garavan, T., Carbery, R., O'Brien, F., & McGuire, D. 2016. Diversity training programme outcomes: A systematic review. *Human Resource Development Quarterly, 27* (1), pp. 95–149.

Allport, G. 1954. *The Nature of Prejudice.* New York: Perseus Books.

Bakan, A. B., & Kobayashi, A. 2004. Backlash against employment equity: The British Columbia experience. *Atlantis: Critical Studies in Gender, Culture & Social Justice, 29* (1), pp. 61–70.

Bakan, A. B., & Kobayashi, A. 2007a. Affirmative Action and Employment Equity: Policy, Ideology, and Backlash in Canadian Context. *Studies in Political Economy, 79* (1), pp. 145–166.

Bakan, A. B., & Kobayashi, A. 2007b. 'The Sky Didn't Fall': Organizing to Combat Racism in the Workplace – The Case of the Alliance for Employment Equity. In G. F. Johnson and R. Enomoto (eds), *Race, Racialization, and Antiracism in Canada and Beyond.* Toronto: University of Toronto Press, pp. 51–78.

Banakou, D., Hanumanthu, P. D., & Slater, M. 2016. Virtual embodiment of white people in a black virtual body leads to a sustained reduction in their implicit racial bias. *Frontiers in Human Neuroscience*, *10*, p. 601.

Beelmann, A., & Heinemann, K. S. 2014. Preventing prejudice and improving intergroup attitudes: A meta-analysis of child and adolescent training programs. *Journal of Applied Developmental Psychology*, *35* (1), pp. 10–24.

Bezrukova, K., Jehn, K. A., & Spell, C. S. 2012. Reviewing Diversity Training: Where We Have Been and Where We Should Go. *Academy of Management Learning & Education*, *11* (2), pp. 207–227.

Bonnett, A. 2000. *Anti-Racism*. London: Routledge.

Bonnett, A. 2006. The Americanisation of Anti-Racism? Global Power and Hegemony in Ethnic Equity. *Journal of Ethnic and Migration Studies.*, *32* (7), pp. 1083–1103.

Brown, R., & Paterson, J. 2016. Indirect contact and prejudice reduction: limits and possibilities. *Current Opinion in Psychology*, 11, pp. 20–24.

Cadenas, G.A., Cisneros, J., Todd, N.R., & Spanierman, L. 2018. DREAMzone: Testing Two Vicarious Contact Interventions to Improve Attitudes Toward Undocumented Immigrants. *Journal of Diversity in Higher Education*, *11* (3), pp. 295–308.

Castelli, L., Carraro, L., Pavan, G., Murelli, E., & Carraro, A. 2012. The Power of the Unsaid: The Influence of Nonverbal Cues on Implicit Attitudes. *Journal of Applied Social Psychology*, *42* (6), pp. 1376–1393.

Czopp, A. M., Monteith, M. J., & Mark, A. Y. 2006. Standing up for a change: Reducing bias through interpersonal confrontation. *J Pers.Soc.Psychol*, *90* (5), pp. 784–803.

Denson, N. 2009. Do curricular and co-curricular diversity activities influence racial bias? A meta-analysis. *Review of Educational Research*, *79*, pp. 805–838.

Dobbin, F., & Kalev, A. 2016. Why diversity programs fail. *Harvard Business Review*, *94* (7), pp. 52–60.

Dobbin, F., Schrage, D., & Kalev, A. 2015. Rage against the Iron Cage: The Varied Effects of Bureaucratic Personnel Reforms on Diversity. *American Sociological Review*, *80* (5), pp. 1014–1044.

Donovan, R. J., & Vlais, R. 2006. *A review of communication components of anti-racism and prodiversity social marketing/public education campaigns*. Melbourne: RJD Consulting Pty Ltd.

Dovidio, J. F., Love, A., Schellhaas, F. M. H., & Hewstone, M. 2017. Reducing intergroup bias through intergroup contact: Twenty years of progress and future directions. *Group Processes & Intergroup Relations*, *20* (5), pp. 606–620.

Falomir-Pichastor, J. M., & Frederic, N. S. 2013. The dark side of heterogeneous ingroup identities: National identification, perceived threat, and prejudice against immigrants. *Journal of Experimental Social Psychology*, *49* (1), pp. 72–79.

Ferdinand, A. S., Paradies, Y., & Kelaher, M. 2017. Enhancing the use of research in health-promoting, anti-racism policy. *Health Research Policy and Systems*, *15* (1), pp. 61.

Focella, E. S., Bean, M. G., & Stone, J. 2015. Confrontation and Beyond: Examining a Stigmatized Target's Use of a Prejudice Reduction Strategy. *Social and Personality Psychology Compass*, *9* (2), pp. 100–114.

Gawronski, B., Deutsch, R., Mbirkou, S., Seibt, B., & Strack, F. 2008. When "Just Say No" is not enough: Affirmation versus negation training and the reduction of automatic stereotype activation. *Journal of Experimental Social Psychology*, *44*, pp. 370–377.

Gulker, J. E., Mark, A. Y., & Monteith, M. J. 2013. Confronting prejudice: The who, what, and why of confrontation effectiveness. *Social Influence*, *8* (4), pp. 280–293.

Hage, G. 2015. Alter-Politics: Critical Anthropology and the Radical Imagination. Melbourne: Melbourne University Publishing.

Hagopian, A., West, K. M., Ornelas, I. J., Hart, A. N., Hagedorn, J., & Spigner, C. 2018. Adopting an Anti-Racism Public Health Curriculum Competency: The University of Washington Experience. *Public Health Reports*, *133* (4), pp. 507–513.

Hameiri, B. Bar-Tal, D. & Halperin E. 2019. Paradoxical Thinking Interventions: A Paradigm for Societal Change. *Social Issues and Policy Review*, *13* (1), pp. 36–62.

Hameiri, B., Porat, R., Bar-Tal, D., Bieler, A., & Halperin, E. 2014. Paradoxical thinking as a new avenue of intervention to promote peace. *Proceedings of the National Academy of Sciences*, *111* (30), pp. 10996–11001.

Hameiri, B., Porat, R., Bar-Tal, D., & Halperin, E. 2016. Moderating attitudes in times of violence through paradoxical thinking intervention. *Proceedings of the National Academy of Sciences*, *113* (43), pp. 12105–12110.

Hewitt, R. 2005. *White Backlash and the Politics of Multiculturalism*. Cambridge: Cambridge University Press.

Hirsh, E., & Cha, Y. 2017. Mandating change: The impact of court-ordered policy changes on managerial diversity. *ILR Review, 70* (1), pp. 42–72.

Igartua, J. J., & Frutos, F. J. 2017. Enhancing Attitudes Toward Stigmatized Groups with Movies: Mediating and Moderating Processes of Narrative Persuasion. *International Journal of Communication*, 11, pp. 158–177.

Johnson, L. M., Antle, B. F., & Barbee, A. P. 2009. Addressing disproportionality and disparity in child welfare: Evaluation of an anti-racism training for community service providers. *Children and Youth Services Review, 31* (6), pp. 688–696.

Kaiser, C. R., & Miller, C. T. 2001. Stop Complaining! The Social Costs of Making Attributions to Discrimination. *Personality & Social Psychology Bulletin, 27* (2), pp. 254–263.

Kalev, A., Dobbin, F., & Kelly, E. 2006. Best Practices or Best Guesses? Assessing the Efficacy of Corporate Affirmative Action and Diversity Policies. *American Sociological Review, 71* (4), pp. 589–617.

Kalinoski, Z. T., Steele-Johnson, D., Peyton, E. J., Leas, K. A., Steinke, J., & Bowling, N. A. 2013. A meta-analytic evaluation of diversity training outcomes. *Journal of Organizational Behavior, 34* (8), pp. 1076–1104.

Kidder, D. L., Lankau, M. J., Chrobot-Mason, D., Mollica, K. A., & Friedman, R. A. 2004. Backlash toward Diversity Initiatives: Examining the Impact of Diversity Program Justification, Personal and Group Outcomes. *International Journal of Conflict Management, 15* (1), pp. 77–102.

Lemmer, G., & Wagner, U. 2015. Can we really reduce ethnic prejudice outside the lab? A meta-analysis of direct and indirect contact interventions. *European Journal of Social Psychology*, 45 (2), pp. 152–168.

Mazziotta, A., et al. 2011. Vicarious intergroup contact effects: Applying social-cognitive theory to intergroup contact research. *Group Processes and Intergroup Relations*, 14 (2), pp. 255–274.

Murrar, S. & Brauer, M. 2018. Entertainment-education effectively reduces prejudice. *Group Processes and Intergroup Relations, 21* (7), pp. 1053–1077.

Noon, M. 2018. Pointless diversity training: Unconscious bias, new racism and agency. *Work, Employment and Society, 32* (1), pp. 198–209.

Paluck, E. L. 2009. Reducing intergroup prejudice and conflict using the media: A field experiment in Rwanda. *J Pers. Soc Psychol., 96* (3), pp. 574–587.

Paluck, E. L. 2010. Is It Better Not to Talk? Group Polarization, Extended Contact, and Perspective Taking in Eastern Democratic Republic of Congo. *Personality & Social Psychology Bulletin, 36* (9), pp. 1170–1185.

Paluck, E. L. 2016. How to overcome prejudice. *Science, 352* (6282), p. 147.

Paluck, E. L., & Green, D. P. 2009. Prejudice Reduction: What Works? A Review and Assessment of Research and Practice. *Annu. Rev. Psychol, 60*, pp. 339–367.

Paluck, E. L., Green, S. A., & Green, D. P. 2018. The contact hypothesis re-evaluated, *Behavioural Public Policy*, 3 (2), pp. 129–158.

Paradies, Y. 2016. Whither anti-racism?. *Ethnic and Racial Studies, 39* (1), pp. 1–15.

Paradies, Y., Chandrakumar, L., Klocker, N., Frere, M., Webster, K., Burrell, M., & McLean, P. 2009. Building on our strengths: a framework to reduce race-based discrimination and support diversity in Victoria: Full report. Melbourne: Victorian Health Promotion Foundation.

Peck, T. C., Seinfeld, S., Aglioti, S. M., & Slater, M. 2013. Putting yourself in the skin of a black avatar reduces implicit racial bias. *Consciousness and Cognition, 22* (3), pp. 779–787.

Pedersen, A., Walker, I., Paradies, Y., & Guerin, B. 2011. How to cook rice: A review of ingredients for teaching anti-prejudice. *Australian Psychologist, 46* (1), pp. 55–63.

Pendry, L. F., Driscoll, D. M., & Field, S. C. T. 2007. Diversity training: Putting theory into practice. *Journal of Occupational and Organizational Psychology, 80* (1), pp. 27–50.

Pettigrew, T. F., & Tropp, L. R. 2006. A Meta-Analytic Test Of Intergroup Contact Theory. *J Pers. Soc. Psychol, 90* (5), pp. 751–783.

Plaut, V. C. 2014. Diversity Science and Institutional Design. *Policy Insights from the Behavioral and Brain Sciences, 1* (1), pp. 72–80.

Rankine, J. 2014. Creating effective anti-racism campaigns: Report to the race relations commissioner. Auckland: Kupu Taea.

Rasinski, H. M., & Czopp, A. M. 2010. The Effect of Target Status on Witnesses' Reactions to Confrontations of Bias. *Basic and Applied Social Psychology, 32* (1), pp. 8–16.

Rodríguez, J., Nagda, B.R.A., Sorensen, N., & Gurin, P. 2018. Engaging Race And Racism For Socially Just Intergroup Relations: The Impact Of Intergroup Dialogue On College Campuses In The United States. *Multicultural Education Review, 10* (3), pp. 224–245.

Rutchick, A. M., & Eccleston, C. P. 2010. Ironic effects of invoking common ingroup identity. *Basic and Applied Social Psychology, 32* (1), pp. 109–117.

Sassenrath, C., Hodges, S. D., & Pfattheicher, S. 2016. It's All About the Self: When Perspective Taking Backfires. *Current Directions in Psychological Science, 25* (6), pp. 405–410.

Schultz, J. R., & Maddox, K. B. 2013. Shooting the Messenger to Spite the Message? Exploring Reactions to Claims of Racial Bias. *Personality and Social Psychology Bulletin, 39* (3), pp. 346–358.

Smith, C. W. & S. Mayorga-Gallo. 2017. The New Principle-policy Gap: How Diversity Ideology Subverts Diversity Initiatives. *Sociological Perspectives, 60* (5), pp. 889–911.

Sonn, C. C., Quayle, A. F., Belanji, B., & Baker, A. M. 2015. Responding To Racialization Through Arts Practice: The Case Of Participatory Theater. *Journal of Community Psychology, 43* (2), pp. 244–259.

Spaaij, R., Magee, J., Farquharson, K., Gorman, S., Jeanes, R., Lusher, D., & Storr, R. 2016. Diversity Work In Community Sport Organizations: Commitment, Resistance and Institutional Change. *International Review for the Sociology of Sport*, 53 (3), pp. 278–295.

Steffens, M. C., Reese, G., Ehrke, F., & Jonas, K. J. 2017. When Does Activating Diversity Alleviate, When Does It Increase Intergroup Bias? An Ingroup Projection Perspective. *PLOS ONE*, 12 (6), pp. e0178738.

Stone, J., Whitehead, J., Schmader, T., & Focella, E. 2011. Thanks For Asking: Self-Affirming Questions Reduce Backlash When Stigmatized Targets Confront Prejudice. *Journal of Experimental Social Psychology, 47* (3), pp. 589–598.

Torino, G. C. 2015. Examining Biases and White Privilege: Classroom Teaching Strategies That Promote Cultural Competence. *Women & Therapy, 38* (3-4), pp. 295–307.

Trawalter, S., Driskell, S. & Davidson, M. N. 2016. What Is Good Isn't Always Fair: On the Unintended Effects of Framing Diversity as Good. *Analyses of Social Issues and Public Policy, 16* (1), pp. 69–99.

Trenerry, B., Franklin, H., & Paradies, Y. 2012. *Preventing race-based discrimination and supporting cultural diversity in the workplace – An evidence review: full report.* Melbourne: Victorian Health Promotion Foundation.

Ülger, Z., Dette-Hagenmeyer, D. E., Reichle, B., & Gaertner, S. L. 2017. Improving Outgroup Attitudes In Schools: A Meta-Analytic Review. *Journal of School Psychology., 67*, pp. 88–103.

Vezzali, L., Stathi, S., Giovannini, D., Capozza, D., & Trifiletti, E. 2015. The greatest magic of Harry Potter: Reducing prejudice. *Journal of Applied Social Psychology, 45* (2), pp. 105–121.

Vittrup, B., & Holden, G. W. 2011. Exploring the Impact of Educational Television and Parent-Child Discussions on Children's Racial Attitudes. *Analyses of Social Issues & Public Policy, 11* (1), pp. 82–104.

Vorauer, J. D., & Sasaki, S. J. 2009. Helpful Only in the Abstract?: IronicEffects of Empathy in Intergroup Interaction. *Psychological Science, 20* (2), pp. 191–197.

Vorauer, J. D. & S. J. Sasaki. 2014. Distinct Effects of Imagine-Other Versus Imagine-Self Perspective-Taking on Prejudice Reduction. *Social Cognition, 32* (2), pp. 130–147.

Watt, S., Maio, G., Haddock, G., & Johnson, B. 2009. Attitude Functions in Persuasion: Matching, Involvement, Self-Affi rmation, and Hierarchy. In W. Crano & R. Prislin (eds), *Attitudes and Persuasion*. New York: Psychology Press, pp. 189–213.

Weech-Maldonado, R., Dreachslin, J. L., Epane, J. P., Gail, J., Gupta, S., & Wainio, J. A. 2018. Hospital Cultural Competency As A Systematic Organizational Intervention: Key Findings From The National Center For Healthcare Leadership Diversity Demonstration Project. *Health Care Management Review, 43* (1), pp. 30–41.

Willard, G., Isaac, K.-J., & Carney, D. R. 2015. Some evidence for the nonverbal contagion of racial bias. *Organizational Behavior and Human Decision Processes, 128*, pp. 96–107.

Wilton, L. S., Apfelbaum, E. P., & Good, J. J. 2019. Valuing Differences and Reinforcing Them: Multiculturalism Increases Race Essentialism. *Social Psychological and Personality Science, 10* (5), pp. 681–689.

Zou, L. X., & Dickter, C. L. 2013. Perceptions of Racial Confrontation: The Role of Color Blindness and Comment Ambiguity. *Cultural Diversity & Ethnic Minority Psychology, 19* (1), pp. 92–96.

17

Anti-racism and everyday life

Kristine Aquino

Introduction

Despite the fact that much of 'the history of anti-racism consists of the actions of ordinary people', studies on 'everyday anti-racism' remain little consolidated in racism and anti-racism theory (Bonnett, 2000: 88). Following from Essed's (1991) seminal work on the concept of 'everyday racism', the term 'everyday anti-racism' has been employed across varied studies to refer to the ways in which individuals respond to racism in interpersonal interactions and spaces of encounter in their day-to-day lives (Bonnett, 2000; Lamont and Fleming, 2005; Pollock, 2008; Mitchell et al.,2011; Nelson, 2015a; Aquino, 2017). This can include the actions of victims confronting perpetrators, witnesses speaking out against racism, practices that bridge cultural difference, material and subjective strategies deployed by those on the receiving end of racism to repair stigmatized identities, and aestheticized expressions through popular culture such as forms of music, youth cultures and media that challenge racism. In this chapter, I review selected works examining anti-racism in everyday life and draw out its key tenets as an area of study with the aim of highlighting how it contributes to broader anti-racism theory and praxis.

The chapter begins with a brief background discussion on how anti-racism debates are bound to older and larger deliberations around the concepts of race and racism which have been characterized by divergences in terms and concepts and dichotomies between the structural/ideological, macro/micro, economic/cultural, leading to calls to better connect theory with lived experience. I then summarize key areas that make up everyday anti-racism literature: the 'micro' dimensions of historical social movements and epochs; 'doing' anti-racism in organizational/institutional contexts; negotiating cultural difference and countering racism in spaces of 'encounter'; and victims developing 'cultural repertoires' to cope with racism. By no means an exhaustive literature review, this chapter instead highlights some of the central objectives of research on everyday anti-racism which involve enhancing understandings of how 'the everyday' is an integral part of the processes that configure and challenge racism. In these works, everyday life is not just seen as the 'setting' where racism and anti-racism happen but applied as a conceptual tool that can problematize taken-for-granted understandings of how race, racism and resistance operate – understandings that have traditionally been predominated by a macro-sociology bias. According to Essed (2001: 188), the everyday does not simply refer to one's immediate sphere, but rather, the *intersection* between micro and macro spheres – the complex of contexts, processes and practices 'present in and activated at the everyday level as well as pre-structured in a way that transcends the control of individual subjects'. In this way, the everyday can involve multifaceted and contradictory processes of reproducing and contesting racism at both the structural and interactional, behavioral and ideological, macro and micro levels. As Essed (1991: 8) argues, 'such analysis demands an eye for detail and challenge the researcher to organize and understand an enormous number of divergent experiences' which has by convention deterred deep scholarly engagement. In reviewing studies of everyday anti-racism, this chapter shows how the 'unruly quality of everyday experience' (Smith, 2014: 1139) in particular can serve a significant function in racism studies, via the ways in which it can 'shake our confidence in the seemingly clear-cut intellectual categories and stories by which we go about making sense of things'. Engaging with the everyday can have a 'monitory effect' (Smith, 2014: 1140) on how analysis is organized in the field – reminding researchers to check tendencies that fix concepts, categories and approaches which may be at odds with the instability of quotidian experience and this attentiveness can help enable racism theory and anti-racism praxis to remain socially and politically engaged.

Race, racism and anti-racism theory: fractures and divisions

At the simplest level, anti-racism can be defined as 'forms of thought and/or practice that seek to confront, eradicate and/or ameliorate racism' and as 'ideologies and practices that affirm and seek to enable the equality of races and ethnic groups' (Bonnett, 2000: 4). The straightforwardness, however, ends there as it remains contested how it is we actually reach this goal. What it means to be 'equal' is fraught with complexity – should we uphold ideals of universalism or particularism as the basis of equality? Do we really mean to address inequality or inequity? And how can we most productively deal with racism – do we focus change on institutions or individuals, systems or interactions, or practices and thinking? Dualistic logic has tended to underline the predominant ways in which anti-racism has been discussed which is bound to the prevalent ways in which the related terms of race and racism have also been debated and theorized. Over the three decades between the 1980s and 2000s, in the English-speaking academy, dichotomous conceptual and methodological approaches came to define race, racism and anti-racism as either cultural or economic concerns, structural or ideological processes, macro or micro phenomena. The fractures, according to some scholars, risked 'over-theorizing' of the field and, moreover, disconnection from social and political engagement (Knowles, 2010). In this section, I outline briefly some of the central issues underpinning these dialogues to set the scene as to how the study of everyday anti-racism has contributed some grounded insights to these debates. The field of study is sizable and I wish to note that I am only able to mention some of the voices in the debate. I also flag that while the conditions of racism and anti-racism are specific to place they also connect across contexts and so the discussion here specifies certain national circumstances but often crosses borders.

As an important starting point Lentin (2000; 2008) reminds us that grappling with the expansive discussion begins with the contested concept of race. In the early twentieth century, the invalidation by science of the biological certainty of racial difference and the challenges posed to racial regimes by social movements made up of long-oppressed racial minorities, threw up questions around the ideological basis of racism and the nature of racist practice, with some scholars calling for the abandonment of the term and concept of race. Gilroy (2002: 253) for example famously called for 'the end to raciology', arguing that the continued theoretical engagement with the discredited concept of race reified essentialisms particularly in the construction of racial or ethnic 'camps' who in their anti-racism politics took up pre-defined positions around 'the Black subject', 'the Asian subject' and so on. Miles (1989) similarly argued against race's persistent autonomy as an analytical category but instead stressed that it was operating to obscure the economic relations that produce racism. The work of other scholars like Taylor (1994), meanwhile, saw a turn to questions around 'ethnicity', 'multiculturalism' and a 'politics of recognition', exemplifying the culturalist discourse that came to ultimately supplant the discourse of race, wherein, 'culture' (customs, ways of life, traditions and so on) was taken up as the more apt marker of difference and posited as departing from the violence of old racial categories.

This 'cultural turn' became integral to giving voice to the experience of those most silenced by racism. For example, feminist accounts by hooks (1992) and Collins (2004) in the US on the experience of black women shed light on the different positionalities of the racialized subject to render understandings of racism more complex, in that, race can be gendered and gender can be racialized. Hall (1992) in his work on 'new ethnicities' in the UK, meanwhile, challenged understandings of migrant identities and positionalities as static and coherent through notions like hybridity and multiplicity which revealed processes of agency and flexibility to rework the fixedness in conceptions of diaspora and nation. Despite being taken up with enthusiasm, however, some scholars were skeptical that discourses of culture were eradicating essentialist ideas of group differences. Balibar (1991) and Taguieff (1990), for instance, writing from the French context, argued that domination was being newly articulated through a 'differentialist racism' and warned that anti-racism projects based on celebrating cultural pluralism would abet the perpetuation of a racism rationalized around the insurmountability of cultural differences. Those writing on Indigenous struggles, for instance in Australia, also pointed out that the focus on questions of culture and ethnicity was very problematic for Indigenous groups who particularly rely on mobilizing the history of race to distinguish their plight as separate from 'ethnic minorities' or 'migrant groups' (Cowlish and Morris, 1997).

Furthermore, structuralists remained persistent in arguing that concerns should be centered on social systems and not in ideological discussions of culture and identity nor questions related to recognition. In part this stemmed from long-held opposition to psychological definitions of racism, wherein, works by Bonilla-Silva (1997) and Goldberg (2002) in the US on racism's systematic nature disputed early understandings that pathologized racism as an individual problem or a mere issue of cultural stereotypes and beliefs. Rather, the structural approach emphasized how histories of colonization and empire, institutions such as the state, and systems like capitalism, were the real sources of racism that needed to be challenged. A particular strand of theorization espoused by scholars like Miles (1987) in the UK, Wilson (1978) in the US, and Morrisey (1984) in Australia, specified that class relations and modes of production determined the limited power held by minority racial groups and positioned racism as the denial of access to resources. Against the latter, cultural studies scholars insisted on the non-reductiveness to race, ethnicity and culture but, as the cultural field became preoccupied with symbols and representation, were continually dismissed for making little progress against ending the material inequalities produced by racism (St Louis, 2002). There was, moreover, a prevailing 'macro-sociological bias' in racism studies according to Essed (1991: 101), that generally paid little serious attention to 'micro-interactional perspectives on racism' nor 'the phenomenological dimensions of racism', denoting a general indifference towards the 'ordinary' and the 'underrating of the insights of "laypersons"' in racism studies.

These debates, Lentin (2000: 101) argues, were not merely semantic, but signal the profound difficulties in finding a language to analyse and understand racism 'without tried and tested concepts' that give meaning to the struggle for anti-racism. Evidenced in the earlier discussion in this chapter, initial analysis of anti-racism chiefly focused on the actions of governments, politicians, international human rights institutions and social movements which took form in public policy, anti-discrimination legislation, affirmative action, and political platforms. At this level, anti-racism has been crucial to addressing broader structures of power – focusing on the re-education of society by targeting institutions of socialization like schools and the media but also attempting to transform the economy, law enforcement, and allocation of resources and services. Yet, at times, under the control of institutions, anti-racism has also proven to be about 'the reproduction of modern economies and the establishment of internationally accepted principles of political legitimacy' (Bonnett, 2000: 26). The politicized interests that governments, institutions, and anti-racism groups have had in anti-racism thus made many initially critical of formal policies, legislation and programs which showed themselves as being pursued in the self-interest of political ideologies and economic outcomes (Gilroy, 2002).

A binary opposition of emphasizing sameness or difference as the basis of 'equality' also surfaced in anti-racism perspectives, simultaneously advancing much needed theoretical engagement with the notion of anti-racism but also began to undermine anti-racist action (Wieviorka, 1997). Equality defined by sameness is rooted in values of universalism and is, for example, embodied in 'color-blind' and 'post-racial' policies in the US which entails positioning 'racial difference' as irrelevant if everyone is to be treated as 'the same'. Equality defined through difference, on the other hand, encourages acknowledging the particularities and pluralities of ethno-racial groups and manifest in policies of multiculturalism in states like Canada and Australia which advocate for 'unity in diversity'. The former was criticized by scholars like Goldberg (2002) and Bonilla-Silva (2017) for invalidating struggles against racism especially masking how racial ideologies continue to permeate social systems. The acknowledgment of difference, meanwhile, produced populist backlash over affirmative action or diversity policies for giving 'preferential' treatment to minorities which Essed (1991) and Beneton (2001), among others, argued demonstrated the failures of cultural pluralism as anti-racism policy in sufficiently addressing the conduct, practice, and ideologies of racism. That pluralism was bearing little fruit in the fight against racism was never enough to give way to embracing universalism. Lentin (2004: 98), for example, argued that more damaging are the enduring universalist ideals of sameness once manifested in colonialism and which persist in assimilationist and integration policies.

Such debates are essential in exploring and exposing the complex contours of racism and its consequences. As Hall (2002: 41) has argued, while theoretical and ideological divisions are often seen as being opposed to each other 'they can also be understood, in many respects, as inverted mirror images of one another. Each tries to supplement the weakness of the opposing paradigm by stressing the so-called "neglected" element' (Hall, 2002: 38). Nonetheless, disputes around theory and approaches, can fall prey to disconnecting from the ordinary lives victimized by racism and their lived struggles fighting racism (Back and Solomos, 2002). Over the last decade or so in racism studies, renewed engagement with 'the everyday' – as a site of empirical investigation, as a concept to inform methodology, as a base from which to build theory – has allayed this risk to add further texture to the field.

Essed's theory of 'everyday racism' for example, while articulated in the past through concepts such as 'infra-racism' (Wieviorka, 1995) or 'interactional racism' (Brandt, 1986), has now been widely adopted as conceptual framework and methodological approach to examine routinized racism in schools, workplaces and public spaces across a range of international contexts. It has stressed the mutual interdependence of macro and micro spheres through analysis of the intersection between social systems and human conduct, illuminating how 'structures of racism do not exist external to agents – they are made by agents – but specific practices are by definition racist only when they activate existing structural racial inequalities in the system' (Essed, 1991: 39). Work by Knowles (2003) on the concept of 'everyday race-making' is a similar mode of social analysis that advocates to close 'the gap between hyper-theorized conceptions of race and the social practices that operate around them' (Knowles, 2010: 26). Using a materialist approach to address the quandary of race as both mythical and real, she engages with 'social texture' by interrogating how the intersection of bodies, space and subjectivities produce or contest racialized privilege and disadvantage.

Understandings of anti-racism too have also been subject to an engagement with the everyday although little consolidated. In the section to follow I identify literature that explore the notion of everyday anti-racism and point out the ways in which these works bridge some theoretical and empirical gaps and disputes in larger debates.

Everyday anti-racism: key themes in the literature

Micro dimensions of historical social movements and epochs

Though not originally conceived within the discourse of 'everyday anti-racism', historical accounts of resisting racism in everyday life have been long documented via the activities of actors or groups directly participating in social movements against racial inequality or, more indirectly, accounting for the tactics of 'everyday resistance' deployed by ordinary people against racial systems set within historical epochs.

The literature on anti-colonial or anti-slavery movements contains some of these stories. For example, Vieira (1995) and Andrew's (1994) writings on resistance from African slaves in colonial Brazil focus on how the abolition of slavery was enhanced through the actions of slaves who escaped from plantations to form self-sufficient communities called *quilombos*, setting up secret societies that enabled the preservation of some African cultural practices in modern Brazil. Moyd (2017) has also described 'everyday colonialism' in Africa and the tactics used to challenge colonial demands in the continent such as Africans employing avoidance methods to escape wartime service or refusing to be recruited for jobs in public works to disrupt economic growth, which set the foundations for organized trade unions in the future. In the US, the work of Aptheker (1992) reports on the period from the eighteenth century to the emancipation of African American slaves, showing how rebellion was in part driven by multiracial coalitions between blacks and whites including arming themselves against slave owners or securing hideouts for escaped African Americans and set precedence to the establishment of multiracial groups like the NAACP (see O'Brien, 2009). Lawson (1991: 457) details scholarship on the civil rights movement between the 1970s and 1980s which shifted focus away from 'leaders' of the movement to grass-roots efforts which shed light on the experience of ordinary people involved. She describes literature by Chafe, Morris, and Killian which looked at the experience of student sit-ins and how these actors were shaped by protest cultures cultivated by churches, civic groups and colleges. Notably, literature in this area has also highlighted intersectionality by documenting the experience of non-white women involved in historical action (Keisha-Khan, 2004; Springer, 2005; Chun et al., 2013). The interest in the ordinary people involved in larger movements are carried through in more recent writings on grass-roots resistance in contemporary racialized urban contexts, for example, in the fight against police racism and the struggle for land rights.

Related scholarship examining what Scott (1990) calls the 'infra-politics' of those unattached to organizations or political movements is also significant to the historical documentation of anti-racism in everyday life. Scott (1990) defines infra-politics as composed of 'hidden transcripts' of the oppressed which mock, criticize and subvert their oppressors. There is much work here on the everyday and popular culture practices of African Americans in the nineteenth and twentieth centuries, such as historical research by Levine (1978) on the jokes, folklore songs and stories used by African Americans to mock white authority, or Kelley's (1994) exposition of black working-class resistance such as foot-dragging on the factory floor, theft from the workplace, and secret practices of 'black-listing' abusive employers among black women working in domestic households. Again, the struggle against colonial domination by the colonized also provides similar stories, for example, Santiago Jr. (2015) has explored how incidents of 'bad manners' such as rudeness, deceitfulness, clumsiness, and insolence among native Filipinos in colonial Philippines were acts of defiance against colonial authority. España-Maram (2006) meanwhile historically accounts for how the zoot-suits worn by Filipino workers in Los Angeles during World War Two in low-brow taxi dance halls enabled a departure from their status as 'servants'. These histories of cultural production 'communicate the expressive and socially challenging content of everyday anti-racism' (Bonnett, 2000: 91) and form the roots of contemporary 'anti-racist popular culture' (Bonnett, 2000: 92) expressed for example in subversive forms of music, leisure practices, and youth fashions today.

The focus on ordinary people in these accounts has widened perspectives that social movements are mostly played out at the legislative or policy stage or that historical change is only orchestrated by national leaders, but rather, that they have equally been driven by struggles engaged by individuals and within communities. This 'history from below' (Scott, 1990) which is the history of ordinary people, and its intersecting focus on 'everyday resistance' in the tradition of scholars like cultural theorist de Certeau or anthropologist Abu-Lughod, are not merely documented to celebrate 'heroic acts' in everyday life but also aim to shed light on how daily actions and practices can amass effect on relations of power both at the micro and macro levels. As well, the fight against racism is proven to be as much about the struggle for recognition and creating new identities for the oppressed as it is about creating structural change and how the latter may not be possible if not fueled by the former.

'Doing' anti-racism in organizational/institutional contexts

Complementing the large body of studies on the anti-racism initiatives and policies of organizations or institutions in societies in the North, is research that explores the experience of people grappling with the challenges of implementing initiatives 'on the ground' within these settings.

By far, the topic of practicing anti-racism in the educational sector forms a large part of the research in this area (Epstein, 1993; Kailin, 2002; Zembylas, 2012). The work of Pollock (2006, 2008, 2017) in particular is associated with furthering the term 'everyday anti-racism' via her edited collection *Everyday Antiracism: Getting Real about Race in School*. The book consists of contributions from researchers, many of whom were former teachers, reflecting on the messiness of practicing anti-racism in the American classroom around top-down directives such as 'color-blindness' or 'race consciousness'. The research explores 'everyday acts' inside the classroom that can perpetuate racial inequality including how teachers talk to and discipline students, the ways in which communities are framed and discussed in curriculum, how papers are graded, how teachers interact with parents, and the manner in which student aspirations are framed. Through these examples Pollock (2008) advances theoretically the concept of 'the everyday' in the term 'everyday anti-racism' by encouraging reflection in routine, taken-for-granted moments of the schooling experience. The collection hopes to function as a practical resource and puts forward four paradoxical points of reflection to facilitate a critical everyday anti-racism in the classroom: rejecting false notions of human difference; acknowledging and engaging in lived experiences along racial lines; building upon and celebrating the differences that racialized groups positively value about themselves; and equipping self and others to challenge racial inequality. These contradictory points aim to inspire routinely contemplating what moves to make and when, in terms of anti-racist practice.

The 'hands-on' challenges and successes of doing anti-racism are also documented in other organizational/institutional contexts such as healthcare and social welfare sectors (Cortis and Law, 2005; Durey, 2010; Pon et al., 2011), corporations (Wrench, 2005), and sporting clubs, bodies and programs (Woodward, 2007; Flintoff et al., 2015). Findings have, in particular, engaged with the status of whiteness of people undertaking the work of anti-racism and the implications around power and disadvantage within these organizational settings. Interestingly, recent focus has also been placed on individuals working in state or local government agencies, NGOs and community organizations who deal directly with ethnic groups, inter-ethnic relations and racism. For example, research by Nelson and Dunn (2017) in Australia discuss the ways in which employees are cognisant of the limitations of 'celebratory' initiatives such as multicultural festivals and 'Harmony Day' in addressing structural racisms but nonetheless deliver them, blaming pressures of a neo-liberal agenda infiltrating the sector which has de-politicized racism and anti-racism. Nelson (2015b) elaborates by describing the difficulties in 'speaking' racism and anti-racism among these workers which can be attributed to things like the government's hesitancy to use the term 'racism' and thus look unfavorably on program funding applications that use this word. Yet, despite actors being constrained by larger institutional pressures or that they must endorse initiatives that often fail to address deep-seated issues, there are still benefits to everyday anti-racism in these spaces. For example, because of the micro context, the successes and failures of the anti-racism can be 'locally owned' which still offers up possibilities to change norms (Nelson and Dunn, 2017).

These studies challenge the institutional/individual binary by reminding us that institutions comprise people and are not independent of them, and that structural racisms are perpetuated or challenged via human action. Moreover, they shed insight into the ambiguities of 'applying' or 'doing' the anti-racism policies of organizations and institutions, accentuating everyday anti-racism as a praxis that is 'complex, conflict ridden and deeply consequential' (Pollock, 2006: 4). Such research has also emphasized the importance of individuals reflecting on one's positioning in terms of race, particularly white privilege, when occupying levels of institutional influence such as the position of a teacher, policy-maker, program coordinator, manager, coach and so on, but also simultaneously signals the risks in research focusing on a white-centric anti-racism.

Negotiating cultural difference and countering racism in spaces of 'encounter'

While not explicitly framed as everyday anti-racism, over the last two decades, a prominent area of literature has looked at the bridging of cultural and racio-ethnic differences in spaces of 'encounter'. Approaches from geography and sociology, particularly from scholarly work in the UK and Australia, predominate in this literature and often focus on routine interpersonal encounters with difference in public or quasi-public spaces, with a growing interest in the private intimate sphere.

The most significant strand of this research looks at how collective civic cultures are forged in shared public spaces. Research on 'everyday multiculturalism' (Wise and Velayutham, 2009), 'everyday cosmopolitanism' (Noble, 2009), 'rubbing along' (Watson, 2009) and 'micro-publics' (Amin, 2008), have shed light on how cultural and racio-ethnic difference is negotiated in a range of spaces people traverse and inhabit such as neighborhood parks and streets, schools, workplaces, shopping centers, cafes, public transport, and leisure and sporting spaces. Perhaps the most taken up in empirical study has been investigation into modes of 'everyday multiculturalism', which Wise and Velayutham (2009: 3) define as a theory that pivots from ideological and policy-based definitions of multiculturalism to instead explaining how multiculturalism is 'lived'. Accordingly, it espouses a grounded approach to studying multicultural communities via ethnographic and qualitative methods. Drawing on theorists such as Latour, Mauss, Massey, Bourdieu and Lefebvre, subsequent studies pay attention to the assemblage of bodies, practice, affect, matter and space that make possible the habits and dispositions for inclusive cohabitation but also those that produce racisms and intercultural conflict. For example, in examining suburban multiculturalism in Sydney, Wise (2005, 2011, 2013) fleshes out the sensory aspects of diversity materialized in shopping streets, wherein, encounters with different bodies and smells of food along with foreign signage can produce encounters of racism but also function as sites to connect across differences. Watson (2017), commenting from superdiverse London, stresses how the physical infrastructure and design of public space can encourage community cohesion and interethnic interaction to reduce negative affect, distrust, fear and antagonism that can feed racist sentiments. Asian cities now also form the basis of analysis, such as navigating ethnically diverse workplaces in Singapore through the use of humor (Wise, 2016), or the use of linguistic resources among diverse workers in restaurants in Tokyo to communicate across difference (Pennycook and Otsuji, 2014).

Investigation into encounters in private spaces, meanwhile, is less ubiquitous but growing, particularly through the work of Valentine who argues that interaction in public spaces are likely prefigured by habits and dispositions 'developed, enacted and contested within "private" spaces of the homes of family and friends' (Valentine and Sadgrove, 2012: 2,051) and so it is pertinent to understand the connection between the two spheres. In looking at family relationships in the UK and European contexts, Valentine et al. (2015) found that diversity experienced within the family through, for instance, the presence of inter-racial relationships, can foster positive attitudes in public life towards the social group the family member represents, but such attitudes are not enough to challenge wider prejudices towards other groups. Nelson (2015a) has taken up the same concerns in her Australian research and adopts Butler's theory of performativity as a means to examining 'whether social change might be enacted through performance' (Nelson, 2015a: 491). She suggests that looking at performative racist talk and practice within families, a key site of socialization, can reveal 'the repetitive and citational practices that both reproduce and potentially subvert discourse' (Nelson, 2015a: 491–3).

The other strand of research that examines negotiating and countering racism in spaces of encounter are emergent studies on 'bystander anti-racism'. The work of Australian scholars makes up recent research on this topic which takes some inspiration from social psychology to define bystander anti-racism as actions taken by people not directly involved or targeted by racism who speak out against or engage others to respond to interpersonal or systemic racism. Nelson et al., (2011), for example, argue for recognizing the potentials of bystander anti-racism in taking some of the burden of combating racism away from the target, decreasing public expressions of racism if more witnesses speak out against racism, potentially educating and changing perpetrators' behaviors when racism is called out, and feelings of personal satisfaction for the bystander for challenging racism. There are though obstacles that can hinder speaking up against racism which they identify as fears of perpetrators turning on the bystander, evaluations of the event as not being 'serious' enough to intervene, or the perceived idea that intervention would be ineffective (Stewart et al., 2014; also see Pedersen et al., 2011).

These literatures on encounter have come a long way from Allport's original conception of the 'contact hypothesis' by illustrating the complexities of engaging with difference in everyday life. Scholarship on everyday multiculturalism has illuminated the textures of modes of inclusion and exclusion in lived experiences and the everyday methods and means through which we learn how to live together across difference. However, critiques are wary of spatial and temporal assumptions that fleeting encounters in public space necessarily alter deep-seated attitudes around racial and ethnic difference and thus the connection between public/private domains is worthy of more attention (Valentine, 2008). This speaks to the general challenge of how it is successful micro-encounters can be 'scaled-up' into successful policy to bring about larger social change (Onyx et al., 2011). Likewise, that the 'bystander' is often framed as a white actor cautions at the limitations of bystander anti-racism in shifting wider arrangements of racialized power (Lentin, 2017).

'Cultural repertoires' of coping with racism

The final noteworthy area of work on everyday anti-racism comes from American sociologist Lamont, who has investigated the 'cultural repertoires' that inform the coping mechanisms deployed by individuals victimized by racism. Lamont's collaborative empirical studies have examined the experience of African American upper and working-class in the US (Lamont and Askartova, 2002; Lamont and Fleming, 2005) and North African immigrants in France (Lamont et al., 2002) and has recently expanded to international comparisons of immigrant and minority responses to racism in the contexts of Israel, Brazil, Sweden and Canada (Lamont and Mizrachi, 2012; Lamont et al., 2016).

Couched in Lamont's long-term interest in using the tools of cultural sociology to understand how ordinary individuals construct and/or bridge group boundaries across race and class, Lamont and Fleming (2005: 31) conceive of everyday anti-racism as 'micro level responses that individuals use to counter racist ideology in their daily life' and unpack the 'cultural repertoires' that inform these responses – the 'tool-kits' of material and non-material devices, 'the symbolic elements … the sets of ideas, stories, discourses, frames and beliefs that people draw on to create a line of action' (Hall and Lamont, 2013: 18). There is a focus on Goffman-esque identity work and understanding the meaning-making processes that go into countering stigmatization, repairing 'spoiled identities' and 'managing the self'. For example, Lamont and Fleming (2005) uncover how upper class African Americans draw on their education, intelligence and competence as anti-racist devices to rebut negative racial stereotypes. On the other hand, non-college educated African Americans see money and consumption practices as providing avenues to respect and 'equal footing' with the dominant group (Lamont, 2002). However, both groups draw on principles of the 'universality of human nature' to understand that everyone, regardless of race and class, ultimately shares the same status as 'children of God' with similar human needs. These findings particularly highlight the situated nature of anti-racism in everyday life, in this case, there is a contextual way ordinary people operationalize values of universalism and particularism to conceive of 'equality' as opposed to seeing them as binary opposites.

Further multi-sited research by Lamont and collaborators expound comparative responses to racism across different stigmatized groups in different national contexts. Research in Israel, for example, indicates national markers of identity as central to the repertoires of marginalized groups compared to the market-oriented repertoires of stigmatized African Americans in the US. Findings from Mizrachi and Zawdu (2012) and Mizrachi and Herzog (2013) show how Ethiopian Jews manage the injuries of phenotypical racism associated with blackness by mobilizing the Zionist nationalist narrative to emphasize their 'belonging' to the nation, Mizrachi Jews play up their Jewishness to negate the low status attached to their arrival from other Arab countries, and Palestinian Arabs seek to maintain their dignity via the status of the 'ultimate other' in the context of ongoing violence between Arabs and Jews in the Middle East. Further away, in Sweden, Bursell (2012) illustrates how Middle Eastern migrants subscribe to a discourse of assimilation by exchanging their foreign-sounding surnames for Swedish-sounding ones to enable them to 'pass' in mainstream society while still remaining attached to their ethnic identity in their private lives. Outside of these collaborations, other scholars have also taken up Lamont's model of everyday anti-racism and, interestingly, have focused on unearthing the experience of middle-class racial minorities. Lacy's (2007) ethnography with suburban middle-class blacks in the US unpacks the 'tool-kits' from which this group draw to navigate their raced and classed positionalities which largely involve conflicted experiences with neo-liberalized choices around the suburbs in which they live or the schools to which they send their children. This is echoed in my own work on middle-class Filipino migrants in Sydney which reveal similar repertoires that feed strategies of social mobility, consumption practices and discourses of middle-class respectability as a means to repair stigmatized racial identities, but that also produce a status of in-betweenness as inclusion remains conditional and revocable (Aquino, 2016). Furthermore, middle-class individualism contrasts to the repertoires of working-class Filipino migrants who tend to draw on notions of solidarity, rights and justice as a means to cope with racism, including coping with the intra-ethnic othering they must endure from their more economically mobile counterparts (Aquino, 2017).

The idea of everyday anti-racism as being composed of 'cultural repertoires' helps reveal 'the active elements in the processes through which actors make sense of their ability to pursue certain lines of action' (Hall and Lamont, 2013: 18). It can draw out the heterogeneity in societies as different contexts make available (and attractive) distinct kinds of resources for resisting racism. The interesting focus on the experience of racial minorities in the middle-class has also complexified reductive structuralist arguments positing that social mobility and economic integration provide a buffer against racism. These actors are positioned in between inclusion/exclusion, equality/inequality which anti-racism dichotomies can fail to take into account. Moreover, anti-racism in these middle-class contexts reveal some problematic strategies to combat racism – such as those based on assimilationist, neo-liberal, individualistic, privatized values – which prompt necessary investigation into what kinds of inclusive membership need to be fostered across different milieus (Lamont and Fleming, 2005).

Conclusion

In recently mapping out the old and new terrains of anti-racism, Paradies (2016: 2–3) states that intellectual differences remain and 'we still lack a shared notion of what is meant by anti-racism' nor do we yet have a 'well developed typology of anti-racist theory and practice anywhere in the academic world', although, 'it is debatable whether distinct types of anti-racism can be distinguished, or more importantly, what the value is in doing so'. Paradies (2016: 2–3) therefore suggests instead for the 'need to recognise the concomitant plurality of anti-racisms' as 'mutual reinforcement across various anti-racisms' may perhaps be the most effective means of addressing racism. Everyday anti-racism, the ways in which individuals respond to racism in their day-to-day lives, can at times focus on resistance from the marginalized and points to the problematic way that the onus to combat racism continues to be mostly taken up by those victimized by racism. Investing in efforts to dismantle racism at the structural level through policy, legal and systemic change that addresses unequal power relations thus remains crucial. This is especially so in light of the resurgence of racisms in societies in the North that accentuate the historically deep-seated problem of racism and its profoundly institutionalized and transnational nature. However, everyday anti-racism is an important arena with which broader anti-racism theory and politics can engage, as it describes the lived and messy struggles against racism 'on the ground'. Studies into everyday anti-racism reveal how racism is not experienced by people as a monolithic system but rather lived out context-ually, necessitating situated strategies to negotiate racism across different temporal and spatial circumstances. It is a 'people-centered' study of racism and anti-racism but attempts to make important links between everyday practice and larger structures and institutions. It delves into questions of 'culture' and 'identity' that, while engaged with symbols, representation and discourse, also attempts to reconnect with questions around the redistribution of power. Furthermore, everyday anti-racism is an imperfect politics – at times engaging problematic strategies to combat racism that do not always aim to achieve 'equality for all' – but nevertheless importantly reveal the hard and complicated labor of fighting racism which must be better taken into account in designing broader anti-racism policy and action.

References

Amin, A., 2008. 'Collective culture and urban public space', *City, 12* (1), pp. 5–24.

Andrews, G. 1994. 'Black political protest in Sao Paulo, 1888-1988', in J. Dominguez (ed) *Race and Ethnicity in Latin America*, New York: Garland Publishing, pp. 303–328.

Aptheker, H. 1992. *Anti-Racism in U.S. History: The First Two Hundred Years*, New York: Greenwood Press.

Aquino, K., 2016. 'Anti-racism "from below": Exploring repertoires of everyday anti-racism', *Ethnic and Racial Studies, 39* (1), pp. 105–122.

Aquino, K. 2017. *Racism and Resistance Among the Filipino Diaspora: Everyday Anti-racism in Australia*, London and New York: Routledge.

Back, L. and Solomos, J. 2002. *Race, Politics and Social Change*, UK: Routledge.

Balibar, E. 1991. 'Is there a neoracism?' In Balibar, E. and Wallerstein, I. (eds) *Race, Nation, Class: Ambiguous Identities*, London: Verso, pp. 17–28.

Beneton, P., 2001. 'On the corruptions of antiracism', *Society*, 30 (1), pp. 83–88.

Bonilla-Silva, E., 1997. 'Rethinking racism: Toward a structural interpretation', *American Sociological Review, 62* (3), pp. 465–480.

Bonilla-Silva, E. 2017. *Racism Without Racists: Color-Blind Racism And The Persistence Of Racial Inequality in America*, Plymouth, UK: Rowman & Littlefield.

Bonnett, A. 2000. *Antiracism*, London: Routledge.

Brandt, G.L. 1986. *The Realization of Anti-Racist Teaching*, London, NY and Philadelphia: Falmer Press.

Bursell, M., 2012. 'Name change and destigmatization among Middle Eastern immigrants in Sweden', *Ethnic and Racial Studies, 35* (3), p. 471–487.

Chun, J.J., Lipsitz, G. and Shin, Y., 2013. 'Intersectionality as a social movement strategy: Asian immigrant women advocates', *Signs: Journal of Women in Culture and Society*, 38 (4), pp. 917–940.

Collins, P.H. 2004. *Black Sexual Politics: African Americans, Gender, and the New Racism*, New York and London: Routledge.

Cortis, J. and Law, I.G., 2005. 'Anti-racist innovation and nurse education', *Nurse Education Today*, 25 (3), pp. 204–213.

Cowlish, G. and Morris, B. 1997. *Race Matters: Indigenous Australians and Our Society*, Canberra: Aboriginal Studies Press.

Durey, A., 2010. 'Reducing racism in Aboriginal health care in Australia: where does cultural education fit?', *Australian and New Zealand Journal of Public Health*, 34, pp. 87–92.

Epstein, D. 1993. *Changing Classroom Cultures: Anti-Racism, Politics and Schools*, UK: Trentham Books, Ltd.

España-Maram, L. 2006. *Creating Masculinity in Los Angeles's Little Manila: Working-Class Filipinos and Popular Culture in the United States*, New York: Columbia University Press.

Essed, P. 1991. *Understanding Everyday Racism: An Interdisciplinary Theory*, Newbury Park: Sage Publications.

Essed, P. 2001. 'Everyday racism: A new approach to the study of racism', In Essed, P. and Goldberg, D. (eds) *Race Critical Theories: Text and Context*, Massachusetts: Blackwell Publishers, pp. 176–192.

Flintoff, A., Dowling, F. and Fitzgerald, H., 2015. 'Working through whiteness, race and (anti) racism in physical education teacher education', *Physical Education and Sport Pedagogy*, 20 (5), pp. 559–570.

Gilroy, P. 2002. 'The end of antiracism', In Essed, P. and Goldberg, D. (eds) *Race Critical Theories*, Massachusetts: Blackwell Publishers, pp. 251–264.

Goldberg, D. 2002. *The Racial State*, Malden, MA: Blackwell.

Hall, Peter A. and Michele Lamont, 2013. 'Why social relations matter for politics and successful societies', *Annual Review of Political Science*, 16 (23), pp. 1–23.

Hall, S. 1992. 'New ethnicities', In Donald, J. and Rattansi, Al (eds) *Race, Culture and Difference*, London: Sage, pp. 252–259.

Hall, S. 2002. 'Race, articulation and societies structured in dominance', in Essed, P. and Goldberg, D. (eds) *Race Critical Theories*, Massachusetts: Blackwell Publishers, pp. 449–454.

hooks, b. 1992. *Black Looks: Race and Representation*, Boston: South End Press.

Kailin, J. 2002. *Antiracist Education: From Theory to Practice*, Maryland: Rowman & Littlefield.

Keisha-Khan, Y.P., 2004. 'The roots of black resistance: Race, gender and the struggle for urban land rights in Salvador, Bahia, Brazil', *Social Identities*, 10 (6), pp. 811–831.

Kelley, R. 1994. *Race Rebels: Culture, Politics and the Black Working Class*, New York: The Free Press.

Knowles, C. 2003. *Race and Social Analysis*, London: SAGE.

Knowles, C. 2010. *Theorising Race and Ethnicity: Contemporary Paradigms and Perspectives*, London: SAGE.

Lacy, K.R. 2007. *Blue-chip Black: Race, Class, And Status in the New Black Middle Class*, Berkeley and Los Angeles: University of California Press.

Lamont, M. and Askartova, S., 2002. 'Ordinary Cosmopolitanisms: Strategies for bridging racial boundaries among working class men', *Theory, Culture and Society*, 19 (4), pp. 1–25.

Lamont, M. and Fleming, C., 2005. 'Everyday antiracism: Competence and religion in the cultural repertoires of the African American elite', *Du Bois Review*, 2, (1), pp. 29–43.

Lamont, M., Morning, A., Mooney, M., 2002. 'Particular universalisms: North African migrants respond to French racism', *Ethnic and Racial Studies*, 25 (3), pp. 390–414.

Lamont, M., Silva, G.M., Welburn, J., Guetzkow, J., Mizrachi, N., Herzog, H. and Reis, E. 2016. *Getting Respect: Responding to Stigma and Discrimination in the United States, Brazil, and Israel*: Princeton University Press.

Lamont, Michele and Nissim Mizrachi, 2012. 'Ordinary people doing extraordinary things: Responses to stigmatisation in comparative perspective', *Ethnic and Racial Studies*, 35 (3), pp. 365–381.

Lawson, S.F., 1991. Freedom then, freedom now: The historiography of the civil rights movement.

Lentin, A., 2000. '"Race", racism and antiracism: Challenging contemporary classifications', *Social Identities*, 6 (1), pp. 91–106

Lentin, A., 2004. 'Racial states, antiracist responses: Picking holes in "culture" and "human rights"', *European Journal of Social Theory*, 7 (4), pp. 427–443.

Lentin, A., 2008. 'After anti-racism?' *European Journal of Cultural Studies*, 11 (3), pp. 311–331.

Lentin, A. 2017. '(Not) doing race: "casual racism", "bystander antiracism" and "ordinariness" in Australian racism studies', in Boerse, M. and Marrota, V (eds) *Critical Reflections on Migration, 'Race' and Multiculturalism: Australia in a Global Context*, UK: Routledge, pp. 125–142.

Levine, L.W., 1978. *Black Culture and Black Consciousness: Afro-American Folk Thought From Freedom* (Vol. 530). Oxford University Press, USA.

Miles, R. 1987. *Capitalism and Unfree Labour: Anomaly or Necessity?* London: Tavistock.

Miles, R. 1989. *Racism*, London: Routledge.

Mitchell, Margaret, Every, Danielle, Ranzijn, Rob., 2011. 'Everyday antiracism in interpersonal contexts: constraining and facilitating factors for "speaking up" against racism', *Journal of Community and Applied Social Psychology*, 21, pp. 329–341.

Mizrachi, N. and Herzog, H. 2013. 'Participatory destigmatization strategies among Palestinian citizens, Ethiopian Jews and Mizrahi Jews in Israel', in Lamont, Michele and Mizrachi, Nissim (eds.) *Responses to Stigmatization in Comparative Perspective*, UK: Routledge, pp. 66–83.

Mizrachi, N. and Zawdu, A., 2012. 'Between global racial and bounded identity: choice of destigmatization strategies among Ethiopian Jews in Israel', *Ethnic and Racial Studies*, 35 (3), pp. 436–452.

Morrisey, M. 1984. '"Migrantness", culture and ideology', in Bottomley, G. and de Lepervanche, M (eds) *Ethnicity, Class and Gender*, North Sydney: George Allen & Unwin Ltd., pp. 72–81.

Moyd, Michelle. 2017. 'Resistance and rebellions (Africa) in 1914-1918', in Ute Daniel, Peter Gatrell, Oliver Janz, Heather Jones, Jennifer Keene, Alan Kramer, and Bill Nasson (eds) *International Encyclopedia of the First World War*, Berlin: Freie Universität Berlin. https://encyclopedia.1914-1918-online.net/article/resistance_and_rebellions_africa. Accessed 4 February, 2019.

Nelson, J. and Dunn, K., 2017. 'Neoliberal anti-racism: Responding to "everywhere but different" racism', *Progress in Human Geography*, 41 (1), pp. 26–43.

Nelson, J.K., 2015a. 'Racism and anti-racism in families: Insights from performativity theory', *Sociology Compass*, 9 (6), pp. 487–498.

Nelson, J.K., 2015b. '"Speaking" racism and anti-racism: Perspectives of local anti-racism actors', *Ethnic and Racial Studies*, 38 (2), pp. 342–358.

Nelson, J.K., Dunn, K.M. and Paradies, Y., 2011. 'Bystander anti-racism: A review of the literature', *Analyses of Social Issues and Public Policy*, 11 (1), pp. 263–284.

Noble, G. 2009. 'Everyday cosmopolitanism and the labour of intercultural community', in Wise, Amanda and Velayutham, Selvaraj (eds.) *Everyday Multiculturalism*, London: Palgrave Macmillan, pp. 46–65.

O'Brien, E., 2009. 'From antiracism to antiracisms', *Sociology Compass*, 3 (3), pp. 501–512.

Onyx, J., Ho, C., Edwards, M., Burridge, N. and Yerbury, H., 2011. 'Scaling up connections: Everyday cosmopolitanism, complexity theory and social capital', *Cosmopolitan Civil Societies: An Interdisciplinary Journal*, 3 (3), pp. 47.

Paradies, Y., 2016. 'Whither anti-racism?' *Ethnic and Racial Studies*, 39 (1), pp. 1–15.

Pedersen, A., Paradies, Y., Hartley, L.K. and Dunn, K.M., 2011. 'Bystander antiprejudice: Cross-cultural education, links with positivity towards cultural "outgroups" and preparedness to speak out', *Journal of Pacific Rim Psychology*, 5 (1), pp. 19–30.

Pennycook, A. and Otsuji, E., 2014. 'Metrolingual multitasking and spatial repertoires: "Pizza mo two minutes coming"', *Journal of Sociolinguistics*, 18 (2), pp. 161–184.

Pollock, M., 2006. 'Everyday antiracism in education', *Anthropology News*, 47 (2), pp. 9–10.

Pollock, M. 2008. *Everyday Antiracism: Getting Real about Race in School*, New York and London: The New Press.

Pollock, M. 2017. *Schooltalk: Rethinking What We Say About and to Students Every Day*, New York: The New Press.

Pon, G., Gosine, K. and Phillips, D., 2011. 'Immediate response: Addressing anti-native and anti-Black racism in child welfare', *International Journal of Child, Youth and Family Studies*, 2 (3/4), pp. 385–409.

Santiago Jr., F., 2015. 'Manners of Resistance: Symbolic defiance of colonial authority in nineteenth century Philippines', *Philippine Sociological Review*, 63, pp. 137–168.

Scott, J. C. 1990. *Domination and the Arts of Resistance: Hidden Transcripts*, New Haven: Yale University Press.

Smith, A., 2014. 'Rethinking the "everyday" in "ethnicity and everyday life"', *Ethnic and Racial Studies*, 38 (7), pp. 1137–1151.

Springer, K., 2005. *Living for the revolution: Black feminist organizations, 1968-1980*, Vol. 114.

St Louis, B., 2002. 'Post-race/'post-politics'? Activist-intellectualism and the reification of race', *Ethnic and Racial Studies*, 25 (4), pp. 652–675.

Stewart, K., Pedersen, A. and Paradies, Y., 2014. 'It's always good to help when possible, BUT … Obstacles to bystander anti-prejudice', *The International Journal of Diversity in Education*, 13 (3), pp. 39–53.

Taguieff, P. A., 1990. 'The new cultural racism in France', *Telos*, 83, pp. 109–122.

Taylor, C. 1994. *Multiculturalism: Examining the Politics of Recognition*, Princeton, New Jersey: Princeton University Press.

Valentine, G., 2008. 'Living with difference: reflections on geographies of encounter', *Progress in human geography*, *32* (3), pp. 323–337.

Valentine, G., Piekut, A. and Harris, C., 2015. 'Intimate encounters: The negotiation of difference within the family and its implications for social relations in public space', *The Geographical Journal*, *181* (3), pp. 280–294.

Valentine, G. and Sadgrove, J., 2012. 'Lived difference: A narrative account of spatiotemporal processes of social differentiation', *Environment and Planning A*, *44* (9), pp. 2049–2063.

Vieira, F. 1995. 'Black resistance in Brazil: a matter of necessity', in B. Bowser (ed) Racism and Anti-racism in World Perspective, Thousand Oaks, CA: Sage, pp. 227–240.

Watson, S. (2009) 'The magic of the marketplace: Sociality in a neglected public space', *Urban Studies*, *46*(8), pp. 1577–1591.

Watson, S., 2017. 'Making multiculturalism', *Ethnic and Racial studies*, *40* (15), pp. 2635–2652.

Wieviorka M. 1995. *The Arena of Racism*, Trans.C. Turner, London: *Sage*.

Wieviorka, M. 1997. 'Is it so difficult to be an anti-racist', in Werbner, P. and Moodood, T. (eds) *Debating Cultural Hybridity: Multi-Cultural Identities and the Politics Of Anti-Racism*, UK: Zed Books, pp. 139–153.

Wilson, W.J., 1978. 'The declining significance of race', *Society*, *15* (2), pp. 56–62.

Wise, A., 2005. 'Hope and belonging in a multicultural suburb', *Journal of Intercultural Studies*, *26* (1-2), pp. 171–186.

Wise, A., 2011. 'Foreign'Signs and multicultural belongings on a diverse shopping street', *Built Environment*, *37* (2), pp. 139–154.

Wise, A., 2013. 'Sensuous Multiculturalism: Emotional landscapes of inter-ethnic living in Australian Suburbia', *Journal of Ethnic and Migration Studies*, 36 (6), pp. 917–937.

Wise, A., 2016. 'Convivial Labour and the "Joking Relationship": Humour and everyday multiculturalism at work', *Journal of Intercultural Studies*, *37* (5), pp. 481–500.

Wise, A. and Velayutham, S. 2009. *Everyday Multiculturalism*, Houndsmill, England: Palgrave Macmillan.

Woodward, K., 2007. 'On and Off the Pitch: Diversity policies and transforming identities?' *Cultural Studies*, *21* (4-5), pp. 758–778.

Wrench, J., 2005. 'Diversity management can be bad for you', *Race & Class*, *46* (3), pp. 73–84.

Zembylas, M., 2012. 'Pedagogies of strategic empathy: Navigating through the emotional complexities of anti-racism in higher education', *Teaching in Higher Education*, *17* (2), pp. 113–125.

18

Formulating a theory in anti-racism activism

Rashawn Ray and Genesis Fuentes

Formulating a theory in anti-racism activism

Canadian comedian and political commentator, Samantha Bee, did a special focusing on racial euphemisms. She noted the lengths to which the media will go to not call a racist act as racism. When racist events happen, the media will often label the incidents as "racially charged" or "racially insensitive." Bee pushed back against these euphemisms and instead suggested that when racialized events happen the media should say, "The racist did racism which was racist." Bee's segment raises an interesting quandary about how to properly tackle racism. This chapter aims to provide some theoretical and practical ways to make engaging in anti-racist activism normative. Drawing upon critical race theory (CRT) and the public health critical race praxis (PHCRP), we establish a racially-inclusive sociological imagination framework to better formulate a typology for addressing structural racism. We use policing in the United States as a case to illuminate the pervasive ways that structural racism permeates a social institution such as the criminal justice system.

The pervasiveness of structural racism: the case of policing

In 2015, Dylann Roof, a self-proclaimed White supremacist, walked into an African American church in South Carolina and murdered nine people. Apprehended days later as an armed and dangerous fugitive of the law, police officers took Roof to eat at Burger King on his way to jail. Many people wondered whether a non-White mass murderer would have been given this type of preferential treatment. Accordingly, some noted the Burger King incident as a lack of respect for Black bodies and a direct affront to racial progress. Furthermore, the presiding judge over Roof's initial hearing was removed due to information indicating that he may hold stereotypical views about Blacks and Whites (McKay, 2015). The judge was previously heard using racial slurs and making derogatory comments about Blacks. Despite these incidents, Roof was ultimately convicted of a slew of hate crime and murder charges, and sentenced to death. The African Methodist Episcopal (AME) Church Massacre was paralleled by another act of domestic terrorism on the campus of the University of Maryland. On May 20, 2017, Army 2nd Lt. Richard Collins III, a graduating Black Bowie State University student, was stabbed to death by Sean Urbanski, a White University of Maryland (UMD) student, on UMD's campus. Urbanski was convicted of first-degree murder in 2019. However, to Bee's point, the judge threw out the hate crime change before the jury had the chance to render a verdict on that count. This decision highlights the normalcy of racism. Authorities discovered Urbanski's ties to White supremacy groups on social media. Over two years later and four stalled motion hearings, Urbanski still has not gone to trial.

When we look at these two events, we see two horrific incidents and how they speak to the prevalence of domestic terrorism and structural racism. Domestic terrorism is when U.S. citizens engage in incidents that use violence or force to intimidate a large segment of U.-S. citizens. Just as foreign attacks of terrorism, such as 9/11, were used to create fear in American lives, domestic terrorist acts are meant to instill fear and terror within the nation-state—in this case Black Americans. Besides demonstrating acts of domestic terrorism, the locations of both of these horrific acts prove to be significant—one was at a church and the other on a university campus. Churches and universities are some of the few places where Blacks have found refuge and the space to learn how to engage in racial uplift activism in order to progress the United States to a more equitable place. Just as the Black community has found solace in these social institutions, both Roof's and Urbanski's behavior were created, supported, and maintained by these same social institutions through their connections to White supremacy.

What is important to understand is that the increase in violence toward Black and Brown communities are not limited to just hate crimes; violence has also increased at the hands of those who are sworn to protect minority communities against White supremacists—police officers. Moreover, structural racism is not only seen through the socialization and domestic terrorist acts of White supremacists, but it is also defined by the racialized acts of police officers. Officer-involved shootings in the United States have increased over the past two decades. After reaching an all-time low in the 1990s and early 2000s, officer-involved shootings have substantially increased. In general, the rate of police involved killings in America is about four times the rate in Canada, 22 times the rate in Australia, and 125 times the rate in England (Zimring, 2017). Race, then, exacerbates the experiences that Whites versus racial minorities have with police. High profile officer-involved killings of Blacks such as Michael Brown, Sandra Bland, Freddie Gray, Tamir Rice, Philando Castille, Koryn Gaines, Eric Garner, John Crawford III, and Laquan McDonald have captured global attention. Among youth, Blacks are 21 times more likely than Whites to be killed by police (Gabrielson, Jones, and Sagara, 2015). Even when exclusively focusing on people who police officers report are not attacking nor have a weapon, we still see huge racial disparities, with Blacks being 3.5 times more likely than Whites to be killed by police.

The rate of police killings in the United States compared to other countries is unfathomable on its own, but when including racial disparities in the understanding of these killings, it is a troubling trend. The criminal justice system has allowed officers to evade punishment and accountability for their actions (Alexander, 2010). In these incidents, there are rarely charges for and even fewer convictions of police officers. Civil lawsuits for unjustified and unlawful deaths fall onto taxpayer dollars. The criminal justice and judicial systems are allowing police officers to kill Blacks at a higher rate, while someone else pays the bill. Some cities like Chicago and Illinois have allocated funds for civil payouts for police brutality settlements. The people who pay the consequences for the actions of the police are the residents of cities and municipalities who end up pay millions of dollars in civil settlements to the families of people killed by police. For example, in 2018, the courts ruled that the first shots fired by a police officer, which killed Korryn Gaines, were unreasonable and violated her civil rights. After the verdict, the City of Baltimore originally settled with the Gaines family for $37 million, which included a large sum of money for Gaines' son who was also shot during the incident. No amount of money can ever replace a person's life, or give back the mother a child lost, but $37 million would go a long way in Baltimore, Maryland to redevelop low-income Black neighborhoods and invest in schools and social programs to improve employment opportunities and health outcomes. Instead, these taxpayer funds are allocated for a settlement for a wrongful killing committed by a police officer.

Structural racism within the criminal justice system does not begin or end with wrongful killings. Officer-involved shootings are just the tip of the iceberg as policies such as 'stop and frisk' disproportionately discriminate and marginalize racial minorities. A study of New York City police stops showed that Blacks and Latinos represented roughly 85% of stops despite making up less than 30% of the city's population. Of these stops, nearly 60% involved frisking and a large percentage involved criminal force. However, only 8% were arrested (with a majority for resisting arrest) with 2% of stops resulted in contraband discovery (see Gilbert and Ray 2016). This means that an overwhelming percentage of people who were stopped were not committing any crimes.

Once in the criminal justice system, Blacks are also more likely than Whites to get convicted and receive longer prison sentences for similar crimes (Alexander, 2010). The enforcement of 'stand your ground' laws also shows racial disparities. Whites are significantly more likely than Blacks to be found not guilty when using stand your ground as a defense. Studies on felony trials for similar crimes also shows similar racial disparities. A study of 700 felony trials in Florida showed that a lack of racial diversity in the jury pool leads to Blacks being significantly more likely to be convicted relative to Whites. Jury selection and how prosecutors, defense attorneys, and judges might corroborate to suppress evidence and maintain the police "blue wall of silence" can be extensive (Gonzalez Van Cleve, 2016).

When people are released from prison, racial disparities continue. Studies show that Blacks with a criminal record face a much more difficult time finding a job relative to Whites with a criminal record. In fact, Pager's (2007) groundbreaking research showed that Whites with a criminal record were more likely to get called back for jobs than Blacks without a criminal record. Well known cities, such as New York City and Baltimore, are not the only places plagued with policing issues. The Department of Justice had to intervene in the Ferguson, Missouri police department for stopping, fining, and arresting Black motorists with the purposes of generating financial revenue for the city government.

So, while Michael Brown became the apex for the Black Lives Matter movement, the structural racism embedded within the Ferguson Police Department and the city was the impetus. These issues are why nearly 85% of Blacks and slightly over 50% of Whites believe there is a difference in the way that police treat Blacks relative to Whites (Pew Research Center 2016). Despite this high percentage of Americans believing there to be racial issues in policing, many people do not actively engage in anti-racist activities to change the system. CRT and PHCRP provide some conceptual insights into these structural and psychological processes.

Critical race theory

We aimed to document above—via policing and the criminal justice system—how pervasive structural racism is in the United States and how it continues to shape life chances and social and economic outcomes. We believe that talking about structural racism is important, but what is more important is discussing how we conceptualize the processes and mechanism that undergird structural racism. Structural racism must be understood on institutional, contextual, and individual levels. To begin the conversation, Whites must be challenged to end structural racism as we know it. Many women's rights activists believe that if sexual harassment, sexual assault, and rape are to decrease, men must take it upon themselves to hold other men accountable for the ways that toxic masculine culture seeps into social institutions to marginalize women. The same logic applies to racism. If structural racism is really going to becoming a thing of the past, Whites must take the onus to ratify a procedural justice perspective.

Critical race theory recognizes that racism is ingrained in the fabric and system of American society (Crenshaw et al., 1995). Now, what is important to understand is that structural racism can be dominant without an individual racist (Bonilla-Silva, 2003). This means we have a racialized society to begin with, creating structurally racist institutions where Whites frequently benefit from social, economic, and cultural privileges not bestowed onto racial minorities. Critical race theory identifies that these racialized power structures are based on White privilege and White supremacy, which perpetuates the marginalization of people of color.

Most people conceptualize racism as static and operating in individuals; however, racism is fluid. It flows through structures that facilitate or inhibit mobility through social institutions (like from a neighborhood to a school to a college to a job). For example, in 2015, a group of Black and Latino teenagers in McKinney, Texas were accosted by police after a group of mostly White adults called about a disturbance. During the encounter, now former McKinney police officer Eric Casebolt was recorded throwing down a 15-year-old girl in a bathing suit. Using its self-insurance risk pool, the city of McKinney settled the case for $184,850 (Uhler, 2018). Former McKinney elementary school teacher Karen Fitzgibbons was fired after stating the following about the incident:

> This officer should not have to resign. I'm going to just go ahead and say it … the Blacks are the ones causing the problems and this 'racial tension.' I guess that's what happens when you flunk out of school and have no education.
>
> *(Klein, 2015)*

If a Black child were sitting in Karen Fitzgibbons' classroom would they be taught equally? As it relates to anti-racism, imagine how many teachers, administrators, and family members knew about Fitzgibbons' racist views and did nothing. These bystanders are complicit in allowing racism to proliferate. As in McKinney, neighborhoods and schools are linked together. Some of the same people who work at the schools live in the local neighborhoods. When incidents with racist intent occur in these two social institutions, they are not isolated or coincidental. They are highly interconnected.

Racism on a structural level is rooted in policies, laws, and legislation that allow differential treatment of individuals based on socially-ascribed racial categories. Unfortunately, policies lead to other teachers, just like some cops, committing one of the ultimate acts of solidary with racists—silence as acceptance. Instead of calling out the racism, racism is dressed up with pretty words through euphemisms and ignored.

Public health critical race praxis

Understanding the importance of how race and racism operate within the broader societal structure is important to understand how the racially violent events discussed above affect minority groups on an individual level. PHCRP is a framework which combines critical race theory and public health theory as a means to best express how to understand and address social and health issues, with the ultimate goal to achieve social justice for marginalized groups (Gilbert and Ray, 2016). The inclusion of PHCRP is important because one cannot talk about the structural racism of our society without also discussing how it is impacting the health of marginalized groups (Ford and Airhihenbuwa, 2010a; 2010b). Violent crimes, such as domestic terrorism, take a significant toll on marginalized groups. By using the PHCRP framework, we aim to move the conversation forward to provide theoretical and policy recommendations.

Looking at the rates of justifiable homicides through the PHCRP lens gives a better understanding of police behavior and how justifiable homicides have increased (Gilbert and Ray, 2016). The PHCRP framework provides principles of: first, utilizing the primacy of racialization principle to illuminate how racial stratification leads to unequal life chances; second, utilizing the race as a social construct and gender as a social construct principles in order to provide researchers with a lens to consider how criminalizing Blacks limits healthy lifestyles; and third, utilizing the race consciousness and interdisciplinary self-critique principles in order to push for policies to better understand five key components that lead to officer-involved shootings:

1. racial biases
2. racial and gender consciousness
3. ways to provide more equitable policing practices
4. the enforcement of legal remedies for those who abuse power
5. the prevention of acts of discrimination by holding individuals culpable who informally police Blacks.

Following the structural determinism principle of PHCRP, Gilbert and Ray (2016) state that policy makers have clear guidelines they should follow to help the growth of anti-racism ideologies and practices surrounding law enforcement behavior. In particular, they note the importance of policy makers relying on valid and reliable research. The next section discusses more direct ways to address "racially charged" incidents such as the ones previously discussed and become more aware of anti-racism ideologies.

Racially inclusive sociological imagination framework

What do we as individuals do to obliterate structural racism and deal with individuals who have the power and influence to make decisions with racist intent that have institutional ramifications?

We suggest employing a "racially inclusive sociological imagination framework." Accordingly, we have three specific suggestions for people aiming to engage in anti-racism activism in their daily lives. First, people can become "racial equity learners" by educating themselves about the reality that racial inequality still exists and permeates every facet of the social world. This is what we aimed to do with policing and criminal justice, above. The unfortunate truth is that even if people think they do not experience race, they live it and may benefit from it. Race affects everyone to such an extent that people who believe they do not experience race maintain it even if they do not feel its tormented wrath directly.

Second, people should not only learn about race and racism, but they should also aim to be a "racial equity advocate" by holding friends, family, and co-workers accountable for what they think, say, and do about inequality. The fact is that in today's society people live highly segregated lives, which means they may never come into contact with marginalized groups, ultimately leading to inequality being fostered because marginalized groups are not present. Speak up for them. Accordingly, being an advocate is much deeper than simply being an ally. Allies can at times populate in silence. Advocacy requires direct action to intervene in racist encounters, frequently by disrupting the normative interaction patterns of the people that we care the most about.

Third, instead of simply asking for quota-type diversity, people can be a "racial equity broker" with their employers, children's schools, churches, and homeowners' associations by aiming to institute more policies and practices that allow for accountability, objective evaluation, and transparency. We must be willing to look at our own institutions to ensure equitable policies and practices within our own neighborhoods, workplaces, and schools. Evaluating and demanding transparency will highlight embedded forms of racial discrimination and their sources that would otherwise not be as overt. When the problem is identified, it makes it easier to rectify by implementing new practices and policies to vehemently attack those sources with solutions to remove racism.

In order to be a racial equity learner, racial equity advocate, and racial equity broker, it is important to implement a "racially-inclusive sociological imagination framework." The racially inclusive sociological imagination framework builds on the work of others who push for the importance of centering racial justice (Meehan, Reinelt, and Perry, 2009; Potapchuk, 2004). We add to this body of knowledge by starting with the fundamental premise that in order to center and engage in racial justice work, procedural justice must be at the forefront of the theoretical model and implementation plan. It is very important for people to begin by understanding and embracing the fact that social justice is "the premise that everyone deserves equal economic, political and social rights and opportunities" (Jiminez et al., 2014: 1). Justice is typically broken down into two main categories—distributive and procedural. On one hand, distributive justice is the belief in equity and fairness; which of course, most people believe in. Procedural justice, on the other hand, is the belief in an equitable procedure to create equitable distributions.

The racially-inclusive sociological imagination framework includes five components: (1) developing a diversity achievement ideology; (2) identifying trust points; (3) reducing implicit bias; (4) creating brave spaces; and (5) engaging in racial uplift activism. These steps help to change our everyday social interactions as well as the policies and practices that augment hate speech and racial discrimination.

Develop a diversity achievement ideology

First, people have to develop a diversity achievement ideology. The diversity achievement ideology includes four important components: (1) self-awareness; (2) social awareness; (3) global awareness; and (4) agency. Self-awareness means an individual must begin to think critically about the ways they view the world and why, and ultimately developing a holistic life perspective. No one can be forced to do this; it is a personal endeavor. People have to come in touch with what they believe morally, spiritually, mentally, emotionally, and physically. They have to confront issues that might not allow them the ability to properly develop a diversity achievement ideology. Often times, this means reflecting on major life events and being able to understand the difference between an individual's actions and the social identities and groups they embody.

Becoming socially aware begins by learning the way that people view social identities. Then, once a person gains the empirical knowledge about how marginalization among these social identities operate, they must think critically and reflexively about how their own social identities influence how others interact with them. The learning process cannot only be knowledge gained; it must invoke a desire for critical analysis of what was learned. Next, people become globally aware by realizing that not all people are treated the same because of their social identities. Finally, people then have to manufacture agency to enact change. Becoming a racial equity learner is really captured by going through this process. It involves much education, reading, studying, learning, and self-reflection.

Identify trust points

Second, people have to identify trust points in order to properly be a racial equity learner. In particular, people have to identify trusted and objective media sites. Admittedly, media is a competing curriculum. The difficulty with competing curricula mean they challenge our ability to obtain empirical data on trends and distorts our power to interpret events as generalizable, valid, and reliable. One way to potentially dilute certain agendas of media outlets is to identify at least three sources about a current event. By having different sources, it allows for the ability to compare and contrast the information being broadcasted. It also helps to relate the learned information back to social theory and empirical trends. Outlets such as *Contexts Magazine: Sociology for the Public* are important sources of information for rigor and empirical analysis.

Altogether, people should not simply trust what they hear and see from only one source. In the current media market, being first and getting ownership credit rather than being correct is premium; viewers must be careful and patient to collect enough information from multiple sources rather than just one. Then, the information gathered can be compiled and analyzed with existing trends to determine if the event is an outlier or within the norm. If this process is not thorough, people are examining events in a vacuum, which can be dangerous.

Mainstream media is not the only competing curriculum, there is also social media. Social media opened the doors of everyday people to generate and contribute to mass communication, but they also created an environment of faux expertise (Ray et al., 2017). Through social media many people believe they are an expert on a topic even when they are not. Additionally, most algorithms on social media platforms operate to give users content based on what they like, click, and read. As a result, social media often reflect people's own belief systems rather than an objective view of social life (Ray and Gilbert, 2018).

Nonetheless, social media can be used as tools for social change to combat prejudicial narratives while also maintain existing power structures. As a result of their unique material history, social media show and tell us what people say and do in real time. They also bring voices to those who traditionally do activist work in silence (Ray et al., 2017). Present day activism has changed because social media circumvent traditional forms of publicity. Power is placed in the hands of individuals who collectively join in solidarity for a common cause or goal. Social media provide a behind-the-scenes look at how people are organizing and communicating to create narratives that survive over time and become engrained in the social consciousness of society (Ray and Gilbert, 2018).

Reduce implicit bias

Third, people need to aim to reduce implicit bias and become better racial equity learners and advocates. Results of implicit association tests (IATs), taken by millions of Americans, show the pervasiveness of prejudice about a host of outcomes (Greenwald, McGhee, and Schwartz, 1998). As it relates to race and skin tone, people are more likely to have positive preference towards Whites and people with lighter skin tones relative to Blacks and people with darker skin tones. Research on IATs also parallels what we see play out in social interactions between police officers and Blacks with people being more likely to have a bias toward Blacks with weapons compared to Whites with weapons.

Create brave spaces

Fourth, people have to transform racist spaces into brave spaces by having candid racial conversations without racist intent. This is often difficult for people, but it is critical if anyone is to be a racial equity advocate. Talking about race is difficult because rarely do people talk about it to someone who is not of their same racial group. Brave spaces mean allowing people to create a space where they can build bridges with people who might have different views than themselves. Though universities mimic the racial segregation that people experience in schools and neighborhoods (Ray and Rosow, 2012), they are one of the rare spaces where people have the ability to (and at times are encouraged to) interact with those who think completely differently than themselves. It is most important to implement brave spaces were different ideas can be shared, especially since people's lives are so segregated by race and class that we rarely have more than superficial conversations with individuals of different social statuses. Converting homogenous spaces into brave spaces is just as important since these are often the spaces where people may have the most impact.

Engage in racial uplift activism

Finally, people have to engage in racial uplift activism. This component of the racially-inclusive sociological imagination framework highlights what it means to be a racial equity broker. There are four main practical approaches to engaging in racial uplift activism. First, people can engage in civil rights by protesting, strategizing, educating and litigating for the rights of individuals/groups. Second, people can engage in public policy by promoting the rights of individuals/groups through acts designed to influence legislative decision making. To make policy changes, people can call and email their local politicians and policy makers; advocate for racially equitable policies, and bring attention to policies that may have racialized (un)intended consequences. For example, a state may want to change the financial thresholds for students qualifying for educational funding or increase the number of months that someone is given as a mandatory minimal sentence. The racial implications for these policies may be grave considering the racial wealth gap and the role of stop and frisk policies in racial disparities in policing. As a citizen, people should express their concerns about racial implications.

Third, people can participate in community service by engaging in hands-on activities to better communities and individuals. Community service is not limited to serving at a local soup kitchen, though that is important. This type of focused community service means identifying thresholds where racial inequality exists and then using one's skill set to help. For example, a person could start a school or community garden. These programs have community and educational benefits by increasing math, science, and reading test scores (Ray, Fisher and Fisher-Maltese, 2016).

Finally, people can engage in philanthropy by raising and giving money to better the lives of others or by raising funds for important causes. Funding can be raised to refurbish the library and recreational centers that community members use for local events. Philanthropy does not always mean giving one's own money if resources are limited. Rather, it may mean thinking of ways to expand how we think about philanthropy to include social and cultural capital. There are a host of potential opportunities for people to make structural differences in people's lives to mitigate structural racism.

Conclusion

This chapter aimed to establish a framework to leverage theories rooted in critical race to think practically about ways to engage in anti-racism activism. By implementing a racially inclusive sociological framework, people can become racial equity learners, racial equity advocates, and racial equity brokers. As Jamelle Bouie (2014) said, "A generation that hates racism but chooses colorblindness is a generation that, through its neglect, comes to perpetuate it." Employing a racially inclusive sociological imagination and being willing to be color brave rather than colorblind helps to embody anti-racism activism.

For people engaging in anti-racism work, it is particularly important to have a theoretical orientation to draw upon and implement. For doing activist work, the racially-inclusive sociological framework is vital. For those engaging in empirical research, critical race theory and the public health critical race praxis are important theories to utilize. All three of these theories have key components that overlap and can be specifically applied to a variety of empirical outcomes to engage in and study scholar-activism. Research on policing, the criminal justice system, and the judicial system is especially fitting. Obviously, the overlap between policing and health care is relevant, in addition to a host of other outcomes.

Potentially more pertinent to this global movement for Black Lives is for scholars to conduct research with and on actual activists. It is some sort of assumption that activists embody ever-present identities rather than people who evolve into their activist selves. Researchers can apply the theories highlighted in this chapter to learn about how people develop an activist identity, how people then pursue their activist work and what we learn from it, and how various strategies used by activists fit within the various components of the racially inclusive sociological imagination framework. Admittedly, some people are better than others at implementing effective activist strategies on the local, state, and federal levels. It is high time for scholars to utilize better theoretical frameworks to make sense of the nuanced ways that activists do their work, and are successful at making anti-racist change. The theories highlighted in this chapter help advance the scholarly and community-based participatory research that informs much of the pursuits of scholar-activists. Advanced technologies allow scholars to do this work in real time rather than waiting to comb through archives. Race scholars must leverage these innovative empirical tools to evaluate social movements as they evolve.

References

Alexander, Michelle. 2010. *The New Jim Crow: Mass Incarceration in the Age of Colorblindness*. New Press: New York City.

Bonilla-Silva, Eduardo. 2003. *Racism Without Racists: Color-Blind Racism and the Persistence of Racial Inequality in the United States*. Rowman and Littlefield Publishers: Lanham, MD.

Bouie, Jamelle. 2014. "Why do Millineals not Understand Racism?" Slate https://slate.com/news-and-politics/2014/05/millennials-racism-and-mtv-poll-young-people-are-confused-about-bias-prejudice-and-racism.html. Accessed on November 12, 2019.

Crenshaw, Kimberle, Neil Gotanda, Garry Peller, Kendall Thomas. 1995. *Critical Race Theory: The Key Writings That Formed the Movement*. New Press: New York.

Ford, Chandra L. and Collins O. Airhihenbuwa. 2010a. "The Public Health Critical Race Methodology: Praxis for Antiracism Research." *Soc Sci Med* 71: 1390–1398. doi:10.1016/j.socscimed.2010.07.030..

Ford, Chandra L. and Collins O. Airhihenbuwa. 2010b. "Critical Race Theory, Race Equity, and Public Health: Toward Antiracism Praxis." *American Journal of Public Health* 100(3): 693–698. doi:10.2105/AJPH.2009.171058.

Gabrielson, R., R.G. Jones, E. Sagara. 2015. "Deadly Force in Black and White: A ProPublica Analysis of Killings by Police Shows Outsize Risk for Young Black Males." *ProPublica.*

Gilbert, Keon and Rashawn Ray 2016. "Why Police Kill Black Males with Impunity: Applying Critical Race and Public Health Theory to Address Determinants of Policing Behaviors and the Justifiable Homicides of Black Men." *Journal of Urban Health* 93(1): 122–140.

Greenwald, Anthony G., Debbie E. McGhee, Jordan L.K. Schwartz. 1998. "Measuring Individual Differences in Implicit Cognition: The Implicit Association Test." *Journal of Personality and Social Psychology* 74(6): 1464–1480.

Jiminez, Jillian A., Eileen Mayers Pasztor, Ruth M. Chambers, Cheryl Pearlman Fujii. 2014. *Social Policy and Social Change: Toward the Creation of Social and Economic Justice (2nd Edition).* Sage: Los Angeles.

King, Jr. Martin Luther. 1963. *Letters from a Birmingham Jail.* African Studies Center. Philadelphia: University of Pennsylvania. Retrieved January 26, 2019. www.africa.upenn.edu/Articles_Gen/Letter_Birmingham.html. Accessed on November 12, 2019.

Klein, Rebecca. 2015. "Texas Teacher Fired After Disturbingly Racist Post in Response to Pool Party Incident." *Huffington Post.* Retrieved January 26, 2019.

McKay, Tom. 2015. "The Charleston Shooter's Judge Has a Shocking History of Racism in the Courtroom." *Mic,* Retrieved January 26, 2019.

Meehan, Deborah, Claire Reinelt, Elissa Perry. 2009. "Developing a Racial Justice and Leadership Framework to Promote Racial Equity, Address Structural Racism, and Heal Racial and Ethnic Divisions in Communities." *Leadership Learning Community.*

Pager, Devah. 2007. *Market: Race, Crime, and Finding Work in an Era of Mass Incarceration.* University of Chicago Press: Chicago.

Potapchuk, Maggie. 2004. "Cultivating Interdependence: A Guide for Race Relations and Racial Justice Organizations." *Joint Center for Political and Economic Studies.*

Ray, Rashawn. 2019. "Forming a Racially-Inclusive Sociological Imagination: Becoming a Racial Equity Learner, Racial Equity Learner, and Racial Equity Broker." In Ray, Rashawn and Hoda Mahmoudi (eds). *Structural Racism and the Root Causes of Prejudice.* Berkeley: University of California Press.

Ray, Rashawn, Melissa Brown, Ed Summers, Neil Fraistat 2017. "Ferguson and the Death of Michael Brown on Twitter: #BlackLivesMatter, #TCOT, and the Evolution of Collective Identities." *Ethnic and Racial Studies* 40(11): 1797–1813.

Ray, Rashawn, Dana Fisher, Carley Fisher-Maltese 2016. "School Gardens in the City: Does Environmental Equity Help Close the Achievement Gap?." *Du Bois Review* 13(2): 379–395.

Ray, Rashawn and Keon Gilbert 2018. "The Evolution of #BlackLivesMatter." Essay 15 In Hunter. M. (ed). *The New Black Sociologists: Historical and Contemporary Perspectives.* New York: Routledge.

Ray, Rashawn and Jason A. Rosow 2012. "Two Different Worlds of Black and White Fraternity Men: Visibility and Accountability as Mechanisms of Privilege." *Journal of Contemporary Ethnography* 41: 66–95.

Survey of U.S. Adults August 16–September 12, 2016. "The Racial Confidence Gap in Police Performance." *Pew Research Center.*

Uhler, Tom. 2018. "Settlement Reached in Viral Video Case of McKinney Police Breaking up Pool Party." *Star-Telegram,* Retrieved January 26, 2018.

Van Cleve, Nicole Gonzalez. 2016. *Crook County: Racism and Injustice in America's Largest Criminal Court.* Stanford University Press: Palo Alto, CA.

Zimring, Franklin E. 2017. *When Police Kill.* Harvard University Press: Cambridge and Massachusetts.

Part VI
Racism and nationalism

Introduction

The chapters in this part explore the complexities of the interrelationships between racism and nationalism. Much of the literature on racism has not engaged much with the wider scholarship on nationalism, but it has become clear in recent years that any rounded account of contemporary racisms has to take a deeper look at nationalism and its expression in various forms in contemporary societies.

The first chapter in this part by Sivamohan Valluvan provides a critical overview of research on nationalism and racism and argues forcefully that it is important to link these two fields of research more closely together. Valluvan seeks, in particular, to show that nationalism is rarely just or even primarily a politics of belonging. Somewhat against the dominant voices in research on nationalism he seeks to show that nationalism often rests on assertions of non-belonging. He argues that in the West this often takes the form of constructing the racialised other as the outsider to be feared and often excluded. From this starting point, Valluvan directs attention to the ways in which contemporary nationalisms have been framed in such a way that they assert the centrality of borders and bordering as a way to protect the nation from the 'others' and 'outsiders' at the other side of the border.

This is followed by Matthew W. Hughey's and Michael L. Rosino's discussion of sociological approaches to race and nationalism. Hughey and Rosino begin their account by discussing four dominant approaches to the sociology of nationalism, exploring both their strengths and weaknesses as analytical frames. Following from this starting point they then seek to outline how a better understanding of the relationship between racism and nationalism is essential to developing a more rounded understanding of the complex manifestations of ethno-nationalism in the contemporary environment.

The next chapter in this part, by Charles Leddy-Owen, is linked in a number of ways to the arguments developed in the first two chapters, although his focus is located more specifically within the context of British society. He argues that much can be gained from developing a conversation that brings postcolonial, racism and nationalism studies together. He frames his discussion around a number of influential texts on nationalism, and he then explores a postcolonial perspective to critique their accounts of nationalism, particularly focusing on their silence about the racialised dimension of modernity. It should be noted, however, that Leddy-Owen is also aware of the limitations of postcolonial perspectives in this field, and a recurring theme of his analysis is that postcolonial theories can learn much from the approaches developed by some scholars of nationalism. In the concluding section of the chapter he focuses on what the 2016 UK referendum on EU membership can tell us about the politics of nationalism. He uses this case study to explore the linkages between racism and nationalism in the context of debates about Brexit.

The final chapter in this part, by James Rhodes and Natalie-Anne Hall, takes up the issue of the relationship between racism, nationalism and the politics of resentment in contemporary English society. Rhodes and Hall identify the key themes that have been viewed by the scholarship as animating the contemporary politics of white resentment in England in order to consider the mutual imbrications of racism and nationalism and their shifting modes of articulation since the turn of the century. They seek to demonstrate how both racism and nationalism operate through processes of othering that necessarily rest upon particular modes of exclusion and inferiorisation. From this perspective, Muslims and migrants emerge as central objects of this process and are presented as threats to the economic, political and cultural integrity of the nation. Rhodes and Hall explore, in particular, how notions of white victimhood and marginalization, racialized conceptions of the working class, and the invocation of a nostalgic and defensive English nationalism are becoming increasingly common. They argue that the recovery of a white English national identity can be seen as indicative of a renewed assertion of racialised discourses of belonging and indigeneity.

19

Nationalism and racism

The racial politics of non-belonging, bordering and disposable humanities

Sivamohan Valluvan

Theorizations of racism as set within the Western context have always run close to reckonings with the idea of nation; formative thinkers like Gilroy (2019), Goldberg (2002) and Yuval-Davis (1997) consistently grapple with the close affinities of the two formations. Racialization and the national imagination respectively are the two major nodes through which hierarchical conceptions of communitarian belonging have been both rendered and circulated within modernity. It palindromically follows that much race-making work will be channeled through conceptions of nationhood and that much nation-making work will be channeled through conceptions of race. Put simply, the two assertions of communitarian identity often act in concert, both discursively and institutionally. It is accordingly this joint expression that will be the focus of this chapter.

The powerful centrality of nation to how Western racisms are articulated has of course become once again, in light of recent electoral trends, a major concern of academic debate. The study of nationalism itself suffered, through the 1990s and 2000s, a brief hiatus. In the immediate wake of the USSR's dissolution, and in line with the complementary analytic trends characteristic of the 'end of history' hubris, nationalism ceased to receive much critical scrutiny. The ills of nationalism were assumed by many to be a matter primarily of the past and/or to have been overstated in the first place. The political consolidation however of nationalism over the last decade, a consolidation that had been germinating over an extended period (Ansell, 1997; Bhatt, 2012; Kundnani, 2007; Lentin and Titley, 2011), has demanded a hasty analytic recourse to the appeal and conduits of nationalism. Whilst this has been partially achieved through a resurgent interest in the toxic politics of the far-right and fascism *proper* (Mondon and Winter, 2019), another line of reawakened analysis has formally centered nationalism as a force of modernity unto itself: requiring in turn measured understanding of how the nation has operated as the preeminent formation by which modern people have both conceptualized and organized their political life. Amidst this reawakening, scholars of race and racism have been insistent about the centrality of whiteness and racialized pathologization to formations of Western nationalism, a centrality that is often absent in more mainstream understandings of the topic.

This chapter will herein profile the different canonical debates through which this relationship between racism and nationalism has been made most productively evident. This discussion will include: first, a summary of classical theorizations of the nation's place within modernity; second, an interrogation, through drawing upon formative works as developed within a critical Cultural Studies tradition, of the Western nation's racial premises; and third, an engagement of a postcolonial theory lens that helps us theorize the nation beyond the particulars of a European modernity. The recurring emphasis of this chapter will be the exclusionary underpinnings and capacities of nationalist politics – racialized exclusionary capacities that are expressed both discursively (e.g. the forms of vilification and outsized political scapegoating of minorities) as well as institutionally (e.g. the suite of citizenship regimes and 'bordering' practices proliferating all around us). The chapter will accordingly argue, contrary to most classical reckonings with the subject, that nationalism is rarely just or even primarily a politics of belonging. It will instead become apparent that its political mandate most often rests on assertions of non-belonging, – wherein nationalism is a politics of exclusion that renders the often racialized Other the oversized object of political anxiety.

Defining and historicizing the nation

The nation was, over an extended period, understood by many academics and popular thinkers alike as something fundamentally natural. But from the 1980s onward, mainstream scholarship realized a more aggressive deconstruction of how nations are themselves specific outcomes of modernity, something that was summoned into existence by the confluence of various historical factors from the 17th century onward. In other words, nation has been ably understood in most contemporary scholarship as being both an institutional and imaginative form unique to modernity.

This does not, however, obviate the truth that nationhood is still conjured in much popular culture as constituting a timeless unit that has always existed – as constituting the natural container by which different peoples are organized historically and culturally. As Tharoor (2018) put it in an entertaining take on what he calls Neflix's 'nationalism problem':

> It is a pity that so many historical films [on the streaming platform] feel so obliged to place the imagined nation at their emotional core. That not only distorts understandings of the past, but it suggests that the past can only be relevant and interesting if it supports conventions of the present. […] Nationalism becomes a kind of virtue that transcends time.

And whilst such popular appeals to an immemorial sense of the nation's character might be easily rebuked, it is worth noting that there are some rather more refined academic schools that still to try to attribute some residual features of premodernity to the emergence of the nation idea. For instance, the influential 'ethno-symbolism' work of the late Anthony Smith (2009) maintains that the myths and symbols of ethnic community that predated the emergence of the modern state are equally vital for situating the longevity and reach of nationalism. Similarly interesting is Llobera's (1996) deep reading of medieval texts in order to historicize the gradual emergence amongst elites of an attachment to nation, an emergence that gradually supplanted the role of formal religion in the political and cultural life of modern societies. His famous remark that nationalism is the 'god of modernity' buttresses the aforementioned Smith's (2001[2010]: 38-39) own claim that, amidst the seeming dissipation of religion's hold on society, it is the idea of nation that constitutes modernity's staging of the 'sacred' – a sacralized sense of nigh metaphysical community whereby nationalism becomes in practice 'a surrogate political religion'.

These tangents aside, the precise emergence of the nation is these days historicized with relative scholarly ease, wherein the vicissitudes and imperatives of early capitalism (intertwined with colonial expansion) and the 19th century era of cultural Romanticism are straightforwardly identified as the two defining stages (Rabinbach, 1974: 127-153). Commonly dated to the 1648 Westphalian Treaty, the nation-state proper, as a form of centralized territorial sovereignty (Anderson, 1983: 7), is now seen as only emerging amidst the debris of the 'religious' wars that tore asunder Europe. It is *modernity* therein – as a particular historical force that 'territorializes' political sovereignty into one centralized unit – that is seen as incrementally promulgating a political belief that the legitimacy of government must always be vested in an idea of the national people that the territory comprises.

This analysis has culminated, in the wake of the cultural and linguistic turn in social theory, with the now famous conception of nation as 'narration' (Bhabha, 1994[2004]), nation as 'discourse' (Calhoun, 1997; Wodak et al., 2009[1999]) and nation as 'a category of practice' (Brubaker, 1996: 15): this being the notion that the idea of the nation – comprising its many myths, its symbols, its nominal values, and also the historical events that it ritualizes as iconic – becomes only something that is told, said, gestured, and performed. Nation is namely only a narration, but a narration with formidable institutional backing and consequences – given that it is in the name of the nation that the modern state is said to exist.

This observation helps prise open the most celebrated accounts of nation and nationalism, the publications of which clustered around the early 1980s. This includes the famous 'imagined communities' account of Benedict Anderson (1983); it includes Gellner's (Gellner, 1983 [2006]) functionalist reading of how nationalisms emerged in accordance to the imperatives of the industrial capitalism; and it also includes the Marxist social formations account of Hobsbawm (1990), Thompson, 1963 [2013]), and also Balibar (1990). A series of canonical concepts took shape here. For instance, Anderson's 'imagined communities' and Balibar's (1990: 349) 'fictive ethnicity' both signposted the manner in which an illusory sense of national community takes concrete shape, cutting across more deeply-worn and materially embedded divisions of geography, gender, politics and, crucially, class (Garner, 2010: 49). Also apparent here is the integral play on temporality. It is often forgotten that national identity is not merely spatial – i.e. an ideal of 'deep, horizontal comradeship' (Anderson, 1983: 7) operating symbolically across a geographic expanse. Nation is also a claim on transhistorical time. As Anderson argued, a sense of 'simultaneous temporality' arises that is affectively intoxicating as well as cognitively satisfying; wherein people, through their investments in prevailing narrations of nation, believe themselves to be joined by historical projection with those who have long been dead alongside those who are yet to be born. After all, it is not at all uncommon to hear in everyday speech claims about how 'we' did this and 'we' did that: how 'we' invented the wheel; how 'we' fought off the Romans; how 'we' invented the number zero; how 'we' built the pyramids; how 'we' defeated the Nazis; how 'we' resisted the Ottomans; and so forth. Central to this memorialization of a 'deep time' that the idea of nation stages is what Hobsbawm and Ranger (1983) coined as being the 'invention of tradition'. The invention of tradition refers here to the important monumentalization of a particular iconic history definitive of the nation. This is namely the selective and often distorted terms by which a particular retrospective understanding of history gets cemented: a history that extolls the nation as constituting an unbroken ethnic coherence, as possessing a shared culture, and as having a distinct political purpose and destiny.

Amidst this expansive academic consensus, there is little scholarly necessity to further establish the specifics of the nation-state's socially constructed historic contingency. The notion of social construct remains after all a truism of contemporary social science, whatever the subject matter being mooted. The more credible and worthwhile critical intervention regarding the specificity of nationalism is accordingly to be had elsewhere. Put differently, it is not the constructed nature of the nation but *how* it is necessarily constructed that critical scholars of nationalism are most inclined to unpack. In other words, it is an interrogation of the process of making in itself, as distinctive to nationalism, which is of more meaningful political value. It is also in this that the nation's story of race and racism will become more immediately visible.

Nation and exclusion

It is not uncommon to encounter claims that either defend the merits of nation and/or exculpate it of its most inconvenient and problematic features. For instance, there are many who see the commitment to nation as testament to a healthy appetite for democratic community. These are the pervasive formulations where a noble patriotism is seen as constituting the basic premise for collective concern and civic duty. There are others of a more Marxist/post-Marxist vintage who see national identity as the basis for the shepherding of popular working class vernaculars around which a critical anti-market, anti-establishment and anti-elite politics can take shape. There are also those of an International Relations disciplinary inclination who press the nation as a necessary practicality by which otherwise anarchic global relations and processes can be pooled into functioning territorial units. This position – famously critiqued by both Ulrich Beck (2007) and by Wimmer and Glick Schiller (2002) as exemplary of 'methodological nationalism' – also marries with certain anthropological intuitions that see nations as the proxy index for culture. This is the inferential tendency to see national identity as corresponding to different cultural formations: say, Swedish versus Italian culture or Australian versus Indian culture. There are then others who see in the collective spirit of nation a crucial antidote to the atomizing, individualizing and excessively rationalized bureaucratic underpinnings of modernity. This more quietly textured orientation sees the binds of nation as returning to people a sense of purpose, attachment and affect that modernity otherwise denies. This is the abiding legacy of Romanticism that, as harnessed to other complementary political programs and temperaments – be it conservative, Marxist, liberal or realist – that continues to vest in the idea of nation a popular validity, pragmatism and spirituality alike.

The treatment of nationalism as informed by a race conscious critical commentary places its emphasis elsewhere. Troubled by these various terms by which the nation continues to leverage a popular credibility, race driven analyses draws its most concerted attention to the exclusionary premises by which the nation obtains its primary and most visceral political mandate. These scholars, particularly those associated with 1980s analyses of the emergent 'new' and 'cultural' racisms, developed an understanding of nation as always being premised on what is often called Othering. Just as Stuart Hall (1992) and Edward Said (1978 [2003]) famously conceived of colonial ideas of the West as being tied to the conjuring of a semiotic Other (be it the 'Orient' or 'the Rest'), critical scholars of nationalism have tended to emphasize the terms by which the emphatic identification of a 'Significant Other(s)' is how the nation itself can be asserted in a substantive manner (Triandafyllidou, 1998). In line with the maxims of structural linguistics underpinning wider analysis of culture and ideology, scholars of the racism/nation nexus have tended to focus on two key fronts of nationalist assertion. First, the respective European nation-state's civilizationist affirmations of difference *vis-à-vis* the colonized elsewhere. But also the terms by which racialized domestic minorities become the negational foil for the majoritarian nation. As regards the latter, the 19th century role of anti-Semitism (McGeever and Virdee, 2017; Mosse, 1978) is seen as a particularly emblematic marker of how nationalist politics has always revolved as much on internal distinction as it has on distinctions as placed at the ostensible frontier.

This more structuralist minded unpacking of the nation's 'self/other' configuration has been further aided by later poststructuralist deconstructions of the very idea of culture that is often indexed to nation – a notion of cohesive cultural identity that is often framed antagonistically against a nation's minorities. It remains a commonplace feature of modern discourse to tie conceptions of cultural difference to mappings of nation and ethnicity. The habitual prevalence of such 'culturalist' (Brah, 1996: 80) logics that nationalisms help uphold was put herein under sustained stress amidst the 'textual turn' in cultural theory; it becoming increasingly apparent that the claims to cultural content as demarcated by the boundaries of nation lacked empirical credibility. To pose a perhaps flippant example, there is very little cultural commonality that can harmonize the dramatic class and geographic contrasts that separate the Liverpool of Wayne Rooney from the Cotswolds shires of Zara Tindall (née Phillips). Culture remains, in other words, too relational, localized, fluid, and unstable a set of practices and orientations to be meaningfully situated at the level of national populations. Conversely, in accordance with some of the globalization oriented analysis of the 1990s and 2000s, the determinations of contemporary culture are often better accounted at the level of a transnational commercial industry as oriented around motifs of Americana and the mythopoesis of the American Dream more broadly. As Hobsbawm and Kertzer (1992: 8) noted in a wry snipe about far-right politics:

> *Culturally*, the most militant gangs who beat up immigrants in the name of the nation belong to the international youth culture and reflect its modes and fashions, jeans, punk-rock, junk food and all. Indeed, for most of the inhabitants of the countries in which xenophobia is now epidemic, the old ways of life have changed so drastically since the 1950s that there is very little of them left to defend. It actually takes someone who has lived through the past 40 years as an adult to appreciate quite how extraordinarily the England of even the 1970s differed from the England of the 1940s, and the France, Italy or Spain of the 1980s from those countries in the early 1950s.

It may well be that the more explicit 'globalization' thesis as hinted at by the authors has become somewhat subdued over the last few years. It is, however, undeniable that an Anglophone social/digital media that supersedes nationally instituted cultural vehicles remains particularly pronounced in the present; this reality lending in turn further weight to the overarching argument that cultural formation is increasingly to be situated along a global scale.

We see herein, in the raw circumstantial specifics of locality on the one hand, and the transnational scale of social/American media on the other, that the indexing of culture to national identity is simply a bankrupt proposition. It follows therefore that the enduring political appeal of nation cannot be naively read as being simply a natural expression of cultural commonality. This is, however, a conceit that has been forcefully institutionalized through various means – after all, it is in the nation's name that the state is authorized. In other words, the belief that one's nation wields an immanent cultural integrity is routinely rehearsed through the institutional mechanisms central to what (Bhabha, 1994[2004]: 212-230) describes as the 'pedagogic' demonstrations of the nation-state. As realized, for instance: through the concerted standardization of a common language, a standardization that proved and continues to prove much more difficult than commonly presumed (Balibar, 1990: 344); through the active intervention in the telling of an official history, particularly in school curriculums (Doharty, 2018); through the preferential institutionalization of state churches/religions or, as in France, the sacralization of a principle of *laïcité*, a principle that is said to be unique to the nation; through the oratorical tropes of figures of state; through the funding and commercial structures of popular culture productions but also academic research financing; and, also, through the more ceremonial rituals that stages national unity (Byrne, 2014) and ethnic custom − rituals that comprise a set of seemingly banal practices that Billig (1995) termed everyday 'flagging'.

In sum, there prevails a significant investment by dominant institutions in the idea of nation. It is, however, also the case that the notion of a nation's well-demarcated cultural cohesiveness is *only* an institutional and discursive insistence that, by its very falsity, is often uneasy and incomplete (Bhabha, 1994 [2004]). As mentioned previously, it is evident that such institutional attempts to 'flag' the nation will always remain fragile, struggling to convincingly account for the marked localisms, the pronounced class fractures, as well as the decidedly global cultural mediations that all cut across such claims to nation. Critical accounts have therein noted that the substantiation of nationalist politics is best sourced elsewhere. As Valluvan (2019) has argued elsewhere, purported investments in national identity are in themselves inadequate to account for the fuller galvanizing force of nationalist politics. Any claim to national identity is in itself too substantively thin, too conceptually unstable, and too affectively illusory to carry all that is generally asked of a politics of nationalism.

It is here that the most distinctive aspect of this chapter's argument becomes visible. Nationalism might, namely, be seen less as a politics of belonging and more as a politics of non-belonging − a politics that takes its cue from the aforementioned processes by which Other figures *vis-à-vis* the nation are summoned into being. Figures that are, of course, frequently racialized. Inspired by the decisive critique issued by Hannah Arendt (1951 [1973]) in her *Origins of Totalitarianism*, a deep body of scholarship has asked us to note the exclusionary terms by which nations obtain symbolic definition and against whom nationalisms orient their political energies. Arendt is particularly helpful here because of her relatively prescient attentiveness to the colonial forms of 'race-thinking' that were in fact feeding into the embryonic nation-state imaginations being contemporaneously cemented within Europe. Arendt (1951 [1973]: 275) famously understood the story of nation-state politics as being the situation, which was played and replayed across the 19th and 20th centuries, where the 'nation conquers the state'. Already primed in the intrinsic logics of the French Revolution itself, nationalism was for Arendt the terms by which the ostensibly egalitarian ideals of the bourgeois revolutions found material and ideational articulation. Put differently, the 'freedom of man' as championed across the revolutionary ecstasies of nation-state formation in Europe was in actuality, the freedom of the nation and its self-declared majoritarian selves. This is the politics of nation where any notional freedom turns fundamentally and necessarily on the unfreedoms and demagogueries as asserted against those peoples understood as being *not* of the relevant nation.

The majestic analysis that Arendt provided here has proved invaluable for so much critical reckoning with the nation-question. As has been widely commented upon, however, she does also remain a somewhat clumsy and uneven observer of these overlapping logics of nation, Othering, and race (Valluvan, 2019: 218). These themes and their joint pivots are herein more efficiently and expansively gleamed through engaging the arguments of various late 20th century scholars, not least those formed in the decorated British cultural studies (CCCS) tradition as well as postcolonial theory's strident remaking of how we understand modernity, belonging and hierarchy.

Racism and nation

It ought to be self-evident to any observer of Western politics that the structures of national Othering germane to its recent memory have rarely been restricted to the simple imperatives of territorial closure. In other words, nationalist agitations are very seldom strictly 'xenophobic' in character – xenophobia as the 'undiscriminating' aversion to all outsiders *sui generis*. Again, except for the acute but generally temporary theatre of regional war, it is apparent that the recent forms of nationalisms typically ascribed to Western Europe have rarely traded on purely national distinctions *vis-à-vis* other nations (Brubaker, 2017: 1211). Instead, these post-war nationalisms have tended to be more exercised by the recurring racialized distinctions that are often expressed along overtly 'civilizational' terms. Put simply, it is not nation contra other nations, but instead, nation contra racialized outsiders that has often engendered the primary fault-lines evocative of Western nationalisms' political traction.

Important to this understanding is the oft-ignored reality that nationalism, as a distinct genre of politics, often tends to take primary issue with its own interior domain. Namely, the national psyche is often most agitated by certain internal minorities that are any given point framed as being iconically problematic. These minorities are certainly of the 'territory', having been in most instances born in the relevant country, but they are still apprehended in the popular imagination as constituting some form of alien community. As Gilroy (Gilroy, 1987[2002]) clarified with searching depth, many nationalist conceptions of fear, threat, decay, excess, and repulsion work through a disavowal of such insider racialized communities. Or, as regards the ascendant nationalist politics of today, consider here the discourses about so-called second and third generation minorities ubiquitous across so much of Europe. As is perhaps most pithily captured in the 'allochtoon'/'autochtoon' (Essed and Trienekens, 2008: 62-63) distinction that governs much Dutch political deliberation of lineage and belonging, racialized minorities often suffer from an asterisked relationship to the nation. An asterisked relationship that renders them vulnerable to extended political scapegoating and handwringing. And even if a round of nationalist assertion is indeed about the border and the foreigner, properly speaking – via, for instance, assorted anxieties about the imminent arrival of immigrants/refugees – this is an anxiety that still hinges in the first instance on a racialized aversion to the insider minority. This is in other words a brand of nationalist disquiet where prospective outsiders (e.g. refugees from Muslim majority countries) threaten to replenish the vilified internal minorities (racialized Muslim communities) who are already perceived as being too many.

Nationalism is herein only rarely about taking issue with external forces in their own right (e.g. the global flow of finance capital, belligerent neighbors, international trade wars, or foreign cultural hegemonies). Though such forms of protectionist defensiveness are always relevant to a nationalist moment, nationalism as a distinct form of contemporary politics can be better defined within tighter parameters. As Valluvan (2019) has argued elsewhere, nationalism is perhaps best understood as the terms by which certain 'constitutive outsiders' as already located *within* the nation becomes the 'overdetermined' object of culpability when accounting for a nation's perceived social, economic, cultural and/or security concerns. Nationalist alarms become herein tightly knotted by the racialized categories of non-belonging so constitutive of Western sociopolitical life. It is namely the racialized outsider who acts as the Western nation's most resonant and fetid constitutive outsider. (Note that the inverse formulation also applies: it is through being impugned as the nation's constitutive outsider that certain communities become further racialized). It is of course true that a nationalist invocation of the Other, to whom a political malaise is ascribed, does not by definition need racialized orientations. But 'race-thinking' does nonetheless act as the complementary logic that either precedes and/or amplifies any such conception of a malignant deluge.

The discursive techniques by which such a conception of deluge finds expression are varied. Most often, these racialized ascriptions often construe the relevant Other as being culturally incompatible with the white majority. This is what Mishra (2017:4) has recently described as being the 'neo-anthropological' speak of contemporary nationalists:

> In [this] vision, cultures rather than biologically defined races were presented as exclusive and unchanging across time and place, with cultural difference treated as a fact of nature – 'rooted' identities, in [David] Goodhart's phrase – that we ignore at our peril. Preferring our own kind, we apparently belong, in defiance of human history, to an immutable community bound by its origins to a specific place, and should have the right to remain distinctive. Hectically naturalising cultural difference, the neo-anthropologists were careful not to preen about their superior origins and heredity as the supremacists of the past had done. They could even claim to be aficionados of racial diversity. 'I love Maghrebins,' Jean-Marie Le Pen declared, 'but their place is in the Maghreb.'

As discussed previously, this increased 'culture talk' (Mamdani, 2002), which scores the fault-line between belonging and non-belonging, does trade on thoroughly disingenuous understandings of culture's relationship to ethnicity and nation. But also looming large within these nationalist harangues are the recurring intimations of a law and order security threat – via prevailing ascriptions of both black and increasingly Roma/Eastern European criminality (Fox, Moroşanu, and Szilassy, 2012), but obtaining a particularly sharp militaristic strain through contemporary discourses regarding terrorism and Muslim fundamentalism. Elsewhere, the threat that the Other poses is imagined along primarily economistic terms. This more left-wing inflected narrative presents the racialized minority/outsider both as a threat to the economic health and work-ethic of the nation, but also as a threat to the 'native' working-class – owing to the purported undercutting of wages and/or crowding out of employment opportunities (Bhattacharyya, 2018; Shilliam, 2018; Virdee, 2019). This latter anxiety, which has become particularly prominent in contemporary nationalist-populisms, also marries with more general concerns about resource scarcity – be if welfare state provisions or access to housing and urban space.

Bordering

As is already likely apparent, much of the nation's racial politics as germane to the contemporary West has been staged via the totemic issue of immigration – an issue that has taken on a nigh unprecedented importance in governing European politics. And whilst the presentation of these anti-immigration anxieties could notionally operate independently of racialized assignations, it is observable that it is this racialized tenor that allows harangues against immigration to operate so viscously and expansively in the public imagination. Put differently, racism lends the charge of both national decay and deluge a decidedly more fetid, rousing and even 'animalizing' (Goldberg, 2015) resonance to the threat being derided.

This attentiveness to how the 'specter of immigration' (Lentin, 2008) organizes contemporary racial nationalisms also draws attention to perhaps the key institutional mechanism through which such nationalisms find material and technical expression. Put bluntly, it is the hardened regimes of bordering multiplying across the world that constitutes the starkest material manifestation of today's nationalisms. Borders represent here the most immediate means by which a nation can police and structure the populations it considers undesirable. A politics that is realized through a suite of interlocking measures – such as increased fortification, the conditioning of citizenship, and the hollowing out of various human rights obligations characteristic of 20th century liberalism. And as will become apparent in this section, the politics of bordering necessarily traffic in a discourse of dehumanization that again harnesses the 'raciologies' (Gilroy, 2000[2004]) and related forms of ethnic chauvinism characteristic of modernity.

Bordering can certainly be as simple as not allowing certain people access to a country. These are the 'death-worlds' (Mbembe, 2003: 40) that have been increasingly normalized in those interstitial spaces that separate borders. The abyssal depths of the Mediterranean Sea and Indian Ocean intertwine with the refugee camps proliferating across various global nodes to produce particularly haunting expressions of such exclusion-cum-indifference; an expression of human expendability as actively engendered by the bordering practices that has become a fixture of modern statecraft (James, 2019; Trilling, 2019). Similarly, bordering also denotes those processes by which suspended zones of national law are brokered: wherein the outsourcing of border-control to other countries and/or the increased recourse to detention centers allows for a more callous domain of legal jurisdiction to be consolidated. Put less abstractly, this is the increasingly normalized scenario where 'outsiders' deemed undesirable can be 'housed', often indefinitely, and without them obtaining the human protections that national regimes of liberal law and supranational treaties would otherwise mandate. Notorious examples of this include the Manus, Nauru and Christmas Island arrangements as overseen by Australia's immigration policy (Davidson, 2017; DW, 2019); mooted proposals in Denmark to convert a facility on a sparsely populated island previously designated for the quarantining of infected farm animals into a migrant detention center (Sorensen, 2018); but also the more general practices by which powerful nation-states and regional entities can outsource, through financial and political incentives, the 'warehousing' of migrants to other countries (the EU arrangements with Turkey, Libya and others having receiving considerable media coverage[Henley, 2018]).

This form of repulsing certain populations, condemning them thereupon to a forcibly sequestered fixity (Mbembe, 2018b), speaks of course to well-established racial scripts by which the dehumanized/'infrahuman' (Gilroy, 2000[2004]) have been rendered disposable (Mongia, 1999). The above constitutes however a fairly conventional, if of course critical, reading of what nationalist bordering constitutes. It is worth noting how bordering also represents those processes by which access to a certain territory is in fact permitted but only in a distorted form. This partial access pertains to those situations where certain denizens' access to resources, rights and protections are either withheld or withdrawn (Back and Sinha, 2018: 138; Jones et al., 2017). Elsewhere, migrant access to the state and territory is characterized by its temporary, fixed-term nature (e.g. the restrictions as applied to non-EU student visas and work-permits). Recent research on deportation and citizenship deprivation has also drawn attention to another particularly stark dimension of today's bordering – wherein those who might initially enjoy rights are then deprived of them (de Noronha, 2019; Kapoor, 2018). This often transpires through a racialized assessment of a putative 'security threat' (e.g. those accused of being 'aligned' (Austin, 2019) to Islamist terrorism) and/or a racialized assessment of criminality (e.g. the ongoing deportation of black Britons to Jamaica). And whilst 'deprivation' might remain a *relatively* marginal feature of contemporary bordering, it not only brings into relief the racial contingency of 'belonging' but it might also constitute a wider portend of the even more diffuse authoritarianism that could await us in a 'mutant, post-judicial future' (Kapoor, 2019).

Fundamentally, as the 'racial state' (Goldberg, 2002; Sharma and Nijjar, 2018) perspective has helped demonstrate, this weaker form of national denizenship allows for the racialized engendering of populations whose presence and activity is always circumscribed – always vulnerable to surveillance and review *vis-à-vis* the expediencies of the state and its attendant nationalist-populisms. But when apprehended from a more avowedly Marxist perspective, bordering of this sort also reveals a striking stratification of labor (Bhattacharyya, 2018). There are namely profound class effects to the engendering of 'multi-status' (de Noronha, 2019) populations. Multi-status denotes here the terms by which a population is fractured by differential legal and political entitlements – including, most acutely, those who are 'undocumented' and therein lack any political recognition whatsoever. Amidst such a formal fragmentation of the polity, people's relationship to labor too becomes differentially conditioned, open therein to different levels of exploitation. For instance, less-than-citizen populations often provide low-wage work but without them being integrated into the complementary protections of the welfare state. Elsewhere, access to work for certain migrants, and those on student or spousal visas, is often dependent on a 'salary threshold'. Another implication of the latter is that should the relevant person suffer a deterioration in their earnings, they then promptly surrender the right to be in the country.

This brief scan of both the sadism but also the classed effects of national bordering helps accordingly foreground the distinctly institutional and material dimensions to the racial politics of the nation-state. This emphasis on bordering attests in turn to a wider shift in emphasis as regards contemporary critical scholarship. Much previous analysis of nationalisms' racial politics, as situated within Western Europe, centered on the theme of integration. Integration was read here as the governmental instruction, often presented within a loosely liberal guise, that the racialized minority and/or migrant community remains in ethnocultural terms a font of dysfunction unless demonstrably altered (Favell, 1998; Lentin and Titley, 2011; McGhee, 2008). It was rightly noted here that much pontification of a nationalist bent traded on some marshaling of such integration agendas/discourses. The critical focus on such integration discourses has however been supplanted of late by the perhaps more explicit theme of bordering (El-Enany, 2019). Given contemporary nationalisms' outsized emphasis on issues of immigration and citizenship, there has been a corresponding analytic push towards surveying the aforementioned materiality of bordering. This being a research program that reminds us that the racial politics of nationalism is never merely a discursive consideration – i.e. how it shapes political deliberation, mobilization and stigmatization (Valluvan, 2019) – but is also about its demonstrably material articulations and cruelties.

The postcolonial perspective

Given the immediate context of my own research experience in Britain and Sweden, much of this discussion has presumed a Western and perhaps even European location. Needless to say, debates about nationalism do extend well beyond the provincialism of Europe, and has indeed been debated far more intensely and generatively in other non-Western contexts. These commentaries, often hosted under the auspices of a wider postcolonial theory conversation, have understandably given the specifics of race and racism only a peripheral analytic berth. These perspectives are instead more inclined towards weighing the putative merits but also the excesses and hazards of the Global South's respective investments in the nation-state form. Particularly relevant here are the wider ethnic chauvinisms and majoritarianisms that have afflicted much of the Global South's attempts at nation-state formation – chauvinisms that very much resemble the majoritarian workings of a racialized inferiorization that I have hitherto attributed to Western nationalism.

This observation helps bring through a conceptual clarification salutary to this chapter's general thesis. Namely, what has been until now understood as the national politics of racialization is itself often acting contiguously to other communitarian formations as construed along ethnic and religious taxonomies. It is, for instance, instructive to remember that the forms of racialized nationalism that Gilroy (1987[2002]) brought to bear in his landmark *There Ain't No Black in the Union Jack* did not operate through an unduly circumscribed conceptualization of racial identity. Indeed, it was his parallel concept of 'ethnic absolutism' (66) that helped properly ground the exclusionary logics that nationalisms turn on. It is therein important, with an eye on the wider insights of postcolonial theory, to understand race and ethnicity as often doing a mutually complementary and often-comparable communitarian work.

The influence of postcolonial theory as regards the question of nation also derives from its formidable attempts to re-historicize the nation-state as well as re-conceptualize its contingent properties. This has involved an attempt to better parse the genealogy of the non-European nation-state. In most authoritative accounts, the nation-state imagination, wherever it might manifest, is largely understood as constituting an inheritance of 'colonial modernity' (Kalra and Purewal, 2019). This remains largely undisputed. But searching questions have been asked about how the nation-state, as subsequently rendered independently of European influence, does partially constitute a cooption of the form. Similarly, in working postcolonial nationalisms away from an analytic reference that is excessively European, there arises also an overarching reevaluation of whether the idea of nation can be salvaged in the charting of anti-imperial futures that are inclusive in form.

This is partly achieved through better affirming how postcolonial nationalisms do embark upon their own histories and contingencies – that they do, in other words, partially escape the determinations of the European nation-state model (Chatterjee, 1986[1993]). McClintock (1993: 67) once derided with a tidy clarity the Eurocentric orthodoxy of formative thinkers like Hobsbawm:

> Nationalisms are invented, performed and consumed in ways that do not follow a universal blueprint. At the very least, the breathtaking Eurocentricism of Hobsbawm's dismissal of Third World nationalisms warrants sustained criticism. In a gesture of sweeping condescension, Hobsbawm nominates Europe as nationalism's 'original home', while 'all the anti-imperial movements of any significance' are unceremoniously dumped into three categories: mimicry of Europe, anti-Western xenophobia, and the 'natural high spirits of martial tribes'.

This insight into the presumptuous arrogance of much European theorization is well observed. But the perhaps more interesting analytic provincializing of Europe is also achieved through noting how postcolonial nation-states produce and authorize their own distinct exclusionary and chauvinistic structures (Anand, 2012; Jayawardena, 1986 [2006]; Mamdani, 2003; Spivak, 1987 [1994]). As much work on South Asia in particular has shown, the autonomy of postcolonial nationalisms is most efficiently established not through expiating it of the sins of nationalism (as is the condescending temptation that still lurks in certain quarters), but instead, through attributing to it its own distinctive violences.

After all, as Mbembe (2018a: 1) recently reminded us in an arresting diagnosis of our current global conjuncture,

> Europe is no longer the center of gravity of the world. This is the significant event, the fundamental experience, of our era. And we are only just now beginning the work measuring its implication and weighing its consequences. Whether such a revelation is

an occasion for joy or cause for surprise or worry, one thing remains certain: the demotion of Europe opens up possibilities – and presents dangers – for critical thought.

In relation to the specifics of my own chapter, such an important observation invites us to demarcate a set of socioeconomic and sociopolitical forces relevant to contemporary postcolonial nationalisms that are no longer merely derivative of the geographic 'West/non-West' relationship. Or as Osuri (2017: 2428) puts it,

> Contemporary colonialisms and imperialisms may be best diagnosed through the lens of identifying forms of sovereignty [as comprising, in part, nation-state logics] rather than relying on the geopolitical framework of West/non-West recognisable in the conceptual vocabulary of postcolonial theory.

And though this is ultimately a call for a 'theorization of the postcolonial nation-state as engaging in its [own] expansionary colonial project' (2432), it also helps to situate the imperatives and violences of the nation-state imagination in the distinctiveness of the present. Put differently, this move helps us better understand how the different nationalisms across the Global South trade in a variety of intersecting exclusions as construed by ethnicity, religion, caste, and race whilst also inhibiting a broader transnational class solidarity as well as the global ecological consciousness so necessary for the present.

Conclusion

The nation remains perhaps the most decisive *political* unit known to modernity – the unit through which moderns have been asked to pool their political goals and imagine their sociopolitical selves. The political allure of nation has accordingly endured across modernity, and is enjoying today yet another revival. This is, needless to say, troubling. As the race-conscious cultural and postcolonial theory surveyed here has made evident, the nation enjoys very little that is benign or redeemable – trafficking necessarily in a whole host of exclusionary assertions that are not only violent (e.g. bordering) and degrading (e.g. pathologisation) but also preclude the possibilities of cosmopolitan and pluralist solidarities that render politics possible and lives inhabitable. The recurring utopian analyses of so many searching anti-racist scholars (such as Fanon, Gilroy, Mbembe and Wynter) appeal in turn to these other memories and possibilities – to realize a transcendent politics that might recover and *affirm* the textures of each other's humanity when less arrested by the myopias, aversions and even hatreds intrinsic to the racial and ethnic politics of nation.

References

Anand, D. (2012) 'China and India: postcolonial informal empires in the emerging global order', *Rethinking Marxism*, 24: 1, 68–146.

Anderson, B. (1983) *Imagined Communities: Reflections on the Origin and Spread of Nationalism*, London: Verso.

Ansell, A.E. (1997) *New Right, New Racism: Race and Reaction in the United States and Britain*, Basingstoke: Macmillan.

Arendt, H. (1951 [1973]) *The Origins of Totalitarianism*, London: A Harvest Book.

Austin, R. (2019) 'Aid worker stranded in Syria after British citizenship revoked', *Guardian*, March 4, www.theguardian.com/global-development/2019/mar/04/aid-worker-stranded-in-syria-after-british-citizenship-revoked

Back, L., and Sinha, S with Bryan, C., Baraku, V., and Yemba, M.. (2018) *Migrant City*, London: Routledge.

Balibar, E. (1990) 'The nation form: history and ideology', *Review (Fernand Braudel Center)*, 13: 3, 329–361.

Beck, U. (2007) 'The cosmopolitan condition: why methodological nationalism fails', *Theory, Culture & Society*, 24: 7-8, 286–290.

Bhabha, H.K. (1994[2004]) *The Location of Culture*, Abingdon: Routledge.

Bhatt, C. (2012) 'The new xenologies of Europe: civil tensions and mythic pasts', *Journal of Cultural Studies*, 8: 3, 307–326.

Bhattacharyya, G. (2018) *Rethinking Racial Capitalism: Questions of Reproduction and Survival*, London: Rowman and Littlefield.

Billig, M. (1995) *Banal Nationalism*, London: Sage.

Brah, A. (1996) *Cartographies of Diaspora: Contesting Identities*, London: Routledge.

Brubaker, R. (1996) *Nationalism Reframed: Nationhood and the National Question in the New Europe*, Cambridge: Cambridge University Press.

Brubaker, R. (2017) 'Between nationalism and civilizationalism: the European populist moment in comparative perspective', *Ethnic and Racial Studies*, 40: 8, 1191–1226.

Byrne, B. (2014) *Making Citizens: Public Rituals and Personal Journeys to Citizenship*, Basingstoke: Palgrave Macmillan.

Calhoun, C. (1997) *Nationalism*, Minneapolis, MN: University of Minnesota Press.

Chatterjee, P. (1986[1993]) *Nationalist Thought and the Colonial World: A Derivative Discourse*, London: Zed Books.

Davidson, H. (2017) 'Manus Island: dark chapter of Australian immigration poised to close', *Guardian*, October 29, www.theguardian.com/australia-news/2017/oct/29/manus-island-dark-chapter-of-australian-immigration-poised-to-close

de Noronha, L. (2019) 'Deportation, racism and multi-status Britain: immigration control and the production of race in the present', *Ethnic and Racial Studies*, doi; 10.1080/01419870.2019.1585559.

Doharty, N. (2018) '"Is it because I'm black?" Personal reflections on Stuart Hall's memoir Familiar Stranger', *Identities*, 25: 1, 14–21.

DW (2019) 'Australia to reopen Christmas Island refugee detention camp', *Deutsche Welle*, February 13, www.dw.com/en/australia-to-reopen-christmas-island-refugee-detention-camp/a-47489714

El-Enany, N. (2019) *(B)ordering Britain: The Migrant, the Refugee and the State*, Manchester: Manchester University Press.

Essed, P. and Trienekens, S. (2008) '"Who wants to feel white?" Race, Dutch culture and contested identities', *Ethnic and Racial Studies*, 31: 1, 52–72.

Favell, A. (1998) *Philosophies of Integration: Immigrant and the Idea of Citizenship in France and Britain*, Basingstoke: Palgrave MacMillan.

Fox, J.E., Moroşanu, L., and Szilassy, E. (2012) 'The racialization of the new European migration to the UK', *Sociology*, 46: 4, 680–695.

Garner, S. (2010) *Racisms: An Introduction*, London: Sage.

Gellner, E. (1983[2006]) *Nations and Nationalism*, Oxford: Blackwell.

Gilroy, P. (1987[2002]) *There Ain't No Black in the Union Jack: The Cultural Politics of Race and Nation*, Abingdon: Routledge.

Gilroy, P. (2000[2004]) *Between Camps: Nations, Cultures and the Allure of Race*, Abingdon: Routledge.

Gilroy, P (2019) 'Still no black in the union jack', *Tribune*, January 1, https://tribunemag.co.uk/2019/01/still-no-black-in-the-union-jack

Goldberg, D.T. (2002) *The Racial State*, Oxford: Blackwell.

Goldberg, D.T. (2015) *Are We All Postracial Yet?* Cambridge: Polity Press.

Hall, S. (1992) 'The West and the rest: discourse and power', In Hall, S. and Gieben, B.. (eds), *Formations of Modernity*, Cambridge: Cambridge University Press, 276–331.

Henley, J. (2018) 'EU migration deal: what was agreed and will it work?' *Guardian*, June 29, www.theguardian.com/world/2018/jun/29/eu-summit-migration-deal-key points

Hobsbawm, E. (1990) *Nations and Nationalism since 1780*, Cambridge: Cambridge University Press.

Hobsbawm, E. and Kertzer, D.J. (1992) 'Ethnicity and nationalism in Europe today', *Anthropology Today*, 8: 1, 3–8.

Hobsbawm, E. and Ranger, T. (eds) (1983) *The Invention of Tradition*, Cambridge: Cambridge University Press.

James, M. (2019) 'Care and cruelty in Chios: The "refugee crisis" and the limits of Europe', *Ethnic and Racial Studies*, 42, 14.

Jayawardena, K. (1986[2006]) *Feminism and Nationalism in the Third World*, London: Verso.

Jones, H., Gunaratnam, Y., Bhattacharyya, G., Davies, W., Dhaliwal, S., Forkert, K., Jackson, E., and Saltus, R. (2017) *Go Home? The Politics of Immigration Controversies*, Manchester: Manchester University Press.

Kalra, V. and Purewal, N. (2019) Bloomsbury.

Kapoor, N. (2018) *Deport, Deprive, Extradite*, London: Verso.

Kapoor, N. (2019) 'Citizenship deprivation at the next of race, gender and geopolitics', *Verso Blog*, February 22, www.versobooks.com/blogs/4250-citizenship-deprivation-at-the-nexus-of-race-gender-and-geopolitics

Kundnani, A. (2007) *The End of Tolerance*, London: Pluto Press.

Lentin, A. (2008) *Racism: A Beginner's Guide*, Oxford: Oneworld.

Lentin, A. and Titley, G. (2011) *The Crises of Multiculturalism: Racism in a Neoliberal Age*, London: Zed Books.

Llobera, J.R. (1996) *God of Modernity*, Oxford: Berg.

Mamdani, M. (2002) 'Good Muslim, bad Muslim: a political perspective on culture and terrorism', *American Anthropologist*, 104: 3, 766–775.

Mamdani, M. (2003) 'Making sense of political violence in post-colonial Africa', *Socialist Register*, 39, 132–151.

Mbembe, A. (2003) 'Necropolitics', *Public Culture*, 15: 1, 11–40.

Mbembe, A. (2018a) *Critique of Black Reason*, Durham, NC: Duke University Press.

Mbembe, A. (2018b) 'The idea of a borderless world', *Africa is a Country*, November 11, https://africasacountry.com/2018/11/the-idea-of-a-borderless-world

McClintock, A. (1993) 'Family feuds: gender, nationalism and the family', *Feminist Review*, 44, 61–80.

McGeever, B. and Virdee, S. (2017) 'Antisemitism and socialist strategy in Europe, 1880-1917', *Patterns of Prejudice*, 51: 3-4, 221–234.

McGhee, D. (2008) *The End of Multiculturalism?*, Maidenhead: Open University Press.

Mishra, P. (2017) 'What is so great about ourselves', *London Review of Books*, 39: 18, 3–7.

Mondon, A. and Winter, A. (2020) *Recationary Democracy: The Rise of the Far Right and the Myth of Populism*, London: Verso.

Mongia, R.V. (1999) 'Race, nationality, mobility: A history of the passport', *Public Culture*, 11: 3, 527–555.

Mosse, G.L. (1978) *Toward the Final Solution: A History of European Racism*, New York: Howard Fertig.

Osuri, G. (2017) 'Imperialism, colonialism and sovereignty in the (post)colony: India and Kashmir', *Third World Quarterly*, 38: 11, 2428–2443.

Rabinbach, A.G. (1974) 'Towards a Marxist theory of fascism and National Socialism', *New German Critique*, 3, 127–153.

Said, E. (1978[2003]) *Orientalism*, London: Penguin.

Sharma, S. and Nijjar, J. (2018) 'The racialized surveillant assemblage: Islam and the fear of terrorism', *Popular Communication*, 16: 1, 72–85.

Shilliam, R. (2018) *Race and the Undeserving Poor*, Newcastle upon Tyne: Agenda Publishing.

Smith, A. (2001[2010]) *Nationalism: Theory, Ideology, History*, Cambridge: Polity Press.

Smith, A. (2009) *Ethno-Symbolism and Nationalism: A Cultural Approach*, London: Routledge.

Sorensen, M.S. (2018) 'Denmark plans to isolate unwanted migrants on a small island', *New York Times*, December 3, www.nytimes.com/2018/12/03/world/europe/denmark-migrants-island.html

Spivak, G. (1987[1994]) 'Can the subaltern speak?', In Williams, P. and Chrisman, L.. (eds), *Colonial Discourse and Post-colonial Theory: A Reader*, New York: Columbia University Press, 66–111.

Tharoor, K. (2018) 'Epic fails: "Outlaw King" and Netflix's nationalism problem', *The Nation*, November 29, www.thenation.com/article/historical-epics-outlaw-king-nationalism/

Thompson, E.P. (1963[2013]) *The Making of the English Working Class*, London: Penguin.

Triandafyllidou, A. (1998) 'National identity and the "other"', *Ethnic and Racial Studies*, 21: 4, 593–612.

Trilling, D. (2019) *Lights in the Distance: Exile and Refuge at the Borders of Europe*, London: Verso.

Valluvan, S. (2019) *The Clamour of Nationalism*, Manchester: Manchester University Press.

Virdee, S. (2019) 'Racialized capitalism: an account of its contested origins and consolidation', *Sociological Review*, 67: 1, 3–27.

Wimmer, A. and Glick Schiller, N. (2002) 'Methodological nationalism and beyond', *Global Networks*, 2: 4, 301–334.

Wodak, R., de Cillia, R., Reisigl, M. and Leibhart, K. (2009[1999]) *The Discursive Construction of National Identity*, Edinburgh: Edinburgh University Press.

Yuval-Davis, N. (1997) *Gender and Nation*, London: Sage.

20

Distinctions, dilemmas, and dangers

Sociological approaches to race and nationalism

Matthew W. Hughey and Michael L. Rosino

Introduction

In the summer of 2018, news broke of South African debates over the African National Congress (ANC) initiative to explore land reform as a form of apartheid-era reparations. Afri-Forum, a South African lobby group supporting white Afrikaner farmers, began circulating a rumor that white farmers would face "genocide" (Chothia, 2018). A British columnist seized upon the debate to make a hyperbolic comment that "The violent, ethnic cleansing of white farmers by armed, black gangs is infuriating & heartbreaking" (in Chothia, 2018), which one South African political scientist saw as an instance of "Afrikaner nationalism" that is "built around farming and language, so they see this as an existential crisis" (in Chothia, 2018). In September 2018, North Korean leader Kim Jong-un received South Korean president Moon Jae-in, for what was described by journalists as the "centerpiece of North Korea's propaganda specialists as they promote an ideology of race-based nationalism that describes North and South Korean people as one nation, temporarily divided" (Klug, 2018). And on the heels of these incidents and many more—from white nationalist rallies in Charlottesville, VA and Washington, DC to the dust-ups over take-a-knee protests against police brutality—Barack Obama broke a tradition of silence about presidential successors to state that the Trump administration appeals to "racial nationalism that's barely veiled, if veiled at all" (in Thiessen, 2018).

What do these intersections of "race" and "nationalism" mean? Alone, these concepts, which contain both a vast sociological literature and pronounced layperson baggage, hold a diffuse and arguably vague denotation to the point of providing as much analytic confusion as clarity. How do they shape each other and create new, *sui generis,* interpretations of phenomena under the umbrella of "racial nationalism"? Terms, methodologies, and theories endemic to each subfield structure a variety of scholarly conversations. Each sociological approach to race and nationalism provides specific strengths and weaknesses. Synthesizing these traditions leaves one with a kaleidoscopic view; at once variegated, attractive, and all-encompassing, and yet, simultaneously fractured, incoherent, and distracting. In what follows, we demonstrate the sociological utility of synthesizing race and nationalism. We then discuss four patterns of their use in contemporary sociology in order to reveal their assumptions, uses, and import.

Race + nationalism = racial nationalism?

The modern concept of race did not exist in the ancient world (cf. Gossett, [1965] 1997; McCoskey, 2012; Snowden, 1970). People categorized and treated people differently based on their social classes throughout the historical record. However, there was no fixed categorical system we would today call "race" until the modern era (McCoskey, 2012). In the eighteenth century, a dominant Eurocentric "scientific" discourse arose to typologize and rank racial groups. "Race" then signified both essentialism and determinism; asserting a biological reality whereby racial groups possess different characteristics that, in turn, result in varied outcomes (cf. Byrd and Hughey, 2015). By the mid- to late-twentieth century, most scholars settled on a social constructionist approach wherein "race" is the product of social forces with a semi-autonomous status (a "social fact"), neither illusion nor reality, but a socially real category with social effects (see Bonilla-Silva, 1999; Omi and Winant, 1994).

Nationalism is the combination of political, social, and economic systems that promote a country's interests, sovereignty, and self-determinism. Nationalism promotes the establishment of a master status based on characteristics such as language, religion, political ideology, and/or common ancestry (Skitka, 2005). It is marked by an "uncritical acceptance of state political authority and belief in the superiority of one's nation compared to others" (Fozdar et al., 2015:321).

Nationalism can take the shape of a "civic" nationalism (Habermas, 1994; Smith, 1991) whereby participants enact a shared commitment to government, civic institutions, and laws as an ordained destiny. It can also be a form of "ethnonationalism" (Gellner, 1996) in which the basis of the nation-state depends on a shared sense of "belonging" rooted in exclusionary access to shared language, culture, traditions and/or history of a particular people. Either can be "banal" (Billig 1995) or become more pronounced via patriotism, and can easily dovetail with xenophobia, Nativism, and jingoism that defines an outgroup as alien, dangerous, and essentially "other" (Turda and Weindling, 2006).

Together, "racial nationalism" is a doctrine in which the "nation," as an imagined community (cf. Anderson, 1983), is composed of a supposedly homogenous or pure racial or ethnic group. As Turda and Weindling (2006:7) write, this ideology puts forth that "the state was a nation-state, and the ethnic majority therein represented the nation." However, the role of the state is also varied and contested. Racial nationalism is often tied to an idealized racialized vision of the nation-state. It can also take on anti-statist discourses as in contemporary fascist movements in the U.S. and Europe who advance anti-Semitic conspiracy theories about Jewish control of the government (Back, 2002).

Racial nationalism as a political-racial project imagines and endeavors to realize an intensely racialized image of the national character. It elevates a particular racialized group as paragon of the nation. It thereby excludes other groups, envisioning and treating them as unbelonging. The conflation of positive and negative physical, moral, and mental characteristics with ethnic groups is endemic to such projects to rationalize dominant ethnic groups as ideal political subjects. For example, in the mid-nineteenth century U.S., Anglo-American imagery of the famine era Irish immigrant depicted the physical and economic impacts of the famine as a set of distinct and inferior natural characteristics and helped justify the extant ethnic social hierarchy (Knobel, 2001).

Given this usage, the term "racial nationalism" meets one of the aims of social scientific knowledge. It is a means to discover and provide a general relationship of social dynamics and human behavior from various contexts. There exist general principles about the operation and variation of racial nationalisms, but explanations for how and why racial nationalism functions remain underdeveloped.[1] There is not a shortage of explanations but rather they are diffuse and contradictory. Below, we review four dominant explanations.

Analytic distinctions, dilemmas, and dangers

The state vehicle of race

A predominant explanation of racial nationalism, particularly in Westernized industrial democracies, is the "racial formation" perspective (Omi and Winant, 2014). Here, racial formation affects all social spheres, but a primary role is assigned to the political level via the idea that the "racial state" is the principal cause of cohesion and/or conflict in a racialized society. Accordingly, a "racial formation" is the "process by which social, economic, and political forces determine the content and importance of racial categories, and by which they are in turn shaped by racial meanings" (Omi and Winant, 1986:61).

State → Race → Nationalism

Well explained by the historian George Mosse (1987, 1975, 1964), such formations take place when the state is able to marshal racial mythologies, symbolism, and political liturgy. The state constructs powerful racial concepts, taking the example of German Nazism, by blending a

> view of Christ with the ideal of force. Germans ... should model themselves upon the medieval bishops who advanced, sword in hand, against their enemies ... By fusing Christ with the life spirit of the Aryan, these men wanted to create a national religion ... This was the "race mysticism" ... Out of this mixture of the romantic and the occult the Aryan arose ... This, however, was not the Darwinian struggle of the survival of the fittest, but rather the good fight of the Aryan who was eternally of the elect
>
> *(Mosse, 1987:210–11)*

Such a "racial formation" can be a powerful tool in the interests of the state. In particular, within this "nation-based paradigm of race," the race concept is a catalyst for the promotion of a blended political and ethno-ontological nationalism, but is not a causal or primary instrument in the creation of that nationalism. Rather, "race" is secondary to the power of the state, which engages in various racial projects to bolster state supportive nationalist sentiment and practice. Alternatively, people can deploy racial projects *qua* nationalism against the state. Omi and Winant (2014:95) write:

> ... the nation-based paradigm of race is an important component of our understanding of race: in highlighting "peoplehood," collective identity, it "invents tradition" (Hobsbawm and Ranger, eds. 1983) and "imagines community" (Anderson, 1983). Nation-based understandings of race provide affective identification: They promise

a sense of ineffable connection within racially identified groups; they engage in "collective representation" (Durkheim 2014). The tropes of "soul," of "folk," of hermanos/hermanas unidos/unidas uphold Duboisian themes. They channel Marti's hemispheric consciousness (Marti 1977 [1899]); and Vasconcelo's ideas of la raza cosmica (1997, Stavans 2011). In communities and movements, in the arts and popular media, as well as universities and colleges (especially in ethnic studies) these frameworks of peoplehood play a vital part in maintaining a sense of racial solidarity, however uneven or partial.

In this explanation, the concept of race is a vehicle marshaled by or against the state toward the fermentation of varied forms of nationalism. The state's monopoly on the legitimated use of physical and symbolic violence is an instrument in contestations over the racialized definitions of the nation and the dispersal of power and resources (see Rosino, 2017a). For instance, Murdocca (2010:369) seeks to illuminate "connections between race, nationalism, and legal violence" via "biopolitical forms of racial governance." Movements work through political efforts to redefine racial categories, have them codified by the state, and produce new racial structures. From this configuration, the racialized image of the nation is shaped by struggles between racial groups which are themselves prefigured by racial categories. For instance, Moreno Figueroa and Tanaka (2016) posit that racism and *mestizaje* becomes a form of nationalism within political contestations in Mexico.

This perspective holds two major limitations. First, "race" becomes a vacant concept that is used or fillable by any political agenda. We are not told why some racial groups (or even particular subgroups) cohere around politically conservative or politically progressive projects. Differing "racial projects" appear as happenstance quarrels over political positions and state power. Second, the spectrum paradigm comes close to race-reduction or conflation in many areas. For instance, the term "racial state" seems to reduce the concept of "race" only to that of the state's ability to mobilize various political agendas, or people's ability to marshal political opposition against the state. It is not clear if race is (or can become) an independent basis of group association and action. The conceptual slippage between race and politics via the state, lends to a reading of racial dynamics as "superstructure" to the materialist "base" of political conflict and state power.

Nationalism builds race

Another branch of scholarship accentuates the causal role of nationalism in constructing or solidifying the salience of racial categories. From this perspective, rising nationalist sentiment corresponds with strengthening ethno-racial boundaries and the significance ascribed to these divisions as markers of authentic national belonging.

Nationalism → Race

For instance, (Cox, 1946:614) wrote:

> The more nationalistic a people, the less will be its tendency to assimilate, the more it will tend to value its culture, especially its non-material culture, its religion. Moreover, when two highly nationalistic groups come into contact, there will be mutual fear, distrust, and intolerance.

From a Marxist standpoint, Cox emphasized how the power of the state can promote and leverage ethnic and racial cleavages and antagonisms for the class interests of capital. From this view, class elites are adept at using ethno-racial prejudices and animus to "dupe" (cf. Hall, 1981) the proletariat against themselves, preventing the formation of cross-racial class solidarity.

The analysis of white nationalism is one prominent area in which this perspective has been applied. For example, Futrell et al. (2006) contend that nationalistic ideals, technology, and state sanctioned "free speech" allows for some lower-socioeconomic whites to find and use the White Power Movement to promote a sense of white racialism and white racial peoplehood:

> U.S. White Power Movement (WPM) activists use music to produce collective occasions and experiences that we conceptualize as the movement's music scene ... We emphasize three analytically distinct dimensions of this scene-local, translocal, and virtual-and specify how each contributes to emotionally loaded experiences that nurture collective identity.
>
> *(Futrell et al., 2006:275)*

More contemporary research pushes back against these interpretations. For instance, Flemmen and Savage (2017) find that elites—not the working class—are more likely to embrace racism in service of the national project, while the working class or "disenfranchised" are more likely to engage with a populist nationalism less attached to notions of race.

> We argue against the view that disadvantaged white working class respondents are especially xenophobic, and show that racist views are not strongly associated with social position. In exploring the clustering of different nationalist and racist sentiments amongst economic and cultural elites, and comparing these with "disenfranchised" respondents with little economic and cultural capital, we show that it is actually the elite who are most likely to articulate "imperial racism". By contrast, the "disenfranchised" articulate a kind of anti-establishment nationalism which is not strongly racist.
>
> *(Flemmen and Savage 201: 233)*

Moving away from class-based arguments, others argue that racial identity claims strengthen and solidify based on accelerations of national and patriotic sentiment. For instance, Foucault (1978:149) came to understand the concept of "race" and "racism" as a particularly "modern" trope of national "power/knowledge" that "took shape at this point (racism in its modern, 'biologizing' statist form)." Here, the state's ability to engage in racial group-making (labeling, counting via census data, and classifying resources based on group-need) can intensify with commitment to state patriotism and nationalism (cf. Burchell et al., 1991; Scott, 1998). Whether "nominating into existence" (Goldberg, 1997:29–30) new racial categories and state sanctioned personhood—such as in the Jim Crow U.S. (Davis, 1991), Nazi Germany (Burleigh and Wippermann 1991) and Apartheid South Africa (Geoffrey and Star 1999)—or in official policies of refusing to acknowledge race—such as the racial backlash against France's recent move toward a refusal to count or acknowledge race (Léonard, 2014)—the practices of (non)recognition driven by nationalist sentiment result in investment in racial identities and group commitment. While such nationalism-driven categories can appear non-consequential, they can easily "cascade" (see Kuran, 1998; Laitin, 1998, 2007) to high levels of racial commitment in response to a variety of intended and unintended conse-quences of nationalism (cf. Brubaker, 2009). Regardless of intent, both the promotion and stifling of racial concepts in the name of the state and its professed values are mechanisms of what Bourdieu called "symbolic violence":

> ...*official naming*, a symbolic act of imposition which has on its side all the strength of the collective, of the consensus, of common sense, ... it is performed by a delegated agent of the state, that is, the holder of the *monopoly of legitimate symbolic violence*".
>
> *(Bourdieu 1991[1982]:239) (emphasis in original)*

In contrast to seeing the state as simply a space of contestation over racial meanings, this perspective plots a more straightforward path between nationalism and race. It contends that nationalism, as a belief in the meaningfulness of the nation as a category of social division, escalates racial conflict and domination. While this strain of theorizing racial nationalism has important contributions, it remains unclear as to whether such an amplified commitment to nationalism is instrumental to the escalation and maintenance of racial domination by elites or a form of false consciousness or psychic wages (cf. Du Bois, 1935) picked up by groups who are disadvantaged by their class position. Moreover, the role of the state as a major institution of promoting national identity in amplifying, silencing, and legitimating forms of racial nationalism deserves more fine-tuned attention from social theorists.

The conflation of nationalism and race

Investigations of the intersection of race and nationalism frequently appear to conflate "nationalism" and "race," which muddles both the two previous models of causality (cf. Brubaker, 2009: 22–23, 25–26). The definitions of these concepts so often are so similar that they are exchangeable; "nationalism" and "race" have been described in equally applicable terms, such as vague and opaque allusions to a shared sense of belonging based on fictive kindship ties and imagined communities that bind one to common interests and a collective identity.

Nationalism = Race

For example, Miles (1987:27) emphasizes how both race and nationalism are subject to similar reifications, whereby analogous formative qualities are ascribed to both:

> the ideas of 'race' and 'nation' are both categories of simultaneous inclusion and exclu-sion. They define certain types of boundary which separate populations into discrete groups which are alleged to be naturally and inevitably distinct ... Herein lies a process of reification because the criteria of inclusion/exclusion are made to appear as the deter-minants of groups' differentiation rather the act of signification, the reproduction of the act of signification, and the ordering of the material world in ways consistent with the act of signification.

While Miles (1987:27) clarifies that the idea of race generally connotes criterion that is "bio-logical, usually phenotypical (e.g. skin colour) but occasionally genetic" while the nationalism refers to criteria that "is usually cultural (e.g. language)", both cases are similar when "those possessing the characteristics are assumed thereby to form a group by natural means." Hence, when the processes of nationalism and race are thought to overlap and converge, they are rarely disentangled and disambiguated.

These conflations appear both empirically and as an artefact of post-hoc analysis. For example, in an analysis of white Australian meaning-making over the Australian flag, Perera (2007:12) cataloged how the Australian flag became "an emblem of racial particularism and aggression" and that politicians and the media failed to distinguish between "deploying the flag as a celebration of 'harmless' nationalist sentiment and deploying it as an emblem of exclusionary violence." In this same vein, Fozdar, et al. (2015: 332) argued that the Australian flag is a processual site where nationalism and race become intertwined:

> Is it possible to conclude that the Australian flag has come to stand for exclusionary nationalism? Not absolutely, for all uses of the flag are contextual. But it seems clear that with the change in uses of the flag, the growth in public 'ownership' of it, and its increasing importance as a symbol aligned with a certain version of Australian identity, there is a danger that it may be becoming so.

In both empirics and evaluation, the flag is interpreted as a symbol of equal parts race and nationalism, divorced from both its history of "White Australia" policies and the future exclusion of people of color, especially the indigenous.

A pitfall of the combined use of terms like "racial nationalism" is how to distinguish between the two concepts (race *and* nationalism) while illuminating what each term either explains: in terms of not only the causes, processes, and outcomes of behavior, but also under what contexts each term might be a better fit for predicting or explaining the same phenomena. For example, Brubaker (2009:24–5) writes that there is an:

> enormous range and heterogeneous causal texture of the phenomena subsumed under the broad rubrics of race, ethnicity, and nationalism … This heterogeneity requires the conjoint use of theoretical resources drawn from a variety of traditions and warrants skepticism about any project of constructing a single unified theory of ethnicity, race, and nationalism … the emerging field [that integrates the concepts] treats race, ethnicity, and nationalism as belonging to a single integrated domain.

Brubaker (2009:26) explains that the integration of these terms does not

> mean that one should treat race, ethnicity, and nationalism as an undifferentiated domain. Distinctions can be drawn on a number of dimensions … grouped for expository purposes into clusters focused on categorization and membership, social organization, and political action.

These concepts rest on sociological assumptions concerning their ability to be descriptive or explanatory. One school of thought sees value in reporting how people's "folk concepts" (about race or nationalism) reflect and give rise to human action and order. A contrasting perspective views such concepts as too vague and murky to serve as precise analytic concepts for sociological explanations (e.g. Alexander 2016; Anderson 1999; Brubaker, 2009; Duneier 1999; Newman 1999; Wacquant 2002).

The first school of thought portrays the specific activities and categories of meaning as providing thick description from which the deeper social relationships and emotions can come through. Fozdar et al. (2015) examined specifically those Australians who fly flags from their cars on Australia Day to understand their perspectives on nationalism and race, finding that flag flyers were more likely to hold racist and exclusionary perspectives of nationalism. Understanding the context-specific meanings that intertwine notions of race and national identity for specific actors can reveal such important insights. From this second perspective, the categories and ideas themselves are not as essential as their analytically generalizable features and processes. For instance, drawing on case studies ranging from the Nazi state to the South African Apartheid Regime, Van Vuuren (2005:60) points out that the common feature of these cases and their escalation into totalitarian violence is "the idealistic self-images of the nation and normative assumptions about its superiority are turned into natural and historical facts."

As Meer (2018:3) writes, "Perhaps the simplest way to put this is to say that social scientists tend to be interested in the dynamic and relational properties of race as both a historical idea and social category." Both perspectives have sociological import but may prove difficult to synthesize while avoiding such conflations as treating race and nationalism as interchangeable. The distinction of these two concepts must be clarified so that precisely what type of features of social reality, relationships between groups, or social processes scholarship seeks to understand when examining "racial nationalism" can truly be unearthed.

The reduction of race into nationalism

Unlike the second paradigm, scholarship of this ilk does not describe race as a phenomenon caused by nationalism. Rather, adherents tend to advocate that nationalism is a larger, more encompassing, (and often better) explanatory concept than race. The race category is simply viewed as a blunt and unsophisticated concept.

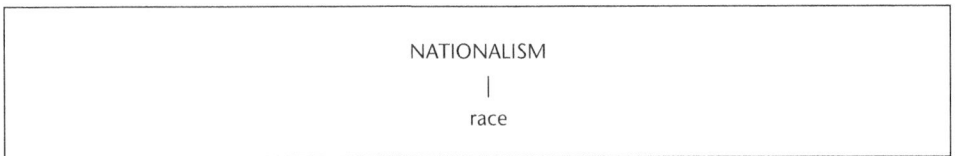

It is popular to reduce or decant "race" into concepts related to the state and nationalism; "race" exists as a second-order concept that lessens in explanatory strength in relation to notions such as a country's "values" (Miah, 2015) or notions of national "sovereignty" (Ware, 2008). While not seen as the direct offspring of nationalism, race is understood as an intellectual stepchild that does not allow its wielder any particular power not already found in the concept of statehood, colonialism, and nationalism. Under this paradigm, the privileging of race (rather than nationalism) presents a serious analytic limitation. Meer (2018:15) points to this trend with an example from how post-colonial scholarship has dealt with the intersection of race and nationalism:

> What I feel is observable across a number of academic outlets are the ways in which race concerns "have metabolized into the twin projects of diaspora identity and something called *post-/de-/colonial/-sim/-ity*" (Bhatt 2016, 398, emphasis in the original). That

is to say, that race scholarship on its own terms is missing. Is this a problem? Yes … since the portrayal of race scholarship can be at some variance from how race scholars conceive it … When, as I have suggested, post-colonial scholarship reduces race to affect or experiential dimensions, it also reduces its role in our understanding of origins and reproductions.

Sites for this particular scholarly logic can be found among attempts to measure how race is "declining in significance" (Wilson, 1978) or amidst those that insist that the using of "race" edges too close to biological essentialism and determinism (Berbrier and Cooper 2001; Gilroy 2000; Loveman 1999). In the former, race matters (and is a real social force), but matters less than nationalism and that state (and their influence over forces like political economy and labor markets). In the latter, race does not (and should not) matter as an intellectual concept among social scientists because it neglects a truly social constructionist approach to how politics and statehood *qua* nationalism form and direct human activity.

Yet, Hanchard and Chung (2004:322) contend that "both constructivist and essentialist arguments operate in arenas of politics in which the race concept in some form is already utilized to serve broader political aims of promoting racial hierarchy, racial egalitarianism, or 'race-neutral' political objectives." So also, Fields (2003:1400) makes a lucid point concerning the misstep of reifying the concepts of the state or nationalism above that of race while relying on the mantra that "race is a social construction":

> identifying race as a social construction does nothing to solidify the intellectual ground on which it totters. The London Underground and the United States are social constructions, so are the evil eye and the calling of spirits from the vastly deep, and so are murder and genocide. All derive from the thoughts, plans, and actions of human beings living in human societies.

Hence, if we accept the notion that "nationalism" and "race" are both products and producers of human activity, then appeals to social constructionism mean little without attention to why and how people actually understand and use both. That is, *a priori* assumptions that "race" is somehow better nested under the umbrella of "nationalism" (or other social forces) may hinder efforts at analysis and illumination. Meer (2018:1–2) again contends:

> race appears to have been traded downwards for sociologies of "development" or "global sociology" (as though race were not central to each) … [some] deem race as marginalized to 'an epiphenomenon to class, or subsumed under ethnicity, or collapsed within what, for some, are wider projects such as cosmopolitanism or social justice and human rights'.

By not treating race and nationalism as variant concepts that may have heterogenous relations across contexts, we foreclose on our ability to distinguish when some groups are constituted more by race or more by nationalism. Kumar (2006:4), for example, contends that English identity and white racial ethnicity were co-constructed via the global imperial relations of the Crown, writing that "it is from the empire that they get their sense of themselves, their identity." Moreover, Berbrier's (1998) examination of "contemporary white supremacist discourse" leads us to consider how varied forms of white pan-ethnicity (based on defined nation-states or imagined nationalities similar to diasporic identities) exist. At times, such discourse aims to present whites as a "pan-ethnic" community of European descendants, whose ethnicity is equivalent to that of established ethnic and minority communities … If indeed there is an emergent pan-ethnic phenomenon among "European-Americans," then it may prove important to recognize when this phenomenon is rooted in white supremacy and when it is not.

(Berbrier 1998:498)

The automatic subsumption of race to nationalism also disallows us from seeing the undulating meeting grounds of race and nationalism. For instance, in Virdee's (2014) examination of working class whites in England, we see moments in which this group both adopted or rejected racial or national belonging as well as when race was used to drive and exacerbate nationalism: "Each time the boundary of the nation was extended to encompass ever more members of the working class, it was accompanied and legitimized through the further racialization of nationalism that prevented another more recently arrived group from being included" (Virdee, 2014: 5).

Perhaps most salient to this trend, the reduction of race ignores the way that race has constructed both nation and nationalism as well as the academic disciplines we use to understand these relations. For example, Winant (2015: 2177) emphasizes that:

nascent social science disciplines [were] core components of running the empires and managing the natives, the slavocracies, and the depredations fundamental to the rise of Europe and the development of the USA, but they were also vital explicators and rationalizers of these systems.

Similarly, Go (2018:446) argues that while post-colonial theory "sees social relations, social structures and institutions as determinant," the theory would help expand our "analytic scope to see those relations, structures and institutions as imperial and hence global, thereby overcoming the methodological nationalism and U.S.-centric (or metropolitancentric) tendencies in some currents of existing sociologies of race."

Conclusion

We outlined four dominant approaches to the sociological intersection of race and nationalism. We drew attention to their analytic shortfalls and implicit theoretical assumptions. Given this chapter's place in the *Routledge International Handbook of Contemporary Racisms*, we have been attentive to the ways in which the race concept has been muted as only an empty signifier or vehicle for nationalism, relegated to secondary variable, conflated with nationalism, or reduced below its explanatory potential. These types are not exhaustive. Nor are any singular one or all of these paradigms inherently flawed. We refrain from a *coup de main* wherein we pronounce one approach correct. The approaches sketched above are not strict types with sharp boundaries. Any heuristic is necessarily troubled, as Weber famously argued, by the imprecision of the categories of race and nationhood (1978[1922]:395, 925). Hence, we advocate for specifying the causes, processes, and outcomes of these terms within their relevant contexts.

In particular, sociology would be well-served by redoubling its efforts to specify the major dimensions of how race—as ideologies, identities, interests, institutions, and interactions (Hughey, 2015)—may overlap, co-vary, or ossify in relation to nationalism within particular social relations. Otherwise, we reify and preclude what we attempt to describe as "racial" as a specific class of people, rather than an action, state, occurrence, or process that can explain why and how human action and order occur as they do.

Race interacts with nationalism in various forms and magnitudes. First, "race" manifests as an *ideologically* laden racial classification system. For example, the development of "multiraciality" in the wake of the 2000 U.S. Census (that allowed for respondents to select more than one race) is particularly double-edged. On the one hand, the rise of a "multiracial" category has legitimated a positive sense of national belonging (*qua e pluribus unum*) among many self-identified multiracial people, which is itself an ideological upheaval of the purity of whiteness which has historically manifested in legal and *de facto* practices such as the "one-drop rule" or "colorism." While on the other,

> both the scientization and politicization of multiraciality in which multiracial people are frequently framed as a utopian blank slate from which actual racist experiences and unequal histories have been scrubbed, multiraciality is increasingly used to signal both the "end of racism" … and to advocate for "color-blind" racist law and policy.
>
> *(Gardner and Hughey, 2019:659)*

Second, racial *identities* rest upon us/them distinctions and "otherness." Consider how centrally racial identities figured in the varied projects of European colonialism. For instance, binary demarcations of morality, health, education, and civilization mapped onto one another to construct a rather robust notion of both belonging and alien national-racial subjects, such as within both France and Holland:

> European nation-states were engaged in programmes of liberal reform to inculcate ideals of civic responsibility as part of a national project. There was a great focus on 'proper' upbringing, schooling and health, combined with widespread fears of (racial) degeneration. In France and Holland, such programmes targeted the poor and 'internal aliens' at home, but also poor whites in their colonies, along with the native population of the colonies to some extent (or more likely a privileged elite of them), and, to varying extent, the colony-born whites, the mixed-bloods offspring of white colonials and natives. 'Proper' (and 'white') sexual morality was restrained and continent, taking place within the family. There were fears that the colonial environment would contaminate and weaken Europeans, especially the poorer men who might live in concubinage with native women. Racial divisions corresponded with sexual-moral ones, such that Asians in the Dutch Indies were seen as licentious, indulgent, sexually uncontrolled and prone to prostitution.
>
> *(Wade, 2001:850)*

Simply put, "Racial identities continue to be central to imaginings of the nation and its destiny" (Wade, 2001:862).

Third, racial *interests* are pursued and protected via group formation and mobilization. Debates over ethnic, racial, and religious "superdiversity" (Vertovec, 2007) in England recently came to a fore in June 2016 referendum to support British withdrawal from the European Union, known informally as "Brexit" (a portmanteau of "British" and "Exit"). Concern that BAME (Black, Asian, and Minority Ethnic) people—particularly immigrants—were unfairly hurting British-born whites through their usurpation of resources and jobs, were a large signal that a White nationalist sentiment was a large part, even core, of Brexit support. As Emejulu (2016) points out,

> In this seemingly "post-race" era, Brexit shows us how whiteness, as a power relation, operates in ways to cast itself as both a "victim" and an "innocent" simultaneously. An unstated

campaign strategy of the Leave campaign was to re-imagine Britain and Britishness (but really Englishness) as white in order to make particular kinds of claims to victimhood … Thus we see whiteness operating as victim—the white working class is being held hostage in their own country by migrants. Any critique of this victimhood further re-enforces a victim status through fulminations that the critic is "the real racist" … whiteness, even in discussions about racism and anti-racism, can intrude, appropriate and colonise these spaces in order to re-enforce an identity of victimhood, whilst at the same time seemingly de-prioritising the interests and experiences of people of colour.

Fourth, racialized *institutions* constrain and enable racialized group relations to social space and resources. All institutions are racialized (Bonilla-Silva, 2014; Feagin, 2006). Moreover, all social institutions such as the economy, the education system, the legal system, or the family serve this latent racial function. One such racialized institution is the complex bureaucracy that deals in issues of immigration and therefore disperses resources such as access to legal rights and status in the United States. As Ngai points out, "the Immigration Act of 1924 constructed a vision of the American nation that embodied certain hierarchies of race and nationality" (2015:23). This policy also produced new institutional mechanisms for mass deportations of those deemed to not to have the proper status or recognition. The new institutional apparatus "constituted undocumented immigrants as criminals" and advanced the nativist vision of racial nationalism via the "goal of expelling immigrants living illegally in the country" (Ngai, 2015:61).

Finally, through racialized *interactions* people engage in boundary maintenance, networks of accountability, and the material and symbolic struggles over, or cooperative endeavors toward, a shared future (Rosino, 2017b). Consider the following account of a British migrant in France:

> Algerians, Moroccans and Tunisians—Maghrebis—and Africans make up the bulk of France's estimated 6.5 million immigrants and they do not appear to have things as easy as I do. It is almost impossible to spend a Saturday afternoon downtown here without seeing some of them—individually or in groups—undergoing random ID checks by the police or riot police, and those without adequate ID have been known to be taken into custody with sometimes fatal results. I see at least one such check a week, although I have never heard of a Brit being checked in that manner.
>
> *(Cosgrove, 2010)*

Alongside ideologies, identities, institutions, and interests, everyday social interactions interconnect with social dynamics of racial nationalism. They provide micro-spaces wherein people continually enact and reshape their sense of the relationship between race and nation.

Note

1 In *The Nature of Social Science*, Homans (1967: 20–21) pens that "when the propositions state relationships between variables, the nature of the relationship, the function, is not very specific … in social science, the greater the generalization, the less its explanatory power."

References

Alexander, Jeffrey. 2016. "Dramatic Intellectuals: Elements of Performance." *International Journal of Politics, Culture and Society* 29:341–358.

Anderson, Benedict. 1983. *Imagined Communities: Reflections on the Origins and Spread of Nationalism.* New York: Verso.

Anderson, Elijah. 1999. *Code of the Street*. New York, NY: W. W. Norton.

Back, Les. 2002. "Aryans Reading Adorno: Cyber-Culture and Twenty First Century Racism". *Ethnic and Racial Studies* 25(4):628–651.

Berbier, Mitch. 1998. "White Supremacists and the (Pan-)Ethnic Imperative: On "European-Americans" and "White Student Unions"". *Sociological Inquiry* 68(4):498–516.

Bhatt, C. 2016. "White Sociology." *Ethnic and Racial Studies* 39(3):397–404.

Billig, Michael. 1995. *Banal Nationalism*. Thousand Oaks, CA: Sage.

Bonilla-Silva, Eduardo. 1999. "The Essential Fact of Race". *American Sociological Review* 64(6):899–906.

Bonilla-Silva, Eduardo. 2014. *Racism Without Racists: Color-Blind Racism and the Persistence of Racial Inequality in Contemporary America*. Fourth Edition. Lanham, MD: Rowman and Littlefield Publishers, Inc.

Berbier, Rogers, and Frederick Cooper. 2001. "Beyond 'Identity.'" *Theory and Society* 29(1):1–47.

Bourdieu, Pierre. 1991 [1982]. *Language and Symbolic Power*. New York, NY: Polity Press.

Brubaker, Rogers. 2009. "Ethnicity, Race, and Nationalism". *Annual Review of Sociology* 35:21–42.

Burchell, Graham, Colin Gordon, and Peter Miller. 1991. *The Foucault Effect: Studies in Governmentality*. Chicago, IL: The University of Chicago Press.

Burleigh, Michael and Wolfgang Wippermann. 1991. *The Racial State: Germany 1933–1945*. New York, NY: Cambridge University Press.

Chothia, Farouk, 2018. "South Africa: The Groups Playing on the Fears of a 'White Genocide'." *BBC News*, 1 September. Accessed: www.bbc.com/news/world-africa-45336840

Cosgrove, Michael. 2010. "In France, all Immigrants are not Equal." *The Guardian*, 23 April. Accessed: www.theguardian.com/commentisfree/2010/apr/23/france-immigrants-discrimination

Cox, Oliver Cromwell. 1946. "The Nature of the Anti-Asiatic Movement on the Pacific Coast". *The Journal of Negro Education* 15(4):603–614.

Davis, F. James. 1991. *Who is Black? One Nation's Definition*. State College, PA: Penn State University Press.

Du Bois, W. E. B. 1935. *Black Reconstruction in America*. New York, NY: Harcourt Brace.

Duneier, Mitchell. 1999. *Sidewalk*. New York, NY: Farrar, Straus & Giroux.

Durkheim, Emile. 2014. *The Rules of Sociological Method: And Seldcted Texts on Sociology and its Method*. Edited by Steven Lukes. New York, NY: Free Press.

Emejulu, Akwugo. 2016. "On the Hideous Whiteness Of Brexit." *Verso Books Blog*. Accessed 5 Feb 2019: www.versobooks.com/blogs/2733-on-the-hideous-whiteness-of-brexit-let-us-be-honest-about-our-past-and-our-present-if-we-truly-seek-to-dismantle-white-supremacy

Feagin, Joe R. 2006. *Systemic Racism: A Theory of Oppression*. New York: Routledge.

Fields, Barbara J. 2003. "Of Rogues and Geldings". *American Historical Review* 108:1397–1405.

Flemmen, Magne and Mike Savage. 2017. "The Politics of Nationalism and White Racism in the UK". *The British Journal of Sociology* 68(S1):233–264.

Foucault, Michele. 1978. *The History of Sexuality, Vol 1*., translated by R. Hurley. New York, NY: Pantheon Books.

Fozdar, Farida, Brian Spittles, and Lisa K. Hartley. 2015. "Australia Day, Flags on Cars and Australian Nationalism". *Journal of Sociology* 51(2):317–336.

Futrell, Robert, Pete Simi, and Simon Gottschalk. 2006. "Understanding Music in Movements: The White Power Music Scene". *The Sociological Quarterly* 47(2):275–304.

Gardner, Sheena K. and Matthew W. Hughey. 2019. "Still the Tragic Mulatto? Manufacturing Multiracialization in Magazine Media, 1961–2011". *Ethnic and Racial Studies* 42(4):645–665.

Gellner, Ernest. 1996. "Ernest Gellner's Reply: 'Do Nations have Navels?'". *Nations and Nationalism* 2(3):366–370.

Bowker Geoffrey and Susan Leigh Star. 1999. *Sorting Things Out: Classification and Its Consequences*. Cambridge, MA: MIT Press.

Gilroy, Paul. 2000. *Against Race: Imagining Political Culture beyond the Color Line*. Cambridge, MA: Harvard University Press.

Go, Julian. 2018. "Postcolonial Possibilities for the Sociology of Race". *Sociology of Race and Ethnicity* 4(4):439–451.

Goldberg, David Theo. 1997. *Racial Subjects: Writing on Race in America*. New York, NY: Routledge.

Gossett, Thomas F. [1965] 1997. *Race: The History of an Idea in America*. New York, NY: Oxford University Press.

Habermas, Jürgen. 1994. "Struggles for Recognition in the Democratic Constitutional State". pp 107–148 in *Multiculturalism*, edited by Amy Gutmann, Princeton, NJ: Princeton University Press.

Hall, Stuart. 1981. "Notes on Deconstructing the Popular". pp 227–239 in *People's History and Socialist Theory*, edited by Raphael Samuel, London: Routledge & Kegan Paul.

Hanchard, Michael and Erin Aeran Chung. 2004. "From Race Relations to Comparative Racial Politics: A Survey of Cross-National Scholarship on Race in the Social Sciences". *Du Bois Review* 1(2):319–343.

Hobsbawm, Eric and Terence Ranger. 1983. *The Invention of Tradition*. Cambridge, UK: Cambridge University Press.

Homans, George Gaspar. 1967. *The Nature of Social Science*. San Diego, CA: Harcourt, Brace, and World.

Hughey, Matthew W. 2015. "The Five I's of Five-O: Racial Ideologies, Institutions, Interests, Identities, and Interactions of Police Violence". *Critical Sociology* 41(6):857–871.

Klug, Foster. 2018. "'Grand Theater': Has N. Korea's Kim Won a Propaganda Coup?" *The Washington Post*, 18 September. Accessed: www.washingtonpost.com/world/asia_pacific/grand-theater-has-n-koreas-kim-won-a-propaganda-coup/2018/09/18/db38684c-bb3c-11e8-adb8-01125416c102_story.html?utm_term=.086708f5bc42

Knobel, Dale T. 2001. "'Celtic Exodus': The Famine Irish, Ethnic Stereotypes, and the Cultivation of American Racial Nationalism". *Radharc* 2:3–25.

Kumar, Krishan. 2006. "Empire and English Nationalism". *Nations and Nationalism* 12(1):1–13.

Kuran, Timur. 1998. "Ethnic Norms and their Transformation through Reputational Cascades". *The Journal of Legal Studies* 27(2):623–659.

Laitin, David D. 1998. *Identity in Formation: The Russian-Speaking Populations in the Near Abroad*. Ithaca, NY: Cornell.

Laitin, David D. 2007. *Nations, States, and Violence*. New York, NY: Oxford University Press.

Léonard, Marie des Neiges. 2014. "Census and Racial Categorization in France: Invisible Categories and Color-blind Politics". *Humanity & Society* 38(1):67–88.

Loveman, Mara. 1999. "Is "race" Essential?". *American Sociological Review* 64(6): 891–898.

Marti, Jose. 1977[1899] *Our America (Nuestra America): Writings on Latin America and the Struggle for Indpendence*. Translator, Elinor Randall, Juan de Onis, and Roslyn Held. New York, NY: Monthly Press.

McCoskey, Denise Eileen. 2012. *Race: Antiquity and Its Legacy*. New York, NY: Oxford University Press.

Meer, Nasar. 2018. "'Race' and 'Post-Colonialism': Should one come before the other?" *Ethnic and Racial Studies* 41(6):1163–1181.

Miah, Shamim. 2015. *Muslims, Schooling and the Question of Self-segregation*. Basingstoke, England: Palgrave Macmillian.

Miles, Robert. 1987. *Capitalism and Unfree Labour. Anomaly or Necessity*. London, UK: Tavistock.

Moreno Figueroa, Monica and Emiko Saldívar Tanaka. 2015. "'We Are Not Racists, We Are Mexicans': Privilege, Nationalism and Post-Race Ideology in Mexico". *Critical Sociology* 42(4-5):515–533.

Mosse, George. 1964. *The Crisis of German Ideology: Intellectual Origins of the Third Reich*. New York, NY: Grosset and Dunlap.

Mosse, George. 1975. *The Nationalization of the Masses: Political Symbolism and Mass Movements in Germany from the Napoleonic Wars through the Third Reich*. New York, NY: Howard Fertig.

Mosse, George. 1987. *Masses and Man: Nationalist and Fascist Perceptions of Reality*. Detroit, MI: Wayne State University Press.

Murdocca, Carmela. 2010. "'There Is Something in That Water': Race, Nationalism, and Legal Violence". *Law & Social Inquiry* 35(2):396–402.

Newman, Katherine. 1999. *No Shame in My Game*. New York, NY: Russell Sage Foundation and Knopf.

Ngai, Mae M. 2015. *Impossible Subjects: Illegal Aliens and the Making of Modern America*. Princeton, NJ: Princeton University Press.

Omi, Michael and Howard Winant. 1986. *Racial Formation in the United States*. New York: Routledge.

Omi, Michael and Howard Winant. 1994. *Racial Formation in the United States: From the 1960s to the 1990s*. Second Edition. New York, NY: Routledge.

Omi, Michael and Howard Winant. 2014. *Racial Formation in the United States*. Third Edition. New York: Routledge.

Perera, Suvendrini. 2007. "'Aussie Luck': The Border Politics of Citizenship Post Cronulla Beach". *Australian Critical Race and Whiteness Studies Association Journal* 3(1):1–16.

Rosino, Michael L. 2017a. "Boundaries and Barriers: Racialized Dynamics of Political Power". *Sociology Compass* 10(10):939–951.

Rosino, Michael L. 2017b. "Dramaturgical Domination: The Genesis and Evolution of the Racialized Interaction Order". *Humanity & Society* 41(2):158–181.

Scott, James C. 1998. *Seeing Like a State: How Certain Schemes to Improve the Human Condition Have Failed*. New Haven, CT: Yale University Press.

Skitka, Linda J. 2005. "Patriotism or Nationalism? Understanding Post-September 11, 2001, Flag-Display Behavior". *Journal of Applied Social Psychology* 35(10):1995–2011.

Smith, Anthony D. 1991. *National Identity*. London: Penguin.

Snowden, Frank M. 1970. *Blacks in Antiquity: Ethiopians in the Greco-Roman Experience*. Cambridge, MA: Harvard University Press.

Stavans, Ilan. *Jose Vasconcelos: The Prophet of Race*. New Brunswick, NJ: Rutgers University Press.

Thiessen, Marc A. 2018. "Look Who's Shattering Presidential Norms Now." *The Washington Post*, September 11. Accessed: www.washingtonpost.com/opinions/democrats-like-to-talk-about-trump-breaking-norms-now-obama-is/2018/09/11/3cb66ef4-b5ff-11e8-a2c5-3187f427e253_story.html?noredirect=on&utm_term=.2e5684f143ad

Turda, Marius and Paul J. Weindling. 2006. *Blood and Homeland: Eugenics and Racial Nationalism in Central and Southeast Europe, 1900-1940*. Plymouth, UK: Central European University Press.

Van Vuuren, Willem. 2005. "Ideologies of Racial Nationalism: The Method in their Madness". *Politikon* 32(1):59–81.

Vasconcelos, Jose. 1997 [1925]. *La Raza Cosmica*. Baltimore, MD: Johns Hopkins University Press.

Vertovec, Steven. 2007. "Super-diversity and its Implications". *Ethnic and Racial Studies* 30(6):1024–1054.

Virdee, Satnam. 2014. *With Racism, Class and the Racialized Outsider*. Basingstoke: Palgrave.

Wacquant, Loic. 2002. "Scrutinzing the Street: Poverty, Morality, and the Pitfalls of Urban Ethnography." *American Journal of Sociology* 107(6):1468–1532.

Wade, Peter. 2001. "Racial Identity and Nationalism: A theoretical view from Latin America". *Ethnic and Racial Studies* 24(5):845–865.

Ware, Vron. 2008. "Towards a Sociology of Resentment: A Debate on Class and Whiteness". *Sociological Research Online* 13(5):9.

Weber, Max. 1978[1922]. *Economy and Society*. Berkeley, CA: University of California Press.

Wilson, William Julius. 1978. *The Declining Significance of Race: Blacks and Changing American Institutions*. Chicago, IL: University of Chicago Press.

Winant, Howard. 2015. "Race, Ethnicity and Social Science." *Ethnic and Racial Studies* 38(13): 2176–2185.

21

Nationalism, postcolonial criticism and the state

Charles Leddy-Owen

Introduction

This chapter explores nationalism and racism by way of a crosspollination of two broad fields of scholarship – postcolonial criticism and nationalism studies – that discuss many of the same social and political patterns, yet generally talk past one another. The first section will introduce postcolonial criticism – as a school of thought that I would suggest is hegemonic in contemporary scholarship of race – which accuses dominant historical and sociological accounts of eliding the central role in modernity played by colonialism and racism. The second section will introduce the nationalism studies literature by way of five of this field's seminal books, before employing postcolonial perspectives to critique their accounts of nationalism and its modern emergence. The lamp will then be turned the other way and some gaps in the postcolonialism literature illuminated by way of insights from the nationalism studies literature regarding political agency and the state in contemporary society. The final main section will bring this discussion to bear on recent analyses of those who voted in favour of Brexit in the UK's 2016 referendum on EU membership. It will be argued that the two dominant academic explanations for these voters' motivations – one positing structural racism, the other a cultural/values divide – could benefit considerably from closer attention to the concept of nationalism in general and, within the field of nationalism studies, to John Breuilly's analysis of nationalism as a form of politics.

In what follows, the term nationalism refers to 'a political principle that holds that the national and political unit should be congruent' (Gellner, 2008/1983, p.1) in relation to which 'the interests and values of [the] nation take priority over all other interests and values' (Breuilly, 1993, p.3). Nationalism thus holds that state and nation should be brought into union and that the nation should be prioritised politically by its members and state. The term is therefore not 'a covering term for objectionable ethnic chauvinism' (Hearn, 2017, p.20) or ideas surrounding national uniqueness and superiority but, rather, something far more mundane and prevalent – what has been described by some scholars (Billig, 1995; Malešević, 2006) as the dominant political ideology of our time.

Postcolonialism

The basic, core argument made in postcolonial criticism is that most social theorists and historians are guilty, to varying extents, of omitting or evading the critically important role of colonialism and racism in shaping societies and political structures, past and present. In particular, they argue that the emergence of modern statehood, new forms of political solidarity and national identities in Europe and the West between the eighteenth and nineteenth centuries must not be portrayed as isolated processes. Such portrayals obscure the 'colonial entanglements' (Bhambra, 2014, p.2) that are fundamental to Western modernity, thereby eliding 'the processes of colonialism, enslavement, dispossession and appropriation that constitute the conditions of [modern Europe's] very possibility' (Bhambra, 2014, p.152). These conditions are partly economically exploitative in character – as Fanon (2001/1961, p.81) famously argues, having 'stuffed herself inordinately with the gold and raw materials of the colonial countries ... Europe is literally the creation of the Third World' – but they also co-constitutively relate to modern subjectivities and the cultural imagination (e.g. McClintock, 1995). In an eighteenth and nineteenth century Europe saturated 'by representations of the imperial world and its peoples' (Hall & Rose, 2006, p.15), racial hierarchies set up 'others' against which constructions of 'home' and emerging national identities could be defined. During this period, '[t]he idea of race ... was to become so widespread as to be part of the "taken-for-granted" world in which the people of the metropole lived their lives' (Hall & Rose, 2006, p.8), as emerging white identities became 'tacitly and emphatically coded by race' (Stoler, 1995, p.7). This was partly achieved through crude racist stereotyping and othering, but also more subtly (from white perspectives at least) through moralising 'Victorian' discourses bound up with bourgeois sexuality and notions of 'self-mastery' (Stoler, 1995, p.8).

From this kind of analytic perspective, therefore, colonialism was crucial for the development of the peculiarly modern forms of 'solidarity, identification and belonging' (Gilroy, 2004, p.158) which Gilroy associates with 'the distinctive institutional ecology of national states' (ibid, p.x). Here, the key role assumed by the increasingly powerful and pervasive state – a role argued to be fundamental to its very development *as* the modern state – was to defend its population from heterogeneity, hybridity and the racial degeneration these were feared to provoke (Stoler, 1995, p.134; Goldberg, 2002). It was through racial frameworks that the state classified and regulated its beholden populations, home and abroad, with women, the working classes, and ethnic and religious minority groups such as Jews and the Irish variously and unevenly racially othered in Western contexts, while similarly intersectional processes rendered the white, bourgeois male explicitly or implicitly racially superior within the national mythology. Though varyingly *racist* in character from instance to instance, the modern European and colonial nation-state was therefore fundamentally *racial* (Goldberg, 2002). Paradigmatically racist manifestations such as Nazi Germany or apartheid South Africa might be qualitatively distinct in the degree of their racism, but it would be a mistake to treat them as 'aberrant offshoots' (Stoler, 1995, p.9) given the racial roots of modern statehood and nationhood.

What postcolonial scholars thus aim to provide is 'a counter-history of modernity which comprehends it in its readily racialised forms' (Gilroy, 2004, p.x). While the mainstream social sciences and humanities have been institutionally and methodologically geared towards 'favouring scholars, questions, theories and concepts derived from a (putatively) European – and "Northern" – experience to make sense of the "Rest"' (Rutazibwa & Shilliam, 2018, p.2), postcolonialism aims to pull the curtain away from such universalist pretensions and Eurocentrism. It critiques the methodological nationalism by which nations are assumed to be 'the natural social and political form of the modern world' (Wimmer & Schiller, 2002, p.302) in favour of more cosmopolitan political and methodological outlooks, and it critiques the methodological whiteness that positions national polities and populations of the West as historically distinct from, rather than formatively related to, the global and multiracial empires from which these states sprung (Bhambra, 2017a, p.224).

Postcolonial criticism therefore poses a significant challenge to the social sciences and humanities. As Rutazibwa and Shilliam (2018, p.1) state,

> At a minimum, postcolonial critique stretches our imagining of what politics does and should entail. At a maximum, postcolonial critique impels us to pluralise, enrich and even rethink the methods, methodologies, concepts, actors and narratives we deploy in order to make sense of global politics.

Many of the above-cited authors can be placed towards the maximal end of the scale. Their conclusions are resoundingly anti-nationalist and cosmopolitan in making future-oriented calls for a more democratic future built on 'new collective endeavours' (Bhambra, 2014, p.156) and a novel, anti-racist political language (Gilroy, 2004, p.335). The normative consequence of postcolonial criticism for the contemporary world is the political requirement for a reconfiguring of state and society, particularly in places where both seem unwilling or unable to reckon with colonial histories and violence. And it is especially by unearthing and enabling the rearticulation (Bhambra, 2014, p.132) of the subordinated histories and knowledges of those who have experienced and resisted the violence of racial hierarchies that alternative social and political imaginaries can come to the surface, whether through indigenous cultures (De Sousa Santos, 2016), critical archival research (Gilroy, 2004) or everyday sociabilities in contemporary multiethnic cities (Nayak, 2003).

Nationalism studies

This section looks at five studies of modern nationalism which are, both in terms of citations and I would argue general influence, the most important book-length contributions to the post-1980's resurgence of academic interest in nationalisms' origins and spread – namely, Benedict Anderson's *Imagined Communities,* Ernest Gellner's *Nations and Nationalism*, Anthony Smith's *The Ethnic Origins of Nations*, Eric Hobsbawm's *Nations and Nationalism Since 1780* and John Breuilly's *Nationalism and the State*. While critiquing these five texts from postcolonial perspectives, and then returning the favour, will not enable a comprehensive treatment of this huge field, I would suggest that even a partial attempt will be useful given the remarkable lack of cross-fertilisation between these areas of study. It is rare for studies concerned with postcolonialism, or racism more generally, to cite scholars of nationalism – other than, occasionally, Anderson – and, as will be demonstrated, this nationalism literature has some apparent gaps in its account of modernity with regard to colonialism. What follows in this section is a necessarily brief summary of these five authors' accounts of what modern nationalism is, how and where it emerged and, when discussed, what some of the social and political legacies of this history are for the present day.

Each of these books is centred in one way or another on analysing how modern revolutions – broadly and roughly those named 'industrial' and 'French', and that concerned with the development of the centralised state – related to emerging nationalist states and identifications from the late eighteenth century. Gellner argues that 'nationalism is a product of industrial social organisation' (Özkirimli, 2010, p.102). The shift from an agrarian to an industrialised society in Europe led to a functional requirement for a national 'high culture' providing 'standardised, literacy- and education-based systems of communication' (Gellner, 2008/1983, p.53) which, with state support, came to pervade and define modern society

(Özkirimli, 2010, p.100). For earlier, more horizontally stratified agrarian societies, absent of the context of industrialisation, nations and their standardised cultures are unnecessary social formations. Anderson similarly lays responsibility for nationalism at the feet of revolutionary economic and technological shifts and their cultural impact. He argues that an emerging 'print capitalism' helped to standardise and diffuse vernacular languages within specific territories among the rising classes therein (Anderson, 1991, Chapter 3), transforming the social perspectives of these populations by enabling the imagination of and identification with national communities most of whose members would never be encountered. With 'religious modes of thought' declining, a sense of the nation moving through history in relation to an immemorial past (despite its radical novelty) provides 'a secular transformation of fatality into continuity, contingency into meaning' (ibid, p.11). Something unique to Anderson's account is the claim that Latin American Creole communities in the late eighteenth and early nineteenth centuries preceded European nationalism.

Hobsbawm (1990, p.14) traces the emergence of nationhood in the West, agreeing with Gellner and Anderson that '[t]he basic characteristic of the modern nation and everything connected with it is modernity'. For Hobsbawm (ibid, p.10), '[n]ations exist … as functions of a particular kind of territorial state or the aspiration to establish one … in the context of a particular stage of [industrial capitalist] technological and economic development'. Any cultural aspects of nationalism are here subordinate to their essential construction (ibid, p.10) 'from above' by manipulative elites, with the masses below not necessarily brought along despite the evident success of the programme on a global scale (ibid, p.192).

Breuilly (1993, p.1) argues that nationalism is 'above and beyond all else, about politics and … politics is about power … [which] in the modern world is principally about control of the state'. He explores the development of nationalism as a form of oppositional politics in the increasingly centralised monarchical states of early-modern Western Europe, before analysing its spread across Europe and the world in the nineteenth and twentieth centuries. In the crucial modern context of a distinct and specialised public sphere of politics, nationalist ideology 'provides a conceptual map' (ibid, p.13) for navigating and potentially solving the 'puzzles' set by modernity (ibid, p.54) such as those relating to the distinctions between public and private, state and society (ibid, p.69). However, nationalist rejections of, or attempts to transcend, these highly complex and incompatible distinctions, through for example a claimed fusion of the political sphere with culturally-conceived nationality, represent mere pseudo-solutions – 'a sleight of hand' (ibid, p.62). For Breuilly, as with Hobsbawm, though nationalism is unquestionably a hugely successful political ideology, its evident triumphs, and apparent popular resonance, can be skewed in the popular and academic imagination alike by the self-understandings and self-representations of nationalists themselves (ibid, p.382; Breuilly, 1985, p.73).

Smith (1986, pp.130–4) agrees that the modern revolutions of Western Europe were central to the emergence and consolidation of nationalism as we know it today but suggests that a key ingredient of nationalism effectively lies outside of and prior to modernity. He argues that the myths and symbols of most successful modern nations draw a special resonance from durable ethnic cultures with pre-modern roots mobilised in the modern era by nationalist politics and intellectuals (ibid, pp.160–1). From this perspective, a pre-existing ethnic cultural core, revivified in modern contexts for modern ends to provide a collective identity and sense of agency, provides the crucial explanatory dimension for modern nationalism's rise and durability.

In summary, therefore, when explaining nationalism and its initial emergence, with the arguable exception of the Latin American element of Anderson's model, modern European colonialism is far from at the heart of these authors' accounts. The focus falls squarely within European territory in relation to the modern revolutions in institutions, politics and the economy set out in classical sociology. The next section will discuss the points where colonialism and imperialism *are* referred to by these authors, thereby further demonstrating how their accounts obscure the fundamentally colonial aspects of modernity described by postcolonial scholars. However, it will also argue that postcolonialism is in danger of downplaying the importance to contemporary politics and society of some of the nationalist inheritances set out within these five books.

Nationalism studies, colonialism and racism

Colonialism is chiefly discussed by these authors in relation to anti-colonial nationalism. Breuilly provides the most sustained treatment of the impact of European empires on colonised lands within the scope of his general analytic model. He argues that it is ultimately the institutions of the colonial state and relationships with these that provide the 'initial determinants' for how an anti-colonial 'nationalist movement develops' (Breuilly, 1993, p.196). Non-Western responses to colonialism were thus bound up with, and expressed in relation to, the revolutionary form of politics introduced by European imperialism (ibid, p.223).

The other authors similarly position anti-colonial nationalisms in relation to their overall hypotheses regarding nationalism's essence and historical origins. For Hobsbawm (1990, p.160), like Breuilly, what is key are not anti-colonial conflicts or identities shaped in relation to ethnicity or nationality but, rather, the institutional and ideological context set by European power. The territories of the states in question were 'overwhelmingly the … creations of imperial conquest' with political movements initiated within a product of an 'adopted … western ideology excellently suited to the overthrow of foreign governments' (Hobsbawm, 1990, p.137). Anti-colonial politicians thus 'spoke the language of European nationalism, which they had so often learned in or from the west' (Hobsbawm, 1990, p.136). For Gellner (2008/1983, p.42; cf. p.84), though anti-colonial nationalisms differed in various ways from their antecedents, ultimately 'the core or essence of nationalism flows from … the premises which were initially laid out' in industrialising European.

Anderson argues that colonial states and capitalism, carried by the technology of the day, provided 'models of nation, nation-ness and nationalism distilled from the turbulent, chaotic experiences of more than a century of American and European history' (Anderson, 1991, p.140) before exploring the effects of late colonial institutions on how postcolonial nations were imagined (Anderson, 1991, Chapter 10). Smith's brief references to anti-colonialism foreground the resonance of ethnic cultures ahead of any political and institutional pathways (1986, pp.146–7). For Smith, the notoriously contrived, imposed borders of postcolonial states and the uneven distribution of ethnic groups within these, immediately sabotages, at the institutional, state level, the potential for a pre-modern ethnic core to form a viable nation. When set alongside destabilising geopolitical conditions, some postcolonial states, particularly in sub-Saharan Africa (ibid, p.212), are therefore considered to lack some of the key elements that enabled the emergence of functioning nation-states in Europe.

This theme of postcolonial intra-state conflict is another relatively common way by which colonialism is touched upon in these books. Gellner (2008/1983, pp.94–5) laments what he refers to as the '"African" type' of national situation 'which arises when the local folk cultures are incapable of becoming the new high culture of the emergent state, either because they are too numerous or too jealous of each other', while Hobsbawm (1990, p.155), specifying the same continent, bemoans 'ethnonational competition and violence … [which has] emerged in relation to societies ill-prepared for the dramatic socioeconomic changes imposed by colonialism'. In explaining such conflicts, Breuilly (1993, p.227) again turns to the state rather than ethnicity and to the 'desperate search for bases of political action in the absence of those appropriate to taking over the colonial state'.

The effects of colonialism on the imperial metropolis are treated very sparely in these books. Gellner (2008/1983, pp.41–2) argues that European colonialism was economically motivated and, generalising from Seeley's famous quip, largely achieved in an absence of mind, but otherwise does not refer to its impact on European society. Anderson (1991, p.150) briefly discusses how colonial hierarchies helped to shore up 'antique conceptions of power and privilege' in England, while Smith's only significant reference to relationships involving colonialism and nationalism in Europe (1986, pp.167–8) refer to 'exclusive' (we might add the more specific designation 'racist') national identities in England 'fuelled by colonial empire' in the late nineteenth century. Anderson's aside (of which more below), race and racism in general do not feature prominently in any of these books. Breuilly (1993, p.60) relates nineteenth-century racism to historicist nationalist thinking in Europe, and in a later analysis of the Third Reich (ibid, pp.310–316) queries the extent to which the Nazis' mass appeal is best understood as motivated by racism rather than specific political conditions and structures relating to modern statehood.

Racism is only otherwise discussed in these texts with regard to urban migrations to and within the West (Smith, 1986, pp.10–11; Hobsbawm, 1990, p.157) or as an important potential trigger for anti-colonial mobilisation (Breuilly, 1993, p.173, p.186; Gellner, 2008/ 1983, p.80). It is contextualised in relation to particular periods and places, and treated as relatively peripheral to the central currents irrigating the history of modernity and European nationalism. These authors date the conditions for nationalism's emergence as *prior to* mid-nineteenth century racial thinking, meaning that the nation-state and racism are considered conceptually distinct rather than fundamentally related. For Anderson (1991, p.149), who dedicates a chapter to comparing the two social formations, 'while racism dreams of eternal contaminations' associated with notions of irredeemable biology, nationalism's more cultural, historical basis renders it far more malleable and open (in principle if not always in practice). Here, though racism can intersect with nationalism, it is what Smith (1998, p.2) in later work describes as a 'darker' force. Racial nationalism is a specific variation (or perversion) of a related but different social formation.

In all five books, therefore, although colonialism features to some extent in each discussion, the authors largely bypass some elements that postcolonial scholars argue should be included in any fuller account of the broad historical period covered (within and outside of Europe), notably the foundational role for conquest, dispossession and exploitation, and the economic, cultural and social impact of colonialism on the imperial metropolis. The 'colonial entanglements' (Bhambra, 2014, p.2) and, crucially, the seam of racism running through the core of modernity that postcolonial narratives aim to bring to the surface remain largely submerged. Where connections and relationships involving colonised lands and peoples become most salient in these books is in relation to the global diffusion of Western modernity, with the subordinated knowledges and epistemologies of colonised peoples, where raised at all, only really discussed with regard to the novel economic and political structures and imaginaries set out by Europe.

This seems to indicate that these books succumb to the Eurocentric maladies diagnosed by postcolonialism. However, I would argue that any such conclusion should be tempered. The extent to which modernity's revolutions were rooted in colonialism remains contested. There is a case for maintaining some focus on the 'generalised condition[s] which made nationalism normative and pervasive' (Gellner, 2008/1983, p.84) and, as part of this, the relatively clearly located geographical origins of these conditions within Europe. In clear contrast to some classical sociological accounts of modernity, the books discussed here certainly do not argue that 'the rest' are catching up to a superior stage of historical development (Bhambra, 2014, p.9). Though their analyses of turmoil in postcolonial Africa might veer towards this narrative, any apparent obscuring of non-European society could be seen as a by-product of these authors' spotlighting of European revolutions which became fundamentally important on a global scale *and* the attempts of populations to reorient themselves in relation to these – particularly vis-à-vis the unprecedented political power of the modern state.

It is particularly with regard to this perspective on modern political agency and the state that the nationalism literature might offer postcolonial criticism something in return. Though such concerns are of course central to postcolonialism in terms of anti-colonial thought and practice, the nationalism literature analyses how a wide variety of social groups, in a much wider variety of social and political contexts than 'the colonial', have attempted (with varying degrees of success) to draw on ideas of nationhood to seize the initiative in challenging political circumstances. Even if we accept (as I, for one, do) that the histories of many nations are fundamentally related to colonialism, when shifting our gaze to the present day, and to postcolonial critics' desire to reframe contemporary politics along radically cosmopolitan lines, we run into a specific and powerful inheritance – the pervasive and enduring structures and institutions of the state and the 'conceptual maps' (Breuilly, 1993, p.13) provided by nationalism. Globalising processes and critiques of methodological nationalism notwithstanding, the nation-state stubbornly remains the dominant source of political sovereignty and the principal enabler and enforcer of resource distribution – as has been conceded by many prominent cosmopolitan thinkers (e.g. Habermas, 1996; Held, 2002). With no significant institutional rival on the horizon, and no serious, popularly resonant anti-nationalist ideological competitor at state level (neo-liberalism aside), it is essential to consider the hugely important existing relationships between the nation-state and 'the continued capacity of political communities to control themselves in the present' (Pocock, 1992, p.388).

Therefore, though they may partially obscure the importance to modern history of colonialism and the racialised power-relations it instituted and bequeathed, I would argue that the perspectives on nationalism and the state set out within the five books analysed here bring us somewhat closer to a level of *contemporary* political understanding of 'the degree of plasticity in our collective fate … [and] the range within which it can, or might be, modified by our own, or others' actions' (Dunn, 2000, p.104). At the risk of being considered conservative or passive with regard to existing political frameworks, I am suggesting that scholars of race should recognise that the ideologies and structures of nationhood and statehood continue to influence our understandings of political peoplehood and public authority so pervasively that viable alternatives can seem almost unthinkable (outside of and within the academy[1]). Without this recognition there is a danger that postcolonial criticism, while justifiably questioning many of the assumptions of nationalist historiographies, is, in its commitment to cosmopolitanism, evading questions about the extent to which nation, state and related identifications have been, are, and will continue to be crucial in shaping politics and society.

Nationalism, racism and 'Leave' voters

To tease these issues out further in relation to a specific contemporary case, this section brings the preceding discussion to bear on academic research regarding the motivations of those who voted 'Leave' in the UK's 2016 referendum on EU membership. The majority of analysis has come from quantitative researchers in political science, with the most prominent voices arguing that, in contrast to those more comfortable with a globalised, cosmopolitan Britain, Leave voters feel their identities and culture are being threatened by an increasingly liberal society and perceptions surrounding unprecedented levels of immigration. Far more saliently than socioeconomic anxieties, the referendum's outcome is therefore best explained by an emerging and entrenched cultural or value divide in the British (especially English) population (Inglehart & Norris, 2016; Kaufmann, 2016; Ford & Goodwin, 2017; Goodwin & Milazzo, 2017). Accounts informed by postcolonial criticism, on the other hand, depict the Leave campaign as 'a proxy for discussions about race and migration' (Valluvan, 2017; Bhambra, 2017b, p.91). The focus, in the media and some political science analysis, on the English 'white working class', 'left behind' voter implicitly constructs 'a new identity politics of race' (Bhambra, 2017a, p.219) in which the 'independent Britain' and 'island nation' depicted by Brexit campaigners represents a historically inaccurate, fantasy depiction of a sovereign (and white) nation, thus eliding the state's multiethnic colonial past and postcolonial present (Bhambra, 2017b, p.92). Here Brexit is, above all, the outcome of a (structurally if not always attitudinally explicit) racist form of English nationalism (Shilliam, 2016; Virdee & McGeever, 2018).

With the exception of Eric Kaufmann – whose PhD supervisor was Anthony Smith – the above-cited scholars almost entirely neglect the nationalism studies literature. Despite the Leave campaign's stated desire to 'take back' sovereignty from the supranational EU, and the referendum result representing perhaps the most starkly nationalist electoral outcome in recent British history, the political science literature has allowed populism and widely discredited classifications of 'civic' and 'ethnic' national identities to stand in for any in-depth analysis (and often any direct mention at all) of nationalism as a principle and ideology (Bonikowski, 2017a, 2017b). In the postcolonial literature, meanwhile, nationalism *is* regularly referred to, but mostly as a synonym or outgrowth for and of racism, with the referendum's outcome seemingly confirming the 'fundamental interplay' between race and nation (Valluvan, 2017, p.238). I would suggest that this lack of engagement with the nationalism literature is depriving these analyses of some valuable analytical perspectives. Kaufmann (2018a) has rightly noted that Smith's critique of globalising and cosmopolitan forces, in the context of his general theory of the durable political resonance of ethnic cultures, foreshadowed the recent upsurge in nationalist populism – though his ethnicist ontology, implicitly accepted in some political scientists' operationalising of national cultures and identities, is unlikely to be adopted by scholars influenced by postcolonialism (see the hostile early response from academics with cosmopolitan political sympathies (Favell, 2019; Özkirimli, 2019) to Kaufmann's (2018b) most recent book). I would, however, suggest that other seminal perspectives on nationalism, particularly John Breuilly's, could add critical insight to both of the broad analytic perspectives on the Leave vote outlined above.

It is instructive, for example, to analyse the 'threatened identities'/'cultural backlash' thesis emerging from political science in relation to Breuilly's discussion of how nationalist ideology maps but also *forms* the very terrain of the political landscape (1993, p.381). From this angle, if we consider the notorious and widespread 'perception gaps' with regard to attitudes towards immigration in Britain, such as wildly exaggerated estimates of the overseas-born population (Duffy & Frere-Smith, 2014), and the extent to which these attitudes are influenced by ideological diffusion or media exposure to particular parties and messages (Bonikowski, 2017a; Murphy & Devine, 2018) – none of which are properly accounted for in the 'threatened identities' research – we might question how much Leave voters' 'identities' were threatened *other than on the terms of nationalism itself*. The attitudes that fuelled this vote might therefore be better explained in terms of the framing and production of a sense of threat through the mobil-isation of nationalist, sometimes racist, political ideology. By bringing the active, fundamentally political dimension of nationalist ideology into the equation in this way we can query claims that somewhat passive, deeply-held and culturally-rooted threatened national identities (still less immigration or ethnic diversity) should be foregrounded in these causal models. We thereby enable some of the historical, structural power-relations highlighted in postcolonial accounts to be brought to the surface – though, importantly, here it is nationalist and not necessarily racist political boundaries that are central.

Breuilly's approach thus both dovetails with and raises questions of postcolonial interpret-ations of the Leave vote. His critique of nationalism's pretensions to offer anything but pseudo-solutions for those wishing to fuse society, culture and state again chimes with postco-lonial scholars' suspicions that even a smooth, successful Brexit would be unlikely to sate the fantasies and anger of many Leave voters. However, crucially, Breuilly's analysis does not encourage much optimism about the supersession of nationalism as a form of politics. Most would concede that cosmopolitan politics, in Britain and globally, remain fragmented, incho-ate and lacking any popularly resonant institutional basis or politically effective identifications. Most would also concede that, as Breuilly and many other nationalism scholars argue, collect-ive and effective political and cultural movements or groups are, in the modern world, difficult to locate or imagine in ways 'distinct from [a] public state' still largely imagined in national terms (1993, p.396). In this context, postcolonial approaches premised on political and meth-odological commitments to cosmopolitanism and radical democratic futures risk bypassing the enduring and resonant structures and identifications of existing political communities. Con-temporary democratic institutions and processes, party politics and elections have, for example, been virtually ignored in recent years by British scholars of race (at least until the referendum result) whose attention has been fixed on micro-level politics, identities and the mapping of increasingly fine-grained hierarchies (Alexander, 2018). While it remains imperative to analyse the anti-racist, anti-nationalist local cultures of England's multiethnic urban areas, and while postcolonial critiques portraying the British state and English nationhood as a bundle of fanta-sies and repressions riddled with structural racism may be phenomenologically accurate, such approaches might also be characterised as conducting a somewhat rhetorical 'righteous demoli-tion' (Pocock, 1995, p.301) on the page rather than contributing as much as they might to urgent debates on collective identifications, viable political action and change.

Conclusion

These two fields draw on very different theoretical influences and utilise different methodo-logical tools for the purposes of somewhat different research questions. However, in the several locations where their interests overlap they have the potential to enrich one other, and the aim of this chapter has been to open up some paths in this direction. I have suggested that the five seminal books from the field of nationalism studies analysed here are, thanks to their elision of modern Europe's foundational relationships with exploitation and racism, vulnerable to some of the central critiques that postcolonialism applies to hitherto dominant historical and socio-logical accounts of modernity. However, I have also argued that the depth to which the his-tory and general concept of nationalism has been researched within the field of nationalism studies might be further drawn upon by scholars influenced by postcolonialism.

In particular, I have argued that crosspollinating nationalism studies and postcolonial criticism bears especially vital – if perhaps from postcolonial perspectives unwelcome – fruit with regard to our contemporary political predicament. While we can find examples of post-national sociabilities and subordinated knowledges in the archives and through ethnographic observation of contemporary society, and while we may succeed in partially destabilising or transcending the nation-state through a commitment to anti-racism and political and methodological cosmopolitanism, the capacity of states to change lives remains institutionally unrivalled and the crux of state politics remains nationalist (cf. Leddy-Owen, 2019). If a key question today for those opposed to nationalism and its many racist manifestations is how to engage with nationhood and the state in order to work towards an anti-racist, cosmopolitan future, then I would suggest that many of the most effective answers will involve working more closely than the postcolonial literature presently implies within the scope of nation-state frameworks and nationalist identifications. Even if our ultimate aim is to abolish the nation-state project, its borders and disagreeable legacies, those postcolonial scholars who emphasise connected histories and contemporary racism are in danger of missing the crucial need to locate some of our most important political analysis and action within the awkward political lines set down in European modernity.

Note

1 See Bartelson's [2001, 185] identification of such patterns within some influential critical scholarship, notably Foucauldian, exploring the state and its relationship with modern power-relations.

References

Alexander, C., 2018. Breaking black: the death of ethnic and racial studies in Britain. *Ethnic and Racial Studies*, *41*(6), pp. 1034–1054.

Anderson, B., 1991. *Imagined Communities: Reflections on the Origin and Spread of Nationalism*. London: Verso Books.

Bhambra, G.K., 2014. *Connected sociologies*. London: Bloomsbury.

Bhambra, G.K., 2017a. Brexit, Trump, and 'methodological whiteness': on the misrecognition of race and class. *The British Journal of Sociology*, *68*(1), pp. 214–232.

Bhambra, G. K., 2017b. Locating Brexit in the pragmatics of race, citizenship and empire. In Outhwaite, W., ed., *Brexit: Sociological Responses*. London: Anthem Press, pp. 91–100.

Billig, M., 1995. *Banal Nationalism*. London: Sage.

Bonikowski, B., 2017a. Ethno-nationalist populism and the mobilization of collective resentment. *The British Journal of Sociology*, *68*(1), pp. 181–213.

Bonikowski, B., 2017b. Nationhood as cultural repertoire: collective identities and political attitudes in France and Germany. In Skey, M. & Antonsich, M., eds., *Everyday nationhood: Theorising culture, identity and belonging after Banal Nationalism*. London: Palgrave Macmillan, pp. 147–175.

Breuilly, J., 1985. Reflections on nationalism. *Philosophy of the Social Sciences*, *15*(1), pp. 65–75.

Breuilly, J., 1993. *Nationalism and the State*. Manchester: Manchester University Press.

De Sousa Santos, B., 2016. A new vision of Europe: learning from the South. In Bhambra, G.K. & Narayan, J., eds., *European cosmopolitanism: Colonial histories and postcolonial societies*. London: Taylor & Francis, 172–183.

Duffy, B. & Frere-Smith, T., 2014. *Perceptions and Reality: Public Attitudes to Immigration*. London: Ipsos MORI.

Dunn, J., 2000. *The Cunning of Unreason: Making Sense of Politics*. London: Harper Collins.

Fanon, F., 2001/1961. *The Wretched of the Earth*. London: Penguin Classics.

Favell, A., 2019. Brexit: a requiem for the post-national society? *Global Discourse: An Interdisciplinary Journal of Current Affairs*, *9*(1), pp. 157–168.

Ford, R. & Goodwin, M., 2017. Britain after Brexit: a nation divided. *Journal of Democracy*, *28*(1), pp. 17–30.

Gellner, E., 2008/1983. *Nations and Nationalism*. Oxford: Blackwell.

Gilroy, P., 2004. *Between Camps: Nations, Cultures and the Allure of Race*. Abingdon: Routledge.

Goldberg, D.T., 2002. *The Racial State*. Oxford: Blackwell.

Goodwin, M. & Milazzo, C., 2017. Taking back control? Investigating the role of immigration in the 2016 vote for Brexit. *The British Journal of Politics and International Relations*, *19*(3), pp. 450–464.

Habermas, J., 1996. The European nation state. Its achievements and its limitations. On the past and future of sovereignty and citizenship. *Ratio Juris*, *9*(2), pp. 125–137.

Hall, C & Rose, S., 2006. Introduction: being at home with the Empire. In Hall, C. & Rose, S.O., eds., *At Home with the Empire: Metropolitan Culture and the Imperial World*. Cambridge: Cambridge University Press, pp. 1–31.

Hearn, J., 2017. Vox Populi: Nationalism, globalization, and the balance of power in the making of Brexit. In Outhwaite, W., ed., *Brexit: Sociological Responses*. London: Anthem Press, pp. 19–30.

Held. D., 2002. Culture and political community: national, global and cosmopolitan. In Vertovec, S. & Cohen, R., eds., *Conceiving Cosmopolitanism: Theory, Context and Practice*. Oxford: Oxford University Press, pp. 48–59.

Hobsbawm, E.J., 1990. *Nations and Nationalism Since 1780: Programme, Myth, Reality*. Cambridge: Cambridge University Press.

Inglehart, R. & Norris, P., 2016. Trump, Brexit, and the rise of populism: economic have-nots and cultural backlash. *Harvard Kennedy School Research Working Paper Series*. No. RWP16-026.

Kaufmann, E., 2016, July 7. It's NOT the economy, stupid: Brexit as a story of personal values [Blog entry]. *British Politics and Policy at LSE*. Retrieved from http://blogs.lse.ac.uk/politicsandpolicy/personal-values-brexit-vote/.

Kaufmann, E., 2018a. The intellectual legacy of Anthony D. Smith. *Nations and Nationalism*, *24*(2), pp. 237–239.

Kaufmann, E., 2018b. *Whiteshift: Populism, Immigration and the Future of White Majorities*. London: Penguin UK.

Leddy-Owen, C., 2019. *Nationalism, Inequality and England's Political Predicament*. Abingdon: Routledge.

Malešević, S., 2006. *Identity as Ideology: Understanding Ethnicity and Nationalism*. London: Springer.

McClintock, A., 1995. *Imperial Leather: Race, Gender, and Sexuality in the Colonial Contest*. Abingdon: Routledge.

Murphy, J. & Devine, D., 2018. Does media coverage drive public support for UKIP or does public support for UKIP drive media coverage? *British Journal of Political Science*. Advance online publication. doi.org/10.1017/S0007123418000145

Nayak, A., 2003. *Race, Place and Globalization: Youth Cultures in a Changing World*. London: Bloomsbury.

Özkirimli, U., 2010. *Theories of Nationalism: A Critical Introduction*. Basingstoke: Palgrave Macmillan.

Özkirimli, U., 2019, Jan 2. White is the new black: populism and the academic alt-right. *Open Democracy*. Retrieved from www.opendemocracy.net/umut-ozkirimli/white-is-new-black-populism-and-academic-alt-right.

Pocock, J.G.A., 1992. History and sovereignty: the historiographical response to Europeanization in two British cultures. *Journal of British Studies*, *31*(4), pp. 358–389.

Pocock, J.G.A., 1995. Conclusion: contingency, identity, sovereignty. In Grant, A. & Stringer, K., eds., *Uniting the Kingdom: The Making of British History*. Abingdon: Routledge.

Rutazibwa, O. & Shilliam, R., 2018. Postcolonial politics: An introduction. In Rutazibwa, O. & Shilliam, R., eds., *Routledge Handbook of Postcolonial Politics*. Abingdon: Routledge.

Shilliam, R., 2016, July 4. Racism, multiculturalism and Brexit [blog entry]. *Robbie Shilliam*. Retrieved from https://robbieshilliam.wordpress.com/2016/07/04/racism-multiculturalism-and-brexit/.

Smith, A.D., 1986. *The Ethnic Origins of Nations*. Oxford: Blackwell.

Smith, A.D., 1998. *Nationalism and Modernism*. Abingdon: Routledge.

Stoler, A.L., 1995. *Race and the Education of Desire: Foucault's History of Sexuality and the Colonial Order of Things*. London: Duke University Press.

Valluvan, S., 2017. Defining and challenging the new nationalism. *Juncture*, *23*(4), pp. 232–239.

Virdee, S. & McGeever, B., 2018. Racism, crisis, Brexit. *Ethnic and Racial Studies*, *41*(10), pp. 1802–1819.

Wimmer, A. & Schiller, N.G., 2002. Methodological nationalism and beyond: nation-state building, migration and the social sciences. *Global Networks*, *2*(4), pp. 301–334.

22

Racism, nationalism and the politics of resentment in contemporary England

James Rhodes and Natalie-Anne Hall

Introduction

Questions of racism and nationalism are once again to the fore of Western social and political life. Across Europe (and beyond), the resurgence of exclusionary forms of nationalistic far right and right-wing populist politics and sentiment have mobilised a range of racialized anxieties centring principally upon immigration, terrorism, the purported limits of multiculturalism, and the perceived economic, socio-cultural and political marginalisation of 'indigenous' white populations (Solomos, 2013; Vieten and Poynting, 2016; Valluvan, 2017). Vieten and Poynting see the rise of 'right wing racist movements' as characterised by 'nationalist, anti-immigration, anti-asylum seeker, anti-Muslim politics' (2016:533). Britain, and England in particular, are no exception to these trends. The first decades of the twenty-first century have been marked by a range of enduring and emergent political preoccupations that are working to sustain and reconfigure the discursive regimes of racism and nationalism. Shifting patterns of migration and racial and ethnic demography, evolving forms of racialization, and altered socio-political contexts shaped by globalisation, economic crisis and austerity, are all informing pronounced shifts in the contours of 'race' and nation. This has been manifest in the rise of far right and radical right-wing populist parties and movements, such as the British National Party (BNP), the EDL (English Defence League), Britain First, and UKIP (UK Independence Party) (Solomos, 2013; Allen, 2014), and the large followings such movements have developed on social media (Davidson and Berezin, 2018).

Most recently, in the referendum on 24 June 2016, the United Kingdom voted to leave the European Union. While the vote enlisted a range of political constituencies and concerns, central to the campaign and the result, were questions of racialized difference and national identity. The Leave.EU campaign, heavily shaped by UKIP, invoked the spectre of a migration 'crisis', the looming threat of terrorism and other purported challenges posed by the Muslim presence, and a nostalgia for the imperial past, as the basis for calls to restore the nation's sovereignty and wrest back control of its borders (Bhambra, 2017; Valluvan, 2017; Virdee and McGeever, 2018). This worked to mobilize sentiments well-established within mainstream popular and media discourses. Indeed, the rise in race-hate crime and the emboldening of racialised expressions of national belonging from both the political margins and mainstream in the aftermath of the result, points to the inseparability of nationalistic and racist politics as well as their widespread allure (Bhambra, 2017; Valluvan, 2017; Virdee and McGeever, 2018).

Drawing on a growing body of scholarship that has sought to delineate the nature of both far-right and radical right-wing populist discourse and sentiment, this chapter identifies the key themes that have been viewed as animating the contemporary politics of white resentment in England. Tracing the nature of these discursive trends provides an analytic lens through which to consider both the mutual imbrications of racism and nationalism and its shifting modes of articulation since the turn of the century. Firstly, the chapter focuses on the production of the 'other' and the 'objects' (Balibar, 1991) of racist and nationalistic discourses, considering the centrality of Islamophobia and anti-immigrant sentiments to contemporary articulations of race, nation and culture. For Balibar, racisms gain particular force in moments of 'crisis', acting as a means of moulding and managing popular anxieties. The 'objects' of such sentiment therefore are revealing of wider contemporary political and cultural anxieties in the current conjuncture. Secondly, it examines how the national 'subject' is articulated through reference to notions of white 'victimhood' and marginalization, drawing upon racialized conceptions of the 'working class' and 'indigeneity', and finding expression through the invocation of an emergent expression of a resentful, nostalgic and defensive English nationalism. The chapter draws on existing literature in situating these trends within the wider politics of 'race' and nation in contemporary England.

Producing 'others': Muslims, migrants and minorities

Central to both the political rhetoric and appeal of right-wing racist movements are the mobilization of notions of both a 'nation' and a 'people', which invariably involve the invocation of notions of ethno-racial difference (Brubaker, 2017; Valluvan, 2017; Vieten and Poynting, 2016). As Balibar (1991) has argued, any appeal to nationalism necessarily rests upon an implicitly exclusionary sensibility in which national subjects are constituted precisely through the designation of particular groups as 'non-nationals'. Such distinctions operate through the construction of a 'fictive ethnicity' generally framed in racial terms. So too Anthias (2010:227) argues that racism is central to this process of 'othering' representing 'a set of discourses and practices that inferiorize, subordinate and lead to outcomes relating to exclusionary group boundaries and hierarchies' (see also Anthias and Yuval-Davis, 1992; Barker, 1981; Gilroy, 1987; Goldberg, 2002; Solomos, 2003). Indeed, throughout the post-war period, far- and right-wing populist movements from the National Front (NF) through to more recent groups like the BNP, EDL, Britain First and UKIP have drawn upon an array of racialized 'others' through which to define the terrains and terms of national belonging.

The enlisting of 'others' serves not only as a means of determining who 'belongs' to the nation, but it also cultivates the purported threat posed by those deemed 'alien'. Valluvan argues that within what he terms the 'new nationalism' evident today, nationalist political sentiments operate chiefly through 'the set of discourses by which primary culpability for significant socio-political problems, whether real or imagined … is attributed to various ethno-racial communities who are understood as not belonging' (2017:233). However, the tenor and forms of 'othering' and the functions they serve are dynamic and subject to both forms of durability and transformation. Stuart Hall (2017) famously viewed both 'race' and the racisms that sustain it as operating as a 'floating' or 'sliding' signifier, as the meanings ascribed to 'race' evolve in relation to prevailing social, historical and political contexts. Gilroy, too, argues for a conceptualization of racism as existing 'in plural form … assuming different shapes and articulating different political relationships. Racist ideologies and practices have distinct meanings bounded by historical circumstances and determined in struggle' (1987:43). As a result, the precise forms of racial othering and the 'objects' of such discursive practices change over time, speaking to and cultivating shifting concerns.

Since the turn of the century there has been a marked shift in the discourses employed by the 'racist right' (Solomos, 2013) within British society. While historically groups such as the NF and the BNP drew heavily and explicitly on conceptions of biological racism, in recent decades racist right movements have instead embraced the language of what has been termed 'new' (Barker, 1981) or 'neo-racism' (Balibar, 1991). Within such formulations, notions of physical difference and hierarchy are disavowed in favour of a set of discursive practices instead focusing on notions of cultural difference and alterity, and the threat that bearers of 'alien cultures' present to the nation (Gilroy, 1987). Framed in this way, Barker argues that racism is imbued with a 'common sense' logic, reformulated as a 'theory of human nature', which posits that 'it is natural to form a bounded community, a nation, aware of its differences from other nations. They are not better or worse. But feelings of antagonism will be aroused if outsiders are admitted' (1981:21; see also Balibar, 1991). Such conceptions of racism have been central to the contemporary re-emergence of the racist right, as various movements have positioned themselves as legitimate guardians of both the security and cultural identity of the nation (Copsey, 2004; Copsey, 2007; Jackson, 2018; Kassimeris and Jackson, 2015; Rhodes, 2010, 2011; Solomos, 2013; Vieten and Poynting, 2016). As Solomos makes clear,

> [these movements] have been able to develop their political language in such a way as to articulate what they perceive as new discourses about race, culture and national identity that have formed the basis of their evolving political strategies and agendas.
>
> *(2013:121)*

Central within the emergent agendas of racist right-wing discourses has been the shifting emphasis from what Anthias and Yuval-Davis (1992) termed 'anti-Black racism' towards anti-Muslim racism and Islamophobia. Indeed, in the early-1990s, in the context of growing anxieties about rising Islamic fundamentalism and the purported dangers posed to British society, they warned that scholars had failed to take religion seriously as a component of contemporary racism. While throughout the postwar period in Britain, across the political right, black and minority ethnic communities have been portrayed as embodying a 'threat to the unity and order of British society' (Solomos, 2013:127), increasingly religion and faith have become key markers of difference and threat and contemporary racist and nationalistic politics increasingly cohere around the figure of the 'Muslim' (Brubaker, 2017; Gupta and Virdee, 2018; Valluvan, 2017; Vieten and Poynting, 2016).

Anti-Muslim racism has manifested itself in a number of ways in the rhetoric and the sentiments of racist right-wing groups, as the 'Muslim' becomes the embodiment of a range of social, cultural and political concerns linked to terrorism, criminality, repressive gender politics, 'troubling' cultural predilections, and sexual pathologies (evident in debates about 'grooming'). In the wake of the 2001 riots in Bradford, Burnley and Oldham, 9/11, 7/7 and more recent terrorist attacks in Manchester and London, as well as the rise of Islamic State (IS), anti-Muslim sentiment has become central to far- and populist right-wing political expression. For the BNP, for instance, the perceived threat posed by Islam and Muslims has been central to its calls for the abolition of immigration and multicultural policies which are seen to facilitate the 'Islamification' of society (John et al., 2006). Here concerns not simply over terrorism, but also about the use of halal meat, veiling practices, self-segregation, challenges to civil liberties and free speech, are all identified as marking a cultural threat to the nation and its Anglo-Saxon and Christian character. The promotion of multiculturalism by state and 'liberals' is seen as compromising the integrity and security of the country (Copsey, 2007; Jackson, 2018; Kassimeris and Jackson, 2015; Rhodes, 2011; Wood and Finlay, 2008). Similarly, the EDL, which emerged as a street-protest movement in 2009, developed with the specific aim of countering what was identified as the inexorable rise of, and existential threat posed by, Islamic extremism (Allen, 2011; Bartlett, Birdwell, and Littler, 2011; Copsey, 2010; Jackson, 2018; Kassimeris and Jackson, 2015; Pilkington, 2016). Here the movement has engaged in protests against 'Islamist' terrorism, but also issues such as Sharia law, child sexual exploitation ('grooming') and the construction of mosques across the country. Within its discourses, Muslims are presented as a particular 'problem', reflecting the asserted irreconcilability of national and 'Muslim' values. Social media and online forums have been identified as particularly significant in the diffusion and mobilization of these sentiments (Awan, 2016; Bartlett, Birdwell, and Littler, 2011; Pilkington, 2016)

Recently, Jackson (2018) has called for a shift in emphasis in the study of anti-Muslim racism and its link to nationalist politics, calling for an analysis not simply of the content but also the functions of Islamophobic discourses. She argues that

> Islamophobia upholds Eurocentrism, the dominant contemporary racialised system where Western-identified subjects are awarded a better social, economic and political 'racial contract' and seek to defend these privileges against real and imagined Muslim demands. Under such a system, Islamophobia is not an 'unfounded hostility', but a rational defence of collective Eurocentric advantages.
>
> *(2018:2)*

Indeed, a number of scholars have argued that the power of anti-Muslim racism lies in its transcendence of narrowly framed nationalistic politics, and the way it instead works through notions of a 'civilizational' rather than simply 'nationalist' threat (Bhatt, 2012; Brubaker, 2017). Brubaker argues that within much European nationalist-populist politics, the 'nation' is being 're-characterized in civilizational terms' (2017:1211). As Brubaker himself acknowledges, however, in Britain the appeal of nationalism endures both through and alongside this formulation and the territorial and symbolic frame of the nation remains central to the appeal of racist and xenophobic discourses. Jackson has argued that for groups such as the EDL and for those harbouring anti-Muslim sentiments in England, Islamophobia is mobilized as a means of articulating the breakdown of the relationship between state, nation, and 'native' citizenry. Drawing on Hage's notion of white nationalistic 'fantasy', she argues that Islamophobic discourses exemplify both a disruption of the 'indigenous' population's position as privileged actors and mark a reassertion of its normative position as guardians and arbiters of the national community. Islamophobia then operates, 'on the one hand to preserve traditional ethno-cultural dominance and privilege, and on the other to contain challenges to this dominance, believed to stem primarily from Muslim communities' (2018:105). Pilkington too, in her ethnographic study of EDL activists and sympathisers, found that, 'expressions of anti-Muslim sentiment … include perceptions that the Muslim "other" constitutes a direct infringement of, or sets itself in a superior position to, respondents' "self"' (2016:144).

The centrality of Islamophobia to the contemporary far- and populist right has also been identified as marking an interesting shift in racist and nationalistic discourse, working as it does to purportedly confound traditional political distinctions of left and right (Brubaker, 2017; Vieten and Poynting, 2016). The EDL, for instance, strongly rejects accusations of racism, casting itself instead as an anti-racist group and a human rights movement, working in defence of secular and liberal values, including mobilising around LGBT issues and asserting an openness to diverse racial and ethnic groups (Copsey, 2010; Bartlett, Birdwell, and Littler, 2011; Busher, 2016; Kassimeris and Jackson, 2015; Pilkington, 2016). Similarly, Burke (2018) showed how Britain First, which had garnered almost two million 'likes' on Facebook by December 2017, strategically constructed its anti-Islam protest activities as in defence of the Jewish minority, in an effort to position itself as 'moderate' and increase its legitimacy. Such discursive strategies are reflected in similar movements across Europe. As Brubaker notes, 'the joining of identitarian Christianism with secularist and liberal rhetoric challenges prevailing understandings of national populism. It questions easy recourse to labels such as 'extreme right' (2017:1210). This is also evident in the rejection of neoliberal policies and the embrace of 'protectionist and pro-welfare' policies and liberal social policies. Here, however, the EDL's disavowal of racism can be seen as symptomatic of the emergence of 'post-racial' discourses (Goldberg, 2006; Lentin and Titley, 2011; Pilkington, 2016), in which distinctions drawn on the basis of religion and culture are seen as 'non-racial' in character. This position has been widely criticized within academic scholarship. Goldberg (2006) argues that it is within the conceptions of Muslims found across European politics that the link between formations of racism and nationalism remain most visible, while the denial of racism becomes a principle mode of racist expression itself (see also Lentin and Titley, 2011). Indeed, scholars examining the EDL have located the movement's rhetoric as rooted in racist ideology and practice. Kassimeris and Jackson (2015), see EDL discourses regarding Muslims as a form of 'cultural racism', and Allen argues that while relative to groups such as the BNP, the EDL 'might be more fluid and reflexive than other far-right organisations, it maintains an ideological premise that is typically discriminatory' (2011:294). Brubaker argues similarly that any claim to possess 'liberal' values is 'strikingly contradictory. Its liberalism is deeply illiberal' (2017:1210).

While this anti-Muslim discourse and sentiment clearly comprise contemporary expressions of racism, these ideas have gained legitimacy through a growing alignment with more mainstream political articulations of the threat posed to race and nation. Since the 2001 riots, successive governments have shifted away from the promotion of multicultural policies, including specific measures to address racialised inequality, in favour of an emphasis on social cohesion, counter-terrorism, and integration and a renewed emphasis on national culture and values. Reflecting what he sees as these policies' proximity to older assimilationist approaches, Kundnani terms such approaches 'integrationism'. Within this political shift, concerns about Muslim communities have become central, traversing the political centre, right, and left, and exemplifying a wider sense of anxiety about the presence of racial and ethnic diversity (Gilroy, 2004; Kundnani, 2007; McGhee, 2008; Lentin and Titley, 2011; Valluvan, 2017; Jackson, 2018). Jackson argues that 'state Islamophobia' has constructed the Muslim 'threat' as a means of reasserting a sense of nationalism, 'through a focus on national identity as the solution to Muslim cultural dysfunction' (2018:32) Similar tendencies are also evident more widely across contemporary British society, in the persistence of negative media representations of Muslims, rising online and offline hate crime. (Runnymede Trust, 2017).

Alongside anti-Muslim sentiment, opposition to immigration remains a key component of the discourses of racist right parties. For EDL supporters, alongside Islamic extremism, concerns over immigration, crime, unemployment and multiculturalism also feature strongly within the politics of white resentment (Bartlett, Birdwell, and Littler, 2011; Goodwin, 2013; Pilkington, 2016). Anti-immigration has been particularly central to the rise of both the BNP and UKIP. Such sentiments have cohered around calls for the restoration of national sovereignty and border controls, as well as invocations of the cultural and economic threats posed by immigrants (Anderson, 2017; Cutts, Ford, and Goodwin, 2010; Ford and Goodwin, 2014; Geddes, 2014; John et al., 2006; Rhodes, 2010; Skey, 2014; Kinvall, 2015). Here, what has been termed 'nativism' or anti-immigrant sentiment within far and populist-right groups is seen as located in concerns for the preservation of 'traditional' culture, values and privileges (Goodwin, 2011). Throughout the postwar period, the political right of all persuasions have consistently articulated a viewpoint in which non-white immigration – rather than racist responses to it – is a threat to the nation. Successive forms of migration from the Indian Subcontinent, the Caribbean, and East Africa formed the basis of right-wing political mobilizations by groups such as the NF (Anthias and Yuval-Davis, 1992; Gilroy, 1987; Solomos, 2003, 2013). From the 1990s, these concerns have been augmented by anxieties about refugees and asylum-seekers, linked to disease, crime, and positioned as the unfair recipients of welfare and housing benefits (Anderson, 2017; Fekete, 2009; Solomos, 2013). Gilroy suggests that in contemporary Britain there exists a 'morbid fixation with the fluctuating substance of national culture and identity', linked to fears of 'Europeanization, and a nonspecific subsumption by immigrants, settlers, and invaders of both colonial and postcolonial varieties' (2004: 13). Within more mainstream politics, this is reflected in emerging forms of border securitization and 'hostile' immigration and citizenship policies since the turn of the century, which have targeted both newer and more established black and minority ethnic groups who continue to be frequently conflated with 'immigrants' (Anderson, 2017; Redclift, 2014).

More recently, the so-called EU migrant 'crisis' of 2015 has been seen to reenergise these concerns, as the arrival of migrants in Europe fleeing war and displacement in countries such as Syria, Iraq, Libya, Yemen, Afghanistan and Kosovo, have been mobilised by far and populist right parties across Europe, with UKIP, for instance, securing over 12 per cent of the vote in the 2015 General Election in the UK (Anderson, 2017; Gupta and Virdee, 2018). Gupta and Virdee argue that these events have compounded concerns around economic recession, neoliberalism and austerity policies, producing a widely-held conception of 'crisis' within Europe that they see as central to the ascendancy of contemporary far right and populist-nationalism. Within the narration of this 'crisis', immigrants are viewed as embodying a range of social, cultural and political problems, and threatening the 'historical authenticity and unitary culture' of the nation (2018:1756). UKIP's 2015 manifesto makes specific links between immigration, 'foreigners', and crime. The fact that most of these migrants were from majority-Muslim countries, reveals the conflation between 'Muslim' and 'migrant', a conflation which discursively links the term 'foreign' with 'terrorist' and 'Islamic', as 'immigration' and 'Islamization' have become symbolically entwined (Gupta and Virdee, 2018: 1756). Here, 'the "cultural" "common-sense racism" of the contemporary moment positions asylum seekers, new migrants and Muslims as the enemies within and without our borders' (Redclift, 2014:579). Indeed, Ghassan Hage (2003) has argued that in the contemporary West, dominant modes of nationalistic expression – what he terms 'paranoid nationalism' – are preoccupied with immigration and border politics, driven by fears of threat and impending decline.

These concerns over immigration were particularly apparent in the EU Referendum, with anti-immigrant sentiment central within the Leave campaign and the attitudes of its supporters (Goodwin and Milazzo, 2017; Virdee and McGeever, 2018). Virdee and McGeever (2018) note how 'migrants' were cast as both an economic threat, through competition for jobs and other key resources and public provisions such as healthcare, as well as a 'security' threat, through links made between immigration and terrorism, and the apparently sexually predatory behaviour of migrants. The EU was charged with failing to protect its member states and citizens, disabling nations from being able to control their own borders and immigration levels. Indeed, central to what has been identified as rising Euroscepticism in Britain over the last decade is the linkage between anti-immigrant and anti-establishment sentiment as the EU is accused of promoting immigration and multiculturalism at the expense of 'native' populations – a claim made by both UKIP and the BNP (Cutts, Ford, and Goodwin, 2010; Ford and Goodwin, 2014; Gest, 2016). Ford and Goodwin, in their study of UKIP and its support, found a strong interrelationship between Euroscepticism, anti-immigrant sentiment, and notions of a 'native' group under threat (2014:188). This is a trend widely observed within the literature exploring far and populist right discourses, as 'immigrants' come to be seen as both the 'symptoms and agents' of the destructive processes of multiculturalism, capitalism, globalization, and the rise of supra-national entities (Holmes, 2000: 114; see also Rhodes, 2010; Gest, 2016; Thorleiffson, 2016; Anderson, 2017).

As mentioned, anti-immigrant sentiments have a long history. What is interesting is the direction of this resentment, not simply towards 'non-white' immigrants but also to migrants from a range of nationalities and regions, including those from other European countries. Analysis of articulations of racism and nationalism in Britain in the 1980s and 1990s, for instance, located this as being oriented towards notions of 'Fortress Europe' which invoked both a sense of shared whiteness, territory, and culture as a basis for exclusion (Anthias and Yuval-Davis, 1992; Gilroy, 1987). Recently, however, scholarship has pointed to the fracturing of this conception, evident particularly in the hostility directed towards Eastern Europeans, in the wake of post-2004 EU accession of states such as Poland, Lithuania, and Romania, targeting 'Roma' populations in particular (Anderson, 2017; Fekete, 2009; Fox, Moroşanu, and Szilassy, 2012; Geddes, 2014). Such hostilities, influenced by hostile immigration policy and tabloid media, racialize these groups based on putative cultural and socio-economic inferiorities, in the process creating hierarchies that render some groups more 'white' than others, despite their shared Europeanness (Fox, Moroşanu, and Szilassy, 2012; see also Rasinger, 2010). Fekete (2009) has conceptualised this development as marking the emergence of a form of 'xeno-racism', which works through 'non-colour-coded' registers in targeting migrants, refugees and asylum-seekers deemed unassimilable to or unwanted within the nation. Indeed, in the wake of the Referendum Virdee and McGeever point to the increase in hate crime directed towards visibly white immigrants, which marks a shift in racism and nationalism: 'What is striking about this wave of racist violence was the way its perpetrators made little attempt to distinguish between black and brown citizens and white European migrants – in their eyes, they were all outsiders (Virdee and McGeever, 2018:1809).

Collectively this anti-immigrant sentiment marks a reassertion of exclusionary forms of nationalism, predicated upon both whiteness and its gradations. Gupta and Virdee note that for racist right organisations, the problematization of immigration has seen calls for both tighter border controls but also more restrictive approaches to citizenship, with an emphasis on the importance of 'indigeneity'. They see such discourses as representing a 'long-term programme for purifying the citizenry', predicated on 'hierarchies of suspicion', in which the emphasis on birth and parentage as a basis for inclusion marks, 'a bid to retrieve an unambiguously racial basis for citizenship' (2018:1758–9). They argue that while explicit reference to 'race' remains rare, with claims instead couched in terms of notions of 'nationality', 'people', 'language', 'culture', and 'values', increasingly 'race is closer to the surface of political discourse now – it is, so to speak, barely coded' (ibid: 1762).

The national subject: whiteness, resentment and nostalgia

If anti-Muslim, anti-immigrant, and anti-minority sentiments animate the 'objects' of contemporary political expressions of racism and nationalism, there have also been interesting shifts in terms of how the national 'subject' is articulated. Recent decades have seen such sentiments narrated through the figure of the beleaguered, besieged and marginalized white 'indigenous' subject. This emergent notion of 'white victimhood' inverts historic processes of racism and racialised inequality and exclusion, arguing instead that white communities represent *the* disadvantaged group, portrayed as being particularly disadvantaged as a result of processes of globalisation, neoliberalism, immigration and multiculturalism and attendant economic and cultural transformations, linked to the decline of manufacturing and the rise of identity politics and a purportedly liberal and cosmopolitan political elite (Holmes, 2000; Hewitt, 2005; John et al., 2006; Ware, 2008; Rhodes, 2010, 2011; Williams and Law, 2011; Oaten, 2014; Gest, 2016; Pilkington, 2016; Mann and Fenton, 2017; Winlow, Hall, and Treadwell, 2017; Mondon and Winter, 2019).

Much of the emergent scholarship in this area has been concerned with tracing the development of this sense of 'white resentment' and its relationship to expressions of racism and nationalism. Roger Hewitt (2005) in his study of the attitudes of white residents in Greenwich and the rhetoric of both the New Right but also local BNP campaigns there in the 1990s identified what he named as an emergent form of 'white backlash' politics. This form of politics – which Hewitt identified as on the rise also in the US and Australia – was predicated on notions of 'unfairness to whites', as processes such as deindustrialization and the dismantling of social housing produced a widely felt sense of insecurity. Alongside this, the rise of multicultural policies deemed to favour 'immigrants' and 'minorities' became entangled with the demise of class-based leftist and Labour politics and the emergence of a new liberal class of politicians, more distant and remote from traditional, white working class communities. Hewitt argues that Enoch Powell had first expressed this notion of white marginalization as a threat to the nation and its 'indigenous' population within his infamous 1968 'Rivers of Blood' speech, but these economic and political developments during the 1980s and 1990s saw it possess an increasing resonance. He argues that while prior to the 1980s racist-nationalist discourses had focused on 'non-white immigration' and the issue of repatriation, since this juncture 'white backlash' politics have become more vociferously felt, expressed and mobilized.

In recent decades, far right and right-wing populist groups have been keen to mobilize and promote such sentiments. Commencing in the 1990s, for instance, the BNP was able to make political gains through campaigns which advocated for 'Rights for Whites' in response to their purported economic, cultural and political marginalization and the existence of 'reverse racism' (Holmes, 2000; Copsey, 2004; Copsey, 2007; John et al., 2006; Rhodes, 2010, 2011; Goodwin, 2011; Solomos, 2013). This strategy saw the party argue that the promotion of globalisation and multiculturalism marked the disenfranchisement of the white population, serving to destabilize 'traditional' white, indigenous communities who are no longer privileged in the distribution of economic resources, public provisions, political rights, or in terms of cultural recognition. Here it is argued for instance that there is a failure to address 'racially-motivated attacks on 'whites', that white 'natives' are no longer allowed to celebrate their own cultural traditions, and that multicultural policies enacted by the political elite mark the disenfranchisement of a form of 'native' disinheritance. The BNP leader, Nick Griffin in 2009 likened multiculturalism to a process of 'bloodless genocide … because it dispossesses the native British of their inheritance fostering a deep sense of grievance that will fester for decades' (cited in Rhodes, 2011:64). The marginalization of the 'indigenous' white population gained purchase through the contrast with the purportedly increased and increasing power of 'minorities' and 'immigrants', particularly Muslims, who it is argued, are favoured by the liberal elite, and benefit through an 'unfair' allocation of resources (Goodwin, 2011; Holmes, 2000; John et al., 2006; Rhodes, 2010; Wood and Finlay, 2008). The EDL also mobilizes similar sentiments, with Oaten (2014) arguing that the movement operates through the production of a sense of 'collective victimhood', with former leader Stephen Yaxley-Lennon ('Tommy Robinson') central to this articulation of the 'cult of the victim', constructed as a hero and martyr willing to risk himself for a defence of the safety and integrity of the nation. Here Oaten argues that while 'victimhood' invokes notions of powerlessness, conversely, it also can become a motivating basis for political mobilization and assertion. Pilkington also found that EDL activists viewed themselves as being 'second class citizens', as a result not simply of the threat posed by Muslims, but due to 'a weak-willed or frightened government that panders to the demands of a minority for fear of being racist'. Within these accounts, whiteness is recast not as a marker of privilege but of victimhood (2016:154; see also Winlow, Hall, and Treadwell, 2017)

Much of the scholarship has focused on the linkages between racism, nationalism and class. If racism and nationalism are increasingly seen to find articulation through notions of white victimhood, the 'white working class' has been mobilised as an archetypal imagined group and subject within these discourses. The BNP and EDL have significantly targeted 'white working class' groups and communities (Copsey, 2004; Goodwin, 2011, 2013; Oaten, 2014; Pilkington, 2016; Rhodes, 2010; Winlow, Hall, and Treadwell, 2017). Within EDL discourse, Oaten notes how the 'white working class' are cast as 'the EDL's ideal victim, vulnerable, helpless and suffering … The EDL requires a steady stream of ideal victims and it focuses on the English working class only in so far as the latter can provide a narrative of victimization that can be embraced within the EDL's collective victimhood' (2014: 342). So too have UKIP and the Leave campaign sought to appeal beyond Eurosceptic conservatives to also engage with 'white working class' voters, with former leader Nigel Farage warning in 2014 that immigration and EU membership threatened a social and political context in which there was a danger of the 'white working class becoming an underclass' (cited in Virdee and McGeever, 2018:1815). Mondon (2017) notes how in a similar vein to other radical right-wing populist parties, UKIP has claimed a purported 'left behind' working class as a symbol of the 'people'. The result is that the notion of the 'people', 'has become the embodiment of a nationalist reactionary wave' (2017:356).

Academic work has also focused on the fact that support for these groups and sentiments has been disproportionately located amongst the 'white working classes' (Cutts, Ford, and Goodwin, 2010; Ford and Goodwin, 2010, 2014; Gest, 2016; Winlow, Hall, and Treadwell, 2017). Justin Gest in his comparative ethnographic study of the US and the UK, notes the way in which collective 'white working class' identities are articulated politically through a sense of 'minoritization' which coheres around notions of becoming demographically out-numbered, being excluded from mainstream political representation, and a belief that they are subject to 'conscious or unconscious prejudgement by members of ethnic minorities, as well as by middle- and upper-class white people' (2016:21–23). Ford and Goodwin (2014), too, in their study of UKIP support, found that the appeal of the party and its xenophobia and anti-immigrant sentiment was located principally within a 'left behind' constituency of older, predominantly male, 'white working class' people located disproportionately in the formerly industrial areas of England. Here it was argued they were responding to deindustrialization and attendant economic insecurity, the breakdown of the link between the working classes, trade unionism and the Labour Party, as well as the rise of what are deemed to be a more cosmopolitan and progressive set of liberal, political values. So too do Winlow et al, in their recent study of EDL supporters, see neoliberalism, austerity and deindustrialization as central to the growing appeal of racist and nationalistic feelings; 'the sentiments and discourses behind the EDL are connected to the concrete localised consequences of the changing economic and cultural circumstances of the white working class' (2017:10).

While much of this work has generated important insights into the shifting articulations of racism and nationalism, there is a danger that this foci risks obscuring more complex relationships between whiteness, class, racism and nationalism. Mann and Fenton (2017), for instance, in their study of the rise of the politics of resentment across the nations of the United Kingdom, argue that rather than being located within any one wide class demographic, the politics of resentment contingently appeals to a range of class fractions and those experiencing downward or insecure class trajectories across a range of social groups. Other studies too have pointed to the cross-class appeal of the sentiments of white 'backlash' and resentment, as support for the BNP, EDL and UKIP all transcend any neat class distinctions. Indeed, analysis of the support for the Brexit vote revealed a broader constituency that was not restricted to the white working classes. Rather, support for Brexit, and nationalist-populist sentiments more generally, appeal to those that feel a sense of economic, but importantly cultural marginalization (Bhambra, 2017; Gidron and Hall, 2017; Mondon, 2017; Mondon and Winter, 2019; Virdee and McGeever, 2018). In his analysis of the EDL, Copsey (Copsey and Macklin, 2011) also argues that it should principally be viewed as an 'identitarian' movement rather than one rooted in material interests, although clearly such sentiments often become difficult to disentangle.

Recently, Bhambra (2017) has identified a problem that she sees as characterising much contemporary political, media, social scientific and other academic discourse exploring the rise of right-wing populism and Brexit. She notes a phenomenon she labels 'methodological whiteness', and identifies this as being problematic in a number of crucial ways; firstly, in limiting racist and nationalistic sentiments to a purported 'white working class', it obscures the appeal of such exclusionary politics to also the middle classes and elites. Indeed, a recent attitudinal study by Flemmen and Savage (2017) revealed that racism and nationalism is also the preserve of sections of the middle classes, who hold racially exclusive conceptions of national belonging. Secondly, Bhambra argues that it also further contributes to a political terrain in which the imputed marginalization of the 'white working class' is explained with an emphasis on the 'white' aspect of this identity, with recourse to multiculturalism and immigration, rather than class-based forms of exclusion and inequality. This can work to limit possibilities for interracial political action, mobilized around issues of inequality (see also Mondon, 2017; Mondon and Winter, 2019; Virdee and McGeever, 2018). Mondon and Winter (2019) warn of the dangers of the 'racialisation of the white working class', in fermenting political conflict along racial and nationalistic lines. Thirdly, Bhambra states that within the discourses forged upon 'methodological whiteness' there is a tendency to 're-centre' 'white interests', marginalizing the concerns of black and minority ethnic communities and ongoing experiences of exclusion and inequality, while at the same time the political grievances of whites are legitimized. Here she argues that within these conceptions, the white working class, the argument goes, has been forgotten – their histories silenced and their claims for a redress of the injustices they face ignored. This has led, in turn, to calls for racial self-interest by the dominant groups to be seen as legitimate and not to be labelled racist.

(2017:S217)

Bhambra points, for instance, to Eric Kaufmann's (2017) report on 'white self-interest', which argued that it was 'natural' for white groups to 'look out for their cultural, economic and demographic interests … [this] does not deserve the racist "appellation"'. For Bhambra, equating the sentiments of whites with other forms of 'minority' political mobilization, ignores the fact that,

claims by minority citizens occurred in the context of conditions of structured racial inequality, a redress argued for in terms of inclusive justice rather than partiality … To be clear, 'white' people are not a minority in Britain who must make claims together as a group in the face of discrimination and marginalization by a majority other.

(2017:S219)

This tendency is more widely observable, and over a decade ago Vron Ware warned of the dangers of legitimizing expressions of 'white resentment'. She argued that politicians have been willing to locate the reasons for rising white resentment in relation to immigration and multiculturalism 'as the trigger for alarming levels of social unease [this] effectively blocks a more rigorous analysis of the material conditions that those communities are facing' (2008:1.7). Indeed, recent decades have seen this notion of 'white victimhood' and marginalization used by politicians across the spectrum. It has been deployed to call for more restrictive immigration legislation, to legitimate the move away from state multiculturalism to integration and, informs a retreat from political mobilizations around more inclusive conceptions of collective class identities (Mann and Fenton, 2017; Rhodes, 2011; Ware, 2008).

If notions of a national 'subject' cast as both white and marginalized have been central to the contemporary politics of racism and nationalism, this has increasingly found expression through the emphasis placed on 'Englishness'. An interesting finding in the wake of the Brexit vote was that those who more strongly identified as 'English' rather than British were much more likely to vote Leave (Bhambra, 2017; Black, 2018; Virdee and McGeever, 2018). While for much of the postwar period, far and populist right-wing parties have mobilized a sense of Britishness and its symbols (i.e. the Union Jack), over recent decades, there has been a marked shift as groups such as the BNP, EDL, and UKIP have both targeted and found greater levels of support in England rather than within Britain more widely (Copsey, 2007; Ford and Goodwin, 2010; Kenny, 2014; Mann and Fenton, 2017; Rhodes, 2010; Wellings, 2010; Winlow, Hall, and Treadwell, 2017). Kenny (2014) too has suggested that 'populist-nationalism' expressions of Englishness, by groups such as UKIP and the EDL, represent one of the key narrations of English nationhood in the contemporary period, forged through hostility towards the political establishment (particularly the EU) and a 'beleaguered English nation' (2014:117). Aughey (2010:506) argues that English nationalism inherently comprises a series of 'political and cultural anxieties', oriented to a lack of sovereignty and a sense of being silenced, and often expressed through a sense of inequity in relation to other forms of British nationalism post-devolution (Aughey, 2010; Black, 2018; Kenny, 2014; Skey, 2012; Wellings, 2010).

In seeking to account for the linkages between Englishness and the contemporary politics of white resentment, Virdee and McGeever note the way in which it increasingly offers a framing and outlet for the expression of economic, social and cultural marginalization, locating, 'contemporary manifestations of Englishness in the structural decline that Britain has undergone during the neoliberal era' (2018:1809). Here,

> Experiences of downward mobility, alongside the persistence of class injuries … have produced a politics of nationalist resentment. Coming in the wake of a momentous working class defeat, Englishness has been reasserted through a racializing, insular nationalism, and it found its voice in the course of Brexit.
>
> *(ibid)*

Mann and Fenton (2017) note an increasingly popular expression of Englishness expressed through a form of 'discontented nationalism', which coheres around a widely felt sense of national decline and deterioration, focusing upon processes such as immigration, ethnic diversity, multiculturalism and European integration, alongside rising economic insecurity and a sense of diminishing public services and cultural and moral values. They note a dominant form of English nationalism both 'defensive' and 'resentful' in its character, invoking a sense of decline and a perception of the inability to legitimately celebrate Englishness. Here also claims to indigeneity through Englishness rest upon a racialised conception of belonging with English identity much more closely linked to notions of whiteness in comparison to Britishness, which is viewed as more 'multi-ethnic' and 'progressive' in its character (see also Leddy-Owen, 2014). Here, the historic subsuming of English nationalism within notions of Britishness, its lack of political articulation vis-à-vis the devolved nations, as well as the tendencies for it to be denounced by elites as rooted in xenophobia and racism, make it particularly amenable to articulate a sense of white resentment and victimhood (Black, 2018; Garner, 2012; Kenny, 2014; Kundnani, 2000; Leddy-Owen, 2014; Mann and Fenton, 2017; Skey, 2012; Virdee and McGeever, 2018).

Kundnani, writing at the turn of the century, noted how in the context of concerns over asylum and immigration, multiculturalism, globalisation, the rise of the EU and devolution, 'Englishness' emerged as a particularly potent political symbol for the right (see also Wellings, 2010; Kenny, 2014; Skey, 2012). These transformations as well as the publication of the Parekh Report which called for a re-envisioning of 'British' national identity and a rejection of a racialised conception of Englishness, produced a response in which the white English were positioned as the most marginalized group. These expressions articulated a view in which, 'if racism is the result of institutions ignoring the specificity of particular racial groups, then surely, the Right argued, the most discriminated against group of all are the English, for they can claim no special privileges' (Kundnani 2000). At the time, Kundnani argued that such sentiments lacked an organised political outlet, with a similar claim also made by Aughey in his statement that Englishness was reflected in a 'mood' rather than a 'movement' (2010:506). However, recent political developments suggest that this has changed. Mann and Fenton link the politicisation of Englishness to the rise of UKIP since 2010, an organization deemed to be the closest to an English nationalist movement there has been (see also Ford and Goodwin, 2014; Kenny, 2014). Commenting on the electoral success of UKIP in the 2015 General Election, Virdee and McGeever argue the party was able to 'gain traction by tapping into a sedimented racist nationalist populism that has been a feature of the English social formation for a number of decades'. Such views gain currency 'not simply through the circulation of racist ideas but because such ideas have been part of the lived habitus of the English social formation for so long' (2018:1812)

Alongside and related to the emergence of Englishness, contemporary discourses of racism and nationalism have also been identified as mobilizing an emergent form of racialised nostalgia, that works through invocations of both the nation's imperial and industrial past (Black, 2018; Kenny, 2017; Mann and Fenton, 2017; Thorleiffson, 2016; Virdee and McGeever, 2018). Virdee and McGeever note 'a striking confluence between English national feeling and the longing for Empire. The ease with which both nation and empire can sit together ... is one of the salient but unspoken dimensions of Brexit and its racist aftermath' (2018:1804; see also Black, 2018). Gilroy famously termed these types of sentiments 'postcolonial melancholia', which he identifies as developing in the postwar and postcolonial period operating through,

> an obsessive repetition of key themes – invasion, war, contamination, loss of identity – and the resulting mixture suggests that an anxious, melancholic mood has become part of the cultural infrastructure of the place, an immovable ontological counterpart to the nation-defining ramparts of the white cliffs of Dover.
>
> *(2004:15)*

Virdee and McGeever note that the Vote Leave campaign mobilized notions of Empire, within the theme of 'Taking Back Control', re-envisioning the colonial era as one of imperial greatness, based on an erasure of its brutality and destruction, as linkages are made between national sovereignty and imperialism (see also Black, 2018; Kenny, 2017). Since the referendum, too, support for Brexit has been articulated with reference to the past, with Bonacchi, Altaweel, and Krzyzanska (2018) illustrating how Facebook users leveraged historical discourses, centred around myths of origin and particularly in relation to the movement of people, to construct pro-Brexit political identities. Indeed, Kenny notes how, 'Politically orchestrated forms of nostalgia appear to be integral features of anti-establishment populism, and have helped project strong objections to liberal elites, and the policies of economic openness, tolerance and cultural diversity associated with them.' (2017:258). For Virdee and McGeever, the entanglements of Englishness, marginalization, and imperial longing, so apparent in the Brexit campaign, mark both the endurance but also potentially the widening appeal of racialized conceptions of nation and citizenship.

Conclusion

This chapter has explored what the contemporary academic literature reveals about the shifting articulations of racism, nationalism and the politics of white resentment in England. Focusing on the political discourses and sentiments associated with far right and populist-nationalist movements such as the BNP, EDL, and UKIP, emergent discursive frames have been delineated which reveal key formations through which the relationship between 'race' and nation is expressed. As asserted, both racism and nationalism operate through processes of 'othering' and forms of negative identification as the 'we' of the nation and its 'people', necessarily rests upon particular modes of exclusion and inferiorization. In terms of the 'objects' of contemporary racism and nationalism, 'Muslims' and 'migrants' emerge as particularly powerful figures, presented as threats to the economic, political and cultural integrity of the nation. These groups – often conflated both with one another and with established black and minority ethnic communities – are seen as abetted by a liberal political elite deemed to be unwilling to protect the 'indigenous' population. Alongside this, the national 'subject' is increasingly narrated through notions of 'white victimhood', with the 'native' population cast as a 'minority', marginalised through processes of globalization, multiculturalism, and immigration. Within these formulations, the 'white working class' has emerged as the archetypal embodiment of the nation's 'people', seen as indicative of the nation's decline and insecurity. Finally, the chapter focused on the emphasis increasingly placed on Englishness rather than Britishness. Here, white resentment finds expression through the reassertion of a form of national identity deemed marginalised. The recovery and reassertion of a white English national identity can be seen as indicative of a renewed assertion of racialised discourses of belonging and indigeneity.

References

Allen, C. (2011) 'Opposing islamification or promoting Islamophobia? Understanding the English Defence League', *Patterns of Prejudice*, 45(4): 279–294.

Allen, C. (2014) 'Britain first: the 'frontline resistance' to the Islamification of Britain', *The Political Quarterly*, 85(3): 354–361.

Anderson, B. (2017) 'Towards a new politics of migration?', *Ethnic and Racial Studies*, 40(9): 1527–1537.

Anthias, F. (2010) 'Nation and post-nation: nationalism, transnationalism and intersections of belonging'. In P. Hill-Collins and J. Solomos (eds) *The Sage Handbook of Race and Ethnic Studies*, London: Sage, pp. 221–248.

Anthias, F. and Yuval-Davis, N. (1992) *Racialized Boundaries: Race, Nation, Gender, Colour and Class and the Anti-Racist Struggle*, London: Routledge.

Aughey, A. (2010) 'Anxiety and injustice: the anatomy of contemporary English nationalism', *Nations and Nationalism*, 16(3): 506–524.

Awan, I. (2016) 'Islamophobia on social media: a qualitative analysis of Facebook's Walls of Hate', *International Journal of Cyber Criminology*, 10(1): 1–20.

Balibar, E. (1991) 'Racism and nationalism'. In E. Balibar and I. Wallerstein (eds) *Race, Class, Nation: Ambiguous Identities*, London: Verso, pp. 37–67.

Barker, M. (1981) *The New Racism: Conservatives and the Ideology of the Tribe*, London: Junction Books.

Bartlett, J., Birdwell, J, and Littler, M. (2011) *Inside the EDL: Populist Politics in a Digital Age*, London: Demos.

Bhambra, G. (2017) 'Brexit, Trump, and "methodological whiteness": on the misrecognition of race and class', *British Journal of Sociology*, 68(S1): S214-2232.

Bhatt, C. (2012) 'The new xenologies of Europe: Civil tensions and mythic pasts', *Journal of Civil Society*, 8(3): 307–326.

Black, J. (2018) 'From mood to movement: English nationalism, the European Union and taking back control', *Innovation: The European Journal of Social Science* (online first).

Bonacchi, C., Altaweel, M., and Krzyzanska, M. (2018) 'The heritage of Brexit: roles of the past in the construction of political identities through social media', *Journal of Social Archaeology*, 18(2): 174–192.

Brubaker, R. (2017) 'Between nationalism and civilizationalism: the European populist moment in comparative perspective', *Ethnic and Racial Studies*, 40(8): 1191–1226.

Burke, S. (2018) 'The discursive "othering" of Jews and Muslims in the Britain First solidarity patrol', *Journal of Community and Applied Social Psychology*, 28(5): 365–377.

Busher, J. (2016) *The Making of Anti-Muslim Protest: Grassroots Activism in the English Defence League*, London: Routledge.

Copsey, N. (2004) *Contemporary British Fascism: The British National Party and the Quest for Legitimacy*, Basingstoke: Palgrave.

Copsey, N. (2007) 'Changing course or changing clothes? Reflections on the ideological evolution of the British National Party 1999-2006', *Patterns of Prejudice*, 41(1): 61–82.

Copsey, N. (2010) *The English Defence League: Challenging our Country and our Values of Social Inclusion, Fairness, and Equality*, London: Faith Matters.

Copsey, N. and Macklin, G. (eds) (2011) *The British National Party: Contemporary Perspectives*, London: Routledge.

Cutts, D., Ford, R. and Goodwin, M. (2010) 'Anti-immigrant, politically disaffected or still racist after all? Examining the attitudinal drivers of extreme right support in Britain in the 2009 European Elections', *European Journal of Political Research*, 50(3): 418–440.

Davidson, T. and Berezin, M. (2018) 'Britain first and the UK independence Party: Social media and movement party dynamics', *Mobilization*, 23(4): 485–510.

Fekete, L. (2009) *A Suitable Enemy: Racism, Migration and Islamophobia in Europe*, London: Pluto Press.

Flemmen, M. and Savage, M. (2017) 'The politics of nationalism and white racism in the UK', *British Journal of Sociology*, 68(S1): S233-2264.

Ford, R. and Goodwin, M. (2010) 'Angry white men: individual and contextual predictors of support for the British National Party', *Political Studies*, 58(1): 1–25.

Ford, R. and Goodwin, M. (2014) *Revolt on the Right: Explaining Support for the Radical Right in Britain*, London: Routledge.

Fox, J. E., Moroşanu, L., and Szilassy, E. (2012) 'The racialization of the new European migration to the UK', *Sociology*, 46(4): 680–695.

Garner, S. (2012) 'A moral economy of whiteness: behaviours, belonging and Britishness', *Ethnicities*, 12(4): 445–464.

Geddes, A. (2014) 'The EU, UKIP and the politics of immigration in Britain', *Political Quarterly*, 85(3): 289–295.

Gest, J. (2016) *The New Minority: White Working Class Politics in an Age of Immigration and Inequality*, Oxford: Oxford University Press.

Gidron, N. and Hall, P. (2017) 'The politics of social status: economic and cultural roots of the populist right', *British Journal of Sociology*, 68(S1): S57-S84.

Gilroy, P. (1987) *There Ain't No Black in the Union Jack: The Cultural Politics of Race and Nation*, London: Hutchinson.

Gilroy, P. (2004) *After Empire: Melancholia or Convivial Culture?* London: Routledge.

Goldberg, D.T. (2002) *The Racial State*, Oxford: Blackwell.

Goldberg, D.T. (2006) 'Racial Europeanization', *Ethnic and Racial Studies*, 29(2): 331–364.

Goodwin, M. (2011) *Right Response: Understanding and Countering Populist Extremism in Europe*, London: Chatham House.

Goodwin, M. (2013) *The roots of extremism: The English Defence League and the counter-jihad challenge*, London: Chatham House Briefing Paper.

Goodwin, M. and Milazzo, C. (2017) Taking back control? Investigating the role of immigration in the 2016 vote for Brexit', *The British Journal of Politics and International Relations*, 19(3): 450–464.

Gupta, S. and Virdee, S. (2018) 'Introduction: European crises: Contemporary nationalism and the language of "race"', *Ethnic and Racial Studies*, 41(10): 1747–1764.

Hage, G. (2003) *Against Paranoid Nationalism: Searching for Hope in a Shrinking Society*, London: Pluto Press.

Hall, S. (2017) *The Fateful Triangle: Race, Ethnicity, Nation*, Chapel Hill: Duke University Press.

Hewitt, R. (2005) *White Backlash and the Politics of Multiculturalism*, Cambridge: Cambridge University Press.

Holmes, D.R. (2000) *Integral Europe: Fast Capitalism, Multiculturalism, Neofascism*, Trenton: Princeton University Press.

Jackson, L. (2018) *Islamophobia in Britain: The Making of a Muslim Enemy*, Basingstoke: Palgrave.

John, P., Margetts, H., Rowland, D. and Weir, S. (2006) *The BNP: The Roots of Its Appeal*, Essex: Democratic Audit.

Kassimeris, G. and Jackson, L. (2015) 'The ideology and discourse of the English Defence League: "Not racist, not violent, just no longer silent"', *The British Journal of Politics and International Relations*, 17: 171–188.

Kaufmann, E. (2017) *'Racial Self Interest' Is Not Racism: Ethno-Demographic Interests and the Immigration Debate*, London: Policy Exchange.

Kenny, M. (2014) *The Politics of English Nationhood*, Oxford: Oxford University Press.

Kenny, M. (2017) 'Back to the populist future?: Understanding nostalgia in contemporary ideological discourse', *Journal of Political Ideologies*, 22(3): 256–273.

Kinnvall, C. (2015) 'Borders and fear: insecurity, gender and the far right in Europe', *Journal of Contemporary European Studies*, 23(4): 514–529.

Kundnani, A. (2000) 'Stumbling on': race, class and England', *Race and Class*, 41(4): 1–18.

Kundnani, A. (2007) 'Integrationism: the politics of anti-Muslim racism', *Race and Class*, 48(4): 24–44.

Leddy-Owen, C. (2014) 'Re-imagining Englishness: "Race", class, progressive English identities and disrupted English communities', *Sociology*, 48(6): 1123–1138.

Lentin, A. and Titley, G. (2011) *The Crises of Multiculturalism: Racism in a Neoliberal Age*, London: Zed Books.

Mann, R. and Fenton, S. (2017) *Nation, Class and Resentment: The Politics of National Identity in England, Scotland and Wales*, Basingstoke: Palgrave.

McGhee, D. (2008) *The End of Multiculturalism? Terrorism, Integration and Human Rights*, Maidenhead: Open University Press.

Mondon, A. (2017) 'Limiting democratic horizons to a nationalist reaction: populism, the radical right and the working class', *Javnost- The Public*, 24(4): 355–374.

Mondon, A. and Winter, A. (2019) 'Whiteness, populism and the racialisation of the working class in the United Kingdom and the United States', *Identities: Global Studies in Culture and Power*, online first.

Oaten, A. (2014) 'The cult of the victim: an analysis of the collective identity of the English Defence League', *Patterns of Prejudice*, 48(4): 331–349.

Pilkington, H. (2016) *Loud and Proud: Passion and Politics in the English Defence League*, Manchester: Manchester University Press.

Rasinger, S.M. (2010) '"Lithuanian migrants send crime rocketing": Representations of "new" migrants in regional print media', *Media, Culture and Society*, 32(6): 1021–1030.

Redclift, V. (2014) 'New racisms, new racial subjects? The neo-liberal moment and the racial landscape of contemporary Britain', *Ethnic and Racial Studies*, 37(4): 577–588.

Rhodes, J. (2010) 'White backlash, "unfairness", and justifications of British National Party support', *Ethnicities*, 10(1): 77–99.

Rhodes, J. (2011) 'Multiculturalism and the subcultural politics of the British National Party', In N. Copsey and G. Macklin (eds) *The British National Party: Contemporary Perspectives*, London: Routledge, pp. 62–78.

Skey, M. (2012) '"Sod them, I'm English": The changing status of the "majority" English in post-devolution Britain', *Ethnicities*, 12(1): 106–125.

Skey, M. (2014) '"How do you think I feel? It's my country": belonging, entitlement and the politics of immigration', *The Political Quarterly*, 85(3): 326–332.

Solomos, J. (2003) *Race and Racism in Britain: Third Edition*, Basingstoke: Palgrave.

Solomos, J. (2013) 'Contemporary forms of racist movements and mobilization in Britain', in R. Wodak, Khosravinik, M. and Mral, B. (eds) *Right-Wing Populism in Europe: Politics and Discourse*, London: Bloomsbury, pp. 121–133.

Thorleiffson, C. (2016) 'From coal to UKIP: The struggle over identity in post-industrial Doncaster', *History and Anthropology*, 27(5): 555–568.

Runnymede Trust. (2017) *Islamophobia: Still A Challenge for Us All*, London: Runnymede Trust.

Valluvan, S. (2017) 'The new nationalism', *Juncture*, 23(4): 232–239.

Vieten, U.M. and Poynting, S. (2016) 'Contemporary far-right racist populism in Europe', *Journal of Intercultural Studies*, 37(6): 533–540.

Virdee, S. and McGeever, B. (2018) 'Racism, Crisis, Brexit', *Ethnic and Racial Studies*, 41(10): 1802–1819.

Ware, V. (2008) 'Towards a sociology of resentment: a debate on class and whiteness', *Sociological Research Online*, 13(5): 117–126.

Wellings, B. (2010) 'Losing the peace: Euroscepticism and the foundations of contemporary English nationalism', *Nations and Nationalism*, 16(3): 488–505.

Williams, S. and Law, I. (2011) 'Legitimising racism: an exploration of the challenges posed by the use of indigineity discourses by the far right', *Sociological Research Online*, 17(2): pp.1–12.

Winlow, S., Hall, S. and Treadwell, J. (2017) *The Rise of the Right: English Nationalism and the Transformation of Working-Class Politics*, Bristol: Policy Press.

Wood, C. and Finlay, W. (2008) 'British National Party representations of Muslims in the month after the London bombings: homogeneity, threat, and the conspiracy tradition', *The British Journal of Social Psychology*, 47(4): 707–726.

Part VII
Intersections of race and gender

Introduction

The intersections between race and gender are the core focus of the chapters in this part of the *Handbook*. This is an area that has attracted much attention from the end of the 20th century onwards, particularly at the conceptual level but also through a wide range of empirical studies that have sought to broaden the coverage of questions of gender within scholarship on race and racism.

The opening chapter by Umut Erel provides an overview of contemporary debates about the intersections of race and gender, arguing that Black feminism and Critical Race Theory have been important influences on the development of this approach. Erel draws on brief examples from the US, the UK, Germany, Turkey and Kurdistan in order to illustrate the impact of intersectional perspectives. She uses these examples to develop a broader conceptual frame that seeks to argue that perhaps the principal contributions of intersectional thought can be found in the ways that it renders visible experiences and positions of those affected by multiple oppressions. She then goes to explore the ways in which intersectionality entails understanding the complexity of multiple oppressions, which are irreducible to each other.

This is followed by Sirma Bilge's chapter, which focuses on the ways in which minority knowledge fields and producers respond to the neoliberal interpellations of the western university, particularly the ways that universities and other institutions have incorporated ideas about difference and diversity. Bilge's critical account of this process of incorporation of diversity highlights the ways in which university efforts in this field are often premised on the recognition of the value of diversity, and they thus seek to promote themselves as spaces that value difference and diversity. But, according to Bilge, it is this process that can have the effect of absorbing and neutralising critical perspectives, among them minority knowledge projects and producers. As an alternative she argues that rather than accepting this process of neoliberal incorporation it remains important to envision other possibilities, alternative forms of relationality and counter-discourse within institutions such as universities.

The next chapter, by Minoo Alinia, is focused on the development of discourses about gender and race in the context of Sweden. She takes a somewhat different angle into this area by exploring how current debates about race and racism in Sweden often include a significant element of arguing in the name of women's rights. Alinia seeks in particular to show that in the current period in Sweden racialising processes have gained a clear gender dimension. Issues of gender equality and women's rights in relation to migrant minorities have become an arena for the production of exclusionary discourses and practices. A strongly dominant discourse constructs notions of so-called honour culture to work as a discursive frame for the construction of otherness.

Anna Korteweg's chapter links up with broader discussions about gendered racialisations, including the arguments of Erel and Alinia. Korteweg focuses in particular on the processes that have led to the construction of 'immigrant subjects'. Her account outlines the conceptual integration of intersectional theory and theories of racialisation to articulate the meaning of gendered racialisations. She then focuses her analysis on specific sites where gendered racialisations are made visible, including veil wearing, the securitisation of borders and other public spaces, as well as educational achievement and labour market participation. From her perspective, gender equality and LGBTQ rights have become, at least in some contexts, tropes fostering gendered racialisation of immigrant communities in contemporary European and North American contexts. receiving nation states. More generally she moves on to discuss the effects that this gendered racialisation has, focusing on the rise of contemporary populism and right-wing nationalism, homonationalism and femonationalism, and European anti-gender movements.

This links up with the final chapter in this part, by Sarah Bracke and Luis Manuel Hernández Aguilar, which focuses on the relationship between biopower, race and sex. They draw on Michel Foucault's account of biopower to explore ways in which sex, sexuality, and sexual differentiation not only established hegemonic notions of femininity and masculinity but were also crafted in terms of the production of race difference. In developing this analysis Bracke and Aguilar emphasise the important role of the state and power relations in shaping race and gender relations. The chapter links up both with the concerns of other chapters in this part and the analysis of the racial state in Chapter 8 by Mills and Chapter 9 by Cook-Martín.

23

Intersections of race and gender

Umut Erel

Introduction

The question of how race and gender oppressions intersect, its effects on individuals and society, and how to challenge, resist and build alternative social and political communities has been a focus of research and activism for a long time. Rooted in Black feminism and Critical Race Theory, intersectional approaches to understanding race and gender oppression can be seen as a 'method and a disposition, a heuristic and analytic tool' (Carbado et al. 2015:303). Intersectional approaches are concerned with analysing, dismantling and challenging institutionalised, structural and interpersonal power relations and oppressions of gender, race, class, sexuality, nation, abilities and others. As this list shows, intersectional approaches go beyond analysing and challenging race and gender oppressions, though race and gender will be the main focus of this chapter. This chapter begins by looking at origins and development of intersectional thought, in particular the emergence of intersectional activist knowledges in the 1970s and 1980s in the US and the UK, and how these were intertwined with academic articulations. It then introduces the different levels of analysis to which intersectional thought has been brought, in particular social ontologies, discursive practice and concrete social relations (Anthias 2012), the matrix of domination, pertaining to structural, disciplinary, hegemonic and interpersonal domains (Collins 2009) and the differentiation between structural, political and representational intersectionality (Crenshaw 1991). The chapter then outlines the principal contributions of intersectional thought as a project to render visible experiences and positions of those affected by multiple oppressions. It also entails understanding the complexity of experiential and structural aspects of multiple oppressions, which should be theorised and understood as irreducible to each other. A key contribution of intersectional thought has been in the arena of epistemology, both as critique of the power structures reproduced in existing knowledge practices and projects of developing new forms and ways of knowing. The chapter then turns to critiques and debates of intersectional thought, in particular about imprecise epistemologies, the marginalisation of issues of sexuality, and the decentring of race, colonial and whitening practices. The final section provides an outlook about the continuing relevance of intersectional thought, in particular in terms of further theoretical and methodological developments through dialogues with decolonial and indigenous approaches, as well as through the cross-over into everyday discourse.

Origins and development of intersectional thought

Intersectional approaches aim at empowering Black women and women of colour, to better understand their experiences of expression, validate their experiences and define themselves.

In this sense, intersectional approaches have also challenged the marginalisation of Black women and women of colour in theoretical debates and social justice movements concerned with single axis analysis and resistance. Kimberlé Crenshaw (1989, 1991) introduced and elaborated the term intersectionality, giving impetus to much future intersectional research. Her critical legal scholarship demonstrates that Black women's experiences of discrimination of gender and race have routinely been rendered incomprehensible in the US legal system that narrowly conceptualised gender discrimination through the experiences of white women, while conceptualising race discrimination through the experiences of Black men. This often meant that Black women were unable to succeed with legal challenges to discrimination. By taking an intersectional approach, Crenshaw challenged the US legal system to take full account of Black women's experiences of discrimination and the structures that created these. While acknowledging that at times these may be similar to white women's experiences of gender discrimination or Black men's experiences of race discrimination, she showed that in other instances, however, Black women experience a unique set of gendered and racialised discrimination. She also challenged feminist and antiracist movements as these can at times produce and legitimise Black women's marginalisation, when they are seen as not fitting in with either white women's articulation of feminism or Black men's articulation of antiracist struggles.

While Crenshaw coined the term intersectionality, Hancock's (2016) intellectual history of intersectionality notes that both Crenshaw (1989, 1991) and Collins (2009, originally published in 1990) developed theories of the intersecting oppressions of race and gender at about the same time. Yet, the concern with understanding and fighting sexism and racism as mutually constitutive systems of oppression is longstanding and has emerged with urgency among political movements and activists. One of the best-known examples of this is Sojourner Truth's oft-cited question 'Ain't I a woman?' in a speech at the Women's Rights Conference in Ohio in 1851, demanding her rights and recognition as both a woman and Black. Yet, she was not alone as Hancock (2015:30) shows, in the 19th century US Black women like Maria Stewart, Anna Julia Cooper and Harriet Jacobs challenged both race and gender oppression. While these early contributions laid the groundwork for later generations of activists and theorists, Hancock suggests taking account of their historical context to view these early voices articulating 'intersectionality-like' arguments. Contemporary understandings of intersectionality were forged in activist communities of women of colour in the US, the UK and the Global South in the 1970s and 80s. The Combahee River Collective noted in their path-breaking text 'A Black Feminist Statement' (1977) that they

> often find it difficult to separate race from class from sex oppression because in our lives they are most often experienced simultaneously. We know that there is such a thing as racial-sexual oppression which is neither solely racial nor solely sexual.
>
> *(Collective orig. 1977, 1982:14)*

The Combahee River Collective articulated this through the notion of 'interlocking systems of oppression'. Other antecedents of the concept of intersectionality included the notions of 'double jeopardy' (Beal 2008, original publication 1970) or 'multiple jeopardy' (King 1988). While the early notion of 'triple oppression' (James 1986) addressed multiple oppressions of race, gender and class, this additive frame did not sufficiently explore the co-constitution of multiple power relations running the risk of instating hierarchies of oppression. Notions of multiple oppression were further explored by Black feminist theorists and feminists of colour interrogating the marginalisation of race and Black women's experiences in the women's movement (Davis 1982; Lorde 1984) and the gendered and racialised social divisions from a global feminist point of view (Mohanty 1988). In the UK, Anthias and Yuval-Davis (1992) highlighted the connections between race, ethnicity and gender, while Lewis (1996) looked at the co-constitution of race and gender in social policy. Brah (1996) explored the concept of diaspora space from a gendered, racialised perspective with particular reference to South Asian diasporas. These theoretical works were closely engaged with and often part of social justice movements. The ground-breaking collection *The Empire Strikes Back*, exploring race and racism in Britain from an emergent Cultural Studies perspective, included two important and influential contributions on racism and sexism, Hazel Carby's (1982) 'White Woman Listen!' which challenged the idea that Black and white women were affected and oppressed in a uniform manner by social institutions, such as the family, and Pratibha Parmar's (1982) contribution exploring the experiences and struggles of Asian women as migrants, workers and in reproduction. The 1984 Feminist Review Special Issue 'Many Voices, One Chant: Black Feminist Perspectives' (Amos et al. 1984) features the London based group Southall Black Sisters who challenged sexism within UK Black and antiracist communities to address domestic violence as well as the silencing of dissenting voices. Also in London, the Organisation of Women of Asian and African Descent, OWAAD, working around the same time, was crucial in developing the British notion of political Blackness, that advocated a cross-ethnic notion of Blackness as a politically resistant, antiracist subject position encompassing African, African-Caribbean and Asian women's alliance building. This combination of scholarly and political concerns has been documented in the collections on Black British feminism (Gunaratnam 2014; Mirza 1997). Debates, theories and understandings of the intersections of race and gender have emerged not simply out of scholarly concerns but in conjunction with activist social justice projects. While varying in different parts of the world, the experiences, activisms and theorising of women of colour and those experiencing racist and sexist oppressions have been key in articulating intersectional knowledge and social justice projects. Often, as in the case of the Combahee River Collective, these debates also included a concern with sexuality as an important social division, reflecting on how their authors' identifications and experiences as lesbian women were key to the articulation of political agendas, as well as understanding the co-constitution of power relations and articulations of resistance and empowerment. Yet, the significance of sexuality as a key social division that contributes to intersectional analysis and politics has been recognised more slowly, and has been contested in social movements (Collins 2009; Erel et al. 2010; Hancock 2016).

Different analytical levels

Intersectionality refers to power relations of racism and sexism. Intersectionality's important contribution is to emphasise that race and gender, as well as racism and sexism, are co-constituted, that is they are inseparable in the social world, both in terms of structure and experience. Yet, it is possible and at times helpful to differentiate various analytical levels. Thus Anthias (2012) argues that intersectionality relates firstly to the constitution of social ontologies as categories of sorting people. While this is a feature of social organisation in general, the constitution of categories of race, class and gender is historically specific and in itself imbued with practices and effects of power. She differentiates between ethnic and racial ontological spaces of constructing collectivities, gender as constructing ontologies of biological reproduction and class as relating to the production of economic life (2012.7). At a second level of abstraction, social categories become categories of discursive practice. While race, gender and class are irreducible to each other, they have certain commonalities as they are concerned with making boundaries and hierarchies. The specific categories to which people are sorted are socially constructed and can change over time and space, yet the issue of categorisation itself remains. The third level of abstraction concerns concrete social relations involving group making processes, where individuals and collectivities negotiate, contest and appropriate the categories with which they are confronted in social life by organisations, institutions and on the interpersonal level. These group making processes are played out in a 'spatial and temporal context and in relation to the operations of power' (2012:9).

Collins also looks at different aspects and levels of intersectionality, arguing that intersectional paradigms are useful to understand the experiences of oppression of different social groups, such as US Black women. They can however also explain how 'Puerticans, US White men, Asian American gays and lesbians, U.S. White women and other historically identifiable groups all have distinct histories that reflect their unique placement in intersecting oppressions' (Collins 2009:245). She further argues that intersectionality goes beyond recognising and validating experiences of oppression. She puts forward the concept of a 'matrix of domination' to describe the 'overall social organisation within which intersecting oppressions originate, develop and are contained' (2009:246). Intersecting systems of oppression are organised in four analytically distinct, though empirically interrelated domains of domination. This refers to (1) the structural domain, including the law and institutions, which organise oppression, (2) the disciplinary domain, consisting of bureaucracy and administration, which manages it, (3) the hegemonic domain, which justifies oppressions through ideology, culture and consciousness, and (4) the interpersonal level that affects everyday life and experience (Collins 2009:295–309).

Crenshaw (1991) differentiates between 'structural intersectionality' and 'political intersectionality'. The former level of analysis refers to the intersection of 'race, gender, and class domination' and the policy responses this requires. For example, in the arena of domestic violence policy, 'intervention strategies based solely on the experiences of women who do not share the same class or race backgrounds will be of limited help to women who face different obstacles because of race and class' (1991:1246). The level of political intersectionality highlights 'that women of color are situated within at least two subordinated groups that frequently pursue conflicting political agendas' (1991:1252). She also refers to 'representational intersectionality' which address the ways in which images of women of colour draw on sexist and racist narratives tropes (Crenshaw 1991). Crenshaw explores in 'particular, how the production of images of women of color and the contestations over those images tend to ignore the intersectional interests of women of color' (1991). Crenshaw looks in particular at legal and social controversies on the alleged 'obscenity' of rap music. She shows how contestations around sexism and racism of the court case against 2 Live Crew did not engage with the experiences or nterests of Black women. She points out how these debates instead formulated antiracist or feminist positions equating anti-racism with Black and feminism with white women's interests. The significance of cultural images of Black women has also been elaborated by Collins (2009), who argues that four key stereotypes of (1) the mule, an uncomplaining hard worker, (2) the jezebel, as highly sexualised, (3) the mammy, the Black woman as loyal domestic worker and (4) the Black lady, who has given up family life in exchange for a career, provide social scripts for Black women to internalise. Against this cultural domination, Black women's self-definition, then, is an important aspect of resistance.

Principal contributions in the study of intersections of race and gender

Intersectional approaches to race and gender have been widely taken up in a range of disciplines and interdisciplinary work, indeed there is a burgeoning of work using and developing and debating intersectional approaches. Work on intersectionality can be broadly distinguished as firstly 'applications of an intersectional framework or investigations of inter-sectional dynamics', secondly 'discursive debates about the scope and content of intersection-ality as a theoretical and methodological paradigm' and thirdly, political interventions employing an intersectional lens (Cho et al. 2013).

Visibility project

Intersectional approaches validate the experiences of those subjected to gender and race oppressions. This 'visibility project' has been key to rendering 'previously invisible, unad-dressed material effects of black women's/women of color's sociopolitical location visible and remediable' (Hancock 2016:623). Much of this work, in particular in the US context, has explored experiences of Black women and women of colour empirically, opening up and developing new fields of study that uncover the historical and contemporary contribu-tions, lifeworlds and political interventions of groups subjected to oppressions on the basis of race, gender, class, sexuality, immigration status, ability and other social divisions (Romero 2017). These studies are important in allowing a fuller and more complete understanding of the social world in itself, and are particularly instructive on the processes by which power relations are constructed, maintained and challenged. Yet, it is important to acknowledge that such intersectional studies have not simply descriptively included a wider range of sub-jects and topics into academic study. By exploring and putting centrally the experiences of intersectionally oppressed groups, intersectional research has further been key in shifting wider theoretical frameworks, concepts and boundaries defining these disciplinary debates. For example, Reynolds (2005) work on Black mothers in the UK challenges neat distinc-tions between concepts of private and public, local and transnational, topics of work, family and community activism while Phoenix and Bauer (2012) make visible the intertwining of class, race, gender and immigration experience as structuring factors in the psycho-social identities and relationships of Caribbean families in Britain. Clarke's (2011) work on how US Black university educated women make decisions about their romantic relationships and family planning shows that in-depth intersectional empirical work is generative of wide-reaching theoretical insights, developing a framework of gendered, racialised and classed stratification in romantic and family relationships. Accounting for the simultaneity of social divisions of race, gender, class, and others thus produces empirical insights and generates new concepts and theories.

Capturing complexity

This gives way to another advantage of intersectional approaches, that is the way it captures experiential and structural complexity. Leslie McCall (2005) differentiates three forms of understanding complexity in intersectional research: Firstly, the intercategorical approach 'focuses on the complexity of relationships among multiple social groups within and across analytical categories' (2005:1786). The intracategorical approach examines complexity within a social group, for example differences among women. Thirdly, the anticategorical approach deconstructs the analytical categories itself, challenging ideas of fixed categories. This com-plexity entails two further aspects, namely the recognition that social identity categories are changeable and specific to time and place (Yuval-Davis 2015). At the same time, one of intersectionality's key contributions is the recognition that aspects of privilege and marginal-isation are not mutually exclusive but features of all social positionings (Collins 2009). Finally, intersectionality's commitment to social justice projects means that this recognition of the complex ways in which social positions and power relations are constructed is not only a scholarly exercise, but intersectionality has a commitment to changing 'the conditions of society such that categories of identity are not permanently linked to sustained inequality in efforts to build a more just world' (Smooth 2013:21). This relates to another important contribution of intersectional analysis, namely, the ways in which it brings together knowledge produced in both activist and academic contexts. As a knowledge project committed to social justice, intersectionality fosters transformative knowledge both within and outside of academia.

Irreducibility

Intersectional approaches view each category, such as race, gender, sexuality, class as irreducible to each other, while also avoiding additive views that see multiple inequalities as simply the sum of its components (Carastathis 2014; Smooth 2013). This issue of irreducibility has generated debate on the methodological approaches to operationalise different categories. Thus, in some quantitative studies, it may be necessary to clearly differentiate factors of race, class, gender in data elicitation, which raises the question whether such a methodological approach is any different from additive approaches. To address this concern it has been suggested that, rather than viewing irreducibility as a methodological feature, it may be best viewed as 'a heuristic to interpret results of quantitative or qualitative research. On this interpretation, irreducibility is a theoretical commitment on the part of the researcher, which informs her analysis of data that may well have been generated using monistic categories' (Carastathis 2014:311).

Smooth (2013) draws attention to the analytic benefit of intersectional approaches in enabling researchers to address both structural and individual aspects of inequality and oppression as evolving in response to resistance strategies. These resistance strategies in turn are understood in the context of institutional processes and historical events 'that can facilitate as well as curtail opportunities for changing categorizations and dismantling dominant frameworks' (2013:26).

Because of its commitment to complexity and the irreducibility of social divisions to each other, Yuval-Davis characterises intersectionality analysis as 'the most valid approach to the sociological study of social stratification because it does not reduce the complexity of power constructions into a single social division, including class, as has been customarily the case in stratification theories' (2015:93–4).

Yuval-Davis' concept of 'situated intersectionality' emphasises the importance of historically contextualising specific power relations and paying attention to their malleability. She highlights the aspects of translocality, that is the different meanings and power of social categories in different spaces; transcalarity, that is the different meanings and power of social divisions when examined at different scales (e.g. households, neighbourhoods, cities, states, regions and globally); and transtemporality relates to 'how these meanings and power change historically and even in different points in people's life cycle' (2015:95).

Yuval-Davis' concept of situated intersectionality underlines that it is applicable to all social groups, beyond the context of Black and women of colour in which it was historically developed. As such, it should be applied to understand the implication of all social groups in multiple power relations. Contributions to a recent edited volume (Jackson 2015) explore how privilege is constructed through the co-constitution of dominant class status and white masculinities (Leek and Kimmel 2015), the articulation of privilege in alternative 'herbivore' masculinities in a Japanese subculture (Charlebois 2015), or the ways in which rural urban

Kurdish women migrants reconstitute their social relationships in Turkish cities (Bahar 2015). While not all engage with the concept of intersectionality, there is a wide range of work contributing to furthering knowledge of the imbrications of race, gender, class, sexuality in various contexts, such as the effects of austerity policies and minority women's resistance in Europe (Bassel and Emejulu 2017), the gendered racialisation of immigrants in the US and Europe (Korteweg, this volume), racialised and gendered effects of design (Onafuwa 2018), or the politics of queer people of colour in urban space (Bacchetta et al. 2015, 2015).

Epistemology

Intersectional debates make a key contribution to wider social sciences on epistemology. Intersectional approaches build on a range of related epistemologies, including standpoint theory (Harding 2004; Hartsock 1983) and Black Feminist thought (Collins 2009), though iterations of intersectional approaches may have distinct emphases and ways of applying and using these. All of these approaches critique the claim to neutrality of dominant, supposedly objective epistemologies, arguing that 'racism and sexism infiltrate ostensibly neutral knowledge practices' (May 2007, quoted in Hancock 2016:81). Hancock argues that intersectional epistemology makes distinct contributions in particular the awareness of multiple systems of oppression challenges a conception of a singular binary of centre and margin. This conceptually shifts understandings of social relations, conceptualising 'reality in a way that takes the politics of subaltern communities as seriously as the politics of mainstream society means that one can no longer self-locate as either on a margin or in a center' (2016:82). Hancock critiques Hartsock's (1983) account of feminist standpoint epistemology for privileging gender as the primary social division, arguing that this tendency has been replicated in some intersectional approaches whose focus is on 'how to theorize intersections between gender/sex and other power differentials based on class, race, ethnicity, sexuality, geopolitical positioning, age, disability and so on' (Lykke 2010, quoted in Hancock 2016:84). In contrast to this, feminists of colour, such as Audre Lorde and the Combahee River Collective, have developed an epistemology that views the relationship between oppressor and oppressed as multivalent and contingent.

A key aspect of intersectional epistemologies draws on Collins' notion of Black Feminist Knowledge (2009), and emphasises that all knowledge projects are not neutral, but sites of political struggle. Because of the societal devaluation of their subject positions and knowledges, Black women had to find alternative ways of self-validating and defining themselves through alternative ways of producing and validating knowledge. While this subjugated standpoint can centrally contribute to an incisive analysis of power relations, others have warned not to take for granted the view that subordinated groups have access to 'greater critical conceptual space' (Narayan quoted in Hancock 2016:92). Yuval-Davis's (2006) concept of the politics of belonging suggests that it is important to differentiate between social locations; identifications and emotional attachments; and ethical and political values, which do not neatly map onto each other.

Intersectionality also intervenes in ontological debates by challenging the idea that social categories and power relations of race and gender can be severed from each other, argues Hancock (2016:105-6). Yet, Yuval-Davis suggests that despite being inseparable in concrete situations, there are indeed different ontological groundings to each social division with '(f)or example, class relations are constructed around notions of production and consumption; gender – those of sexuality and reproduction; race/ethnicity as constructed by particular phenotypical or cultural boundaries; ability around the notion of "the normal" etc' (2015: 94).

An important ontological contribution of intersectional approaches is that it 'deexceptionalizes the processes and structures of racism, sexism, homophobia, classism, imperialism, nativism, ableism, and a host of other stratifications' (Hancock 2016:107) instead viewing these power relations as constitutive of social reality.

Critiques and debates

While some critiques have come from those who do not see themselves as scholars of intersectionality, a lot of debate and contestation has taken place among authors whose work applies and theorises intersectional approaches. While the concept of intersectionality has been extremely successful in travelling across geographical contexts and disciplines, there have been concerns that this process has gone hand in hand with a loss of meaning, rendering it merely a 'buzzword' (Davis 2008) or a 'meme' (Hancock 2015), emptying it of critical and transformative potential.

Epistemological imprecision

The proliferation of work referencing intersectionality, has at times meant that authors use the term without addressing its full analytic potential, often simply enumerating in a 'list' the range of multiple power relations (Erel et al. 2010). This has given rise to the critique that intersectional approaches are epistemologically imprecise: 'Intersectionality tells us … that the condition and subjectivity of and hence the legal treatment of Black women is not simply the sum of Blackness and femaleness, but it does not shed much light on what it is nevertheless' (Kwan 2000:687).

A response to Kwan's critique may be that there is not a single epistemological framework within intersectional approaches. Rather, a number of connected, though distinct knowledge projects work with different epistemological assumptions and ontological frameworks. While his description is fair in regard to some intersectional authors, it does not do justice to the important body of work on epistemology within the intersectional field of scholarship (see above).

Marginalising sexualities

There are contestations between proponents of intersectional scholarship who would 'mainstream' the approach and those committed to a 'critical intersectionality' engaging with concerns of marginalised and oppressed people (Carastathis 2014:306).

One element of this has been criticised as marginalising those affected by multiple oppressions, instead fostering alliances between privileged members of different groups. For example, at times the empirical and analytic centrality of issues of sexuality and gender identification have been neglected, resulting in marginalising trans people's experiences, views and contributions to theory and activism. Related to this, though distinct, has been the argument that projects professing to engage in intersectional engagements of different groups tend to use the experiences and political agendas of the most privileged members of each group as a basis for alliance building, theorising and knowledge projects 'For example, white lesbians are invited to share discursive power with racialised men, or white gay men with heterosexual migrant women … this frequently goes at the expense of racialised gays, lesbians and bisexuals' (Erel et al. 2010:276).

Decentring race, colonising and whitening

An important debate relates to the place of Black women as subjects of study, originators of knowledge and theory. While some critique the idea that intersectionality is closely bound up with researching and understanding the subject position of Black women as limiting its analytic purview (Wiegman 2012) and the ways in which women of colour's experiences are addressed (Puar 2012); for others, 'intersectionality research must be properly understood as the purview of scholars investigating women of color' (Alexander-Floyd: 19), suggesting that scholars researching other groups should develop a distinct conceptual and theoretical vocabulary.

These debates are however not limited to the question of subject of study, but engage more broadly with the centrality of race to intersectional approaches. In particular within feminist debates on intersectionality, there is contestation around the significance of race and racism. While for some authors, intersectionality should normatively involve a commitment to social justice, centrally including recognition of racism, commitments to race equality and anti-racism, for other feminist scholars intersectionality offers a way of describing and analysing social differences, where race is but one difference among others. In some instances, scholars would argue that race should be displaced as a meaningful category of analysis. This relates to critics who have charged intersectional approaches with reifying race-based identity politics in potentially essentialist ways (e.g. Prins 2006; Staunaes 2003). Related to this is the question whether critical race theory as articulating within intersectional approaches can be applied to contexts outside the US, particularly in continental Europe where debates on race are often considered taboo (Lutz et al. 2011). This is in part due to national legislation criminalising data collection on the basis of 'race', such as in France (Mugge et al. 2018); in part, however, it is due to marked contrasts in scholars' political outlook.

Rebuffing these arguments, other authors critique (European) feminist intersectionality discourse for (neo) colonising and whitening the concept. Barbara Tomlinson (2013) focuses her analysis on European feminist critiques of intersectionality which partake in 'racial Europeanization' (Goldberg 2006), that is the denial of the continuing existence and centrality of race and racism to the make up of Europe, resulting in the suppression of debate and reflection on race and racism, as well as tools to fight racism. She rebuts some European feminist critiques of US conceptions of intersectionality as overly identitarian, overemphasising and essentialising race, showing how key arguments of Black feminist US scholars are misrepresented through the strategies of 'depersonalizing', 'collectivizing' and 'fixing' 'the nature of the Black feminists who introduced the concept of intersectionality as a theoretical tool' (2013:254). Tomlinson shows how diverse theoretical, epistemological and political engagements of Black intersectional theorists are mis-recognised, as the Black feminist theorists are treated as a homogenous group, and the nuance of their arguments is ignored. These strategies, she suggests, are akin to what Albert Memmi identified as colonial racism. She argues that this is an expression of unacknowledged white racial privilege and calls on feminists to 'transform the terms of reading and writing to take responsibility for the ways feminist discourses function as technologies of power' (Tomlinson 2013: 254). Alexander-Floyd argues that two key strategies are part of this attempted colonisation of intersectionality debates: 'universalizing' and 'bait and switch'. The universalising tendency refers to activists' claims that an issue goes beyond the experience of women of colour, 'the effect of which is to typically highlight the plight of white women and not that of black women' (2012:8), while in the 'bait and switch' rhetorical strategy, 'black women are focused on, but only to make visible white female suffering' (Alexander-Floyd 2012:9). Both strategies result in disappearing the experiences, subjectivities, and intellectual legacies of Black women. In a related vein, Bilge (2013:414) critiques the whitening of intersectionality studies, arguing that the decentring of race from intersectional approaches allowed white feminism to appropriate intersectionality and disregard the intellectual origins of intersectionality in Black feminism. This emphasises the stance that 'feminists have theorized intersectionality from many perspectives' (Lykke 2010, cited in Bilge 2013:414) and reduces the intellectual and political role of Black and women of colour's feminist thought to 'just "another perspective"' (Bilge 2013:414), thereby denying the central role of Black and women of colour in generating the theoretical framework, as well as decentring race as a central element of intersectional thought. Bilge thus draws attention to the politics of knowledge production, arguing that '"whitening intersectionality" refers to ways of doing intersectional work in the political economy of genealogical and thematic re-framings, in the citational practices, and in the politics of canonicity' (Bilge 2013:412).

While this debate is often cast as one between white European feminist race avoidance and US Black and women of colour feminism, Lewis points out that an attempt to void intersectionality of engagement with race and racism affects racialised women in Europe, rendering them 'uncomfortable and silenced':

> In such circumstances speaking from that location—as an embodied-sentient subject who knows she is raced—felt risky because it might expose one to the risk of being deemed too emotional or of being reinscribed as knowing only about race.
>
> *(Lewis 2013:883-4)*

This furthermore sidesteps meaningful engagement and critique of whiteness as a racialised social position. While these debates about the centrality of race and the role of Black and women of colour feminists in conceptualising intersectionality have not been resolved (Mugge et al. 2018), it is important to challenge the notion that

> Black women are too different to stand in for a generalizable theory about power and marginalization. The travels of intersectionality belie that concern. Actors of different genders, ethnicities, and sexual orientations have moved intersectionality to engage an ever-widening range of experiences and structures of power. At the same time, the generative power of the continued interrogation of Black women's experiences both domestically and internationally is far from exhausted.
>
> *(Carbado et al. 2013:305)*

One of the questions raised in this debate is whether and how the concept of intersectionality can be applied to contexts outside of Black US women's experiences without emptying it of meaning, in particular without devoiding it of its antiracist critique. A number of scholars have proposed ways to bring in the knowledges of racialised activists and intellectuals from a range of geographical contexts. The idea that race has no relevance in the European context is reinforced by marginalising, silencing and ignoring the contributions of scholars of colour within Europe (Bacchetta et al. 2015; Erel et al. 2010; Petzen 2012). Yet, within continental Europe, there are important ways in which activists and scholars commit to, and develop further, intersectional understandings of race and racism and have done so for decades, even where these are routinely ignored in the literature (e.g. Bassel and Emejulu 2018 for recent activism; for the German context, cf. e.g Apostolidou 1980; Kalpaka and Räthzel 1985; Oguntoye et al. 1986; Roig 2018). An example from two contrasting studies on the Kurdish and Turkish context demonstrates the importance of political values, as suggested in Yuval-Davis' reflections on the politics of belonging (2006), rather than geography and cultural specificity for the ways in which the concept of intersectionality is applied. Bahar (2015) argues that gendered oppression by kin and ethnic group is key to understanding the subordination of Kurdish women migrants to Turkish cities, disavowing the structural racism and internal colonialism to which Kurds in Turkey have been subjected. In contrast to this, Al-Rebholz's (2013) study on Kurdish and Turkish feminists emphasises the importance of an analysis of racism in Black feminist texts for Kurdish women's engagement with feminism, as it was this engagement with racism that allowed Kurdish women to make feminism relevant to their own intersecting experiences of racist and sexist oppression.

This debate between White 'disciplinary feminism' (Bilge 2013) and intersectional scholars for whom race is central to the constitution of intersectionality, has not been resolved and is ongoing. Some of the positions within this debate are that intersectional research should focus on Black women and be delimited as such (Alexander-Floyd (2012). Others, such as Tomlinson (2013) and Bilge (2013) call on white feminist researchers to recognise and challenge their own racially privileged positioning in their research practice, which would involve actively desisting from appropriating and depoliticising the notion of intersectionality. Bilge (2013) argues that in some instances intersectional knowledge production may step back from claiming the term intersectional, if this would result in empowering subordinated groups without marginalising other subordinated groups. Another proposition for moving the debate forward is Hancock's (2015:624) call to conceive of authors and activists' relationship to the concept of intersectionality beyond the idea of ownership and appropriation through the notion of stewardship. She borrows the term stewardship from Indigenous women in Canada to denote the complex practices of engaging in interpretive communities of intersectionality. Yet, this debate remains unresolved and is likely to continue as long as the centrality of race and racism as forms of oppression, inequality and exploitation to the constitution of the social world are denied or minimised in academic as well as public debates.

Continuing relevance of intersectionality

As current societal developments in many parts of the world point to the continuing importance of racism, nationalism and gender oppression, intersectional approaches to understanding and challenging these will continue to be relevant. Three key points seem particularly important for future developments. One is the ways in which intersectional thought links with related methodological and theoretical projects; second, this particularly challenges intersectional thought to engage with global and transnational social justice projects; and third, intersectionality has been able to cross over beyond academia into social movements and everyday life.

Intersectional epistemologies recognise that knowledge is situated and partial (Collins 2009), and a closer engagement with related social justice knowledge projects such as decolonial approaches (Hancock 2016; Lugones 2007), participatory methods (e.g. Chmielewski et al. 2016), Indigenous methodologies (Smooth 2013) or theoretical frames of assemblages (Puar 2012) is likely to prove fruitful. Further developing a transnational understanding of the locally specific but globally constituted intersections of race and gender oppressions can contribute to bringing into being new political alliances, subjects and ways of knowing (Collins 2009). While intersectional approaches to gender and race have had immense influence in various academic disciplines and transnational contexts, they have also crossed over into mainstream debates and inspired a wide range of engagements by activists, social movements and wider readers. For example, Hancock (2016:13-4) notes that the citation figures of Crenshaw (1989, 1991) and

Collins (2009, originally published in 1990) key works range between 9,948 and 12,002 which are exceptional for academic publications, testifying to the authors' wide-ranging influence. Yet, in the first quarter of 2015 alone, Wikipedia's entry on intersectionality has been viewed 86,734 times, demonstrating that debates on intersectionality have become part of debates beyond academia. This engagement is invigorated by recent publications from scholars who address an introductory or general readership (e.g. Collins and Bilge 2016; Romero 2017). As such, we can expect many more engagements, debates and developments of intersectional approaches in the future.

References

Alexander-Floyd, N. G. 2012. Disappearing acts: reclaiming intersectionality in the social sciences in a post-Black feminist era. Feminist Formations, pp. 1–25.

Al-Rebholz, A. 2013. Gendered subjectivity and intersectional political agency in transnational space. The case of Turkish and Kurdish women's NGO activists, in: A. Wilson (ed.) *Situating Intersectionality. Politics, Policy, and Power*. New York: Palgrave Macmillan, pp. 107–130.

Amos, V., Lewis, G., Mama, A. and Parmar, P. 1984. Editorial, *Feminist Review*, 17, pp. 1–2.

Anthias, F. 2012. Transnational mobilities, migration research and intersectionality.

Anthias, F. and Yuval-Davis, N. 1992. *Racialized Boundaries: Race, Nation, Gender, Colour and Class*. London: Routledge.

Apostolidou, N. 1980. Für die Frauenbewegung auch wieder nur 'Arbeitsobjekte?' *Informationsdienst Zur Ausländerarbeit*, 2, pp. 143–146.

Bacchetta, P., El-Tayeb, F. and Haritaworn, J. 2015. Queer of colour formations and translocal spaces in Europe, *Environment and Planning D: Society and Space*, 33(5), pp. 769–778.

Bahar, O. S. 2015. Kurdish migrant women negotiating the complex web of gender, class and ethnicity in the city, in: S. A. Jackson (ed..) *Routledge International Handbook of Race, Class and Gender*. Abingdon: Routledge, pp. 73–83.

Bassel, L. and Emejulu, A. 2017. *Minority women and austerity, Survival and Resistance in France and Britain*. Bristol: Policy Press.

Beal, F. M. 2008. Double jeopardy: to be black and female, *Meridians*, 8(2), pp. 166–176.

Bilge, S. 2013. Intersectionality undone: saving intersectionality from feminist intersectionality studies, *Du Bois Review: Social Science Research on Race*, 10(2), pp. 405–424.

Brah, A. 1996. *Cartographies of Diaspora: Contesting Identities*. London: Routledge.

Carastathis, A. 2014. The concept of intersectionality in feminist theory, *Philosophy Compass*, 9(5), pp. 304–314.

Carby, H. 1982. White Woman Listen! Black Feminism and the Boundaries of Sisterhood. *The Empire Strikes Back: Race and Racism in 70s Britain*. London: Hutchinson, pp. 212–235.

Carbado, D. W., Crenshaw, K. W., Mays, V. M., Tomlinson, B. 2013. Intersectionality: Mapping the Movements of a Theory, *Du Bois Rev,*;10(2), pp. 303–312. doi:10.1017/S1742058X13000349.

Centre for Contemporary Cultural Studies (ed.), 1982, *The Empire Strikes Back: Race and Racism in 70s Britain*. London: Centre for Contemporary Cultural Studies.

Charlebois, J. 2015. Herbivore masculinity opposition or accommodation to hegemonic masculinity, in: S. A. Jackson (ed..) *Routledge International Handbook of Race, Class and Gender*. Abingdon: Routledge, pp. 117–127.

Chmielewski, J. F., Belmonte, K. M., Fine, M. and Stoudt, B. G. 2016. Intersectional inquiries with LGBTQ and gender nonconforming youth of color: participatory research on discipline disparities at the race/sexuality/gender nexus, in: *Inequality in School Discipline*, New York: Palgrave Macmillan, pp. 171–188.

Cho, S., Crenshaw, K. W. and McCall, L. 2013. Toward a field of intersectionality studies: theory, *applications, and praxis. Signs: Journal of Women in Culture and Society*, 38(4), pp. 785–810.

Clarke, A.Y., 2011. *Inequalities of love: College-educated Black women and the barriers to romance and family*. Durham, NC: Duke University Press.

Collective, C. R. orig. 1977, 1982. A black feminist statement, in: G. T. Hull, P. B. Scott and B. Smith (eds..) *All the Women are White, All the Blacks are Men, but Some of Us are Brave*. New York: The Feminist Press, pp. 13–22.

Collins, P. H. 2009. *Black Feminist Thought: Knowledge, Consciousness, and the Politics of Empowerment.* Abingdon: Routledge.

Collins, P. H. and Bilge, S. 2016. *Intersectionality.* Cambridge: Polity Press.

Crenshaw, K. 1989. University of Chicago legal forum, *Demarginalizing the Intersection of Race and Sex: A Black Feminist Critique of Antidiscrimination Doctrine, Feminist Theory and Antiracist Politics*, 139, pp. 139–167.

Crenshaw, K. 1991. Mapping the margins: intersectionality, identity, and violence against women of color, *Stanford Law Review*, 43~6, pp. 1241–1300.

Davis, A. 1982. *Women, Race and Class.* London: Women's Press.

Davis, K. 2008. Intersectionality as buzzword: a sociology of science perspective on what makes a feminist theory successful, *Feminist Theory*, 9(1), pp. 67–85.

Erel, U., Haritaworn, J., Rodríguez, E. G. and Klesse, C. 2010. On the depoliticisation of intersectionality talk: conceptualising multiple oppressions in critical sexuality studies, in: Yvette Taylor, Sally Hines and Mark E. Casey (eds) *Theorizing Intersectionality and Sexuality.* Houndmills, London: Palgrave Macmillan, pp. 56–77.

FeMigra, Akin, S., Apostolidou, N., Atadiyen, H., Güran, G., Gutiérrez Rodríguez, E., Kanat, A., Kutz, L. and Mestre Vives, L.) 1994. Wir, die Seiltänzerinnen, in: C. Eichhorn and S. Grimm (eds.) *Gender Killer.* Amsterdam and Berlin: Edition ID-Archiv, pp. 49–63.

Goldberg, D. T. 2006. Racial europeanization, *Ethnic and Racial Studies*, 29(2), pp. 331–364.

Gunaratnam, Y. 2014. Black British feminisms: many chants, *Feminist Review*, 108(1), pp. 1–10.

Gutiérrez Rodríguez, E. 1999. *Intellektuelle migrantinnen: Subjektivitäten im zeitalter der globalisierung, Eine Dekonstruktive Analyse Von Biographien Im Spannungsverhältnis Von Ethnisierung Und Vergeschlechtlichung.* Opladen: Leske & Budrich.

Hancock, A. M. 2015. Intersectionality's will toward social transformation, *New Political Science*, 37(4), pp. 620–627.

Hancock, A. M. 2016. *Intersectionality: An Intellectual History.* Oxford: Oxford University Press.

Harding, S. G. (ed.), 2004. *The Feminist Standpoint Theory Reader: Intellectual and Political Controversies.* London: Psychology Press.

Hartsock, N. 1983. *Money, Sex and Power.* Boston: North eastern University Press.

James, S. 1986. *Sex, race and class, pamphlet series – Centrepiece 1, housewives in dialogue*, London.

Jackson. S. A. (ed.), 2015. *Routledge International Handbook of Race, Class and Gender.* Abingdon: Routledge, pp. 73–83.

Kalpaka, A. and Räthzel, N. 1985. Paternalismus in der Frauenbewegung?!, *Informationsdienst Zur Ausländerarbeit*, 3, pp. 21–27.

King, D. K. 1988. Multiple jeopardy, multiple consciousness: the context of a black feminist ideology, *Signs*, 14(1), pp. 42–72.

Kwan, P. 2000. Complicity and complexity: cosynthesis and praxis, *DePaul Law Review*, 49, pp. 687.

Leek, C. and Kimmel, M. 2015. Conceptualizing intersectionality in superordination: masculinities, whitenesses and dominant classes, in: S. A. Jackson (ed..) *Routledge International Handbook of Race, Class and Gender.* Abingdon: Routledge, pp. 3–9.

Lewis, G. 1996. Situated voices: 'Black women's experience' and social work, *Feminist Review*, 53(1), pp. 24–56.

Lewis, G. 2013. Unsafe travel: experiencing intersectionality and feminist displacements, *Signs: Journal of Women in Culture and Society*, 38(4), pp. 869–892.

Lorde, A. 1984. *Sister Outsider: Essay and Speeches.* Berkeley: Freedom.

Lugones, M. 2007. Heterosexualism and the colonial/modern gender system, *Hypatia*, 22(1), pp. 186–219.

Lutz, H., Vivar, M. T. H. and Supik, L. 2011. Framing intersectionality: an introduction, in Lutz Helma, Maria Teresa Herrera Vivar and Linda Supik (eds) *Framing Intersectionality: Debates on a Multi-faceted Concept in Gender Studies*, Farnham: Ashgate, pp. 1–22.

Lykke, Nina 2010. *Feminist Studies: A Guide to Intersectional Theory, Methodology and Writing.* New York: Routledge.

McCall, L. 2005. The complexity of intersectionality, *Signs: Journal of Women and Culture in Society*, 30(3), pp. 1771–1800.

Mirza, H. S. (ed.), 1997. *Black British Feminism: A Reader.* London: Taylor & Francis.

Mohanty, C. T. 1988. Under western eyes: feminist scholarship and colonial discourses, *Feminist Review*, 30(Autumn 1988), pp. 61–88.

Mugge, L., Montoya, C., Emejulu, A. and Weldon, S. L. 2018. Intersectionality and the politics of knowledge production, *European Journal of Politics and Gender*, 1(1-2), pp. 17–36.

Oguntoye, K., Opitz, M. and Schultz, D. 1986. *Farbe Bekennen: Afrodeutsche Frauen Auf Den Spuren Ihrer Geschichte*. Berlin: Orlanda Frauen Verlag.

Onafuwa, Dimeji 2018. Allies and Decoloniality: A Review of the Intersectional Perspectives on Design, Politics, and Power Symposium, *Design and Culture*, 10(1), pp. 7–15.

Parmar, P. 1982. Gender, race and class: Asian women in resistance, in: Centre for Contemporary Cultural Studies (ed.), *The Empire Strikes Back: Race and Racism in 70s Britain*. London: Centre for Contemporary Cultural Studies.

Petzen, J. 2012. Queer trouble: centring race in queer and feminist politics, *Journal of Intercultural Studies*, 33(3), pp. 289–302.

Phoenix, A. and Bauer, E. 2012. Challenging gender practices: intersectional narratives of sibling relations and parent-child engagements in transnational serial migration, *European Journal of Women's Studies*, 19 (4), pp. 490–504. doi:10.1177/1350506812455994

Prins, B. 2006. Narrative accounts of origins: a blind spot in the intersectional approach? *European Journal of Women's Studies*, 13(3), pp. 277–290.

Puar, J. K. 2012. "I would rather be a cyborg than a goddess": becoming-intersectional in assemblage theory, *PhiloSOPHIA*, 2(1), pp. 49–66.

Reynolds, T. 2005. *Caribbean Mothers: Identity and Experience in the UK*. London: Tufnell Press.

Roig, E. 2018. Intersectionality in Europe: a depoliticized concept? Völkerrechtsblog, 6 March 2018, doi: 10.17176/20180306-142929.

Romero, M. 2017. *Introducing Intersectionality*. New Jersey: John Wiley & Sons.

Smooth, W. G. 2013. Intersectionality from theoretical framework to policy intervention, in: Angelia R. Wilson (ed.) *Situating Intersectionality: Politics, Policy, and Power*, New York: Palgrave Macmillan, pp. 11–41.

Staunæs, D. 2003. Where have all the subjects gone? Bringing together the concepts of intersectionality and subjectification, *NORA: Nordic Journal of Women's Studies*, 11(2), pp. 101–110.

Tomlinson, Barbara 2013. Colonizing Intersectionality: Replicating Racial Hierarchy in Feminist Academic Arguments, *Social Identities*, 19(2), pp. 254–272.

Wiegman, Robyn 2012. *Object Lessons*. Durham, NC: Duke University Press.

Yuval-Davis, N. 2006. Belonging and the politics of belonging, *Patterns of Prejudice*, 40(3), pp. 197–214.

Yuval-Davis, N. 2015. Situated intersectionality and social inequality, *Raisons Politiques*, 58(2), pp. 91–100.

24

We've joined the table but we're still on the menu

Clickbaiting diversity in today's university[1]

Sirma Bilge

As some may have noticed, my intervention's title alludes to a present-day maxim, "if you're not at the table, you're on the menu"[2] – the liberal inclusive mantra that suggests once at the table, self-representing, it gets better, or at least we won't be eaten alive. I beg to differ. Against the promises of the integrationist dictum, I make another argument: *we've joined the table, but we're still on the menu* – which amounts to say that, in a way, we (racialized scholars working in the western academy) are eating ourselves. I develop "who/what is being eaten by whom to do what?" under the term of *diversity clickbaiting*, which is a double entendre in that the contemporary university clickbaits diversity to enlist scholars assigned to embody diversity into its hegemonic project, at the same time, these "diversity scholars" become the bait used by the institution to attract new "clienteles", i.e. students, that would become future generations of experts governing difference for the state and capital. As in the end the bait is that which is eaten by others, some might wonder why I mentioned eating ourselves, or self-cannibalizing. Then, consider this.

Writing in the mid 1990s, a period of (neo)liberal multicultural revamp in Canadian higher education, Bengali-Canadian scholar Himani Bannerji, a Marxist antiracist feminist, gives a poignant account of the violence of being included in a white institution. After locating herself as "perhaps one of the oldest non-white women teachers in Ontario universities", teaching in a field (gender, race and class) that is simultaneously fetishized and marginalized, and has even become an orthodoxy in academic feminist theory (1995: 97), Bannerji argues, "[t]he social relations of teaching and learning are relations of violence for us, those who are not white, who teach courses on 'Gender, Race and Class,' to a 'white' body of students in a 'white university'". (102). In front of the white gaze fixing meaning onto her small-framed brown female body, she interpellated to occupy the professor's authoritative space in a predominantly white classroom to teach contentious subjects: colonialism, racism, patriarchy, and capitalism. Enduring this violence makes her dissociate from her corporeality, while at the same time she stages it as her teaching tool, articulating what I call a *self-cannibalizing pedagogy*.

[W]hile I am lecturing on "bodies" in history, in social organization of relations and spaces, constructed by the gaze of power, I am actually projecting my own body forward through my words. I am in/scribing rather than erasing it. First I must draw attention to it, focus this gaze, let it develop me into a construct. Then I take this construct, this "South Asian" woman and break it up piece by piece. In every sense they are learning on my body. I am the teacher, my body is offered up to them to learn from, the room is an arena, a stage, an amphitheatre, I am an actor in a theatre of cruelty …

(101–2)

Bannerji counters the racializing gaze by using her body as a bait to capture her audience's attention, body turned into an empty vessel carrying an inflicted construct, a stereotype. The body becomes the principal site of representation in an attempt to make the stereotypes work against themselves (Hall 1997: 274) and return the gaze. This is violent practice implying dismemberment.

I dissociate from my own presence in the room. But I signify, symbolize, embody a construct and teach on it. […] this body, along with centuries of "knowing," of existential and historical racism, is my "teaching" presence and tool. […] I am offering up piece by piece my experience, body, intellect, so others can learn. Unless I am to die from this violence of the daily social relations of being a non-white South Asian woman, in a white Ontario, Canada classroom – I have to dissociate.

(102–3)

Yet, violently subjecting the self to the white university's racialized governmentality is also a process of subjectivation. Her account of a slowly sublimated anger – how she processes it into teaching and research material in and through institutional interventions such as containment and formalizing, closely resonates with the Foucauldian nexus of subjection/subjectivation, the constitutive relationship between the process of being subordinated by power and that of the subject formation. Bannerji's self-cannibalizing pedagogy is her way of constructing subject out of an object status, a subject that subverts and contests. It is a "choice" under not self-selected circumstances, as Marx would say – nonetheless a contribution to freedom dreams.

But there is another way to understand my distress, my dissociation. Fear of the gaze, my presence in the theatre of cruelty, the sacrifice of my body to a white pedagogic god, is not the entire story. I am an object. But also I am a subject. My dissociation has also much to do with that. My pedagogic choice to teach at all, in this country, and what I insistently teach about, have something to do with de-colonization of myself and other, the innermost need to fight patriarchal, imperialist racism.

(104)

I am aware of doing violence to myself by choosing this pedagogic path. […] And yet I choose to do this violence to myself. Because I choose to de-colonize, to teach anti-racism, not only for myself but for others as well. This slow, long, extended anger of a method, perspective, theories, ideology, instances, political economy and history – these hours of lectures, examinations and essays, are my spontaneity, my anger, formalized, expanded and contained, occasioned and stymied by the regulations of a white university. Subversion, protest, not revolutionary yet, or perhaps will never be. Yet a stream moving on its way, a little tributary to join what I dream of – a real socialist revolution, feminist, antiracist, Marxist, anti-imperialist. [...] The mediation of my anger cuts me into two. But here in my actual, immediate work of teaching, I am not silent. At least not that.

(105–6)

Bannerji's embodied auto-analysis brings invaluable insights to my argument that racialized peoples are differently interpellated into the neoliberal white university, especially when they are hired to teach and research race, and expected to embody diversity. Being "diversity" can be exhausting, as Sara Ahmed (2009) stresses, for our arrival is taken as evidence that university has arrived, that whiteness has been undone. In a way, our presence in the institution undermines our teachings that "still" problematize white supremacy and institutional racism. We are thus consigned to an untenable position: teaching racism to people and institutions that read our very presence in that space as a testament that the problem has been overcome. Ahmed (2009: 41) argues,

> The turn to diversity is often predicated on the numbers game, on getting more of us, more people of colour, to add colour to the white faces of organisations. [...] We symbolise the hope or promise that whiteness is being undone. Our arrival is read as evidence of commitment, of change, of progress. [...] I am speaking of whiteness in a seminar and someone in the audience says, "but you are a professor", as if to say if Black women become professors then the whiteness of the world recedes. If only we had the power we are imagined to possess, if only our proximity could be such a force. If only our arrival was their undoing. I was appointed to teach "the race course", I reply. I am the only person of colour employed on a full-time basis in the department. I hesitate. It becomes too personal. *The argument is too much to sustain when your body is so exposed*, when you feel so noticeable. I stop, and do not complete my answer to the question. [My italics.]

The body consigned to embody diversity is again overexposed and objectified. Racialized professor in the white university finds herself again in the impossible subject-object position of being both at the table and on the menu – position crafted and sustained by the academic appetite for diversity, repurposing minority knowledge projects and producers to buttress hegemony under neoliberalism, which constitutes, following Ferguson (2008: 162), "the latest expression of contemporary globalization's effort to *cannibalize difference* and its potential for rupture" (my italics).

Rarely is such "cannibalizing" more acute than in the academic management of Black feminism and Black feminist scholars. While the neoliberal white university's institutional arrangements make an array of minority thought projects desirable as extractable resources to uphold an image of diversity and multicultural progress, it also sequesters them to the margins (Crawley 2018: 10), the fate of Black feminism and Black women scholars calls for particular attention. Aware of this fatal fondness early on, Black feminist scholars made critical interventions. Writing a quarter century ago, Ann duCille called out the academic appetite for a kind of Black difference emptied of actual Black bodies – an academy ardent to "have that 'signifying Black difference' without the difference of significant blackness" (1994: 600). The same year, Barbara Christian cautioned: "It would be a tremendous loss, a distinct irony, if some version of Black feminist inquiry exists in the academy to which Black women are not major contributors" (1994: 173). With hindsight, one cannot but be in awe how farsighted these Black feminist academics have been in their grasp of the stakes involved in institutionalising minority knowledge fields/producers, particularly Black feminist scholarship. In their prescient interventions, they painted "a powerful picture of a bleak and ironic future, one in which the university's fetishization of black feminism as intellectual inquiry does not render impossible, and indeed in some ways facilitates, its systemic violence against black women" (Hong 2008: 96). This "double move of *hailing* and *failing*" (Bilge 2013) is part and parcel of contradictory and toxic interpellations of the neoliberal academy, and was identified by Bannerji from the onset, when she pointed out how "her" field "has become *trivialized and sanctified at the same time* as the 'mantra,' or perhaps a hegemonic device for teaching a certain kind of feminist theory in the universities, namely 'Gender, Race and Class'" (1995: 97, my italic). While "black feminism has sustained African American cultural theory at the same time as it has grounded the institutional existence of black studies for the last few decades" (Weheliye 2014: 5), it has continually faced cruel ironies of hailing and failing, when it is not outright disavowed. This failing can be literally lethal, as Grace Hong's long list of Black feminist academics who met with premature death in an extractivist academy acutely marked by a "pathological hatred of Black women" (Walcott 2018: 96) demonstrates. Consider the damning evidence Rinaldo Walcott gives about anti-black-womanness permeating Canadian academy:

> In my various positions over 20 years in the academy, I have witnessed how colleagues respond to Black women's presence in the academy. In almost every instance that a Black woman is mentioned, there is an attempt to move on to something else, to delegitimize, or to blatantly ignore. This position can only be understood in light of the ways in which Black women's feminist politics have retained the most significant critique of state and institution of any contemporary feminist politics. This insistence is one that consistently uncovers the ruses of diversity and inclusion as ongoing forms of violence, meant to incorporate a few at the expense of the many.
>
> *(ibid)*

Following unique insights from Black, women of colour and Indigenous feminist writings, along with queer of colour scholarship, I seek to interrogate here the ways in which minority knowledge fields and producers respond to neoliberal interpellations of the western university, particularly to its newfound fondness for difference that opens up toxic opportunities for them. My intervention aims to contribute to the growing literature on envisioning collectively other possibilities, alternative forms of relationality and counter-institutionality within the neoliberal white university. But first, I briefly situate my speaking position.

In unpacking power's operations through academic incorporation of minority knowledge projects/producers, including our own multifarious involvements in these processes as scholars working in these fields that routinely extract knowledge from minoritized communities, I am guided by Black feminism, which, as an intellectual project, reminds us the significance of being always clear about the social location from which we ask questions and provide criticism (Cooper 2017). This requires awareness of my own embeddedness in what I critique and of my own positioning in the circuits of power of the neoliberal university, as well as of my subjective positionality forged by and through these structural positions. I am a settler woman of colour, a first-generation immigrant academic with structural privileges of being tenured, almost white passing, and working in a top-five Canadian research-intensive university. I work in minority knowledge fields organized as subfields within the disciplinary structure of a sociology department in a French-speaking university where where I was for 14 years (till June 2019) the only fulltime faculty of non-European descent, the only non-white. Yet, it bears mentioning that I did not grow up as the ethnic/racialized Other of my origin society, Turkey. As Frankenberg reminds, in her conversation with Lata Mani, in the US context, "[t] his fundamental difference in life experiences [...] between those of us from the geographical Third World and those of us who came to adulthood as people of color in the West" must be taken into account to avoid problematic amalgamations between groups

> with very different relations to the US power structure. We need to be wary of the possibility that university affirmative action or diversity agendas might be met by filling positions with people trained elsewhere, a strategy common in the business world.
>
> *(1993: 297)*

Moreover, teaching undergraduate and graduate level courses on sociology of race and ethnic relations, gender and sexualities, intersectionality, and postcolonial/decolonial approaches, I am, incontestably, one of the agents of academic incorporation of these minority knowledge fields, serving doubly the institution: as a person embodying diversity – as someone "from diversity", as they like to call us here in Québec, who also teaches and researches these "object" matters.

Politics of minority knowledge

The term *minority* in *minority knowledges* doesn't refer to a statistical sense of less numerous, but a sociological one of *less power*, of being *minoritized*. Minority knowledge fields are the areas of scholarly work that emerged from the emancipatory social movements of the 1950s and 1960s and entered the western university through institutional compromise and devising which entail forms of containment and governance of dissent. As Ferguson (2008: 163) portrays, the historic beginning "in the late 1960s signifies a profound change within modern institutions in the West. Administrative power had to restrict the collective, oppositional, and redistributive aims of difference" while concurrently asserting it to signify institutional progress. For him, this validation does not only encode encouragement but also subjugation, concealing some forms of difference while asserting others. Incorporating differences entails hence a power calculus to assess their transformative and "ruptural capacities". Calling "this incorporation of modes of difference and the calculus that seeks to determine the properties and functions of those modes" the *will to institutionality*, Ferguson stresses how it doesn't only absorb institutions and modern subjects, but is itself a mode of subjection. (*ibid.*)

From the onset, there is tension between unsettling and settling down, between the desire to unsettle university's dominant frames of knowledge production, which reduce minorities to "objects of study" and serve to subjugate and govern them, and the push to conform to established disciplinary conventions and norms, to "take a seat" and become proper science, i.e. leave the politics out. This created an important conundrum, for these oppositional knowledge projects were never "simply about coming up with a better truth," but always comprised "an immanent critique of power/knowledge and disciplinarity" directed to disrupt "the machinery of knowledge from within the very institutions of knowledge" (Ferguson 2015: 45). Disrupting from within is far from easy. Several decades after the entry of minority knowledge projects and scarce numbers of racialized scholars to the university, their objectives are still to be met. These projects often face a double bind: being "enfolded into the neoliberal institutional mandates of the university through a particular proliferation as commodified and domesticated 'difference' that performs the ideological and material labor of buttressing late-capitalist mantras such as 'diversity and excellence' and 'global citizens'", and at the same time being "rendered vulnerable and periodically threatened with eradication within a university structure that is surrendering to the twin pressures of increased corporatization and economic duress" (Elia et al. 2016: 2–3).

If institutionally, "minority studies have been made up by necessity of whatever has been excluded from the canon and the mainstream work of the disciplines, the afterthought of the academy, if thought at all", as Alcoff and Mohanty argue, their academic reception has been equivalently depreciating: "these bodies of knowledge have been doubly devalued, or minoritized, within the academy: associated with scholars who face a general intellectual discrimination [...] , and attacked as inquiry that fails to achieve the ideal of academic disinterestedness" (2006: 7–8). One may notice the similarity between "minority knowledge" and Foucault's notion of "subjugated knowledge" defined as "a whole series of knowledges that have been disqualified as non-conceptual knowledges, as insufficiently elaborated knowledges: naïve knowledges, hierarchically inferior knowledges, knowledges that are below the required level of erudition and scientificity" ([1976]2003: 7). It must not go unmentioned that Foucault understood genealogy as a way to "desubjugate historical knowledges, [...] to enable them to oppose and struggle against the coercion of a unitary, formal, and scientific theoretical discourse" (11), which indicates how illusory is to think we can desubjugate these knowledges through dominant paradigms. Indeed, a major issue at stake in their entrance to the university revolved around the questions of the "collective knowledge of marginal peoples and the recovery of alternative, oppositional histories of domination and struggle" (Mohanty 1990: 184). The power of self-definition was central to debates about knowledge production and legitimation, particularly to "the pedagogical projects of fields such as women's studies, black studies, and ethnic studies" (*ibid*). Questions of self-representation and self-definition, and power to do so, were hence at the forefront of struggles waged to bring minority knowledge formations into the academy, as the frequency of terms such as "owning one's narrative", "agency" and "voice" evidences. But the knowledge politics of these critical new domains did not stop at self-definition/representation, for they also (ideally) entail a radical critique of knowledge itself, including knowledge produced in these new domains, what Cornel West calls a radical self-inventory of our own academic practices (1987). Our practices are constituted by and constitutive of the governmental rationalities, techniques and affects through which the neoliberal university is made and maintained. Unpacking how we contribute to hegemonic rearticulations is vital to act otherwise, to be able to envisage other relationships. It is a high stake seldom attained in by now disciplined minority knowledge formations, and it is not because of lack of knowledge, as many of the stakes were clearly identified by the late 1980s. Chandra Mohanty captures the double criticality these new, "often heretical", knowledges ought to articulate thusly:

> It is only in the late twentieth century, on the heels of domestic and global oppositional political movements, that [...] new analytic spaces have been opened up in the academy, spaces that make possible thinking of knowledge as praxis, of knowledge as embodying the very seeds of transformation and change. The appropriation of these analytic spaces and the challenge of radical education practice are thus to involve the development of critical knowledges (what women's, black, and ethnic studies attempt), and simultaneously, to critique knowledge itself.
>
> *(1990: 184–5)*

But the knowledge politics of these new projects, particularly their claims to self-representation and self-definition frontally clashed with mainstream scientific claims of objectivity, distance and axiological neutrality – a clash still very current, as the extent of present-day student protests for decolonising university/curricula around the world and the backlash to their claims in the name of scientificity, testify. Consequently, instead of radical transformation, a liberal inclusive approach putting forward being added as subject matters to extant disciplinary frames, sans attendant transformative epistemologies and methodologies, has become the most travelled path in the journey of minority knowledge integration. The push for "scientific" cloning is not simply an internal academic issue, but also comes from outside. Constant attacks from both the right and the left on identity politics ascribed to minority struggles and knowledge formations have forced scholars to distance themselves from their "organic" bases. These projects have lost to a large extent their relevance to communities and movements they claim to represent/serve and neglected their second task: criticism of knowledge itself, the one they produce. What's more, under the pressure to comply with narrowly defined scientific methods and disciplinary conventions, many either turned away from co-producing knowledge with their communities, or turned them into object of study. Seeking to increase one's value on the academic market, to be considered "properly scientific" are costly aspirations for minority scholars with community ties; the risk of exploiting one's community and morphing into an ethnic broker or curator is real.

However, there is always the route of refusal, refusing institutionality, power and recognition that come from being science. Instead of disciplining insurgent knowledges into science, shouldn't we rather ask ourselves the question, following Foucault ([1976]2003: 10), "about the aspiration to power that is inherent in the claim of being a science". Some minoritized knowledge fields resist better than others this siren's song and ensuing depoliticization; there is much to learn from a better grasp of context-specific conditions underlying their success. Sometimes, the tradition upon which a field is (seen to be) built consolidates or hinders its capacity of resisting neoliberal evisceration. For example, the history of the race and ethnic studies[3] field is dominantly narrated as squarely sitting with the sociological establishment, particularly the Chicago school and the work of Robert Park[4], rather than being associated to civil rights and ensuing freedom movements of the 1950s–1960s. Such lineage understands the field as a subfield of sociology or anthropology, instead of a counter-hegemonic knowledge project seeking to transform the terms and structures of what is considered science. An outcome of this is the perpetuation, under the new clothes of a "progressive" field, of the conventional scientific gaze that makes racially or ethnically othered groups an object of inquiry, which differs from the post-insurgent movement approach to them as *knowing subjects* producing valid knowledge about their own life-worlds – an approach also asserting the imperative of hiring minority scholars with ties to communities to teach and research these matters. In contrast, Black studies traces its origins on Black radical tradition and Black protest, which does not make it immune to be ingested as neo/liberal diversity, but provides to the collectivity a radical theoretical and activist memory to inspire and prod current practices. As Kelley (2016) argues:

> Black studies was conceived not just outside the university but in opposition to a Eurocentric university culture with ties to corporate and military power. Having emerged from mass revolt, insurgent black studies scholars developed institutional models based in, but largely independent of, the academy. In later decades, these institutions were – with varying degrees of eagerness – incorporated into the university proper in response to pressure to embrace multiculturalism.

The problem is not only the desubstantiation of radically transformative orientations of these fields, but also how their incorporation provides mainstream, business-as-usual, academic practices a new "politically-engaged" edge. A case in point is the tenacity of scientism in academic events pretending to unsettle knowledge hierarchies. Consider these examples. In a recent international conference on intersectionality, a plenary speaker exhorts the audience, among them many graduate students, to "enjoy the field! Go and have fun!" Projected at the backdrop, is the in/famous black and white photograph of Malinowski, towering in his all white attire on half-naked and crouched black bodies. Nobody contests the call and its dehumanising colonial gaze. Another place, another international conference: a keynote speaker asserts, in a 2017 North-American sociology and anthropology conference on in/disciplines and unsettling knowledges, that if one works *on* one's group it's not anthropology, and goes on with the tired routine of distance and objectivity, to then tell gleefully how he refused supervising a graduate student of Armenian descent who wanted to work on her family trauma related to genocide, advising her instead to go into therapy! This also goes unchallenged. "Incidents" like these are too numerous to list here; but their regularity and the lack of any significant challenge when they unfold tell something important about the inertia in our scholarly communities – inertia as if "[c]ollectively all of us – all we liberal academics – were struck with a paralysis of will as the system not only grew around us, but built us into its own body-walls" (Thompson 1970: 303).

But then how does one get built into the system's body-walls? Alongside Thompson's incisive remark, we might take on board Derrida's, that our intellectual work itself is integral to institutional immurement: "An institution is not merely a few walls or some outer structures surrounding, protecting, guaranteeing, or restricting the freedom of our work; it is also and already the structure of our interpretation" (2004: 102). Our academic practices and values, relationships to institutionality, which are understudied in the otherwise critical scholarships of our critical fields, prove to be at the heart of the matter. Although there is enough work lamenting the adverse effects of institutionalisation on minoritized knowledge fields, research is lacking on the specific terms and structures through which these fields have been institutionalized and with what consequences. Same negligence applies to symbolic and material conditions that forge and organize our meaning-making within "our" fields. Neglecting these issues hinders our ability to grasp how much the parameters of what we do within these fields, how we produce knowledge, understand equity, justice and so on, are affected by the techniques, arrangements and rationalities governing the institutionalising of our initially insurgent fields and selves. As Chandan Reddy puts it: "the terms and structures through which institutionality [of ethnic studies] is achieved become the basis for the meaning and appearance of racial equality" (2011: 30). In fine, by overlooking these dimensions we also overlook, following Derrida, the fact that the institution is also and already the structure of our interpretation, that the conduits and mechanisms of institutionalization also impact the meaning-making within these epistemic communities carrying minoritized difference.

Clickbaiting diversity

It would hardly be an exaggeration to say that the neoliberal university's embrace of minority difference, repackaged as diversity – "our difference becomes their diversity" (Ahmed 2009: 43), is mainly driven by corporate interests; it is "neither antiracist nor redistributive, instead it seeks to generate surplus value out of diversity or desire for the surplus value produced by diversity" (Roediger 2017: Kindle). Moreover, as several scholars and student movements argue, the limited integration of racialized elites effectively conceals the domination of masses under neoliberal multiculturalism and its white supremacist foundations (Reddy 2019). Under the university's neoliberal administrative regime, "diversity, inclusion, and multiculturalism are each used with varied intensities to leave the racialist logics in play and place" (Crawley 2018: 10), which disciplinary ordering is integral to. Often, we/BIPOC scholars working in minority knowledge fields get built into the neoliberal western university's body-walls as diversity – when we are immured as diversity, the university's walls become diverse through us, projecting outside a happy, colourful face (Ahmed 2009). Yet, this process does not forbid alternative ways of responding to neoliberal interpellations that disrupt rather than comfort the hegemonic project, for hegemony is never complete and its contradictions breed the means of its own contestation. As Ferguson posits,

> [a]s the university figured and figures prominently in the critical and dominant production of minority difference and in all of these aspects of liberal and neoliberal multiculturalism, the university also becomes a site of struggle and contestation, a site in which minority difference can be maneuvered against liberal and neoliberal social practices.
>
> *(2015: 48)*

The neoliberal university's embrace of diversity may take multiple forms – creating minority knowledge programmes in ethnic studies or WGS, commissions to launch and govern institutional equity, diversity and inclusion (EDI) agendas, hiring (in ridiculously low numbers) minority knowledge producers; but rarely do they lead to any significant transformation in the university's power structure. They are not designed for that. Quite the contrary! Some scholars tackled this phenomenon from the angle of "commodification of difference", which has led to categorical stances equating commodification with unequivocal dispossession of insurgent knowledges from their emancipatory projects. I feel ambivalent vis-à-vis commodification when used as the primary analytical angle for three main reasons: first, its reading of hegemonic co-optation (dispossession) obscures how hegemonic rearticulations are instable processes with cracks, contradictions, and contesting/subverting actors from within. Second, it often romanticises minority knowledge fields as inherently insurgent, even "safe" spaces unencumbered by power, and curtails the self-critique imperative – foreclosing thereby interpretive possibilities of the "historical coincidence" between the rise of these knowledge projects and the neoliberal reconfiguration of power alignments between the state, capital and the academy (Hall 1991; Ferguson 2012). Third, commodity no longer constitutes the core of our current capitalist moment; neoliberal reason's complexity and its ambiguous relationship to difference cannot be adequately captured by putting the commodity relation as the model of all social relations and by making neoliberalism synonym for ruthless commodification of society as a whole (Dardot & Laval 2013). Several analysts concur that commodity's centrality has been replaced by something else; for many, the successor is credit (or debt). These shifts and their impacts need to be accounted for. For one, there is substantial difference between the classical liberal market and the new financial neoliberal market: The former viewed all individuals as potential traders having something to sell, whereas for the latter we are all investment-seeking projects (Feher 2017). We are hence hailed in asking ourselves constantly "what is my credit value" and seeking to increase our "human capital" value, which provides a promising inquiry line to think neoliberal academic subjectivities at large, and those of POC academics interpellated as diversity in particular. Ultimately, neoliberal capitalism interpellates us differently as subjects than classic capitalism did, and this difference makes a difference on the transformation of our relationships to our academic work, to each other and to ourselves.

Accordingly, Dardot and Laval's proposition is more useful and generative than the commodification of difference angle. Engaging Foucault's work, they argue that neoliberalism is not merely an ideology or economic policy, but is first and foremost a new rationality – a governmental one. This new rationality deploys the market logic "as a generalized normative logic, from the state to innermost subjectivity" (2013: Kindle Loc425). Far from being "the spontaneous expansion of the commodity sphere and the field of accumulation" (188), neoliberalism "tends to structure and organize not only the actions of rulers, but also the conduct of the ruled" (110), and deploys to that end "unprecedented techniques of power over conduct and subjectivities" (188) and advances by incorporating its own critiques. In fine, these readings provide better tools to address the ambiguities and contradictions of a phenomenon that is only partially-captured by the commodification of difference. Stuart Hall's work holds a peerless position among them. Discussing capital's newfound interest in difference, Hall explains how globalized neoliberalism couldn't keep its hold without learning to live with and work through difference, but also, to that end, tried to resignify, incorporate, and govern difference:

> [I]n order to maintain its global position, capital has had to negotiate [...] had to incorporate and partly reflect the differences it was trying to overcome. It had to try to get hold of, and neutralize, to some degree, the differences. It is trying to constitute a world in which things are different [...] but the differences do not matter.
>
> *(1991: 32–3)*

For Hall, this new form of economic power "lives culturally through difference and [...] is constantly teasing itself with the pleasures of transgressive Other" (31), while absorbing and partially neutralising disruptive difference, turned into governable, benign difference. Disruptive difference brought to the forefront by emancipatory social movements was not only a challenge for ruling power, but also an opportunity to refurbish hegemony by institutionalising difference. For Ferguson (2012: 42), this meant a new societal contradiction: minority self-affirmation, undertaking a radical critique of hegemony, also becomes a site, through its institutionalisation, of unprecedented opportunities for power to rearticulate its hegemony. Initially critical of "the presumed benevolence of political and economic institutions", these differences were absorbed "within an administrative ethos that recast [them] as testaments to the progress of the university and the resuscitation of a common national culture" (Ferguson 2008: 162–3). Significantly, the terms and structures of their institutionalisation intruded into the theoretical structures, interpretive frames and thinking tools of these fields, transforming their meanings – which illustrate Hall's point about how neoliberalism incorporates, partly reflects and resignifies the differences it tries to overcome, turning them into differences that don't make any difference, into diversity which is difference without adversity. As Reddy argues,

> With historical hindsight, we can see the liberal institutionalization of race within which ethnic studies programs were often forcibly contextualized – or made into pure context – in their emergence on college and university campuses. [...] [W]e see that liberal institutionalization has sought from ethnic studies not a genealogical critique of the modern university within racial capitalism, but the development of a representative cross-racial class within the educational institution whose appearance and restricted space of effort it promotes as exhausting the meaning of racial equality.
>
> *(2011: 30)*

Yet, hegemonic (re)articulations are never absolute, given hegemony's instability and contradictions, which house possibilities for disruption, counter-hegemonic rearticulation or subversive subterranean coexistence. The absorption of minoritized difference by the state, capital, and the university does not only "produce anew the occasion for white self-ordering" (Crawley 2018: 11), and provide opportunities for hegemony's renewal, but also encompasses unpredictable fissures and fault zones for its destabilization. In this light, Bannerji's autophagy qua pedagogy constitutes an instance of such subversion – one that may join bigger streams of refusal flowing within and eroding the neoliberal white settler university.

Learning from Black and Indigenous refusals

Viewing neoliberalism as "a postpolitical discourse that progressive scholars also inhabit" (Blalock 2015: 73), rather than merely a conservative ideology, provides a wider angle for assessing how the neoliberal university interpellates us all. Yet, we are also interpellated differently along the lines of differentially intersecting axes of power – axes that are both irreducible (the principle of non-equivalence) and inseparable (Bilge 2015). Moreover, our responses to neoliberal interpellations are highly dissimilar, even among BIPOC academics. As noted above, interpellated into the white academy as a "South Asian woman" teaching race, Bannerji retorts by subverting her dehumanized object status through a pedagogy of self-cannibalizing which enables her to survive and resist. She collectivizes her anger and struggle, anchors them to a multigenerational lineage between those who march with us and those who will come after: "Undoing history soils us, cuts us up. We are in the front line. Others are coming along with and behind us, someday we will be whole" (1995: 106).

Others may respond to them by becoming ethnic intermediaries and making their insider knowledge and cultural competencies available to the institution in the pursuit of noble and less noble motives – from promoting racial equality within the institution to personal gain. Investing the institution, putting faith in it attracted sizeable criticism from BIPOC scholars for some time now. Notably, Cornel West took issue with "minority canon formation" which, he charged, "principally reproduces and reinforces prevailing forms of cultural authority" (1987: 198). To answer his mordant questions, "what does it mean to engage in canon formation at this historical moment? [...] what role do the class and professional interests of the canonizers play in either the enlarging of a canon or the making of multiple, conflicting canons?", West proceeds through "a critical self-inventory of [his] own intellectual activity as an Afro-American cultural critic" (193). Decoding the debates over Afro-American canon formation through the rise of liberal multiculturalism in the 1980s US academy, West tackles not only the class interests of Black scholars who "become the academic superintendents of a segment of an expanded canon or a separate canon", but also how their inclusion is "held up as evidence for the success of prevailing ideologies of pluralism" (197) – a still valid argument as recent debates confirm. Thus, three decades later, Kelley argues that liberal multiculturalism has never been about remedying "the historical legacies of racism, dispossession, and injustice" but rather "bring[ing] some people into the fold of a 'society no longer seen as racially unjust'" (2016). Likewise, Walcott (2018) urges us to refuse the liberal inclusive path that integrates few racialized elites to the detriment of the masses while perpetuating structural oppression and underlines our responsibility as scholars to refuse individual enticements that such path offers. Such incentives are integral to what I call *diversity clickbaiting*, which is a double entendre in that institution clickbaits diversity to enrol scholars "from diversity" to its hegemonic project, while at the same time, scholars "from diversity" become the bait used by the institution to attract new "clienteles" (students) that would become future generations of experts governing difference for the state and capital. Refusing to celebrate individual "success" as if it is collective, Walcott stresses that "compensatory individualism that characterizes our present moment requires a rigorous refusal", and pursues:

> Make no mistake about it, current logics of anti-racism, equity, and even social justice have as their other the Black subject. We never collectively benefit from their institutional performativity. The benefit is reserved for those closer to white – white not only as phenotype, but as instituted antiblackness and thus white supremacist logics.
>
> *(2018: 93)*

These scholars urge us to see the inclusive performativity unfolding in today's university for what it is: cosmetic reformism that colludes with the forces of oppression. Yet, this heated debate about whether to invest or divest the university is not the whole story, as some divest even this debate; they refuse its terms and choices (pro/contra). Instead, they propose no less than sedition and maroonage, arguing that we can only hide from neoliberal interpellations in fugitive spaces. Fred Moten and Stefano Harney articulate this latter journey as "undercommons":

> [t]he only possible relationship to the university today is a criminal one. […] it cannot be denied that the university is a place of refuge, and it cannot be accepted that the university is a place of enlightenment. In the face of these conditions one can only sneak into the university and steal what one can. To abuse its hospitality, to spite its mission, to join its refugee colony, […] to be in but not of – this is the path of the subversive intellectual in the modern university. […] After all, the subversive intellectual came under false pretenses, with bad documents, out of love. Her labor is as necessary as it is unwelcome. The university needs what she bears but cannot bear what she brings. And on top of all that, she disappears. She disappears into the underground, […] into the *undercommons of enlightenment*, where the work gets done, where the work gets subverted, where the revolution is still black, still strong.
>
> *(2013: 26)*

Harney and Moten's work struck a sensitive nerve with academic public, spreading "like wildfire among the PhD precariat and radical-thinking graduate students. For many young scholars cobbling together a life adjuncting, [their] critique of the university spoke an essential truth" (Kelley 2016). Their refusal to view the university as an enlightened place made sense to many, particularly to those facing its racialized, classed, gendered, ableist and heterosexist structures. The undercommons they propose, says Kelley (2016), "is a fugitive network where a commitment to abolition and collectivity prevails over a university culture bent on creating socially isolated individuals whose academic skepticism and claims of objectivity leave the world-as-it-is intact."

There is much to learn from reading, alongside this Black radical refusal, another major refusal praxis developed by Indigenous scholars (Simpson 2007; Grande 2018). Building on Indigenous land-based pedagogies and resistance against settler colonialism, this refusal also addresses extractivism, particularly academic extractivism which was and still is integral to larger sets of extractivist relationships attempting to subjugate Indigenous peoples (Smith 2012). As Michi Saagiig Nishnaabeg writer, musician, and "recovering academic", Leanne Betasamosake Simpson puts it:

[T]he extractivist mindset isn't about having a conversation and having a dialogue and bringing in Indigenous knowledge on the terms of Indigenous peoples. It is very much about extracting whatever ideas scientists or environmentalists thought were good and assimilating it … put it onto toilet paper and sell it to people. There's an intellectual extraction, a cognitive extraction, as well as a physical one. […] there's a responsibility on the part of mainstream […] society to figure out a way of living more sustainably and extracting themselves from extractivist thinking.

(quoted in Klein 2013)

Indigenous critique of academic extractivism ought to be carefully engaged, as it tackles a central problem and is not itself immune to misappropriation. Despite ubiquitous gesturing to power-knowledge nexus and lip-service to "decolonize knowledge" across minority knowledge fields, community responsibility remains elusive. Our fields are yet to do their radical self-inventories about extractivist research and teaching practices where knowledge taken from minoritized communities and students is not used in their terms and do not benefit them. As our programmes do not include mandatory courses on decolonial epistem-ologies and non-extractivist research practices (they never will), we have to smuggle these counter-methods and knowledges into mandatory and optional courses; otherwise our teach-ing also produces the next generation of researcher-extractivists. In many institutional con-texts, we, the professoriate, have still that latitude. We can take our cues from alternative practices such as the "convivial[5] research" practiced in the Universidad de la Tierra, a multisite alternative university in Mexico rooted in "vernacular" knowledges. Convivial research is not only a research about a minoritized community, but a research "grounded in that community in the interest of the preservation and survival of that community", a research also "predicated on the notion that knowledge already exists within that commu-nity, and it's about trying to figure out exactly how to understand and to honor that know-ledge" (Moten in Cooper et al. 2018: 167–8). We can take our cues from the ethical refusal framework that Quechua scholar Sandy Grande proposes – framework bridging the Black radical and Indigenous theories for co-resistance against the white settler university and towards emancipatory futures. Built on three main commitments – collectivity, reciprocity, and mutuality, this framework urges us to refuse individual enticements and personal brand-ing to collectivise knowledge production; to practice community responsibility and establish relationships of deep reciprocity that make ourselves "answerable to those communities we claim as our own and those we claim to serve" and also "being answerable to each other and our work" (2018: 61). And last, the commitment to mutuality relates to reciprocity but is more encompassing; it asserts connection particularly to land and intergenerational com-munity and fosters "the development of social relations not contingent upon the imperatives of capital – that refuses exploitation" (*ibid.*).

Coda

Is there a way out of the lived paradox of being interpellated as accomplices of a university system that usurps radical liberation struggles and their attendant knowledge projects to refur-bish and rearticulate neo/liberal arrangements that govern and extract profit from difference, from us? Is there a way out of the university system that clickbaits diversity and lures us into baiting ourselves qua diversity – which amounts to saying that we end up eating ourselves? If "the fully racialized social and epistemological architecture upon which the modern uni-versity is built cannot be radically transformed by 'simply' adding darker faces, safer spaces, better training, and a curriculum that acknowledges historical and contemporary oppressions" (Kelley 2016), then what? There is enough evidence that criticism of the university from within can be enfolded into the neoliberal project and aligned with hegemonic ends, so much so that the criticality itself, the professionalized critical academic, becomes a cornerstone holding the edifice in place (Harney & Moten 2013: 31). These are the contradictions of our times we ought to work with and through. While there is no one-size -fits-all strategy, it matters that we seize on these contradictions and widen institutional crevices to nest our fugitive spaces. The university "lulls us into believing that politics – to lobby for access to, or control over, such institutions – is our only salvation" (Kelley 2016). Far from being our salvation, this path proves to be our damnation[6]. The violence of sitting at the table of neo/liberal inclusion while being simultaneously displayed on the menu is real. Other paths exist – knowingly uncleared paths interconnecting under the radar, where the ungovernable work, useless for the administrative power, still gets done

Notes

1 This chapter builds on my on-going (SSHRC-funded) research on minority knowledges and the neoliberal academy.
2 The saying's origins are unclear. "Many seem to believe it originated in Washington, DC somewhere around 2000". Carol Bush, "If You're Not at the Table, You're on the Menu" www.oncnursing news.com/nurse-blogs/carol_bush/1213/if-youre-not-at-the-table-youre-on-the-menu 30 Dec 2013.
3 The "field" is organized differently in different academic and national contexts. In the US, ethnic studies often serves as an umbrella term encompassing specific minority knowledge projects such as Black, African-American, Asian-American, Latinx, Native/Indigenous, Arab-American, Puerto-Rican studies, so on. In Canada, the history of established programs and degrees in Black studies is much shorter, and its geography across provinces smaller – there is no Black studies in Francophone universities. Also, Black and Indigenous studies are not subsumed under ethnic studies; the latter often forms a subfield in sociology and anthropology departments. It is likely that inclusion as a subfield into an established discipline such as sociology, which is still ridden with Eurocentric epistemology to say the least, renders race and ethnic studies more vulnerable to disciplinary cloning and domestication.
4 Park intentionally obscured the seminal work of WEB DuBois, who is still denied his status as a founding figure of American sociology (Morris 2015).
5 It is worth noting the etymological meaning of convivial, from the Latin convivere, living together.
6 This is a rather belated realization for me, as I've put my faith for too long in a vision that considers reformist endeavours as complementary and not oppositional to insurgent ones. Like recent converts becoming over-zealous, my remarks may reflect such flaws, which I own for they also reflect where I am now in my academic journey vis-à-vis institutionality.

References

Ahmed, S 2009, Embodying diversity, *Race Ethnicity and Education*, 12:1, 41–52.
Alcoff, L & Mohanty, S 2006, Reconsidering identity politics. In L Alcoff et al (ed.), *Identity politics reconsidered*, (1–9), New York: Palgrave-Macmillan.
Bannerji, H 1995, *Thinking Through*, Toronto: Women's Press.
Bilge, S 2013, Intersectionality undone, *DuBois Review*, 10:2, 405–424.
Bilge, S 2015, Le blanchiment de l'intersectionnalité, *Recherches féministes*, 28:2, 9–32.
Blalock, C 2015, Neoliberalism and the crisis of legal theory, *Law and contemporary problems*, 77:4, 71–103.
Christian, B 1994, Diminishing returns. Can Black feminism(s) survive the academy? In DT Goldberg (ed.), *Multiculturalism: A Critical Reader*, (168–179), Oxford: Blackwell.
Cooper, A, Walcott, R & Hughes, L 2018, Robin DG Kelley and Fred Moten in conversation, *Critical Ethnic Studies*, 4:1, 154–172.
Cooper, B 2017, *Beyond Respectability*, Urbana: University of Illinois Press.

Crawley, A 2018, Introduction to the academy and what can be done? *Critical Ethnic Studies*, 4:1, 4–19.

Dardot, C & Laval, P 2013, *The New Way of the World*, London: Verso.

Derrida, J 2004, *Eyes of the University*, Stanford: Stanford University Press.

DuCille, A 1994, The occult of true Black womanhood, *Signs*, 19:3, 591–629.

Elia et al 2016, Introduction: a sightline. In *Critical Ethnic Studies: A Reader*, (2–15), Durham: Duke UP.

Feher, M 2017, *Le temps des investis*, Paris: Découverte.

Ferguson, R 2008, The will to institutionality, *Radical History Review*, 100, 158–169.

——— 2012, *The reorder of things*, Minneapolis: University of Minnesota Press.

——— 2015, University, *Critical Ethnic Studies*, 1:1, 43–55.

Foucault, M [1976]2003, *Society must be defended*, New York: Picador.

Frankenberg, R & Mani, L 1993, Race, 'postcoloniality' and the politics of location, *Cultural Studies*, 7:2, 292–310.

Grande, S 2018, Refusing university, In E Tuck & KW Yang (eds.), *Toward What Justice?* (47–65), New York: Routledge.

Hall, S 1991, The local and the global, In AD King (ed.), *Culture, Globalization and the World-System*, (19–39), Minneapolis: University of Minnesota Press.

——— 1997, The spectacle of the 'other', In S Hall (ed.), *Representation*, (223–279), London: Sage.

Harney, S & Moten, F 2013, *The Undercommons*, Wivenhoe/New York/Port Watson: Autonomedia.

Hong, G 2008, 'The future of our worlds': Black feminism and the politics of knowledge, *Meridians*, 8:2, 95–115.

Kelley, RDG 2016, Black study, black struggle, *Boston Review* (March 7). http://bostonreview.net/forum/robin-d-g-kelley-black-study-black-struggle

Klein, N 2013, Dancing the world into being: a conversation with Idle-No-More's Leanne Simpson. *Yes Magazine* (March 5). http://Black.yesmagazine.org/peace-justice/dancing-the-world-into-being-a-conversation-with-idle-no-more-leanne-simpson

Mohanty, C 1990, On race and voice, *Cultural Critique*, 14, 179–208.

Morris, A 2015, *The Scholar Denied*, Oakland: University of California Press.

Reddy, C 2011, *Freedom from Violence*, Durham: Duke UP.

——— 2019. Neoliberalism then and now: Race, sexuality, and the black radical tradition, *GLQ*, 25:1, 150–155.

Roediger, D 2017, *Class, Race, and Marxism*, London: Verso.

Simpson, A 2007, On ethnographic refusal: Indigeneity, 'voice' and colonial citizenship, *Junctures*, 9, 67–80.

Smith, LT 2012, *Decolonizing Methodologies*, Sydney: Zed Books.

Thompson, EP 1970, The business university, *New Society*, 386, 301–304.

Walcott, R 2018, Against social justice. In E Tuck & KW Yang (eds.), *Toward what justice?* (85–99), New York: Routledge.

Weheliye, A 2014, *Habeas Viscus*, Durham: Duke UP.

West, C 1987, Minority discourse and the pitfalls of canon formation, *Yale Journal of Criticism*, 1:1, 193–202.

25

Racial discrimination in the name of women's rights

On contemporary racism in Sweden

Minoo Alinia

In recent years, a celebration of "Swedish values" and "Swedish culture" has been one of the most frequent themes in the speeches and articles of many politicians and opinion formers. This became so prevalent during the annual political week in Sweden, known as *Almedalsveckan*,[1] in 2016 that Gunnar Hökmark—a politician whose party is a member of the centre-right coalition —was moved to note that values are constantly changing, and that people should instead be talking about the rules and laws on which we all agree (Hökmark's blog 8 June 2016). This nationalist discourse or rhetoric was not an isolated or occasional phenomenon. It was preceded and followed by other examples that demonstrate a clear pattern. For example, in her speech delivered on Sweden's national day (6 June 2016), Anna Kindberg Batra, the former leader of the Moderate Party (*Moderatema*) and former leader of the opposition, used words and phrases such as Swede and Swedish values 86 times—once every 20 seconds (Opinion Almedalen, 9 June 2016, SVT, interview with Anna Kindberg Batra). Such statements used to be limited to those positioned on the right and centre of Swedish politics but they have gradually become more acceptable and normalized across all political blocs. Ylva Johansson, the former labour market minister (2014–2019) in the Social Democrat government, has made a number of statements where she raises "Swedish values", suggesting, for example, a "strengthened orientation towards Swedish values for new migrants" (*Dagens Nyheter* 2017-12-11).

In little more than two decades a discourse that defines violence against women in relation to migrant communities as their "culture" has gained currency and the authority to define the problem and set the agenda, even though marginalized, critical opinions also exist. The problems with culturalization and the way it racializes society have been addressed in a number of studies in Sweden (e.g. Alinia, 2011, 2013, 2019; Baianstovu, 2012; Carbin, 2010; Gruber, 2007; Mulinari and Lundqvist, 2018; NCK, 2010, 2013; Pérez, 2014) and elsewhere (e.g. Al-Ali, 2008; Keskinen, 2009; Razack, 2004; Korteweg and Yurdakul, 2010: 40–41; Wallach Scott, 2007; Welchman and Hossain, 2005; Werbner, 2007). This article aims to shed light on the discourses and practices of racialization and social exclusion in Sweden that occur at the intersection of gender and ethnicity. Racialization of non-western minorities and especially those from Muslim majority countries is not entirely a Swedish phenomenon. Nor is the interplay between gender and race/ethnicity in these processes exclusively Swedish. However, each country and each context has its own specificities. Sweden can be distinguished by its dominant and fairly normalized culturalist discourse, which I call honour discourse. According to this discourse, people who originate from Muslim-majority societies, especially the Middle East, are driven by "honour culture" and therefore violence against women is a natural part of their behaviour (see Alinia, 2011, 2013; Baianstovu, 2012; Carbin, 2010; Gruber, 2007; Keskinen, 2009; Pérez, 2014). For example, in 2016 some neighbourhoods in southern Stockholm began campaigning to stop refugees moving to their areas. In expressing their concerns and fears in letters and emails of protest to the local authorities, campaigners referred in particular to issues of sexuality (*SVT Nyheter*, 10 May 2016; Björn af Kleen 2016). The notion of honour constitutes a dividing line that separates "we" from "them" and as Eduards (2007) puts it, honour is today at the core of the construction of Swedish identity.

Cultural pathology and the construction of otherness: a contextual background

When it comes to the discourse and policy on violence in the name of honour in Sweden, it is possible to talk about before and after Fadimeh Sahindal, a young woman from Turkey with a Kurdish background who was killed by her own father in 2002. She was shot dead because she refused to enter into a forced marriage with a cousin and instead fell in love with the "wrong" man. Although it was not the first case of murder of this kind, it attracted huge media attention and made violence against women in migrant settings highly visible. Before 2002, domestic violence against women with a migrant background was more or less tolerated, or ignored, by society and its representatives. Perpetrators were seen as victims of their culture and therefore received lesser punishment (Carbin, 2010; Eldén, 1998: 91; Ertürk, 2009; Westerstrand and Eldén, 2004). The violence was regarded as cultural in those countries and regions from which the victims and perpetrators or their families originated. Thus, instead of seeing it as criminal acts that should be punished according to existing legislation, the violence was regarded as people's belief and behaviour. The outcome of this different treatment of gender-based violence was discrimination against women with a migrant and Muslim background.

In the aftermath of the murder of Fadimeh Sahindal, strong and justified criticism was directed at the previous policy of silence and tolerance, including from a number of politicians and opinion formers. The problem, however, was that the majority of the criticism was not directed at the ideologies and politics that were behind the silence and tolerance, that is, culturalization of gender-based violence (Alinia, 2013). Instead, it was diversity, difference and the coexistence of differences that came to be questioned in many ways (Alinia, 2011; Carbin, 2010; Eduards, 2007). Hence, instead of accusing the "culturalization of politics" (Brown, 2006; Žižek, 2009) that motivated a culturalization of gender-based violence and led to a politics of silence and tolerance of the violence, it was people from certain backgrounds, mainly Muslims, who were identified as the problem. Thus, the politics of difference continued in a new form as tolerance was replaced by aversion and hatred (see Brown, 2006). Ever since, the notion of "honour culture" and "honour violence" has constituted a major dividing line between "we" and "them", that is those with a "Swedish culture" and those with an "honour culture" (Alinia, 2019). Mona Sahlin, who at the time was the Minister for Integration, told the newspaper *Dagens Nyheter* on 8 June 2001: "Everybody must follow Sweden's view on freedom and equality … If people refuse to adapt we must find ways to enforce Swedish values" (Cited by Lernestedt, 2006: 288).

This must be seen in a wider global political context. The murder took place in February 2002, only a few months after "9/11" and within the discursive and political climate of the "war on terror" and the "clash of civilizations", at a time when the whole idea of diversity and coexistence across cultures and differences was being questioned. In such a discursive and political climate, the murder provided more fuel for the arguments against previous multicultural policies and above all against the idea of diversity and the mixing of people (Alinia, 2011, 2013, 2019; Carbin, 2010; Keskinen, 2009). In fact, the multicultural society that had been official policy in Sweden since the 1970s had been problematic, as despite its excellent intentions, it gave rise to ethnic enclaves and ethnic segregation in Sweden (Ålund and Schierup, 1991). However, what was questioned by culturalist opponents were not the problems with certain aspects of multiculturalism, but the whole idea of diversity and the coexistence of difference.

To sum up, the culturalization of violence against women within migrant communities has not proved able to contribute to a just society free from violence and oppression. This is because it can only offer two equally discriminatory approaches: tolerating violence against women with a migrant background in the name of culture, and thereby discriminating against women and normalizing violence against them; or racializing people with a migrant background in the name of gender equality by ascribing to them an "honour culture" and "honour violence", and thereby excluding them from society and social power. Currently, it is the latter that is in the foreground and still dominant despite the existence of an active, albeit marginalized, opposition. These two discriminatory approaches do not differ essentially, but they are the two poles of what Werbner (2007) calls a "racial discourse of cultural pathology" and as such are able to replace each other whenever the political context demands or allows it.

Theoretical and methodological positioning

The power of knowledge and the violence of discourse

The broad concept of violence used here is not limited to subjective and directed violence, but includes symbolic and structural violence (Žižek, 2009). The focus of this article is the symbolic violence committed through the exclusionary and racializing discourses and practices of everyday life. The production of knowledge, perceptions and "truth" in society is conducted through language, discourse and ideology. Hence, the study of discourses and ideologies, and their social and political effects should also consider the symbolic violence that is inherent within them (see Fairclough, 2015; van Dijk, 1993) and the everyday racism (Essed, 1991) to which they contribute. Access to resources such as status and authority imply the right to define a problem, give the discourse legitimacy and authority, and make it appear "the truth". It is in this regard that the elite's discourse and its importance to the production of social knowledge must be understood (van Dijk, 1993).

Illiberal treatment in the name of liberal values

To understand the Swedish discourse and policy on gender-based violence within migrant communities and its variations, I employ Wendy Brown's conceptualization of tolerance and aversion (Brown, 2006). From this perspective, the policy of tolerance must be understood as a "tool for managing" differences that are construed as "essential" and therefore as "non-political" (ibid.: 24). As Brown notes:

> Tolerance, a beacon of civilization, is inappropriately extended to those outside civilization *and* opposed to civilization; violence, which tolerance represses, is the only means of dealing with this threat and is thereby self-justifying. (2006: 179)

Tolerance, depoliticization and culturalization are elements of a "civilizational discourse" that Brown argues has a dual function. It not only defines the superiority of western civilization, but also:

> Legitimize[s] liberal policies' illiberal treatment of selected practices, peoples, and states. They sanction illiberal aggression toward what is marked as intolerable without tarring the 'civilized' status of the aggressor. (2006: 179)

The politics of difference: rights, experience and agency

An important aspect of the culturalist honour discourse concerns its notion of difference, which implies othering, objectification and essentialization. Violence against women is universal but women's experiences of violence and oppression vary strongly depending on their different histories and different socio-economic and political contexts. The problem with cultural explanations is the lack of attention paid to different local histories and contexts, to relations of domination and subordination, and to the multidimensionality of experiences of gender-based violence. As Mohanty (2003) puts it, the greatest challenge in a diverse society is to historicize and explain our differences in terms of historicity and agency in a way that makes it possible to understand each other and build solidarity across dividing lines (ibid.: 219; see also Collins, 2009). It is, however, as Mohanty notes, not enough just to "acknowledge" differences. The idea of differences as natural, essential and unbridgeable is highly problematic and racializing. This "culturalization of politics" hides the mechanisms of power and domination, and depoliticizes, "naturalizes" and "neutralizes" social conflict and difference by presenting them as cultural (Žižek, 2009: 119; Brown, 2006: 15). The idea of difference as a set of benign variations or diversities, where conflicts, struggles and contradictions are totally erased, is also problematic as according to Mohanty, this evokes an image of a harmonious and empty pluralism (2003: 220).

Construction of Sweden and its other

Colonial and Orientalist conceptions of "the Other" have always been gendered (Said, 1978). However, notions of the sexualized "Other" have shifted over time according to different discursive and political circumstances. In the new century, and in the post-9/11 political climate (Keskinen, 2009; Wallach Scott, 2007; Yuval-Davis, 2011), it is no longer promiscuity but chastity, "honour culture" and "honour violence" that are associated with the notion of the Other. The idea of essentially and naturally different worlds is an example of a fundamentalist positioning represented and justified by the honour discourse, and normalized and reproduced in everyday discourses and practices (Alinia, 2013, 2019). Racial notions of the West and its "Others" as hierarchically organized cultural worlds are not something abstract. Nor are their connections to the Swedish discourse limited to those who explicitly adhere to racist ideologies. They are also demonstrated in what might appear to be "innocent" and "well-intentioned" comments (See Essed, 1991), as is illustrated below.

"Swedish values", "we" and "the Other"

In her speech at *Almedalsveckan* on 6 July 2016, Ebba Busch Thor, the leader of the Christian Democrats (*Kisdemokraterna*), said the following:

> Sweden, Sweden, my beloved country. I love you, not because your strawberries are the most delicious, not because your meadows, your fields and your archipelagos are the most beautiful. I love you because you are my home. [...] We who live here shape our life on grounds that we have inherited from our ancestors and those who have been living here and residing here before us. [...] We have much to be proud of but there is also much that needs to change and improve. Sweden is in a crisis of values. Those values that have built our home strong, such as trust, freedom, equality and equal value for all human beings, are under threat. Many people wonder where our society is going. We see people who ignore people in need. Women cannot go to festivals without fear of sexual outrages and molestation. Youth gangs batter a lonely old man. And people travel to Syria to fight for IS. These are obvious signs of a deep crisis of values that our society is caught in. Such things break down and weaken. They do not equip us for future challenges. These things create insecurity in our home—Sweden.

This speech was given in a context of intensely negative public opinion on and fear and securitization of migration and migrants. One issue that was loudly discussed was the sexual assaults and outrages committed by two groups of refugees in Stockholm and Cologne in 2014 and 2015. This was presented as a phenomenon that had not existed before but arrived with recent migration. The perpetrators were presented as representative of their countries' people, moral values and culture, which was described as "honour culture".

Anna Kindberg Batra, mentioned above, was interviewed after her speech at *Almedalsveckan* (9 July 2016). Asked to explain why it was so important to talk about "Swedish values" now, she replied that it was important because:

> We have sexual outrages at music festivals, we have outrages in asylum camps, we have had discussions about whether we should shake hands with people of the opposite sex in public spaces, and different similar small and big issues of various kinds. [...] And I think we should do so because perceptions of right and wrong change as our surrounding world changes and challenges arise. Sweden is really such a good society and gender equality is part of this; and we should try to ensure that it remains that way.

Kindberg Batra repeatedly used the phrase "doing the right thing" (*göra rätt för sig*). She was then asked by the interviewer whether this was a typical "Swedish value". She replied that:

> It is a typically good value and I wish it existed everywhere in the world. But right now I am working in Sweden and wish to build a government here. It is typical for us that we have a strong society that in order to work actually demands that everybody should work and do the right thing. It demands that everybody works and pays taxes

She was then asked whether it is non-Swedish to not do the right thing, and in addition: "When you say we in Sweden are like this, must we be defined against something else, as if it is unique to us". She replied:

> I think that if one thinks that it is right to live at others' expense even though one has the ability to work, or to skip paying taxes, this is to betray society and our common resources.

Pressed one final time on whether she meant that doing the right thing was a typical Swedish value, Kindberg Batra confirmed: "Yes I think so".

The debate about sexual assaults on and outrages against women at music festivals in Stockholm and Cologne in 2014 and 2015 provided a constant and noisy discursive background throughout the spring and summer of 2016. These discussions took place within the discursive frame of "honour culture", a term which as noted above is used in Sweden as a demarcation line to separate "us" from "them". Putting the discourse on "Swedish culture and values" in this context, it becomes obvious that gender and sexuality are at the centre of racializing processes. In addition, the notion of Swedish values is implicitly defined and shaped in contrast to migrant Others' culture and values, and vice versa.

"Honour culture", Sweden and the Muslim Other

Elisabeth Höglund, a prominent and experienced Swedish journalist, now retired, portrayed the perpetrators of outrages at festivals as representative of people from the Middle East and North Africa as a whole. She defined people from these regions collectively as bearers of a so-called honour culture. In her blog, she wrote:

> Of course it is not just migrant boys who offend women. Swedish men can be as much bastards as them. However, it is wrong to deny that there are cultural differences between some refugee groups' views on women and so-called ethnic Swedish men's views on women. We should dare to shout about these culture clashes. (13 January 2016, translated by the author)

Höglund presents violence against women committed by native Swedish men as an individual phenomenon while presenting violence against women committed by migrant Muslim men as cultural. This proves what Eduards (2007) suggests: that the honour discourse is at the core of the construction of Swedishness (see also Alinia, 2011; Baianstovu, 2012; Carbin, 2010). Höglund explains the popularity of the Sweden Democrats—an anti-immigration and anti-Muslim party with Nazi roots that has steadily grown since it entered parliament in 2010—as a consequence of "our" silence about "honour violence" and cultural differences in Sweden. She therefore encourages journalists to talk about cultural differences and clashes. She means that there are problems related to migrants from the Middle East and North Africa about which mainstream opinion is silent while, according to her, the Sweden Democrats discuss such matters. She presents this as a reason why they have gained so much support.

In an interview with Swedish Television, Birgitta Ohlsson, a prominent Swedish politician, a member of the Liberal Party and a former Minister for the European Union and democracy, celebrated "Swedish culture and values" which she connected to gender equality and women's rights. At the same time she described people from the Middle East and North Africa in a collective sense as exactly the opposite. She was very determined to point out that the people who were committing the sexual assaults were not Swedish. It was important for her to cleanse the notion of Swedishness from its Other. Departing from an essentialized perspective on and a hierarchical notion of culture and cultural differences, Ohlsson singled out people from Muslim majority regions and especially mentioned Iran, Afghanistan and Morocco as bearers and reproducers of so-called honour culture, and also inferior to the superior Swedish nation. The journalist asked her why she believed that it is important to discuss cultural differences in regard to sexual assaults. Ohlsson replied:

> There are men who are bastards in all societies and cultures but different cultures have different degrees of acceptance of them and also of respect for women and girls' rights. … I think we must dare to say that different cultures have different degrees of progress when it comes to respect for girls and women and their rights.
>
> (SVT Nyheter 12 January 2016)

Of course, there are huge differences between countries when it comes to women's rights and gender equality and the problem is primarily and strongly political and historical. Of course, too, there is also a cultural dimension that is very important. To reduce the problem to only a matter of culture, however, and exclude the political aspect, power structures, historical context and so on is to adopt an ideological position. She argued that violence against women among native Swedes is committed by individual, sick men while in the countries she mentioned such violence is a cultural issue. When the journalist asked whether it is possible to see sexual harassment as a matter of sexuality, meaning that we should not involve ethnicity or culture, Ohlsson replied:

> No I do not agree with that and I think that is to spit on the feminist struggle that has made it possible for us to live in such a fantastic country where women have fought to reach the level of gender equality that we have. It is to equate Sweden, which has a gender equality level like this [she lifts her hand to almost the level of her head], and compare it with countries such as Iran, Afghanistan and Morocco [she brings her hand down when she mentions these countries] where respect for women is much less and of course it informs the behaviour of people in these countries. […] We talk very much about school, education and jobs and the importance of language but we talk too little about values.
>
> (ibid.)

In other words, what she meant was that sexual harassment, when committed by people from countries such as Iran, Afghanistan and Morocco, is not an issue of gender and sexuality, but one of ethnicity and culture. She lumped together three different countries and peoples and labelled them collectively bearers of so-called honour culture, and opponents of and a negative counterpart to Swedish culture and values, in which gender-based violence is either absent or trifling. To talk about law and legislation in these countries, or about political systems, states and their gender policies, is one thing. Assigning sexual harassment to the culture of entire countries or nations, however, is something entirely different. Such statements are strongly ideological. Europe, including Sweden, as Morley and Robins (1995) assert, is not just a geographic place. It is also an idea that is strongly connected to the myth of the superiority of Western civilization in relation to the colonized Other (ibid.: 5). Notions of Swedishness/non-Swedishness and their effects on those who are defined as "Other" in the current Sweden must be understood within this historical frame of reference.

Racial violence for the sake of women

In 2005, the Liberal Party (*Libralerna*) awarded the former Dutch politician, Ayaan Hirsi Ali, a democracy prize at the same time as she was closely collaborating with and openly paying tribute to prominent Islamophobic and anti-Semitic individuals such as the Dutch film director, Theo van Gogh, a close friend and supporter of the Dutch right wing populist and anti-Muslim politician, Pim Fortuyn (Alinia, 2011).[2] The prize was justified with reference to Hirsi Ali's struggle for women's rights, but Hirsi Ali's struggle for women is not above ideological and political projects. Hirsi Ali has equated Islamic symbols such as the minaret and the half-moon with the swastika (Gardell, 2015; see also Hirsi Ali 2009). As a voice of the post-9/11 global anti-Muslim discourse, Hirsi Ali, inspired by Samuel Huntington's idea of the clash of civilizations, asserts that Islam and the West cannot coexist (Hirsi Ali 2010). She stands for an ideology according to which the west represents civilization and progress while the rest and especially the so-called Muslim world represent barbarism and backwardness (Brockes 2010). Referring to Hirsi Ali—or other non-white women—as Africans, Muslims, and so on, who "have their own experiences" is the best way to deliver a message that a white person cannot deliver so easily. Hence, Hirsi Ali and other migrant women who adhere to the culturalist discourse have become the perfect spokespersons for "us" in the battle against "them" (ibid.; see also Alinia, 2011).

Another example of how women's rights excuse racial violence is the case of a politician from the Left Party (*Vänsterpartiet*) in April 2016. Amineh Kakabaveh—a member of the *Riksdag* (Swedish Parliament), and herself from a migrant background—is known as one of the loudest proponents of the culturalist honour discourse in Sweden. Despite her membership of the Left Party she has been much closer to the right-wing populist discourses and also to liberal feminists in discriminating against people of migrant and Muslim backgrounds and racializing society in the name of gender equality and women's rights. For this reason and despite protests she was finally excluded from the Left Party in August 2019. In 2016 she spread blatantly racist propaganda in the form of a film on her Facebook page. The film was "propaganda based on blatantly Afrophobic and Islamophobic notions of rape, drugs and an alleged hidden agenda to change Swedish legislation to legalize rape" (*Expo Idag* 18 March 2016; see also Karlsson 2016). When, later the same day, it became clear that the film, which had a Swedish Television logo on it, was a fake that had in reality been made by *Nordisk Ungdom* (Nordic Youth), a fascist organization, she deleted it. She did not properly apologize, however, and nor did she express regret for her own comments[3] on the film (*Expo Idag*, 29 April 2016). Later, when the pressure of critical opinion from inside her party became more acute, she gave a half-hearted apology that contained no serious degree of self-criticism or genuine regret (*Expo Idag*, 29 April 2016; see also Karlsson 2016). Opinion was divided even inside her own party. However, despite internal demands, the party was in 2016 unable to exclude her because she received support from many politicians from left and right, and from many other powerful people both inside and outside the Left Party who thought she was acting for the sake of women and their rights (Karlsson 2016). In December 2016 she was appointed as the 'Swede of the Year' by the Swedish news magazine Focus (*Fokus*) and the appointment was motivated as follows·

> By bringing attention to radicalization, and tribal and honour oppression Amina Kakabaveh uncovers in action and speech the Swedish unwillingness to touch all too sensitive subjects.

> *(15 December 2016)*

Comparing the way she was treated with other cases of insult and discrimination raises many questions. For example, the high school minister, Aida Hadzialic, resigned immediately on 12 August 2016 having been caught drink-driving. She had driven a car four hours after drinking two glasses of wine, and 0.10–0.15 mg of alcohol was found in her system. She was highly apologetic and strongly regretful and self-critical, and her resignation was accepted by the Prime Minister even though some of her colleagues and others saw the offence as insignificant. Another case that attracted even more attention was the case of a Muslim politician, Yasri Khan of the Swedish Green Party, who for religious reasons had refused to shake hands with a female journalist who was interviewing him. He chose instead to greet her in his own way, by putting his hand on his chest. This gave rise to a fervent debate to which even the Prime Minister, Stefan Löfven, contributed (*Svenska Dagbladet* 21 April 2016). Yasri Khan was forced to resign shortly afterwards because his refusal, according to majority social norms, was seen as offensive to the journalist and as an offence against gender equality. While Hadzialic and Khan lost their positions as a consequence of their offensive actions, Kakabaveh by contrast received more support than criticism. The only penalty imposed on her was a one-month break from public political activities.

Final remarks

Previous studies on Sweden have shown that racial hatred and different forms of violence towards migrants are always preceded by racializing discourses and politics. The story of two Swedish serial killers illustrates this statement. In 1991–1992, John Ausonious, known as the laser man, shot and killed several people in Stockholm (Tamas, 2005). In 2010 Peter Mangs did the same in Malmö (Gardell, 2015). These events took place at different times and in different places but there are significant similarities. The victims in both cases were people of colour. In both cases the crime took place in a political climate permeated by racial hatred where non-European migrants and refugees were continually portrayed as problems, economic burdens, security risks and dangers by the media and politicians. Based on interviews with each perpetrator, the studies suggest that these killers were driven by racial hatred and felt that something must be done and someone had to act to "save" the nation from undesirable people (Gardell, 2015; Tamas, 2005).

Lutz, Phoenix and Yuval-Davis noted in 1995 that the boundaries between Europe and the rest of the world were constantly being strengthened, and Europe more than ever before was seeking to legitimize measures to exclude "waves of foreigners". They meant that measures to exclude Others go hand-in-hand with the construction of cultural, religious and racial otherness (1995: 5–8). What they concluded more than 20 years ago feels very current today. However, the difference is that in the new century the construction of otherness and racial exclusion is strongly, and significantly, gendered. While this is not entirely new, what is new is the way in which gendered racism (Essed, 1991), that is the construction of otherness at the intersection of racism and sexism, has become normalized in everyday social relations and has become part of public perceptions and consciousness. One arena in which these illiberal discourses and politics operate and are justified is gender equality and women's rights issues. To racialize in the name of women's rights and gender equality is not new either. Arruzza, Bhattacharya, and Fraser (2019) suggest that "the history of feminism when it comes to the issue of race is not uplifting" (ibid.: 52). They write:

> The leading suffragettes in the USA dedicated themselves to explicit racist campaigns after the civil war when black men achieved the right to vote while white women did

not. Even in the 20th century leading British feminists defended the colonial occupation of India with racial and 'civilizational' arguments—they claimed that British rule was necessary in order to "lift the brown women out of their miserable situation".

(ibid.: 52–53)

The examples highlighted in this article show that similar thoughts and statements have been normalized and legitimized in such a way that sanctions the illiberal treatment, racialization and social exclusion of certain groups in society. Today's feminism is much more powerful and influential than it was in the early 20th century. Especially in countries like Sweden where issues of women's rights and gender equality constitute a hegemonic discourse—even though the #MeToo movement has shown that the reality is very different—they have a great impact on society and politics. Hence, given the historical and current experiences of the relationship between feminism and racism, it is of central importance always to pose certain questions. To prevent women's rights from being taken hostage and used as a battering ram to serve racism, it is crucial to ask: whose feminism? from what position? And from whose perspective?

Notes

1 Almedalsveckan or politikerveckan is an annual week-long event that takes place in early June in Visby, on the island of Gotland. It began in 1968 and has continued and expanded since to become an important forum for Swedish politics. All the political parties, major politicians and other social and political actors participate to present their programmes, lobby, promote their ideas and politics, and discuss current social and political issues.
2 According to van der Veer, van Gogh had "a long-established reputation for being a provocateur that included insulting the Jewish community and more recent references to Muslims as 'the secret column of goat-fuckers'" (2006:111); van Gogh was killed by a Muslim fundamentalist and Fortuyn was killed by an animal rights activist.
3 She wrote: "Congratulations Sweden for establishing an Islamic State and a Kalifat soon in several suburbs. This has been made possible thanks to the Swedish 'integration policy'—an idiotic polity …"(*Expo Idag*, 29 April 2016).

References

Al-Ali, Nadje (2008) "Iraqi women and gender relations: Redefining difference", in *British Journal of Middle Eastern studies*, 35(3), pp. 405–418.

Alinia, Minoo (2011) "Den jämställda rasismen och de barbariska invandrarna: hedersvåld, kultur och skillnadens politik", Carina Listerborn, Irene Molina and Diana Mulinari (eds), *Våldets topografier: Betraktelser över makt och motstånd*. Stockholm: Atlas. pp. 287–329.

Alinia, Minoo (2013) *Honor & Violence Against Women in Iraqi Kurdistan*. New York: Palgrave Macmillan.

Alinia, Minoo (2019) "Etnisk särbehandling i regeringens genuspolitik - utmaningar for socialt arbete i - storstadens mångfald", In i Alinia & Songur (red.), *Socialt arbete i i storstaden: villkor och praktik*. Stockholm: Liber. pp. 45–59.

Ålund, Alexandra and Schierup, Carl Ulrik (1991) "Prescribed multiculturalism in crisis", In Alexandra Ålund and Carl-Ulrik Schierup, *Paradoxes of Multiculturalism: Essays on Swedish Society*. Avebury: Aldershot. pp. 1–21.

Arruzza, Cinzia; Bhattacharya, Tithi; Fraser, Nancy (2019) *Feminism för de 99 procenten*. Stockholm: Tankekraft.

Baianstovu, í Runa (2012) *Mångfald som demokratins utmaning: En studie om hur socialtjänsten som välfärdsbyråkrati och moralisk samhällsinstitution förstår och hanterar kulturell mångfald*. Diss.. Örebro: Örebrouniversitet.

Brown, Wendy (2006) *Regulating Aversion: Tolerance in the Age of Identity and Empire*. Princeton: Princeton University Press.

Carbin, Maria (2010) *Mellan tystnad och tal – flickor och hedersvåld i svensk offentlig politik*. Stockholm: Stockholm University.

Collins, Patricia Hill (2009) *Black Feminist Thought*. New York: Routledge.

Eduards, Maud (2007) *Kroppspolitik: om moder Svea och andra kvinnor* [The body politic: On Mother Svea and other women]. Stockholm: Atlas.

Said, W. Edward (1978) Orientalism. London: Routledge & Kegan Paul Ltd.

Eldén, Åsa (1998) "'The killing seemed to be necessary': Arab cultural affiliation as an extenuating circumstance in a Swedish verdict", *NORA*, 6(2), pp. 89–96.

Ertürk, Yakin (2009) "Towards a post-patriarchal gender order: Confronting the universality and the particularity of violence against women", *Sociologisk forskning*, 46(4), pp. 61–70.

Essed, Philomena (1991) *Understanding Everyday Racism: An Interdisciplinary Theory*. Newbury Park: SAGE Publications.

Fairclough, Norman (2015) *Language and Power*. New York: Routledge. London & New York: Routledge..

Gardell, Mattias (2015) *Raskrigaren: Seriemördaren Peter Mangs*. Stockholm: Leopard förlag.

Gruber, Sabine (2007) *I skolans vilja att åtgärda "hedersrelaterat" våld: etnicitet, kön och våld*, Report 2007: 1, Linköping University.

Keskinen, Suvi (2009) "'Honour-related violence' and Nordic nation-building", In Suvi Keskinen, Salla Tuori, Sari Irni and Diana Mulinari (eds), *Complying with Colonialism: Gender, Race and Ethnicity in the Nordic Region*. England, USA: Ashgate. pp. 237–257.

Korteweg, Anna C. and Yurdakul, Gökçe (2010) *Religion, culture and the politization of honour-related violence: A critical analysis of media and policy debates in Western Europe and America*. United Nations Research Institute for Social Development, Gender and development programme paper number 12.

Lernestedt, C. (2006) "Kulturellt försvar", In likhet och diskriminering. I: Jerzy Sarnecki (ed.), *Är rättvisan rättvis? Tio perspektiv på diskriminering av etniska och religiösa minoriteter inom rättssystemet*. SOU 2006: 30. Stockholm: Regeringskansliet. pp. 283–321.

Lutz, Helma; Phoenix, Ann, and Yuval-Davis, Nira (eds.) (1995) *Crossfires: Nationalism, Racism and Gender in Europe*. London: Pluto Press.

Mohanty, Chandra Talpade (2003) *Feminism utan gränser: avkoloniserad teori, praktiserad solidaritet*. Stockholm: Tankekraft.

Morley, David and Robins, Kevin (1995). *Spaces of Identity: Global Media, Electronic Landscapes and Cultural Boundaries*. London/New York: Routledge.

Mulinari, Diana and Lundqvist, Åsa (2018)" Genus, kultur och välfärd: Migrant kvinnor i jämställdhetspolitiska diskurser", In Aleksandra Ålund, Carl-Ulrik Schierup and Anders Neergard (eds), *Nation i ombildning: Essäer om 2000-talet Sverige*. Umeå: Boréa. pp. 121–143.

NCK, Nationellt Centrum för Kvinnofrid (2010) *Hedersrelaterat våld och förtryck – En kunskap- och forskningsöversikt*. Uppsala: Uppsala universitet.

NCK, Nationellt Centrum för Kvinnofrid (2013) *Delrapport 3: Nationell kartläggning om hur mäns våld mot kvinnor, hedersrelaterat våld och förtryck samt våld i samkönade relationer beaktas i myndigheters fortbildning*. Uppsala: Uppsala Universitet.

Pérez, E. (2014) *Vad vet vi om de insatser socialtjänsten gör i hedersrelaterade konflikter inom familjen?* Malm: Malm.hgskola.

Razack, Sherene H. (2004) "Imperilled Muslim women, dangerous Muslim men and civilized Europeans: Legal and social responses to forced marriages", *Feminist Legal Studies*, 12, pp. 129–174.

Tamas, Gellert (2005) Lasermannen: en berattelse om Sverige. Stockholm: Ordfront.

van der Veer, Peter (2006) "Pim Fortuyn, Theo van Cogh, and the politics of Tolerance in the Netherlands" *Public Culture*, 18(1), pp. 111–124.

van Dijk, Teun A. (1993) *Elite Discourse and Racism: Sage series on Race and Ethnic Relations, Vol. 6*. London: Sage.

Wallach Scott, Joan (2007) *Slöjans politik [The politics of the veil]*. Stockholm: Tankekraft.

Welchman, Lynn and Hossain, Sara (2005) "Introduction: 'Honour', rights and wrong", In Lynn Welchman and Sara Hossain (eds), *"Honour": Crimes, Paradigms, and Violence Against Women*. London & New York: Zed Books. pp. 1–22.

Werbner, Pnina (2007) "Veiled interventions in pure space: Honour, shame and embodied struggles among Muslims in Britain and France", *Theory, Culture & Society*, 24(2), pp. 161–186.

Westerstrand, Jenny and Eldén, Åsa (2004) "Hederns försvarare. Den rättsliga hanteringen av ett hedersmord", I *Kvinnovetenskaplig Tidskrift*, Nr, 3, 2004, pp. 35–56.

Yuval-Davis, Nira (2011) *The Politics of Belonging: Intersectional Contestations.* London, Los Angeles, New Delhi, Singapore, Washington DC: Sage.

Žižek, Slavoj (2009) *Violence.* London: Profile Books LTD.

Reported sources

Af Kleen, Björn (2016) *Frågan om Hells Angels kvinnosyn ställs på sin spets i Nacka.* Hämtat från: www.dn.se/nyheter/sverige/bjorn-af-kleen-fragan-om-hells-angels-kvinnosyn-stalls-pa-sin-spets-i-nacka/.

Brockes, Emma. "Why are Muslims so hypersensitive?" Published, 2010-05-08. Accessed on 2018-11-17, at: **www.theguardian.com/world/2010/may/08/ayaan-hirsi-ali-interview**

Expo Idag (18 mars 2016) *De patrullerar som Soldiers of Odin – högerextrema och rovt kriminella.* Hämtat från: http://expo.se/2016/de-patrullerar-som-soldiers-of-odin–hogerextrema-och-grovt-kriminella_7043.html

Expo Idag, (29 April 2016) *Befogad kritik mot Kakebaveh.* Accessed at: http://expo.se/2016/befogad-kritik-mot-kakabaveh_7082.html

Fokus, (15 December 2016) *Årets svensk.* Accessed at: www.fokus.se/2016/12/arets-svensk–4/

Hirsi Ali, Ayaan (2009) "Maktens torn", *Expressen,* 5 December 2009.

Hirsi Ali, Ayaan (2010) *Nomad: From Islam to America: A personal Journey Through the Clash of Civilizations,* New York: Free Press.

Höglund, Elisabeth (2016) *Fortsätt skräck i Sverige att tala om invandrarmäns kränkningar av kvinnor.* Hämtat från Höglunds blogg: https://elisabethoglund.se/blogg/fortsatt_skrack_i_sverige_att_tala_om_invan drarmans_krankningar_av_kvinnor/.

Hökmark, Gunnar (2016) I Sverige råder svensk lag. Hämtat från Hökmarks blog: http://hokmark.eu/i-sverige-rader-svensk-lag/

Dagens Nyheter, debatt, published: 2017-12-11. Accessed 2018-11-17 at: www.dn.se/debatt/stark-orien tering-om-svenska-varderingar-for-nyanlanda/

Karlsson, Per (2016) *V-veteran lämnar partiet – efter hårda konflikten.* Hämtat från: www.aftonbladet.se/nyh eter/samhalle/article23424744.ab

Svenska Dagbladet, 21 April 2016, acced 2018-11-17 at: www.svd.se/folj-fragestunden-med-stefan-lofven,

SVT Nyheter 12 januari 2016 22.02: www.svt.se/nyheter/inrikes/ohlsson-l-vi-maste-kunna-diskutera-olika-kulturers-kvinnosyn.

SVT Nyheter, 10 maj 2016. Accessed 2018-11-17 at: www.svt.se/nyheter/lokalt/stockholm/protester-i-saltsjo-boo-mot-flyktingboenden

26

Gendered racializations

Producing subordinate immigrant subjects, discrimination, and oppressive feminist and queer politics

Anna Korteweg

Introduction

This chapter starts from the intersectional premise that race is always gendered and gender is always raced (Glenn 1999; Crenshaw 1990; Collins 2002; Choo and Ferree 2010; McCall 2005; Yuval-Davis 2006, see also Erel, this *Handbook*). From that vantage point, I first outline the process of gendered racialization and identify migration as a primary site in which that process takes place. Specifically, contemporary gendered racializations shape the understanding of large scale contemporary migrations into (western) Europe and North America. As people who moved to Europe and North America in the last fifty years have become permanent residents and citizens, these places have become home. However, immigrants' membership is too often not recognized by those who claim the label "native" or who see membership in the nation-state they live in as a natural birthright rooted in a history of presence, even when that presence is settler-colonial (Shachar 2009; Thobani 2007; Yuval-Davis 2011). This continued failure of recognition is enacted, in part, through the gendered racialization of immigrants.

Yet, gendered racialization is not solely a process experienced by immigrant communities, all processes of racialization are gendered as the literature on for example African Americans in the United States shows. While immigrants become newly racialized in gendered ways when they move across borders, racialization is an ongoing process of the continuous reinforcement and rearticulation of supposed racial gendered difference. This chapter focuses more heavily on those labeled Muslims, as the contemporary immigrant group that most clearly illustrates gendered racialization, and starts by unpacking the mechanisms underlying the gendered racialization of those labeled immigrant and/or Muslim (see Spielhaus 2006 for an analysis of how immigrants from North Africa and the Middle East were reclassified from "guest worker" to "Muslim"). Where possible, however, the chapter brings in examples from other racialized peoples to show the continuous process of gendered racialization. In addition, the chapter highlights literature that queers these gendered racializations.

The chapter proceeds as follows: After outlining what gendered racialization entails, it focuses on the experiences of gendered racialization, honing in on sites in which gendered racializations are made visible, including veil wearing, the securitization of borders and other public spaces, as well as educational achievement and labor market participation. The next section of this chapter draws on research that illustrates the link between gendered racialization and discrimination in these sites. Third, the chapter turns to work by scholars who have observed that both gender equality and LGBTQ rights have become tropes fostering gendered racialization of immigrant communities in contemporary European and North American contexts (Eid 2015; Keskinen 2018; Korteweg 2017; Verloo 2018; Yurdakul and Korteweg 2013). The literature illustrates how these tropes are used to simultaneously reinforce a distinction between those labeled immigrants and "native" populations, while downplaying continuous concerns regarding the limited achievement of gender equality and LGBTQ rights within immigrant-receiving nation-states. These gendered racializations have an effect as evidenced in the rise of contemporary populism and right-wing nationalism (Geva 2018), "homonationalism" (Puar 2013) and "femonationalism" (Farris 2017), and European "anti-gender" movements (Verloo 2018). Furthermore, this last section shows how these gendered racializations impact politics beyond the ultra-right, highlighting feminist and LGBTQ movements' complicity in these processes (Jivraj and De Jong 2011; Keskinen 2018).

What is gendered racialization? Experiences of gendered racialization

Omi and Winant's define racialization as "*the extension of racial meaning to a previously racially unclassified relationship, social practice or group*" (2014, 111, italics in original). For the purposes of this chapter, I add that racialization should be understood as the process of attributing racial meaning to relationships, social practices, or groups that are already classified as racial. Furthermore, I argue, following Selod (2019), that the process of racialization is not solely rooted in an interpretation of (presumptions about) biology but extends to bodily comportment and embodiment as well as cultural and religious practices, as, for example, the racialization of Muslim hijab-wearing women shows (see also Korteweg and Yurdakul 2014; Parvez 2017; Scott 2009). Thus, while being mindful of Murji and Solomos (2005) warning that racialization is at times overused to the point of banality, I argue that the concept enables a focus on the *process* of categorization of difference that continues to be critical to understanding how inequalities are produced and structural violence is perpetrated against groups constituted through this process of racialization.

In addition, racialization needs to be understood from an intersectional perspective. Intersectionality in this context captures the co-constitutiveness of categories of difference, in which each dimension gives meaning to all others (Glenn 1999). In other words, rather than decoupling different dimensions of subjectivity and inequality, such as race, gender and sexuality, an intersectional vantage point argues that the meaning of these categories of differentiation are always created in the interaction between such categories. The resulting intersectional categorizations in turn generate hegemonic definitions of subjectivity, operate through institutional mechanisms, and structure complex inequalities (Glenn 1999; Yuval-Davis 2006; see also Erel, this volume). In particular, gender interacts critically with racialization, as a similarly interpreted biological marker. And, as with race, gender is socially constructed in reference to a presumed underlying biological difference and as with race the biological is overdrawn and often imputed from non-biological markers (Butler 2011; Meadow 2017; Phoenix 2017). In 1851, former slave Sojourner Truth famously asked a group of white women agitating for women's liberation, "ain't I a woman?" (see Erel, this volume). What we learned from her question was that gender is socially constructed in reference to race just as race is constructed in reference to gender (with other differences including class, religion, physical ability, and so on, becoming salient at different moments in time; see Glenn 1999; Yuval-Davis 2006). In the contemporary period, ongoing racial classifications of, for example, African Americans or Blacks in Britain, are inflected by gender, as the construction of dangerous masculinity in racialization of street crime or gang violence shows (Murji and Solomos 2005, 3; Contreras 2009). As these examples suggest, it is imperative that we do not focus solely on the unmarked of the race-gender continuum and understand the workings of masculinity in reference to race, just as we should analyze the construction of whiteness in relation to gender.

The literature also shows that we need to queer the ways in which we understand the gendered racialized production of subjectivities. Reflections from Black feminist lesbians were critical to the initial articulations of intersectional theory: the Combahee River Collective's statement, written by a collective of radical lesbian Black feminists and published in 1977, was one of the texts critical to Kimberle Crenshaw's 1990 articulation of intersectionality (Crenshaw 1990; see also Erel, this volume). Nonetheless, Jin Haritaworn (2012), Fatima El-Tayeb (2012), Sarah Bracke (2012), and Jasbir Puar (2013) have all shown from different perspectives that in much work "Europeans are generally presumed to be homogeneously white, while racialized subjects are generally presumed to be uniformly straight and cis" (Bacchetta, El-Tayeb, and Haritaworn 2018, 150). Generally, hegemonic gendered racializations have produced understandings of sexuality and embodiment that render the lived experience of gendered racialized LGBTQs invisible in our scholarship and social policies, though potentially dangerously hypervisible in everyday life (see Amar 2011 on hypervisible Muslim masculinities). At the same time, a narrow interpretation of "gay liberation" has associated support for a white hegemonic gay/lesbian existence with the west's progressive approach to human rights in ways that erases the complexities of queer life globally.

Studies of the experiences of Muslims in the global north make processes of gendered racialization visible. In her ethnographic study of the racialization of Muslims in the United States, Atiya Husain (2019) compares the experiences of 28 Black and white Muslims and finds that Blackness, whiteness and Muslimness are co-constructed. This means that whites, normally the unmarked racial category (Frankenberg 1993), become racialized when they are discernably Muslim. White Muslims experience a degree of denial of white privilege but, as Husain (2019) shows, some also deny their own whiteness, arguing that being Muslim cancels out being white, something not accepted by African Americans who point out that white privilege is still at play even when one is also Muslim (Husain 2019, 600). African American Muslims by contrast experience a complex interaction between being racialized Black versus Muslim, with the categories reinforcing each other in ways that produce different kinds of racializations depending on which racialized category is made salient in any given encounter.

Husain (2019) does not explicitly theorize the gendered aspects of racialization, but in separating out experiences of women and men, she shows how African American women try to avoid being racialized Muslim by wearing their headcover in a style associated with being African American rather than Muslim. Similarly, wearing the hijab racializes white women (who are often converts), where the hijab confronts them with being seen as foreign (Husain 2019, 596). White women wearing a headscarf are talked to slowly, asked where they learned English, and presumed to be unfamiliar with expected "American" cultural interactional modalities (Husain 2019, 595). African American men experience that being Muslim can at times redirect attention away from Blackness (as in the example when an officer let an African American man go when he discovered that the man was Muslim). In general, Husain shows how in the US context, Muslim is racialized brown and foreign and that this affects both African American and white Muslims differently as it intersects with the gendered racialization of whiteness and Blackness to produce differently racialized identities and experiences that are also distinctly gendered.

Where Husain (2019) speaks to the US context, research on the regulation of the headscarf shows how gendered racializations are nationally and locally specific. Work on France, where the hijab as well as the niqab have been heavily politicized, shows how gendered racializations of Muslim's women's expressions of religiosity and subjectivity inform highly exclusionary laws that ban headscarf wearing in schools, and niqab wearing in any public space (Bowen 2007; Laborde 2008; Laxer 2018; Parvez 2017; Scott 2009). Other European countries regulate veiling less through the legal system but nonetheless attribute meaning to the practice of veiling that suggests an absence of individual agency on the part of women wearing it and a disregard for women's ability to control their own bodily comportment as they see fit (Elver 2011; Moors 2009; Rottmann and Ferree 2008; Sauer 2009). As a result, headscarf wearing women are not interpreted as independent subjects but rather as objects of a repressive practice perpetrated by violent men. In the process, Muslim women and men confront the gendered racialization of religious practices.

These gendered racialized constructions also become visible in the experiences and interpretations of Muslim converts. Esra Özyürek (2014) shows how German converts respond attempts to deny their belonging to the German nation by reinforcing the racialization of "immigrant" Muslims. Özyürek (2014) analyzes the presence of Islam in Germany over the past 100 years and shows how as conversion moved from a rare, elite endeavor, to one that is more widespread but far less elite, it became more threatening to the German nation. German converts to Islam manage the tensions that their chosen religion brings to the fore by rejecting what they claim are the cultural trappings of a Turkish, North-African, or Middle Eastern Islam for what they see as a true Islam, which they claim epitomizes European values. German converts to Islam thus end up reinforcing the current discourses of racialization, but not of all Muslims but of those who converts see as failing to ground their religiosity in European identity. Özyürek (2014) thus shows how anti-Muslim racism gets constituted in the contemporary European context not only by non-Muslims but also by Muslims. This process is gendered insofar as Muslim converts assert what they see as values of gender equality usually not attributed to Islam.

Finally, a similar process occurs vis-à-vis queer Muslims in the global North. For example, Jivraj and De Jong (2011) critically assess a Dutch policy to make LGBTQ identities "speakable" or discussable within Dutch Muslim communities. They show how this fosters the creation of a dichotomy between a form of liberation based on speech rather than action (I am gay, rather than I do gay), while also positioning Muslim communities as inherently hostile to LGBTQ rights (Jivraj and De Jong 2011). Similarly, Bracke (2012) shows how the strong impulse to rescue both Muslim women and Muslim gays from "their" culture structures presumably liberatory politics, particularly in the Netherlands but also in Europe more generally, in ways that limit the articulation and recognition of a queer Muslim subject and practice in everyday politics and society.

Gendered racialization: discrimination and the production of complex inequalities

To discriminate can mean to discern difference, in and of itself not necessarily a negative process. However, gendered racializations turn the discernment of difference into hierarchy and various forms of exclusionary violence that can be grouped under the header "discrimination." Farris and de Jong (2014, 1507) usefully define discrimination as the "subordination and exclusion that are experienced by individuals on the basis of certain characteristics they either possess, or with which they are associated." Pager and Shepherd (2008), in their discussion of racial discrimination, argue that discrimination can result from differential treatment based on arbitrary distinction as well as from differential impact of actions that do not have "any explicit racial content but that have the consequence of producing or reinforcing racial disadvantage" (2008, 182). In short, an analysis of discrimination focuses "on behavior" (Pager and Shepherd 2008, 182). In what follows, I look at literature, which suggests that gendered racializations inform a number of discriminatory practices. The literature on education, labor market outcomes, and surveillance all clearly show the discriminatory impact that processes of gendered racialization can have.

Farris and de Jong (2014) advance the concept of intersectional discrimination. They argue that discrimination is an intersectional construct, where they define intersectionality as "a specific interplay between different 'axes' that cannot be reduced to the sum of its parts" (Farris and de Jong 2014, 1507). They argue that intersectional discrimination occurs on three dimensions: structural, institutional and discursive (this in line with much intersectional theorizing, see Choo and Ferree 2010; Yuval-Davis 2006). In the language deployed in this chapter, each of these dimensions of intersectional discrimination is also always a site of gendered racialization – systemic gendered raced formations that are also inflected by class and religion, bureaucratic organizations that operationalize these formations, and discursive forms of gendered racialization or the stereotyped intersectional representation of subject positions.

Farris and de Jong (2014) turn to six European countries to show how gendered racializations result in immigrant girls performing better in school than immigrant boys but worse than non-immigrant girls. They argue that this outcome is the result of gendered familial expectations and gendered societal expectations that position girls as the cultural bearers of social success. At the same time, this relative educational success does not translate into labor market success as institutional discrimination on racialized gendered lines is widespread across Europe. Farris and de Jong pay particular attention to headscarf wearing girls, coming to the conclusion that the penalty for wearing the headscarf is both real and high (Farris and de Jong 2014, 1517–18). This penalty affects both first and second-generation young women.

Research that adds sexuality as an intersectional difference in the analysis of occupational discrimination shows that such gendered racialized impacts are structural elements of workplace bureaucracies. For example, white and Asian women who present as gender-fluid or identify as LGBTQ fare better in the California tech industry than women perceived as normatively heterosexual but in ways that ultimately reinforce male dominance in the field (Alfrey and Twine 2017). The positive impact of non-normative feminine gender representation does not extend to racially non-dominant women, including queer Black women, in the industry. They are not seen as offering the same skills or capacities as their numerically more common white or Asian counterparts.

Gendered racializations also affect LGBTQ refugees, who as research shows have to demonstrate their identity as gay, lesbian, or bisexual rather than providing support for the fact that they faced persecution if they are to be granted asylum (Rehaag 2017). Focusing on the Canadian case, Rehaag (2017) shows that refugee determinations hearings tend to affirm gendered understandings of queerness based on western stereotypes. Dhoest (2018), in his analysis of gay Muslim men's refugee claims, presents a similar finding for Belgium, which he describes as a country generally seen as open to refugee claims based on sexual orientation and gender identity. Here, too, gay men have to adopt a "coming out" gay narrative to make their claim stick. As Dhoest (2018) also points out, this does not allow for alternate understandings and experiences of queerness. Thus accessing rights of refugees depends on enactments of LGBTQ identity that do not necessarily reflect the sense of subjectivity queer refugees bring to their encounter with state agents involved in refugee status determination.

Scholars focusing on the workings of intersectionality have often observed the role that invisibilization plays in producing discriminatory outcomes. Bassel and Emejulu (2017) cite extensive research demonstrating the racialization of poverty and labor market attainment (pp. 190–91), with minority populations in both France and Britain having poverty rates double those of non-minorities. However, the ways in which statistics are collected juxtapose ethnicity/race and gender and thus fail to highlight the intersectional effects of these two categories of difference. The failure to analyze such intersections is also evident in Dutch programs to further the labor market integration of ethnic minority women (Korteweg and Triadafilopoulos 2013; Roggeband and Verloo 2008). These programs treat all racialized women on the template of Muslim women without paying attention to the fact that in the Dutch case, women from the Caribbean and Surinam participate on par with or exceed the labor market participation of white Dutch women (Korteweg and Triadafilopoulos 2013; Roggeband and Verloo 2007). Similarly, Bassel and Emejulu (2017) observe, in their research on austerity, that much other work treats 2008 as a break point. However, for Black and minority ethnic women the 2008 moment is just one in what Bassel and Emejulu call "routinised crises" (2017).

These institutional and structural discriminatory effects are also reflected in everyday informal interaction. For example, there has been an uptick in the harassment of headscarf wearing women in France after the implementation of the niqab and burqa-ban (Korteweg and Yurdakul 2014). Similarly, the 2018 Interim Report of the British organization Tell MAMA, which measures anti-Muslim attacks, reported a sharp rise in street-level anti-Muslim attacks, with those identified as women more likely to be the victim than those seen as men (https://tellmamauk. org/gendered-anti-muslim-hatred-and-islamophobia-street-based-aggression-in-cases-reported-to-tell-mama-is-alarming/).

Gendered racialization also interacts with particular constructions of masculinity. Stereotypes of violence attributed to racialized men (or those seen as men) have a negative impact on their capacity to participate in the labor market and increase their risk of incarceration. Border securitization is one site in which racialized masculinity becomes particularly salient. Research on securitization of the border shows how gendered racializations impact movement and creates new and reinforces old inequalities of mobility, particularly for those understood to be Muslim (Selod 2019). Yet, control of borders is not only aimed at masculinized Muslim bodies – hijab-wearing women are subjected to intensified scrutiny as well.

Gendered racialized practices of border securitization also affect those trying to cross borders to settle elsewhere. Gina Marie Longo (2018) shows how women and men marrying foreign nationals navigate a US immigration system that continuously focuses on the genuineness of the relationship in ways that generate gendered barriers to entry for racialized persons. The same process occurs in Canada (Bhuyan, Korteweg, and Baqi 2018). Ironically, Canadian evidence suggests that greater scrutiny is placed on couples who do not conform to a normatively white heterosexual hierarchies, for example, couples in which women are more highly educated or higher earners than the foreign men they are trying to marry. Similarly, research on the regulation of marriage migration in Canada shows that couples seen as non-normative in their country of origin face greater scrutiny of immigration officials (Satzewich 2015). Longo (2018) shows that those engaged in marriage across borders reinforce white heterosexual normativity as they provide advice to others trying to navigate the US immigration system.

Politics and social movements: enacting and countering gendered racialization

Gendered racializations often work through the trope of "gender equality". As I have written elsewhere, gender equality functions as an empty signifier, notoriously difficult to define yet easily deployed to accuse others of not achieving it (Korteweg 2017). This idea of the malleability of gender equality is also reflected in various empirical studies. For example, Rothing and Bendsen (2011) in a study of Norwegian high school textbooks argue that gender equality and support for gay rights is used to mark Norwegianness. Furthermore, a profession of adherence to gender equality and gay rights is positioned as a prerequisite of symbolic belonging to the Norwegian nation (Rothing and Bendsen 2011). Discussing the hijab, Eid (2015) observes how "the hijab has increasingly come to be regarded in the West as an unambiguous symbol of female oppression. Such an orientalist framework rests upon a feminist rhetoric using gender equality as a vehicle for the racialization of Muslims" (2015, 1902; see also Razack 2007; Korteweg and Yurdakul 2014). Eid further argues that a simultaneous movement of Muslim clerics to position the hijab as a rejection of the west and a form of "religious nationalism" renders the hijab so laden with symbolism as to make it difficult for Muslim women produce their own "social meanings" (Eid 2015, 1903). However, the young Muslim women he interviewed were quite capable of "engag[ing] reflexively with the dominant gender roles into which they were socialized" (Eid 2015, 1913). Eid concludes that we need to reject "the misconceived notion that racialized minorities are solely motivated by culture whereas free choice is confined to Western people" (Eid 2015, 1913; see also Volpp 2000).

Research on so-called honor killing forcefully brings home the impact of the portrayal of Muslims as disregarding gender equality to the point of murder (Abu-Lughod 2011; Razack 2007; Yurdakul and Korteweg 2013). This research shows how this use of gender equality activates the trope of cultural backwardness (Razack 2007). The resulting gendered racializations make it more difficult to address gendered violence in Muslim communities (Korteweg 2014). As this work suggests, the issue of gender equality is particularly salient in the gendered racialization of Muslim immigrants in Europe and North America. It is also reflected in research on MENA countries that addresses support for gender equality, research which is clearly motivated by the political debates around the presumed incompatibility between Islam and gender equality in the global north (see for example Glas, Spiering, and Scheepers 2018).

As a growing number of scholars have pointed out, the call for gender equality, and a concomitant emphasis on support for LGBTQ rights, has informed increasingly exclusionary politics of gendered racialization. Verloo (2018) shows how right-wing political parties in the Netherlands uses the gender equality and LGBTQ rights tropes to promote racist anti-immigrant politics. Analyzing both party statements and political positions, Verloo (2018) clearly demonstrates that for Geert Wilders' Party for Freedom (PVV), which was the second largest party in the Dutch elections of 2017, and also for newer ultraright-wing party, Forum for Democracy, led by Thierry Baudet, which entered parliament with two seats that same year, gender equality and LGBTQ rights are Dutch achievements under threat by "Islamization". In this narrative, gender equality is already achieved by "native" Dutch. Thus, these parties' positions reflect a complete absence of support for furthering gender or queer rights unless the proposal at hand is framed as a way to safeguard those presumably achieved rights from Muslims or Islam. Yet, neither Netherlands, nor any other European nation, has achieved gender equality or full support for LGBTQ rights. Such appeals thus have a dual function: they make addressing continuing issues around gender and gender equality in the general population appear unnecessary, while facilitating the exclusion of racialized others. Farris (2017), in her work on femonationalism, drives this point home forcefully, as does Puar's earlier work on homonationalism (Puar 2007).

This literature also show how processes of gendered racialization are not confined to the ultra- or anti-immigrant right. Rather the notion that gender equality and queer rights are an achievement of the west that can and should be spread to the rest is present across the political spectrum (see Keskinen 2018; Laxer and Korteweg 2018). This also affects the assessment of gendered racialized persons' capacity to be politically active. Bassel and Eme-julu (2017) highlight how gendered racializations structure what counts as activism:

> voting, being a political party or trade union activist, taking part in demonstrations and standing for election are usually what counts as legitimate political action. Because minority women are underrepresented in these traditional political spaces it appears as if minority women are absent from politics, or worse, operate largely as apolitical agents. It is only when we redefine 'what counts' as politics and political behaviour that the diverse ways in which minority women undertake political action becomes visible
>
> *(189)*

This gendered racialized visibility/invisibility dynamic translates into feminist movement activity, where organizations apply an implicit or explicit rank ordering of the potential constituencies they represent and the possible issues they address. The literature shows that feminist movement organizations struggle with the multiplicity of "gender equality" in finding ways to counter gendered racializations but at times enact their own gendered racializations as work by Lépinard (2014), Luna (2016) and Rottmann and Ferree (2008) shows. This work addresses feminist organizing and focuses on the degree to which organizations engage deeply with intersectionality. In other words, these scholars ask to what extent women's organizations are willing and able to take into account the impact of diverse forms of gendered racializations. This work identifies difficulties that feminist organizations continue to have in recognizing the differences between women as they make claims for the recognition of gendered inequalities. Eleonore Lépinard (2014) shows that French practices of denying racialization under the call of republican citizenship informs a repertoire of feminist organizing that puts the category of "women" over and above any specificities that attach to that category through gendered racialization. By contrast, in Canada, there is more room for the recognition of gendered racialization in a context where multiculturalism informs an understanding of recognition for different group rights (Lépinard 2014). Rottmann and Ferree (2008) show that German feminist organizations (run by non-immigrant German women) privilege gender over other differences with respect to both anti-discrimination law and the regulation of headscarf wearing. Feminists failed to see common interests between "women" and those marginalized in employment, education, and so forth on the basis of immigration status or religion as well as gender. As Rottmann and Ferree state, German feminist organizations were not willing to "define 'women's interests' as also intersecting those of their wider ethnic and religious communities" and failed "to form a strategic alliance that did not privilege 'Germanness'" (2008, 487). While German feminists seemed to have limited stamina for protecting German Muslim women's labor rights, they were deeply engaged with the regulation of the headscarf in ways that suggested a desire to, paraphrasing Lila Abu-Lughod (2011) "save Muslim women from Muslim men." Difficulties in feminist organizing around differences between women can extend to organizations led by racialized women. Zakiya Luna (2016) finds that an important, broad, national umbrella organization focusing on gender, race and reproductive health in the United States, nonetheless homogenizes gendered racialization under a "women of color" label that ultimately fails to recognize the specificities of gendered racialization faced by different (groups of) women. Finally, similar processes occur around LGBTQ rights, with EU and North American organizations fostering a recognition of gendered racializations' intersection with LGBTQ subjectivities and practices. However, these recognitions are limited when they reinforce particular understandings of pathways to and realizations of liberation that are patterned on US or European history.

Discussion and conclusion

This chapter has provided a non-exhaustive discussion of processes of gendered racialization with a particular focus on Muslim immigrants in the global north, who following Omi and Winant's definition, experience *"the extension of racial meaning to a previously racially unclassified relationship, social practice or group"* (2014, 111, italics in original). European countries witnessed how a group of immigrants, who as Spielhaus shows, were initially classified by country of origin, have increasingly been imagined through the label Muslim (Spielhaus 2006). This label, in turn, is attached to embodied practices, such as wearing a veil, a beard, or a skull cap. Furthermore, this label is also attached to purported religious values, beliefs and resulting practices that are seen as threats to established nation-states and a politics of (nominal) support for gender equality and LGBTQ rights. In this chapter, I argue that both the ways in which "Muslim" becomes the most salient identity marker for the group thus conceived and the ways in which that label is attached to threat and danger comes about through a process of gendered racialization. Furthermore, this process results in discriminatory practices that do both material and symbolic harm. At the same time, gendered racializations are not limited to Muslims in the global north. Rather, analyzing the positioning of those inhabiting that subject position can be a point for reconceptualizing the ways in which gendered racializations produce complex inequalities across multiple societies.

After illustrating how gendered racializations produce intersectional discrimination, the last part of the chapter turns to political action informed by gendered racializations. I hone in on the ways in which two particular tropes, that of a poorly defined "gender equality" as well as that of "LGBTQ rights," become the vehicle for a particular type of gendered racialization. These tropes are not only taken up in ultra-right politics but across the political spectrum. I also look at how feminist organizations navigate gendered racializations in feminist work. The literature shows feminist movements continue to have difficulty with a genuine recognition of intersectionality that is captured by the concept of gendered racialization.

This chapter barely scratches the surface of work that could be done to analyze the construction and effects of gendered racialization. This chapter offers an overview of work that takes seriously the co-constitution of two categories that both navigate complex ideas about biology and embodiment. The chapter also makes a modest attempt to incorporate a large literature on the LGBTQ dimensions as part and parcel of contemporary gendered racializations. A critical absence in this chapter suggests the need to address the erasure of Indigeneity in the work on gendered racialization and take seriously the ways in which settler colonialism informs ongoing processes of gendered racialization (Glenn 2015; A Simpson 2014; L Simpson 2017).

References

Abu-Lughod, L., 2011. Seductions of the "honor crime". *Differences*, 22(1), pp. 17–63.
Alfrey, L. and F. W. Twine, 2017. Gender-Fluid Geek Girls: negotiating inequality regimes in the Tech industry. *Gender & Society*, 31(1), February 2017 pp. 28–50. 10.1177/0891243216680590

Amar, P., 2011. Middle East masculinity studies: Discourses of "men in crisis," industries of gender in revolution. *Journal of Middle East Women's Studies*, 7(3), pp. 36–70.

Bassel, L. and Emejulu, A., 2017. *Minority Women and Austerity: Survival and Resistance in France and Britain*. Bristol: Policy Press.

Bhuyan, R., Korteweg, A.C. and Baqi, K., 2018. Regulating Spousal Migration through Canada's Multiple Border Strategy: The Gendered and Racialized Effects of Structurally Embedded Borders. *Law & Policy*, 40(4), pp. 346–370.

Bowen, J.R., 2007. *Why the French Don't Like Headscarves: Islam, the State, and Public Space*. Princeton, NJ: Princeton University Press.

Bracke, S., 2012. From "saving women" to "saving gays": Rescue narratives and their dis/continuities. *European Journal of Women's Studies*, 19(2), pp. 237–252.

Butler, J., 2011. *Gender Trouble: Feminism and the Subversion of Identity*. Abingdon: Routledge.

Choo, H.Y. and Ferree, M.M., 2010. Practicing intersectionality in sociological research: A critical analysis of inclusions, interactions, and institutions in the study of inequalities. *Sociological Theory*, 28(2), pp. 129–149.

Collins, P.H., 2002. *Black Feminist Thought: Knowledge, Consciousness, and the Politics of Empowerment*. Abingdon: Routledge.

Contreras, R., 2009. "Damn, Yo—Who's That Girl?" An Ethnographic Analysis of Masculinity in Drug Robberies. *Journal of Contemporary Ethnography*, 38(4), pp. 465–492.

Crenshaw, K., 1990. Mapping the margins: Intersectionality, identity politics, and violence against women of color. *Stan. L. Rev.*, 43, pp. 1241.

Dhoest, A., 2018. Learning to be gay: LGBTQ forced migrant identities and narratives in Belgium. *Journal of Ethnic and Migration Studies*, pp. 1–15.

Eid, P., 2015. Balancing agency, gender and race: how do Muslim female teenagers in Québec negotiate the social meanings embedded in the hijab?. *Ethnic and Racial Studies*, 38(11), pp. 1902–1917.

Bacchetta, P., F. El-Tayeb, and J. Haritaworn. 2019. Queers of Colour and (De)Colonial Spaces in Europe. In *Global Racialities: Empire, Postcoloniality, and Decoloniality*, Bacchetta, P. Maira, S., and Winant, H. (eds). New York: Routledge, pp. 150–178, https://doi.org/10.4324/9780429402203.

El-Tayeb, F., 2012. "Gays who cannot properly be gay": Queer Muslims in the neoliberal European city. *European Journal of Women's Studies*, 19(1), pp. 79–95.

Elver, H., 2011. *The Headscarf Controversy: Secularism and Freedom of Religion*. Oxford: Oxford University Press.

Farris, S. F. and S. de Jong, 2014. Discontinuous intersections: second-generation immigrant girls in transition from work to school. *Ethnic and Racial Studies*, 2014, 37(9), pp. 1505–1525. http://dx.doi.org/10.1080/01419870.2013.774033

Farris, S.R., 2017. *In the Name of Women's Rights: The Rise of Femonationalism*. Durham, NC: Duke University Press.

Frankenberg, R., 1993. *The Social Construction of Whiteness: White Women, Race Matters*. Abingdon: Routledge.

Geva, D., 2018. Daughter, Mother, Captain: Marine Le Pen, Gender, and Populism in the French National Front. In *Social Politics: International Studies in Gender, State & Society*.

Glas, S., N. Spiering, and P. Scheepers, 2018. Re-Understanding Religion and Suppor for Gender Equality in Arab Countries. *Gender & Society*, 32(5), pp. 686–712. 10.1177/0891243218783670.

Glenn, E.N., 1999. The social construction and institutionalization of gender and race. *Revisioning Gender*, pp. 3–43.

Glenn, E.N., 2015. Settler colonialism as structure: A framework for comparative studies of US race and gender formation. *Sociology of Race and Ethnicity*, 1(1), pp. 52–72.

Haritaworn, J., 2012. Women's rights, gay rights and anti-Muslim racism in Europe: Introduction. *European Journal of Women's Studies*, 19(1), pp. 73–78.

Husain, A., 2019. Moving beyond (and back to) the black–white binary: a study of black and white Muslims' racial positioning in the United States. *Ethnic and Racial Studies*, 42(4), pp. 589–606.

Jivraj, S. and A. De Jong, 2011. The Dutch homo-emancipation policy and its silencing effects on queer Muslims. *Feminist Legal Studies*, 19(2), pp. 143.

Keskinen, S., 2018. The "crisis" of White hegemony, neonationalist femininities and antiracist feminism. In *Women's Studies International Forum*, Vol. 68. Pergamon, pp. 157–163.

Korteweg, A.C., 2014. "Honour Killing" in the Immigration Context: Multiculturalism and the Racialization of Violence against Women. *Politikon*, 41(2), pp. 183–208.

Korteweg, A.C., 2017. The "what" and "who" of co-optation: gendered racialized migrations, settler nation-states and postcolonial difference. *International Feminist Journal of Politics*, *19*(2), pp. 216–230.

Korteweg, A.C. and Triadafilopoulos, T., 2013. Gender, religion, and ethnicity: Intersections and boundaries in immigrant integration policy making. *Social Politics*, *20*(1), pp. 109–136.

Korteweg, A.C. and Yurdakul, G., 2014. *The Headscarf Debates: Conflicts of National Belonging*. Stanford: Stanford University Press.

Laborde, C., 2008. *Critical Republicanism: The Hijab Controversy and Political Philosophy*. Oxford: Oxford University Press.

Laxer, E., 2018. "We are all republicans": Political Articulation and the Production of Nationhood in France's Face Veil Debate. *Comparative Studies in Society and History*, *60*(4), pp. 938–967.

Laxer, E. and Korteweg, A.C., 2018. Party competition and the production of nationhood in the immigration context: particularizing the universal for political gain in France and Québec. *Ethnic and Racial Studies*, *41*(11), pp. 1915–1933.

Lépinard, É., 2014. Doing intersectionality: Repertoires of feminist practices in France and Canada. *Gender & Society*, *28*(6), pp. 877–903.

Longo, G.M., 2018. Keeping It in "the Family": How Gender Norms Shape US Marriage Migration Politics. *Gender & Society*, *32*(4), pp. 469–492.

Luna, Z., 2016. "Truly a Women of Color Organization" Negotiating Sameness and Difference in Pursuit of Intersectionality. *Gender & Society*, *30*(5), pp. 769–790.

McCall, L., 2005. The Complexity of Intersectionality. Signs: Journal of Women in Culture and Society, *30*(31), pp. 1771–1800.

Meadow, T., 2017. Whose chosenness counts? The always-already racialized discourse of trans–response to Rogers Brubaker. *Ethnic and Racial Studies*, *40*(8), pp. 1306–1311.

Moors, A., 2009. The Dutch and the face-veil: The politics of discomfort. *Social Anthropology*, *17*(4), pp. 393–408.

Murji, K. and Solomos, J., 2005. *Introduction: racialization in theory and practice* (pp. 1–27). Oxford University Press.

Omi, M. and Winant, H., 2014. *Racial Formation in the United States*. Abingdon: Routledge.

Özyürek, E., 2014. *Being German, becoming Muslim: Race, religion, and conversion in the new Europe*. Vol. 56. Princeton, NJ: Princeton University Press.

Pager, D. and Shepherd, H., 2008. The sociology of discrimination: Racial discrimination in employment, housing, credit, and consumer markets. *Annu. Rev. Sociol*, *34*, pp. 181–209.

Parvez, Z.F., 2017. *Politicizing Islam: The Islamic Revival in France and India*. Oxford: Oxford University Press.

Phoenix, A., 2017. Unsettling intersectional identities: historicizing embodied boundaries and border crossings. *Ethnic and Racial Studies*, *40*(8), pp. 1312–1319.

Puar, J., 2013. Rethinking homonationalism. *International Journal of Middle East Studies*, *45*(2), pp. 336–339.

Puar, J.K. 2007. Introduction: Homonationalism and biopolitics. In *Terrorist Assemblages: Homonationalism in Queer Times*, Puar, J.K. (ed.). pp. 1–36.

Razack, S., 2007. *Casting Out: The Eviction of Muslims from Western Law and Politics*. Toronto: University of Toronto Press.

Rehaag, S., 2017. Sexual Orientation in Canada's Revised Refugee Determination System: An Empirical Snapshot. *Canadian Journal of Women and the Law*, *29*(2), pp. 259–289.

Roggeband, C. and Verloo, M., 2007. Dutch women are liberated, migrant women are a problem: The evolution of policy frames on gender and migration in the Netherlands, 1995–2005. *Social policy & administration*, *41*(3), pp. 271–288.

Rothing, A. and Svendsen, S.H.B. 2011. Sexuality in Norwegian textbooks: constructing and controlling ethnic borders?. *Ethnic and Racial Studies*, *34*(11), pp. 1953–1973.

Rottmann, S.B. and Ferree, M.M., 2008. Citizenship and intersectionality: German feminist debates about headscarf and antidiscrimination laws. *Social Politics*, *15*(4), pp. 481–513.

Satzewich, V., 2015. *Points of Entry: How Canada's Immigration Officers Decide Who Gets In*. Vancouver: UBC press.

Sauer, B., 2009. Headscarf regimes in Europe: Diversity policies at the intersection of gender, culture and religion. *Comparative European Politics*, *7*(1), pp. 75–94.

Scott, J.W., 2009. *The Politics of the Veil*. Princeton, NJ: Princeton University Press.

Selod, S., 2019. Gendered racialization: Muslim American men and women's encounters with racialized surveillance. *Ethnic and Racial Studies*, *42*(4), pp. 552–569.

Shachar, A., 2009. *The Birthright Lottery: Citizenship and Global Inequality*. Cambridge, MA: Harvard University Press.

Simpson, A., 2014. *Mohawk Interruptus: Political Life Across the Borders of Settler States*. Durham, NC: Duke University Press.

Simpson, L.B., 2017. *As We Have Always Done: Indigenous Freedom through Radical Resistance*. Minneapolis: University of Minnesota Press.

Spielhaus, R., 2006. Religion and Identity. How Germany's foreigners have become Muslims. *Internationale Politik Transatlantic Edition*, 8(2), pp. 17–23.

Thobani, S., 2007. *Exalted Subjects: Studies in the Making of Race and Nation in Canada*. Toronto: University of Toronto Press.

Verloo, M., 2018. Gender knowledge, and opposition to the feminist project: Extreme-right populist parties in the Netherlands. *Politics and Governance*, 6(3), pp. 20–30.

Volpp, L., 2000. Blaming culture for bad behavior. *Yale JL & Human.*, *12*, pp. 89.

Yurdakul, G. and Korteweg, A.C., 2013. November Gender equality and immigrant integration: Honor killing and forced marriage debates in the Netherlands, Germany, and Britain. In *Women's Studies International Forum*, Vol. 41. Pergamon, pp. 204–214.

Yuval-Davis, N., 2006. Intersectionality and feminist politics. *European Journal of Women's Studies*, *13*(3), pp. 193–209.

Yuval-Davis, N., 2011. *The Politics of Belonging: Intersectional Contestations*. London: Sage.

27

Racial states – gendered nations

On biopower, race, and sex

Sarah Bracke and Luis Manuel Hernández Aguilar

Introduction[1]

When Michel Foucault (1990) began interrogating biopower in *History of Sexuality Vol. 1*, the category of sex occupied a critical position in this thinking as it linked the microphysics of power aimed at disciplining the body with the larger project of control and regulation of the population. Sex thus figured at the juncture of the body and the population, pertaining both to the life of the body as well as to the life of the species. When Foucault (1997; see also: Foucault, 2007; Foucault, 2008) subsequently further developed his thesis of biopower in the lecture series *Society must be Defended*, he was concerned with thinking about the state, historical discourse as a weapon of power, and the category of race in the frame of biopower. Here, the critical category of sex receded to the background of his analysis. Moreover, most of Foucault's work has avoided or failed to attend to the question of sexual differentiation (Braidotti, 1994; Grosz, 1994). In this contribution, we revisit and critically engage with a biopolitical analytic of power in a way that attends to not only to how race and racial differentiation are situated at the heart of biopower, but equally engages sex and sexual differentiation.

We do so in order to address the scholarly lacuna identified by David Goldberg (2002), i.e. the historical co-definition of race and the state in its modern manifestations. According to Goldberg (2002: 2), the growing literature on state formation has avoided dealing with the implication of race within processes of state formation, while research on race and racism has circumvented, to a large extent, the function of the state in the formation of racial configurations and exclusions. Yet race, as Goldberg argued,

> is integral to the emergence, development, and transformations (conceptually, philosophically, materially) of the modern nation-states … racial configuration fashions the terms of the founding myth, the fabrication of historical memory, necessary (as Charles Tilly insist) to both the discursive production and ideological rationalization of modern state power.
>
> *(Goldberg, 2002: 4)*

Furthermore, racial states have elaborated, circulated, and predicated a linkage between the notion of race and a conceptualization of homogeneity defined in national terms. In other words, states have defined, invested, and promoted projects of racial homogeneity, which also necessitated and operated through sexual differentiation, as we will argue. In this contribution, we take Foucault's theoretical and methodological elaboration on race and the state as a fruitful starting point to bridge the gap identified by Goldberg regarding the co-definition of race and the state. Moreover, we also contend that this analysis should proceed by taking into account the way in which race and the state are also co-defined by sex and sexual differentiation. The argument thus proceeds as follows. First, we briefly sketch Foucault's methodological approach toward institutions and the state which we will apply in our analysis. Second, we rehearse the thesis of biopower and lay out the centrality of race and racism within the biopolitical analytic. Finally, we (re-)engage sex and sexual differentiation – including various arguments positioning gender at the core of the production and reproduction of nationalism – at the heart of biopower. Following Kyla Schuller (2018), we make an argument for recovering the centrality of sex within the context of biopower in order to understand how the state, through biopolitical power, effects and works upon caesuras on racial and sexual differentiation. For its functioning as the mechanism of power granting life and letting die, biopower crafts not only a racial caesura determining the parameters of who lives and who is left to die, but also necessitates power techniques oriented toward reproducing the life of that segment of population deemed racially superior. Sex differentiation in the form of binary heteronormativity then appears precisely as that technique inciting and seeking to secure the reproduction of the nation.

Approaching the state: suspending universals

While Foucault has often been charged with lacking a detailed and elaborated method (Gutting, 2001), in the lecture series *Security, Territory, Population* (Foucault, 2007) he outlined three methodological procedures with which he undertook his de-centered analysis of institutions – including the state – articulated with power-knowledge relations. The first analytical procedure involves a displacement outside the institution, "moving off-center in relation to the problematic of the institution or what could be called the 'institutional-centric' approach" (Foucault, 2007: 116). Rather than focusing on institutions, Foucault seeks to uncover techniques and procedures generating the institutions, that is to say, the discourses, subject formations, and social relations that are codified, condensed, and reproduced by institutions. The second methodological movement outside the institution consists of analyzing its purpose. According to Foucault (2007: 117), the history of institutions is not determined by the failure or success of their imputed functions. The examination of the expected purpose of an institution should therefore be suspended, and the institutional setting should be inserted into the general economy of power relations. And finally, the third strategy can be found in the refusal to put an already defined object at the center of analysis; "instead, it involved grasping the movement by which a field of truth with objects of knowledge was constituted through these mobile technologies" (Foucault, 2007:118).

The method outlined by Foucault proposes an alternative view on how to think of and analyze institutions (and one may even argue categories of analysis) by moving outside the institutions, and thereby releasing power relations from their institutional constraints in order to analyze them from the advantageous point of view of the technologies of power. These methodological procedures, one might argue, emanate from the epistemological point of departure which Foucault captured in the phrase: "Let's suppose that universals do not exist" (Foucault, 2008:3). Suspending universals operates as a critique of the kind of sociological analysis that deduces concrete problems on the basis of prefigured universal categories such as the state, civil society or the market. And we might add, stretching Foucault's argument, that it also questions analyses that take prefigured categories of race, class, and gender as their point of departure (see also: Puar, 2012). The incitement to "suppose that universals do not exist" entails a theoretical and methodological position which shifts the analytical focus to the practices sustaining and shaping those universals. That is to say, it urges us to consider the state – and also race and gender for that matter – as an effect of power/knowledge relations and technologies of power such as discipline (the modality of power that produces docile bodies), biopolitics (the power to manage life and its reproduction), and governmentality (the rational strategy to conduct conducts).

In this sense, the state should be interpreted neither as a given fact nor as a singular event, but rather "as a contingent political process" (Lemke, 2007: 46), subjected to continual conflicts, stabilizations, and transmutations,

> Rather, the state is conceptualized as a 'transactional reality' [réalité de transaction] (Foucault, 2004: 301), that is to say a dynamic ensemble of relations and syntheses that at the same time produces the institutional structure of the state and the knowledge of the state ... The assumption that the state does not exist is followed by the question of how different elements and practices made it possible that something like the state possesses a historical reality and structural consistency over a longer period of time.
>
> *(Lemke, 2007: 48)*

The relevance of Foucault's method for analyzing the state resides in not taking for granted what is usually apprehended as such, and instead investigating the power relations and mechanisms that create the categories in first place, a principle that also applies to Foucault's inquiry into race and racism, and its function within the biopolitical technology of power.

Biopower, race, and racism

Foucault began developing his biopower thesis in the last chapter of his interrogation of the history of sexuality, an analytic move that took him from the micro toward the macrophysics of power. Yet this purportedly sudden turn from the microphysics of power towards the governmentalized state, as Bob Jessop (2013: 140) has pointed out, might also be seen as a smooth transition from the study of institutions and modalities of power toward a wider frame, namely, the techniques with respect to state forces: biopower and governmentality.

In the *History of Sexuality*, Foucault (1990: 145) considered the configuration of "sex as a political issue" in a twofold manner. First, sex was part of the arrangements of disciplinary techniques directed at the body, and second, sex was also deployed in the regulation and management of the social body, the population. Sexuality thus constitutes the link between regulatory power and discipline. On the one hand, discipline operating at the level of the body, and on the other hand, biopower working at the level of the production, control, and regulation of populations. Sex linked the life of the individual body to the life of the species as a whole and became the axis of micro and macro technologies of power. In the words of Foucault (1990: 147 [emphasis in the original]), "Through the themes of health, progeny, race, the future of the species, the vitality of the social body, power spoke of sexuality and *to* sexuality".

This is the point where race entered biopower's analytics. According to Stoler, what links Foucault's *History of Sexuality* with the 1976's lectures is the argument "that the emergence of biopower inscribed modern racism in the mechanism of the normalizing state" (Stoler,

1995: 55). In his lectures, Foucault focused on the modern state and the emergence of state racism as a part of it. Biopower, in this view, was a crucial feature of racism, in the same vein as racism was a crucial feature of biopower.

Foucault was, however, not interested in the break of modern racism with what could be seen as previous and older forms of the phenomenon. Rather, his concerns centered on the discursive bricolage whereby an old discourse of race was recovered, reactivated, modified, and embedded in new forms, thus crafting new statements and relations (Stoler, 1995). In this vein, and drawing upon a Foucaultian perspective, Kyla Schuller proposes us to think race in terms of a palimpsest, in which one meaning and conceptualization of race is inscribed upon the other – older – one in such a way that each contemporary notion of race always carries visible traces of those earlier inscriptions (Schuller, 2018: 97). Such an approach to race is consequential when it comes to understanding racism. Following Foucault, Stoler (2002: 376) argues that "polyvalent mobility" represents one of racism's defining features, namely, racism's discursive capacity to renew itself, to be used in different ways and for diverse purposes, e.g. by the state or by actors opposing the state. Racism can be a narrative of state power, but also a counter-narrative opposing the state (Stoler, 2002: 376).

It is, therefore, possible to talk about a dynamic racism – a racism of expansion having different historical moments, conjunctures, and varieties. Stuart Hall (1971, 2000)) developed a similar argument, reasoning that racial formations have been produced and molded by specific and historical relations of power thereby developing different and in-situ historiographies. Thus, when analyzing a specific socio-historical reality, instead of *racism* the more appropriate label would be *racisms* (Hall, 2000: 11).

The polyvalent mobility of racism highlights its capacity to draw from old racial vocabularies while aligning its arguments with contemporary political claims. It also underscores the flexibility of racism in its different configurations productively incorporating and refashioning categories such as religion, culture, class, sexuality, and gender intertwined in the process of fixing ontologies and creating hierarchies between them, influencing processes of inclusion and exclusion, violence, discrimination, establishing privileges, but also producing and being produced by state projects of homogeneity. Racism and its meanings are neither immutable nor final.

Thus, the main task when analyzing racist discourses does not reside in determining their newness or oldness, but in exploring how they are produced, reproduced, and utilized. In other words, the task consists of unpacking which power relations created these racist discourses, and what are racism's political consequences in a particular context. Likewise, we should be looking at how racist discourses produce consent and legitimacy between groups and individuals with dissimilar access to resources and in different positions. One might also wonder about the relation between the spread of racial statements and their use as a means to legitimate policies, stricter measures of surveillance and control, exclusionary practices and consent about their implementation. Last but not least, the analysis of racial discourses should inquire not only about the racially characterized subjects that they manufacture, but also about the relational aspect of such a process, that is, how the dominant identity is imagined and reified as the positive counterpart of the racialized representation of the Other.

If the state might be approached as a "transactional reality" and racism as a "polyvalent discourse", biopower, according to Foucault, represents the technology of power inscribing racism in the mechanisms of the state (1997: 254), thus establishing the distinction between what must live from what must die, by producing a set of differences and hierarchies among the continuum of the human race, this will allow power to treat the population as a mixture of races, or to be more accurate to treat the species, to subdivide the species it controls, into the subspecies known as races. That is the first function of racism, to create caesura within the biological continuum addressed by biopower.

(Foucault, 1997: 255)

The first function of racism within the biopolitical scheme posits the idea that society must defend itself. It has to be purified from the permanent threat posed by its own internal dangers – the inferior races within. Racism creates the need to protect the society, allowing the inscription of this principle in the state's mechanisms, which enacted different techniques in the name of defending the social body whereby

we see the appearance of a State racism: a racism that society will direct against itself, against its own elements, and its own products. This is the internal racism of permanent purification, and it will become one of the basic dimensions of social normalization.

(Foucault, 1997: 62)

This first function is complemented by a second one, the warfare relation, which entails the recoding of the discourse on war as a means to understand power relations and its working in dividing the social body, in which in order to live you must kill, for racism the sentence is translated into "if you want to live, the other must die" (Foucault, 1997: 255). In the words of Foucault,

racism justifies the death-function in the economy of biopower by appealing to the principle that the death of others makes one biologically stronger insofar as one is a member of a race or a population, insofar as one is an element in a unitary living plurality.

(Foucault, 1997: 258)

Henceforth, the work of racism in a biopolitical state enables, on the one hand, the elimination of the biological menace, and on the other hand, the improvement of the race. Racism makes killing acceptable.

The fact that the other dies does not mean simply that I live in the sense that his death guarantees my safety; the death of the other, the death of the bad race, of the inferior race (or the degenerate, or the abnormal) is something that will make my life in general healthier and purer.

(Foucault, 1997: 255)

Improving by eliminating, eliminating to improve,

In this light, the systematic genocidal campaigns mounted by a political state such as Nazi Germany must, Foucault suggests, be seen as consistent with the emergence of biopower in modernity. To the extent that the purity of blood – and of race defined in terms of genetic heritage – is the primary reason used for the extermination of those who are branded as unclean, racial discrimination is a logical manifestation of biopower, the point of which, it should be emphasized, is not simply to kill but to generate life, to manage and optimize it, to make it better for the future of the human species.

(Chow, 2002: 7)

In this sense, according to Stoler (1995: 84), biopower established "a *positive* relation between the right to kill and the assurance of life. It posits that 'the more you kill [and] … let die, the more you will live'." Henceforth, racism reactivated the discourse of permanent war in a novel way by "establishing a biological confrontation between my life and the death of others" (Stoler, 1995: 85).

Killing in Foucault's terms also refers to political death, which does not entail a direct act of extermination or murdering, but denotes the rejection and expulsion of the inferior races from the political body. In other words, biopower equally manifests itself through mechanisms of segregation, exclusion, and discrimination. Thus, racism works as the principle that justifies the death function of the technology of power aimed at the population by direct or indirect killing.

The peculiarity of modern racism therefore resides in its linkage and articulation with the technology of biopower. Racism thus is linked to the functioning of the state, which uses race as the principle for purifying the society from its internal enemies; as such, biopower marks a transition from sovereign power, "which either put to death or let live" towards the biopolitical frame where the state "let die and granted life" (Lemke, 2019: 137). The conceptualization of the state entails a collective body that should manage life, "racism is intrinsic to the nature of all modern, normalizing states and their biopolitical technologies" (Stoler, 1995: 88).

Revisiting biopower and sexual differentiation

This administration and management of life, however, begs the question of social and biological reproduction, which is not only the reproduction of life but also of race, of life that is reproduced – or prevented from reproducing – as racial difference. This is where sex is central to biopolitics, as a technology of reproduction: sex and its fertility had to be administered, and emerged as a result of the deployment of sexuality (Foucault, 1990). While Foucault understood sex to be crucially situated at the intersection of the life of the body and the life of the population or species, he avoided or failed to think sexual differentiation (Braidotti, 1994; Grosz, 1994).

Stoler, moreover, makes a similar suggestion in relation to the nation and also empire. She criticizes Foucault's lack of engagement with the significance of the discourse of nation and empire and its gender-specificity, since "Europeanness was not only class-specific but gender coded" (Stoler, 1995: 115). Foucault's account of the cultivation of the bourgeois-self remained rooted in Europe, as if the West functioned as a self-contained entity (Spivak, 1994), a narration that is rebuked by the history of colonialism and imperialism. In addition, the cultivation of the bourgeois-self transpired through a wider world of Manichean distinctions, where the non-European Others provided the contrast positing the racially characterized colonized body as the negative counterpart to the European "healthy vigorous bourgeois body" (Stoler, 1995: 8). Foucault's lack of analysis of how biopower, race, sexuality, and sex were articulated in the colonies, obscured the crafting of subjugated bodies crucial for the development of his history of sexuality, for as Stoler (1995: 15) points out, the colonies functioned as "laboratories of modernity" in which the technologies of power were rehearsed.

Furthermore, as Schuller (2018: 20) has recently documented, biopower also operated and was deployed through the regulation of "sentiment and affect as sites of Imperial control". These critiques and further elaborations of Foucault's biopower do not discard the analytics of power put forward by the French philosopher; rather, they open new venues of analysis, while complementing the ubiquitous operations of a technology of power that has not respected national borders. One of these venues pertains to the co-constitutive relation between the inscription of race in the state on the one hand, and the operations of gender in the production of nationalisms as well as the function of sexual differentiation within the biopolitical frame on the other. Racial states, as Goldberg noted, are also gendered states. This means that the inscription of race in the mechanisms of the state or the configuration of the state through racial principles is tied up with the production of gendered identities. But gender, following Anne McClintock (1995: 352), has, in different ways, been coupled with the other part of the dyad of the nation-state. "All nationalisms are gendered," McClintock has argued (1995: 352), which entails the dependence of nations upon the social construction of race and gender for the reproduction of the imagined community, and the crafting of gendered national identities and their reproduction. Nationalisms have been played out to draw, circulate, and reify symbolic boundaries and distinctions between men and women. The gendered character of the nation and nationalism has been investigated by Floya Anthias and Nira Yuval-Davis (1993; Yuval-Davis, 1997), who argue that the implication of women in the gendered reproduction of the nation and its relation with state practices can be analytically distinguished in five categories (Anthias and Yuval-Davis, 1993: 115). First, women are situated as the subjects reproducing the ethnic group and the nation in biological terms – a reproduction which has more recently been rethought as "regeneration", as non-heteronormative modes of the reproduction of life have found their place within the folds of the nation (see Puar, 2007 on homonationalism; Schuller, 2018). Second, women have been cast as the subjects who delimit the ethnic boundaries (see also: Stoler, 1995). Third, still according to Anthias and Yuval-Davis, women have been positioned as active conveyors of national culture. On a symbolic level, moreover, women have been seen as vehicles for the reproduction of national identities, which constitutes a fourth way in the nation is gendered. And finally, women have been "as participants in national, economic, political and military struggle" (Anthias and Yuval-Davis, 1993: 115). These distinct albeit interrelated dimensions affirm that process of nation-building are profoundly sexually differentiated, and sexually differentiating, projects. Projects, in other words, that produce national gender identities.

Additionally, McClintock (1995: 355) argues that nationalisms are produced by and reproduce gendered discourses intertwined with dislocated projections of time, in which the nation comprises contradictory narratives about past and future, which are

> resolved by figuring the contradiction in the representation of times as a natural division of gender. Women are represented as the atavistic and authentic body of national tradition (inert, backward-looking and natural). Men, by contrast, represent the progressive agent of national modernity (forward-thrusting, potent and historic) embodying nationalism's progressive, or revolutionary principle of discontinuity.
>
> *(McClintock, 1995: 359)*

These various analyses affirm that, within a biopolitical analytic, sexual differentiation, and indeed the gender categories resulting from this differentiating, are crucial for the nation-state. Biopower divides the population into who lives and who doesn't live in other words, biopower establishes racial taxonomies and hierarchies, and race "stabilizes the economic and biological health of the population", according to Kyla Schuller, (2018: 16), which in turn enables the development of civilization. The stabilization of civilization, Schuller continues, occurs through sexual differentiation. Schuller develops this argument through an investigation of "impressibility" as a "key measure of racially and sexually differentiating the refined, sensitive, and civilized subject, who was embedded in time and capable of progress" (Schuller,

2018: 8). Sex difference, she argues, divides the civilized body into two halves, with a more susceptible female half that thus relieves the other, male, half of the burden of embodiment and too much susceptibility, and thereby establishes the male connection to reason. Rationality, in other words, which operates as a key-component of civilization, is made possible because of sexual difference. "Binary sex is both the cause and effect of reason," Schuller argues, that is to say, it represents a division of sexual labor that secures reason to be on the side of men (Schuller, 2018: 16).

In this vein, the purported lack of rationality among the "less civilized" is the expression of another, more fundamental, lack, i.e. sexual difference. In her work on sex and secularism, Joan Scott (2018) demonstrates that "the presumed natural difference of the sexes was the social foundation of modern Western nation-states", as sexual difference was deployed to establish the racial superiority of the West (Scott, 2018: 18). In a conception and self-understanding of modernity as a social formation based on increased (functional) differentiation, sexual differentiation understood as an ontological distinction between the sexes was taken to be a sign of modernity, both in its association with the West as well as in its implementation by colonial powers (Scott, 2018: 27). This point has been further elaborated by scholars seeking to decolonize gender. In her critical examination of Western gender discourses from an African standpoint, Oyèrónké Oyěwùmí, (1997) has argued that a rigid binary understanding of sex, tightly connected to gender, was not an organizing principle of Yoruba society prior to Western colonization. Thinking from a Latin American context, María Lugones (2010) has argued that the Western "gender system is not just hierarchical but racially differentiated" (Lugones, 2010: 748), in a way in which the hegemonic gender taxonomy serves racial differentiation which not only denies humanity to the colonized, but indeed also gender. Put differently, the denial of "proper" sexual differentiation, and subsequent gendered identities, among the colonized was a crucial way in which the humanity of the colonized was denied. Or in words that resonate with Foucault's lectures: in a modern Western context sexual differentiation developed as a "defense" strategy, defending the social body and the racial differentiation that defines it, including what Foucault refers to as the permanent purification of internal racism.

In her study on the biopolitics of feelings, Schuller suggests that we should understand sexual difference as a function of race (Schuller, 2018: 17). Binary sexual differentiation, together with "civilized sexuality", "linking the two halves [of the population] under strict conditions of reproductive monogamy" (Schuller, 2018: 108) has come to accomplish the biopolitics of racial differentiation, not only through "reproducing the nation" but also reproducing civilization as a means of racial hierarchy. Sexual difference, in other words, as it has emerged in the context of Western modernity, is also racial distinction. Racial power, as Schuller puts it, has delineated the notion of "woman", and their corresponding physical attributes and affective capacities (Schuller, 2018: 133), and regulates who has access to (claim) femininity. The notion of woman, in other words, emerged as a biopolitical subjectivity conceived within racial hierarchies of civilization (Schuller, 2018: 103).

Conclusion

The biopolitical analytic, as put forward by Foucault and critically elaborated by many others – notably with the aim of incorporating colonialism and empire within the analytic (Stoler, 1995) as well as thinking necropolitics (Mbembé, 2003) – remains very apt, we insist, to account for the endurance of race and racisms and their functioning within modern states. Yet at the heart of this biopolitical analytic lies a notion of sex, which operates as the juncture between the (disciplined) body and the (regulated) population, and a process of sexual differentiation, which accounts for the reproduction of race and racial differentiation, along the construction of national identities and myths.

To put this in a different way all together, we might argue that *History of Sexuality* is (also) an account of the emergence of modern race in Western Europe. Yet while Foucault has left us with a seminal account of modern sex and sexuality, sexual differentiation remains undertheorized within this biopolitical analytic. Elaborating a biopolitical focus on sexual differentiation, as the work of Schuller (2018) does, enables a better understanding of how deeply racialized hegemonic notions of femininity and masculinity are, and the significant extent to which patterns of sexual differentiation are indeed patterns of racial differentiation.

Considering sexual difference in terms of the production of race difference might suggest that sexual difference can be relegated to a secondary role, or an analogical effect of racial formation (Schuller, 2018:17). Yet this biopolitical analytic holds a different analytical promise. It recognizes that sexual difference is at the heart of racial formation and indeed racism, while, conversely, race is inscribed at heart of the Western gender system with its tenets of binary sex and heteronormativity. It also questions *certain* more recent understandings or applications of intersectionality in which gender and race are understood as prefigured categories which subsequently intersect with each other – an understanding of intersectionality which has been critiqued in various manners (see notably Puar, 2012, but also Bilge, 2013). The biopolitical analytic invites us to, at least temporarily, suspend any ontological, prefigured or descriptive nature to categories of analysis such as race, sex, and gender. Instead, it proposes to inquire about the power relations, forces, and mechanisms at play in the formation of these categories and social ontologies. Suspending the existence of these categories is not equivalent to denying their effects in the social world, but often analyses investigating such effects grant a certain degree of stability to these categories. What we have proposed so far is taking a step back and interrogating those discourses, relations, and mechanisms of power creating the conditions of appearance of categories such as race, gender, class, and one may add religion and class as well. Here we might return to and paraphrase Foucault; our analyses might benefit from supposing that race, sex, and gender do not exist.

Note

1 This work was developed in the context of the research programme *EnGendering Europe's Muslim Question* with project number 016.Vici.185.077, which is financed by the Dutch Research Council.

References

Anthias, F. & Yuval-Davis, N., 1993. *Racialized Boundaries: Race, Nation, Gender, Colour and Class and the Anti-Racist Struggle*, London: Routledge.

Bilge, S., 2013. Intersectionality Undone: Saving Intersectionality from Feminist Intersectionality Studies. *W.E.B. DuBois Review*, 10(2), 405–424.

Braidotti, R., 1994. *Nomadic Subjects. Embodiment and Sexual Difference in Contemporary Feminist Theory*, New York: Columbia University Press.

Chow, R., 2002. *The Protestant Ethnic and the Spirit of Capitalism*, New York: Columbia University Press.

Foucault, M., 1990. *The History of Sexuality. Volume 1: An introduction*, New York: Vintage.

Foucault, M., 1997. *Society must be Defended*, New York: Picador.

Foucault, M., 2007. *Security, Territory, Population*, New York: Picador.

Foucault, M., 2008. *The Birth of Biopolitics*, New York: Picador.

Goldberg, D.T., 2002. *The Racial State*, Massachusetts/Oxford: Blackwell Publishers.

Grosz, E., 1994. *Volatile Bodies: Toward a Corporeal Feminism*, Bloomington: Indiana University Press.

Gutting, G., 2001. *French Philosophy in the Twentieth Century*, Cambridge: Cambridge University Press.

Hall, S., 1971. Race, articulation and societies structured in dominance. In P. Essed & D. T. Goldberg, eds. *Sociological Theories Race and Colonialism*. Paris: Unesco, 305–345.

Hall, S., 2000. Rassismus als ideologischer Diskurs. In N. Räthzel, ed. *Theorien über Rassismus*. Hamburg: Argument Verlag, 7–16.

Jessop, B., 2013. *State Power*, Manchester: Polity Press.

Lemke, T., 2007. An indigestible meal? Foucault, governmentality and state theory. *Distinktion: Scandinavian Journal of Social Theory*, 8(2), 43–66.

Lemke, T., 2019. *Foucault's Analysis of Modern Governmentality. A Critique of Political Reason*, London & New York: Verso.

Lugones, M., 2010. Toward a Decolonial Feminism. *Hypatia*, 25(4), 742–759.

Mbembé, A., 2003. Necropolitics. *Public Culture*, 15(1), 11–40.

McClintock, A., 1995. *Imperial Leather. Race, Gender and Sexuality in the Colonial Contest*, New York: Routledge.

Oyěwùmí, O., 1997. *The Invention of Women, Making an African Sense of Western Gender Discourses*, Minneapolis & London: University of Minnesota Press.

Puar, J.K., 2012. "I would rather be a cyborg than a goddess" Becoming-Intersectional in Assemblage Theory. *PhiloSOPHIA*, 2(1), 49–66.

Schuller, K., 2018. *The Biopolitics of Feeling, Race, Sex, and Science in the Nineteenth Century*, Durham and London: Duke University Press.

Scott, J.W., 2018. *Sex & Secularism*, Princeton: Princeton University Press.

Spivak, G.C., 1994. Can the Subaltern Speak?. In P. Williams & L. Chrisman, eds. *Colonial Discourse and Post-colonial Theory. A Reader*. New York: Columbia University Press, 66–111.

Stoler, A.L., 1995. *Race and the Education of Desire. Foucault's History of Sexuality and the Colonial Order of Things*, Durham and London: Duke University Press.

Stoler, A.L., 2002. Racial Histories and Their Regimes of Truth. In D. T. Goldberg & P. Essed, eds. *Race Critical Theories*. Malden & Oxford: Blackwell Publishers, 369–391.

Yuval-Davis, N., 1997. *Gender and Nation*, London: Sage.

Part VIII
Racism, culture and religion

Introduction

The focus of the two chapters that make up this part is on the interactions between racism, culture and religion. Among the issues that have come to the fore in recent scholarship on race and racism questions about culture and religion are perhaps the most important. The events of 9/11 and wider developments in the two decades that followed have helped to shape the study of culture and religion in quite fundamental ways. In particular it has led to a focusing of attention on Islam and on Muslim communities in the West. We have seen growing bodies of scholarly research and debate about Islam, forms of religious fundamentalism, the role of terrorist movements such as Al-Qaida and ISIS, Islamophobia, the position of Muslim minorities in the West and related questions. This growth of scholarship has been evident in a number of fields of research, ranging from sociology, politics, international relations, law and the humanities. In addition, we have also seen intense media and public policy debates about Islam, particularly in the context of electoral politics and debates about multiculturalism.

In this part of the *Handbook* we have two chapters that explore key facets of this phenomenon. Nasar Meer's chapter takes a broad sweep and asks the question of what characterises the evolving relationship between modernity, race and religion. Meer's chapter seeks to cover a wide range of issues and he argues that it is important for scholars of racism to develop both a historical and contemporary understanding of the relationship between race and ethnicity and religion. He traces out a number of historical examples in order to develop the core argument that underpins the chapter as a whole, namely that the category of race was not only co-constituted with religion, but pre-constituted with religion. He follows this up with an exploration of the complex mechanisms through which the formation of racial ideologies in the racialisation of religious subjects. In particular, he seeks to question the ways in which many of the classic accounts of the emergence of modes of racial thinking elide the historical role of Islam and Muslims in the making of European racial thought. His overarching argument is then developed through a number of examples that explore the role of religion in processes of race making.

Meer's more historically based approach is followed by Riva Kastoryano's chapter, which sets out to explore the mechanisms through which religious *otherness* helps to define the boundaries of contemporary racism. She bases her argument on the key idea that religion and race often interact and provide alternative elements to national identities and to nationalisms. Much of the chapter is focused on the current situation in Europe, and Kastoryano provides a detailed discussion of the ways in which Muslim migrants have been framed through a specific lens that questions the compatibility of Islam with secularism and universal democratic values. But she also extends this account in order to highlight the ways in which we have seen in the contemporary period the emergence of Islam as a transnational political force that forms a form of political community guided by a de-territorialised imagined geography that gives rise to a form of transnational nationalism around religion. She suggests that ideas about religion and otherness are playing an increasingly important role in developing political and civil society discourses about cultural and civic diversity. In developing this analysis, she seeks to outline the increasingly important role of transnational forms of religious mobilisation and the role of diasporas and networks of political mobilisation.

Taken together, these two chapters provide an overview of some of the key issues that need to be addressed in developing a more rounded account of the ways in which discourses about religion and culture become embedded with questions about race and racism. They are also suggestive of the need for more detailed analysis of the role of religious and cultural identities in shaping contemporary expressions of racism.

28

Modernity, race and religion

Nasar Meer

Introduction

This chapter will consider the relationship between race and modernity, and examine how the historical status of Islam and Muslims can cast light on this. The discussion begins with what is sometimes characterised as the standard account of how modernity generated categories of race, before challenging this reading with an argument about the racialisation of Islam and Muslim minorities in Europe. In this first section the argument traces the rise of modernity interalia the emergence of race, following which this reading is historicised in section two by taking into consideration pre-modern articulations of race. In section three, the racio-relgious character of modernity is drawn out to illustrate the continuity between pre-modern and modern racialisation of religion. The conclusion then returns us to the objective of the prevailing discussion, which is not to refute the standard account, but instead to invite readers to think more critically, and indeed historically, about the form and content of religion in processes of race making.

When is modernity, and how is it related to race?

'Modernity', the great Frankfurt School author Theodore Adorno once argued, 'is a qualitative, not a chronological, category' (1978: 218). That is to say, modernity is a process of experience as much as it is a period of time. In this chapter what is meant by modernity relies on both a temporal frame as well as an experiential one, and dates from the historical period from the late fifteenth century in Europe that was bolstered by the Renaissance and European Enlightenment. These grand historical terms fold together a series of *both* processes and temporal developments, summarised by Giddens (Giddens, 1998: 94) as, firstly, 'a certain set of attitudes towards the world, the idea of the world as open to transformation, by human intervention', secondly, 'a complex of economic institutions, especially industrial production and a market economy', and thirdly 'a range of political institutions, including the nation-state and mass democracy'.

Modernity therefore needs to be understood as both *experiences* and *events*, which might be brought together and described through a 'periodised' account. For example, Berman (1982) distinguished between 'early modernity', roughly from the late fifteenth century when Columbus landed in the Americas and the Catholic *Reconquista* re-captured the Muslim Iberian Peninsula, up to the French Revolution. Then, 'Classical modernity'

(1789–1900) and the long nineteenth century which saw the birth of industrial capitalism in Europe and the colonial adventure and imperial systems of wealth and labour extraction from the Global South. Lastly, 'late modernity' (1900 onward) which comes to name bulk of the twentieth century and probably beyond. The colonial feature of modernity, however, is something often overlooked yet is central to the story of race, and is one reason for the term 'colonial modern', which signals the desire for 'a reconstructed understanding modernity inclusive of its colonial histories and their consequences' (Bhambra, 2015: 13).

Perhaps the most conventional reading of race in this characterisation is to make it the *explanandum* and modernity the *explanans*. To frame it in these terms borrows from Hempel and Oppenheim (1948: 152) who wanted to use these terms to understand events 'by virtue of the realization of certain specified antecedent conditions'. In this respect, the *explanandum* ('what is the contemporary provenance of race?') meets the response of the *explanans* ('the activity of modernity'). Take, for example, Quijano (2000: 534) for whom the idea of race 'does not have a known history before the colonization of America', since 'the racial axis has a colonial origin and character' (Quijano, 2000: 533). Elsewhere Feagin (2014: 8) argues that 'European colonialism and imperialism … reached much of the globe and *created a global racial order*, which has had severe consequences for the world's peoples for centuries' (my emphasis). Or the argument proposed by Bonilla-Silva (2015) that racial theory should have been 'rooted in the experiences of the first peoples who experienced racialisation [by which is meant colonisation] … We would be in a better explanatory position today to understand not only race in the world system, but even developments in the United States and Europe, if we were to go back and … begin at the beginning'. For Mignolo (2010: 24) too, 'the racial classificatory logic' is anchored in a colonial 'historical foundation [that] can be traced back to the end of the fifteenth century in Spain', and that 'Racism, as we sense it today, was the result of … conceptual inventions of imperial knowledge' (Mignolo, 2009: 19).

What these readings share in common is not only that coloniality is the crucible of race, but also that the race concept is most substantively forged in modernity, or in Gilroy's (2004: 56) terms: 'modernity transformed the ways "race" was understood and acted upon'. One possible example of the difference strands being brought together, though not necessarily in a linear sequence, is Goldberg's (2006: 331) study 'mapping the racial contours of contemporary European self-conception, historically understood'. In this he traces 'the European imaginary of the European, the Black, the Jew, and the Muslim' (Goldberg, 2006: 331) to argue that while 'the relational frame for thinking through race in the European context has usually been ordered in dualistic terms … there is a third major artery' (Goldberg, 2006: 362). This comprises 'The Muslim' (Goldberg, 2006: 344), which, in Bleich's (2006: 17) terms, 'has all the earmarks of classic racialization', namely 'the classification of such a group as inherently dangerous and inferior' (Bleich, 2006: 17). As with the thrust of my argument, what these examples make manifest are the compositions contained in working references to racial and religious antipathy, but also that modern biological racism has some roots in pre-modern religious antipathy. There are a number of literatures which might develop this point. Paul Gilroy is an interesting example as there are several places in his repertoire where this might be taken up. Perhaps strangely, his majestic *Black Atlantic: Modernity and Double Consciousness* (1993) does not make this an explicit focus, concentrating specifically on the ways in which 'the social and political subordination of blacks and other non-European peoples does not generally feature in debates about … modernity'. That book then is one – very compelling – corrective to the oversight. It is instead elsewhere in *Between Camps* (2004) where Gilroy's fullest elaboration of the points raised above arguably come through. This includes his reading that: 'Although it is not acknowledged as often as it should be, the close connection between "race" and modernity can be viewed with a special clarity if we allow our understanding of modernity to travel, to move with the workings of the great imperial systems' (2004: 58). So there is what we can call an elective affinity between empire, race and modernity. Incidentally, this trafficking of the race concept across modernity and colonialism was a tendency shared by Foucault (1978: 149), especially his reading of how the race concept came to take a distinctly 'modern' form somewhat later, 'in the second half of the nineteenth century' when race 'took shape at this point (racism in its modern, "biologizing" statist form)'.

What came before the 'new'?

One response to these characterisations of the relationship between modernity and race is not to deny that modernity has a particular formulation of race, but simply to suggest this is a formulation that is underwritten and made possible by pre-modern characteristics that are pulled through, and that without these the modernist conception of race cannot hold. As Bethencourt (2015: 3) has argued, '[n]otions of blood and descent already played a central role in medieval forms of collective identification, while the modern ethnic and racial divide was largely inspired by traditional religious antagonism'.

It would be intellectually fruitful in this respect to register how modernity therefore offers 'one of many reorganisations and re-articulations of the meaning of race that have occurred throughout the centuries' (Winant, 2001: 21). There are two parts to this recognition. One is to note that that race bears pre-modern antecedents. The other is to grasp how these have retained a currency *despite* modernity. Beginning with the former issue, what might these antecedents resemble? Christian symbolism, for example, long portrayed 'white' as synonymous with purity, which in turn was contrasted with 'black' impurity, in a way that suggests it is insufficient to accept the prevailing view that while the precise content to race was at best ambiguous, it was certainly distinct to how it later became known. By the time the Atlantic slave trade was well under way, Christian theologians would seek religious justification for hierarchies between whiteness and blackness, that mapped onto these colonised populations. As Garner (2011: 13) summarises, this they did so by among other things pointing to the story of Canaan (Son of Ham) in the Book of Genesis (9:18–27), which told of a punishment to Canaan of servitude and blackness. There are multiple examples to sustain this view and both Hund (2006) and Isaac (2004) dwell on this at some length (though they disagree on the geographical provenance of race).

If one shares the view that modernist formulations of race are in part assembled from pre-modern components, 'the neatness of the present periodization will have to be given up', and as 'a corollary, the case for making race a subject of inquiry across various disciplines would be greatly strengthened and made more urgent' (Mills, 2011: 61). Perhaps the broader issue compels us to register that there is a longstanding methodological (and indeed philosophical) question as to whether 'the possession of a concept can predate the possession of a corresponding word' (Thomas, 2010: 1739). Without seeking to resolve this, if one is persuaded that language is both constitutive and reflective, we can see evidence of racialisation prior to the creation of racial categories through plantation slavery and Enlightenment informed colonial encounters from the sixteenth century.

Indeed, when Islam is first encountered in Europe, 'the Prophet Mohammed (with his Jewish parents and Nestorian/heretical teacher)' is embodied as a dark-skinned, satanic menace (Matar, 2009: 217). The race concept then has long been saturated with cultural portrayals of religious minorities too, further challenging the Atlantocentric view of the race concept, in so far as European religious minorities too were endowed with characteristics that offered 'reassurance that their difference could be easily identified by Christians' (Thomas, 2010: 1747).

There is an analogous point that could be made about the ways other imperial config-urations of ideas of insider and outsider required race to become a modern activity. The very idea of citizenship, for example, has contained, since it earliest formulations, a dialectical tension between notions of inclusion and exclusion, for the citizenship of cer-tain types of people implies the non-citizenship of others. This is to say that citizenship is a relational idea that is identified in as much by what it is not as by that which it is. As Bethencourt (2015: 13) has argued:

> The discussion of lineage and autochthony developed by the Athenians, who held that they had always occupied the same land and were of pure ancestry, was projected by the Greeks and Romans onto other peoples, shaping their attitudes. The idea of descent became crucial in two ways: as a link between blood and soil, which reinforced the perception of an identity based appearance, language, and custom in the creation of an essential definition of peoples (*gentes*); and as a guarantee of the reproduction among a people of characteristics shaped by their original environment.

Here, however, there is a further contention, that in addition to the argument that who is in and who is not racialised needs to factor in a prior notion of race that is re-assembled in modernity, it is the very idea of modernity is itself that is reliant not only colonialism but within that a racialisation of religion.

A christian modernity?

'Islam has forever vanished from the stage of history at large, and has retreated into Oriental pose and repose'. So declared the 'great sorcerer' (Voegelin, 1972) better known to us as Georg W. F. Hegel, in his *Philosophy of History* (written between 1830 and 1831). Since all ideas are forged in social and political contexts, it is useful to under-stand that this philosopher's claim was made against the presence (and anticipated decline) of the Ottoman Empire, perhaps Europe's perennial 'other' which at one time spanned from Southeast Europe, Western Asia, the Caucasus, and from the North to the Horn of Africa. There are several ways in which Hegel's claim is helpful to our discus-sion of race and modernity.

The first thing to register is how for Hegel, as for many European observers, Islam was often synonymous with the Ottoman Empire. We find this conflation throughout the Euro-pean Enlightenment, not least in the works of in the works of other seminal German thinkers including Leibniz, Kant, Herder, Goethe, Schlegel and of course Marx (Almond, 2011). In this respect at least, our foremost philosopher of 'spirit' very much understood Islam in *geopolitical* rather than *theological* terms. The second observation is that Hegel's pre-diction of decline was not an act of great clairvoyance. After six centuries of Ottoman ascendency, internal nationalist movements, as well as British and Russian imperial ambi-tions, were taking their toll.[1] The Ottoman Empire nonetheless continued to head an Islamic *Caliphate* which reached well inside the European landmass of the day, and even further within the contemporary boundaries of the European Union. It is striking, therefore, that in the writings of Hegel, as noted by Turner (2013: 132), it was Europe alone that remained 'the telos of history', where civilisation 'is finally realised'.

As we learn below, to what extent this confidence flowed from a certain idea of modernity, and to what extent it reflected a reading of Islam is difficult to separate. But it is striking that the idea of Islam in the West 'occupied the peculiar place of historical opposition to both European Christianity *and* modernity' (Almond, 2008: 153). If we fast forward to the end of the twentieth century we easily find continuities in the way these two tendencies are run together. Perhaps the most well-known is Samuel Huntington's (1996) thesis on a clash of civilisations. This is a much less opaque discussion about world history and consciousness, for it succinctly posits that 'the West was West long before it was Modern' (ibid. 69), specifically in so far as 'Western Christianity … is historically the single most important characteristic of Western civilisation' (ibid. 70). Taken together, these sets of observations provide a useful illustration because they drive home the importance with which our concepts of Islam and Modernity have very much relied upon underlying frames of geopolitical decline and European advance, and in which Christianity is a prevailing reference point.[2] This rather simple observation is worth holding on to, for the relationship between Islam and modernity has generated and rich but complex literature. While competing accounts sometimes appear incommensurable, there is at least some convergence on the view that Islam and modernity reflect an unsettled encounter. For some this is self-evident because the relationship rests on contested foundational questions, not least: whose modernity and which Islam? For others it is a less a theoretical and more a historical issue, in so far as there has been a process underway in which Islam has proved slow in 'catching up'.

It is striking that much of the framing scholarship on the relationship between Islam and modernity arrives quite late in prevailing accounts of modernity itself, and specifically commences in the eighteenth and nineteenth centuries onwards with the institutionalisation of the academic study of Islam in Europe's universities. In addition to the Germanic scholarship listed above, one might think of the parameters developed in works such as Ernest Renan's (1862) *De la part des peoples semitiques dans l'histoire de la civilisation* and Max Weber's (1920) *Gesammelte Aufsatze sur Religionssozologies* which continue to cast an illustrative (though often indirect) shadow over subsequent inquiry. One might further say that a prevailing theme of this this work is that the formative periods of Islam locate it 'in a mould from which it cannot escape' (Zubaida, 1995: 153). If this is true of the analysis of Islam's relationship to modernity however, it is also true of the relationship of this work to itself. Hence it is no accident that the argument of Bernard Lewis (1988), penned from a North American context, would be familiar to Renan writing over a century before:

> The Distinction between Church and State, so deeply rooted in Christianity, did not exist in Islam, and in classical Arabic and other languages drawing their intellectual and political vocabulary from classical Arabic, there are no pairs of words reflecting the distinction between spiritual and temporal, the lay and the ecclesiastic, the religious and the secular.
>
> *(quoted in Filali-Ansar, 1999: 126)*

So the drivers of modernity therefore are more constrained in Islamic traditions, it is claimed, than in Christian ones. Perhaps the fullest scholarly elaboration of this view is Ernest Gellner's (1983) work contrasting the political economy (as well as morals and social organisation) of Western societies with – in the title of his book – *Muslim Society* (in the singular).[3] In a number of respects Gellner relied on the framing of Renan and Weber to propose that when it comes to discerning what kinds of authority are sovereign, there is a common (secularism resistant) pattern of social organisation across different Muslim societies. This he said was borne of Islam's over-reliance on scripture, in contrast to Christianity's dualism (between church and state). This kind of intellectual inheritance displays some important tendencies. The first sees the relationship between Islam and Modernity as an unlikely one. Or, more precisely, that the differentiation of state and religious power that facilitated *European Modernity* could not easily be replicated in Islamic polities where a certain doctrinal rigidity limits space for critical innovation. 'Islam was never really a religion of salvation' wrote Max Weber (1965: 28), but much more 'a warrior religion' to be contrasted to the inner-worldly rationality of Calvinism and Protestantism more broadly. Some of this is a reflection of first principles, in Weber's (1965: 75) account, because the basis of membership 'contented itself with confessions of loyalty to god and to the prophet, together with a few practical and ritual primary commandments'.

Weber is not here selected at random. While it is important not to overstate any one author's contribution, according to Salvatore, 1999: 11), 'Weberian theory … provides a basic repertoire for the formation of the toolkit for the categories we still use for making sense of the relationship between Islam and Modernity'. What to my mind is especially striking is how little in what Weber offers do we find sociological or political or economic analyses. Perhaps most obviously he overlooks the early forces of mercantile capitalism in Muslim societies. For as Turner, 2013: 31) describes, there is indeed evidence for this, especially in how early modern Muslim societies were 'primarily urban, commercial and literate'. Here continues:

> Mecca was strategically placed on the trade routes between the Mediterranean and the Indian Ocean; Muhammed's own tribe, the Quraysh, had achieved a dominant political position based on their commercial strength in the region. [...] The Qu'ran itself is steeped in a commercial terminology. There has been continuous conflict in Islam between the dominant urban piety and the values of the desert, but this conflict was also economic. [...] Islam was thus as much a triumph of town over desert as Arab over Persian and Christian.

If one tendency has been to view the relationship between Islam and Modernity as an unlikely one, another – perhaps already apparent – is to locate Islam on the same historical trajectory forged both implicitly and explicitly by Christianity. Starting in pre-history, yet carrying its mark through Antiquity via the Middle Ages, to the Wars of Religion and Reformation, what Jaspers (1953) called the 'Axial Age' (from the initial establishments of settled communities and spread of literacy) is the implicit course for transformations in European social and political life, and the latter processes are precisely what are deemed lacking in Islam's encounter with modernity. While Islam is not excluded from the story of the socio-cultural formations that the axial age seeks to capture, it is not clear if Islam is an add-on or is capable of charting its own course.[4] The prevailing judgement is that while the 'the European pattern … fosters eventual secularization, accompanying the processes of modernisation and modernity, the Muslim case is just the opposite: not only resistant to secularization, but pursuing its modernity through religion' (Zubaida, 1995: 156). Both of these tendencies encourage what might be called the deficit model in conceptualising the relationship between Islam and modernity, perhaps most affectively put in Bernard Lewis's (2002) book – focusing exclusively on the Middle East as a short hand for the entire Muslim story – *What Went Wrong?*

In this respect these authors promulgate a view that Muslim innovation falls outside of the framing of modernity is that a particular conception of what is modern is the standard.

As John Gray (2000) identified in his seminal public lecture on 'Three Mistakes about Modernity', this model of modernity assumes convergence and seeks out symmetry. As he describes, since the earliest articulations in European social and political theory, there have been an assumption of:

> A universal convergence in all modern societies on a particular worldview essentially embodying a universal civilisation grounded on secular rationalist values and norms. The Positivists believed that as societies came to be more dependent on society and technology they would become more alike in giving up their religious and traditional differences.

A rather definite illustration of this is found in Gellner (1983: 4) where he understands that Islam 'was the partial victim, not the progenitor, of the modern world'. Such a statement overlooks the possibilities of 'many modernities' and leaves even less space to grasp the 'ways in which science and technology can be absorbed into different cultures', maintains Gray (2000):

> As societies become more modern and as they, therefore, become more similar in some respects, so at the very same time they are likely to and have become more different in other respects.

> *(ibid.)*

Perhaps the main reason for the oversight is that Islam's relationship to modernity has come to serve as a methodological tool, in being contrasted with notions of Western conceptions of human progress. The narrative arc of Western modernity has come to predict that any given society's norms and values would move away from the types of traditional rationality exemplified in Muslim polities. As Turner (2013: 126) puts it, 'the Oriental divide was an important precondition for the decisive definition of politics as a division between friend and foe in European reactionary modernism'.

Conclusions

This chapter has argued that the relationship between race and modernity is best understood by grasping the racialisation of religion before, during and since modernity. What this means is that the category of race was not only co-constituted with religion, but pre-constitued with religion. The resurrection of this genealogically therefore profoundly implicates the formation of race in the racialisiation of religious subjects. To this end the discussion began with what is sometimes characterised as the standard account of how modernity generated categories of race, which the chapter challenged by examining the historical status of Islam and Muslims in European racial thought. In the opening sections the argument was presented that in actual fact the rise of modernity curates a particular category of race that relies itself on the prior racialisation of religious subjects. This argument is then drawn out at length through a historicised reading which does not seek to refute the standard account, but instead to invite readers to think more critically, and indeed historically, about the form and content of religion in processes of race making. The final substantive section makes this argument with the example of Islam in Europe. If nothing else, it shows us the continuity between pre-modern and modern racialisation of religion. The implications of this argument are not hermetically sealed to a discussion of race, but as the chapter shows, is in fact linked to the constitution of modernity too.

Notes

1 During the period Hegel was writing plans were underway for an ultimately unsuccessful Ottoman *Tanzimât* (or reorganisation) (Gelvin, 2008). Marshall-Hodgson (1974: 134) begins his story of decline sooner and broadens it out from that of the Ottoman Empire. 'In the general history of pre-Modern civilisations, a single century is a very brief period. In the fifty some generations of Muslim history, three or four hardly suffice to indicate any long term trend. Yet the depression of Islamicate social and cultural life in the late seventeenth and eighteenth centuries does stand out it retrospect. […] With the nineteenth century came utter collapse of the strong Muslim posture in the world: that nothing was done in the eighteenth century to forestall this smacks of inexplicable weakness or folly'.

2 The complicating factor is that this also has a racial logic to it (Meer, 2013). The historical literature on whiteness provides an understanding of the ways in which 'the history of whiteness is one of transitions and changes' (Bonnett, 2008: 18), as well as the ways in which this history also serves as 'a geography' of the West (ibid.). While 'white' and 'Western' are often conflated in contemporary discussion, according to Bonnet the idea that the 'West' has a coherent unity, something resembling an 'ethnocultural repertoire' of whiteness, is a relatively novel conception that owes much (though not necessarily in a straightforward manner) to late nineteenth-century writers who anxiously debated the 'decline' of white dominance (ibid. 23). Amongst others, Bonnett (2008) identifies Benjamin Kidd's *Social Evolution* (1894) and *Principles of Western Civilisation* (1902), each of which prefigure the current theories of *Eurabia* and European decline discussed elsewhere (see Meer, 2014).

3 A title that would perhaps face Mohammed Arkoun's (1989) question: 'Who would dare to describe all European societies under the heading 'Christianity and its Civilisation' or 'The Civilisation of Classical Christianity'.

4 At an elementary level, measuring Islam by a Christian tape was very much found in the 'analogical' tendency to assume that 'Mohammed was to Islam as Christ was to Christianity, hence the "Mohammedanism"' (Said, 1978: 60).

References

Adorno, T. (1978) *Minima Moralia: Reflections from Damaged Life*, trans. E.F.N. Jephcott. London: Verso.

Almond, A. N. A. A. (2008) *Islam and the Secular State: Negotiating the Future of Shari'a*. Cambridge, MA: Harvard University Press.

Almond, I. (2011) *The History of Islam in German Thought: From Leibniz to Nietzsche*. New York: Routledge.

Arkoun, M. (1989) *Overtures sur L'Islam*. Paris: Johnson.

Berman, M. (1982) *All that Is Solid Melts into Air: The Experience of Modernity*. New York: Simon and Schuster.

Bernard, L. (1988) *The Political Language of Islam*. Chicago: University of Chicago Press.

Bethencourt, F. (2015) *Racisms: From the Crusades to the Twentieth Century*. Princeton: Princeton University Press.

Bhambra, G. (2015) *Connected Sociologies*. London: Bloomsbury.

Bleich, E. (2006) 'On Democratic Integration and Free Speech', *International Migration* 44 (5): 18–22.

Bonilla-Silva, E. (2015) 'More than Prejudice: Restatement, Reflections, and New Directions in Critical Race Theory', *Sociology of Race and Ethnicity* 1 (1): 73–87.

Bonnett, A. (2008) 'Whiteness and the west', in C. Dwyer and C. Bressey (eds), *New Geographies of Race and Racism*. Aldershot: Ashgate, 17–28.

Feagin, J. R. (2014) *Racist America: Roots, Current Realities, and Future Reparations*. London: Routledge.

Filali–Ansar, A. (1999) 'Islam and secularism', in G. M. Martin (ed.), *Islam, Modernism and the West*. New York: I. B. Tauris.

Foucault, M. (1978) *The History of Sexuality Volume 1: An Introduction*. London: Allen Lane.

Garner, S. (2011) *Racisms*. London: SAGE.

Gellner, E. (1983) *Muslim Society*. Cambridge: Cambridge University Press.

Gelvin, J. L. (2008) *The Modern Middle East: A History*, 2nd ed.). Oxford: Oxford University Press.

Giddens, A. (1990) *The Consequences of Modernity*. Stanford: Stanford University Press.

Giddens, A. (1998). *Conversations with Anthony Giddens: Making Sense of Modernity*. Stanford, Calif.: Stanford University Press.

Gilroy, P. (1993) *Black Atlantic: Modernity and Double Consciousness.* London: Verso.

Gilroy, P. (2004) *Between Camps.* New York: Routledge.

Goldberg, T. (2006) 'Racial Europeanization', *Ethnic and Racial Studies* 29 (2): 331–364.

Gray, J. (2000) 'Three Mistakes about Modernity', Public Lecture, 2 March, available at http://fathom. lse.ac.uk/Features/2187/gen.html (accessed 2 January 2015).

Hempel, C. G. and Oppenheim, P. (1948) 'Studies in the Logic of Explanation'. *Philosophy of Science* 15 (2): 135–175.

Hodgson, M. (1974) *The Venture of Islam: Conscience and History in World Civilisation*, Volume 3. Chicago: University of Chicago Press.

Hund, W. D. (2006) *Negative Vergesellschaftung: Dimensions Der Rassismusanalyse.* Munster: Westfälisches Dampfboot.

Huntington, S. (1996) *The Clash of Civilizations and the Remaking of the Modern World.* New York: Simon & Schuster.

Isaac, B. (2004) *The Invention of Race in Classical Antiquity.* Princeton, NJ: Princeton University Press.

Jaspers, K. (1953) *The Origin and Goal of History*, trans. Michael Bullock. London: Routledge & Kegan Paul.

Lewis, B. (2002) *What Went Wrong?* London: Weidenfeld and Nicolson.

Matar, N. 2009. 'Britons and Muslims in the Early Modern Period: From Prejudice to (a Theory of) Toleration'. *Patterns of Prejudice* 43 (3–4): 212–231.

Meer, N. 2013. 'Race, Culture and Difference in the Study of Antisemitism and Islamophobia'. *Ethnic and Racial Studies* 36 (3): 385–398.

Meer, N. (ed.) (2014) *Racialization and Religion.* London: Routledge.

Mignolo, W. (2009) 'Epistemic Disobedience, Independent Thought and De-Colonial Freedom', *Theory, Culture & Society* 26 (7–8): 1–23.

Mignolo, W. (2010) 'Islamophobia and Hispanophobia: How They Came Together in the Euro-American Imagination', *Arches Quarterly* 4 (7): 24–38.

Mills, C. (2011) 'Artificial persons, natural sub-persons: Hobbes's aristotelian contractarianism', in I. Wigger and S. Ritter (eds), *Racism and Modernity, A Festschrift for Wulf D. Hund.* Berlin: LIT Verlag, 55–67.

Renan, E. (1862) *De La Part Des Peoples Semitiques Dans L'histoire De La Civilisation.* Paris: Levy.

Quijano, A. 2000. 'Coloniality of Power, Eurocentrism, and Latin America'. *Nepantla: Views from South* 1 (3): 533–581.

Ritter, S. (2011) 'Natural equality and racial systematics: Selected aspects of blumenbach's anthropology', in I. Wigger and S. Ritter (eds), *Racism and Modernity, A Festschrift for Wulf D. Hund.* Berlin: LIT Verlag, 102–116.

Said, E. W. (1978) *Orientalism.* New York: Pantheon.

Salvatore, A. (2009 [1999]) 'Tradition and modernity', in K. M. Massud and A. Salvatore (eds), *Islam and Modernity: Key Issues and Debates.* Edinburgh: Edinburgh University Press, 3–35.

Thomas, J. M. (2010) 'The Racial Formation of Medieval Jews: A Challenge to the Field', *Ethnic and Racial Studies* 33 (10): 1737–1755.

Turner, N. (2013) 'Islam, capitalism and the weber theses', in B. Turner and K. M. Nasir (eds), *The Sociology of Islam: Collected Essays of Bryan S. Turner.* Farnham: Ashgate, 53–70.

Voegelin, E. (1972). 'On Hegel – A study in sorcery', in J. T. Fraser, F. Haber and G. Muller (eds), *The Study of Time.* New York: Springer-Verlag, 418–451.

Weber, M. (1920) *Gesammelte Aufsatze Sur Religionssozologies.* Tubingen: J. C. B. Mohr.

Weber, M. (1965) *The Sociology of Religion.* London: Mathuen.

Winant, H. (2001) *The World Is a Ghetto: Race and Democracy Since World War II.* New York: Basic Books.

Zubaida, S. (1995) 'Is There a Muslim Society? Ernest Gellner's Sociology of Islam', *Economy and Society* 24 (2): 151–188.

29

Religious otherness
Defining boundaries of contemporary racism

Riva Kastoryano

Religion, race or ancestors provide alternative elements to national identities and to nationalisms. They constitute, in different contexts, in different times and in different ways elements of inclusion and exclusion. When Aristide Zolberg and Long Litt Woon asked in an article published in 1999, "Why Islam is like Spanish", they referred to two ways of designing otherness on both sides of the Atlantic: religion in Europe, language in the United States. The authors justify these two otherness with "the passions awakened by the Rushdie affair in the United Kingdom and the headscarf affair in France denote a simmering confrontation between 'Christian' Europe and 'intruding' Islam". In the United states, they argue that the referendum on bilingual education in California points to an equally dramatic tension between "Anglo America" and the "invading" Spanish language (Zolberg & Woon, 1999). Although religion, conceptualized as civil religion, in the United States succeeded in eliminating political conflicts in the public space and avoided religious discrimination, in Europe "it is viewed as problematic area" (Foner & Alba, 2008). The visibility of religion in public space of post-colonial migrants in Europe, Muslims comprising a large majority, have created a tension between the established and non-questioned principle of secularism, and the management of diversity in Europe.

Many studies and analyses have underlined the unprecedented character of Muslim migration to Europe in comparison with other waves of migration. Muslims who are citizens in the west today have been outside the history of the relationship between church and state that shaped western national character. Their settlement as a new minority goes along with the expression of an ethno-religious collective identification and claims, which blurs the accepted boundaries between private and public and creates differentiations among cultures, source of social and racial inequality. On a national level these boundaries find an institutional echo with the representation of the Other in terms of religious identities, along with a narrative that reflects the difficulties to legitimize its inscription as Otherness into a political and juridical account along with the principles of secularism.

Religion as opposed to secular power is not only a phenomenon that appears in a minority situation. The renewal of the sacred in general and its public expression as belonging (Davie, 2007) has become one of the characteristics of globalization. "Public religion" as empirical evidence according to Casanova is at the core of the "theory of differentiation" of the religious and secular sphere (Casanova, 1994). In the case of Muslims in Europe, the demand for public recognition and representation of Islam within national institutions and societies tests the principle of secularism in the context of diversity and pluralism expressed in terms of religion. If Islam in the United States constitutes one element of ethnic pluralism in European nation-states it figures instead as a "minority religion" (Kastoryano, 2004).

In countries where Islam is the religion of the majority of the population, states' discourses and strategies target both economic growth and nationalism with an emphasis on an "ethnonational-religious-pride" in opposition to secularism of the west. Moreover, the emergence of Islam as a transnational political force, as a global religion, redefines new boundaries of Otherness on a global level leading to tensions and rejection on a national level in European countries as well as in home countries. Both fight against "globalized Islam" (Roy, 2014); home countries praise "diaspora politics" linking religion and nationalism abroad and European countries aim at nationalizing minority religions as a part of inclusive diversity.

Ethnicization of religion

They are a variety of established secularism in different European countries (Kuru, 2004). However almost all European countries are facing same controversies based on the visibility of Islam (Göle, 2015): the headscarf and its variations (burka ban), construction of mosques, the height of the minaret and the degree of their visibility, religious instruction and more specifically the instruction of Islam in public school, instruction of imams, slaughtering, gender equality, or political values, liberalism, secularism or human rights, all questioning the "compatibility" of Islam with the secular West. Such questions generate urban violence, political violence, and linguistic violence. They all lead to feelings of fear, mistrust, and rejection that characterize the relationships between European societies and polities and their Muslim populations. It is in these terms that the presence of Muslims in Europe has settled at the heart of national debates as a major political issue and a challenge with respect to questions of equality (social and cultural), recognition (institutional and cultural) and secularism, making of religion considered as "contested category with the Enlightenment" a dominant narrative in politics (Manelli & Wilson, 2017).

Since the 1980s much research has focused on state policies concerning the governance of increasing religious pluralism (Koenig, 2007; Kastoryano, 2002, 2004; Minkenberg, 2007; Soper & Fetzer, 2007). Curiously, notes Miriam Schader, migrant and minority religions other than Islam have received far less scholarly attention, especially when it comes to analyzing the relationship between the religious and the political (Schader, 2017). A statement that José Casanova interprets as

> "Immigration and Islam are almost synonymous. The overwhelming majority of immigrants in most of the European countries are Muslim and the overwhelming majority of Western European Muslims are immigrants. This entails a superimposition of different dimensions of Otherness that exacerbates the issue of boundaries, accommodation and incorporation. The immigrant, the religion, the racial and the socio-economic disprivileged 'other' all tend to coincide".[1]

Indeed Islam challenges the principle of secularism as basis for equality and neutrality that rejects the domination of one religion of the national majority over other religions in a *de facto* minority situation. Since 9/11, religion as Otherness around Islam has been focused on the question on security creating amalgamation between migration, Islam and terrorism.

The boundaries of Otherness have thus shifted from a cultural or racial category to a religious one in studying the politics of immigration and integration, pluralism and diversity. It had become obvious that the visibility of religion and public claims for its recognition have changed the parameters of policies with regard to integration once defined in terms of social and economic markers into religious markers. While in the 1960s or 1970s, immigrants expressed their interests in terms of class, the younger generations now express their concern in terms of culture or religion, or any identity reinterpreted in interaction with the cultural and political environment and mobilization. Islam has been defined then in terms of practice, tradition, and moral values. Its perception as a "permanent difference" – both by immigrants and by public authorities – marked a step toward the construction and recognition of an ethnic group, generating an "awareness of belonging" with religion as the emergent ethnicity in Europe (Kastoryano, 2004).

In 1989, the headscarf issue in France and the Rushdie affair in Britain placed Islam at the center of public opinion and of claims made by Muslims migrants from North Africa in France and from South East Asia in Britain. Both cases situated Islam at the core of negotiations challenging the relationship between state and religion in France (Kastoryano, 2002), and of equal treatment of religions and multiculturalism in Britain. In France, state resistance to *laïcité* on the one hand, and mobilization for claims for institutional representation of Islam on the other reinforced identification of the Muslim population over generations and of diverse nationality who made religious identity paramount over that of national origins. Islam is thus perceived as a source of pride for identification and action and has strengthened the mobilization for representation of a community taking shape around a religious identity, as have ethnic groups in the United States. In France the primacy of religious identification is the result of the interactions between public opinion, public authorities and immigrant groups, rather than the result of a generational process of assimilation as in the United States (Kastoryano, 2004). Recent research in France on "trajectories and origins" of migrants shows how implicitly or explicitly Islam (without being mentioned at all) crosses all the themes that are analyzed: relation to the country of origin, way of life, values, discrimination, secularism, and so on. It emphasizes that nationality does not eliminate the perception of exclusion and rejection, and sends the image of "origin" to the second generation. In general the research shows, without naming it, how religion is transformed into a "minority identity", or "minority culture" or "origin" in France (Beauchemin, Hamel & Simon, 2016).

In Britain, a country where the Anglican Church represents the state religion, questions of separation and representation are not all posed in the same terms as in France. The United Kingdom considers that Islam should be respected on the same footing as other religions. That implies extending the blasphemy law that applies to Christianity to Islam.[2] Salman Rushdie's novel *The Satanic Verses* sparked indignation among the Muslim population, which found the content offensive and blasphemous to Islam and its prophet. Part of the diaspora thus appropriated a Muslim identity that had become politicized, demanding justice, equal rights, representation and recognition (Werbner, 2000). Similar demands were heard in the wake of caricatures of Prophet Mohammed that were published in a Danish newspaper in 2005.

The Rushdie affair thus triggered an identity movement drawing on multiculturalist policies to demand the inclusion of Islam within this framework. According to Tariq Modood, Muslims are not considered as an ethnic group in equality legislation or in anti-discrimination laws, whereas religion is an essential element of the ethnic identity of British citizens of Asian origin. This political indifference to Islam, or rather, its exclusion from the "politics of recognition," works to Islam's detriment and puts it on the sidelines of public debate (Modood, 2005). Furthermore, even though multiculturalism policy aims to guarantee equal opportunity in education and employment, a large body of research shows young people of South Asian origin, particularly from Pakistan and Bangladesh, the majority of them Muslims, to be disadvantaged from a socio-economic standpoint. In Britain, the definition of the other in racial terms and the fight against discrimination had placed "black identity" on the political agenda of antiracist activists. In fact, "in 1982, the Commission for Racial Equality, well aware that Asians disagreed, had categorized all minorities as 'black,' because that was 'the conventional way now of regarding all those who suffer from the particular disadvantage related to colour'"(Joppke, 1998). Activists intended to make "political blackness" the center of antiracist mobilizations at the European level. This was not, however, an identity South East Asian populations identified with, as they define themselves more as Muslim and Asian, in other words in terms of religion and nationality or ethnicity, often related (Modood, 2005). The current debate over multiculturalism in Britain thus raises the question of redefining "race" so as to include Muslims in the populations that need to be protected against discrimination. According to Tariq Modood, Asians are the "Other" and pose "complex empirical questions" that he analyzes in terms of cultural rather than racial exclusion (Modood, 2005). In the United Kingdom, as in France, there has been an "ethnicization" of religion, expressed by demands for cultural and institutional recognition (Kastoryano, 2004).

Neither British nor German Enlightenment are hostile to religion. The *Aufklärung* (Enlightenment philosophy) was not really against religion, just as rationality was not against Protestant piety; it meant both modernization and secularization. Beyond nationalism, religion plays an important role in the search for social cohesion, mainly in the definition of solidarities. After the formation of the German state, the *Kulturkampf* was, as in France, characterized by an effort to guarantee social cohesion by minimizing the role of the Catholic Church while limiting Protestant influence on politics as well. After the state was created, churches organized into associations, and pressure groups influenced the establishment of the "welfare state." With regard to Islam, in Germany it is nationality (Turkish in this case) that has been for a long time the primary source for ethnicity. The cleavages in terms of religion in France and in terms of nationality in Germany correspond to these states' understandings of difference and ethnicity. From the perspective of migrant populations, their identities as minorities within Europe appear to be contiguous with their collective identities with their home countries where national and religious identities are closely related. Claims for religious recognition in the new country of citizenship have turned the *Türken Problem* into a "Muslim question" in Germany (Schader, 2017).

Diversity and the institutionalization of religious otherness

Obviously, if religion appears empirically as the main cleavage, its recognition in European countries is translated in terms of institutional setting with regard to the relationship between state and religion of each country. Public recognition of identities reinforces the inventive character of identities, an awareness of belonging to a specific group that asserts its difference with regard to its cultural, social and economic environment. It imposes also the adoption of new features of identity that seem relevant and legitimate in a minority situation. While the political and normative issue remains justice and equality, the social issue has become the ethnicization of a "religious minority", with Islam as the main identity element, thus cementing a "legitimate community" to institutionalize. Its recognition on the same register as other institutionalized religions in different European countries has become fundamental for equal treatment of all religions. The process implies the reshaping of existing institutions so as to provide for the general recognition of Islam or, as Bhikhu Parekh suggests, to extend these institutions to include the newly emerging Islam in European societies (Parekh, 2000). What is at stake is the contemporary acceptance of Islam as part of Europe's historical continuity, to place Islam as a new religion represented and recognized in relation to the established principles that govern the interaction between church and state in the history of each country. Recognition of a new religion has thus spawned a general revision of the place of religions in the public sphere, challenging the concept of secularism with regard to pluralism and equal representation. Researchers in European countries, as if to assert historic continuity, developed normative "inclusionist" perspectives along with liberal democratic principles.

In France, *laïcité*, an important element of national history, is related to the institutional setting of religion and its contextual accommodations. The separation of church and state confers institutional legal status on the Catholic clergy, the Protestants of the National Federation of Protestant Churches of France, and the Jews governed by the Consistory created under Napoleon. With Islam as an emerging religion, the extension of institutional recognition for equal representation defined as a pluralist promotion of diversity had the objective that such an institutional representation lead to "an official recognition which in its turn would lead to the institutionalization of differences" (Lochack, 1989). This process clearly aims to develop an Islam which will express itself and grow within the framework of national institutions. The latter assumes its liberation from foreign influences, especially those of the homeland.

In Britain, a new vision of multiculturalism for Tariq Modood is to extend the privileges of the Church of England, an "institutional figure of England's and British national identity," to other faiths in order to achieve a "multicultural nationalism" (Modood, 2017). Non-denominational state schools should also include compulsory religious education of all faiths as a part of a national curriculum. It seems that two different national histories, and different relationships between Church and State, lead to different perspectives of equal representation of religion within the institutional settings of each nation, and the understanding of the public sphere.[3]

In Germany, the same question regarding the public recognition of Islam affects in a more complex way the status of Turks as an ethnic minority, based on both a Turkish national identity and a Muslim religious identity. Therefore, recognition by public authorities of a "Muslim community" was broadly proclaimed as a means of integrating Turkish immigrants into German society. The argument was firmly based on the official place of religion in German public space and the role of churches in taking care of foreigners in the manner of a "religious society" (*Religionsgesellschaft*). Recognition, within the legal framework of the corporate body of public law (*Körperschaft des öffentlichen Rechts*) from which other religions in Germany benefit, has raised questions about the place of Islam in public instruction, just as with the Christian faiths. Despite different approaches Germany has emphasized the "dialogue" with the creation of the *Deutsche Islam Konferanz* in 2006. Local, regional and federal authorities are involved in the formation of "German Muslims", that is to install Islam as a part of religious pluralism in Germany and to control extremist activities. The expressed objective is that a "mutual comprehension among religions will lead to a better integration of Muslims, and a better communication and respect of liberal democratic values in which modern Islam can grow and develop in Germany."

All European countries work on the liberation of Islam from foreign influences, especially those of the homeland, with the idea of "nationalizing" Islam. Belgium and the Netherlands also integrated Islam into the religious "pillarization" of their respective countries very early on. Spain launched a petition for Islam to be officially recognized alongside Protestantism and Judaism in 1989.

Despite different national histories, interpretations, and definitions of social cohesion, distinctions between private and public and the neutrality of the state regarding religion are both sources of contradictions when states confront Islam. Although Islam constitutes one element of pluralism and diversity among ethnic groups in the United States, Islam emerges as a "minority religion" in European nation-states. Such a conceptual difference is reflected in the different understandings of the recognition of diversity in European countries and the United States. The general trend clearly aims to organize a transition from Islam *in* different European countries to a "European Islam," from the simple presence of Muslims and their visible practices to an Islam which will express itself and grow within the framework of national institutions. By institutionalizing Islam, states, "nationalize" the new religion established on their territory. The process would liberate Islam from home countries' nationalisms and from globalized forces.

The question of institutional setting is not only a compensation of religious inequality and response to claims for equal representation of an ethno-religious minority; it aims also to promote values as a basis for cultural and religious recognition as a way to integrate "otherness", in everyday life and in "mentalité." The debate opens the way obviously to variations on the theme of secularism and religious diversity from a normative perspective. Overcoming religious discrimination is at stake. If the principle of secularism refers indeed to the neutrality of the state before religions, its reconceptualization is required to overcome its internal paradoxes, source of tensions and differentiations. The issue is not the resistance of secularism but its redefinition.

However, whatever the ideology and the objective of policies of integration (social, cultural or institutional), states are confronted with the transnational actions of the activists who try to bypass states in order to reach a global perspective of their mobilization. After 9/11, the question of secularism and religious integration are focused on security, which comes to extend the boundaries of otherness beyond national territories.

Religious boundaries beyond borders

Even though empirically the political identity of Muslim immigrants has been shaped and developed primarily according to their specific relations with each state, the international agenda for Muslims is expressed through transnational networks throughout Europe and beyond. Their scope is broad and expansive with regard to nationality of origin, regional identity, and even denominations. Such networks are built on common interests defined and formulated at the European level in terms of equality of rights expressed beyond nation-states, before supranational institutions. The elaboration of transnational structures clearly reveals multiple references and allegiances: to the host country, to the home country, to the constructed transnational community and to the European Union as a democratic space for claims and participation as well as for free circulation. Whether or not immigrants are citizens, their loyalty to the host country comes from sharing in its social and political institutions. The home country, despite its cultural and ethnic heterogeneity, provides emotional support and identity resources. A transnational community combining both host and home country ties represents a new reference of involvement that gives rise to the formation of a transnational identity as inspiration for political action and as an instrument for cultural and religious purposes beyond national borders.

From this perspective, Islam in Europe has provided a basis for trans-state and transnational organization, with the common identification and experience of being Muslim in Europe. According to Steven Vertovec, religion is better adapted to transnationalism than other forms of identity, since it acquires the indices of transformation in modes of religiosity, enabling it to follow the evolution of the importance of religion in the country of origin (Vertovec, 2002). Religious communities have always been stimulated by secularization to organize themselves into pressure groups and to take action in the domain of international relations, as demonstrated in treaties governing minorities from the 1648 treaties of Westphalia until the 1878 Berlin Conference, partially resumed by the League of Nations after World War I (Preece, 1998).

Above all, a transnational community founded on religion is in essence a multiethnic community, and religion nonetheless provides a common identity for a minority formation in Europe. For Muslims in Europe, their identities fragmented from within by various home and host national identities and denominations, Islam represents increasingly a unifying identity for asserting collective interest and structuring a transnational community that transcends the boundaries. In Europe, the internal fragmentation is centralized around norms and values diffused by supranational institutions in their fight against racism and discrimination and inclusive discourses elaborated by transnational activists on human rights and equal citizenship. The same internal diversity is recentralized also around a common identity element, to wit, religion, which is transnational both in essence and *de facto*. The process is promoted by international organizations that re-activate the religious loyalty of Muslim populations living in different European countries.

Moreover, diffusion of debates about the current issues involving Muslims, such as the Rushdie affair or the headscarf affair in Europe, or, more broadly, the war in Iraq and the Israeli-Palestinian conflict, made Islam into a "refuge", a source of identification with causes "agitating the world" both at local and at transnational/global level. This identification can be seen in the violence perpetrated in the name of a cause that directly or indirectly affects an Islam which is perceived as a "global victim", an image that is reinforced by the rhetoric of humiliation and domination by the West propounded by its militants. Pnina Werbner points out that "imagining their different diasporas, local Pakistanis tended to position themselves imaginatively as the heroes of global battles", and argues that "diasporas are transnational communities of co-responsibility" (Werbner, 2002). In an "imagined global diaspora" where individuals and groups and transnational communities are connected in global networks, the traditional *diaspora* loses its territorial bases in which home is an imagined place to express precisely "co-responsibility" without a territorial reference as "home". But at the same time, rhetoric surrounding Islam, both localized and non-territorialized, appears as the underpinnings of a "liberation" movement, a new movement of national emancipation, with the effects of identification with a new entity.

These references produce an identity that is not linked to the immediate space but to a non-territorial community, which becomes a refuge for a young generation that is looking for a cause and identification through political action. The process gives rise to the formation of a transnational identity as inspiration for solidarity and religious and cultural mobilization beyond national borders. Their claim is de-nationalized (with regard to the country of origin) and de-territorialized, with reference to a new understanding of a nation that is a transnational nation that creates new expressions of belonging and political engagement (Kastoryano, 2007, 2018). Transnational nationalism leads to a new imagined community that goes against the unified community that is the basic principle of a territorialized political project. The "transnational nation" is imagined on the basis of a religion or an ethnicity that encompasses linguistic and national differences and breaks away from the territorialized nationalist project to assert itself beyond national borders, without geographical limits, as a de-territorialized nation in search of an inclusive (and exclusive) center, around an identity or an experience constructed out of immigration, dispersion and a minority situation. Reflecting to the states their "deficiency" in human rights, or citizenship as a foundation of democratic equality, the actors seek to channel the loyalty of individuals from territorialized political community towards a non-territorialized political community, thus redefining the terms of belonging and allegiance to a "global nation." The unity of such a transnational community is sustained by the desire to belong to a "people" through a process of nominal appropriation of its actions and discourses, a sense of participation in its "destiny." This gives birth to new subjectivities which accompany the imagined geography of the "transnational nation".

Transnational nationalism, or nationalism without territory, appears to be the result of a historical evolution *a priori* linked to what has become a global market, to the emergence of a so-called global space and the rising influence of supranational institutions, in short, to changes related to what is known as the process of globalization. The territorial boundaries of these communities are not disputed; on the contrary, their non-territorial boundaries follow formal and/or informal network connections that transcend the territorial limits of states and nations, thus creating a new form of territorialization – invisible and unbounded – and, consequently, a form of political community within which individual actions become the basis for a form of non-territorial nationalism that seeks to strengthen itself through speeches, symbols, images and objects. This reflects the nationalization of communitarian sentiments of religion guided by an "imagined geography"(Kastoryano, 2018).

Some of the activists categorized by Robert Leikin as "Europe's Angry Muslims" are drawn into a single narrative of belonging to the *umma*, the reimagined worldwide Muslim community in which national, religious and worldly attachments are all mixed up (Leikin, 2015). Of course the term is reinterpreted in such a way as to reframe all the internal diversity into an "imagined transnational community", or an "imagined global diaspora", or even an "imagined global nation" that defines itself as a cultural nation, giving rise to a form of nationalism which can be viewed more as cultural nationalism than as ideological or state nationalism. Such nationalism would be based upon a sense of belonging to a culture that sees itself as being "uprooted", which leads to a redefining of it in a new environment. Its adaptation or resistance as well as its radicalization lends it a new scope and a new content in which nationalities, ethnicities and religion are blended, thereby cultivating a culture which presents itself as "different" from the environment.

It is not only via immigration that Islam contributes local and non-local elements of identification. And it is not only Islam that develops non-territorial modes of belonging. Non-territoriality is part of a globalization process which more generally affects religions on the whole. Davie refers to "global ecumenism," a value for global solidarity (Davie, 2007) and Peter Beyer sees in religion a mode of social communication in globalization, a new potential for voluntary activities through networks (Beyer, 1994). With regard to Islam, its politicization since the 1980s has been expressed in various ways throughout the world. Discourses exceeding national limits are developed in a similar fashion both in countries where Islam constitutes the religion of the majority and in diaspora where it emerges as a minority religion. The rhetoric surrounding both territorialized and non-territorialized Islam seems to be the basis for a liberation movement or a new national emancipation movement, with a semblance of identification with a new entity. A form of nationalism arises when they mobilize beyond national borders, and this phenomenon reinforces the interdependency between internal political developments and the involvement of transnational actors in the international political system.

New religious boundaries, de-nationalized and de-territorialized, challenge the Westphalian understanding of state and nationhood. Non-territorial although localized religious boundaries in various parts of the world where networks have reach recalls pre-Westphalian conceptions of territory. The path taken is in reverse, however. In 1648, the treaty gave religion territorial value – the sovereign's territory – and matched political compartmentalization with religious compartmentalization in both law and fact. Territory is thus, according to the geographer Jean Gottmann, at the root of "the differentiation of space" (Gottmann, 2007) in which community and identity overlap, moving from sovereign territorial states to a new geography based on religious divisions.

A reaction to "globalized religions" increasingly producing countries where national and religious identities are combined, are those who are also active in transnational politics, called "*diaspora politics*" as a means of maintaining the loyalty of the citizens on both their territory of settlement and "abroad." The main objective is to fight against "global Islam" by re-territorializing and re-nationalizing their belonging, expressed in terms of religion and in control of their citizenry and loyalty abroad as a resource for the transnationalization of the state. The objective then is to counter non-territorial solidarity expressed in global religious terms, which attracts the young generation, who reject any or all national identification, and develop a new "ethnic" pride, a sense of community whose attributes are drawn out of a global religious identification.

Diaspora politics integrates states in the process of globalization and allows them to compete with transnational and global forces. The extension of state nationalism along with an extra-territorial citizenship as translated by *diaspora* politics confronts a non-territorial, transnational nationalism, de-territorialized and de-nationalized. It aims at redefining solidarity, in order to influence identity expression and mobilization beyond national boundaries, and respond to a nationalism that is extra-territorial as a reaction to a nationalism that is de-territorialized. These reflect the paradox of globalization. If space replaces territory, it re-localizes extra-territorial references and redefines identity boundaries with new inclusions and exclusions. The expansion of state sovereignty beyond its borders generates a new power relationship between the mobility of individuals and the capacity of states to control individuals in movement within and without their borders and leads to a clash of nationalisms on a global scale: national state and territorial nationalism versus transnational religious nationalism, creating new boundaries of otherness beyond borders.

Notes

1 José Casanova (2006), Religion European Secular Identities and European Integration, In Baynes, T.A. & P.J. Katzenstein (eds.) *Religion in Expanding Europe*, New York, Cambridge University Press, pp. 65–92, cited by Mavelli, L. and Wilson, Erin K. (eds.), *The Refugee Crises and Religion. Secularism, Society and Hospitality in Question*, London, NY, Rowman and Littlefield, 2016, p. 76.
2 The British law considering blasphemy a crime dates back to the 17th century. It was only abolished in 2008.
3 A perspective that agrees with Andreas Wimmer's and Nina Glick Schiller's argument in "methodological nationalism", the way it has influenced studies on migration – its relations to states, societies, politics and sovereignty. See Andreas Wimmer and Nina Glick Schiller, Methodological Nationalism, the Social Sciences and the Study of Migration: An Essay in Historical Epistemology, *International Migration Review*, Fall 2003, Vol. 37, No.3, pp. 576–610.

References

Beauchemin, C., Hamel, C., & Simon, P. (eds) (2016), *Trajectoires Et Origines. Enquête Sur La Diversité Des Populations En France*, Paris: Grandes Enquêtes, INED.
Beyer, P. (1994), *Religions and Globalization*, New York: Sage Publications.

Casanova, J. (1994), *Public Religions in the Modern World*, Chicago: Chicago U. Press.

Davie, G. (2007), *The Sociology of Religion*, London: Sage Publications.

Foner, Nancy, & Alba, Richard D. (2008) Immigrant Religion in the U.S. and Western Europe: Bridge or Barrier to Inclusion? *International Migration Review* 42, 2: 360–392.

Göle, N. (2015), *Musulmans Au Quotidien. Une Enquête Européenne Sur Les Controverses Autour De L'islam*, Paris: La Découverte.

Gottmann, J. (2007), *La Politique Des Etats Et Leur Géographie*, Présenté par Luca Muscara, Paris: Editions du CTHS.

Joppke, C. (1998), *Immigration and the Nation State. The United States, Germany and Great Britain*, New York: Oxford University Press.

Kastoryano, R. (2002), *Negotiating Identities. Immigrants in France and Germany*, Princeton: Princeton U. Press.

Kastoryano, R. (2004), Religion and Incorporation. Islam in France and Germany. *International Migration Review* 38, 3: 1234–1255.

Kastoryano, R. (2007), Transnational Nationalism: Redefining Nation and Territory. In Benhabib, S., I. Shapiro & D. Petranovic (eds) *Identities, Affiliations, and Allegiances*, Cambridge: Cambridge University Press, pp. 159–181.

Kastoryano, R. (2009a), Negotiations beyond Borders: States and Immigrants in Europe. *Journal of Interdisciplinary History* 41, 1: 79–95.

Kastoryano, R. (2018), *Burying Jihadis: Bodies between State, Territory, and Identity*, London and New York: Hurst & Company and Oxford University Press.

Koenig, M. (2007), Europeanising the Governance of Religious Diversity: An Institutionalist Account of Muslim Struggles for Public Recognition. *Journal of Ethnic and Migration Studies* 33, 6: 911–932.

Kuru, A. (2004), *Secularism and State Policies Towards Religion: The United States, France and Turkey*, New York: Cambridge University press.

Leikin, R. (2015) *Europe's Angry Muslims*, second edition. New York: Oxford University Press.

Lochack, D. (1989), Les minorités dans le droit public français: du refus des différences à la gestion des différences. In *Les minorités et leur droit depuis 1789*, CRISPA-GDM, Paris: L'Harmattan.

Manelli, L., & Wilson, E.K. (eds) (2017), *The Refugee Crisis and Religion. Secularism, Security and Hospitality in Question*, London: Rowman & Littlefield.

Minkenberg, M. (2007), Democracy and Religion: Theoretical and Empirical Observations on the Relationship between Christianity, Islam and Liberal Democracy. *Journal of Ethnic and Migration Studies* 33, 6, August 2007: 887–909.

Modood, T. (2005), *Multicultural Politics: Racism, Ethnicity and Muslims in Britain*, Minneapolis: University of Minnesota Press.

Modood, T. (2017), Must Interculturalists Misrepresent Multiculturalism? *Comparative Migration Studies* 5, 1: 1–17.

Parekh, B. (2000), *The Future of Multi-ethnic Britain. The Parekh Report*, London: Profile Books.

Preece, J.J. (1998), *National Minorities and the European Nation-State System*, London: Oxford University Press.

Roy, O. (2014), *Globalized Islam*, New York: Columbia University Press.

Schader, M. (2017), *Religion as a Political Resource: Migrants from Sub-Saharan Africa in Berlin and Paris*, London: Springer.

Soper, J.C., & Fetzer, J.S. (2007), Religious Institutions, Church-State History and Muslim Mobilisation in Britain, France and Germany. *Journal of Ethnic and Migration Studies* 33, 6: 933–944.

Vertovec, S. (2002) *Religion in Migration, Diasporas and Transnationalism, Research on Immigration and Integration in the Metropolis*, Vancouver Center of Excellence, 33p. (Working Paper Series, no. 02–07).

Werbner, P. (2000), Divided Loyalties, Empowered Citizenship? Muslims in Britain. *Citizenship Studies* **4**, 3: 307–324.

Werbner, P. (2002), Theorising Complex Diasporas: Purity and Hybridity in the South Asian Public Sphere in Britain. *Journal of Ethnic and Migration Studies* 30, 5: 895–911.

Zolberg, A., & Woon, L. (1999), Why Islam Is like Spanish: Cultural Incorporation in Europe and the United States. *Politics and Society* 27, 1: 5–38.

Part IX

Methods of studying contemporary racisms

Introduction

The expansion of research on contemporary forms of racism has highlighted the need to develop a better understanding of the methodological challenges that we face in this field. Some of these methodological challenges have been discussed in other sections of the *Handbook*, but the two chapters in this part are focused on this issue. The first chapter, by Yasmin Gunaratnam and Hannah Jones, addresses key dilemmas faced by researchers who are working on racism and migration in the contemporary conjuncture. They explore in particular how empirical research can engage with and intervene in the intimacies between race and immigration discourses and practices. They use the case of a collaborative multi-method study about migration in the UK to illustrate some of the methodological dilemmas that are faced. They explore in particular the ways in which the study sought to use survey questions and focus groups as methodological tools. They discuss how the methods can produce and/ or elicit linkages between racism and xenophobia. In the concluding part of the chapter, Gunaratnam and Jones discuss the limits and possibilities of critical methodologies in the present conjuncture of British race and immigration politics.

The following chapter by Sarah Neal is focused particularly on the challenges of developing research in the field of everyday multiculture. Drawing on examples from research that involves researchers in everyday interactions with people who live in culturally diverse places, Neal argues that it is important to reflect on the dilemmas of doing research in such locations. The chapter argues that research on race and racism remains by and large marginal in mainstream research methods literature and training even as social and demographic worlds becomes more diverse and heterogenous. Using reflexive narratives and vignettes from previous research project experience, the chapter suggests that co-production approaches can resonate with older anti-racist critiques of social research and reposition research methods in this field. Neal notes that while post-structuralist, feminist and anti-racist and participatory research critiques have helped to break new ground in thinking about this style of research, there still remain important challenges that researchers need to address. In particular she suggests that researchers working in communities need to address more fully the methodological challenges of co-production in research.

30

Same difference? Researching racism and immigration

Yasmin Gunaratnam and Hannah Jones

> In the sectors we studied – different aspects of employment, housing and the provision of services – there is racial discrimination varying in extent from the massive to the substantial. The experiences of white immigrants, such as Hungarians and Cypriots, compared to black or brown immigrants, such as West Indians and Asians, leave no doubt that the major component in the discrimination is colour.
>
> *(Daniel, 1968: 209)*

That race and racism are deeply entangled in British immigration politics is in part what our epigram encapsulates. The quotation is from one of the first large studies of "Racial Discrimination in England" (Daniel, 1968), carried out in the late 1960s. Full of fascinating insights into the methodological demands of researching post-war immigration, the study used "colour" discrimination as a proxy for racism that could be separated empirically from anti-immigrant discrimination. The research used a mix of quantitative and qualitative methods, including covert "situation tests", where the research team sent people with the same qualifications but of "different colours and countries of origin to apply for jobs, houses, mortgages, insurance or hotel rooms … [to] find out what happened to them" (p.20). The research design assumes an ontology of racism as psycho-social, made up of material practices and complicated emotions. The researchers argued that those discriminated against were not always aware of the extent of the racism they were subject to, while "practising discrimination either caused … some feelings of guilt or at least exposed [those practising it] to the possibility of censure from certain quarters" (p.25). For the lead researcher W.W. Daniel, these charged effects of racism could result in dissimulation or pre-emptive apology. The latter was a discursive manoeuvre that was epitomised for the researchers in the wording of housing adverts, "*Sorry,* no coloureds" (p.25, emphasis in original).

Today in Britain, direct and indirect discrimination on the basis of race, including colour, ethnicity, national origin or faith, is against the law. Yet, critical accounts attest to the on-going effects of the racist and colonial inflections of immigration policies. At the same time there is a persistent denial by most mainstream politicians that racism is embedded in immigration policies and rhetoric (see Virdee and McGeever, 2018; Sirriyeh, 2018). Similar – but geographically and historically specific – dynamics can be seen in other countries, including the USA, Australia, and Western Europe (for examples see Galis and Summerton, 2018;

Sirriyeh, 2018). For some scholars, and despite variations in contemporary Western European racisms and anti-immigration discourses (El-Tayeb, 2011), the cosmopolitan aspirations of European states has failed to come to terms with the colonial past and pluricultural present (Bhambra, 2015; Gilroy, 2004).

Here, we discuss how empirical research can engage with and intervene in the intimacies between race and immigration discourses. We are mindful of the shape-shifting incarnations of race as a "floating signifier" (Hall, 1996) in British immigration politics (for a review of race and immigration research see Erel, Murji, and Nahaboo, 2016), and the continuing affective charge of being seen to be racist that Daniel identified over five decades ago. Our examples come from a recent collaborative multi-method study, "Mapping Immigration Controversy".[1] Looking specifically at how we worded survey questions and the focus group method, we show how the methods can produce and/or elicit some of the eerie relations between racism and xenophobia, where the eerie is characterised by "a *failure of absence*"(Fisher, 2016: 61, original emphasis). An example of the eeriness of racism is that the attribution of intent often relies on speculation. We can be offered hurt innocence or outright denial that racism is at play; "evidence" and "proof" can be difficult to assemble. It is clear to us that the period we were researching to the time of writing is a time marked by a shift towards the normalisation of different modes of hostility, including racism and xenophobia (Venn, 2019) that demands critical empirical investigation.

To better ground these concerns, we will introduce our study, the research questions and the research project as a whole, including some of the concepts that informed our research design. We then discuss (1) how the shaping of survey questions helped us to investigate and also intervene in the holding apart of matters of racism from immigration; and (2) the insights we gleaned from the focus group method. We conclude by reflecting on the role of critical methodologies in the present conjuncture of British race and immigration politics, marked by huge political and economic uncertainty and upheaval.

The research: Operation Vaken and mapping immigration controversies

In mid-July 2013, the British Home Office launched "Operation Vaken", a pilot campaign targeting information at irregular immigrants to "encourage" them to leave the country voluntarily (voluntary returns do not incur the increased cost of seeking out individuals for enforced removal). One element of the campaign drew public and media attention: two advertising vans that were driven through six of London's most ethnically diverse boroughs, with a billboard reading: "In the UK illegally? Go Home or Face Arrest". The billboard included a telephone number to call, a close-up photograph of a border guard's uniformed arm holding handcuffs, and a claim that there were "106 arrests last week in your area". National and local commentators were quick to point out that the injunction *Go Home*, now the strapline of a tax-payer funded advertising campaign, had roots in slogans of the far-right, with *Go Home* being a common racist catcall in the 1970s.

Operation Vaken included an increase in highly visible immigration enforcement checks at train and underground stations, and immigration advice surgeries at community and religious centres. During the same period, the Twitter account of the Home Office – the government department responsible for immigration control – shared images of enforcement raids and individuals being put into the back of secure vans with the hashtag #immigrationoffender, and "There will be no hiding place for illegal immigrants with the new #immigrationbill". The campaign turned out to be short-lived, running for one month (the vans were stopped after two weeks). Vaken caused controversy in the national press and was condemned by the Advertising Standards Authority for using inaccurate information; the Authority found that the claim "106 arrests in your area" was fabricated (Jones et al., 2017).

Not surprisingly, Vaken sparked public and policy conversations on whether immigration policies and rhetoric were racist. The government response to the public renaming of the *Go Home* van as the #RacistVan on Twitter and in some national newspapers, came from the then Minister for Immigration, Mark Harper. Writing in a tabloid newspaper, Harper, (2013) described being "astonished" by the reactions of the "Left and pro-immigration industry" that had denounced Vaken as racist. "Let me clear this up once and for all", Harper wrote,

> It is not racist to ask people who are here illegally to leave Britain. It is merely telling them to comply with the law. Our campaign targets illegal immigrants without any discrimination at all between them. By no stretch of the rational imagination can it be described as "racist".
>
> *(n.p.)*

At the time of Vaken, we were part of a group of academics and activists who came together to challenge this mode of government public engagement campaigns, which mobilised racist tropes while denying that they were racist. We hoped that as social researchers, we could play a role in stopping such campaigns and contribute to conversations on the dis/articulation of racism and immigration. In this case, we decided to take the minister at his word. Harper's claim was that government campaigns on "illegal immigration" should matter only to those "in the UK illegally". Others should not worry. We began to investigate this rationale by researching the effects of government immigration campaigns on the public.

To develop our research questions, we worked with civil society organisations that were already engaged with the effects of these campaigns, including local migrant support groups and national anti-racist charities. This collaborative working unfolded organically, as we had already made contact with such groups through initial oppositions to Vaken. Through our partnerships, we were able to identify areas where empirical evidence would be of use to anti-racist campaigners. We were also prompted to think outside our comfort zones. A vital perspective that a civil society partner asked us to include in the study was the impact of immigration campaigns on self-identified "white working class" groups, and supporters of anti-immigration political parties, who were worried about increasing immigration (discussed further below).

In brief, our locality-based research was carried out in partnership with civil society organisations in six areas of the UK. The organisations helped to recruit participants for qualitative interviews and focus groups, and organised local public meetings where we discussed our emerging findings. These local engagements were combined with interviews with national policy-makers, and a large-scale national quantitative survey. In overview, our study consisted of:

- 13 focus groups with 67 people (including new and long-settled migrants, ethnic minority and white British citizens);
- 24 one-to-one interviews with local activists;
- interviews with eight national policy-makers about the intentions and thinking behind immigration enforcement campaigns;
- a survey commissioned from Ipsos MORI that investigated awareness of and attitudes to immigration enforcement. Questions were placed on the Ipsos MORI Omnibus (Capibus)

amongst a nationally representative quota sample of 2,424 adults (aged 15 and over). Interviews were conducted face-to-face in respondents' homes between 15 August and 9 September 2014. All data are weighted to the known national profile of adults aged 15+ in Great Britain;

- participation in and documentation of online debates on Twitter about key elements of Vaken and related campaigns, and reactions to them;
- presenting and discussing interim findings with the communities and organisations with whom we had done the initial research, and including their responses in the findings;
- fieldnotes of interviews and ethnographic observation that we used to help us develop more multisensory and reflexive insights.

It is important to point out that methodologically, racism and immigration are considered "sensitive topics" (Brannen, 1988; Gunaratnam, 2003; Lee, 1993). Sensitive topics are those that constitute levels of threat to research participants and/or the researchers. Lee, (1993) has identified three main forms of threat: "intrusive", where research investigates issues felt to be private; threat that carries the possibility of sanction; and threat that is political. We encountered all of these types of threat and in varying combinations, depending on who was involved in any particular research interaction. The methodological demand of researching sensitive topics for Lee is how to manage or mitigate threat, "but without compromising the research itself or limiting the overall scope of the research to address important features of contemporary society" (1993:16).

Fast moving times

As well as the sensitive nature of our research topics, another methodological challenge was that the campaigns we were studying continued to unfold during the funded project (2013–2015). Despite high profile opposition to Vaken, the drive to immigration communications campaigns by national government (ostensibly targeted at migrants but directed at an audience of the general public) continued. In the following two years, related government initiatives included an increased visibility of branded Home Office immigration enforcement vans carrying out immigration raids throughout the UK; signs in doctors' waiting rooms declaring "The NHS is not free for everyone", highlighting limited access to "universal" healthcare for some migrants; and press releases and ride-alongs on immigration raids for local and national journalists (Jones et al., 2017).

So our study had to come to grips with a fast-changing political climate. The government's "hostile environment" policies were intensifying (see Hill, 2017; Venn, 2019). Race and immigration were also becoming a central focus of the Brexit referendum debates (Gietel-Basten, 2016) and political campaigning from 2014/5, and in the run-up to the 2014 Scottish Independence referendum. Although we captured initial public responses to Vaken through an unfunded street survey in August 2013,[2] most of our research happened months later. The time-lag meant that our methods became quasi-archives, storing, compressing and re-introducing Vaken images and discourses in multiple iterations, against the backdrop of other campaigns. This created new *in situ* affective encounters and responses to Vaken, distanced in space and time from the original events and framed by a more heightened politicisation of immigration.

To better understand the flows between anti-migrant narratives and racism in our project, it is important to say something about contemporary modes of race-making or racialisation and their imbrication with racism and anti-immigrant hostility.

Racialisation, racism and xenologies

Racialisation or the creating of classifications and interpretive repertoires where race can become a proxy for, be splayed across, or subsume other social differences is not the same as racism. Although the terms can be used interchangeably, some researchers believe that while the concept of racialisation is helpful in identifying a diversity of race-based narratives, it risks obfuscating the historical and structural underpinnings of racism and white privilege (Song, 2014). In our analysis, we follow Gail Lewis (2007) in recognising the interplay between racialisation and racism. Racialisation becomes racism for Lewis, when "racial categorization acts to define the terms of inclusion in, modes of relation among, and the horizons of the racialized social" (Lewis, 2007: 874).

To address the complexity and fissuring of these relationships, we add two further points. First, the importance of recognising the indeterminacy of race as a category. More than acknowledging categories of race and racism as fluid and situational, indeterminacy flags up the instabilities of race *per se* as a *queer* signifier; that is, how race can fix, blur, breach and subvert categorical distinctions and couplets. Second, we are mindful of recent discussions of the diverse forces and supranational alliances that constitute contemporary nationalisms and right-wing populism (Bhatt, 2012; Puar, 2007). Chetan Bhatt uses the term "new xenologies" to evoke the "complicated assembly of claims associated with civilization, religion, and culture as well as race, ethnicity, and nationalism", suggesting that the word:

> draws promiscuously from each precisely because older "racial" and "cultural" discourses of animosity have become problematic. Xenologies constitute whatever is considered the stranger as an object for politics and they render other political possibilities inconceivable: By "xenology", we are largely speaking about xenomisia, animosity that is vitalized towards the stranger, hostis as hostility.
>
> *(2012: 310)*

Where anti-immigrant hostility is shuffling and confusing all manner of identities, so that certain bodies are read as being strangers, regardless of citizenship or migration (El-Tayeb, 2011; Tudor, 2017), we suggest that critical social thought does not as yet have a strong sense of how methodologies might themselves not only attune to such dynamics but also intervene in them. This point has been elaborated in the more recent exploration of "Live" (Back and Puwar, 2012) "inventive" (Lury and Wakeford, 2012) and "activist" (Ambikaipaker, 2018) methods. In these approaches, methods are recognised as more than neutral devices for tracing, probing and describing a research problem but are approached as "ways to introduce answerability into a problem" that, "should not leave the problem untouched" (Lury and Wakeford, 2012: 3).

As we will show, our methods also had to take account of the seemingly different, and often paradoxical ways in which racialisation and xenologies become racism in British government policies and popular narratives. While racialisation can still centre whiteness as normative (Hesse, 1997), we are interested in examining how signifiers of belonging – tied to matters as diverse as skin colour, faith, language, cultural competence and gendered dress – can stand in for, confuse or camouflage race in defining "the terms of inclusion in, modes of relation among, and the horizons of the racialized social" (Lewis, 2007: 874). Anti-immigration rhetoric and hostility, we argue, is enfolded into the terms of national belonging, while overt racism remains socially unacceptable. This distancing is based on two premises. The first is the acknowledgement that the category "immigrant" (and indeed, "asylum seeker" and "refugee") includes people of diverse phenotype, ethnicities and heritage, who cannot therefore be thought of as a single group. Second, is the idea that the nation (in this case Britain) is not ethnically homogenous, and many ethnic minorities and people with migrant heritage are British; and indeed some of these British citizens can align themselves with anti-immigration policies and rhetoric as recent discussions of what is sometimes called "brown Brexit" – the relatively large numbers of people from South Asian ethnicities who voted to leave the European Union in 2016 – have suggested (Ehsan, 2017).

Topic threat in research

For some of our migrant, refugee and asylum seeker research participants of colour, the political threat that Vaken posed was read as undeniably racist. Lucee,[3] a refugee from Sierra Leone, worried that the *Go Home* vans would exacerbate local "racial tension". In a focus group with asylum seekers and refugees that Hannah facilitated in Bradford in the North of England, Lucee anticipated how immigration publicity campaigns like Vaken could invigorate racism where she lived:

> there had been a few racist things going on ... these are people who obviously don't care whether I've got my stay or not ... every time they've seen me they've always told me to go back to my country. So imagine if they saw this they'd probably call them [the Home Office], pick me up [laughs], do you know?

We found that those subjected to xenologies and racism were acutely aware of the many ways in which immigration and racism were co-constitutive in political and media discourses and vernacular imaginaries. In similar ways, in a one-to-one activist interview between Yasmin and Amaal, a community worker in Barking in East London, the *Go Home* vans were storied as inflaming racism in the borough. "'Go home', that sentence," Amaal said,

> that is the sentence people are really angry about and feel quite violated. If someone says to them "go home" and for the Government to come up with that ... that is a green light for others to use [it] as well.

Consciousness of the imbrications of racism and immigration in everyday narratives had very different effects in our focus groups with supporters of far-right and anti-immigration political parties. In these groups, the topic threat of being seen as racist was somewhat de-jeopardised. Despite qualifications ("I'm not racist, but ..."), there seemed to be little embarrassment or shame in voicing xenological views and sceptical support for the theatricality of Vaken, where the *Go Home* vans were seen as making local white residents "happy". Because of our mixed-method approach, we were able to further explore these qualitative findings in our survey research. In the survey, we found that attitudes towards immigration control changed when we worded and framed a question to include racial profiling. That is, when we made connections between immigration policing and racism.

Talking about race and immigration: large-scale survey design

Overall, respondents to our survey found the implementation of border policing, including in its more violent forms in immigration raids, tolerable or even desirable. Yet, when we asked for their opinions on reports that the checks were being carried out on the basis of skin colour, they did not endorse these types of practices in public places such as train stations. We asked,

> Some people have suggested that white people are less likely to be questioned during checks or raids on suspected irregular/illegal immigrants. How acceptable or unacceptable do you think it would be if immigration officers carried out checks on the basis of someone's skin colour?

Responses to the question were significantly different according to the broad racial categories of "white" and "non-white" used by the survey company to categorise respondents. With this question, the survey found that:

- 60% of the sample said that it was fairly or very unacceptable for immigration officers to carry out checks on the basis of someone's skin colour.
- 24% had no opinion either way on this issue (and 2% said they did not know).
- 14% considered it acceptable.
- 45% (n= 214) of "non-white" and 42% (n=794) of "white" respondents found this "very unacceptable".
- 10% (n=50) of "non-white" and 19% (n=365) of "white" respondents found this "fairly unacceptable".

One interpretation of the finding is that by connecting immigration checks to racism in the wording of the question, we increased the topic threat of respondents showing that they supported racist practices. In this mode of thought, the refusal to mitigate the topic threat of supporting racist practices led to dissimulation and an underreporting of support for the practices. Another interpretation by Gargi Bhattacharyya (2015), offered in the vein of inventive methods, has particular implications for researchers. It suggests that we need to make efforts *not* to disarticulate matters of racism from immigration in research. "Quarantining talk of racism", Bhattacharyya believes, "has the effect of silencing concerns about the racist and violent impact of everyday immigration control" (n.p).

We see such attempts to separate out talk of immigration from racism as an integral part of contemporary rhetorical strategies, named by critical discourse analysts as "disclaimers" (van Dijk, 1992). Disclaiming racism can take the form of disassociation, distancing, blaming, the reversal of accusations of racism and more recently, attempts to detoxify the words "racism/racist" by putting them under semiotic duress, dispersing them into a less politicised vocabulary. An example of the latter can be seen in calls to replace the word racism with terms such as discrimination, prejudice, insensitivity (Goodhart, 2014) and racial self-interest (Kaufmann, 2017). David Goodhart (2014), a British centre-right journalist, has sought to reclassify racism as *extreme* hatred, overlooking its multiplicity. From this perspective, Goodhart claims that racism has been in decline over several decades, so that Britain has become "a much more racially open society, if not a post-racial one" (p.251). At the core of Goodhart's argument is the call for what he sees as greater "race literacy"; clarity and nuance in concepts and terminology, so that a spectrum of hostilities, insensitivity, prejudice and within-group identifications do not carry the social stigmatisation that accompanies what is in his view "proper" racism (p.257).

Drawing from the findings of our focus group interviews, we suggest that attention to disclaiming is a particularly fruitful site for the mapping of the mundane contexts, trajectories and inter-relations between racialisation, racism and new xenologies. Contrary to Goodhart, we found that participants *were* race literate and agile in how they used disclaiming to simultaneously mediate the stigmatisation of being viewed as racist *and* express racist and xenological views. Because interactions are the key feature of the focus group method, as we discuss further below, the groups helped us to trace the interpersonal effects of disclaiming.

Talking about immigration – focus groups

In our 14 focus groups – held in Barking and Dagenham, Bradford, Cardiff, Glasgow, Ealing and Hounslow, Birmingham and Coventry – we showed local residents photographs of the *Go Home* vans and a Home Office tweet of an "immigration offender" being led into a van. We asked what the images brought to mind and allowed conversations to develop among the group. We chose to use focus groups because they have been seen as reducing topic threat, especially when research participants have something in common. In our study, the commonality was living in the same area, supporting the same political party and/or being a user of a particular community resource. Focus groups are also claimed to be more democratic than one-to-one interviews, because with lesser steering by the facilitator, there are more opportunities for participants to control the topics discussed (Wilkinson, 1998, 1999). In practice, we found a tension in our rationale for recruiting focus group participants with shared characteristics in order to lessen topic threat and how the method allows participants to take control of topics. When participants hold racist and xenophobic views, there is less opportunity for these views to be challenged. Indeed, the focus group method might even embolden and normalise the public expression of racism, qualified by disclaiming strategies.

The following extract is from the beginning of a focus group interview with supporters of the far-right, racist British National Party in Dagenham (East London). The transcript shows how race, ethnicity and immigration were introduced by participants early on in the interview and in response to a general opening question, "could you just give me a general idea, a flavour of what it's like to live here?". Alan responded to the question with "Not very nice at all". We join the conversation as it moved quickly to the subject of local parking problems:

JOE: You have to pay to park out in the front.
ALAN: The front, but the service road people are parking down there and because it's an African shop, they all park down there and don't get charged.
JOE: Yeah.
ALAN: Well, that's another thing, where I live on S, it was a very close-knit community, but they've built a big wall round it now and it's like being in Colditz, do you know what I mean? But the thing is there's a lot of youngsters that have grown up there while I've been there, children of my friends and they've applied for houses on the estate and the houses have come empty, immigrants have got them and they've had to move out, they've gone to Clacton and other places and it's like you said, there's a lot of the elderly people, when their houses become too big for them, as their families have grown up, they've had to move away, because they've not offered even, they've not offered any smaller houses within the vicinity and the children, as they're growing up are meeting people and getting their own families, they can't stay within their own family, like their mothers and fathers to help them, because all the houses have been snatched up by immigrants.
JOE: That's right, that's right, so it's splitting our families up.
ALAN: Yeah.

JOE: Isn't it? And the council say, oh no, our people get housed first, but they pull the wool over our eyes. We can see what's happening. It's the immigrants that are getting the houses.

ALAN: They always say that there's a long waiting list and yet an immigrant can come over here and get a house within a couple of weeks, do you know what I mean?

JOE: Exactly, yes, and a house, not a flat, a house, yeah.

In this conversation, a personal story of parking permits and restrictions becomes part of a highly condensed exchange of meaning on the local effects of race and immigration. The rapid flow of the conversation and turn-taking serves to build shared identifications through moral prescriptions, seemingly about immigration but with slippages into racial categorisation. Because our recruitment of participants was place-based, the groups often elicited talk about the singularities of local histories and multicultural living. What is noteworthy with this group, all supporters of the far-right British National Party, was the level of comfort among the white British, working class participants in expressing a range of racist and xenophobic views with a middle-class researcher of colour.

For us, the apparent lack of topic threat offers insights into the imbrication of new xenologies and racism. With immigrants it is a fundamental incommensurability of lifestyles and values that was talked about as a problem rather than skin colour; a discursive formation that social scientists have referred to as second-degree, culturalist or neo racism (Balibar and Wallerstein, 1991). Cultural racism can be a way of avoiding the social stigmatisation of being seen as a racist. It is also possible that because Yasmin appeared to be British Asian rather than a recent immigrant, talking through cultural racism was desensitised. Yet, despite participants belonging to an overtly racist political party, they also used disclaimers, "I'm not racist", which served to anticipate and neutralise social censorship while building rapport that encouraged the further expression of racism. In this instance, the disclaimer was part of a narrative of victimhood wherein "white working class" communities[4] were depicted as being reduced to "nobodies"; a discourse that dovetails with Hochschild's, (2016) "strangers in their own land", (a narrative of loss and of being "left behind" among seemingly homogeneous rural white populations who voted for Donald Trump):

JOE: I joined the BNP because the council weren't listening to the people in the borough, that was the only people you could join because they won't listen to the local people. If you weren't in favour of Labour you was an outcast and that's the way we got treated, you know? I've got black people in my family, right? I'm not racist, because when I go to hospital I expect the nurse, whatever colour she is to treat me with kindness. There's a lot of people that's coming in in the last year that's got no charisma at all, they don't even say, if you open a door for them, they don't say thank you.

CAROL: No morals.

ALAN: No bedside manner as they call it.

JOE: No bedside manner, no and this is what gets up a lot of people's noses. You'll be queuing up in the Post Office, I've seen so many people arguing in the Post Office where immigrants just walk in and walk straight up to the desk.

CAROL: Straight up, yes.

JOE: Where there's a line, they don't realise they have rules.

CAROL: They do realise, but they think they can always do what they want.

ALAN: They do it in the cars, they chop you up and they think they're doing the right thing.

CAROL: That's it.

JOE: : Yeah.

ALAN: It's as though they've never had a driving licence, you know what I mean? But you know, they have this attitude that they are the important people and we are second to none.

CAROL: We're nobody.

Disclaimers such as "I'm not racist" are a part of a spectrum of conversational strategies. Yasmin Jiwani and John Richardson (2011: 245), drawing from the work of Teun van Dijk, have identified a sub-category of racist "apparent disclaimers". Apparent disclaimers are conversational sleights of hand. They include, "apparent denial" ("I have nothing against immigrants, but ..."), apparent concession ("Of course some Muslims are tolerant, but generally ..."), apparent empathy ("Of course asylum seekers endure hardships, but ..."), apparent ignorance ("Now, I don't know all the facts, but ...") and transfer (e.g. "of course I have nothing against them but my customers ..."). The transfer strategies that we heard in our focus groups included indirect xenology and racism through ventriloquism: voicing anti-immigrant feelings on behalf of others that proved especially powerful when the person ventriloquised was from a racially minoritised group. An underlying logic here is that those from racialised minorities cannot be racist.

The following extract is from Jackie, a supporter of the anti-immigration UK Independence Party (UKIP). What is interesting about this exchange is how the indeterminancy of racial signifiers is simultaneously problematised and mobilised, a feature of the new xenologies highlighted by Bhatt, (2012). It is a duality that can accommodate an array of political and affective responses and alliances. The excerpt comes at the beginning of the focus group, where Jackie is responding to another participant, who had prefaced her description of the "problems" of Barking (in East London) with the disclaimer "I'm not racist by any means, OK?". For this participant, Barking is a place with "all the immigrants, so we've got Muslims, Asians, Somalis, every race you can think of is now in the borough". The extract below begins with Jackie's response to this description:

JACKIE: Well, back in the 50s you had a lot of immigration from lots of places, but the people that came over then, they had to integrate, they had to work hard, they'd no benefits, nothing was handed out on a plate and now [they] resent this far more than we ever do, because if people see a black face they don't know whether that person's integrated into society, they just are wary of them, whoever they are and they really, really do hate it, because I used to go to an exercise class and there were a lot of them there and they used to talk about it all the time.

YASMIN: So what sort of things did they say?

JACKIE: They resented the fact that a lot of them get everything for nothing, that a lot of them get free travel where they didn't until they were over sixty. It's all sorts of things, they just don't like the fact that in their words they're ruining our society, because these people that came over with their families back then to all intents and purposes they're English, because they live the English way of life. They haven't come like the people that have come over now, you've got mosques springing up all over the place. More than that, in our area, we back onto an industrial area and every unit that comes empty, in fact anywhere in this borough it's taken over by the, I use the term loosely, black African churches and the people that come to them, they're busting from all over the place, so they're not local residents and it just doesn't seem there can ever be enough of these places, everything they're trying to take over and that's causing an awful lot of resentment, particularly from the Muslims who can't get somewhere to have as their own, well, they just ask for a community centre at the moment where the council seem to be supporting the African churches and yet they get no revenue from them whatsoever. So that is causing a problem anyway, we've got lots and lots of Eastern Europeans, they make no attempt to speak English and people I've spoken to that are teachers say that causes a huge problem, because if a child, you know, you need to speak to the parent, the parent doesn't speak English and so they obviously don't seem to push their children, like the Asians do definitely, I think a lot of the Africans probably do, but where the Eastern Europeans don't and the fact that they do not speak English, they all work for themselves, advertise only Polish workers or Lithuanian, that is causing a lot of resentment and also they're nocturnal people, so when you're in bed at night you can hear them outside having conversations at the top of their voices.

There are many themes in Jackie's narrative. For brevity we highlight the merging and interchangeability of racial and cultural signifiers, where animosity to recent migrants on one axis of differentiation is mediated by a valorising of settled migrants and a see-sawing between being pro and anti-Muslim. "Cultures of racism have frequently, if not always, scaled and ranked human diversity", Les Back and colleagues have written, "often conferring the status of 'contingent insiders' on some migrants while unloading hate and derision on other migration groups" (Back and Sinha, 2018: 139).

Notably, Jackie's neoliberal version of citizenship is one where good/successful/enterprising immigrants take responsibility for themselves (and their children) and integrate into communities. It is a familiar narrative that can be found across political parties and media and public discourses. For example, in a one-to-one interview with an activist in Birmingham, Kirsten Forkert was told about xenologies across different immigrant and racially minoritised groups:

I remember going in and it was a corner shop run by an Asian guy, I guess probably of Pakistani or Bangladeshi heritage, was having a row with a Somali customer and as she walked out he said, "I fucking hate Somalis." It is bizarre. I don't know how much of a pain in the arse that woman is but she wasn't all of Somalia, you can't actually … but it is interesting because I hear, and not across the board that wouldn't be fair or accurate to say, but I hear people from second generation migrant communities my age or younger talking about new migrant communities in much the same way as my parents spoke about their parents. It is kind of interesting to me that a lesson hasn't been learned somehow, you know?

The conversations that we sparked in response to Operation Vaken evoke something of the tenor, paradoxes and ambivalence of contemporary British racial and immigration imaginaries. Talking about immigration and immigration control has become a way of showing knowledge of the terms of national belonging, especially as citizenship and belonging became more prominent following the "Brexit" referendum in June 2016. For some of our discussants, and sometimes regardless of ethnicity or migrant heritage, to belong is to be anti-immigrant but not racist. Such public performance of race sensitivity runs counter to the rationale of the claims made by David Goodhart,

if we are unable to become more discriminating in the way we talk about discrimination, parts of the population will become desensitised to the language of racism – or, worse, they will find the all-encompassing definition of racism so much at odds with their own definition that they will start to self-identify as racist as a form of protest.

(p.257)

Being seen to be racist, we suggest, is still socially unacceptable in Britain, but this does not mean that racism and its material effects have gone away. Rather, we see the ideological promiscuity of new xenologies (Bhatt, 2012) as offering capacious spaces of thinking, speaking and acting that are utterly entwined with the complexity and paradoxes of race. This became most palpable to us in the sharing of views in our focus groups, where as researchers we had less control over topics and their framing than in our one-to-one qualitative interviews or survey research.

Conclusion

The mixed methods that we used in our study have helped us to discern how racist exclusions, hostility and denigration are produced and performed as a part of xenologies, at the same time that racism is denied or disassociated from in contemporary British immigration politics. And while our quantitative methods allowed us to trace some of the affective aftermath of Vaken, they also allowed us to examine the extents to which methods can be inventive in luring methodologies and empirical materials into posing their own problems (Lury and Wakeford, 2012). As we have pointed out, through our survey, we were able to experiment with the wording of survey questions as an empirical affordance that can be used to support and/or resist the holding separate of racism from immigration discourses that characterises government rhetoric.

Our focus groups offered other insights. Because we wanted to encourage free-flowing dialogue, we exerted less control over the direction and development of conversations. The interactional momentum of focus groups helped us to better understand how xenological and racist discourses are social and situated, in the sense that conversations are located in, but also respond to and anticipate interpersonal and wider political debates and controversies. We were privy to how the everyday material, media and affective landscapes that our participants inhabited became resources in how the imbrications between racism and xenologies were produced and storied.

More broadly, in the focus groups, we were able to see and hear how the logic of immigration campaigns that we have outlined – that anti-immigration narratives cannot be racist because migrants and refugees are racially diverse and the British nation is multiracial/multicultural – has extended into the everyday. Some people, who have migrant heritage in living memory themselves, or who are racialised as ethnic minorities and see latter-day immigration as a problem argue that they do not see being part of an ethnic group associated with recent migration, as a social concern (Jones et al., 2017). But they may still see newly arrived migrants, or migrants from particular places, as problems, because of behaviours seen as unsuitable within British life. A simplistic sense of racism (white=good, not-white=bad) is therefore still articulated as wrong, but has been replaced by a more complex and temporalised xenology (integrated/established=good, insular/newer=bad), which because of different migration trajectories and interethnic mixing can realign and settle along more varied lines of ethnicity and national origin.

There is a "civic task" at stake in how we use our sociological imaginations in social research and analysis, Alberto Toscano, (2012) has argued. For our research team, this civic task included trying to make visible the interrelations between racism and xenologies, as well as exploring the extent to which research methods can challenge or even displace attempts to depoliticise and recalibrate racism. Some evidence of this first ambition can be seen in the project's contribution quoted in the report of the United Nations Special Rapporteur on

Racism on her mission to the UK, in which she directly quotes our work as demonstrating harassment on the basis of immigration status, based on racialising logics (Achiume, 2018).

We hope that our collaborative approach not only produced scholarly knowledge, but also enabled access to this knowledge for those directly affected by immigration control, providing resources for them to build their own engagements. We see this, for example, in a conversation between our co-investigator Sukhwant Dhaliwal and Pragna Patel, Director of Southall Black Sisters (SBS), one of our research partners, which is shared in full in the monograph of our research (Jones et al., 2017: 29–37). On behalf of SBS, a not-for-profit organisation established in 1979 to meet the needs of Black (Asian and African-Caribbean) women, Patel says: "The research enabled the women to see their own experiences as connected to others around the country" (p30), "it gave us space to make the connections" (p.32). Significantly, for Patel, the women's involvement in our project was "part of a process, a continuation of work we were already doing with service users. And after the focus group sessions we continued some of those debates" (p.31). She added that some of the women "eventually went on to speak at public events about their experiences" (p.34).

The role of research "is not to create pacifying knowledge", Toscano writes, but to provide "a realistic estimate of the powers necessary to alter, however minimally, the course of history" (2012: 68).

Notes

1 The Mapping Immigration Controversy research project ran between 2013 and 2015, and was funded by the Economic and Social Research Council (grant reference ES/L008971/1). The co-investigators were Gargi Bhattacharyya, William Davies, Sukhwant Dhaliwal, Kirsten Forkert, Yasmin Gunaratnam, Emma Jackson, Hannah Jones and Roiyah Saltus.
2 Before the Mapping Immigration Controversy project began, we were also part of a wider team of researchers that conducted a quick-turnaround street survey in response to the *Go Home* van in July and August 2013. See https://aarx.wordpress.com/
3 All the names of our research participants are pseudonyms.
4 A related trope in the UK is one that positions the working class as only white, so that when racist ideas are attributed to "the white working class", the white middle classes are without racism (Haylett, 2001).

References

Achiume, E. T. (2018) "End of Mission Statement of the Special Rapporteur on Contemporary Forms of Racism, Racial Discrimination, Xenophobia and Related Intolerance at the Conclusion of Her Mission to the United Kingdom of Great Britain and Northern Ireland", *United Nations Human Rights Office of the High Commissioner*, www.ohchr.org/EN/NewsEvents/Pages/DisplayNews.aspx?NewsID=23073&LangID=E Last accessed 7 March, 2019.
Ambikaipaker, M. (2018) *Political Blackness in Multiracial Britain*. Philadelphia: University of Pennsylvania Press.
Back, L., Sinha, S. with Bryan, C., Baraku, V. and Yemba. M. (2018) *Migrant City*. London and New York: Routledge.
Balibar, E. and Wallerstein, I. (1991) *Race, Nation, Class, Ambiguous Identities*. London: Verso.
Bhambra, G.K. (2015) Whither Europe? Postcolonial versus neocolonial cosmopolitanism, *Interventions* 18(2): 187–202.
Bhatt, C. (2012) The new xenologies of Europe: Civil tensions and mythic pasts, *Journal of Civil Society* 8(3): 307–326.

Bhattacharyya, G. (2015) Immigration control, racism and public opinion, *Mapping Immigration Controversy blog*, 7 January 2015, https://mappingimmigrationcontroversy.com/2015/01/07/290/Last accessed 17 December 2018.

Brannen, J. (1988) The study of sensitive subjects, *Sociological Review* 36(3): 552–563.

Daniel, W.W. (1968) *Racial Discrimination in England*. Harmondsworth: Penguin Books.

Ehsan, R. (2017). *The British Asian vote for Brexit contains a few surprises*, LSE Brexit blog, 20 February 2017 http://blogs.lse.ac.uk/brexit/2017/02/20/the-british-asian-vote-for-brexit-contains-a-few-surprises/ Last accessed 17 December, 2018.

El-Tayeb, F. (2011) *European Others: Queering Ethnicity in Postnational Europe*. Minneapolis and London: University of Minnesota.

Erel, U., Murji, K and Nahaboo, Z. (2016) Understanding the contemporary race–migration nexus, *Ethnic and Racial Studies* 39(8): 1339–1360.

Fisher, M. (2016) *The Weird And The Eerie*. London: Repeater Books.

Galis, V. and Summerton, J. (2018) We are all foreigners in an analogue world: cyber-material alliances in contesting immigration control in Stockholm's metro system, *Social Movement Studies* 17(3): 299–317.

Gietel-Basten, S. (2016) Why Brexit? The toxic mix of immigration and austerity, *Population and Development Review* 42(4): 673–680.

Gilroy, P. (2004) *Between Camps*. New York: Routledge.

Gilroy, P. (2014) *Postcolonial Melancholia*. New York: Columbia University Press.

Goodhart, D. (2014) Racism: Less is more, *The Political Quarterly* 85(3): 251–258.

Gunaratnam, Y. (2003) *Researching "Race" and Ethnicity*. London: Sage.

Hall, S. (1996) *Race: The Floating Signifier*. Northampton, MA: Media Education Foundation.

Harper, M. (2013) Racism? It is not racist to ask people who are here illegally to leave Britain, *Daily Mail*, 29 July 2013 www.dailymail.co.uk/news/article-2381051/MARK-HARPER-Racism-It-racist-ask-people-illegally-leave-Britain.html#ixzz3pUKlqpJ3, last accessed 25 November 2018.

Haylett, C. (2001) Illegitimate subjects? Abject whites, neoliberal modernisation, and middle-class multiculturalism, *Environment and Planning D: Society and Space* 19(3): 351–370.

Hesse, B. (1997). White Governmentality – Urbanism, nationalism, racism. In: Westwood, S. and Williams, J. (eds) *Imagining Cities: Scripts, Signs, Memory*. London: Routledge, pp. 86–103.

Hill, A. (2017) Hostile environment the hardline home office policy tearing families apart, *The Guardian*, 28 November 2017 www.theguardian.com/uk-news/2017/nov/28/hostile-environment-the-hardline-home-office-policy-tearing-families-apart Last accessed 12 December 2018.

Hochschild, A. R. (2016) *Strangers in Their Own Land: Anger and Mourning on the American Right*. New York: New Press.

Jiwani, Y. and Richardson, J.E. (2011). Discourse, ethnicity and racism. In: van Dijk, Teun A. (ed) *Discourse Studies: A Multidisciplinary Introduction*. London: Sage, pp. 241–263.

Jones, H., Gunaratnam, Y., Bhattacharyya, G., Davies, W., Dhaliwal, S., Forkert, K., Jackson, E. and Saltus, R. (2017) *Go Home? The Politics of Immigration Controversies*. Manchester, UK: Manchester University Press.

Kaufmann, E. (2017) *"Racial Self-Interest" Is Not Racism*, London: Policy Exchange https://policyexchange.org.uk/wp-content/uploads/2017/03/Racial-Self-Interest-is-not-Racism-FINAL.pdf webpage last accessed 3 December 2018.

Lee, R. (1993) *Doing Research on Sensitive Topics*. London: Sage.

Lewis, G. (2007) Racialising culture is ordinary, *Cultural Studies* 21(6): 866–886.

Lury, C and Wakeford, N. (Eds) (2012) *Inventive Methods: The Happening of the Social*. Abingdon, London: Routledge.

Puar, J.K. (2007) *Terrorist Assemblages: Homonationalism in Queer Times*. Durham and London: Duke University.

Sirriyeh, A. (2018) *The Politics of Compassion: Immigration and Asylum Policy*. Bristol: Bristol University Press.

Song, M. (2014) Challenging a culture of racial equivalence, *British Journal of Sociology* 65(1): 107–129.

Toscano, A (2012) Seeing it whole: staging totality in social theory and art, *The Sociological Review* 60(S1): 164–183.

Tudor, A. (2017) Dimensions of transnationalism, *Feminist Review* 117: 20–40.

van Dijk, T.A. (1992) Discourse and the denial of racism, *Discourse and Society* 3(1): 87–118.

Venn, C. (2019) How neoliberalism is normalising hostility, *Open Democracy* 11 February 2019, www.opendemocracy.net/en/opendemocracyuk/how-neoliberalism-is-normalising-hostility/, last accessed 17 March 2019.

Virdee, S. and McGeever, B. (2018) Racism, crisis, Brexit, *Ethnic and Racial Studies* 41(10): 1802–1819.

Wilkinson, S. (1998) Focus groups in feminist research: Power, interaction and the co-construction of meaning, *Women's Studies International Forum* 21(1): 111–125.

Wilkinson, S. (1999) Focus groups: A feminist method, *Psychology of Women Quarterly* 23(2): 221–244.

31

Researching racisms, researching multiculture

Challenges and changes to research methods

Sarah Neal

Introduction

Anyone engaged in social research and based in a university will be familiar with the requirement to obtain ethical approval for the research project as well as the standard list of topic areas which are identified as being 'sensitive' and which you are required to highlight if your project relates to any of the area. Race and ethnicity are on this list. Each time I tick the little square box on the form on my screen and indicate 'Yes, this is an area with which this project engages' I am always struck by the range of contestations, contradictions and politics that constitute research around race and the inadequacies of labelling research relating to race with the word 'sensitive'. This sanitised labelling of race as a sensitive subject area in universities' ethics processes is perhaps not surprising given the institutional context of ethical approval. Yet being badged in this way resonates with what France Winddance Twine and Jonathan Warren (2000: 4) have suggested is the profound marginalisation of race politics in wider research methods literature and approaches. It is noteworthy that almost two decades since Twine and Warren's observation, race is still a minimal presence or even entirely absent in many of the most popular and well used research methods textbooks. And while some may argue that research that investigates race is a specialised and particular field the ways in which race unevenly shapes the social world and individual lives means, as Twine and Warren suggest that all social research including that which is not necessarily or primarily about race will encounter issues of race and racism in some form and at some point.

Similarly, as urban populations in most national contexts become increasingly diverse and heterogeneous, the ways in which ethnic and cultural difference, processes of racialisation and racism can emerge, be felt, spoken of and experienced demand that social researchers are able to respond to the ways in which narratives of race might be shaping experiences and perspectives. The acknowledgement and problematisation of the ethnic and cultural contexts of research and the diversity of those populations who participate in social research need to occupy a much more central place in social science research investigations whether or not the immediate research focus is on race. Research training and methods literatures need to recognise and respond to these new realities and the requirement to decolonise research methods. There are research methods books that focus on social research in racialised contexts and a range of methods accounts and discussions of research projects which have researched questions of race and this overview will engage with a number of these. But it is also important to acknowledge that in higher education institutional research processes race continues to be a research area which is routinely presented as both specialised and 'sensitive' while in under- and postgraduate methods training race is *still* too often not a visible or a core area of consideration (Twine 2000).

On race and ethnicity

Decolonialising social research involves a recognition of the tension between the ways in which race was positioned at the empirical centre of the historical development of social thought and knowledge production (Tuhiwai-Smith 2012) even as black scholars' work was invisibilised, as the marginalisation of W. E. B. Du Bois's 19th century development of urban sociology based on the large scale empirical investigations of racism and poverty in Philadelphia demonstrates (Back and Tate 2015; Bhambra 2014). The erasure of scholars of colour from social science and the role of race science in developing colonial social and scientific knowledge is a dynamic which has shaped sociology's disciplinary development and requires sociologists to engage with this legacy and its current iterations and implications. Research on race is bound into an ongoing series of tensions, divisions, ambivalence and contradictions.

Core to these are the essentialising categorisations of the phenomenon of race. Late 20th century shifts in social science which have argued that race has no biological basis but is a social concept, fetishising the corporeal, have repositioned it from the hierarchical terrains of the genetic to the more uncertain but equally hierarchical terrains of the cultural. The idea that race is a social category as been influential and in part has pushed a shift towards the use of the term ethnicity as a less indicted and politically saturated concept. The impact of this has been significant, with race often being avoided in many official conexts and replaced with a focus that is much more exclusively on ethnicity, multiculturalism and racism (Song 2018). However, as a number of scholars have pointed out, the ways in which race impacts the social world and everyday lives means that the arguments that emphasise the unreality of race are challenging not least because of its experiential and divisive impacts but also because as social scientists continue to research and speak of race (Nayak 2006). As Song (2018) argues, [e]ven when people articulate the idea that race is socially constructed, such assertions can be eclipsed or counteracted by evidence that many people still, 'deep down', subscribe (whether consciously or not) to the idea that human beings are racially different in meaningful and consequential ways. Replacing race with ethnicity – or diversity – might de-racialise cultural and corporeal difference but it is not quite the 'get out card' that might be imagined. Ethnicity itself becomes biologised as well as culturalised and evokes the same essentialising and hierarchical orderings implied by categories of race.

And so race has not disappeared. Nayak (2006) and St Louis (2005) have mapped the paradox of race being defined as a social construct while continuing to be widely used in academic and non-academic contexts as an ontological category. To focus on what race does and achieves is one approach for managing the tensions between researching a social category that has been assigned naturalised meanings and corporeal associations. Writing with Alice Bloch and John Solomos, we argued (Bloch, Neal, and Solomos 2013) that race remained a necessary focus as it worked as a line of social division producing inequalities around core social resources and goods as well as creating erasures from collective identities and belongings and exclusions from processes of recognition and entitlement. Race can, in other words, be approached as a social division, but it is important to acknowledge its multiple and mutable forms – that its meanings change, can be assigned and self-identified, embodied and disembodied, a focus of political mobilisation and a focus for political rejection. As Murji argues 'putting forward an argument that race is merely an idea or just a social construct might make social scientists seem detached from reality when viewed against the backdrop of national and global events of recent years' (2017: 18). The mutability of race and its powerful status demands that any engagement with research on race requires dexterity and recognition of the ambivalences, harms, divisions and political intensities and associated with the concept.

It is in this context that this chapter provides an overview of some of these contestations and dilemmas that are presented by – and encountered when – conducting social research that is focused on multicultural social worlds and diverse research populations.

The political nature of racism research

Today, one of the key tenets of the ethics of social research focuses on the need for it to have social impact and benefit, or, as a minimal threshold, to do no harm, to not be deceptive, to be based on ongoing consent and project transparency. This means that research that addresses race is going to be intensely demanding given that race does harm, race is a deception and race is usually as far from open and transparent. This means that quantitative and qualitative research that investigates issues and questions of race has to acknowledge and reflect the political nature of the field of inquiry and the political nature of the particular research project. As Back and Solomos (1993: 196) noted from their research experiences while conducting research on race and local politics in the UK city of Birmingham in the early 1990s, it is impossible for research on racism not to be political in some way (see also Back and Sinha 2018; Phoenix 1994). Given that research which generates data and findings in relation to race, social relations, social resources and social processes will also generate intended and unintended impacts and interpretations in the social worlds the challenge is not only to acknowledge this but also to find ways of engaging with and managing research relating to race in highly political terrains.

Qualitative research in particular now has an embedded and more explicit commitment to reflexivity and the recognition both that social research is necessarily partial and that research can be neither politically neutral nor value-free. This paradigm shift in qualitative research approaches is largely a result of feminist and post-structuralist critiques of research methodologies that emerged in the 1970s and 1980s. The shift has been profound and, while the feminist critique has been widely recognised for its questioning of methods, focus, approach, positionality and research relationships, what is less acknowledged is the significance and the contributions that anti-racist approaches made to these debates. While research approaches that emerged directly from gender considerations are now at the heart of conventional qualitative research methodology (see above) the arguments and issues raised by anti-racist research debates are much less present.

This unevenness is striking given the extent to which there was a significant amount of shared ground in the two positions. For example, both feminist and anti-racist critiques have emphasised the partial, exclusionary and essentialising nature of social knowledge and the powerful if contradictory dynamic which either completely neglects difference and the experiences and perspectives of marginalised groups or, if there is a focus on minoritised groups, then it often problematically reinforces assumptions, labels and stereotypes (Lawrence 1982). These overlapping concerns also underpinned a commitment to a shared agenda for doing social research differently. The ontological and epistemological repositionings that this involved also meant that a range of methodological demands became core considerations and these ranged from questions of knowledge production and wider political agendas – what and who got researched – to a focus on research relationships, what the purpose of social research on race and racism was, the ways in which research questions were framed through power and hierarchy, questions about what researchers should be doing in and with research and a recognition of researcher effect as well as more prosaic but still profound methods questions around access, rapport and trust. These were questions raised in the UK nearly four decades ago and yet they remain as pertinent and contemporary today as they were in the 1980s.

Methods challenges for researching difference

One of the key areas of dicussion and overlap were the arguments for the development of standpoint or the 'matched' co-identities in social research relationships between researchers and research participants. As feminists made the case for the importance for women to research and interview women participants so the same case was made for the importance of black and Asian researchers conducting research with black and Asian research participants. However, the rationale and practice of ethnic matching in research interview settings has not been widely taken up and a number of black and South Asian scholars have problematised the concept and limitations of standpoint research (Gunaratnam 2003; Twine 2000). Phoenix (1994: 6) has similarly argued against the idea that there may be a 'unitary truth about respondents lives that matched researchers are most effectively able to get to' and highlights the variety of identities and biographical and situational experiences that disrupt as much as confirm apparent sameness (see also Puwar 1997). Although Gunaratnam (2003) is sympathetic to what she calls 'broad matching' in contexts of co-production and participatory research, like Phoenix she too questions the ways in which standpoint methods neatly fix and essentialise categories of identity. While ethnic matching does create agentic spaces for different research agendas, priorities and dialogue, as both Phoenix and Gunaratnam warn, matching also creates routes for white researchers to avoid engaging with questions of race and marginalising both black and minority ethnic researchers and participants in a narrowed down field of race research which gets done by black, Asian and minority ethnic researchers, while they are effectively sidelined from research on other areas of social life.

But if standpoint research is problematised it it may still be worth reflecting on how and why it works in those situations where it may be appropriate. When I was involved in a recent project researching the 'patterns of intergenerational adults' and children's friendships across ethnic and social difference (Vincent, Neal, and Iqbal 2018) I was part of an ethnically diverse research team. Humera Iqbal identifies as British Pakistani and Carol Vincent and I would both identify as white British. In one interview situation with Kaleb – an Ethopian parent participant who had lived in London since his asylum status was secured – the interview conversation covered experiences of the difficulties of settling in a new country, cultural challenges and reflected on enagaing in practices of belonging while being attached to elsewhere and, speaking to Humera directly, Kaleb said 'you understand this'. I was struck immediately by the significance of this brief exchange as it was the explicit if still coded articulation of the, until then, unspoken ways in which race, ethnic difference and connections circulated in the interview setting. This was not ethnic matching between

Humera and Kaleb in any straightforward sense but was rooted more in an intersectional sense of recognition and a summoning of sameness in the experience of difference and dislocation. This momentary exchange seems to me to speak to the urgency of thinking through the dynamics and complexities as to how ethnically and culturally diverse researchers interview across ethnic and social difference and the impact that these non-essentialised differences have in interview settings and in the co-productive processes of data generation.

These challenges become more acute given the complexities, contradictions and increasingly heterogenous demographic profile of those people who become the research populations of research projects that are focused on race questions. But research that is not about race issues also needs to engage with this non-essentialised diversity and show how and in what ways sampling strategies incorporate ethnic diversity into their logics. Again, the paucity in discussion of social difference and race in mainstream methods training and literature is striking. The late 20th century feminist and anti-racist arguments around standpoint interviewing need space for ongoing discussion but also resituating in the context of approaches that recognise the significance of intersectionality and focus 'on the complexity of relationships among multiple social groups within and across analytical categories and not on complexities within single social groups, single categories or both' (McCall 2005: 1786). There is also a need to extend these debates to the increasing range of quantitative and qualitative research methods and in both online and offline research environments. Even with traditional and core methods such as ethnography there is still surprisingly little methods discussion of, or guidance on, researcher immersion and observation of social settings and the people within them.

I have written with colleagues about the challenges of multicultural ethnography (Neal et al. 2015; 2018) in which the core ethnographic research process of interpreting and recording micro descriptions of the social world in which you are located as a researcher can become problematic and troubling. The research project, *Living Multiculture*, used a range of qualitative research approaches to respond to and examine the increasing complex social geographies of ethnic diversity in contemporary urban England. Based in three distinct geographies the project focused on a variety of key social spaces – such as schools, parks, cafes and leisure organisations – which would be likely to have local multicultural populations and in which everyday and routine social relationships and interactions might be reasonably expected to occur. It was in these spaces, in different geographical locations, that we hung out, spending time observing and participating. However, we became quickly unnerved by the gap between being immersed in and surrounded by superdiverse, composite, context specific and multiple identities and what we found ourselves writing in our fieldnotes as these were written in worryingly singular and essentialising ways as they tried to capture the complexity we were seeing.

In short, our fieldnotes were tending to 'fix'/secure populations within categories of difference, of ethnicity, of national and non-national identity. Writing about seeing difference in ways which meant that perhaps we were not being nuanced and attentive but rather doing archaic 'difference work', reducing people to their visible characteristics and emphasising/defining (their) difference on this basis. Our fieldnote descriptions of the people in the social worlds that we were part of had a UK census-like feel to them as we wrote of there being white British, black British, South Asian, Muslim, Turkish, Eastern European, black African and Jewish people in the places we were spending time. There is a paradox in the process of looking at social practices, interactions, atmospheres and exchanges but then also relying on the corporeal and cultural signs (skin colour, dress, language, accent) that make these significant and assigning unitary ethnicity categories to identify and understand difference in order then to identify how difference may have been disrupted – or not (Gunaratnam 2003). In our attempts to change the objectification of what we described our fieldnotes became filled with questions marks and tentative writing – lots of 'perhaps' and 'appears to be'. This experience highlights the retreat to a sort of phenotypical and cultural reading, relying on descriptive ethnic classifications and the assigning of people to those in ethnographic writing but also of the centrality of the ethnographer in the ethnographic process. The challenge of how to respond to these contradictions is to design research with the limitations and challenges of any singular method in mind.

Participation, conversation and a multiple (and mobile) interviewing process can help to counter some of the ways in which the visual may become essentialised as the intersectional biographies and narratives of the participants undo identity categories as well as decentering us as ethnographic researchers. And while the role of the ethnographer as the interpretive core of the research process has been problematised, their role in relation to race and difference has received less attention, despite the very present dangers that ethnographic representations of social worlds can be more about the assumptions of the ethnographer than the 'exotic Others we colourfully stitch into our richly embroidered texts' (Nayak 2006: 413). While there is some reflective and political scrutiny of this it tends to be confined to monographs, papers, and the few specialist methods books on race and social research such as Winddance Twine and Warren (2000), Gunaratnam (2003) and Nayak (2006). There needs to be a more integrated approach and acknowledgement of racialised positionalities, intersectionality and the meanings and implications of these for 'mainstream' research methods training and literature.

Research on race is not always or necessarily about research with participants who are marginalised but may also involve engagement with powerful actors and elites. An example of this comes from a research project which involved interviewing participants who had been members of the Future of Multi-Ethnic Britain Commission in the UK in the early 2000s. While the commissioners, themselves a highy multi-ethnic group, were elites in that they were all very successful, influential and often high profile professionals, academics, civil servants, media figures and policy leaders, their expereinces of co-authoring a report which had been very negatively received by the then UK Labour government and by the mainstream media disrupted this status, revealing the ways in which racism reshaped social standing. The Commissioners' retelling of their experiences for the project also reshaped our experience of conducting interviews with elite participants (see Neal and McLaughlin 2009). The racialised identities and situational experience of the commissioners destablised their elite status and illustrates the complexities of researching race in situtational contexts and the importance of an intersectional approach in social research. Such an intersectional approach not only attempts to recognise and incorporate – in a non-additive way – a range of social divisions but recquires researchers to recognise what McCall (2005) defines as 'intercategorical complexity'. It involves researchers being aware of the ways in which people's identities, situations and biographies are likely to be multidimensional, social and relational as the stories of the Commission members and of Kaleb and Humera both demonstrate. This means that ethnic symmetries and categorisations are unlikely to provide any easy or straightforward answers to who should be doing research investigating race and racism but intersectionality also means that broader or partial ethnic matching might sometimes be appropriate to the research context (Gunaratnam 2003).

The dilemmas of research attention

This emphasis on intersectionality is not just because there is a need for more research to be conducted with communities of colour and marginalised groups. One of the key concerns is to recognise and acknowledge the broader role and presence of race politics and racism within social research. As I argued earlier there is a profound contradiction between the history, nature and extent of research on race and the paucity of research on racism, the politics of race and racialisation. While the colonial production of race knowledge can seem like a danger of the past, it would be politically naïve not to see that the interests in race science and the representations of minority, problematised and subjugated groups reinforces and reproduces widely established labelling, stereotypes and assumptions in policy, public and everyday discourse. Both quantitative and qualitative research may be implicated in this. The seminal text *Policing the Crisis* by Stuart Hall and colleagues (1979) showed how this happened through the media but also through academic research.

Others from Birmingham's Centre of Contemporary Cultural Studies (where Hall was based) highlighted the ways in which white researchers directly contributed to these processes pathologising young black and South Asian people as 'problems or victims', as lost between two cultures and in cultural crisis or locked into sub cultural deviances and criminal behaviours (Carby 1982; Lawrence 1982). For anti-racist social researchers writing in the context of race politics in the UK in the 1980s, the concerns about academic research were not only about a neglect of racism and marginalisation of black people's experiences and perspectives nor about the ways in which the disproportionate focus of research attention on black, Asian and minority ethnic people reinforced racialised stereotypes and cultural misrepresentations but above all on how 'their "theories" about black people help to shape public policy at every level, from the exalted heights of the Home Office to the humbler ranks of the school staff room' (Lawrence 1982: 97). This concern about the impact of academic research converges with wider questions about the politics and purpose of social research – and the extent to which so much of social research involves a 'downwards' gaze with an over-research of marginal and powerless groups and the places in which they are located. More recent social research which problematises cultural difference through an association with social conflict and 'segregation' continues to contribute to rather than challenge dominant racialising discourses or, more mundanely, but just as insidiously, may simply be extractive, taking experiences, perspectives and knowledge from participants without generating any benefit for them.

This concern with the over-research of certain groups highlights the dangers of representation and political positioning. This has meant that racialised and marginalised communities and populations have long been concerned about the role of research and researchers and research agendas that have a 'research on' rather than a 'research with' orientation. It is not enough to recognise the research scrutiny to which black, migrant and minority communities, Muslim communities and refugee groups are subject. The legitimacy of such a research gaze must be questioned given that research has reinforced damaging assumptions, pathologies and stereotypes and because, despite high levels of research attention, there is far too little evidence of positive change or policy intervention that is felt or experienced by those populations or in those places (Beebeejaun et al. 2013; Clarke 2008). Repeated attention results in participants literally getting tired of answering similar questions from successive cohorts of researchers without then seeing any benefits. For example, talking of Liverpool, Moore (1996) recounts how 'research fatigue had set in in certain well studied zones as the local residents were only too willing to tell the fieldworker'.

Social researchers may be 'outsiders' with only a rudimentary knowledge of the localities or communities on which their research is focused and so appear spatially naïve or detached, reinforcing the sense that they are driven by different agendas to the people they are researching. Particular places as well as populations become problematised through research as well as media and policy attention. How places become presented, conceptualised and identified has a lasting outcome that continues to exist after the field work is concluded. Beyond the research encounter itself research produces a series of written artefacts that circulate in different networks. In re-studies in particular it was knowledge of the first round of studies by the communities concerned that prompted anxiety towards later studies (Charles and Crow 2012). Some places particularly attract research attention. The East End of London and nearby Hackney, an ethnically diverse borough in North East London, for example, have consistently attracted social researchers. Hackney's research allure can be understood through what Karner and Parker (2010) call 'reputational geographies'. Hackney has a long history of different migrant flows and settlements, a tradition of oppositional politics, urban disorder and its high levels social and ethnic diversity, recently accelerated by gentrification dynamics. All of this has drawn the research gaze. For example a (non-exhaustive) list of academic research about and/or based in Hackney would include (Butler and Hannett 2011; Jones 2014, 2015; Kulz 2013; Neal et al. 2015; Vincent 1996; Rhys-Taylor 2013; Wessendorf 2014; Wright 1985) and show how multicultural places like Hackney can come to resemble 'research labs' for social researchers.

My own presence as member of a research team in the borough as part of the *Living Multiculture* project also contributed to this overcrowding as we joined this long list of scholars not to mention social commentators, writers, and artists drawn to researching in and on Hackney. Over and under-researched geographies raise political questions especially given the correlation between over-researched places and levels of social deprivation, migration, conflict, decline, gentrification and so forth. In this context it is important to understand that 'knowledge production needs to be collaborative and relational [and] process-based rather than outcome-based inquiry' (de Leeuw, Cameron, and Greenwood 2012: 182) so that research agendas are orientated towards co-productive approaches which 'destablise academia as a privileged site for the production and dissemination of knowledge' (Bell and Pahl 2018: 107). Instead of privileging the researcher it becomes necessary to recognise the significance of the knowledge brought by participants to research teams, as data is generated through the active collaboration of researched-researcher interaction and dialogue (Sinha and Back 2013; Back and Sinha 2018; Beebeejaun et al. 2013).

But research participants are, in any case, rarely as passive as 'extractive' models imply. So, for example, Sukarieh and Tannock (2013) note, in the context of the over-research in the Shatila refugee camp, that minor subversions took place as participants acknowledged purposefully 'lying' to researchers to protect themselves and their communities. Rankin (2009) too has also examined how research participants resisted the external agendas of development professionals at the same time as using the political resources made available by external interventions. Sustained interactions with researchers can create participant 'know how' to make such demands. By framing the issue as one of 'extraction' of information the over-research arguments conceals more uneven dynamics and power relations within the research process. This highlights the co-productive nature of research relationships and chimed with the extent to which the Hackney participants in the *Living Multiculture* project were often confident and assertive in negotiations over their participation in the project reflecting a knowledge and 'know how' about social research processes. Participants negotiated access and set out expectations and participation rules with the team in some settings because key participants were familiar and confident enough with research ethics and research relationships to do this. In another dimension of this we encountered a critical approach to social research voiced by some of the policy-related participants whom we interviewed. For example, in one of these policy interviews a local authority participant directly raised the issue of the number of social researchers working in Hackney:

[w]ithout wanting to sound awkward or anything, but we get a lot of people who come in and want to research Hackney, but what sort of legacy do they leave apart from wanting to come in and publish and then take to a different academic community? But there are lots of groups which could benefit from access to research expertise that cannot pay for it.

The concern expressed here relates to the academic extraction of data from a particular place and population without longer-term reciprocity but it is also reflects an awareness that social research is a potentially valuable co-productive process and resource. This participant's critique of the social research being undertaken in Hackney was not targeted at the project research team *per se* (and these were people who were willing to engage with our project) but that it was raised in the interview conversation is significant. This questioning of 'what gets delivered back?' from high levels of research activity in particular places and with particular populations reflects a concern with over-research as well as the key requirements of research ethics i.e. that social research should be a socially beneficial process. This awareness of social research extended into the confident and critical engagements we had with the policy and organisation related participants. While the challenges raised around disproportionate research have understandably problematised the direction of the research gaze on particular populations in places rather than on the places themselves, we suggest that these are co-constituted and the places in which research participants live also require an ethics of care and research responsibility.

Some reflections

Being attentive to situated and placed lives echoes concerns raised by earlier post-structuralist, feminist, anti-racist and participatory research critiques which set some of the agenda four decades ago. More recently these are developed through the 'co-productive turn' in mainstream academic research environments. The 'understand[ing]that useful and critical knowledge is dispersed throughout society and to seek to activate, expand and apply this knowledge to effect change [and] empower co-producers to shape the world in which they live' (Bell and Pahl 2018: 107) is a fundamental building block in developing a more open and engaged approach to the practices of social research. There may be dangers of the translation and the depoliticisation of this commitment as co-production becomes incorporated and institutionalised. But at its heart co-production problematises social research processes and intentions and re-works research relationships. With its commitment to not doing research that is 'about us without us', and its emphasis on democratising the research process, decentring the researcher and prioritising participants' experience and knowledge, co-production can be seen to respond to and reflect the anti-racist critiques of social research. In contexts in which particular individuals, groups, communities and the places in which they live have a history of being stigmatised, marginalised or pathologised then research approaches which are orientated towards collaborative arrangements like these can shift research relationships into what Back and Sinha describe as being a more 'sociable methods [which are] participatory and dialogic' (2018).

The need to prioritise and cultivate multicultural research skills and competencies which are able (and adept) in making methods decisions and recognise increasingly ethnically diverse and socially differentiated populations within research design and collaborative data generation becomes profoundly important. Putting questions of race and cultural difference and intersectionality at the centre of research methods training and practice is part of the decolonising process. To understand the real/unreal contradiction of race as a social set of relations given that 'international belief in race as real [is what] makes race real in its social consequences' (Bonilla-Silva and Zuberei 2008: 7) is why research on race and ethnicity needs to more than be simply listed as a sensitive research area in universities' ethical approval processes and instead needs to be integral part of core social research methods literature as well as methods teaching and learning.

References

Back L., and Sinha S. with C., Bryan, V., Baraka and M. Yemba (2018) *Migrant City*, Oxford: Routledge.

Back L. and Solomos J. (1993) 'Doing research, writing politics: the dilemmas of political intervention in research on racism', *Economy and Society*, vol. 22, pp. 178–199.

Back L. and Tate M. (2015) 'For a Sociological Reconstruction: W.E.B. Du Bois, Stuart Hall and Segregated', Sociology *Sociological Research Online*, vol. 20, 15, no. 3, pp. 1–12.

Beebeejaun Y., Durose C., Rees J., Richardson J. and Richardson J. (2013) 'Beyond text: exploring ethos and method in co-producing research with communities', *Community Development Journal*, vol. 49, no. 1, pp. 37–53.

Bell D.M. and Pahl K. (2018) 'Co-production: towards a utopian approach', *International Journal of Social Research Methodology*, vol. 21, no. 1, pp. 105–117.

Bhambra G. (2014) 'A sociological dilemma: race segregation and US sociology', *Current Sociology*, vol. 62, no. 4, pp. 472–492.

Bloch A., Neal S. and Solomos J. (2013) *Race, Multiculture and Social Policy*, Basingstoke: Palgrave Macmillan.

Bonilla-Silva E. and Zuberei T. (2008) *White Logic, White Methods: racism and methodology*, Maryland: Rowman and Littlefield Publishers.

Carby H. (1982) 'Schooling in Babylon' in CCCS (ed.), *The Empire Strikes Back*, London: Hutchinson.

Butler T. and Hamnett C. (2011) *Ethnicity, Class and Aspiration: Understanding London's New East End*, Bristol: Policy Press.

Charles N. and Crow G. (2012) 'Community re-studies and social change', *The Sociological Review*, vol. 60, no. 3, pp. 399–404.

Clarke T. (2008) 'We're over-researched here! Exploring accounts of research fatigue within qualitative research engagements', *Sociology*, vol. 42, no. 2, pp. 953–970.

de Leeuw S., Cameron E. and Greenwood M. (2012) 'Articipatory and community based research, indigenous geographies and the spaces of friendship: a critical engagement', *The Canadian Geographer*, vol. 56, no. 2, pp. 180–194.

Du Bois W.E. B. (1899, 2007 reprint) *The Philadelphia Negro: a social study*, New York: Oxford University Press.

Gilroy P. (1987) *There Ain't No Black in the Union Jack*, London: Unwin Hyman Publishers.

Gunaratnam Y. (2003) *Researching 'Race' and Ethnicity. Methods, Knowledge and Power*, London: Sage.

Jones H. (2014) 'The best borough in the country for cohesion! Managing place and multiculture in local government', *Ethnic and Racial Studies*, vol. 37, no. 4, pp. 605–620.

Jones H. (2015) *Negotiating Cohesion, Inequality and Change: Uncomfortable Positions in Local Government*, Bristol: Policy Press.

Karner C. and Parker D. (2010) 'Reputational geographies and urban social cohesion', *Ethnic and Racial Studies*, vol. 33, no. 8, pp. 1451–1470.

Kulz C. (2013) 'Structure liberates? Mixing for mobility and the cultural transformation of 'urban children' in a London academy', *Ethnic and Racial Studies*, vol. 37, no. 4, pp. 685–701.

Lawrence E. (1982) *In The Abundance Of Water the Fool is Thirsty: Sociology and Pathology in CCCS the Empire Strikes Back*, London: Hutchinson.

McCall L. (2005) 'The complexity of intersectionality', *Signs*, vol. 30, pp. 1771–1800.

Moore R. (1996) 'Crown Street revisited', *Sociological Research Online*, vol. 16, no. 3, p. 12. http://www.socresonline.org.uk/16/3/12.html.

Murji K. (2017) *Racism, Policy and Politics*, Bristol: Policy Press.

Nayak A. (2006) 'After race: ethnography, race and post-race theory', *Ethnic and Racial Studies*, vol. 29, no. 3, pp. 411–430.

Neal S, Bennett K, Cochrane A and Mohan G. (2018) *The Lived Experiences of Multiculture: The New Spatial and Social Relations of Diversity*, Abingdon: Routledge.

Neal S., Bennett K., Jones H., Cochrane A. and Mohan G. (2015) 'Multiculture and public parks: researching super-diversity and attachment in public green spaces', *Population, Space and Place*, vol. 21, no. 5, pp. 463–475.

Neal S. and McLaughlin E. (2009) 'Researching up? Interviews, emotionality and policy making elites', *Journal of Social Policy*, vol. 38, no. 4, pp. 689–707.

Puwar N. (1997) 'Reflections on interviewing wormn MPs', *Sociological Research Online*, vol. 2, no. 1, p. 4. http://www.socresonline.org.uk/2/1/4.

Phoenix A. (1994) 'Practising feminist research: the intersection of gender and 'race' in the research process', In M. Maynard and J. Purvis (eds) *Researching Women's Lives*, London: Taylor and Francis, pp. 49–71.

Rankin K. (2009) 'Critical development studies and the praxis of planning', *City*, vol. 13, no. 2-3, pp. 216–226.

Rhys-Taylor A. (2013) 'The essences of multiculture: a sensory exploration of an inner city street market', *Identities: Global Studies in Power*, vol. 20, no. 4, pp. 393–406.

Sinha S. and Back L. (2013) 'Making methods socialble: dialogue, ethics and authorships in qualitative research', *Qualitative Research*, vol. 14, no. 4, pp. 473–487.

Song M. (2018) 'Why we still need to talk about race', *Ethnic and Racial Studies*, vol. 41, no. 4, pp. 1131–1145.

St Louis B. (2005) 'The difference sameness makes: racial recognition and the 'narcissism of minor differences', *Ethnicities*, vol. 5, no. 3, pp. 343–365.

Sukarieh M. and Tannock S. (2013) 'On the problem of over-researched communities: the case of the Shatila Palestinian refugee camp in Lebanon', *Sociology*, vol. 47, no. 3, pp. 494–508.

Tuhiwai-Smith L. (2012) *Decolonizing Methodologies: research and indigenous Peoples*, 2nd edition, London: Zed Books.

Twine W. F. (2000) 'Racial ideologies and racial methodologies', In W. F. Twine and J. Warren (eds) *Racing Research, Researching Race*, NYC: NY University Press, pp. 1–34.

Twine W. F. and Warren J. (eds) (2000) *Racing Research, Researching Race*, NYC: NY University Press.

Vincent C. (1996) *Parents and Teachers: Power and Participation*, London: Routledge.

Vincent Ca., Neal S. and Iqbal H. (2018) *Friendship and Diversity, Class, Ethnicity and Social Relations in The City*, Basingstoke: Palgrave Macmillan.

Wessendorf S. (2014) *Commonplace Diversity: Social Relations in a Super-diverse Context*, Basingstoke: Palgrave Macmillan.

Wright P. (1985) *On Living in an Old Country*, Oxford: Oxford University Press.

Part X
The end of racism?

Introduction

In this concluding part of the *Handbook* we return to an issue that has been touched upon in other parts, but which has not been explored fully as yet: namely the question of how we can begin to think beyond racism. In the previous nine parts of this volume we have been able to explore key facets of contemporary racisms, but we wanted in this part to look forward more in the direction of how we can begin to think beyond the realities of contemporary racisms. The three chapters seek in one way or another to address the question of likely future trends in the articulation of racism.

The first chapter by Michel Wieviorka is centrally concerned with the ways in which racism, anti-Semitism and anti-racism are being reconfigured in the current conjuncture. Wieviorka's account provides an exploration of the ways in which racism and anti-semitism persist in older pre-existing or classical forms but also in newer and changing expressions that are the product of contemporary processes. Wieviorka argues that in the past few decades new expressions of racism have been shaped to some extent by the role of social media and other communication technologies that have enabled the articulation of new forms of racialised ideologies. His chapter also explores the contradictory forms through which anti-racist ideas are expressed in the contemporary conjuncture. In developing this part of his analysis, he argues that anti-racism is in practice not a singular phenomenon and can take a variety of forms. It is also important to note that Wieviorka's chapter highlights the ways anti-semitism has found new means of expression in the contemporary conjuncture.

This is followed by Kevin Durrheim's chapter, which explores the development of the concept of racism in the social sciences and includes some reflections about the possible end of racism. Durrheim traces the origins of the idea of racism and then explores the ways that it became firmly established as a focus for research in the social sciences. His account suggests that the social sciences played an important role in developing our understanding of racism in modern societies. He concludes the chapter by exploring the ways in which contemporary debates have tended to involve to some extent as denial of racism and even claims that the perpetrators of racism are actually the victims of some forms of racism themselves.

The final chapter by Philomena Essed seeks to provide a nuanced and challenging account of how we can research and think beyond racism. In doing so she highlights the need for researchers to address more fully than they have done hitherto the role of strategies of humiliation, dehumanisation and the quest for dignity. Essed argues that dehumanisation and humiliations are at the heart of all forms of structural inferiorisation and marginalisation. On the basis of this argument she argues that struggles against racism should not be seen through the lens of single-issue mobilisations, since in practice it is interrelated to other structural social injustices and inequalities. In contrast to other anti-racist perspectives Essed seeks to identify how mobilisations against racism need to focus centrally on issues of social injustice and dehumanisation more generally if they are to counter racism more effectively (see also Chapter 14 by Bojadžijev).

The three chapters together raise important issues for further reflection and research about both the contemporary forms of racism and how to develop both our understanding of them and how to move beyond racism.

32

Metamorphoses of racism, anti-semitism and anti-racism today

Michel Wieviorka

Racism, and the hatred of Jews – anti-Semitism is a term only in use since the end of the 19th century – are phenomena which are constantly changing. Thus towards the end of the 1960s we witnessed profound transformations in both, indicative of a change which had begun at the end of World War II and which on the whole seemed to point to their decline.[1]

The movements for civil rights and decolonisation on one hand, and the awareness, albeit belated, of the specifically genocidal dimensions of Nazi barbarism to which hatred of the Jews had led on the other had suggested that, until then, support for racism and anti-Semitism was declining considerably in strength. Of particular note at the time were the significant efforts made by UNESCO which had the ability then to mobilise the most prestigious intellectuals, in the first instance Claude Lévi-Strauss; these efforts resonated with this evolution and strengthened it, culminating in particular in the resounding *Declaration on Race and Racial Prejudice* (1978).

But in fact, instead of regressing, racism was taking new paths to remain in existence: it continued, or was revealed, in what some American specialists referred to as 'covert' or 'veiled' forms. It was apparently an integral part of institutional structures or mechanisms and not consciously implemented by those who practised it.

The acknowledgement of this change can be found, at an early date, in the book by Carmichael and Hamilton, published in 1967, entitled *Black Power*,[2] which attracted significant media attention.[3] In this book, the two militants of the American Black Power movement envisage the modalities of action appropriate to dealing with the 'systemic' or 'subtle' racism characteristic of the established and respected forces in the society and which they analyse. The idea of a racism which will be described as structural, or institutional is there. It is based on the existence of modalities of prejudice or of discrimination which do not need to be manifested by explicitly racist individuals to function perfectly well. It is the institution and the structures which are racist; those who belong to it are not necessarily required to be racist themselves. The phenomenon seems to be a property of the system and not of the actors.

At the end of the 1970s a second change in direction was observed in the first instance by American specialists in the study of racism (in particular psychologists) which at this point was perceived as 'symbolic'. The new racists considered that Black people were not capable of adapting to the American '*credo*' or 'way of life' which focuses on work and family. The Black population was said to be culturally different, preferring social welfare to employment and contributing to the break-up of the family rather than to its promotion. Here also, all over the world, an extensive literature took up this observation under various denominations: cultural racism, differentialism, new or neo-racism, the idea being that Black people (then other groups) are not necessarily inferior as such in their physical characteristics but that they are irredeemably different and, as such, a threat to traditional values (family, work) but also to the identity of the society (the nation or the dominant religion for example). From being 'natural', the racists now considered race to be 'cultural'. In the wake of the United States, the debate was launched in the UK (Barker, 1981) as from 1981; in France, Etienne Balibar (Balibar, 1981) and Pierre-André Taguieff (Taguieff, 1988) popularised this theme in the second half of the 1980s.[4]

Similarly, the question of anti-Semitism was relaunched in the 1970s with the success of the 'negationist' theses (the claim that the gas chambers had never existed), followed by the extension of the theme of the 'Shoah business' – which is simply a softer version of the negationist themes (the claim being that today the Shoah is a 'business', a source of profit and wealth for the Jews). In the same context, there was a rise in hostility and hate toward the state of Israel and in radical identification with the Palestinian cause and/or Islam and Islamism in their cultural 'shock' with the West.[5]

Thus, at the end of the 20th century, racism would have seemed to have started to cast off its traditional guise and to be becoming less assertive. The very idea of race seemed to be losing its influence while that of cultural or religious difference was gaining in strength. The Jews were no longer described in terms of race by anti-Semites, contrary to what culminated in Nazism, so much so that some intellectuals questioned whether it would not be more appropriate to find another term for hatred of the Jews, and speak for example of the new 'Judeophobia'. When apartheid was ended in South Africa in 1991, then when for the first time in the history of the United States a Black American, Barack Obama, was elected president in 2008, the idea of a world which had done away with racism began to acquire credibility. President Obama described America as being 'post-racial'.

But it must be admitted, as Obama himself said in his farewell speech in February 2017, at the end of his second term as President, that this vision had never been 'realistic' and that in fact, racism and anti-Semitism today are in no way on the decline.

This is true for the English-speaking world but these countries are not alone. It is also the case in France, or in Latin America and the countries in the Northern Hemisphere, but also in India or in South America. The question of racism and anti-Semitism, and from there, that of anti-racist action, calls for a fundamental intellectual and perhaps, even, a scientific *updating*, and in its wake, political support.

As we shall see the new institutional, cultural and post-colonial forms of racism and anti-Semitism intertwine with classical and even archaic forms of these phenomena; at the same time they are also the outcome of a number of ambiguities in anti-racism.

A clean bill of health for classical racism

At the outset, we must state emphatically that any idea of a post-racial society must be abandoned for the moment, whether it be a question for example of the United States or South Africa. We must also be wary of the idea of a decline in racism and anti-Semitism, or of a softening up process whereby racism can only advance in disguise, by stealth, indirectly, losing any charge of explicit essentialisation, or naturalisation of people and thus becoming cultural and therefore not racial, or at least less so. This idea is totally belied by the facts.

In the United States, the Black Americans who are shot by the police without having committed the slightest crime, or the least offence, are victims of a direct, flagrant racism which has nothing in the slightest 'cultural' or 'symbolic'. This racism exists at the core of institutions like the courts, the police or the penitentiary system but this does not mean to say that it is only 'institutional', at least if we give this adjective the meaning which it acquired in the 1970s referring, as we said, to unobtrusive, non-explicit mechanisms acting apparently independently of the awareness of the actors. The white supremacists act in broad daylight, setting the stage for murderous violence, as on the occasion of their rally at Charlottesville in August 2017. Above all, wholesale racism, targeting Blacks but also Mexicans or Indians, has risen to the highest political level, with President Trump showing great understanding with respect to some of those who in one way or another profess it.

In South Africa, fierce campaigns on social networks compare the Black population to monkeys. In particular since 2015, university campuses have been disrupted by challenges in the name of the Black population and the 'coloured people' denouncing the cost of enrolment fees and also the still over present marks of the past of colonisation and Apartheid. For example, there have been demands for the removal of the statue of Cecil Rhodes (a leading figure in the colonial domination of the country) from Cape Town University. National reconciliation is very far from being a reality and the majority of observers speak of a deterioration in 'race relations', which is confirmed by the surveys.

Throughout Europe, populist and nationalist movements are developing intense xenophobic and racist campaigns which are in no way concerned by cultural niceties. Black football players are greeted by monkey chants from the stands. Political figures like Christiane Taubira in France, Minister for Justice from 2012 to 2015, are also publicly compared to monkeys, or even to a female monkey – which adds a particularly vulgar sexism to the racism.

Discrimination, which we readily described as systemic, indirect and institutional also remains explicit in particular in employment. In many democratic countries, the law, the legislation and the anti- racism institutions in no way prevent racial assignation, particularly in firms, when hiring or in promotion and advancement.

Anti-Semitism, weighted with old anti-Judaic themes, is back and thriving in Europe in its classical forms, unmistakable and rapidly brutal even deadly. In France, Islamist terrorists have killed Jewish people (Mohammed Merah murdered three Jewish children and a teacher in Toulouse in March 2012, and Amedi Coulibaly took as hostages the personnel and clients of a kosher hypermarket in Paris in January 2015 – four people were killed). Anti-Semitic crimes with no political or religious backing also occur, as when Youssouf Fofana and his 'gang of barbarians' captured and left for dead a young Jewish man, Ilan Halimi, for reasons which amalgamate villainy and prejudice – the Jews have money, he thought, they will pay a ransom. In the United States, the vitality of the anti-Semitic campaigns, fraught with intimidation and even violence, and imbued with prejudice about which there is nothing new, is patent, viral thanks to the Internet and the social networks and driven by the new right, the 'alt right' (or alternative right) discussed by Jonathan Weisman[6] as distinct from that of the 'neo-Cons'. It also thrives in the evangelical sectors which their hatred of Jews in no way prevents them from actively supporting the politics of the State of Israel.

It must be recognised that in numerous countries there is a persistence, and even a revival of a form of racism and anti-Semitism supported by the old cornerstones of racial hatred, and medieval prejudices from far before the innovations constituted in the 1970s and 1980s by institutional and cultural racism.

This persistence is in action at a time when an important specificity characterises the potential targets of this blatant racism or at least some of them: they are less hesitant than in the past in internalising the racialisation or ethnicisation aimed at them, and much less hesitant in choosing to assert a real visibility, to describe themselves for example as Black or Jewish, including in the public sphere. The self-declaration of an identity then leads to discussions and challenges in which race becomes, along with other cultural, social or religious differences, a category of reference for the racists but also for those whom they target.

This observation should not prevent others from being formulated: these issues are in a process of renewal well beyond the transformations observed in the 1970s and 1980s.

The technological density of institutional racism

Recently in the United States and the United Kingdom, researchers, either in academic circles or in relation with these, possibly along with militant organisations from movements for example like Black Lives Matter[7] have been developing work showing the links which may exist between digital tools and, in particular, racist forms of discrimination. Algorithms are not inherently neutral; they are liable to duplicate the biases and prejudices at work within society. Digital platforms and social media which operate increasingly as online communities, often quite remote from any universalism, are also prone to reproducing the racism which traverses society, or even to reinforce it.

Similarly, artificial intelligence is far from neutral, which leads us to question the implicit racist assumptions at the core of some of its developments (Buranyi, 2017).[8] Racism transits through worlds in which digital technology, the Internet, new technologies and social networks may reproduce it; it operates like an additional layer or a supplementary screen between the prejudices which circulate in society and their implementation, in particular in the form of discrimination. From this point on, racism becomes invisible, apparently neutralised by resort to technologies which in fact strengthen it by appearing to be neutral.

This is a highly original version of institutional racism, a 'digitalisation' of the phenomenon which offers it immense perspectives, given that today digital technologies are central to our community lives. Whence the importance of the research in the humanities and social sciences on the possible abuses of artificial intelligence which could produce the racial, or other, for example, sexist prejudices, embedded in our culture with no questions asked. The same applies to research on the methods used by firms to hire personnel which discriminate against the members of certain groups, unaware of the implications associated with resort to digital procedures. Anti-racist mobilisation is itself under tension here: should it be exercised in the name of groups of victims, focusing on their racial specificity, in the name of cultures which are especially targeted or, instead, in the name of individual human rights with no consideration for any collective specificity? Or should there be a combination of both approaches? Should the campaign be anti-racist or more broadly-based, for example by pleading for legislation and institutions capable of regulating the new media environment created by digitalisation, along the lines chosen by some countries to regulate the press at the end of the 19th century (Frau-Meigs, 2018)?[9]

The analysis of the link between racism and digital technology must on one hand consider digital technology as it actually functions, criticising the idea of its technological neutrality. On the other hand, it must consider the instrumental, deliberate use of digital technology in racist strategies, for example in the misuse of tools and massive resort to social accounts and networks in spreading the discourse of hate. These are immense issues for discussion, research and polemics.

Anti-Semitism is concerned by these issues not only in the same way as any other form of racism, but also more particularly for reasons linked to the present-day culture of immediate communication and the inter-activity facilitated by the Internet and digital technologies. Limits to freedom of expression are reviled in this culture. However, action against anti-Semitism demands that these limits be defined; to curb the expression of incitement to racial or religious hatred, the glorification of crime, discriminatory remarks, the search for scapegoats, etc. The Jews are accused of being particularly vociferous in their demands for restriction of freedom of expression and the imposition of barriers on Internet specifically for their protection. This is perhaps the newest aspect of present-day hatred of Jews – these images which make of them enemies of this freedom. Thus, in January 2018, when Editions Gallimard postponed the re-editing of Céline's anti-Semitic pamphlets, some social networks attributed this renunciation to Jewish influence – the CRIF, the Israeli Embassy, and important Jewish personalities had effectively intervened in the request. But they were not alone.

The second aspect of cultural racism

To evaluate the extent of the changes in cultural racism, we have to bear in mind the overall context at the end of the 1960s and in the 1970s. At the time, in Western societies, and in others, the idea of universalism was beginning to be challenged while, at the same time, specific identities were beginning to emerge in the public sphere.

Until then, cultural minorities had either been rejected or poorly treated, or else invited, if not to assimilate, and therefore to become invisible in the general population, at least not to attract attention. Subsequently various movements began to make demands for recognition which at times were quite radical and were backed up by memories usually fraught with suffering historically: some also demanded the independence of a country. Alex Haley's best-seller *Roots*, published in 1976, is an American expression of this global phenomenon. The challenges grew in number; some purely and simply broke with the universal values of the rule of law and reason, others sought negotiable solutions, and yet others somewhat confusedly appealed to both registers. The challenges included cultural dimensions, focusing on a language, a history, a national identity and possibly a social or economic input. They were frequently 'victim-orientated', recalling in these instances the suffering endured by the minority concerned: genocide, slavery, victims of mass violence or plundering, etc. As from the 1980s, these challenges also included references to religion, in particular to Islam. There was even talk of competition amongst victims (Chaumont, 1997).[10]

Confronted with the rise in these identities, the political responses varied. Some minimised the impact and attempted to keep alive the conception of the Universal, inherited from the Enlightenment. France represents an extreme example in this respect; the majority of intellectuals and political leaders staunchly demand respect for the Republic, which is the national representation of the Universal, totally refusing any recognition of specific identities: from a republican perspective '*à la française*' only individuals 'free and equal before the law' can be considered in the public sphere and there is no question of minorities. Others have endeavoured to promote different variants of a multiculturalism with two interactive aspects. One aspect is a demand for recognition of the cultural specificities of the group concerned, their language, their traditions, their history, music, ways of thinking, etc. The other aspect is the expectation for social justice which should be regulated by Affirmative Action measures which compensate for the structural inequalities to which the members of the group are subjected.

On this basis the question of racism is posed in different terms. On becoming visible, a minority group would be likely to advance demands for recognition, while at the same time witness some of its members benefitting from specific resources, for example for admission to university. This led to discussions but also to tensions, even violence linked to the rise in the number of identities asserted and the challenge this represented to the political and social structure in the societies concerned.

The cultural racism described by researchers and anti-racist militants in the 1980s and 1990s and even in 2000 was primarily that of members of the majority group accusing members of minorities of being completely different so much so that they did not wish to accept the values of the nation and thus posed a threat to cultural integrity: it became more complex as from the point at which those targeted came to understand that the issuewas precisely their difference which they themselves valorised, that it was their dignity and cultural being which was being called into question. As soon as they put forward their own culture and their contribution to the nation, to society, even to the world at large, these minorities found a resource to counter a racism which in fact denied them the access to the values which the dominant group vaunted. Cultural fragmentation forged ahead and with it, relativism.

The cultural racism of the 1980s or 1990s sees in those it targets a refusal to integrate the dominant culture. There is no questioning of the content of the difference which it in fact reduces to a refusal, or an incapacity, to adhere to its universalist credo as defined by the dominant group. Henceforth, in addition we have the fear and the contempt towards the minority cultures themselves devalued, or even forbidden, and in all instances inadequately recognised, but which are now gaining in confidence. Now, cultural racism not only challenges the capacity of those targeted to access universal values, but also invalidates their history, language, contribution to philosophy, forms of art, of literature, of music, etc.

There are therefore two sides to cultural racism, depending on whether the focus is on the presumed refusal of those targeted to integrate, or whether it stigmatises their identity.

But let's take one step further. There are times when, by bringing to the fore a cultural identity, but also, as we shall see later, a racial identity, victims of racism themselves become liable to develop racist arguments as regards members of other groups, including the majority group. For example, minorities of colour may develop the theme of 'anti-white racism' targeting white people. The racism which some anti-racist discourse does today describe, even if it is not necessarily contradictory, does differ from classical racism and even from that of the 1980s and 1990s. The cultural and racial fragmentation which classical universalism tempered or countered, is spreading.

Post-colonial, anti-racist mobilisation

Post-colonial approaches have for long been critical of the negative or ignorant images associated with the formerly colonised countries and peoples. Edward Saïd's book, *Orientalism* is a landmark here (Saïd, 1978); his analysis of the way in which the imperialist West has represented the Orient since the Middle Ages contributed to opening the way to post-colonial studies. But contemporary critics may well take another direction.

In the United States, following the research of a feminist academic, Kimberlé Crenshaw, since the beginning of the 1990s particularly dynamic trends have been pleading in favour of putting 'intersectionality'[11] at the centre of the analysis of racial discrimination. Behind this concept, which has become a rallying cry for various critical trends, one can find the idea that research should be located at the point where those who cumulate discrimination perceive it. From this perspective, the 'intersection' or the overlapping of different forms of injustice, exclusion, violence experienced, lack of respect of all sorts, is more than the simple addition of difficulties concerning certain people and certain groups: to be a woman, homosexual, poor and coloured, for example, means an accumulation of characteristics that shape a situation which cannot be reduced to the mere sum of its parts.

From there, discussions – at times heated – develop, particularly in the universities. The theme appears in the discourse of the Black Lives Matter movement but while this movement does also act in defence of homosexuals, it is primarily mobilised against the 'framing' of Black Americans by the police and the violence targeting Blacks, whether on the part of the police or from other sources. It focuses primarily on classical racism, in areas where trends open to 'intersectionality' or the overlapping of forms of discrimination develop different perspectives, in particular those which are more open to post-colonial themes.

In the United Kingdom, where 'intersectionality' is also all the rage, and where some movements claim to act on behalf of Black Lives Matter, an initiative originating in University College (London) demanded: #WhyIsMyCurriculumSoWhite? This movement challenged white domination as it is manifested in teaching, particularly, of history and literature. In September 2016, nine militants from Black Lives Matter chained themselves together on the runway at London City Airport. They explained to the BBC that

> only a small elite was able to travel from London City Airport. In 2016, 3,176 migrants were drowned or disappeared in the Mediterranean … Black people are the first to die and not the first to fly. The global warming crisis is a racist crisis. Lets reduce greenhouse gas emissions. Let's open the borders.

In France, in August 2016, a '*décolonial* summer camp' not open to white people, an 'Afro-feminist' festival organised in May 2017 and a trade-union training course organised by Sud-éducation93 were all issues which led to controversy and polemics as they offered activities to which access, if only partially, was on an ethnic and racial basis. This approach opposed 'state racism', sometimes described as 'institutional racism'. They spoke in terms of categories which, till then, were unheard of in discussion in France, such as 'racialised' and 'whitened'. It was primarily a question of organising a campaign in which those who were, or felt, 'racialised' started thinking about, anti-racist action then possibly participating therein, on the basis of this 'racialisation'. They were constituting themselves as subjects not on the basis of the colour of their skin, or any other racial attribute, but in function of the perception of the society which had racialised them. In this instance, 'race' is a social construction and not a natural attribute. In this approach, combating racism and discrimination calls for consideration which only those who have actually experienced it are supposed to be able to implement appropriately. Racism, in the words of Sihame Assbague, one of the organisers of the 'decolonial summer camp','has its roots in slavery and colonialism'. From this perspective, only those who have been victims of discrimination are able to analyse it adequately. For this reason, some activities or groups and workshops were reserved to the 'racialised' 'completely on their own, with no tutor, no observers and no interpreter', said Assbague; the principle has sometimes been compared to the thinking behind the organisation of 'Alcoholics Anonymous' or 'Weight Watchers'.

The challenge also concerns conceptions of teaching which are still imbued with former domination at once racial, white, and colonial or possibly Western and Euro-centric. We have referred to the 'Rhodes Must Fall' movement when describing these challenges in South Africa.

The protest targets Western universalism which is considered to be just another form of post-colonial domination. It is part of the approaches in which local, national, regional and global dimensions are all intertwined and which, when they are academic, or in the university, may be associated with academic disciplines. Economists request consideration for approaches other than *mainstream*; sociologists and social anthropologists plead for the contribution of the *Global South* to be valorised in the social sciences; philosophers and historians intervene in their own right. With the help of 'intersectionality', in this discourse, race overlaps with and interacts with other themes, beginning with those of gender and *feminist studies* on one hand, poverty and social injustice on the other.

Thus the worlds of higher education and research are outstanding terrains for protests and challenges which are anti-racist in intention and which target, amongst others, the very functioning of the University. Hence Boaventura de Sousa Santos, one of the pioneers of the promotion of the idea of the 'Global South', a professor at the University of Coimbra in Portugal (de Sousa Santos, 2018b) speaks of *Decolonising the University*.[12]

An analysis of the transformations in the university system and its opening up in the 1970s and 1980s to newcomers from communities more discriminated than others could shed useful light here; disappointments and economic difficulties are acute for those who, originating in these backgrounds, have difficulty today, or may no longer hope to accede to higher education as students, researchers or teachers. This explains their radicality; conservative or reactionary sociology would describe it as 'relative frustration'.

Criticism of universalism is frequently the driving force behind post-colonial anti-racism and is the basis of its approach to racism. Universalism, understood as a mode of domination of the West over the rest of the world, of whites over peoples of colour, or of men over women is said to prevent the existence of traditional, indigenous or pre-colonial forms of thinking. It leads in Rajeev Bhargava's telling words to 'epistemic injustice',[13] that is, to unequal access to knowledge and the possibilities of spreading it; and is a sharp reminder of the injury inflicted on those whom it deprives of access to the pre-colonial past and its cultural, literary, philosophical and historical resources. This criticism could be perceived as a call for intellectual openness of the kind personified by the economist Amartya Sen when he explains that the West does not have the monopoly of the invention of democracy nor that of justice.[14] It could then be a source of cultural enrichment for societies opening up to traditions from elsewhere. But it may equally well turn into identitarian closure, withdrawal, rejection of so-called Western values and lapse into obscurantism.

The more radical the criticism, the more it tends to relativism. When anti-racism reaches this stage, it contributes to processes of fragmentation and the withdrawal of groups or nations into themselves with no communication, or less and less, with others, especially if these are Western, 'whites', Americans, etc.

A tipping point is reached in these processes when the victims of racism, or their spokespersons present themselves in the public sphere as 'racialised', and not only as individuals or citizens. 'Race' is now turned against the oppressors. This 'embodiment' of race, (or auto-racisation) for those who wish to uphold the universal values of law and reason, may constitute an invitation to rethink these values, to convert them into human rights and to associate them with a struggle for emancipation without which they might effectively serve as legitimation for various modalities of domination. But by upholding a racial and ethnic image of community life, as had been the case for their own group, this 'embodiment of race' or auto-racisation, may equally well lead to a 'race war', reviving the perspective of serious or violent clashes arising from the *Rassenkampf* described by Ludwig Gumplowitz in 1883. If human groups define themselves in racial terms and no longer in social, cultural or political termsthis will eventually lead to a racial clash.

Present-day anti-Semitism is no stranger to these trends especially when hatred of Jews is the result of criticism which goes well beyond the policy of the Israeli government. Thus it took the form of radical anti-Zionism when it was expressed in September 2001 in Durban during the World Conference against Racism, Racial Discrimination, Xenophobia and Intolerance. Symmetrically, Jewish institutions have developed hyper-community approaches which have contributed to the fragmentation of societies.

Ambivalence in anti-racism

The subjectivity at work in present-day anti-racist campaigns has two dimensions which are as likely to blend as they are to oppose each other. On one hand it refers to subjects who have no rights to existence as human beings, or individuals and on the other to historic or cultural communities which are in part destroyed or deprived of the right to exist and who desire to focus on its continuity, to establish or re-establish it or save it from disappearance.

To be banned from humankind, generally speaking, and rejected in the name of 'race' from the universal to which everyone wishes to belong is one thing; to be affected by racism because one belongs to a culture, traditions, ways of thinking different from the majority, is quite another. Some, as we have seen, demand a discussion amongst victims of what they share, to have a better analysis of their experience, which leads ultimately to a collective demand attracted by separatism and, for example, to demands for spaces reserved for specific racialised groups. The collective identity which may thus be forged originates in the experience of racism and not in a reference to a specific pre-existing culture.

In contrast, those who invoke a collective identity which has been destroyed, threatened or altered, a past, or non-Western ways of thinking, may grant less importance to 'race' and 'racialisation' in defining themselves since it is primarily a question for them of reconnecting with traditions in the assertion of the elements of a culture not recognised by the West.

In both cases, whether or not there be a cultural and historical identity in the references of the actors, the campaign against various forms of discrimination and injustice, at the outset those which are of a racist nature, strengthens the rationales of fragmentation, directly racial in the first case and cultural in the other instance. These processes rapidly become hybrid and the term 'ethnicity' is convenient to describe the outcome since it enables the maintenance of a degree of imprecision between categories of nature and those of culture. To put it clearly: whenever processes of this sort get going, protests and demands may well give way on the part of the actors (despite their being mobilised against racism, ignorance and lack of understanding on the part of others) to radical discourse and even to violence. Hatred, distance, fear or contempt may thus originate in the racism experienced: the new anti-racism may well bear within it renewed forms of racism.

Racism is a phenomenon which is ever changing and diversifying, as we have said: in a way, as Pierre-André Taguieff (Taguieff, 1988) has stated, anti-racism is its clone, (cf the sub-title of his book).

As we have seen, the old colonial, physical, biological racism lives on; this is not the target of the new anti-racism which is primarily successful in educated circles and, in particular, in universities. Its primary function is not to act against the most flagrant forms of racism, police violence, or the most unrefined forms of prejudice, segregation, direct discrimination. The new anti-racism is a separate issue, which does not mean to say that it is indifferent. It tends to be sectorial, specific to actors who are quite well defined, in the world of research and in academia, in the media, culture and intellectual life where it can be counter-offensive and demanding, more easily than when the issue is one of confronting classical and brutal or explicit forms of racism. Loaded with demands for recognition, references to cultures and ways of thinking which may come from various parts of the world or which should be of interest or concern to the world at large, if only through groups in diaspora, by challenging the way in which migrants are treated all over the world, this globalised anti- racism can develop its own global credos.

Nor is post-colonial anti-racism the direct extension of the demands of multiculturalism, whether it be demands for multi-culturalism, whether it be, as we have seen, for Affirmative Action or cultural recognition – for a history, a language, a literature, a music, traditions, etc., individually, or in articulated fashion.

The multiculturalism thus conceived and implemented does have a counterpart. Those who benefit from it must accept what justifies this policy: belonging to a group, possibly visible, by virtue of the colour of one's skin, for example, and the desire to belong to a society, by sharing its values, including the most individualist.

The innovation is that today, some of those who promote anti-racism are far more likely to maintain hyper-critical positions of suspicion and denunciation than to endeavour to obtain results and progress in integration.

Anti-racism is, on the whole, a multifaceted phenomenon within which tensions, if not contradictions, may appear. It can, for example, contribute to an academic system which is more just and richer in content, sensitive to qualities which are not those usually valorised, open to teachers and researchers from underprivileged backgrounds, to ways of thinking, authors, philosophical or literary traditions which usually are only of interest to a few specialists in specific 'cultural areas'. An academic system also capable of not remaining smug and even less sanctimonious when confronted with the progress of artificial intelligence and digital technology, even though technologies are liable to reproduce racism. But, and this is the other side of the coin, this new anti-racism may also contribute to increasing the rationales of fragmentation and ethnicisation of community life which are destructive including, to continue with our example, intellectually and scientifically, within institutions for teaching and research. In these instances, the new anti-racism is likely to produce the opposite of what is desired: a world which is not more just, but on the contrary, even more unjust and in which the attraction of relativism reinforces inequalities and fuels hate speech and practices.

We have therefore entered a new historical era in which both racism and anti-racism are assuming new forms while at the same time the more classical forms persist. In this evolution, anti-racist campaigns are also changing and it sometimes happens that these changes are linked to a relativism which is never itself far from racism.

Notes

1 We shall not discuss here the issue of whether anti-Semitism should be considered a form of racism amongst many, or on the contrary, as is the case in this article, considered apart – cf. in particular my book *La tentation anti-Semite* (2005). Paris: éd Robert Laffont.
2 Carmichael, S., Hamilton, C., (1967). *Black Power: The Politics of Liberation in America.* New York: Random House. (Stokely Carmichael was later known by the name of Kwame Ture).

3 Thereafter an extensive literature analysed the concept of institutional racism and applied to various sphere of community life, housing, education, employment, justice, the penal system, migration policies, etc. or to demonstrate how it could be used for groups other than black people.

4 Barker, M., (1981). *The New Racism: Conservatives and the Ideology of the Tribe*. London: Junction Books. Balibar, E., Wallerstein, E., (1988). *Race, nation, classe. Les identités ambiguës*. Paris: Editions La Découverte Taguieff, Pierre-André, (1988). *La force du préjugé. Essai sur le racisme et ses doubles*, Paris: Editions La Découverte.

5 The reader will permit me to refer here to the research which I directed. Wieviorka M. et al, (2007). *The Lure of Anti-Semitism*. Leiden, Boston: Brill.

6 Weisman, J., (2018)*(((Semitism)))*. *Being Jewish in America in the Age of Trump*, New York, Saint Martin's Press.

7 (a movement set up in 2013, after the acquittal of the assassin of a Black adolescent in Florida)

8 The Inequality Project, supported by the Ford Foundation, is specialised in the critique of these developments. Cf. the article by Stephen Buranyi, « Rise of the racist robots – how AI is learning all our worst impulses », *The Guardian*, 8-8-2017.

9 Divina Frau-Meigs, « Fake news: engager enfin un débat confisqué … », *The Conversation*, 8 January (2018)

10 Chaumont, J. M., 1997. *La concurrence des victimes*. Paris.: La Découverte.

11 https://www. ted.com/talks/kimberle_crenshaw_the_urgency_of_intersectionality#t-647129

12 Boaventura de Sousa Santos, (Sousa Santos, 2018b). *Decolonising the University. The Challenge of Deep Cognitive Justice*. Cambridge: ScholarsPublishing.

13 Rajeev Bhargava,, « Pour en finir avec l'injustice épistémique du colonialisme », *Socio,* 1, (2013), pp.41–76

14 Amartya Sen, *L'idée de justice*, Paris, Flammarion, (2012); *La Démocratie des autres: pourquoi la liberté n'est pas une invention de l'Occident*, Rivages poche, (2006)

References

Balibar, E., Wallerstein, E. 1988. *Race, nation, classe. Les identités ambiguës*. Paris: Editions La Découverte.

Barker, M. 1981. *The New Racism: Conservatives and the Ideology of the Tribe*. London: Junction Books.

Bhargava, R. 2013. Pour en finir avec l'injustice épistémique du colonialisme. *Socio*, 1, pp. 41–76.

Buranyi, S. 2017. *Rise of the Racist Robots – How AI is Learning All Our Worst Impulses*. London: The Guardian, 8-8-2017.

Carmichael, S. Hamilton, C., 1967. *Black Power: The Politics of Liberation in America*. New York: Vintage. (Stokely Carmichael was later known by the name of Kwame Ture).

Chaumont, J. M. 1997. *La concurrence des victimes*. Paris: La Découverte.

de Sousa Santos, B. 2018b. *Decolonising the University. The Challenge of Deep Cognitive Justice*. Cambridge: Scholars Publishing.

Frau-Meigs, D. 2018. Fake news: engager enfin un débat confisqué … , *The Conversation*, 8 January 2018 (Online Journal).

Saïd, E. W. 1978. *Orientalism*. New York: Pantheon Books (PLACE).

Sen, A. *La Démocratie des autres: pourquoi la liberté n'est pas une invention de l'Occident*. Paris: Rivages poche. 2006.

Sen, A. 2012. *L'idée de justice*. Paris: Flammarion.

Taguieff, P.-A. 1987b. cf. the sub-title of his book, *La force du préjugé. Essai sur le racisme et ses doubles*, *op. cit*. Paris: Gallimard.

Taguieff, P.-A. 1988. *La force du préjugé. Essai sur le racisme et ses doubles*. Paris: Editions La Découverte.

Weisman, J. 2018. *(((Semitism)))*. *Being Jewish in America in the Age of Trump*. New York: Saint Martin's Press.

Wieviorka, M. et al, 2007. *The Lure of Anti-Semitism*. Leiden and Boston, MA: Brill.

33

The beginning and the end of racism – and something in-between

Kevin Durrheim

Racism is a historical fact and ongoing reality. Any visit to a slavery, Holocaust or apartheid museum should provide evidence enough. If not, walk through a post-apartheid city, examine the racial disparities in spatial and economic data, or hear the pain and protest of those who have borne the brunt of 400 years of brutality and unfreedom. We might call this Racism with a capital R.

And yet, despite its brute reality, racism is also a social construction, a subject of discourse. Call this 'racism' with scare quotes (which I will use only where necessary). Of course, we should be wary of overdrawing the distinction between Racism and 'racism' – the raw reality and the cultural cooked constructions (Derrida, 1970). Nonetheless, the crude distinction can help sharpen our focus on the way racism has become cooked, mythologized, and to what ends.

At first, Racism didn't know itself as 'racism'. The word did not exist. It was unselfconscious. For most of its history, what we now call racism was known by other names: trans-Atlantic trade, slavery, abolitionism; the white man's burden, governance, colonialism, the will of God, separate development, democracy, the natural order of things, and so on.

It was only in the 1930s that the word sprang into circulation. There were recorded isolated uses of the word racism dating from as early as 1902 (Oxford English Dictionary; Demby, 2014), but it was only with the rise of Nazism that the word gained currency and traction (Safire, 2006). On the one hand, it was used to discredit the Nazis' belief in race differences. Frederickson (2002) says that Hirschfeld's (1938) posthumously published book, *Racism*, 'first gave real currency to the term "racism"' (p. 162). On the other hand, 'racism' was also used as an emblem of identity, 'popularised through Mussolini's public embrace of razzismo (racism) in the second half of 1938' and worn with nationalistic pride by his followers (Myburgh, 2016).

Although many argue that Racism existed before the word was coined and popularized, its appearance did mark a momentous change. Frederickson (2002) observes that 'the concept of racism emerges only when the concept of race, or at least some of its applications, begin to be questioned' (p. 156). 'Racism' emerges when the political and oppressive use of race categories become conscious of themselves as Racism. Interestingly, this momentous shift occurs at home in Europe, to problematize the way the Nazis had drawn racial distinctions between citizens of Europe in the quest to isolate an Aryan essence of the Caucasian race. European anti-Semitism (and other Otherings) might have been ancient and contested (Arendt, 1973), but it was only after the political project built on race science that it became 'racism'.

At the end of the war, the defeat of fascism sounded the death knell for a celebratory identification with nationalistic racism. Racism was to become a mark of shame, an object of scientific investigation, and (later) a subject of government and social administration.

Authoritative definitions of racism

The horrors of the Holocaust quickly led to the judgment that racism was a prejudice, irrational at its heart. In one generation, social science had shifted from studies of race to studies of racism. Samelson (1978) describes the *volte-face* in psychology. In the 1920s, 'most psychologists believed in the existence of mental differences between races; by 1940, they were searching for the sources of "irrational prejudice"' (p. 265). The slew of prejudice research after the war had one thing in common: race was treated as an unreality, and belief in race difference was deemed to be prejudice. Klineberg (1951, p. 505) describes national stereotyping as 'autistic thinking'. Adorno et al. (1950) described anti-Semitism as both social disease and mental pathology. Perhaps most famously, Allport (1954) says the antipathy stems from 'faulty generalization'.

It is not an exaggeration to say that nearly the whole of the social sciences and the humanities – the postwar liberal tradition – has been opposed to prejudice and racism. Racism was something that others practiced. It was a problem to be understood and eradicated.

Although much writing about racism assumes that the nature of the problem is self-evident, close inspection of the theoretical and empirical literatures shows that this is far from true. The definition of racism has been hotly contested both within and between disciplines. Definitions have changed over time and across contexts, both because of differences in the phenomenon itself and the differing politics of the writers.

In the postwar context of the 1950s and the 1960s, research in the social sciences focused on the irrational nature of prejudice, stereotyping, and myths about race differences. The first three UNESCO statements on 'the race question' sought to show that the idea of race differences lacked scientific validity, and holding such beliefs was thus not justified. It was only in their forth statement in 1967 – written some 17 years after the first statement – that the UNESCO committee first problematized "racism", which they defined as 'antisocial beliefs and acts which are based on the fallacy that discriminatory intergroup relations are justifiable on biological grounds' (UNESCO, 1969, p. 51). This definition of racism as false beliefs was 'incorporated directly into the social sciences in the 1960s and 1970s' (Miles and Brown, 2003, p. 60).

The consensus that racism was irrational prejudice was short lived. Already by 1971 social psychologists were suggesting that a new form of racism had arisen. David Sears and Donald Kinder found that a sample of liberal Californian suburbanites opposed a black mayoral candidate on nonracial grounds, not out of unjustifiable beliefs about biological differences (Sears and Kinder, 1971). Across the Atlantic and the Academy, writers began heralding the advent of a new racism – one that supported racial equality and desegregation in principle, but that used arguments about culture, fairness and pragmatics rather than biology to justify discrimination in practice (e.g. Barker, 1981; Gaertner and Dovidio, 1986; Katz and Hass, 1988; Balibar, 1991).

Disciplinary backgrounds also contributed to the contested definition of racism. Wieviorka (1995) identifies three kinds of definitions of racism: as prejudice, as ideology and as practice. Traditionally, psychologists had viewed racism as a manifestation of underlying prejudice, with cognitive or motivational roots whereas sociologists tended to view racism systemically as an ideology. By the 1990s, an inability within either tradition to uncover a 'deep unity of racism' led scholars like Wieviorka (1995, p. 37) to define racism in terms of practices such as segregation, discrimination and violence – or in the discourse and political and legal relations that justified such practices (see also Goldberg, 1993; Omi and Winant, 1995).

Diverging political perspectives have also contributed to the contested definition of racism. For example, writing in Britain in the 1990s, Gilroy (1992) argued that the 'moralistic excesses practiced in the name of antiracism' required urgent and radical critique. A version of racism had become institutionalized and defended by a bureaucratic class and the black petit bourgeoisie, shrouded in a 'spurious cloak of legitimacy' (p. 587) and invested in a limiting view of blacks as victims. In that context, racial justice and the unlocking of human potential required an alternative definition of the problem. The anti-racism of one generation had become troubling to the next (see Donald and Rattansi, 1992; Solomos and Back, 1994).

In the varieties of authoritative discourse there are many divergent definitions of racism and a contested politics of anti-racism. Occasionally these different points of view clashed, resulting in heated exchanges, especially when definitions demanded that the specific contents of racism be identified in a specific context (see Durrheim, 2014). Psychologists, for example, clashed over whether or not opposition to affirmative action or liberal welfare policies or implicit biases are racist (Tetlock, 1994; Tetlock and Arkes, 2004; Jussim et al., 2015). Similar contestations have arisen in specifying which ideological contents are racist. An interesting instance of a familiar refrain was aired in the media in the wake of #RhodesMustFall protests at the University of Cape Town in 2015. Economists, Seekings and Natrass (2015) argued that affirmative action should target economic disadvantage and that a race-based policy bordered on racism itself. Sociologist, Xolela Mangcu (2015), countered that this class-based argument amounted to a motivated ignorance of the singular reality of anti-black racism and the experience of black pain, which he implied was definitive of racism itself.

Academic discourse works towards authoritative definitions of racism. Each theory and each measure of the phenomenon includes some contents in the category 'racism' and excludes others. Is racism irrational or can it be rational? Does it involve beliefs specifically about biological differences? Which practices, policies, beliefs and biases are properly labeled racist? Can blacks be racist and whites anti-racist? And who can legitimately speak to and decide on these issues? Whose is the final voice of authority regarding 'racism'? Seventy years of academic research and writing about racism has taught us that it is exceedingly difficult to tease the truth of racism from the interests, politics and disciplinary perspectives of the authors. Each contribution to the sciences is also a reflection of a socially situated point of view.

Racism as an everyday concept

The category of racism soon migrated from science to everyday use. It was especially useful for oppressed groups and targets of discrimination to frame their experiences. Philomena Essed's (1991) groundbreaking work sought to develop a 'new approach to the study of racism'. She was less interested in the 'mechanisms of racism' that had been studied by social scientists than 'Black definitions of racism' which she suggested would be 'interesting as an object for academic inquiry' (pp. 1–2). Racism had become self-conscious in a new way. Whereas it might have been transmitted in practices and routines that the dominant group deemed to be normal – an invisible knapsack of privilege, unrecognized, unacknowledged and unproblematized (McIntosh,

2008) – racism had become a powerful tool for oppressed groups to describe their experiences and to formulate action. Essed shone the torch of analytic scrutiny on the 'real racial drama … the fact that racism is an everyday problem' (p. 10).

The everyday use of 'racism' was not restricted to oppressed groups. Racial dramas were unfolding in other settings, which required the objectification and problematization of racism. As the human sciences took a discursive turn, researchers were ready to begin 'mapping the language of racism' (Wetherell and Potter, 1992). A large body of research quickly emerged to show how racism had become impressed on commonsense and was expressed in everyday conversations and talk in institutional settings (e.g. Van Dijk, 1987a; Goldberg, 1993; Teo, 2000; Reisigl and Wodak, 2005). *Everyday racism* included beliefs, opinions and arguments, both subtle and blatant, 'that directly or indirectly contribute to the dominance of the white group and the subordinate position of minorities' (van Dijk, 1993, p. 5; Augoustinos and Every, 2007).

It was soon discovered that the hallmark of everyday racism was its refusal to recognize itself as such. As the social taboos against racism strengthened, those accused of racism were able to formulate their own definition of the concept, excuse themselves, deny racism, and make counteraccusations of racism (Cohen, 1992; van Dijk, 1992; Augoustinos and Every, 2007; Billig, 2012). The discursive work of accusation and denial depended on contrasting commonsense understandings of racism that were developed to counter each other (Durrheim, Quayle, and Dixon, 2016).

This work on everyday racism has been profoundly important. Not only did it show that racism occurred in everyday micro-sociological interaction, where the great forces of history and ideology, psychological motive, and cognitive deficiency took hold in concrete contexts of social life. More important even, it showed that these historical, sociological and psychological agents reflexively understood their lives and actions in terms of the category 'racism' and participated in life in its terms. Ordinary people and elites were lay critics and lay scientists as they argued about the reality or unreality of *both* race and racism. As in authoritative writings about racism, in everyday life, racism acquired a dialogical character. It was something that others practiced, and each definition was shaped in part by alternative definitions that were deemed to be wrong.

Although the discursive tradition of scholarship was critical of 'mainstream' treatment of racism in academic work and governance (see e.g. Gilroy, 1987; Condor, 1988), it remained part of the tradition of liberal social science, opposed to racism and presuming to know what racism is (see Durrheim, 2016). Researchers went to great lengths to show that categories of 'race' were potent social constructions, but they seldom subjected the category 'racism' to the same treatment. Of course, scholars recognized that the concept was pejorative and used as an epithet (Banton, 1970) or as a 'coat-of-paint' to color one's opponents (Gilroy, 1987). Discourse analysts also showed how versions of racism were developed by ordinary people, treating these as social constructions (Wetherell and Potter, 1992; Reisigl and Wodak, 2005). However, the work conveys a strong sense that the authors know what the problem of racism really is, and against which the other definitions (especially of people characterized as 'racists') can be judged to be limited, wrong, or ideological. Studies of everyday racism have continued to be exercises in authoritative discourse, mapping the language of Racism

'Racism' as a social accomplishment

Only relatively recently has research on everyday racism taken the final step in conceptualizing racism a social construction. The critical factor here is not so much the authoritative model of racism that any instance conforms to or not, but the implicit or explicit agreements that can be garnered for one or other definition of the concept. Addressing the psychological literature on prejudice, Condor and her colleagues argued that what counts as prejudice is a 'social accomplishment' whose nature 'ultimately depends upon its acceptance or rejection on the part of an audience' (Condor et al., 2006, p. 458). 'Racism' is here cut free from any predefined content. Anything can be 'racism' or 'not-racism' depending on what is allowed to stand as such in any social context. Expressions of hate *and* sympathy, acknowledgment *or* denials of bias, belief in the existence *or not* of biological categories, and support for equality and inclusion *or* inequality and exclusion can all count as either 'racist' or 'not-racist' in particular situations among specific audiences (cf. Durrheim, 2017; Greenland et al., 2018). In ordinary, institutional and academic conversations and debates, participants are alert to conceptions of what *could count* as racism and they work hard to ensure that what *does count* as racism does not fatally rupture social interaction. Collectively they cultivate agreements and disagreements about the meaning of racism and develop relationships with friend and foe as they live and argue about their experiences, events, politics and social change.

This thoroughgoing constructionism is practiced most consistently by conversation analysts, who refuse to orient their readings of discourse around authoritative definitions by which researchers know and recognize racism and reach judgments about what is racist or not. To the contrary, their focus is strictly limited to participant-developed understandings of racism. Stokoe (2015) adopts as a starting point, not racism, but the 'possible-ism', something that is marked by the speaker or audience as possibly racist.

Possible-isms can be difficult to pin down, and whether the possible-ism ends up being regarded as racism or not depends on how it is treated by the participants; whether it is deleted, topicalized, supported or challenged.

Possible racism is an ambiguous event. In contrast to the certainty of authoritative discourse and other definitive judgments of racism, possible-isms are barely recognizable. Sometimes they pass through a conversation silently as unmarked implications (see Durrheim, 2012; Durrheim and Murray, 2019). On other occasions, they may be tacitly recognized and marked with 'parenthetical inserts' and other subsidiary activities (e.g. hedges, disclaimers, qualifications) that treat an expression as a possible racism that could be challenged (Whitehead, in press) and that orient to prospective problems and lay the foundation for repair (see Schegloff, 1992). However, the ambiguity of the possible racism is preserved, keeping race and racism implicit and the potentially problematic expression deniable (Stokoe, 2012; Whitehead, in press).

Hearers of a possible racism (including its author) face a dilemma regarding how to react: will they ignore the racism, support it, collude, or challenge it? Agreeing with or ignoring a possible racism exposes the hearer to the moral judgment of complicity, whereas challenging the possible racism is a disaffiliative act that has the potential to threaten rapport and lead to conflict (Stokoe, 2015; Whitehead, 2015). Intricate maneuvers are often needed to manage this fine moral economy. Once again, conversation analysts have shown how tacit evaluations can be used to signal a repairable possible hearing of a possible-ism.

The investments of both speakers and hearers in avoiding interactional trouble means that explicit expressions and hearings of racism are often dispreferred. Possible-isms are therefore designedly ambiguous, 'slippery' (Durrheim and Murray, 2019), 'hard to capture cases in social life' where 'talk that looks like a possible-ism might turn out not to be' (Stokoe, 2015, p. 443). What counts as racism in any concrete instance is developed in '(re)negotiation by participants in the moment-by-moment unfolding of interactions' (Schegloff, 2006, cited in Stokoe, 2015, p. 429). What then stands as 'racism' are the specific expressions and hearings that are either treated implicitly as such or rise to the surface as such in social interaction.

'Racism' is thus forged in the fires of 'participant-administered accountability' (Whitehead, 2017) through which participants themselves decide on what counts as racism and manage the moral accountability of making such attributions.

'Racism' as identity performance

There is a sharp contrast between the authoritative anti-Racism of scholars like Miles, Banton, Omi/Winant, Essed, and many others, and the tentative constructionist studies of 'racism' undertaken by Condor, Stokoe, Whitehead, and others. The former are self-confident in knowing what is wrong with the world and saying what needs to be done. The latter are focused solely on instances of micro-interaction and on fleeting representations of what counts as racism in the immediacy of the cut and thrust of social interaction. The constructed, contested and changing nature of 'racism' definitions that are apparent in everyday and academic interactions raise challenging questions about the foundations of authoritative discourse. The constructionist perspective suggests that all definitions of racism – expert and lay, authoritative and everyday – are social accomplishments whose authority rests on social agreements. However necessary this anti-foundationalism might appear, it comes with one great challenge: how to recover a critical, systemic and political treatment of racism upon which to found an anti-racism (cf. also Hoyt, 2012)?

Discursive social psychology offers a potential solution. A great body of literature now shows how social constructions can gain purchase in social life by way of (1) the functions that such constructions perform in concrete instances of deployment, and (2) the fact that particular versions of racism gain authority by their use in shared and enduring routines (Potter and Wetherell, 1987; cf also Fairclough, 1992). Shared depictions of racism – what Wetherell and Potter (1988) call 'interpretative repertoires' – develop because they are effective pragmatically in resolving particular kinds of interactional trouble that arise in a particular society (cf. Cohen, 1992). For example, the idea that black people were ineducable was used to defend segregated, unequal education in apartheid South Africa as a non-racist policy (Dubow, 1991)! But such categorical depictions of difference lost their currency and needed to be replaced by alternative depictions of racism that could regulate inter-racial encounter and exchange in the post-apartheid context (Durrheim and Dixon, 2005; Durrheim, 2014).

In an effort to give shape to critical constructionist anti-racism, researchers have attempted to specify in more detail the functional aspects of shared racism representations that arise in particular societies to fulfill the interactional accountability demands needed there. Durrheim and his colleagues proposed that 'racism' constructions be treated as 'identity performances' (Durrheim, Quayle, and Dixon, 2016; Durrheim, 2017; Durrheim et al., 2018). This draws analytic attention to three related functions of 'racism' and the routines by which they are accomplished: identification, explanation, and mobilization. An analysis of racism-related identity performances can help understand the force and function of racism constructions. These are collectively and dialogically produced as moral foundations in various forms and instances of social interaction.

1. **Identification**
    All the work reviewed thus far shows that racism is a moral field (cf. Garcia, 1997; Miles and Brown, 2003; Whitehead, 2017). The moral high ground is occupied by those who are able to develop definitions that paint others as racists and that normalize and excuse their own practices. At its heart then, the social accomplishment of developing a successful definition of racism is an identity project (Klein, Spears, Reicher, 2007) in which the 'moral community' of the prejudiced are differentiated from the irrational, bigoted world of the racists (cf. Tileagă, 2007; Billig, 2012).

The role that racism constructions play in identity performance may be illustrated by Montgomery's (Montgomery, 2005) analysis of Canadian high school history textbooks. Textbooks published in the 1960s represented racism as 'exceptional ideas or occurrences contained to the distant past or to non-Canadian spaces' (p. 430). The moral high ground that Canadians occupied was developed by way of contrast with racist others: hooded Klansmen, Americans, Adolf Hitler and apartheid South Africa. Although textbooks published after 2000 acknowledged racism within Canada, these were portrayed as 'isolated occurrences confined to exceptionally flawed individuals or to unusual times' (p. 437).

Accusations of racism and depictions of racist others are means for claiming the moral high ground, but they also risk rejection and reversal, portraying the racism critic as instrumentally playing the race card or manifesting real racism and intolerance (see Augoustinos and Every, 2010; Goodman, 2010; Goodman and Burke, 2010; Durrheim et al., 2018). Heated contestations can result, pitting one version of racism against another, in a form of discourse in which each party displays an uncompromising belief in the correctness of their views and the wrongness of the opposing view. This is a Manichean field of belief and morality developed around identity categories of the real racist that are deployed in accusation and denial as different parties seek to occupy the moral high ground. In each corner, like-minded fellows agree what the problem is and sneer at the racists and their sympathizers in the other corner.

The contestation rests on two sets of common ground. First, the idea that racism is wrong is typically accepted by all parties. Second, there is a shared and limited set of core representations of the prototypical racist that revolve around the image of the irrational bigot (Billig, 2012), the momentary, explicable lapses of reason and control (see Figgou and Condor, 2006), or as a slip of the tongue (Burford-Rice and Augoustinos, 2018). This common ground, together with the differences of positioning and strategies it supports are all part of the field of identification that is our object of study.

2. Explanation

The politics of identity described above is thoroughly imbricated with the politics of social change. 'Racists' and 'anti-racists' find themselves at loggerheads over concrete current issues: migration, school and housing policy, policing, welfare, employment equity, government, sports team selections, and so on. All these debates revolve around a defense or critique of the status quo. In each instance, constructions of racism are deployed as explanations for some social ill. In particular, 'racism' explains why people would promote or support a flawed – racist – program or policy.

The use and political functioning of 'racism' constructions have become increasing evident with the rise of populist movements across the globe. Durrheim et al. (2018) studied one such contestation that emerged in the campaigning toward the UK referendum to leave or remain in the European Union. Days before the referendum, the populist UKIP party launched a media campaign supporting the Leave vote by depicting migrants pouring into the UK. The campaign, the party, and the leader, Nigel Farage, were branded racists by most mainstream politicians and commentators, even those that supported the Leave campaign. They were accused of 'disgusting racism', using Nazi imagery of racial others to whip up fears of foreigners. Farage defended the campaign as an 'undoctored' depiction of the immigration crisis facing the UK, and his supporters rallied around him, arguing that it was the political mainstream, invested in the status quo, that were 'playing the racism card' in order detract attention away from the real challenges that immigration posed.

To be sure, the accusations, denials and counteraccusations of racism were identity performances which (re)drew boundaries around who belonged to the moral community of the unprejudiced and provided instantiations of such identification. At the same time, they were developed as explanations of what was wrong with the world and what needed to be done about it.

3. Mobilization

As explanations, the discourse of racism is directed at the social accomplishment of persuasion. 'Racism' is developed in a rhetoric that seeks to convince an audience that one way of depicting the world is based on reality while another is based on racism. But, as political discourse, constructions of racism cannot rest content as persuasive discourse. They also need to move audiences to action (see Reicher, 2012). The mobilizing function of racism constructions emerge from the two other functions. Individuals and collectives can be mobilized to action by persuasive explanation of social wrongs that interpellate categories of people and place them on the moral high ground, supporting a righteous indignation.

The mobilizing functions of anti-racism can be found in the contemporary rise of populism. While the anti-immigrationism, policing, hardening of borders, and the self-glorifying nativism of populist movements is regarded as racism by their ideological opponents, proponents and adherents certainly do not view themselves as racists. To the contrary, a common theme in their discourse is the idea that they are victims of prejudice. In the debate over Brexit studied by Durrheim et al. (2018), Farage's supporters complained of being victims of prejudice by the mainstream establishment, and that fallacious portrayals of them as racists should be embraced with scorn and worn as an emblem of resistance. Schröter (2019) has similarly shown how anti-PC discourse functions in Germany to portray the liberal consensus and political elite as silencing free speech and using this constructed victim-status as a means of rallying support for ideas regarded as social taboos, including an implicit (or even explicit) defense of Nazism.

Accusations of racism made against leaders may thus be turned to political advantage as they seek to portray themselves as victims of powerful others and the prejudiced anti-racism orthodoxies they hide behind. There may thus be mileage to be gained from inviting such criticisms by making extreme and provocative comments, and meeting the inevitable chorus of execration with the mobilizing response: 'see how they treat us as a "basket of deplorables"'. This positioning as a victim against scripted accusations of racism can help leaders to position themselves as prototypical members of an oppressed class of those wrongly regarded as 'racists'.

The identity category of the racist is therefore not only a tool for managing participant administered accountability, it is also a tool for enacting category prototypicality around which leaders can mobilize others (Haslam, Reicher, and Platow, 2011).

In sum, identity performance theory focuses attention on the way particular versions of 'racism' are constructed to serve three interrelated functions: identification, explanation, and mobilization. 'Racism' is not the aberration it seeks to depict. It is a kind of social glue that cements the meeting of hearts and minds, constructing patterns of agreement (and disagreement) about which versions of racism can be deemed acceptable and pass through social interaction. Agreements about racism affect the direction of micro interactions, but also gain purchase by affecting the individual and collective agents who identify themselves and act in its terms. In so doing, racism discourse begins to construct the world in its image as opposing camps of 'racists' and 'decent people' take formation in social life and politics.

Kevin Durrheim

Conclusion – the end of racism

It is a significant fact that the word racism entered into circulation only when the horrors that European nations had practiced against colonized others began to be applied to citizens at home in Europe. In a sense, this marked the beginning of the end of racism. Racism became self-conscious of itself as 'racism' and in the process it became a tool to define itself out of existence by the slippery and endlessly shifting process of dialogical distancing, attributing racism to others.

For most of its history, because of the liberal consensus in postwar society and the social sciences, authoritative versions of Racism have held sway, capturing the imagination of progressives and proponents of anti-racist projects of all kinds. Together, they collectively forged a new morality – one of the last vestiges for foundational moralizing discourse in a secularizing world.

Yet, as the liberal consensus has broken down, as the world has become more unequal, divided, and insecure, the moral currency of anti-racism has entered a cycle of inflation that threatens to expose its fragile foundations, constructed on the shaky ground of social identification and political maneuver. As the legacy of colonial violence has spilled back into the old white world of Europe and North America by way of terrorism and immigration, criticisms of racism have become shriller. The muscular critique of racism from the traditional left is something of a last stand. 'Racism' has become unmoored from Racism. The centre cannot hold as historically privileged groups portray themselves as racism's victims. In the USA and Europe, but also in Asia, Africa and Latin America, brutal nationalisms of all kinds are now being developed as bulwarks against racism, rather than its expressions.

The success of 'racism' as a moral framework for identification, explanation and mobilization may have provided the seeds of its own undoing. Political discourse has become a cacophony of racism versus racism. Social media interaction, identification with opinion-based groups (McGarty et al., 2009), and the information glut have promoted social fragmentation in which broad-based social movements and pockets of homophilous interest groups use constructions of racism to practice the politics of identity and social change and vie with each other for the moral high ground.

References

Adorno, T. W., Frenkel-Brunswik, E., Levinson, D. J., & Sanford, N. (1950). *The Authoritarian Personality*. New York: Harper.
Allport, G.W. (1954). *The Nature of Prejudice*. Garden City, NY: Doubleday.
Arendt, H. (1973). *The Origins of Totalitarianism*. New York: Harcourt Brace Jovanovich.
Augoustinos, M., & Every, D. (2007). The language of "race" and prejudice: A discourse of denial, reason, and liberal-practical politics. *Journal of Language and Social Psychology, 26*, 123–141. doi:10.1177/0261927X07300075.
Augoustinos, M., & Every, D. (2010). Accusations and denials of racism: Managing moral accountability in public discourse. *Discourse & Society, 21*, 251–256. doi:10.1177/0957926509360650.
Balibar, E. (1991). Is there a neo-racism? In E. Balibar & I. Wallerstein (eds) *Race, Nation, Class: Ambiguous Identities* (pp. 17–28). London: Verso.
Banton, M. (1970). The concept of racism. In S. Zubaida (ed) *Race and Racialism* (pp. 17–34). London: Tavistock.
Barker, M. (1981). *The New Racism: Conservatives and the Ideology of the Tribe*. London: Junction Books.
Billig, M. (2012). The Notion of "Prejudice": Some Rhetorical and Ideological Aspects. In J. Dixon & M. Levine (eds) *Beyond Prejudice: Extending the Social Psychology of Conflict, Inequality, and Social Change* (pp. 139–157). Cambridge, UK: Cambridge University Press.

Burford-Rice, R., & Augoustinos, M. (2018). 'I didn't mean that: It was just a slip of the tongue': Racial slips and gaffes in the public arena. *British Journal of Social Psychology*, *57*, 21–42.

Cohen, P. (1992). "It's racism what dunnit": Hidden narratives in theories of racism. In J. Donald & A. Rattansi (eds) *Race, Culture and Difference* (pp. 62–103). Newbury Park, CA: Sage.

Condor, S. (1988). "Race stereotypes" and racist discourse'. *Text*, 8, 69–91.

Condor, S., Figgou, L., Abell, J., Gibson, S., & Stevenson, C. (2006). 'They're not racist … ' Prejudice denial, mitigation and suppression in dialogue. *British Journal of Social Psychology*, *45*, 441–462.

Demby, G. (2014). The ugly, fascinating history of the word 'racism'. www.npr.org/sections/codeswitch/2014/01/05/260006815/the-ugly-fascinating-history-of-the-word-racism

Derrida, J. (1970). Structure, sign, and play in the discourse of the human sciences. In Richard Macksey & Eugenio Donato (eds) *The Languages of Criticism and the Sciences of Man: The Structuralist Controversy*. Baltimore, MD: Johns Hopkins University Press, pp. 247–272.

Donald, J., & Rattansi, A. (eds.). (1992). *Race, Culture and Difference*. Newbury Park, CA: Sage.

Dubow, S. (1991). Mental testing and the understanding of race in twentieth-century South Africa. In T. Meade & M. Walker (eds) *Science, Medicine & Cultural Imperialism* (pp. 148–177). New York: ST Martin's Press.

Durrheim, K. (2012). Implicit prejudice in mind and interaction. In J. Dixon & M. Levine (eds) *Beyond the Prejudice Problematic* (pp. 179–199). Cambridge: Cambridge University Press.

Durrheim, K. (2014). Two histories of prejudice. In C. Tileagă & J. Byford (eds) *Psychology and History: Interdisciplinary Explorations* (pp. 205–222). Cambridge University Press.

Durrheim, K. (2016). 'Race stereotypes' as 'racist' discourse. In C. Tileagă & L. Stokoe (eds) *Discursive Psychology: Classic and Contemporary Issues* (pp. 257–270). London: Routledge.

Durrheim, K. (2017). Race trouble and the impossibility of non-racialism. *Critical Philosophy of Race*, 5, 320–338.

Durrheim, K., & Dixon, J. (2005). *Racial Encounter: The Social Psychology of Contact and Desegregation*. Hove: Routledge.

Durrheim, K., & Murray, A.J. (2019). Conclusion: Topographies of the said and unsaid. In A.J. Murray & K. Durrheim (eds) *Qualitative Studies of Silence: The Unsaid as Social Action* (pp. 270–289). Cambridge: Cambridge University Press.

Durrheim, K., Okuyan, M., Twali, M. S., García-Sánchez, E., Pereira, A., Portice, J. S., Gur, T., Wiener-Blotner, O., & Keil, T. (2018). How racism discourse can mobilize right-wing populism: The construction of identity and alliance in reactions to UKIP's Brexit "Breaking Point" campaign. *Journal of Applied and Community Social Psychology*, *28*, 385–405. doi:10.1002/casp.2347.

Durrheim, K., Quayle, M., & Dixon, J. A. (2016). The struggle for the nature of "Prejudice": "Prejudice" expression as identity performance. *Political Psychology*, *37*, 17–35. doi:10.1111/pops.12310.

Essed, P.J.M. (1991). *Understanding Everyday Racism*. Newbury Park, CA: Sage.

Fairclough, N. (1992). Discourse and social change. Cambridge, MA: Polity.

Figgou, L., & Condor, S. (2006). Irrational categorization, natural intolerance and reasonable discrimination: Lay representations of prejudice and racism. *British Journal of Social Psychology*, *45*, 219–243. doi:10.1348/014466605X40770.

Frederickson, G. M. (2002). Racism: A short history. Princeton, NJ: Princeton University Press.

Gaertner, S. L., & Dovidio, J. F. (1986). The aversive form of racism. In J. F. Dovidio & S. L. Gaertner (eds) *Prejudice, Discrimination and Racism* (pp. 61–89). New York: Academic Press.

Garcia, J. A. (1997). Current conceptions of racism: A critical examination of some recent social philosophy. *Journal of Social Philosophy*, *28*, 5–42.

Gilroy, P. (1987). *There Ain't No Black in the Union Jack: The Cultural Politics of Race and Nation*. London: Hutchinson.

Gilroy, P. (1992). The end of antiracism. In J. Donald & A. Rattansi (eds) *Race, Culture and Difference* (pp. 49–61). Newbury Park, CA: Sage.

Goldberg, D. T. (1993). *Racist Culture: Philosophy and the Politics of Meaning*. Cambridge, MA: Blackwell.

Goodman, S. (2010). "It's not racist to impose limits on immigration": Constructing the boundaries of racism in the asylum and immigration debate. *Critical Approaches to Discourse Analysis across Disciplines*, *4*, 1–17.

Goodman, S., & Burke, S. (2010). "Oh you don't want asylum seekers, oh you're just racist": A discursive analysis of discussions about whether it's racist to oppose asylum seeking. *Discourse and Society*, 21, 325–340. doi:10.1177/0957926509360743.

Greenland, K., Andreouli, E., Augoustinos, M., & Taulke-Johnson, R. (2018). What constitutes 'discrimination' in everyday talk? Argumentative lines and the social representations of discrimination. *Journal of Language and Social Psychology*. doi:10.1177/0261927X18762588.

Haslam, S. A., Reicher, S. D., & Platow, M. J. (2011). *The New Psychology of Leadership: Identity, Influence, and Power*. New York: Psychology Press.

Hirschfeld, M. (1938). *Racism*. London: Gollancz.

Hoyt, C. (2012). The pedagogy of the meaning of racism: Reconciling a discordant discourse. *Social Work: A Journal of the National Association of Social Workers*, 57, 225–234. doi: 10.1093/sw/sws009.

Jussim, L., Crawford, J. T., Anglin, S. M., & Stevens, S. T. (2015). Ideological bias in social psychological research. In J. Forgas, K. Fiedler, & W.D. Crano (eds) *Social Psychology and Politics* (pp. 91–109). New York: Taylor & Francis.

Katz, I., & Hass, R. G. (1988). Racial ambivalence and American value conflict: Correlational and priming studies of dual cognitive structures. *Journal of Personality and Social Psychology*, 55, 893–905.

Klein, O., Spears, R., & Reicher, S. (2007). Social identity performance: Extending the strategic side of SIDE. *Personality and Social Psychology Review*, 11, 28–45.

Klineberg, O. (1951). The scientific study of national stereotypes, *UNESCO Social Science Bulletin III*, 3, 505–511.

Mangcu, X. (2015, April 2). Race transcends class in this country: A response to Seekings and Nattrass. Retrieved from www.groundup.org.za/article/race-transcends-class-country-response-seekings-and-nattrass_2806

McGarty, C., Bliuc, A.-M., Thomas, E. F., & Bongiorno, R. (2009). Collective action as the material expression of opinion-based group membership. *Journal of Social Issues*, 65, 839–857. doi:10.1111/j.1540-4560.2009.01627.x.

McIntosh, P. (2008). White privilege: Unpacking the invisible knapsack. In P. Rothenberg (ed.) *White Privilege: Essential Readings on the Other Side of Racism* (pp. 123–127). New York: Worth.

Miles, R. & Brown, M. (2003). *Racism*. London: Routledge.

Montgomery, K. (2005). Imagining the antiracist state: Representations of racism in Canadian history textbooks. *Discourse: Studies in the Cultural Politics of Education*, 26, 427–442. doi: 10.1080/01596300500319712.

Myburgh, J. (2016). How the word "racism" was born, and why it's important. www.politicsweb.co.za/news-and-analysis/on-the-origins-of-racism

Omi, M., & Winant, H. (1995). *Racial Formation in the United States: From the 1960s to the 1990s* (revised edn). New York: Routledge.

Potter, J., & Wetherell, M. (1987). *Discourse and Social Psychology*. London: Sage.

Reicher, S. (2012). From perception to mobilization: The shifting paradigm of prejudice. In J. Dixon & M. Levine (eds) *Beyond the Prejudice Problematic* (pp. 27–46). Cambridge: Cambridge University Press.

Reisigl, M., & Wodak, R. (2005). *Discourse and Discrimination: Rhetorics of Racism and Anti-Semitism*. London: Routledge.

Safire, W. (2006). *Safire's Political Dictionary*. Oxford: Oxford University Press.

Samelson, F. (1978). From "race psychology" to "studies in prejudice": Some observations on the thematic reversal in social psychology. *Journal of the History of the Behavioral Sciences.*, 14, 265–278.

Schegloff, E. A. (1992). Repair after next turn: The last structurally provided defense of intersubjectivity in conversation. *American Journal of Sociology*, 97, 1295–1345.

Schegloff, E. A. (2006). On possibles. *Discourse Studies*, 8, 141–157.

Schröter, M. (2019). The language ideology of silence and silencing in public discourse: Claims to silencing as metadiscursive moves in German anti-political correctness discourse. In A. J. Murray & K. Durrheim (eds) *Qualitative Studies of Silence: The Unsaid as Social Action* (pp. 165–185). Cambridge: Cambridge University Press.

Sears, D. O., & Kinder, D. R. (1971). Racial tensions and voting in Los Angeles. In W. Z. Hirsch (ed) *Los Angeles: Viability and Prospects for Metropolitan Leadership* (pp. 51–88). New York: Praeger.

Seekings, J. & Nattrass, N. (2015, March 31). Rhodes and the politics of gain. Retrieved from http://groundup.org.za/article/rhodes-and-politics-pain_2796

Solomos, J., & Back, L. (1994). Conceptualising racisms: Social theory, politics and research. *Sociology*, 28, 143–161.

Stokoe, E. (2012). Moving forward with membership categorization analysis: Methods for systematic analysis. *Discourse Studies*, 14, 277–303.

Stokoe, E. (2015). Identifying and responding to possible '-isms' in institutional encounters: Alignment, impartiality and the implications for communication training. *Journal of Language and Social Psychology*, *34*, 427–445.

Teo, P. (2000). Racism in the news: A critical discourse analysis of news reporting in two Australian newspapers. *Discourse & Society*, *11*, 7–49.

Tetlock, P. E. (1994). Political psychology or politicized psychology: Is the road to scientific hell paved with good moral intentions?. *Political Psychology*, *15*, 509–529.

Tetlock, P. E., & Arkes, H. R. (2004). The implicit prejudice exchange: Islands of consensus in a sea of controversy. *Psychological Inquiry*, *15*, 311–321.

Tileagă, C. (2007). Ideologies of moral exclusion: A critical discursive reframing of depersonalization, delegitimization and dehumanization. *British Journal of Social Psychology*, *46*, 717–737. doi:10.1348/014466607X186894.

UNESCO (United Nations Educational, Scientific and Cultural Organization). (1969). *Four Statements on the Race Question*. Paris: UNESCO.

van Dijk, T. A. (1992). Discourse and the denial of racism. *Discourse & Society*, *3*, 87–118.

van Dijk, T. A. (1993). *Elite Discourse and Racism*. Newbury Park, CA: Sage.

Van Dijk, T. A. (1987a). *Communicating Racism*. Newbury Park, CA: Sage.

Wetherell, M. & Potter, J. (1988). Discourse analysis and the identification of interpretative repertoires. In C. Antaki (ed) *Analysing Everyday Explanation: A Casebook of Methods* (pp. 168–183). London: Sage.

Wetherell, M., & Potter, J. (1992). *Mapping the Language of Racism: Discourse and the Legitimation of Exploitation*. Hertfordshire: Harvester Wheatsheaf.

Whitehead, K. A. (2015). Everyday antiracism in action: Preference organization in responses to racism. *Journal of Language and Social Psychology*, *34*, 374–389.

Whitehead, K. A. (2017). Managing the moral accountability of stereotyping. *Journal of Language and Social Psychology*, 1–22. doi:10.1177/0261927X17723679.

Whitehead, K. A. (in press). The Problem of Context in the Analysis of Social Action: The Case of Implicit Whiteness in Post-Apartheid South Africa. *Social Psychology Quarterly*.

Wieviorka, M. (1995). *The Arena of Racism* (Transl. C Turner). Thousand Oaks, CA: Sage.

34

Humiliation, dehumanization and the quest for dignity
Researching beyond racism

Philomena Essed

Thinking through and beyond racism

Racism research can build on a solid body of work relating the experiences of generations, synchronously and over time. Increasingly, scholars have broadened their scope beyond national confines to compare, integrate and relate racism across the globe (Reilly, Kaufman and Bodino, 2003; Bulmer and Solomos, 2004; Goldberg, 2009; Romm, 2010; Essed et al., 2018). The past two decades witnessed also the proliferation of critical analyses of the identity politics of whiteness (Levine-Rasky, 2016; Wekker, 2016), while extreme right ideologies are taking more comfortable seats at European and US political tables. National identity crises and discontent about politicians, democracy and government policies (Mounk, 2018) are normalizing into fear-mongering immigrant blaming (Postelnicescu, 2016), thereby stirring the quietness of the public secret that white supremacy and nationalism are deeply rooted in European and American histories (Serwer, 2019). Moral tension is hardening in Western countries around sentiments of white entitlement and supremacy on the one hand, and on the other, democratic and humanistic values majorities also subscribe to. The contradiction between international human rights commitments and the economization of whether and how to respond to global human tragedy has been referred to as one of the current century's 'greatest tests to humanity' and 'moral leadership' (Abbasi, Patel and Godlee, 2015:351). Indeed, humanitarian crises in many areas of the world have moved high numbers of people across regions and borders, seeking safety from wars, political and religious prosecution, racism, tribalism, genocide, terrorism, rape, gang violence, environmental depletion, homophobia, unemployment, starvation, human unworthy living conditions, and futures void of hope (Gale, 2004; Carrera et al., 2015; Guild et al., 2015; Ostrand, 2015; Hage, 2017; Esses, Hamilton and Gaucher, 2017; Leach, 2003; Greussing and Boomgaarden, 2017). These and other violations of equality, equity and human dignity in a global context are not just a list. They are related (Noble, 2015; Adams and Bell, 2016).

How different systems of dominance converge is, among others, at the heart of intersectionality (Kimberlé Crenshaw, 1989) with its initial emphasis on race and gender. Probing into a related, often overlooked, direction Ghassan Hage (2017) explored the relation between the ecological crisis and racism as inherently related social phenomena. His work reveals at a deeper level how systems develop through and inside each other, from similar roots, validating the subjugation and exploitation of nature to the will and power of human as more deserving of life than non-human animals. The fundamental principle of dehumanization, more or lesser degrees of being considered 'human' versus closer to 'animals' (or other parts of nature), accommodates the ranking of Others and their (imagined) ways of life. Fuller and Gerloff (2008) captured this in more popular terms as 'rankism'. Whether dehumanizing metaphors directly refer to aggressive animals or despised animalistic behavior, they involve humiliations (Haslam, 2006; Nussbaum, 2006, 2009; Keith and Keith, 2013; Hage, 2017). This points to the assumption, central to this chapter, that dehumanization and humiliations help sustain most if not all of forms of structural inferiorization and marginalization, even when experienced also differently on local and individual levels. Implications are that the impact of *one issue struggles* – like racism – is bound to be curtailed because it operates through most if not all other structural social injustices and inequalities. While the insight of relatedness is not new, I hope to add to the conversation a different take. Rather than the paradigm of overlapping systems of domination, my approach seeks to identify shared experience across (imagined) borders and boundaries as a basis for social justice and for liberating practices that also honor the integrity of nature and life itself. Because this is too large a mission for this chapter, I simply take on the challenge of thinking through and beyond racism in order to counter racism more effectively. But more about this later. First I further elaborate on some of the moral implications of humiliating the racialized Other as if doing so is a natural right.

Entitlement racism as humiliation

The new millennium has brought surging populist support for the acclaimed right to defend white, national, European, and related exclusive entitlements. The slogan of 'never again' has faded with the rapidly decreasing numbers of World War II survivors who carried a critical moral consciousness. There are concerns about the negative impact of strong polarization on the trust among people (Rapp, 2016), much of which gets to be expressed in the public sphere of political, social and traditional media reporting. Overemphasis on conflict, rather than what people share, fuels anxieties and fears among hosting populations imagining or living cultural and societal changes. Exposure to refugee stories through global media also brings closer to home, in rich countries, the kind of existential insecurities and survival challenges the majority of the world faces. At the same time, in the US, Europe and other white dominated countries (racialized, ethnicized, and zipcode) economic inequality has increased (Sayer, 2015) along with stress, a sense of loss and insecurity. The current mode of rudeness, offensive language, openly racist discourse, among politicians, in social media, or in street demonstrations, signals a more general trend of moral erosion (de Gaay Fortman, 2016). In the new millennium, the limitless symbolic violence against Muslims, a form of *cultural character assassination* (Essed, 2009), became a fertile ground as well for the return of unashamed explicitly anti-black, sometimes called Afrophobic, discourse and images. What I have coined *entitlement racism* (Essed, 2013; Essed and Muhr, 2018) points to the insistence on the right to use any discourse and images as freedom of expression, also when racially offensive. Entitlement racism presumes that whites are entitled to priority, deserve more space, are more human than people of color, and the license to openly claim this. Entitlement racism has different connotations than the racial bigotry before and during the Civil Rights era of the previous century, when the universal rejection of racism was relatively new and modern democracies were still in the making. Today, the claim of 'white innocence' has lost credibility (Wekker, 2016). The grace of the benefit of the doubt depletes when racist discourse, presented as freedom of expression, gets to be licensed in spite of the universal right to live free from discrimination. In the information society few, if any, with access to television, mobile phones, computers, tablets, libraries, free E-news papers, search engines, or the financial means to shop at physical or E-bookstores, can claim that they do not have any access to publications or programs, blogs, and other social media, to know when discourses, symbols and images are racially humiliating. Entitlement racism must also be seen against the background of the celebration of neo-liberal individualism to speak your mind; that anything 'me-me-me' wants to say 'should be possible'.

Case in point, the Dutch Black (faced) Pete (Zwarte Piet). This Sambo-esque figure with exaggerated African features, servant of the Saint Nicholas who traditionally visits the Netherlands in early December, has become a prime example of entitlement racism. Not so in its initial stage of racialization, the mid 19th century, when Black Pete first came to resemble a 'negro', with exaggerated Black African features, in the aftermath of the abolition of slavery. In spite of three decades of protests, which intensified over the past ten years, pro-Black Pete groups, representing significant parts of the population, still feel entitled to claim the right to 'their' Black Pete (Essed and Hoving, 2014; van der Pijl and Goulordava, 2014; Hilhorst and Hermes, 2016; Rodenberg and Wagenaar, 2016). As recently as November 2018[1] pro-Black Pete figures, apparently including children cheered by their parents, threw eggs, beer cans and dirt while scandalizing with racist and sexist slurs against black (and other) 'kick out Black Pete' advocates. The inclusion of sexist slurs suggests the relatedness to other forms of domination[2], which will be addressed later in this chapter. In light of these and other developments, the question of 'end of racism?' sounds rhetorical. Although the 'Black Pete = Racism' slogan is inevitably gaining more support, the viciousness of 'keep your hands off Black Pete' proponents and the deep emotions involved, including death threats, suggests that advocacy for the Black face cannot simply be reduced to racism (only). Families, friends, the whole country are highly polarized. But they also share something significant. Both pro- and anti-Black-Pete camps feel humiliated, be it for different reasons and seen from different power positions. The former, who draw from the power of entitlement as white Dutch, feel infuriated and humiliated by what they see as immigrants and national 'traitors' disrespectfully ripping apart their Saint Nicholas celebration, 'accusing' them of racism and demanding that they should do without the Black Pete. Those who reject the racism the celebration invokes, have been exposed to verbally and physically violent forms of humiliating and dehumanizing attacks in their struggle for national celebrations that can honor the dignity of all, including Black Dutch. The pain of feeling disrespected and humiliated is universal, regardless of the cause. Mutual recognition of violation of dignity as a member of a social group, what I would call *dignity hurt*, can become the rope for a possible bridge across divides, even when initially narrow and shaky (Hicks, 2011).

In the course of this chapter I make an effort to focus more specifically on these two universal mechanisms sustaining racism and other forms of oppression and domination: humiliation and dehumanization. I also suggest that a human made and destructive universal phenomenon, *dignity hurt*, urges a universal healing response, one that draws from constructive human capabilities to enable, restore and honor that dignity is a universal need (Fuller and Gerloff, 2008). I hope to inspire consideration that new directions in researching racism might be more effective when thinking and acting broader than racism as a standalone.

To date, one of the most accessible and potentially transformative approaches in this context has been intersectionality.

Are we all intersectional now?

The 1974 Combahee River Collective's much cited 1977 statement was a wake up call:

> The most general statement of our politics at the present time would be that we are actively committed to struggling against racial, sexual, heterosexual, and class oppression, and see as our particular task the development of integrated analysis and practice based upon the fact that the major systems of oppression are interlocking.
>
> *[http://circuitous.org/scraps/combahee.html]*

But ideas do not develop in isolation. Across countries and continents feminist pioneers urged recognition of the simultaneity of oppression, including Hull, Scott and Smith (1982), Audre Lorde (1984) and Adrienne Rich (1979, 1984) from the US; Pratibha Parmar (2004) and Hazel Carby (1985) in the UK. Their work made explicit the epistemological power of positioning as a basis for identifying knowledge gaps, while transforming the relation between experience and theory.

In my own case, a critical article about racism in the (Dutch) feminist movement, contesting the homogeneity of the generic 'we and us women' (Essed, 1982) preluded the concept of *everyday racism*, based on the gendered and racialized experiences of Black women in the Netherlands and the US (Essed, 1984). Kim Crenshaw's introduction of *intersectionality* (Crenshaw, 1989) became the most influential breakthrough for theories of simultaneous oppression. With this metaphor she reached from within theory and social movements into the professions, notably the legal system.[3] Together with notable legal scholar Dereck Bell and others Crenshaw became founder of Critical Race Theory, a frame that has proliferated into a rich body of work (Crenshaw, 2010; Bonilla-Silva, 2015). As an intervention in legal studies, CRT problematized the US failure, in spite of the Civil Rights Movement, to improve the political, social and economic conditions of African Americans. CRT called out the neglect, denial and indifference in legal studies when it came to addressing, studying and countering racism. Moreover, Crenshaw (1989) revealed the erasure of black women's experience in Courts where it was and often still is not possible to consider both racial and gender discrimination in the same complaint. You had to make a choice, usually at the expense of black women's voice and experience. As a notion, concept, activist tool, analytical frame, policy instrument and more, intersectionality has gained popularity and, arguably, societal acceptance, beyond expectations.

Theory is one thing, but how intersectional analysis can work in everyday life is a domain still under-researched in the area of race critical studies (Essed and Goldberg, 2002; Solomos and Collins, 2010). The following example, a personal anecdote, can probably illustrate the complexity of interpretation when different modes of domination are latent or actively operative at the same time. An everyday example can also call attention to some of the unresolved conceptual tensions underlying the very idea of multiple, but still separate, factors as intersectional in occurrence.

The other day I went to a nearby supermarket in the small mall adjacent to a university campus in Southern California. Bright sunny day, at noon. In order to enter you have to cross the driveway in front of the supermarket, where cars are supposed to go very slow, and where they have to give way to pedestrians. Walking towards the entrance, a car, silver compact, approaches from my right looking as if it had no intention of stopping and is about to hit me when I call out last second: "Heh!" The driver, who had been looking at something in his lap, lifts his head, steps on the brake, and makes eye contact, apparently taken by surprise. My brains make a quick assessment based on his appearance: a guy, maybe olive skin, maybe white with tan – hard to see skin color in the summer underneath elaborately tattooed arms, baseball cap, sunglasses. Traditional student age, probably a student indeed – remember this is almost on the premises of a university campus. The professor-educator in me is right there. I urge him to scroll down his window, point at the smartphone he had quickly squeezed in between the two front seats, commenting, "You're not supposed to do that, emailing while driving." Agitated, he barks back: "What the *fuck* do *you* know?" Flabbergasted, I respond, "You almost *hit* me!" But he is already driving off. My immediate thoughts: how rude! Why? What's wrong with these young people? Donald Trump effect? Social media entitlement to say whatever you want? Racism? Only to notice that he stops again, ten meters further at the far left of the supermarket facade, where a young woman, black, decidedly walks towards his car, opening the door to take a back seat. She might have come from one of those small snack or nail polish places behind her.

Girlfriend? I guess so. 'The' girlfriend? Interracial dating is not very common in the US, but possible. Hmm… maybe this was not really about race, but iGen or Generation Z who do not want to be lectured, certainly not a testosterone charged male having a lady, one or two generations his senior accuse him of doing an 'oh so 20th century' thing as *emailing* when, in retrospect, his ear phones, I had also noticed, suggest he might have been browsing music collection, Facebook or whatever apps. He probably knows it is against the law to be on a smartphone while driving. So, was it necessary to 'educate' on top of that? I could have just left him with a little touch of shock about what *could* have happened. The imagined litigation due to injury of pedestrian might have touched him sufficiently to cause a little scare. But then this rude language and not even apologizing… no politeness, no sense of dignity.

So far the 30 seconds of the event include hasty interpretation, scratching the surface of layers in an ordinary everyday encounter. Mind you, even olive skin with black girlfriend could still make it a case of rudeness inclusive of racism. And this could also have been an Uber or Lyft driver collecting a passenger, which could explain her taking the back seat and might suggest that he was doing a last minute smartphone check for info about the passenger or pick-up space when his car almost hit a pedestrian…

The initial quick interpretation draws from generalized, arguably, quite stereotypical, profiling: the woman as possibly coming from the corner nail studio; the relation to the 'young, student, white' driver constructed in terms of a hetero-normative scenario: if a young man picks up a young woman they must be friends or maybe dating. The other scenario projects what an Uber or Lyft driver might be doing with their smartphone.

While the above intersectional interpretation attempts to be inclusive in terms of possibly relevant identity factors, it remains a question of reductionism, be it not to one factor (racism) but to various simultaneously (e.g. racism, ageism, sexism). Reductionism usually works at the expense of nuance in terms of 'truth' value, even when multiple reductions are acknowledged at the same time. Life experiences and frames of interpretation cannot simply be reduced to generalizable categories as if we would only live according to what racial, gender, economic or other parts of positionality would dictate. This immediately highlights the tension between the fact that any experience is uniquely received in the context of a unique constellation of life experiences (this particular event, that particular location, these specific actors involved) but also shared, because at a higher level of abstraction an event like this (white male verbal aggression against female of color) fits a standard scenario of gendered everyday racism (Essed, 1991). Different than gender *and* racism, the notion of *gendered racism* assumes that race is modified, co-constructed, or fused with gender, class and the other way around. It contests the existence of 'pure' racism, pure sexism, pure ageism, or pure xenophobia, for that matter. The theoretical principle of experiencing race through another modality is not new. The 1970s/80s had also been the era of critiquing sociological and economic reductionism, notably through the notion of articulation (Hall, 1980).

The story, so far, is fairly apolitical, not much at stake, indicating how intersectionality, a concept grounded in generations of political protest and struggle, has evolved to come to cover the more general idea of multiple dimensions of identity, including style preference (baseball cap and tattoos), lifestyle (silver car) and professional status (professor and student) (Fuller and Gerloff, 2008).

But, one can also make the story more political. Suppose the car had hit the pedestrian indeed, who, given the fairly slow speed, would have survived, probably with some injuries. The subsequent 911 call would have activated already latent and also additional issues of power and (health-legal) politics. The police, ambulance, hospital, insurance policies, are imbued with different and oppositional issues of interest, and hence, social power inequalities would be activated to become highly relevant. The pedestrian would still be a university professor, but also a woman of color, which might chip away at the status of being a professor (Henry and Tator, 2009); and the driver might have been 'just' a student, but white male and maybe also the son of a wealthy white lawyer, which might 'upgrade' his version of the story the police and maybe, later, a judge would hear and take into consideration. Each of the considerations, race, ethnicity, gender, class, sexual orientation, national status, age have their own set of empowering or disadvantaging characteristics, none of which works in isolation. Fusing the factors could look like this: the driver is not just young, but let's say a particular young man, namely a *white* young man, not a black young man, and then white, middle class able-bodied young, which is a quite different white young person than say, a white lower class young man or a white highly educated middle class *blind* young man (Adams, 2019).

The story could have been just a dinner table entertainment story about 'almost got hit by a car the other day'. But analyzing the story can reveal the complexity of interpreting that and most other interactive situations in life. The interpreter not only inserts into the story socially constructed categories, but also acts upon those projections. I was interpreting on the basis of prototypes *and* my particular personal experiences with those categories. For instance, coming from the Netherlands, where, unlike the US, gun ownership is unusual, it was probably risky to ask the driver to scroll down his window. He clearly got agitated and could have drawn a gun and fired. The face saving excuse that he felt threatened could have been acceptable as it fits a standard US racism scenario of criminalizing ordinary black and brown people.

This dramatic fictional turn introduces yet another approach to the event: Apparently, the driver felt *entitled* to use offensive language against someone who is, on face value to him, an able-bodied, generationally older woman of color immigrant – given my 'foreign' accent most Americans seem to detect after two words – or whatever 'Othering' projections might have been on his mind. The sense of entitlement is embedded in his being a whole person. Agitated, annoyed, irritated or otherwise negatively emotionally impacted, he somehow feels authorized to express these feelings. This kind of empowerment is grounded in the lived experience of entitlement in a societal system that attaches premium worthiness to masculine *whiteness* and white (American, middle-classed, able-bodied, heterosexual) *masculinity*.

The above fusions of premium values and characteristics around human worth prompted me to redefine racism to acknowledge the key role of questioning the 'worthiness' of the Other as a human being:

> **Racism** is about the creation of **hierarchies of worthiness** attached to groups of people identified as different in terms of (attributed) racial, or cultural (ethnic) factors. It is a historically anchored ideology, structure and process, where one racial or ethnic group privileges its members on the basis of attributed preferred values and characteristics, in order to legitimate the disadvantaging of other groups. These values and characteristics are used to assess the worthiness of **human beings** and **ways of being** in terms of related degrees of entitlement to 'be', to be validated, and to develop.

My definition purposefully intends universal or multi-applicability. Because you can change race for gender, sexual orientation, physical and mental ability, religion or other, it creates the opportunity to address fused forms of domination.

The shared experience of dignity hurt

Dominated groups will seek, sooner or later, acknowledgment of the injustices done to them, while dominating groups might defend themselves or deny. Fellow teachers in the area of race and racism studies may be familiar with the situation where teaching about the topic could trigger emotions of recognition and empowerment, but also anger, resentment, race-fatigue, humiliation, shame, defensiveness, self-silencing, guilt, or powerlessness, depending on the identities involved. There could be those who felt unseen in their hurt, based on violations of what they felt was primarily not race but class, gender, disability, religious or another part of their experience. There would be those who felt seen in their dominated racial identity, but denied or only marginally seen in their LGBTQ identity. Whether (fused) gender, class, sexual orientation or other systems or domination involved, all operate, among other things, through humiliation and dehumanization; the creation of hierarchies of (human) worthiness attributing a lesser degree or complete absence of human-ness to one or more particular groups. The purpose of humiliation in systems of oppression is to discourage potential protest and to punish or retaliate against actual rebellion. Without resistance there will be no change.

With the emergence of the 'Black Lives Matter' movement, the discourse of hierarchies of worthiness in terms of 'ways of being' and 'of being human' has become tragically explicit again, since the (pre) Civil Rights Movement. The very name of the movement, a 21st century reminder that black people are human and equally worthy of life, reminds, like a déjà vu, of abolition movements of the 19th century. Going back to basics as if (formal) democracy never happened: some are less deserving than others for being seen as (fully) human. The BLM movement rises up against the widely spread phenomenon in the US (and increasingly in Europe) that black and brown people can be beaten, kicked, strangled, dragged, smashed, shot, stamped upon, and killed without repercussions, in particular by the hands of Law Enforcement. The moral crisis around discourse in the social media and the renewed respectability of hate infused populism, has also emboldened openly racist verbal aggression whites feel entitled to take ownership of again. At this point in time there is an endless list of everyday entitlement racism one can read about in the (social) media, where racially offensive discourse freely violates the right of black people to 'be'. Tags are floating around social media, such as: driving while black; having a barbeque in a park while black; going to Starbucks while black; trying to enter your own apartment building while black male; taking a seat on a Ryan airplane while black female, and so on. Add the examples you have read, heard about, witnessed or been exposed to yourself.

History is rife with the use of humiliation in personal and group conflict – without exception including all of the structural forms of domination. In a groundbreaking study Donna Hicks (2011) analyzed the role of dignity in conflict resolution. Drawing from decades of expertise as a mediator, she discovered that even long standing historical enemies were able to share the same table and start a dialogue, on the basis of the mutual recognition of shared experiences when they had felt violated in their sense of dignity by the other party. I would like to rephrase this as the recognition of *dignity hurt*, as a way of acknowledging the subjectivity of social, cultural or ethnic-racial pain involved (Essed, 2009). The focus should not be on the (often contested) 'facts' of violated dignity or humiliating, – she said versus he said – but on the shared experience that people feel pained or violated when they are humiliated as a member of a group perceived in terms of 'They and Them'. The point of departure then becomes the way words, discourses, (physical) acts, practices, are received and interpreted, and why/how this causes a sense of feeling hurt in their (social identity) dignity. It is exactly the interpretative, that is, subjective, painful, often also shameful, space, that makes *dignity hurt* often being overlooked as an essential part of power, dominance and resistance. Earlier, Cynthia Cockburn (1998) had been successful in Participative Action Research projects that brought together women from different national, religious, ethnic enemy groups who shared deeply felt, often traumatic, experiences of (violent, often sexual) humiliation as women, across warring parties. Because they could face *dignity hurt* as shared experience across historical divides, there was a space to build mutual understanding and more. Both authors draw from a negative and a positive account of human dignity. A negative account explains what dignity is not – how it is being violated in terms of physical, social, economic, and cultural humiliations and forms of dehumanization. Focusing on the shared experience of dignity hurt is invaluable as a way of acknowledging as well as transcending multiple and interrelated systems of oppression/domination. Without an in-depth understanding of the inherent role of dignity hurt in sustaining oppression, it is too easy to embrace a positive account of 'dignity'. Who could not be for dignity? An easy 'yes' to dignity would be vulnerable to missing the point that systems of domination reserve dignity for some only, over the backs of many. Therefore, one cannot really appreciate and understand the depth of what dignity stands for without understanding even better what it means to be denied equal human worth and the right to live in dignified circumstances.

Although humiliation often serves to coerce or reconfirm respect for the superior status of the humiliating party, there might be a negative impact on the latter's dignity in the eyes of others (Dillon, 2013). Denying respect to people of color, questioning their humanity, or trying to strip away the dignity of disabled people, invariably implies undignified behavior from the side of the actor (Margalit, 1996). Yet, few people would think of themselves as having compromised or lost their dignity in the process of humiliating others, practices including: all acts of sexual harassment; acting out racial and sexual disgust towards anyone; laughing about the abuse of transgender sex workers; all parties involved when one bullies a colleague by mimicking his 'Asian English' or her physical disability in order to humor the audience of peers who crack up about it; punishing your child with a belt, and so on. More about the meaning of dignity will follow, but simply click on a YouTube video: focused observation of the humiliator/s might be revealing.

Loss of dignity is not bounded by class or by social status. The most privileged are known to degrade themselves: impulsively twittering state or company presidents, cursing CEOs, yelling directors losing self-control, or authoritarian supervisors bossing workers around, are not uncommon.

There are two sides of the interactional coin between actors and targets with regards to humiliating the Other. First, the earlier mentioned disregard of actor decorum. Second, the force by which the target may try to maintain dignity in spite of humiliations (Moody-Adams, 2013). Having said this, it should be seen as well that continuous attacks on your sense of human worth and dignity throughout years, lives and generations can damage or destroy the sense of self as a worthy human being, worthy family, community or people (Moody-Adams, 2013).

How humiliation dehumanizes

Dehumanization involves degrees of humanness measured along dominant group based normative or idealized values and traits, which are culturally sensitive and more generously attributed to the 'we-us' group. Values determining the degree of human superiority scoring high in Western (capitalist) societies, such as control over nature, progress, profit, rationality, autonomy, and productivity translate into desired traits, including intelligent, civil, developed, self-made, invulnerable, competitive, stable, independent, able-bodied, or born to lead, which are often associated, implicitly, with and thereby naturalizing superiority attached to white middle class males. Not surprisingly, because these dominant values and traits are and have been produced through, and with the purpose of sustaining a nature destroying, growth obsessed, patriarchal, racist, and exploitative system of power relations. Lower on the scale of importance are, for instance, love for the earth, sharing, compassion, care, kindness, sacrifice, vulnerability. Dehumanization takes two main forms: full or partial exclusion of being considered part of the human race. Full exclusion is often expressed in terms of the animalization of the 'they-them' group. Examples are African descent people compared to monkeys, or Jews being called rats. Not being considered fully human finds expression in terms of the target group being seen, for instance, as less rational – women as a group; as less civilized – African and indigenous communities in particular; as less intelligent – women as a group; certain races and ethnicities; as 'stupid' – people with cognitive disabilities; as culturally 'backward' – Muslims portrayed in Dutch and other European discourse.

The phenomenon of dehumanization has been theorized and studied in relation to various social domains, including gender, disability, criminal offenders, and others, but most often in relation to race, war, and genocide, that is, as the denial of the humanness of the racial, ethnic, national or religious other (Haslam, 2006; Bain, Vaes and Leyens, 2014). The pervasiveness of dehumanization (Nussbaum, 2009; Kaufmann et al., 2010) makes the cry for respect and the struggle to maintain dignity essential to dominated groups (Lamont, 2000; Moody-Adams, 2013; Lamont et al., 2016).

Towards cultures of dignity

Dignity is difficult to define but most people know, intuitively, what it means. It is

> a need so strong that people will give up their freedom to have it met; an inner drive so insistent that it can move people to shocking acts of revenge when the attempt to achieve it is thwarted; a human value so critical to happiness and well-being that people sometimes value it more than life itself.
>
> *Fuller and Gerloff (2008, Kindle locations 50–52)*

Though included in the UN declaration of human rights, the meaning of dignity is contested. It has been associated, among other things, with rank and position, used alternatively as equal to self-respect, as paying respect and giving honor, as unique and inherent to being human or something that can be cultured and achieved (Dillon, 2013). For the purpose of this essay dignity is seen as a universal desire and/or need. Because of its universal significance, even when the exact interpretation can vary, the search for dignity in itself has unifying potential that transcends personality and group differences: race, ethnicity, class, gender, physical-cognitive ability, sexual orientation and others.

On a personal or dispositional level, having dignity is not inherent to being human. Who is not familiar with images of undignified living conditions, with comments or observations that so-and-so have 'lost' their dignity or behaves in an undignified way? Dignity can be seen as 'a potential that has to be fulfilled and self-actualized by the persons in question themselves', but the circumstances under which this happens can be 'precarious' (Pollmann, 2011:233). Undignified conditions can, but do not necessarily, take away your dignity. However, supportive social, legal, economic, political, cultural, and other societal conditions, can make it easier to maintain the full potential of dignity.

Dignity can be manifest in at least three, related, areas:

> Personal/dispositional (traits)
> Relational (behavior towards others)
> Environment (human or 'life' worthy living, working, learning conditions)

Manifestations of dignity as a quality or disposition are culturally sensitive and there is no agreement on what these qualities are. For instance, Immanuel Kant would see dignity as inherent in being a *rational* person. Aurel Kolnai (1976), another much cited Western philosopher, explains that dignity as a quality is manifest in 'such characteristics as composure, calm self-control, serenity, and quiet invulnerability' (Dillon, 2013: 22). Drawing from Bontekoe (2010), Bolton (2007), Sayer (2007) and others, I suggest that dignity, as a potential personal quality, represents related principles of leading the self towards aims beyond self-interest:

- *Moral integrity* assumes consistency in living up to moral principles, including social justice, honesty and truthfulness.
- *Whole person approach.* Acknowledging that we are all fully human, that is, with capabilities and vulnerabilities, can prevent patronizing, pathologizing and dehumanization.
- *Humility.* This opens up to see, hear, and value others, while countering self-aggrandizement. It can also contribute to a degree of emotional stability, relevant to appreciate critique.
- *Emotional self-control* combined with *responsible risk taking* in the pursuit of justice. The discussion of entitlement racism illustrated the importance of 'think before you say it' because of the damaging impact on others. This does not mean that one cannot show anger or firmness in rejecting injustice.
- *Self-direction* while acknowledging *interdependence.* The usual term used in the context of dignity is 'autonomy'. Because of the (masculine) connotations of (heroic) acting alone, I prefer the notion of self-direction in *thinking* and deciding about *acting.* Recognizing interconnectedness between all human beings and our natural environment enables recognition of (the needs of) others and acknowledging their contributions. Human achievements always imply the direct or indirect, synchronous or past, seen or unseen, work of others, including self-direction with the trusted help of someone else in case of challenged physical or cognitive facilities.

The above qualities are not meant to be comprehensive or conclusive, but as a step into the direction of reflecting on dignity as a disposition in everyday life.

Dispositional qualities are not relevant in themselves but in the way they can enable and foster dignity in interpersonal relations, which, drawing from Donna Hick's 'essential elements' of dignity in interpersonal relations (Hicks, 2011:25–26) can include: freedom from social prejudice; providing a mutual sense of belonging; absence of physical harm and humiliation; mutual (critical) appreciation of each other's talents and capabilities; fairness and belief in each other's moral integrity, for instance by giving the other the benefit of the doubt (Hicks, 2011).

Personal qualities and interpersonal relationships with dignity contribute to creating dignified working and living environments or *cultures of dignity*. What could a culture of dignity mean, for instance, as applied to dignity in the workplace? Key theories and empirical explorations of dignity at work (Hodson, 2001), the dignity of workers as moral experience (Michele Lamont, 2000), organizational and relational dimensions of dignity at work (Sharon Bolton, 2007) and dignity as humanistic leadership and management (Kostera and Pirson, 2017) agree that dignity at work goes beyond mere formal rights.

In a global world where the exploitation of nature services to compete for the fastest productivity growth, one of the most basic, but difficult, ways of honoring the dignity of people at work is to challenge workplace (and other) instrumentalism.

The reign of capitalism and corporate culture, the global primacy of economic goals, the legitimacy of greed, the widely shared pursuit of profit and cultures of constant assessments, reduce employees to mere instruments – a pair of hands or a set of brains. Humanistic leadership and management (Kostera and Pirson, 2017) could contribute to environments where employees, supervisors and leaders feel seen, heard, and understood as embodying many capabilities, vulnerabilities and life experiences, rather than foremost as being instrumental to profit and brand value for the organization. Employees would likely feel trusted with a degree of self-direction, which increases work satisfaction, motivation and pride. In addition, one could imagine the following workplace suggestions with dignity in mind, as including but certainly not restricted to:

- Respect for employee rights and interests
- Freedom from chronic or serious conflict with managers or peers
- Work that can make you feel meaningful, proud, and which can be a source of growth
- Worker citizenship, including flexible working hours, but without the burden or 24/7 availability that often undermines family and other private commitments
- Self-direction in moving around in the workplace, making friends, building networks (Hodson, 2001)
- Competent leaders who feel comfortable with a dignity disposition (see above) and ability to relate in a dignified way with others (see also above)
- Teamwork and collaboration rather than competitive individualism
- Working spaces designed with the employee as a whole person in mind, not just the performer of a particular function in a particular physical space. Dignity design speaks to the body, spirit, and senses, such as the human need for pleasing aesthetics, including direct or indirect contact with nature (Mannen and McAllister, 2017).

Summarizing from the above, it means that in cultures of dignity interpersonal relations are interdependent and participants are recognized as a whole person with (potential) capacities who is equally worthy to be. They would neither be boxed, overvalued or undervalued in terms of specific elements of identity – race, gender, disability or other – nor reduced to human capital or followers as if lacking responsibility and relevant agency. All forms of social injustice, including and beyond racism, can be addressed at the same time when people are seen, heard, understood, valued, and critically supported in their (potential) capabilities and vulnerabilities (Nussbaum, 2011).

This brings us back, full circle, to countering (fused forms of) racism as embedded in the pursuit of social, cultural, economic and environmental justice. If dignity is truly a universal desire, its pursuit can be considered a potentially strong motivation to unite in common pursuit of cultures of dignity as a mode of thinking through while thinking beyond single issues.

Notes

1 News item in the daily newspaper PAROOL, 18 November 2018. www.parool.nl/binnenland/ actiegroep-kick-out-zwarte-piet-gemeenten-hebben-gefaald~a4607853/
2 A news item from the RTL Nieuws indeed reports infiltration among Black Pete of extreme right representatives dressed up like Black Pete. www.rtlnieuws.nl/editienl/artikel/4490091/extreemrechtse-pieten-liepen-mee-met-intocht-dit-provocatie
3 www.newstatesman.com/lifestyle/2014/04/kimberl-crenshaw-intersectionality-i-wanted-come-every day-metaphor-anyone-could

References

Abbasi, K., Patel, K. and Godlee, F. 2015. Europe's refugee crisis: An urgent call for moral leadership. *BMJ (Clinical Research Ed.)*, **351**, p. h4833.

Adams, K. 2019. Journeys through rough country: An ethnographic study of blind adults successfully employed in American Corporations.

Adams, M. and Bell, L.A. 2016. *Teaching for Diversity and Social Justice*. New York: Routledge.

Bain, P.G., Vaes, J. and Leyens, J. eds, 2014. *Humanness and Dehumanization*. New York: Psychology Press.

Bolton, S. (ed.) 2007. *Dimensions of Dignity at Work*. Amsterdam: Elsevier.

Bonilla-Silva, E. 2015. More than prejudice: Restatement, reflections, and new directions in critical race theory. *Sociology of Race and Ethnicity*, **1**(1), pp. 73–87.

Bontekoe, R. 2010. *The Nature of Dignity*. Lanham, MD: Lexington Books.

Bulmer, M. and Solomos, J. 2004. Introduction: Researching race and racism. In: M. Bulmer and J. Solomos eds, *Researching Race and Racism*. London: Routledge, pp. 13–27.

Carby, H.V. 1985. "On the threshold of woman's era": Lynching, empire, and sexuality in black feminist theory. *Critical Inquiry*, **12**(1), pp. 262–277.

Carrera, S., Blockmans, S., Gros, D. and Guild, E. 2015. The EU's response to the refugee crisis: Taking stock and setting policy priorities. *Ceps Essay*, (20/16).

Cockburn, C. 1998. *The Space between Us: Negotiating Gender and National Identities in Conflict*. London: Zed Books.

Crenshaw, K. 1989. Demarginalizing the intersection of race and sex: A black feminist critique of antidiscrimination doctrine, feminist theory and antiracist politics. *University of Chicago Legal Forum*, **1989** (1/8), pp. 139–168.

Crenshaw, K.W. 2010. Twenty years of critical race theory: Looking back to move forward. *Connecticut Law Review*, **43**, pp. 1253–1354.

de Gaay Fortman, B. 2016. *Moreel Erfgoed: Koers Houden in Een Tijd Van Ontwrichting (Moral Heritage: Keeping Course in A Time of disruption)*. Amsterdam, The Netherlands: Bert Bakker.

Delgado, R. and Stefancic, J. 2000. *Critical Race Theory: The Cutting Edge*. Philadelphia, PA: Temple University Press.

Delgado, R. and Stefancic, J. 2017. *Critical Race Theory: An Introduction*. New York: New York University Press.

Dillon, R.S. 2013. *Dignity, Character and Self-respect*. New York: Routledge.

Essed, P. 1991. *Understanding Everyday Racism: An Interdisciplinary Theory*. Newbury Park, CA: Sage.

Essed, P. 2009. Intolerable humiliations. *Racism Postcolonialism Europe*, **6**, p. 131.

Essed, P. 2013. Entitlement racism: License to humiliate. In: *European Network against Racism, Recycling Hatred: Racism (S) in Europe Today*. Brussels: ENAR.

Essed, P., Farquharson, K., Pillay, K. and White, E.J., Relating worlds of racism.

Essed, P. and Goldberg, D.T. 2002. *Race Critical Theories: Text and Context*. Malden, Mass: Blackwell Publishers.

Essed, P. and Hoving, I. 2014. *Dutch Racism*. Amsterdam: Rodopi.

Essed, P. and Muhr, S.L. 2018. Entitlement racism and its intersections: An interview with Philomena Essed, social justice scholar. *Ephemera: Theory & Politics in Organization*, **18**(1), pp. 183–201.

Esses, V.M., Hamilton, L.K. and Gaucher, D. 2017. The global refugee crisis: Empirical evidence and policy implications for improving public attitudes and facilitating refugee resettlement. *Social Issues and Policy Review*, **11**(1), pp. 78–123.

Fuller, R.W. and Gerloff, P. 2008. *Dignity for All: How to Create a World without Rankism*. San Francisco, CA: Berrett-Koehler Publishers.

Gale, P. 2004. The refugee crisis and fear: Populist politics and media discourse. *Journal of Sociology*, **40**(4), pp. 321–340.

Goldberg, D.T. 2009. *The Threat of Race: Reflections on Racial Neoliberalism*. Malden, MA: Wiley-Blackwell.

Greussing, E. and Boomgaarden, H.G. 2017. Shifting the refugee narrative? An automated frame analysis of Europe's 2015 refugee crisis. *Journal of Ethnic and Migration Studies*, **43**(11), pp. 1749–1774.

Guild, E., Costello, C., Garlick, M. and Moreno-Lax, V. 2015. *The 2015 Refugee Crisis in the European Union*. Belgium: Centre for European Policy Studies Brussels.

Hage, G. 2017. *Is Racism an Environmental Threat?* Cambridge: Polity Press.

Hall, S. 1980. Race, articulation, and societies structured in dominance. *Black British Cultural Studies.Chicago: University of Chicago Press*, **16**, p. 60.

Haslam, N. 2006. Dehumanization: An integrative review. *Personality and Social Psychology Review*, **10**(3), pp. 252–264.

Henry, F. and Tator, C. 2009. *Racism in the Canadian University: Demanding Social Justice, Inclusion, and Equity*. Toronto: University of Toronto Press.

Hicks, D. 2011. *Dignity: The Essential Role It Plays in Resolving Conflict*. New Haven: Yale University Press.

Hilhorst, S. and Hermes, J. 2016. 'We have given up so much': Passion and denial in the Dutch Zwarte Piet (Black Pete) controversy. *European Journal of Cultural Studies*, **19**(3), pp. 218–233.

Hodson, R. 2001. *Dignity at Work*. Cambridge: Cambridge University Press.

Hull, G.T., Scott, P.B. and Smith, B. 1982. *All the Women are White, All the Men are Black, But Some of Us are Brave*. New York: Feminist.

Kaufmann, P., Kuch, H., Neuhaeuser, C. and Webster, E. 2010. *Humiliation, Degradation, Dehumanization: Human Dignity Violated*. Dordrecht: Springer.

Keith, H. and Keith, K.D. 2013. *Intellectual Disability: Ethics, Dehumanization, and a New Moral Community*. Chichester: John Wiley & Sons.

Kolnai, A. 1976. Dignity. *Philosophy*, **51**(197), pp. 251–271.

Kostera, M. and Pirson, M. 2017. *Dignity and the Organization*. London: Palgrave Macmillan.

Lamont, M. 2000. *The Dignity of Working Men: Morality and the Boundaries of Race, Class, and Immigration*. New York: The Russell Sage Foundation.

Lamont, M., Silva, G.M., Welburn, J., Guetzkow, J., Mizrachi, N., Herzog, H. and Reis, E. 2016. *Getting Respect: Responding to Stigma and Discrimination in the United States, Brazil, and Israel*. Princeton, NJ: Princeton University Press.

Lawson, A. 2016. *European Union Non-Discrimination Law and Intersectionality: Investigating the Triangle of Racial, Gender and Disability Discrimination*. New York: Routledge.

Leach, M. 2003. "Disturbing practices": Dehumanizing asylum seekers in the refugee "crisis" in Australia, 2001–2002. *Refuge*, **21**(3), pp. 25–33.

Levine-Rasky, C. 2016. *Whiteness Fractured*. Farnham: Ashgate.

Lorde, A. 1984. *Sister Outsider*. Trumansburg. NY: Crossing.

Mannen, D. and McAllister, L. 2017. Dignity by design: A shift from formalistic to humanistic design in organizations. In: M. Kostera and M. Pirson eds, *Dignity and the Organization*. London: Palgrave Macmillan, pp. 221–244.

Margalit, A. 1996. *The Decent Society*. Cambridge, Massachusetts London: Harvard University Press.

Moody-Adams, M.M. 2013. Race, class, and the social construction of self-respect. In: R.S. Dillon ed, *Dignity, Character and Self-Respect*. Kindle edn. Routledge, pp. 271–289.

Mounk, Y. 2018. *The People Vs. Democracy: Why Our Freedom Is in Danger and How to Save It*. New York: Harvard University Press.

Noble, D.J. 2015. Pratfalls, pitfalls, and passion: The melding of leadership and social justice. *Creighton Journal of Interdisciplinary Leadership*, **1**(2), pp. 107–119.

Nussbaum, M.C. 2006. *Frontiers of Justice: Disability, Nationality, Species Membership*. Cambridge, Massachusetts: Belknap Press.

Nussbaum, M.C. 2009. *Hiding from Humanity: Disgust, Shame, and the Law*. Princeton, NJ: Princeton University Press.

Nussbaum, M.C. 2011. *Creating Capabilities: The Human Development Approach*. Cambridge, Mass.: Belknap Press of Harvard University Press.

Ostrand, N. 2015. The Syrian refugee crisis: A comparison of responses by Germany, Sweden, the United Kingdom, and the United States. *Journal on Migration and Human Security*, **3**(3), pp. 255–279.

Parmar, P. 2004. Gender, race and class: Asian women in resistance. In: Centre for Contemporary Cultural Studies, ed. *Empire Strikes Back*. London: Routledge, pp. 235–274.

van der Pijl, Y. and Goulordava, K. 2014. Black pete,"smug ignorance," and the value of the black body in postcolonial Netherlands. *New West Indian Guide/Nieuwe West-Indische Gids*, **88**(3–4), pp. 262–291.

Pollmann, A. 2011. Embodied self-respect and the fragility of human dignity: A human rights approach. In: P. Aufmann, H. Kuch, C. Neuhaeuser and E. Webster eds, *Humiliation, Degradation, Dehumanization: Humand Dignity Violated*. Dordrecht: Springer, pp. 232–253.

Postelnicescu, C. 2016. Europe's new identity: The refugee crisis and the rise of nationalism. *Europe's Journal of Psychology*, **12**(2), pp. 203–209.

Rapp, C. 2016. Moral opinion polarization and the erosion of trust. *Social Science Research*, **58**, pp. 34–45.

Reilly, K., Kaufman, S. and Bodino, A. 2003. *Racism: A Global Reader*. Armonk, NY: ME Sharpe.

Rich, A. 1979. *Disloyal to Civilization: Feminism, Racism, Gynephobia (1978)*. New York: WW Norton.

Rich, A. 1984. Notes towards a politics of location. In: R. Lewis and S. Mills eds, *Feminist Postcolonial Theory: A Reader*. New York: Routledge, pp. 29–42.

Rodenberg, J. and Wagenaar, P. 2016. Essentializing 'Black Pete': Competing narratives surrounding the Sinterklaas tradition in the Netherlands. *International Journal of Heritage Studies*, **22**(9), pp. 716–728.

Romm, N. 2010. *New Racism: Revisiting Researcher Accountabilities*. Dordrecht: Springer Science & Business Media.

Sayer, A. 2007. What dignity at work means. In: S. Bolton, ed. *Dimensions of Dignity at Work*. Kindle edn. Amsterdam and New York: Elsevier and S. Bolton, pp. 17–29.

Sayer, A. 2015. *Why We Can't Afford the Rich*. Bristol: Policy Press.

Serwer, A. 2019. *White Nationalism's Deep American Roots*. Magazine: The Atlantic.

Solomos, J. and Collins, P.H. 2010. *The SAGE Handbook of Race and Ethnic Studies*. Los Angeles, CA: SAGE Publications.

Wekker, G. 2016. *White Innocence: Paradoxes of Colonialism and Race*. Durham: Duke University Press.

Index

Page numbers in *italics* denote a figure **bold** denotes a table and n, an endnote.

Printed in Great Britain
by Amazon

22939918R00271